# The Christian Tradition

# The Christian Tradition

A History of the Development of Doctrine

Jaroslav Pelikan

## 4  Reformation of Church and Dogma (1300-1700)

The University of Chicago Press

Chicago and London

The University of Chicago Press, Chicago 60637
The University of Chicago Press, Ltd., London

© 1984 by The University of Chicago
All rights reserved. Published 1983
Paperback edition 1985
Printed in the United States of America

00 99 98                                    9 8 7

**Library of Congress Cataloging in Publication Data**

Pelikan, Jaroslav Jan, 1923–
    The Christian tradition.

    Includes bibliographies and index.
    CONTENTS: v. 1. The emergence of the Catholic tradition
(100–600).—v. 2. The spirit of Eastern Christendom
(600–1700).—[etc.]—v. 4. Reformation of church and dogma
(1300–1700).
    1. Theology, Doctrinal—History.
BT21.2.P42        230          79-142042
ISBN 0-226-65376-5 (vol. 4, cloth); 0-226-65377-3 (vol. 4, paper)

# Contents

# Preface

This fourth volume of *The Christian Tradition* has taken me back to the period of the history of Christian doctrine with which my scholarly work began: my dissertation, in 1946, dealt with the doctrinal relations between the Hussite Reformation of the fifteenth century and the Lutheran Reformation of the sixteenth; my first scholarly article, in 1947, was on the thought of a seventeenth-century theologian of Protestant orthodoxy; and my first book, in 1950, described the connections between theology and philosophy in the age of the Reformation and beyond. Even then, of course, I was conscious of the many ways in which the thought of the Reformation reflected the vocabulary and the thought patterns of the patristic and medieval periods. But coming to the doctrines of the Reformation now, after having rehearsed the doctrinal development of those periods in great detail, I am still more impressed with the importance of understanding the sixteenth century in the light of its continuity and discontinuity with the history of church doctrine since the second century. Despite their protestations of "sola Scriptura," the Reformers showed that the "Scriptura" has never been "sola." I would urge, moreover, that the readers of this volume take seriously its context as part of the history of the Christian tradition.

It may be appropriate as well to explain its relation to the next and final volume of the work. The periodization of a historical narrative is always arbitrary; nor do the events of the narrative always conform themselves to the neatness of the title or table of contents of the book. As the last chapter of this volume indicates, the account in volume 5 will begin with

Pietism, Puritanism, and Jansenism, which, together
with contemporaneous developments in Eastern Orthodoxy, represented "the crisis of orthodoxy East
and West." Therefore the doctrinal significance of those
movements, while adumbrated here, will receive more
substantial treatment there (even though a considerable number of the sources antedate 1700). Once again,
it will be the context in the history of the Christian
tradition that will determine the selection and the arrangement of those developments.

Another feature of the present volume that should
be explained is bibliographical. It was during the period covered here that printing was invented, and thus
for the first time in this work the publication of a
book in printed form could happen during the lifetime
of the author. In the case of many of the authors cited,
that first edition was also the last. As a glance at the
list of "Authors and Texts" will show, I have therefore
provided the facts of publication within that list rather
than as part of "Editions and Collections," which
would have been both inconvenient and pedantic. This
period is likewise the time in the history of the West
when surnames gradually came into common use: although he was often called "Doctor Martin," it was
as "Martin Luther" that the German Reformer was—
and is—usually referred to. I have attempted to take
account of this change in devising the abbreviations
catalogued under "Authors and Texts." While I have,
to be sure, not listed nearly all of the sources I have
read, I have included in that catalogue some that have
not been cited specifically in the notes. In quoting my
sources, I have, as is my wont throughout this work,
felt free to adopt and adapt translations, including my
own, without attribution. Since this is the first volume
with any significant number of English sources, I
should also state that I have translated most of those
as well into twentieth-century usage and orthog-
raphy.

It remains only to express my gratitude for all the
assistance and courtesy without which I could never
have written this book. Various lectureships in the
United States, Canada, Europe, and Australia have
given me the opportunity to try out most of this material on an audience before committing it irrevocably

to print; among these, let me mention explicitly the Gauss Lectures at Princeton University, which permitted (and compelled) me to straighten out my presentation of what is now the second chapter. Ironically, the closer I come to the present, the more dispersed the sources are. Therefore there has been a quantum increase in the number of libraries I have had to use, and in the depth of my thanks to their directors and staffs: the Catholic University of America; the University of Chicago; Concordia Theological Seminary in Saint Louis; the Folger Shakespeare Library; Harvard University; the University of Iowa; the Library of Congress; the Lutheran Theological Seminary in Philadelphia; the New York Public Library; the University of Notre Dame; the University of Oxford, especially the Bodleian Library; the University of Pennsylvania; Princeton Theological Seminary; Princeton University; Stanford University; the University of Toronto, including the Pontifical Institute of Mediaeval Studies; Union Theological Seminary in New York; the Biblioteca Apostolica Vaticana; Yale University; and the Zentralbibliothek of Zurich. My thanks are due as well to Ruth Mazo, who helped with verifying references in the first two chapters, and to Mary Whitney, who typed the first five chapters.

# Primary Sources

## Authors and Texts

xi

*Ep.Jo.XXIII.*                   Epistle to Pope John XXIII
*Ext.schism.*                    Extermination of the Schism
*Fals.proph.*                    False Prophets
*Indoct.*                        Whether Someone Not Learned in the Law of God Can Rightly
                                 Preside over the Church [*Utrum indoctus in jure divino possit
                                 juste praeesse in ecclesiae regno*]
*Inst.ut.*                       Useful Instruction
*Leg.*                           Whether the Church of Peter Is Subject to Law
*Lib.creat.*                     The Liberty of the Rational Creature before and after the Fall
*Mat.*                           The Matter of a General Council
*Nec.ref.*                       The Necessity of Reformation
*Prop.Mont.*                     Proposition against John of Montesono
*Recom.*                         The Recommendation of Holy Scripture
*Ref.eccl.*                      Reformation of the Church
*Reg.*                           Whether the Church of Peter Is Governed by a King
*Serm.*                          Sermons. Strasbourg, 1490
*Tract.*                         Tractates. Strasbourg, 1490
*Trin.*                          Whether the Trinity Is Incommunicable to Creatures
Alst.                            Johann Heinrich Alsted
*Theol.cat.*                     Catechetical Theology. Frankfurt, 1616
*Theol.schol.*                   Scholastic Theology. Hanau, 1618
*Alt.paup.*                      Treatise on the Highest Poverty [*Tractatus super altissima paupertate*]
Alt.                             Johannes Altenstaig
*Voc.theol.*                     Vocabulary of Theology. Hagenau, 1517
*Voc.voc.*                       Vocabulary of Words [*Vocabularius vocum*]. Hagenau, 1508
Alv.Pel.                         Alvaro Pelayo
*Ep.*                            Epistles
*Planc.eccl.*                    Lament of the Church [*De planctu ecclesiae*]
Ambr. Cath.                      Ambrosius Catharinus Politus
*Apol.ver.*                      Apology for the Truth of the Catholic and Apostolic Faith [*Apol-
                                 ogia pro veritate*]
*Clav.*                          Two Keys for Opening or Understanding the Holy Scriptures
                                 [*Claves duae, ad aperiendas intelligendasve Scripturas Sacras*].
                                 Lyons, 1543.
*Comm.*                          Commentaries [*Commentaria ... im omnes Divi Pauli et alias
                                 septem canonicas epistolas*]. Paris, 1566
*Consid.*                        On Consideration. Venice, 1547
*Excus.disp.*                    Excuse for the Disputation against Martin. Florence, 1521
*Immac.*                         Disputation for the Immaculate Conception of the Mother of God.
                                 Lyons, 1542
*Sac.*                           Oration on the Priesthood [*Oratio ... de officio et dignitate
                                 sacerdotum*]. Saint Vincent, 1537
Ambr.Trav.                       Ambrose Traversari
*Ep.*                            Epistles and Prefaces to Translations
*Or.Bas.*                        Oration at the Council of Basel
*Or.Sig.*                        Oration before Emperor Sigismund
*Vers.Chrys.Prov.*               Translation of John Chrysostom. "On the Providence of God"
*Vers.Joh.Clim.*                 Translation of John Climacus
*Vers.Joh.Mosch.*                Translation of John Moschus
*Vers.Man.Cal.*                  Translation of Manuel Calecas
*Vers.Pall.*                     Translation of Palladius. "The Life of Chrysostom"
Ames.                            William Ames [Guilelmus Amesius]
*Bell.*                          Bellarmin Unnerved [*Bellarminus enervatus*]. Oxford, 1629

| | |
|---|---|
| Coron. | Conclusion to the Conference at the Hague [*Coronis ad collationem Hagiensem*]. 6th ed. London, 1632 |
| Marr. | *The Marrow of Sacred Divinity.* London, 1642 |
| Scrip. | *Theological Disputation on the Perfection of Holy Scripture.* Cambridge, 1646 |
| Ams.Vict. | Nicholas Amsdorf. *Statement on the Declaration of Victorinus* [*Strigel*] |
| Amyr. Thes. | Moïse Amyraut. *Theses* |
| And.Brd. | Andreas de Broda |
| Orig.Hs. | *Origins of the Hussites* |
| Utraq. | *Against the Communion of the Common People under Both Kinds* [*Contra communionem plebis sub utraque specie*] |
| Andr.Per. | Andrew of Perugia |
| Ed.Bav. | *Against the Edict of* [*Emperor Louis IV*] *the Bavarian* |
| Andrs. | Jacobus Andreae |
| Ang.Cat. | *Anglican Catechism* |
| Ang.Clar. | Angelus Clarenus |
| Alv.Pel. | *Epistle in Response to Alvaro Pelayo* |
| Ep. | *Epistles* |
| Ep.excus. | *Excusatory Epistle* |
| Ang.Pasch.Trad. | Angelus Paschalis Illyricus. *Unwritten Traditions* |
| Ans. | Anselm of Canterbury |
| Conc. | *On the Harmony of the Foreknowledge, Predestination, and Grace of God with Free Will* [*De concordia praescientiae et praedestinationis et gratiae dei cum libero arbitrio*] |
| Cur d.h. | *Why God Became Man* [*Cur deus homo*] |
| Lib.arb. | *On the Freedom of the Will* [*De libertate arbitrii*] |
| Ps Ans. | Pseudo Anselm |
| Concept.BVM. | *On the Conception of the Blessed Virgin Mary* |
| Ant.P.Conf. | Antoninus Pierozzi. *Confessional.* Rome, 1490 |
| Apol.Conf.Aug. | *Apology of the Augsburg Confession* |
| Arch. | Filippo Archinto |
| Aret. | Benedictus Aretius |
| Act. | *Commentary on the Book of Acts.* Geneva, 1590 |
| Ev. | *Commentary on the Four Gospels.* 2 vols. Geneva, 1587 |
| Loc. | *Loci.* Geneva, 1617 |
| Arn.Hist. | Gottfried Arnold. *Nonpartisan History of the Church and of Heretics from the Beginning of the New Testament to 1688* [*Unparteyische Kirchen- und Ketzerhistorie von Anfang des Neuen Testaments bis 1688*]. 2 vols. Frankfurt, 1699–1700 |
| Art.XXXIX. | *The Thirty-Nine Articles* |
| Art.Ang.(1552). | *The Forty-Two Articles of the Church of England* |
| Art.Ratis. | *Regensburg* [*Ratisbon*] *Articles* |
| Ast.Can.paen. | Astesanus of Asti. *Penitential Canons* |
| Aug. | Augustine of Hippo |
| Bapt. | *On Baptism against the Donatists* |
| Civ. | *City of God* [*De civitate dei*] |
| Conf. | *Confessions* |
| Corrept. | *On Rebuke and Grace* [*De correptione et gratia*] |
| Ep. | *Epistles* |
| Ep.fund. | *Against the Epistle of Manicheus Called Fundamental* |
| Ev.Joh. | *Exposition of the Gospel of John* |
| Grat. | *On Grace* |

| | |
|---|---|
| *Hept.* | Questions on the Heptateuch |
| *Parm.* | Against the Epistle of Parmenianus |
| *Pecc.merit.* | On the Merits and the Remission of Sins [De peccatorum meritis et remissione] |
| *Pelag.* | Against Two Epistles of the Pelagians |
| *Persev.* | On the Gift of Perseverance |
| *Praed.sanct.* | On the Predestination of the Saints [De praedestinatione sanctorum] |
| *Ps.* | Exposition of the Psalms |
| *Serm.* | Sermons |
| *Spir. et litt.* | On the Spirit and the Letter [De spiritu et littera] |
| *Trin.* | On the Trinity |
| Ps.Aug. | Pseudo-Augustine |
| *Praed. et grat.* | Predestination and Grace |
| Aug.Alf. | Augustin von Alfeld |
| *Babst.stl.* | The Papal Throne [Von dem Babstlichen stuhl]. Leipzig, 1520 |
| *Malag.* | Poultice [Malagma]. Leipzig, 1520 |
| *Salv.Reg.* | Salve Regina |
| *Witt. Abg.* | Against the False God of Wittenberg, Martin Luther [Wyder den Wittenbergischen Abgot Martin Luther] |
| Aug.Rom. | Augustine of Rome |
| *Sacr.unit.* | The Sacrament of the Unity of Christ and the Church |
| *Serm.mag.* | Magisterial Sermon on the Ave Maria |
| Aug.Tr. | Augustine [Triumphus] of Ancona |
| *Dup.pot.* | The Twofold Power of Prelates and of Laymen [De duplici potestate praelatorum et laicorum] |
| *Pot.coll.* | The Power of the College [of Cardinals] when the Pope Has Died [De potestate collegii mortuo papa] |
| *Pot.eccl.* | Summa on the Power of the Church [Summa de potestate ecclesiae]. Augsburg, 1473 |
| *Temp.* | On the Templars |
| Aur.Rocc. | Aurelius of Rocca |
| *Avis.Sig.* | Advisory Recommendation Addressed to the Emperor Sigismund at the Time of the Council of Constance |
| Bai. | Michel Baius |
| *Eccl.* | On the Church |
| *Infall.* | On the Infallibility of the Roman Pontiff |
| *Just.* | On Righteousness [De justitia] |
| *Lib.arb.* | On Free Will [De libero arbitrio] |
| *Mer.op.* | On the Merits of Works [De meritis operum] |
| *Pecc.orig.* | On Original Sin [De peccato originis] |
| *Prim.just.* | On the Original Righteousness of Man [De prima hominis justitia] |
| *Sacr.* | On the Sacraments |
| Bald. | Friedrich Balduinus |
| *Anath.* | On Anathemas. Wittenberg, 1700 |
| *Art.Smal.* | Twenty-Two Disputations in Support of the "Smalcald Articles." Wittenberg, 1605–6 |
| Ban. | Domingo Báñes |
| *Apol.* | Apology [against Molina] |
| *Conc.* | On the True and Legitimate Harmony of Free Will with the Aids to the Grace of God [De vera et legitima concordia liberi arbitrii cum auxiliis gratiae] |
| *Mont.* | On the Thesis of Father Prudencio de Montemayor |

| | |
|---|---|
| Barth.Bon. | Bartholomew of Bologna [Bartholomaeus de Bononia] |
| Assump. | Questions on the Bodily Assumption of the Blessed Virgin Mary |
| Barth.Pis. | Bartholomew of Pisa [Bartholomaeus de Rinoncino] |
| Conform. | The Conformity of the Life of Saint Francis with the Life of the Lord Jesus |
| Quad. | Lenten Sermons on Despising the World [Quadragesimale De contemptu mundi]. Milan, 1498 |
| V.Mar. | The Life of the Blessed Virgin Mary. Venice, 1596 |
| Bas.Spir. | Basil of Caesarea. On the Holy Spirit |
| Bek.Zur. | Zurich Confession [Warhaffte Bekanntnusz der dieneren der kirchen zu Zürych] |
| Bell. | Robert Bellarmine |
| Bai. | Refutation of Baius |
| Brev.apol. | Brief Apologia for His Book on the "Book of Concord" |
| Cont. | Disputations on the Controversies over the Christian Faith against the Heretics of This Time |
| Dich.dott.cris. | A More Complete Statement of Christian Doctrine [Dichiarazione più copiosa della dottrina cristiana] |
| Dott.cris.brev. | A Brief Statement of Christian Doctrine [Dottrina cristiana breve] |
| Imag. | Refutation of a Book on the Cult of Images |
| Indulg. | On Indulgences |
| Lib.Conc. | Judgment of the So-Called "Book of Concord" [Judicium . . . de libro, quem lutherani vocant, Concordiae] |
| Scrip.eccl. | The Writers of the Church [De scriptoribus ecclesiasticis] |
| Vulg. | On the Vulgate |
| Ben.XIII.Ep. | Pope Benedict XIII. Epistles |
| Berg.Calov. | Georg Conrad Berg. Response to Abraham Calovius. 2d ed. Berlin, 1657 |
| Bert. | Pietro Bertani |
| Bez. | Theodore Beza [Théodore de Bèze] |
| Cast. | Response to the Calumnies of Sebastian Castellio |
| Coen. | On the Lord's Supper [De coena Domini] |
| Coll.Mont.Bell. | Answer to the Colloquium of Montbéliard. Heidelberg, 1588 |
| Conf. | Confession of the Christian Faith |
| Ep.theol. | Theological Epistles. 2d ed. Geneva, 1575 |
| Flac. | Against Matthias Flacius Illyricus |
| Praed. | On Predestination |
| Bgn. | Johann Bugenhagen |
| Annot. | Annotations on Ten Epistles of Paul. Basel, 1524 |
| Bed. | Some Christian Reflections on the Mass and Other Ceremonies [Etlich christliche Bedencken von der Mess und andern Cerimonien]. Wittenberg, 1525 |
| Chr.gl. | On the Christian Faith [Von dem Christlichen glauben]. Nuremberg, 1527 |
| Conjug.episc. | On the Marriage of Bishops [De conjugio episcoporum]. Wittenberg, 1525 |
| Ind. | Indexes of the Gospels. Wittenberg, 1524 |
| Kind. | On Unborn Children and on the Children Whom We Cannot Baptize [Von den ungeborn kindern und von den Kindern die wir nicht teuffen können]. Wittenberg, 1557 |
| Luth. | Funeral Sermon for Doctor Martin Luther. Wittenberg, 1546 |
| Off. | A Beautiful Revelation of Antichrist [Ain schöne Offenbarung des Endchrists]. Augsburg, 1524 |

| | |
|---|---|
| *Ps.* | *Interpretation of the Book of Psalms.* Basel, 1524 |
| *Sac.* | *Response to a Question about the Sacrament.* Wittenberg, 1525 |
| *Sum.Sel.* | *Summary of Salvation [Summa der Seligkeit].* Augsburg, 1525 |
| *Unt.* | *Instruction for Those in Illness and Peril of Death [Unterricht (Underricht) derer, so in Kranckheiten und Todesnöten liegen].* Wittenberg, 1527 |
| Bill. | Eberhard Billick |
| Blngr. | Heinrich Bullinger |
| *Alb.* | *Response to Albert of Brandenburg.* Zurich, 1532 |
| *Antib.* | *Brief Response to Cochlaeus [Brevis Antibole].* Zurich, 1554 |
| *Assert.orth.* | *Orthodox Assertion of Both Natures in Christ.* Zurich, 1534 |
| *Coen.* | *Sermon on the Lord's Supper [De coena Domini sermo].* Zurich, 1558 |
| *Conc.* | *On Councils.* Zurich, 1561 |
| *Dec.* | *Five Decades of Sermons.* Zurich, 1552 |
| *Eliz.* | *Refutation of the Papal Bull against [Queen] Elizabeth.* London, 1571 |
| *Ev.Joh.* | *Commentary on the Gospel of John.* Zurich, 1543 |
| *Ggn.* | *The Opposition of Evangelical and Papal Doctrine [Gägensatz . . . der Euangelischen und Bäptischen leer].* Zurich, 1551 |
| *Grat.just.* | *The Grace of God that Justifies Us for the Sake of Christ through Faith Alone, without Good Works, while Faith Meanwhile Abounds in Good Works.* Zurich, 1554 |
| *Luc.* | *Commentary on Luke.* Zurich, 1546 |
| *Nacht.* | *On the Holy Supper [Von dem heiligen Nachtmal].* Zurich, 1553 |
| *Or.err.miss.* | *The Origin of the Error of the Mass.* Basel, 1528 |
| *Perf.* | *The Perfection of Christians.* Zurich, 1551 |
| *Resp.Brent.* | *Response to Show that the Doctrine of Heaven and of the Right Hand of God Should Not Be Overthrown by the Contrary Doctrine of Johann Brenz.* Zurich, 1562 |
| *Resp.Coch.* | *Response to the Book of Johannes Cochlaeus on the Canonical Scripture and the Catholic Church.* Zurich, 1544 |
| *Scrip.auth.* | *On the Authority of Holy Scripture.* Zurich, 1538 |
| *Sum.* | *Summa of the Christian Religion.* Zurich, 1556 |
| *Test.* | *A Brief Exposition on the Unique and Eternal Testament or Covenant of God.* Zurich, 1534 |
| *Ver.* | *Persecution [Veruolgung].* Zurich, 1573 |
| Bon.VIII. | Pope Boniface VIII |
| *Un.sanct.* | *Unam sanctam* |
| Bonagr. | Bonagratia of Bergamo |
| *Paup.* | *On the Poverty of Christ and the Apostles* |
| Bonuc. | Agostino Bonuccio |
| Boss. | Jacques Bénigne Bossuet |
| *Def.trad.* | *Defense of the Tradition of the Holy Fathers* |
| *Hist.var.* | *History of the Variations of the Protestant Churches* |
| Br.Comp. | Johann Wilhelm Baier. *Compendium of Positive Theology* |
| Brad.Caus. | Thomas Bradwardine. *The Cause of God, against Pelagius* |
| Brd.Clr. | Bernard of Clairvaux |
| *Cons.* | *On Consideration* |
| *Ep.* | *Epistles* |
| *Grat.* | *On Grace and Free Will* |
| *Laud.Mar.* | *In Laud of Mary* |
| *Praec.et disp.* | *On Precept and Dispensation* |

| | |
|---|---|
| Ps.Brd.Clr. | Pseudo-Bernard of Clairvaux |
| *Laud.Virg.* | *In Laud of the Glorious Virgin Mother* |
| *Pass.Chr.* | *On the Passion of Christ and the Sorrows and Laments of His Mother* |
| Brn. | Johannes Braunius |
| *Doct.foed.* | *The Doctrine of Covenants* [*Doctrina foederum*]. Amsterdam, 1688 |
| Buc. | Martin Bucer |
| *Caen.* | *On the Lord's Supper* [*De caena dominica*] |
| *Ec.* | *Refutation of the "Loci" of Eck* |
| *Ep.apol.* | *Apologetic Epistle* |
| *Flor.pat.* | *Patristic Florilegium* |
| *Regn.Chr.* | *On the Reign of Christ* |
| *Rom.* | *Commentary on Romans.* Basel, 1562 |
| Bucan. *Inst.* | Guilelmus Bucanus. *Theological Institutes.* 5th ed. Geneva, 1625 |
| Burm.*Synop.* | Frans Burmann. *Synopsis of Theology.* 2 vols. Maastricht, 1687 |
| Caj. | Cajetan (Tommaso de Vio) |
| *Apol.* | *Apologia on the Comparative Authority of the Pope and the Church.* Rome, 1513 |
| *Concept.* | *On the Conception of the Blessed Virgin* |
| *Euch.* | *Errors touching the Sacrament of the Eucharist* |
| *Ev.* | *Commentaries on the Gospels.* Venice, 1530 |
| *Indulg.* | *On Indulgences* |
| *Miss.sac.* | *The Sacrifice of the Mass* |
| *Mos.* | *Commentaries on the Five Books of Moses.* Paris, 1539 |
| *Nov.Test.* | *Breakfasts from the New Testament* [*Novi Testamenti Jentacula*]. Lyons, 1530 |
| *Opusc.aur.* | *Golden Opuscules* [*Opuscula aurea*]. Paris, 1511 |
| *Pont.* | *On the Divine Institution of the Pontificate of the Roman Pontiff* |
| *Purg.* | *On Purgatory* |
| *Ref.eccl.* | *Counsel Given to the Supreme Pontiff concerning the Reformation of the Christian Church* |
| *Resp.Luth.* | *On Seventeen Responses That Appear to Favor the Assertions of Martin Luther* |
| *Summul.* | *Brief Summa on Sins.* Lyons, 1530 |
| *Utraq.* | *On Communion under Both Kinds* [*De communione sub utraque specie*] |
| Calov. | Abraham Calovius |
| *Art.fid.* | *Demonstration of the Articles of Faith Solely from Passages of Scripture.* Lüneburg, 1684 |
| Calv. | John Calvin |
| *Admon.Paul.III.* | *Paternal Admonition of* [*Pope*] *Paul III with Comments* |
| *Anab.* | *Brief Instruction against the Anabaptists* |
| *Ant.* | *Acts of the Synod of Trent with the Antidote* |
| *Astrol.* | *Warning against Astrology* |
| *Bland.* | *Response to the Questions of George Blandrata* |
| *Br.admon.* | *Brief Admonition to the Polish Brethren* |
| *Carol.calumn.* | *Defense against the Calumnies of Peter Caroli* |
| *Cn.* | *Short Treatise on the Holy Supper* [*Petit traicté de la saincte cene*] |
| *Conc.acad.* | *Academic Sermon* [*Concio academica*] |
| *Ep.du.* | *Two Epistles* |
| *Ep.Pol.* | *Epistle Confirming the Recently Issued Admonition to the Poles* |
| *Form.pr.* | *Forms of Prayers* |

| | |
|---|---|
| Frat.Pol. | Response to the Polish Brethren |
| Harm.ev. | Commentary on the Harmony of the Evangelists |
| Hes. | A Clear Explanation of the Sound Doctrine of the True Partici- pation of the Flesh and Blood of Christ in the Holy Supper, in Refutation of the Nebulous Ideas of Heshusius |
| Inst. | Institutes of the Christian Religion |
| Inv.rel. | Inventory of Relics |
| Nec.ref. | On the Necessity of Reforming the Church |
| Nob.Pol. | Response to the Polish Nobles |
| Occ.prov. | On the Occult Providence of God |
| Opt.rat. | The Best Way of Achieving Concord [Optima ineundae concor- diae ratio] |
| Ord.eccl. | Ordinances of the Church |
| Pac.et ref. | The True Method of Giving Peace to Christendom and Reforming the Church |
| Psych. | Soul Sleep [Psychopannychia] |
| Resp.neb. | Brief Response to the Calumnies of [Sebastian Castellio] the Scoundrel [Brevis responsio ad diluendas nebulonis cujusdam calumnias] |
| Rom. | Commentary on Romans |
| Sad. | Reply to Sadoleto |
| Scand. | On Scandals |
| Theol.Par. | Against the Articles of the Theologians of Paris |
| Trin. | Defense of the Orthodox Faith about the Holy Trinity |
| Usur. | On Usury |
| West. | Replies to Joachim Westphal |
| Calx. | Georg Calixtus |
| Conc.eccl. | Desire and Zeal for Concord in the Church. Helmstedt, 1655 |
| Epit.theol. | Epitome of Theology. Helmstedt, 1661 |
| Pr.Vinc.Ler. | Preface to Vincent of Lérins "Commonitory." Helmstedt, 1629 |
| Camp. | Lorenzo Campeggio |
| Depr.stat.eccl. | On the Depraved State of the Church |
| Cap. | Petrus Paulus Caporella |
| Car.Mal. | Carlo Malatesta |
| Ep. | Epistles |
| fr. | Fragment |
| Caraf. | Joannes Petrus Carafa |
| CAraus.(529) | Council of Orange [Concilium Arausicanum] |
| Can. | Canons |
| Card.leg. | Cardinal legates at the Council of Trent |
| Ep. | Epistles |
| Cas. | Thoms Caselli |
| Cast.Calv. | Sebastian Castellio [Sébastien Châteillon]. Against Calvin. Am- sterdam, 1562 |
| Castr. | Alphonsus de Castro |
| Ep.Hebr. | On the Epistle of Paul to the Hebrews |
| Haer. | Against All Heresies. Paris, 1571 |
| Cat.Gen. | Geneva Catechism |
| Cat.Heid. | Heidelberg Catechism |
| Cat.Rac. | Racovian Cathechism |
| Cat.West.Maj. | Larger Westminster Catechism |
| Cat.West.Min. | Westminster Shorter Catechism |
| Cauc. | Jacobus Caucus Venetus |

CBas.(1431–39)          Council of Basel
CConst.(1414–17)        Council of Constance
Cen.                    Ricardus Cenomanus
Cerv.*Ep.*              Marcello Cervini (Pope Marcellus II). *Epistles*
CFlor.(1438–45)         Council of Florence
  *Decr.Arm.*         *Decree on the Armenians*
  *Decr.Copt.*        *Decree on the Copts*
Chas.V.*Ep.*            Emperor Charles V. *Epistles*
Chauc.*Cant.*           Geoffrey Chaucer. *Canterbury Tales*
Chel.                   Peter Chelčický
  *Boj.*              *On Spiritual Battle* [*O boji duchovním*]
  *Crk.*              *The Holy Church* [*O církvi svaté*]
  *Post.*             *Postil*
  *Repl.*             *Reply to Bishop Nicholas*
  *St.vr.*            *The Net of Faith* [*Síť víry*]
Chem.                   Martin Chemnitz
  *Du.nat.*           *On the Two Natures in Christ* [*De duabus naturis in Christo*]. Leipzig, 1580
  *Exam.CTrid.*       *Examination of the Council of Trent*
  *Loc.*              *Theological Loci.* 3 vols. Frankfurt, 1604
  *Osndr.*            *The Status of the Controversy between Andreas Osiander and Dr. Joachim Morlinus*
Chil.                   William Chillingworth
  *Rel.Prot.*         *Religion of Protestants a Safe Way to Salvation.* 9th ed. London, 1727
Chrys.*Heb.*            John Chrysostom. *Homilies on the Epistle to the Hebrews*
Chyt.                   David Chytraeus
  *Pecc.orig.*        *Judgment on the Controversy over Original Sin* [*Censura de controversia peccati originis*]
Civ.Prag.*Ep.*          City of Prague. *Epistles*
CLater.(1215)           Fourth Lateran Council
  *Const.*            *Constitutions*
Clicht.                 Josse van Clichtove [Jodocus Clichtoveus]
  *Annun.*            *On the Dignity and Excellence of the Annunciation of the Blessed Virgin Mary.* Paris, 1519
  *Antiluth.*         *Anti-Luther.* Paris, 1524
  *Bell.pac.*         *On War and Peace* [*De bello et pace*]. Paris, 1523
  *Cec.*              *On the Praises of* [*Saint*] *Cecilia.* Paris, 1516
  *Concept.*          *On the Purity of the Conception of the Blessed Virgin Mary.* Paris, 1513
  *Eluc.eccl.*        *Ecclesiastical Elucidation.* Basel, 1517
  *Hom.*              *Homiliary.* Cologne, 1535
  *Hymn.*             *Hymns and Sequences.* Venice, 1555
  *Improb.Luth.*      *Improbation of Luther.* Paris, 1533
  *Oec.*              *On the Sacrament of the Eucharist, against Oecolampadius.* Paris, 1526
  *Prop.eccl.*        *Defense of the Church against the Lutherans* [*Propugnatio Ecclesie adversus Lutheranos*]. Cologne, 1526
  *Ven.sanct.*        *On the Veneration of the Saints.* Paris, 1523
  *Vit.sacer.*        *On the Life and Morals of Priests* [*De vita et moribus sacerdotum*]. 2d ed. Paris, 1520
Clvs.                   Joannes Calvus
  *Libr.can.*         *Apologia for the Canonical Books* [*Apologia pro libris canonicis*]

| | |
|---|---|
| Cocc.*S.T.* | Johannes Cocceius. *Summa of Theology.* Amsterdam, 1665 |
| Coch. | Johannes Cochlaeus |
|   *Aeq.dis.* |   *Discussion of Equity* |
|   *Luth.art.* |   *Reply to the [Smalcald] Articles of Luther* |
|   *Obsc.vir.* |   *Against Obscure Men* |
|   *Patr.parv.* |   *Defense of Infants [Patrocinium parvulorum]* |
|   *Phil.* |   *Four Philippics against the "Apology" of Philip Melanchthon.* Leipzig, 1534 |
| Coll.*Lips.* | *Leipzig Colloquy* |
| Coll.*Mont.Bell.* | *Colloquium of Montbéliard [Acta Colloquii Montis Belligartensis].* Tübingen, 1588 |
| Conc.*Witt.* | *Wittenberg Concord* |
| Conf.*Aug.* | *Augsburg Confession [Confessio Augustana]* |
| Conf.*Aug.Var.* | *Variata of the Augsburg Confession* |
| Conf.*Bas.* | *First Basel Confession of Faith* |
| Conf.*Belg.* | *Belgic Confession* |
| Conf.*Boh.*(1535) | *Bohemian Confession of 1535* |
| Conf.*Boh.*(1575) | *Bohemian Confession of 1575* |
| Conf.*Gall.* | *Gallic Confession* |
| Conf.*Gen.* | *Geneva Confession* |
| Conf.*Helv.post.* | *Second Helvetic Confession [Confessio Helvetica posterior]* |
| Conf.*Helv.pr.* | *First Helvetic Confession [Confessio Helvetica prior]* |
| Conf.*Mans.* | *Confession of the Theologians of Mansfeld* |
| Conf.*Remon.* | *Remonstrant Confession.* Harderwijk, 1622 |
| Conf.*Scot.* | *Scots Confession* |
| Conf.*sent.Wit.* | *Confession and Declaration of the Wittenbergers about Free Will [Confessio et sententia Wittenbergensium de libero arbitrio]* |
| Conf.*Tetrap.* | *Tetrapolitan Confession* |
| Conf.*Ung.* | *Hungarian Confession* |
| Confut.*Conf.Aug.* | *Confutation of the Augsburg Confession [Confutatio pontificia]* |
| Conr.*Meg.* | Conrad of Megenberg |
|   *Guil.Oc.* |   *Against William of Ockham* |
|   *Planc.eccl.* |   *Complaint of the Church against Germany [Planctus ecclesiae in Germaniam]* |
|   *Trans.imp.* |   *The Transfer of the Roman Empire* |
| Cons. | Joannes Consilii |
| Cons.*Brem.* | *Bremen Consensus* |
| Cons.*Gen.* | *Geneva Consensus* |
| Cons.*Helv.* | *Helvetic Consensus* |
| Cons.*rep.* | *Repeated Consensus of the Truly Lutheran Faith.* Wittenberg, 1666 |
| Cons.*Send.* | *Consensus of Sandomierz* |
| Cons.*Tig.* | *Zurich Consensus [Consensus Tigurinus]* |
| Consid.*Cat.Heyd.* | *[Remonstrant] Consideration of the Heidelberg Catechism [Consideratio Catechismi Heydelbergensis]* |
| Consid.*Conf.Belg.* | *[Remonstrant] Considerations of the Belgic Confession [Considerationes Confessionis Belgicae]* |
| Cont. | Gasparo Contarini |
|   *Confut.* |   *Confutation of the Articles or Questions of the Lutherans* |
|   *Just.* |   *Epistle on Justification* |
|   *Pot.pont.* |   *On the Power of the Pontiff [De potestate Pontificis]* |
|   *Praed.* |   *On Predestination* |
| Cor. | Jacobus Coriesius [Cortesius] |
| Corp.*Jur.Can.* | *Corpus Juris Canonici* |

| | |
|---|---|
| Decr.Grat. | Decree of Gratian |
| Decr.Greg.IX. | Decree of [Pope] Gregory IX |
| Extrav. | Extravagantes |
| Corr. "Quaest." | Correctorium "Quaestione" |
| Corr. "Quare." | Correctorium "Quare" |
| Cost. | Bonaventura Pius Costacciaro |
| Cpr. | Nicolaus Audetus Cyprius |
| Cran. | Thomas Cranmer |
| Gard. | An Answer unto . . . Stephen Gardiner |
| Cresc. | Marcello Crescenzio |
| Crll.Op.exeg. | Johann Crell. Exegetical Works [Opera exegetica] |
| Crz. | Antonio de la Cruz |
| CTrid. | Council of Trent [Concilium Tridentinum] |
| Act. | Acts |
| Can. | Canons |
| Decr. | Decrees |
| Decr.just. | [Draft] Decrees on Justification |
| Decr.min. | Draft Decrees of the Congregation of Non-Prelate Theologians [Decreta theologorum minorum] |
| CVien.(1311–12) | Council of Vienne |
| Cypr. | Cyprian of Carthage |
| Bon.pat. | On the Good of Patience [De bono patientiae] |
| Ep. | Epistles |
| Laps. | On the Lapsed |
| Dan.Haer. | Lambertus Dannaeus [Lambert Daneau] Refutations of Heretics [Elenchi haereticorum]. Geneva, 1580 |
| Dant. | Dante Alighieri |
| Inf. | Inferno |
| Mon. | On the Monarchy |
| Par. | Paradiso |
| Dav.Def. | Francis Dávid. Defense |
| Decl.cler.Gall. | The Four Gallican Articles [Clerici Gallicani de Ecclesiastica potestate Declaratio] |
| Decl.Thor. | Declaration of Thorn |
| Deutsch.Ang. | Johann Deutschmann. Anti-Calvinist Disputation concerning the Origin, Nature, and Status of the Angels. Wittenberg, 1659 |
| Diet. | Johannes Dietenberger |
| Cat. | Catechism. Cologne, 1545 |
| Phim. | Muzzle of Scripture Passages for the Mouths of Heretics [Phimostomus scripturariorum . . . contra haereticos]. Cologne, 1532 |
| Salv.Reg. | Ground and Explanation for How the Holy Canticle of Mary "Salve Regina" Is Being Neglected. Cologne, 1526 |
| Dion.Ar. | Pseudo-Dionysius the Areopagite. |
| D.n. | On the Divine Names |
| Myst. | On Mystical Theology |
| Dir. | Sigismund Diruta |
| Disp.Lips. | Leipzig Disputation |
| Disp.Vinar. | Weimar Disputation [Disputatio de originali peccato et libero arbitrio inter Matthiam Flacium Illyricum, et Victorinum Strigelium publice . . . Vinariae . . . 1560 . . . habita]. 2d ed. N.p., 1563 |
| Disp.Zof. | Zofingen Disputation [Handlung oder Acta gehaltner Disputation und Gespräch zü Zoffingen inn Bernner Biet mit den Widertöuffern]. Zurich, 1532 |

| | |
|---|---|
| Dnk. | Hans Denck [Johannes Denk] |
| Bek. | Confession [Bekenntnis] |
| Bös. | Whether God Is a Cause of Evil [Ob Gott eyn ursach sei des bösens] |
| Ges. | On the Law of God [Vom Gesetz Gottes] |
| Lieb. | On True Love [Von der wahren Liebe] |
| Mic. | Exposition of the Prophet Micah |
| Ord. | The Ordinance of God |
| Wid. | Retraction [Widerruff] |
| Dns.Scot. | John Duns Scotus |
| Ord. | Commentary on the Sentences [Ordinatio] |
| Ox. | Oxford Commentary on the Sentences [Opus Oxoniense] |
| Prim.princ. | On the First Principle [De primo principio] |
| Quaest. | Question whether the Blessed Virgin Was Conceived in Original Sin |
| Quodlib. | Quodlibeta |
| Rep.Par. | Paris Commentary on the Sentences [Reportatio Parisiensis] |
| Doct.Prag.Ep. | Doctors of Theology at Prague. Epistles |
| Dom.Domen. | Domenico de Domenichi |
| Pot.pap. | On the Power of the Pope and Its Terminus |
| Sang. | On the Blood of Christ [De sanguine Christi]. Venice, 1557 |
| Dried. | John Driedo [Jean Driedoens] |
| Concord. | On the Harmony of Free Will and Divine Predestination [De concordia liberi arbitrii et praedestinationis divinae]. Louvain, 1537 |
| Cap. | On the Captivity and Redemption of the Human Race. Louvain, 1534 |
| Eccl.scrip. | The Writings and Dogmas of the Church [De ecclesiasticis scripturis et dogmatibus]. Louvain, 1533 |
| Grat.lib.arb. | On Grace and Free Will [De gratia et libero arbitrio]. Louvain, 1537 |
| Lib.christ. | On Christian Liberty. Louvain, 1540 |
| Drk.Phil. | Dirk [Dietrich] Philipsz |
| Enchir. | Enchiridion |
| Drp.Ep. | Marten Dorp. Epistles |
| Dur.P. | Durandus of Saint-Pourçain |
| Hab. | Treatise on Habitudes |
| Nat.cog. | Question on the Nature of Cognition |
| Orig. | On the Origin of Powers and Jurisdictions |
| Dz.Luc. | Juan Bernal Díaz de Luco [de Lugo] |
| Eben. | Thomas Ebendorfer |
| Consid. | Considerations |
| Diar. | Diary at the Council of Basel |
| Or.Bas. | Oration at the Council of Basel |
| Ec. | Johann Eck [Eccius] |
| Dial. | Elements of Dialectic. Augsburg, 1517 |
| Disp.Vien. | Vienna Disputation |
| Dion.Ar. | Commentary on the "Mystical Theology" of Saint Dionysius the Areopagite. Dillingen an der Donau, 1610 |
| Eleg. | Elegy [Elegia . . . contra Petri Lempergii Gorlicensis calumniam]. Ingolstadt, 1544 |
| Enchir. | Enchiridion [Enchiridion locorum communium adversus Lutherum et alios hostes ecclesiae] |

| | |
|---|---|
| *Ev.* | *Sermons on the Gospels.* Ingolstadt, 1530 |
| *Imag.* | *Defense of the Images of Christ and the Saints.* Ingolstadt, 1522 |
| *Mal.Luth.* | *Response to Luther's Malicious Hunting Down of the Epistle of Emser.* Ingolstadt, 1519 |
| *Ps.20.* | *Explanation of Psalm 20 [21]* |
| *Rep.art.Zw.* | *Repulsion of the Articles of Zwingli.* N.p., 1530 |
| *Rit.* | *Defense against the Ritian Attacks [Defensio adversus invectiones Ritianas].* Augsburg, 1519 |
| Edw. | Jonathan Edwards |
| *Fr.Wll.* | *Freedom of the Will* |
| *Orig.Sn.* | *Original Sin* |
| *Rel.Aff.* | *Religious Affections* |
| *Emd.Kat.* | *Emden Catechism* |
| Ems. | Hieronymus Emser |
| *Disp.Lips.* | *On the Leipzig Disputation* |
| *Ven.Luth.* | *Assertion of the Wild Goat against Luther the Hunter [A venatione Luteriana aegocerotis assertio]* |
| Episc. | Simon Episcopius. *Opera theologica.* 2d ed. Amsterdam, 1678 |
| *Camer.* | *Examination of John Cameron* |
| *Inst.* | *Theological Institutes* |
| *Jud.* | *Two Sermons on the Causes of the Unbelief of the Jews* |
| *Lib.arb.* | *On Free Will [De libero arbitrio]* |
| *Quaest.* | *Response to Sixty-Four Questions* |
| *Wad.* | *Response to Two Epistles of Peter Wadding* |
| Eras. | Desiderius Erasmus |
| *Adnot.* | *Annotations on the New Testament* |
| *Apol.Pi.* | *Apologia against A. Pius* |
| *Aug.* | *Edition of Augustine* |
| *Ep.* | *Epistles* |
| *Hier.* | *Edition of Jerome* |
| *Hyp.* | *Hyperaspistes* |
| *Inq.fid.* | *Inquiry concerning Faith [Inquisitio de fide]* |
| *Iren.* | *Edition of Irenaeus* |
| *Lib.arb.* | *On Free Will [Diatribe de libero arbitrio]* |
| *Nov.inst.* | *New Testament [Novum instrumentum]* |
| *Obsec.Virg.Mar.* | *Petition to the Virgin Mary [Obsecratio sive oratio ad Virginem Mariam in rebus adversis]* |
| *Pn.Virg.Mat.* | *Paean to the Virgin* |
| *Pr.Vall.* | *Preface to Lorenzo Valla* |
| *Pseudev.* | *Against the Pseudoevangelicals* |
| *Stun.blasph.* | *Against the Book of Jacobus Stunica Entitled "The Blasphemies and Impieties of Erasmus"* |
| Esc. | Andrés de Escobar |
| *Avis.* | *Advisory Recommendations concerning Holy General Councils [Avisamenta sacrorum conciliorum generalium]* |
| *Can.poen.* | *Penitential Canons.* Rome, [1491]. |
| *Gub.conc.* | *Governance of Councils* |
| *Mod.conf.* | *The Manner of Confessing [Modus confitendi].* Rome, [1495–98]. |
| Esq. | Didacus de Alaba y Esquivel |
| *Fabr.Praep.* | Johannes Fabri [Heigerlein]. *Preparation for a Future Universal Council* |
| *Feur.Grh.* | Justus Feurborn. *Oration in Honor of Johann Gerhard.* Jena, 1638 |

| | |
|---|---|
| Fil. | Robert Filheul [*Antonius Filholi*] |
| Fill. | Guillaume Fillastre |
|   *Gest.conc.Const.* | *History of the Council of Constance* [*Gesta concilii Constantiensis*] |
| Fish. | [Saint] John Fisher |
|   *Clicht.* | *Refutation of the Defense of Jodocus Clichtoveus.* Louvain, 1520 |
|   *Confut.* | *Confutation of Luther's "Assertion."* Antwerp, 1523 |
|   *Corp.* | *On the Reality of the Body and Blood of Christ in the Eucharist* [*De veritate corporis et sanguinis Christi in Eucharistia*]. Cologne, 1527 |
|   *Def.* | *Defense of the King's "Assertion" against the "Babylonian Captivity."* Cologne, 1525 |
|   *Pen.Ps.* | *The fruytfull saynges of Davyd the kynge and prophete in the seven penytencyall psalmes.* London, 1508 |
|   *Sac.* | *Defense of the Holy Priesthood against Luther* [*Sacri sacerdotii defensio contra Lutherum*] |
| Flac. | Matthias Flacius Illyricus |
|   *Admon.* | *Amicable, Humble, and Devout Admonition to Correct the Holy Canon of the Mass.* Magdeburg, 1550 |
|   *Bew.Osndr.* | *Proof that Osiander Holds and Teaches that the Divinity Dwells in the Believers in the Same Way as in the Humanity of Christ Itself* [*Beweisung das Osiander helt und leret das die Gottheit eben also in den rechtgleubigen wone wie in der menschheit Christi selbst*]. Magdeburg, 1553 |
|   *Clar.not.* | *Certain Clear Notes of True and False Religion.* Magdeburg, 1549 |
|   *Clav.* | *Key to Holy Scripture* [*Clavis Scripturae Sacrae*]. [4th ed.] Basel, 1628 |
|   *Conc.* | *Explanation of the Shameful Sin of Those Who Are Falling Away to Antichrist through the Council, the Interim, and the Adiaphora.* 2d ed. Magdeburg, 1551 |
|   *Essent.imag.* | *The Essence of the Image of God and of the Devil.* Basel, 1570 |
|   *Gegn.* | *Quotations from Luther against Osiander* [*Tröstliche Gegensprüch . . . Doctoris Martini Lutheri . . . wider . . . Osiandri*]. Magdeburg, 1552 |
|   *Hist.* | *A Frightful History.* Magdeburg, 1549 |
|   *Sum.* | *Brief Summaries of the Religion of Jesus Christ and of Antichrist.* Magdeburg, 1550 |
| Fon. | Juan Fonseca |
| *Form.Conc.* | *Formula of Concord* |
|   *Epit.* | *Epitome* |
|   *S.D.* | *Solid Declaration* |
|   *Sum.* | *Summary Formulation* |
| Fosc. | Egidio Foscarari |
| Fr.Mayr. | Francis of Meyronnes [Mayronis] |
| Fr.Per. | Franciscus Toti [Coti] of Perugia |
|   *Bav.* | *Against* [*Emperor Louis IV*] *the Bavarian* |
|   *Sent.* | *Commentary on the Sentences* |
| Frnk.*Br.* | Sebastian Franck. *Epistle* [*Brief*] |
| Frth. | John Frith |
|   *Disp.purg.* | *A disputacion of purgatorye.* [London, 1531] |
| Gabr.Bl. | Gabriel Biel |
|   *Can.miss.* | *Exposition of the Canon of the Mass* |
|   *Epit.can.miss.* | *Epitome of the Exposition of the Canon of the Mass.* Tübingen, 1499 |

| | |
|---|---|
| Fest.Chr. | Sermons on the Festivals of Christ. Tübingen, 1499 |
| Fest. Mar. | Sermons on the Festivals of the Glorious Virgin Mary. Tübingen, 1499 |
| Just. | Questions on Justification |
| Obed.apost. | In Defense of Apostolic Obedience |
| Pass.Dom. | Historical Sermon on the Passion of the Lord [Passionis Dominicae sermo historialis]. Hagenau, 1515 |
| Sanct. | Sermons on the Saints. Tübingen, 1499 |
| Sent. | Commentary on the Sentences |
| Serm. | Sermons. Tübingen, 1499–1500 |
| Gers. | Jean de Gerson |
| Appell. | Whether It Is Permissible to Appeal to the Pope in Matters of Faith |
| Auct.conc. | The Authority of a Council Representing the Universal Church |
| Aud.conf. | On the Art of Hearing Confessions [De arte audiendi confessiones] |
| Aufer. | The Removability of the Bridegroom from the Church [De auferibilitate sponsi ab ecclesia] |
| Br.int. | Brief Introduction to the Holy Christian Faith |
| Cant. | Exposition of the Song of Songs |
| Conc.un.obed. | On a Council of One Obedience |
| Cons. | The Consolation of Theology |
| Consil.ev. | On the Evangelical Counsels and the State of Perfection |
| Consid. | Considerations on the Restoration of Obedience |
| Consid.Jos. | Considerations on Saint Joseph |
| Cur.st. | Against Curiosity [Contra curiositatem studentium] |
| Desp. | For the Feast of the Betrothal of Our Lady [Pour la fête de la desponsation Notre Dame] |
| Dial.spir. | Spiritual Dialogue |
| Dist.rev. | On the Distinction between Genuine Revelations and False Ones |
| Ep. | Epistles |
| Exam.doct. | On the Examination of Doctrines |
| Fuss. | Against Matthew de Fussa |
| Glor. | On the "Gloria in Excelsis" |
| Joh.Mont. | Against John of Montesono |
| Jos. | Discussions of Joseph |
| Jur.episc. | Eight Conclusions on Episcopal Jurisdiction in Definitions of Faith |
| Jur.spir. | On Spiritual Jurisdiction |
| Lull. | On the Doctrine of Raymond Lull |
| Magn. | Commentary on the Magnificat |
| Mat.fid. | On Protesting regarding a Matter of Faith |
| Mat.schism. | Trialogue on the Matter of the Schism |
| Mend.spir. | Spiritual Mendicancy |
| Mir.am. | The Mirror of the Soul [Le miror de l'âme] |
| Mod.hab. | On How to Conduct Oneself in a Time of Schism [De modo se habendi tempore schismatis] |
| Mon. | Harmony of the Gospels [Monotessaron] |
| Mont.cont. | The Mountain of Contemplation |
| Myst.theol.prac. | On Practical Mystical Theology [De mystica theologia practica] |
| Not.Dion. | Notes on "The Celestial Hierarchy" of Dionysius the Areopagite |
| Nov.pos. | New Position |
| Nupt. | On the Nuptials of Christ and the Church |
| Or.priv. | On Private Prayers [Contra fraticellum, de orationibus privatis fidelium] |

| | |
|---|---|
| Pap.cont. | On the Contenders for the Papacy |
| Petr.Lun. | Against Pedro de Luna [Antipope Benedict XIII] |
| Pot.eccl. | On Ecclesiastical Power |
| Prop.Ang. | Proposition for the English |
| Remem.agend. | Instructions for Visitations [Rememoratio agendorum durante subtractione] |
| Rép.cr. | Response to Criticisms of the University's Proposition for Peace |
| Repl. | Replies |
| Rest.ob. | On the Restoration of Obedience |
| Schism. | On the Schism |
| Schol.myst. | On the Scholastic Elucidation of Mystical Theology |
| Sens.lit. | On the Literal Sense of Holy Scripture |
| Serm. | Sermons |
| Sim. | On Simony |
| Stat.eccl. | Protest concerning the State of the Church |
| Styl.theol. | Eight Rules about Theological Style |
| Sub.schism. | On Ending the Schism [De subtractione schismatis] |
| Sup. | Against Superstition |
| Theol.myst. | Six Lectures on Mystical Theology |
| Union.eccl. | The Union of the Church |
| Unit.eccl. | The Unity of the Church |
| Ver.cred. | Which Truths Are Necessary to Believe for Salvation [Quae veritates sint de necessitate salutis credendae] |
| Vit.cont. | On the Comparison of the Contemplative with the Active Life |
| Vit.spir. | On the Spiritual Life of the Soul |
| Utraq. | Against the Heresy of Communion by the Laity under Both Kinds [Contra haeresim de communione laicorum sub utraque specie] |
| Giac. | Giacomo Giacomelli |
| Gl.ord. | Glossa Ordinaria |
| Gr.Arim.Sent. | Gregory of Rimini [Gregorius Ariminensis]. Commentary on the Sentences. Venice, 1522 |
| Gr.M.Ep. | Pope Gregory the Great. Epistles |
| Gr.Paw. | Gregory Paul [Grzegorz Paweł z Brzezin] |
| Praw.smr. | On True Death, Resurrection, and Eternal Life [O prawdziwej śmierci, zmartwychwstaniu i żywocie wiecznym] |
| Roz.ter. | On Contemporary Controversies [O rożnicach teraźniejszych] |
| Gr.XII.Mod. | Pope Gregory XII. Modes of Achieving Union |
| Grh. | Johann Gerhard |
| Conf.cath. | Catholic Confession. 2 vols. Jena, 1662 |
| Disp. | Theological Disputations. Jena, 1655 |
| Hom. | Homilies |
| Interp. | On the Legitimate Interpretation of Holy Scripture. Jena, 1663 |
| Loc. | Theological Loci |
| Med. | Meditations. Oxford, 1633 |
| 1 Pet. | Commentary on the First Epistle of Peter. 3d ed. Hamburg and Leipzig, 1692. |
| Grop. | Johann Gropper |
| Antididag. | Lesson in Opposition [Antididagma]. Venice, 1547 |
| Buc. | Reply to Bucer. Cologne, 1545 |
| Cap.inst. | Chapters of Instruction for Piety. Cologne, 1549 |
| Enchir. | Enchiridion of Christian Instruction. Rev. ed. Paris, 1547 |
| Leyb. | On the True, Essential, and Abiding Presence of the Body and Blood of Christ [Vonn warer, wesenlicher, und pleibender Gegewertigkeit des Leybs und Bluts Christi]. Cologne, 1556 |

| | |
|---|---|
| Grot.*Sat.* | Hugo Grotius. *Defense of the Catholic Faith concerning the Satisfaction of Christ against Faustus Socinus of Siena* |
| Gualt.Cast. | Walter of Château-Thierry [Gualterus de Castro Theodorici] |
| *Assump.* | *Question on the Bodily Assumption of the Blessed Virgin Mary* |
| Guer. | Petrus Guerrerus de Logrono |
| Guib.Tour. | Guibert of Tournai |
| *Scand.eccl.* | *On the Scandals of the Church* |
| Guid.Terr. | Guido Terrena of Perpignan |
| *Mag.infall.* | *Question on the Infallible Magisterium of the Roman Pontiff* |
| *Quodlib.* | *Quodlibeta* |
| Guid.Vern. | Guido Vernani |
| *Repr.mon.* | *Condemnation of [Dante] "On the Monarchy" [De reprobatione monarchiae]* |
| Guidic. | Bartolomeo Guidiccioni |
| *Eccl.emend.* | *On the Church and the Correction of the Ministers [De ecclesia et emendatione ministrorum]* |
| Guil.Crem. | William Amidani of Cremona |
| *Repr.err.* | *Condemnation of the Errors [of Marsilius of Padua] [Reprobatio errorum]* |
| Guil.Mar. | William de la Mare |
| *Corr.Thom.* | *Correctorium of Brother Thomas [Aquinas]* |
| *Var.sent.Thom.* | *Declarations or Examinations of Various Sentences of Saint Thomas Aquinas* |
| Guil.Oc. | William of Ockham |
| *Ben.* | *Treatise against Pope Benedict XII* |
| *Brev.* | *Brief Statement on the Tyrannical Principate [Breviloquium de principatu tyrannico]* |
| *Corp.* | *On the Body of Christ [De corpore Christi]* |
| *Dial* | *Dialogue* |
| *Ep.frat.min.* | *Epistle to the Friars Minor* |
| *Imp.et pont.* | *On the Power of Emperors and Pontiffs* |
| *Jn.* | *Against Pope John XXII* |
| *Op.XC.dier.* | *Work of Ninety Days* |
| *Pot.pap.* | *Eight Questions on the Power of the Pope* |
| *Praed.* | *Predestination and the Foreknowledge of God* |
| *Sacr.alt.* | *On the Sacrament of the Altar* |
| Guil.War. | William of Ware |
| *Quaest.* | *Question whether the Blessed Virgin Was Conceived in Original Sin* |
| Han.*Conc.* | Johannes Haner. *On Councils* |
| Hav.*Majest.* | Michael Haveman. *Whether or Not the Divine Majesty Is Truly and Really Communicated to the Human Nature in Christ.* Jena, 1658 |
| Heid. | Johann Heinrich Heidegger |
| *Corp.theol.* | *Corpus of Christian Theology.* 2 vols. Zurich, 1700 |
| Henr.VIII. | King Henry VIII |
| *Assert.* | *Assertion of the Seven Sacraments against Martin Luther.* Rome, 1521 |
| *Coerc.Luth.* | *On Coercing the Lutheran Faction.* Leipzig, 1523 |
| Henr.Crem. | Henry of Cremona |
| *Pot.pap.* | *On the Power of the Pope* |
| Henr.Gnt.*Quodlib.* | Henry of Ghent. *Quodlibeta.* Paris, 1613 |
| Henr.Kalt. | Heinrich Kalteisen |
| *Err.Amed.* | *The Errors of the Amedists* |

| | |
|---|---|
| *Lib.praedic.* | *On the Free Proclamation of the Word of God [De libera prae-dicatione verbi Dei]* |
| Henr. Lang. | Henry Heinbuche of Langenstein |
| *Concept.* | *Against the Disputes and Contradictory Preaching of the Men-dicant Friars concerning the Conception of the Blessed Virgin Mary.* Strasbourg, 1516 |
| *Cons.pac.* | *Epistle of Counsel on Peace* |
| *Tel.* | *Against the Prophecies of Telesphorus the Hermit about the Last Times* |
| Henr. Oyt. | Henry Totting of Oyta |
| *Scrip.* | *Question on Holy Scripture* |
| *Ver.cath.* | *Question on Catholic Truths [Quaestio de veritatibus catholicis]* |
| Henr. Wrl. | Henry of Werl |
| *Imac.* | *On the Immaculate Conception of the Blessed Virgin Mary* |
| Herb. *Enchir.* | Nicholas of Herborn. *Enchiridion against the Heresies of This Time* |
| Hes. | Tilemann Heshusius |
| *Anal. Vict.* | *Analysis of the Declaration of Victorinus [Strigel]* |
| *Confut.Syn.* | *Confutation of the Arguments of the Synergists* |
| Herv. Nat. | Hervaeus Natalis |
| Hier. | Jerome [Hieronymus] |
| *Hebr.nom.* | *The Interpretation of Hebrew Names* |
| *Pr.ep.can.* | *Prologue to the Seven Canonical Epistles* |
| Hier. Prag. | Jerome of Prague |
| Hier. Syr. | Jerome of Syracuse |
| Hinc. R. | Hincmar of Reims |
| *Opusc.Hinc.L.* | *Opusculum against Hincmar of Laon* |
| Hkr. *Eccl.pol.* | Richard Hooker. *Of the Laws of Ecclesiastical Polity.* 2 vols. Lon-don, 1594–97 |
| Hn. *Ep.chr.* | Cornelius Hoen [Honius]. *Christian Epistle* |
| Holl. *Exam.* | David Hollaz. *Examination of Theology.* Rev. ed. Stockholm and Leipzig, 1763 |
| Hon. Aug. | Honorius of Autun [Honorius Augustodunensis] |
| *Oct.quaest.* | *Eight Questions about the Angels and Man* |
| Hpk. *Pms.* | Gerard Manley Hopkins. *Poems* |
| Hs. | John Hus |
| *Coll.* | *Sermons Called "Collecta"* |
| *Corp.* | *On the Body of Christ [De corpore Christi]* |
| *Eccl.* | *On the Church* |
| *Err.* | *On Six Errors* |
| *Exp.dec.* | *Exposition of the Decalogue* |
| *Post.ad.* | *Adumbrated Postil* |
| *Sanct.* | *Sermons on the Saints* |
| *Sang.* | *On the Blood of Christ [De sanguine Christi]* |
| *Sent.* | *Commentary on the Sentences* |
| *Svat.* | *Books on Simony [Knížky o svatokupectví]* |
| Hub. | Balthasar Hubmaier |
| *Ax.* | *Axioms* |
| *Bn.* | *On Christian Excommunication [Von dem christlichen Bann]* |
| *Ent.* | *A Brief Apology [Eine kurze Entschuldigung]* |
| *Erb.* | *An Earnest Christian Petition [Eine ernstliche christliche Erbietung]* |
| *Form.Nacht.* | *Form of the Lord's Supper [Form des Nachtmals]* |
| *Form.Tf.* | *Form of Baptism [Form zu taufen]* |

| | |
|---|---|
| *Gespr.Zw.* | *A Discussion of Zwingli "On Baptism"* [*Ein Gespräch auf Zwinglis Taufbüchlein*] |
| *Ketz.* | *On Heretics and Those Who Burn Them* [*Von Ketzern und ihren Verbrennern*] |
| *Kind.* | *On Infant Baptism* [*Von der Kindertaufe*] |
| *Lr.* | *Catechism* [*Christliche Lehrtafel*] |
| *Rech.* | *Statement of Faith* [*Rechenschaft des Glaubens*] |
| *Schl.* | *Conclusions* [*Schluszreden*] |
| *Schw.* | *On the Sword* |
| *Str.* | *On Fraternal Discipline* [*Von der brüderlichen Strafe*] |
| *Sum.* | *Summary* |
| *Tf.* | *On the Christian Baptism of Believers* [*Von der christlichen Taufe der Gläubigen*] |
| *Unt.* | *Simple Instruction* [*about the Lord's Supper*] [*Einfaltiger Unterricht*] |
| *Urt.* | *Judgment of the Teachers* [*Der Lehrer Urteil*] |
| *Will.* | *On the Freedom of the Will* |
| *Zwlf.Art.* | *The Twelve Articles* [*Die Zwolf Artikel*] |
| Hug.*Man.* | Jakob Hüglin. *Diary at the Council of Basel* [*Manuale mei . . . super actis et gestis in concilio Basiliensi*] |
| Huls. | Johann Hülsemann |
| *Vet.nov.test.* | *On the Nature of the Old and the New Testament* [*De Veteris et Novi Testamenti natura.*] Rev.ed. Leipzig, 1714 |
| Hunn. | Aegidius Hunnius |
| *Just.* | *The Doctrine of Justification.* Frankfurt, 1590 |
| *Pers.Chr.* | *The Person of Christ.* Frankfurt, 1590 |
| *Trin.* | *The Doctrine of the Trinity.* Frankfurt, 1589 |
| Hutt.*Conc.* | Leonhard Hutter. *Defense of the "Book of Concord"* [*Concordia Concors*]. Frankfurt and Leipzig, 1690 |
| *Impug.Aeg.* | *Attacks on Giles of Rome for His Contradictions of Thomas* [*Impugnationes contra Aegidium Romanum contradicentem Thomae super Primum Sententiarum*] |
| Inn.III. | Pope Innocent III |
| *Sacr.alt.* | *The Mystery of the Sacrament of the Altar* |
| *Serm.div.* | *Sermons on Diverse Occasions* |
| Inn.IV. | Innocent IV |
| *Ep.Fred.II.* | *Epistle to Frederick II* |
| *IPM* | *Peace of Westphalia* [*Instrumentum Pacis Monasteriense*] |
| *Ir.Art.Rel.* | *Irish Articles of Religion* |
| Iren.*Haer.* | Irenaeus of Lyons. *Against Heresies* |
| Jac.Cerr. | Jacobus de Cerretanis |
| *Lib.gest.* | *Chronicle* [*of the Council of Constance*] [*Liber gestorum*] |
| Jac.Mis. | Jakoubek ze Stříbra |
| *Com.parv.* | *On Infant Communion* [*De communione parvulorum*] |
| *Corp.* | *On the True Existence of the Body of Christ in the Sacrament of the Altar* [*De existencia vera corporis Christi in sacramento altaris*] |
| *Purg.* | *On the Purgatory of the Soul* |
| *Rem.* | *On Remanence* |
| *Salv.* | *Our Savior* [*Salvator noster*] |
| *Utraq.* | *Defense against Andreas de Broda of the Communion of the Laity under Both Kinds* [*Vindiciae contra Andream Brodam . . . pro communione plebis sub utraque specie*] |

| | |
|---|---|
| Ven.sacr. | Final Treatise against Those Who Heretically Oppose the Venerable Sacrament |
| Zjev. | Commentary on the Revelation of Saint John [Výklad na Zjevenie svatého Jana] |
| Jac.Parad. | Jakob von Jüterbog [Jacobus de Paradiso] |
| Sept.stat. | On the Seven States of the Church Described in the Apocalypse |
| Jac.Vit. | James of Viterbo [Jacobus Viterbiensis] |
| Quodlib. | Quodlibeta |
| Reg.chr. | On Christian Government [De regimine christiano] |
| Jac.Vor. | Jacob of Voragine |
| Def. | Defense against Those Who Impugn the Friars Preachers |
| Leg.aur. | Golden Legend [Legenda aurea] |
| Jaj.Trad.eccl. | Claude Le Jay [Claudius Jajus]. On Ecclesiastical Traditions |
| Jans.Aug. | Cornelius Jansen. Augustinus. 3 vols. Berthelin, 1643 |
| Joach.Apoc. | Joachim of Fiore. Exposition of the Apocalypse. Venice, 1527. Facsimile edition. Frankfurt, 1964 |
| Joh.XXII. | Pope John XXII |
| Cum inter. | Cum inter nonnullos |
| Serm. | Sermons |
| Joh.Brev. | Johannes de Brevi Coxa [Jean Courtecuisse] |
| Tract. | Treatise on Faith, the Church, the Roman Pontiff, and the General Council |
| Joh.D.Fo. | John of Damascus. The Orthodox Faith |
| Joh.Lutt. | John Lutterell |
| Guil.Oc. | Against the Doctrine of William of Ockham |
| Joh.Maur. | Johannes Mauroux |
| Prop.Const. | Proposition at the Council of Constance |
| Super. | On the Question of Superiority between the Council and the Pope |
| Joh.Mont. | John of Montesono |
| Prop.dam. | Condemned Propositions |
| Joh.Neap. | John of Naples |
| Immac. | Questions on the Immaculate Conception of the Blessed Virgin Mary |
| Joh.Pal. | John of Palomar |
| Civ.dom. | On the Civil Dominion of Clerics |
| Dial. | Dialogue between James and John |
| Hist. | History of the Beginning of the Conflicts between the Council and the Pope |
| Quaest.par. | The Question of Who Is to Be Obeyed [Quaestio . . . cui pariendum est] |
| Joh.Par. | John of Paris |
| Apol. | Apologia |
| Conf. | On Hearing Confessions |
| Corp. | Determination concerning the Mode of Existence of the Body of Christ in the Sacrament of the Altar [Determinatio . . . de modo existendi corpus Christi in sacramento altaris] [1304]. London, 1686 |
| Corr. | Correctorium |
| Pot. | On Royal and Papal Power |
| Joh.Pol. | Johannes de Polliaco [Pouilly] |
| Immac. | Question on the Immaculate Conception of the Blessed Virgin Mary |

| | |
|---|---|
| Joh.Rag. | John of Ragusa [Johannes Stojković of Dubrovnik] |
| Auct.conc. | Six Considerations on the Authority of the Council |
| Bas.conc. | The Beginning and Continuation of the Council of Basel |
| Boh. | How the Bohemians Were Restored to the Unity of the Church |
| Eccl. | On the Church |
| Ep. | Epistles |
| Graec. | How the Greeks Were Restored to the Unity of the Church through the Council of Basel |
| Miss.CP. | Mission to Constantinople |
| Utraq. | Oration [at Basel] on Communion under Both Kinds [Oratio de communione sub utraque specie] |
| Joh.Rok. | John of Rokycana |
| Ep. | Epistles |
| Sanct.com. | Reply on the Holy Communion |
| Utraq. | The Position that Communion under Both Kinds Is Necessary and Commanded by the Lord our Savior [Positio . . . : Communio . . . sub utraque specie . . . est necessaria, et a Domino praecepta Salvatore] |
| Joh.Rup. | John de la Rochelle [Johannes de Rupella] |
| Serm. | Sermons |
| Joh.Schel. | Johannes Schele |
| Avis. | Considerations of Reformation [Avisamenta reformationis] |
| Joh.Var. | Joannes de Varennis |
| Ep.Ben.XIII. | Epistle to Pope Benedict XIII |
| Ep.Card. | Epistle to the Cardinals of the Holy Roman Church |
| Joh.Vit. | Juan Vidal [Johannes Vitalis] |
| Concept. | Treatises on the Immaculate Conception |
| Joh.Z.Tract. | Jan Němec ze Žatce [Johannes de Zacz]. Short Tractate [Tractatulus] |
| Jul.Ces. | Giuliano [Julianus] Cesarini |
| Disp.Bas. | Disputation at the Council of Basel |
| Sim. | Draft Decree on Simony |
| Just.Dial. | Justin Martyr. Dialogue with Trypho |
| Juv. | Roger Juvenis |
| Keck.Syst. | Bartholomaeus Keckermann. System of Sacred Theology. Cologne, 1611 |
| Krom.Trad. | Hieronymus Kromayer. On Traditions. Leipzig, 1665 |
| Lact.Inst. | Lactantius. Divine Institutes |
| Lain. | Diego Laínez [James Laynez] |
| Disp.Trid. | Tridentine Disputations |
| Las. | Jan Łaski [Johannes a Lasco] |
| Coen. | Epistle on the Lord's Supper [Epistola de coena] |
| Hos. | Response to Cardinal Stanislaus Hosius |
| Inc. | On the Incarnation, against Menno |
| Sacr. | Brief Tract on the Sacraments of the Church of Christ |
| Sum.cont. | Summary of the Controversies over the Lord's Supper |
| West. | Response to Westphal |
| Lat. | Bartholomaeus Latomus [Steinmetz] |
| Def.Buc. | Defense against Martin Bucer |
| Resp.Buc. | Response to Martin Bucer |
| Latom. | Jacobus Latomus [Jacques Masson] |
| Conf.secr. | On Secret Confession |
| Ling. | Dialogue on the Reason for Three Languages and Theological Study |

| | |
|---|---|
| Laur.Reich. | Laurentius [Vavřinec] of Reichenbach |
| Diurn. | *Diary on the Deeds of the Bohemians at the Council of Basel* [*Liber diurnus de gestis Bohemorum in concilio Basiliensi*] |
| Lec. | Sebastiano Leccavella de Chio |
| Leo.M.*Ep.* | Pope Leo the Great [Leo Magnus]. *Epistles* |
| Leo X. | Pope Leo X |
| Cum post. | *Cum postquam* |
| Ex.Dom. | *Exsurge Domine* |
| Leon. | Vincentius de Leone |
| Leys.*Exor.* | Polycarp Leyser. *A Christian Consideration of Exorcism at Baptism.* N.p., 1591 |
| Lib.Conc. | *Book of Concord* [*Liber Concordiae*] |
| Lib.Ratis. | *Regensburg Book* [*Liber Ratisbonensis*] |
| Lip. | Luigi Lippomani |
| Lomb. | Hieronymus Lombardellus |
| Ltmr. | Hugh Latimer |
| Lud.Pal.*Resp.* | Louis Count Palatinate. *Responses to Emperor Sigismund and Pope Gregory XII* |
| Lun. | Vincentius Lunellus |
| Luth. | Martin Luther |
| Ab.Chr. | *Confession concerning Christ's Supper* [*Vom Abendmahl Christi, Bekenntnis*] |
| Alb.Pr. | *Open Letter to Prince Albert of Prussia* |
| Ambr.Cath. | *Response to the Book of Master Ambrosius Catharinus* |
| Anb. | *The Adoration of the Sacrament* [*Vom Anbeten des Sakraments*] |
| Antinom. | *Against the Antinomians* |
| Bisch. | *Example of How to Consecrate a True Christian Bishop* |
| Br.Wink. | *A Letter concerning His Book on Private Masses* [*Ein Brief D. M. Luthers von seinem Buch der Winkelmessen*] |
| Capt.Bab. | *The Babylonian Captivity of the Church* |
| Dav. | *The Last Words of David* |
| DB | *German Bible* [*Deutsche Bibel*] |
| Dec.praec. | *The Ten Commandments Preached to the People of Wittenberg* [*Decem praecepta Wittenbergensi praedicata populo*] |
| Def.Ec.jud. | *Defense against the Wicked Judgment of Johann Eck* |
| Decl.Gen. | *Sermons on Genesis* [*In Genesin Declamationes*] |
| Dict.Ps. | *Lectures on the Psalter* [*Dictata super Psalterium*] |
| Disp.Heid. | *Heidelberg Disputation* |
| Disp.indulg. | *Ninety-Five Theses* [*Disputatio pro declaratione virtutis indulgentiarum*] |
| Disp.just. | *Disputation on Justification* |
| Disp.schol.theol. | *Disputation against Scholastic Theology* |
| Dol. | *On Translating and on the Intercession of the Saints* [*Von Dolmetschen und Fürbitte der Heiligen*] |
| Dtsch.Kat. | *Large Catechism* [*Deutscher Katechismus*] |
| Dup.just. | *Two Kinds of Righteousness* [*De duplici justitia*] |
| Ehsach. | *On Marital Matters* [*Von Ehesachen*] |
| Eis. | *Against Johann Agricola* [*Wider den Eisleben*] |
| Ep.Joh. | *Lectures on the First Epistle of John* |
| Ev.Joh.1–2 | *Sermons on the Gospel of John 1–2* |
| Ev.Joh.6–8 | *Sermons on the Gospel of John 6–8* |
| Ev.Joh.14–15 | *Sermons on the Gospel of John 14–15* |
| Feg. | *Disavowal of Purgatory* [*Widerruf vom Fegfeuer*] |

| | |
|---|---|
| *Gal.* (1519) | *Commentary on Galatians* (1519) |
| *Gal.*(1535) | *Commentary on Galatians* (1535) |
| *Gen.* | *Lectures on Genesis* |
| *Grnd.Urs.* | *Defense and Explanation of All the Articles* [*Grund und Ursach aller Artikel*] |
| *Gut.Werk.* | *Treatise on Good Works* [*Sermon von den guten Werken*] |
| *Henr.* | *Against King Henry VIII of England* |
| *Himm.Proph.* | *Against the Heavenly Prophets* [*Wider die himmlischen Propheten*] |
| *Hspost.* | *House Postil* |
| *Inst.min.* | *Concerning the Ministry* [*De instituendis ministris ecclesiae*] |
| *Jak.* | *Sermon on Saint James* |
| *Jes.* | *Lectures on Isaiah* |
| *Jud.* | *That Jesus Christ Was Born a Jew* |
| *Kirchpost.* | *Church Postil* |
| *Kl.Kat.* | *Small Catechism* [*Kleiner Katechismus*] |
| *Konz.* | *On the Councils and the Church* |
| *Latom.* | *Against Latomus* |
| *Ld.* | *Hymns* [*Lieder*] |
| *Magn.* | *Commentary on the Magnificat* |
| *Matt.5–7* | *Commentary on the Sermon on the Mount* [*Das 5., 6. und 7. Kapitel Matthaei gepredigt und ausgelegt*] |
| *Menschlehr.* | *That Doctrines of Men Are to Be Rejected* [*Von Menschenlehre zu meiden*] |
| *Oper.Ps.* | *Commentary on the Psalms* [*Operationes in Psalmos*] |
| *1 Pet.* | *Commentary on 1 Peter* |
| *Pr.Brent.Amos* | *Preface to Johann Brenz "Exposition of Amos"* |
| *Pr.op.lat.* | *Preface to His Latin Works* |
| *Pred.* | *Sermons* [*Predigten*] |
| *Pred.2 Mos.* | *Sermons on Exodus* |
| *Ps 51* | *Commentary on Psalm 51* |
| *Ps.90* | *Commentary on Psalm 90* |
| *Ps.147* | *Commentary on Psalm 147* |
| *Ps.grad.* | *Commentaries on the Fifteen Psalms of Degrees* [*In quindecim psalmos graduum commentarii*] |
| *Res.disp.indulg.* | *Resolutions of the Disputation concerning the Value of Indulgences* |
| *Res.Lips.* | *Resolutions of His Propositions at the Leipzig Disputation* |
| *Res.pot.pap.* | *Resolution concerning the Power of the Pope* |
| *Rom.* | *Scholia on the Epistle to the Romans* |
| *Schmal.Art.* | *Smalcald Articles* |
| *Serm.poen.* | *Sermon on Penance* |
| *Serm.sacr.* | *Sermon on the Sacrament* |
| *Serv.arb.* | *The Bondage of the Will* [*De servo arbitrio*] |
| *Stras.* | *Letter to the Christians at Strasbourg* |
| *Sup.ann.* | *Computation of the Years of the World* [*Supputatio annorum mundi*] |
| *Symb.* | *The Three Symbols or Creeds* |
| *Thes.Antinom.* | *Theses against the Antinomians* |
| *Ti.* | *Table Talk* [*Tischreden*] |
| *Vor.N.T.* | *Prefaces to the New Testament* [*Vorreden zum Neuen Testament*] |
| *Wied.* | *On Rebaptism* [*Von der Wiedertaufe*] |
| *Worm.* | *Diet of Worms* |
| *Wort.* | *That These Words of Christ, "This Is My Body," Still Stand Firm against the Fanatics* |

| | |
|---|---|
| Zn.Geb. | Exposition of the Ten Commandments [Auslegung der zehn Gebote] |
| Lymp. | Balthasar Lympus |
| Madr. | Cristoforo Madruzzo |
| Marb.Art. | Marburg Articles |
| Mars.Pad. | Marsilius of Padua |
| Def.min. | Defensor minor |
| Def.pac. | Defender of the Peace [Defensor pacis] |
| Mart. | Braccio Martelli |
| Martn.Sum.op. | Matthias Martinius. Summa of Works [Summa operum, seu Commentarius in legem duarum divinarum tabularum]. Bremen, 1612 |
| Mass.Diar. | Angelo Massarelli. Diaries |
| Matt.Crac. | Matthew of Cracow |
| Squal. | On the Squalors of the Roman Curia |
| Matt.Mayn. | Matteus Maynage [Matthaeus Meynage] |
| Avis. | Advisory Recommendation |
| Maz. | Lorenzo Mazochi |
| Mel. | Philip Melanchthon |
| An. | On the Soul [De anima] |
| Annot.Rom. | Annotations on Romans |
| Cat.puer. | Children's Catechism [Catechesis puerilis] |
| Coen. | Opinions of Several Ancient Writers concerning the Lord's Supper [Sententiae veterum aliquot scriptorum de coena Domini] |
| Comm.Rom. | Commentary on Romans |
| Disp.part.poen. | Disputation on the Parts of Penance |
| Doct.Paul. | On the Study of the Doctrine of Paul |
| Ep. | Epistles |
| Ev.Joh. | Exposition of the Gospel of John |
| Eccl. | On the Church and the Authority of the Word of God |
| Enarr.Rom. | Exposition of Romans [Enarratio epistolae Pauli ad Romanos] |
| Enarr.Symb.Nic. | Exposition of the Nicene Creed [Enarratio Symboli Niceni] |
| Explic.Symb.Nic. | Explanation of the Nicene Creed [Explicatio Symboli Niceni] |
| Loc. | Loci |
| Post. | Postil |
| Pot.pap. | Treatise on the Power and Primacy of the Pope |
| Ref.abus.coen. | Refutation of the Abuses of the Lord's Supper [Refutatio abusuum coenae Domini] |
| Thes.bacc. | Theses for the Baccalaureate |
| Torg.Art. | Torgau Articles |
| Men.Gerecht. | Justus Menius. Righteousness [Gerechtigkeit]. Erfurt, 1552 |
| Menn. | Menno Simons |
| Bek. | Confession [Bekentenisse] |
| Belyd. | On the Trinity [Een vermanende belydninge, van den drie-eenigen, eeuwigen, ende waren Gott] |
| Chr.gl. | On the True Christian Faith [Van het rechte Christen Geloove] |
| Doop. | Explanation of Christian Baptism [Verklaringe des christelycken Doopsels] |
| Excom. | Excommunication |
| Fund. | The Foundation of Christian Doctrine |
| Geest.Ver. | On the Spiritual Resurrection [Van die Geestelijke Verrijsenisse] |
| Gell.Fab. | Reply to Gellius Faber |
| Jan.Leyd. | Against John of Leiden |
| Las. | Confession against Jan Laski |

| | |
|---|---|
| Nw.Geb. | On the New Birth [*Van de Nieuwe Geboorte*] |
| Ont. | Apology and Reply [*Ontschuldinge ende verantwoordinge*] |
| Oors. | My Reason [*De Oorsake, waerom dat ich Menno Symons niet af en late te Leeren, ende to Schrijven*] |
| Ps.25. | Meditation on Psalm 25 |
| Sup. | Supplication |
| Verm. | Admonition [*Een lieflycke Vermaninge of Onderwysinge*] |
| Mentz. | Balthasar Mentzer |
| Thes.theol. | Theological Theses. Giessen, 1612 |
| Milt.Par.L. | John Milton. *Paradise Lost* |
| Mir. | Bartholomaeus de [Carranza] Miranda |
| Mol. | Louis Molina |
| Conc. | The Harmony of Free Will with the Gifts of Grace [*Liberi arbitrii cum gratiae donis . . . concordia*] |
| Grat. | Treatise on Grace |
| Praed. | On Predestination |
| Sum.haer.maj. | Larger Summary of Heresies [*Summa haeresium major*] |
| Mont. | Giovanni Maria Ciocchi del Monte [Pope Julius III] |
| Mor. | Thomas More |
| Apol. | Apology |
| Bod. | Treatise on the Blessed Body |
| Comf. | Dialogue of Comfort against Tribulation |
| Her. | Dialogue concerning Heresies |
| Luth. | Response to Luther |
| Pass. | Treatise on the Passion |
| Trist. | On the Sadness of Christ [*De tristitia Christi*] |
| Tyn. | Confutation of Tyndale's Answer |
| Morl. | Joachim Mörlin |
| Leg. | The Third Use of the Law [*Disputationes tres pro tertio usu legis*] |
| Obed. | The Proposition that Perfect Obedience of the Law Is Necessary for Salvation |
| Resp.Pont. | Response to Pontanus |
| Mrl. | Joannes Morellus [Massarello] |
| Pecc.orig | On Original Sin [*De peccato originali*] |
| Mrtr. | Coriolanus Martiranus Consentinus |
| Mus.Utraq. | Johann Musaeus. On Communion under Both Kinds [*De communione sub utraque specie*]. Jena, 1654 |
| Muss. | Cornelio Musso |
| Myl. | Georgius Mylius |
| Naus. | Friedrich Nausea [Grau] |
| Cat.cath. | Catholic Catechism. Vienna, 1542 |
| Misc. | Miscellanies |
| Nav. | Andreas Navarra |
| Nicol.Bisk. | Nicholas Biskupec [Mikuláš Biskupec z Pelhřimova] |
| Nicol.Cl. | Nicholas of Clamanges [Clémanges] |
| Ruin.eccl. | On the Ruin and the Repair of the Church |
| Nicol.Cus. | Nicholas of Cusa [Nicolaus Cusanus] |
| Abscond. | On the Hidden God [*De deo abscondito*] |
| Alchor. | The Sifting of the Koran [*Cribratio Alchoran*] |
| Apol. | Apologia for Learned Ignorance |
| Conc.cath. | Catholic Concordance |
| Dat.patr.lum. | On the Gift of the Father of Lights [*De dato patris luminum*] |
| Doct.ign. | On Learned Ignorance [*De docta ignorantia*] |

| | |
|---|---|
| *Ep.* | *Epistles* |
| *Ep.Joh.Seg.* | *Epistle to John of Segovia* |
| *Fil.* | *On the Filiation of the Son* |
| *Gen.* | *On Genesis* |
| *Pac.fid.* | *Reconciliation between the World Religions [De pace fidei]* |
| *Poss.* | *On Possibility and Being in God [De possest]* |
| *Quaer.* | *On Searching for God [De quaerendo deum]* |
| *Sap.* | *On Wisdom [Idiota de sapientia]* |
| *Serm.* | *Sermons* |
| *Ult.* | *Conjecture about the Last Days [Conjectura de ultimis diebus]* |
| *Vis.* | *On the Vision of God* |
| Nicol.Dr. | Nicholas of Dresden [Mikuláš Drážďanský] |
| *Utraq.* | *Apologia for the Communion of the Laity under Both Kinds [Apologia pro communione plebis sub utraque specie]* |
| Nun.*Conc.* | Diego Nuño. *Judgment of Molina. "Harmony" [Censura de la Concordia de Molina]* |
| Ob.Phil.*Bek.* | Obbe Philipsz. *Confession [Bekentenisse]* |
| Oec. | Johannes Oecolampadius |
| *Antisyn.* | *Reply to the "Syngramma" of the Swabian Clergy [Antisyngramma]. Zurich, 1526* |
| *Bill.Ant.* | *Reply to Luther's Foreword to the "Syngramma" [Billiche Antwurt . . . uff D. M. Luthers Bericht des Sakraments]. Basel, 1526* |
| *Conf.* | *That Confession Is Not Onerous to Christians. Basel, 1521* |
| *Corp.* | *The Genuine Exposition of the Words of the Lord, "This Is My Body" [De Genuina verborum Domini, "Hoc est corpus meum" . . . Expositio]. Basel, 1525* |
| *Dial.* | *Dialogue Showing What the Ancient Doctors of the Church, both Greek and Latin, Thought about the Eucharist. Heidelberg, 1572 [1530]* |
| *Dign.euch.* | *On the Dignity of the Eucharist. Zurich, 1526* |
| *Ev.Joh.* | *Annotations on the Gospel of John. Basel, 1533* |
| *Luth.* | *Judgment about Doctor Martin Luther. N.p., 1521* |
| *Mis.* | *That Dr. M. Luther's Misunderstanding of the Eternally Valid Words, "This Is My Body," Cannot Stand. Basel, 1527* |
| *Resp.post.* | *Second Response to Willibald Pirckheimer [De eucharistia . . . responsio posterior]. Basel, 1527* |
| *Rom.* | *Annotations on Romans. Basel, 1526* |
| *Theob.Bill.* | *Reply to Dieboldt Billican. Zurich, 1526* |
| Oliv. | Peter John Olivi |
| *Infall.* | *Question on the Infallibility of the Roman Pontiff* |
| *Post.Joh.* | *Postil on the Gospel of John* |
| *Ren.pap.* | *On the Renunciation of the Pope* |
| Opic.Can. | Opicinus de Canistris |
| *Spir.imp.* | *On the Preeminence of the Spiritual Imperium* |
| Ord.Zür. | *Christian Order of Service at Zurich* |
| Osndr. | Andreas Osiander |
| *Apol.* | *Apologia. N.p., 1545* |
| *Conject.* | *Conjecture about the Last Times. Nuremberg, 1544* |
| *Hild.* | *The Prophecy of Saint Hildegard about the Papists. N.p., 1527* |
| *Mar.* | *Report on the Marburg Colloquy. [Augsburg], 1529* |
| *Schatz.* | *Against Caspar Schatzgeyer. Nuremberg, 1525* |

| | |
|---|---|
| Ott. | Luciano degli Ottoni |
| Pach. | Pedro Pacheco |
| *Paen.Med.* | *Milanese Penitential [Paenitentiale Mediolanense]* |
| Pasc. | Blaise Pascal |
| *Aug.* | *Opinions of Saint Augustine, the Pelagians, and Calvin about the Problem of Grace* |
| *Pens.* | *Pensées* |
| *Poss.com.* | *On the Possibility of the Commandments* |
| *Prob.gr.* | *Summary Exposition of the Problem of Grace* |
| *Prov.* | *Provincial Letters* |
| Pasch. | Angelus Paschalis Illyricus |
| Patav.*Just.* | Christophorus Patavinus. *On Justification* |
| Paul.III. | Pope Paul III |
| *Init.* | *Initio nostri hujus Pontificatus* |
| Paul.IV. | Pope Paul IV [Johannes Petrus Carafa] |
| *Luth.haer.* | *On Repressing the Heresy of the Lutherans and Reforming the Church* |
| Paul.V.*Form.* | Pope Paul V. *Formula for Ending the Disputes about the Aids to Grace* |
| Pch. | Andrew Poach |
| *Def.* | *Defense* |
| *Ep.* | *Epistles* |
| *Resp.* | *Reply [to Mörlin]* |
| Per.*Trad.* | Martin Pérez de Ayala. *On Divine, Apostolic, and Ecclesiastical Traditions*. Cologne, 1562 |
| *Perf.am.* | *Treatise on Perfect Love [Tractatus de perfecto amore]* |
| Pet. | Petrarch |
| *Fam.* | *Letters to Intimates [Familiares]* |
| *Ign.* | *On His Own Ignorance and That of Many Others* |
| *Ot.rel.* | *On the Repose of the Religious [De otio religioso]* |
| *Secr.* | *My Secret* |
| *Sen.* | *Letters of Old Age [Seniles]* |
| Petr.Aur. | Peter Aureoli |
| *Comm.* | *Commentary on the Entire Bible [Aurea ac pene divina totius sacre pagine commentaria]*. Venice, 1507 |
| *Reper.* | *Reply to the Adversary of the Innocence of the Mother of God [Repercussorium editum contra adversarium innocentiae Matris Dei]* |
| *Sent.* | *Commentary on the Sentences* |
| *Tract.* | *Tractate on the Conception of the Blessed Virgin Mary* |
| Petr.Br. | Peter of Brussels |
| Petr.Brun. | Peter Bruneti |
| *Act.conc.Bas.* | *Acts of the Council of Basel* |
| Petr.Cand. | Petrus de Candia [Antipope Alexander V] |
| *Immac.* | *Treatise on the Immaculate Conception* |
| Petr.Cell. | Peter of Celle |
| *Ep.* | *Epistles* |
| Petr.Lut. | Petrus de Lutra [Kaiserlautern] |
| *Lig.frat.* | *An Alliance of Brethren [Liga fratrum]* |
| *Pont.emin.* | *On the Eminence of the Supreme Pontiff* |
| Petr.Pal. | Peter of La Palu [Paludanus] |
| *Pot.pap.* | *Treatise on the Power of the Pope* |

| | |
|---|---|
| Petr.Verb. | Petrus de Verberia |
| Brd. | Declaration of the Belief of Saint Bernard concerning the Conception of the Virgin Mary [1338]. Mainz [1490] |
| Pez.Lib.arb. | Christoph Pezel. On Free Will [De libero arbitrio] |
| Pg. | Albert Pighi |
| Cont. | Explanation of the Controversies by which the Faith and Religion of Christ Are Now Being Disturbed. 2 vols. Venice, 1541 |
| Mosc. | On Moscow, to Pope Clement VII. Venice, 1543 |
| Pgn. | Sebastiano Pighino |
| Pi.V.Ex om. | Pope Pius V. Ex omnibus afflictionibus |
| Pinar. | Antonius Frexius Pinaroliensis |
| Pisc. | Johannes Piscator [Fischer] |
| Grat. | Treatise on the Grace of God. Herborn, 1614 |
| Praed. | Theological Disputation on Predestination. 2d ed. Herborn, 1598 |
| Pol. | Reginald Pole |
| Conc. | On the Council. Rome, 1562 |
| Disc.pac. | Discourse on Peace [Discorso di pace]. [Rome, 1555] |
| Ep. | Epistles |
| Henr.VIII. | To Henry VIII. Rome, 1536 |
| Just. | A Treatise of Justification. Louvain, 1569 |
| Sum.pont. | On the Supreme Pontiff. Louvain, 1569 |
| Test. | A Truly Christian Testament. [N.p.], 1559 |
| Polan. | Amandus Polanus of Polansdorf |
| Syntag. | System of Christian Theology [Syntagma theologiae Christianae]. Geneva, 1617 |
| Prael.Germ.Ep. | Prelates of Germany. Epistles |
| Přib.Tract. | Joannes de Příbram. Tractate on the Eucharist against Nicholas the False Bishop of the Taborites |
| Prof.fid.Franc. | Profession of the Catholic Faith in the Church of Exiles at Frankfurt |
| Prosp.Auct. | Prosper of Aquitaine. Official Pronouncements of the Apostolic See on Divine Grace and Free Will [Praeteritorum episcoporum sedis apostolicae auctoritates de gratia dei et libero voluntatis arbitrio] |
| Ptol.Luc. | Bartholomew of Lucca [Ptolemaeus de Lucca] |
| Ann. | Annals |
| Det.comp. | Compendious Determination concerning the Jurisdiction of the Empire |
| Quen.Theol. | Johann Andreas Quenstedt. Didactico-Polemical Theology. 2 vols. Leipzig, 1715 |
| Ramb.Bol. | Rambert of Bologna |
| Apol.ver. | Apologia for the Truth against the "Corruptorium" [Apologeticum veritatis contra corruptorium] |
| Rav. | Ottaviano Raverta |
| Rdly. | Nicholas Ridley |
| Br.decl. | A Brief Declaration of the Lord's Supper |
| Conf.Ltmr. | Conferences with Hugh Latimer |
| Ep. | Epistles |
| Imag. | A Treatise on the Worship of Images |
| Lam. | A Piteous Lamentation of the Miserable Estate of the Church in England |
| Rej.Post. | Mikołaj Rej. Postil |
| Remon. | Remonstrance |
| Rep.Anh. | The Repetition of Anhalt |

| | |
|---|---|
| Resp.Lib.Ratis. | Responses to the *"Regensburg Book"* [*Responsiones ad Librum Ratisbonensem*] |
| Rich.S.Laur. | Richard of Saint Lawrence |
| Laud.Mar. | *In Laud of the Blessed Virgin Mary* |
| Robt.Bas. | Robert of Basevorn |
| Form.praedic. | *The Form of Preaching* [*Forma praedicandi*] |
| Robt.Orf. | Robert of Orford [de Colletorto] |
| Corr. | *Correctorium* |
| Repr.Aeg. | *Reproof of Giles of Rome* |
| Rog. | Thomas Rogers |
| Cath.Doct. | *The Catholic Doctrine of the Church of England* |
| Roll. | Robert Rollock |
| Voc.eff. | *Treatise on Effective Vocation*. Edinburgh, 1597 |
| Rov. | Philos Roverella of Ferrara |
| Rup.Matt. | Rupert of Deutz. *Commentary on Matthew* |
| Sad. | Jacopo Sadoleto |
| Genev. | *To the Genevans* |
| Orat. | *Oration* |
| Sal. | Juan de Salazar |
| Salm. | Alfonso Salmerón |
| Sanfel. | Tommaso Sanfelice |
| Sarac. | Giovanni Michele Saraceni |
| Sarr. | Petrus Sarra |
| Schatz. | Kaspar Schatzgeyer |
| Scrut. | *Scrutiny of the Divine Scripture* |
| Seg. | John of Segovia |
| Diff. | *Difficulties Raised by the Ambassadors of the Sacred Council of Basel* |
| Diff.pot. | *On the Difference of Powers* |
| Eccl. | *On the Insuperable Holiness of the Church* [*De insuperabili sanctitate ecclesiae*] |
| Gabr. | *Justification of the Sentence Pronounced against Gabriele* [*Condulmaro*], *Formerly Pope Eugenius IV* |
| Gl.Eug. | *Gloss on the Bull of the Former Pope Eugenius* |
| Hist.Conc.Bas. | *History of the Events of the General Council of Basel* |
| Mat.haer. | *On the Matter of Heresy* |
| Mod. | *The Mode and Form by which the Council Allowed the Ambassadors of the Pope to Preside* |
| Narr.conf. | *Narrative of the Conflict between the Council of Basel and Pope Eugenius IV* |
| Neutr. | *On the Matter of the Neutrality of Princes* |
| Prop.sec. | *Second Proposition* |
| Regn. | *On the New Kingdom, which is the Church* [*De novo regno, quod est ecclesia*] |
| Sept.not. | *Seven Notable Facts concerning the Matter of Heresy* |
| Sim. | *On Simony* |
| Utraq. | *Proofs that Communion of the Laity under Both Kinds Is Not Necessary by Divine Command* [*Allegationes, quod communio sub utraque specie non est de necessitate divine praecepti quantum ad plebem*] |
| Sent.Remon. | *Statement of the Remonstrants* [*Sententia Remonstrantium*] |
| Serip. | Girolamo Seripando |
| Concup. | *On Concupiscence* |

| | |
|---|---|
| *Decr.just.form.alt.* | *Second Form of His Draft Decree on Justification* [*Decreti de justificatione forma altera per eundem*] |
| *Decr.just.form.prim.* | *First Form of His Draft Decree on Justification* [*Decreti de justificatione forma prima per F. Hieronymum Seripandum*] |
| *Just.* | *On Justification* |
| *Libr.Scrip.* | *On the Books of Holy Scripture* [*De libris sacrae scripturae*] |
| *Pecc.orig.* | *On Original sin* [*De peccato originali*] |
| *Sacr.* | *On the Sacraments* |
| *Trad.* | *On Traditions* |
| *Serm.conc.Const.* | *Sermons Delivered during the Council of Constance* |
| Serv. | Michael Servetus |
| *Dial.* | *Two Dialogues on the Trinity* |
| *Ep.Calv.* | *Epistles to Calvin* |
| *Fid.just.* | *On Faith and the Righteousness of the Kingdom of Christ* [*De fide et justitia regni Christi*] |
| *Trin.* | *On the Trinity* |
| *Trin.err.* | *On the Errors of the Trinity* |
| *Sevrl.Comm.* | Ercole Severoli. *Diary at the Council of Trent* [*De concilio Tridentino commentarius*] |
| *Sib.Art.* | *Schleitheim Confession* [*Brüderliche vereynigung etzlicher kinder Gottes siben Artickel betreffend*] |
| Sib.Bek. | Siebert de Beka |
| *Repr.err.* | *Reproval of Six Errors* [of Marsilius of Padua] |
| *Sig.Ep.* | Emperor Sigismund. *Epistles* |
| Sixt.IV. | Pope Sixtus IV |
| *Cum praeex.* | *Cum praeexcelsa* |
| *Grav.* | *Grave nimis* |
| *Snds.Serm.* | Edwin Sandys. *Sermons* |
| Soc. | Faustus Socinus [Fausto Sozzini] |
| *Auct.Scrip.* | *On the Authority of Holy Scripture* |
| *Cat.* | *Catechism* |
| *Cat.fr.* | *Fragments of the Catechism* |
| *Conc.Chr.* | *Commentary on the Sermon on the Mount* [*Concionis Christi quae habetur capite 5., 6., et 7. apud Matthaeum Evangelistam, Explicatio*] |
| *Ep.Joh.* | *Commentary on the First Epistle of John* |
| *Prol.Ev.Joh.* | *Explanation of the Prologue of the Gospel of John* |
| *Resp.Dav.* | *Response to Francis Dávid* |
| *Rom.7.* | *On a Passage in the Seventh Chapter of the Epistle of Paul the Apostle to the Romans* |
| *Serv.* | *Jesus Christ the Savior* [*De Jesu Christo Servatore*] |
| *Var.loc.* | *Explanation of Various Passages of Holy Scripture* [*Explicatio variorum Sacrae Scripturae locorum*] |
| Sol. | Antonius Solisius |
| *Speng.Ld.* | Lazarus Spengler. *Hymns* [*Lieder*] |
| Staph. | Joannes Lucius Staphyleus |
| Stapl. | Thomas Stapleton |
| *Ant.ev.* | *Evangelical Antidote against the Heresies of These Times.* Lyons, 1595 |
| *Apol.* | *Apologia for the Catholic King Philip II of Spain.* Constance, 1592 |
| *Count.* | *A Counterblast to M. Hornes Blaste against M. Feckenham* |
| *Fort.* | *A Fortresse of the Faith First Planted Among Us Englishmen* |

| | |
|---|---|
| Pr.Bed. | Preface to "The History of the Church of Englande" Compiled by Venerable Bede, Englishman. Antwerp, 1565 |
| Ret. | A Returne of Untruthes upon M. Jewelles Replie |
| Tr.Thom. | Three Thomases. Douai, 1588 |
| Steph.Sest. | Stephanus a Sestino |
| Stl. | Tommaso Stella |
| Stoeck.Ep. | Ulrich Stöcklin. Epistles |
| Strig. | Victorinus Strigel |
| Decl. | Declaration |
| Hum.vir. | The Doctrine of Human Powers or Free Will [Locus de humanis viribus seu libero arbitrio] |
| Suar. | Francisco de Suárez |
| Div.sub. | On the Divine Substance |
| Grat. | On Grace |
| Praed. | On Divine Predestination and Reprobation |
| Sacr. | On the Sacraments |
| Succ.Anabap. | Anabaptist Succession |
| Syn.Bern. | Doctrinal Articles of the Synod of Bern |
| Syn.Dord. | Synod of Dort [Dordrecht] |
| Can. | Canons |
| Rej.err. | Rejection of Errors |
| Sess. | Sessions |
| Tab. | Nicolaus Trecensis Gallus Taborel |
| Tap.Orat. | Ruard Tapper. Orations |
| Tel. | Telephorus of Cosenza |
| Pr.schism. | On the Causes, State, Knowledge, and End of the Present Schism |
| Vet.Nov. | The State of the Church in the Old and New Testaments [Qualiter fuit status Ecclesiae in Veteri et Novo Testamento] |
| Tert.Marc. | Tertullian. Against Marcion |
| Thdrc.Nm. | Dietrich of Nieheim [Theodericus de Nyem] |
| Avis. | Advisory Recommendations on the Union and Reform of Members and Head |
| Conc. | The Council |
| Convoc. | On Convoking General Councils |
| Int.pac. | Introduction to Peace and Union |
| Invect. | Invective against Pope John XXIII |
| Mod. | On the Modes of Uniting and Reforming the Church in a Universal Council |
| Nem.un. | The Grove of Union [Nemus unionis] |
| Not. | Notification to Each and All |
| Schism. | On the Schism |
| Thes.Bern. | Bern Theses |
| Thes.Laus. | Lausanne Theses |
| Thos.Aq. | Thomas Aquinas |
| S.T. | Summa Theologica |
| Sent. | Commentary on the Sentences |
| Thos.Cel. | Thomas of Celano |
| Vit.prim. | First Life [of Francis of Assisi] [Vita prima] |
| Thos.Kemp. | Thomas à Kempis |
| Cant. | Songs [Cantica] |
| Disc.cl. | On the Discipline of the Cloistered |
| Doct.juv. | A Book of Doctrine for Juveniles |
| Epit.mon. | Epitaph for Monks |

| | |
|---|---|
| *Fid.disp.* | *On a Faithful Dispenser* |
| *Im.Chr.* | *The Imitation of Christ* |
| *Inc.* | *Meditation on the Incarnation of Christ* |
| *Mort.vit.* | *On Life Mortified for Christ* [*De mortificata vita pro Christo*] |
| *Orat.* | *Prayers* [*Orationes*] |
| *Rec.frag.* | *On the Recognition of One's Own Fragility* |
| *Serm.Dom.* | *Sermons on the Life and Passion of the Lord* [*Sermones de vita et passione Domini*] |
| *Serm.frat.* | *Sermons to the Brethren* [*Sermones ad fratres*] |
| *Serm.nov.* | *Sermons to Novices* |
| *Soliloq.* | *Soliloquy* |
| *Spir.ex.* | *Book of Spiritual Exercise* |
| *Tr.tabern.* | *On Poverty, Humility, and Patience: On the Three Tabernacles* |
| *Vall.lil.* | *The Valley of the Lilies* |
| *Vit.Chr.* | *Prayers and Meditations on the Life of Christ* [*Orationes et meditationes de vita Christi*] |
| Thos.Sut. | Thomas of Sutton |
| *Quodlib.* | *Quodlibeta* |
| Thos.Wal. | Thomas Waleys |
| *Comp.serm.* | *On the Way to Compose Sermons* |
| Tit. | Gerhard Titius |
| *Calx.* | *Funeral Sermon for Georg Calixtus.* Helmstedt, 1656 |
| *Eccl.* | *On the Church* |
| Tok. | Heinrich Toke |
| *Eccl.* | *On the Church* |
| *Neutr.* | *On the Preservation of Neutrality* |
| Toss.*Praed.* | Daniel Toussain [Tossanus]. *The Doctrine of Predestination.* Hanover, 1609 |
| Trel. | Lucas Trelcatius |
| *Schol.inst.* | *Scholastic Institutes of Sacred Theology.* Oxford, 1606 |
| Trith. | Johannes Trithemius |
| *Scrip.eccl.* | *On Ecclesiastical Writers* [*De scriptoribus ecclesiasticis*]. Paris, 1512 |
| Trtn.*Inst.* | Francis Turrettini. *Institutes.* 2d ed. 3 vols. Geneva, 1688–89 |
| Turr. | Juan de Torquemada [Johannes de Turrecremata] |
| *Auct.* | *On the Authority of the Supreme Pontiff and of the General Council* |
| *Aug.Rom.* | *Reply to Augustine of Rome* |
| *Or.primat.* | *Oration on the Primacy* |
| *Vot.avis.* | *Evaluation of the Advisory Recommendation* [*Votum super avisamento*] |
| Ub.Cas. | Ubertino of Casale |
| *Arb.vit.* | *The Tree of the Crucified Life of Jesus* [*Arbor vitae crucifixae Jesu*] |
| *Declar.* | *Declaration* |
| *Decr.* | *Decretal* |
| *Rot.* | *Little Wheel* [*Rotulus iste*] |
| *Sanct.ap.* | *Apostolic Holiness* [*Sanctitas apostolica*] |
| *Sanct.vest.* | *Your Holiness* [*Sanctitas vestra*] |
| *Tr.scel.* | *On the Three Crimes of Damascus* [*Super tribus sceleribus Damasci*] |
| Univ.Par. | University of Paris |
| *Avis.conc.* | *Advisory Recommendations for a General Council* |
| *Ep.* | *Epistles* |
| Urs. | Zacharias Ursinus |

| | |
|---|---|
| Admon. | Admonition |
| Apol.Cat. | Apologia for the Heidelberg Catechism |
| Aug.Conf. | The Doctrine of the Augsburg Confession and the Apology |
| Ex.ver.doct. | Exegesis of the True Doctrine of the Supper of Our Lord Jesus Christ [Exegesis verae doctrinae de sacra Domini nostri Jesu Christi coena] |
| Expl.Cat. | Explanations of the Heidelberg Catechism |
| Fract.pan. | On the Rite of Breaking Bread in the Holy Supper [De ritu fractionis panis in S. Coena] |
| Loc.theol. | Theological Loci |
| Vall. | Lorenzo Valla |
| Annot. | Annotations on the New Testament |
| Don.Const. | On the Donation of Constantine |
| Enc.Thos.Aq. | Encomium of Thomas Aquinas |
| Euch. | Sermon on the Mystery of the Eucharist |
| Lib.arb. | On the Freedom of the Will [De libero arbitrio] |
| Prof.rel. | On the Profession of the Religious |
| Volup. | On Desire, and on True Good [De voluptate, ac de vero bono] |
| Vauch. | Robert Vauchop |
| Veg. | Andreas de Vega |
| Form.decr.just. | Formula for the Decree on Justification |
| Opusc.just. | Opusculum on Justification, Grace, and Merits. Venice, 1546 |
| Trid. | Exposition and Defense of the Tridentine Decree on Justification. Venice, 1548 |
| Vig. | Marco Vigerio della Rovere |
| Vinc.Ler. | Vincent of Lérins |
| Comm. | Commonitory |
| Visdom. | Franciscus Visdominus [Vicedominus] |
| Vit.Furn. | Vital du Four [Vitalis de Furno] |
| An. | On the Soul and Its Powers [De anima et ejus potentiis] |
| Quodlib. | Quodlibeta |
| Rer.princ. | On the First Principle of Things [De rerum principio] |
| Vos. | Melchior Vosmedianus [Bosmedianus] |
| Walp.Art. | Peter Walpot. The Book of Articles |
| West. | Joachim Westphal |
| West.Conf. | Westminster Confession of Faith |
| Wic. | Georg Witzel [Wicelius] |
| Apol. | Apologia. Leipzig, 1535 |
| Aug. | Saint Augustine "On the Christian Life." Leipzig, 1539 |
| Cat.eccl. | The Catechism of the Church. Leipzig, 1535 |
| Cred. | In What Ways the Word "Believing" Is Used in Holy Writ [Quibus modis credendi verbum accipiatur in Sacris literis]. Leipzig, 1535 |
| Euch. | On the Holy Eucharist or Mass. Leipzig, 1534 |
| Hag. | Hagiology. Mainz, 1541 |
| Hom.orth. | Orthodox Homilies. Mainz, 1546 |
| Luth.art. | Answer to the [Smalcald] Articles of Martin Luther |
| Purg. | On the Question of the Fire of Purgatory. Cologne, 1545 |
| Pus. | On Penance, Confession, and Excommunication [Von der Pusse, Beicht und Bann]. Leipzig, 1534 |
| Ret.Luth. | Exposure of Lutheranism [Retectio Lutherismi]. Leipzig, 1538 |
| Wolf. | Johannes Wolfius |

| | |
|---|---|
| *Eut.Luth.* | Proof that the Charge of Eutychianism against the Lutherans Is a Specter. Wittenberg, 1680 |
| Wm.S.Th. | William of Saint-Thierry |
| *Ep.frat.* | Epistle to the Brethren [*Epistola ad fratres de Monte Dei*] |
| Wyc. | John Wycliffe |
| *Apost.* | On Apostasy |
| *Ben.inc.* | On the Blessed Incarnation [*De benedicta incarnacione*] |
| *Civ.dom.* | On Civil Dominion |
| *Comp.hom.* | On the Composition of Man [*De compositione hominis*] |
| *Dial.* | Dialogue |
| *Eccl.* | On the Church |
| *Euch.* | On the Eucharist |
| *Serm.* | Sermons |
| Zab. | Francesco Zabarella |
| *Ben.XIII.* | Report of the Commission on Pope Benedict XIII |
| *Schism.* | On the Schism of His Time |
| *Zür.Einleit.* | Zurich Introduction [*Züricher Einleitung*] |
| Zw. | Ulrich Zwingli |
| *Act.* | Action, or the Usage of the Lord's Supper |
| *Amic.exeg.* | Amicable Exegesis |
| *Apol.Arch.* | Apologia for the Beginning and the End [*Apologeticus Archeteles*] |
| *Art.LXVII.* | The Sixty-Seven Articles |
| *Bek.* | Reply to Luther's "Confession concerning Christ's Supper" |
| *Bgn.* | Reply to an Epistle of Johann Bugenhagen |
| *Can.miss.* | On the Canon of the Mass |
| *Ec.* | Replies to Johann Eck |
| *Ems.* | Reply to Hieronymus Emser |
| *Fid.rat.* | Statement of Faith [*Fidei ratio*] |
| *Gen.* | Annotations on Genesis |
| *Ger.* | On Divine and Human Righteousness [*Von göttlicher und menschlicher Gerechtigkeit*] |
| *Hub.* | Reply to Balthasar Hubmaier's "Book on Baptism" |
| *Klar.* | The Clarity and Certainty or Power of the Word of God |
| *Mar.* | A Sermon on Mary the Pure Mother of God |
| *Ord.* | Ordinance of the Christian Church in Zurich |
| *Pecc.orig.* | On Original Sin [*De peccato originali*] |
| *Prov.* | On the Providence of God |
| *Schl.* | Explanation and Proof of the Conclusions or Articles [*Uszlegen und gründ der schluszreden oder artickeln*] |
| *Speis.* | On Freedom in Matters of Food [*Von Erkiesen und Freiheit der Speisen*] |
| *Subsid.* | Support and Conclusion concerning the Eucharist [*Subsidium sive coronis de eucharistia*] |
| *Supplic.Hug.* | Supplication to Bishop Hugo of Constance |
| *Tf.* | On Baptism [*Von dem Touff*] |
| *Unt.* | A Clear Instruction about Christ's Supper [*Eine klare Unterrichtung vom Nachtmahl Christi*] |
| *Val.Comp.* | Reply to Valentin Compar |
| *Ver.fals.rel.* | Commentary on True and False Religion [*Commentarius de vera et false religione*] |
| *Vorschl.* | Proposal regarding Images and the Mass [*Vorschlag wegen der Bildern und der Messe*] |

Wort.      *That These Words, "This Is My Body" Will Always Have Their Ancient Meaning*

# Editions and Collections

| | |
|---|---|
| *Act.Remon.* | *Acta et scripta synodalia Dordracena ministrorum remonstrantium.* Harderwijk, 1620. |
| *Act.Syn.Dord.* | *Acta Synodi . . . Dordrechti habitae.* Dort, 1620 |
| *AFH* | *Archivum Franciscanum historicum.* 1909–. |
| Alberigo-Jedin | Alberigo, Giuseppe, and Jedin, Hubert, eds. *Conciliorum oecumenicorum decreta.* 2d ed. Basel, 1962. |
| *ALKGMA* | *Archiv für Literatur- und Kirchengeschichte des Mittelalters,* edited by Heinrich Denifle and Franz Ehrle. 7 vols. Berlin and Freiburg, 1885–1900. |
| Allen | Allen, Perry Stafford, ed. *Opus epistolarum Des. Erasmi Roterodami.* 12 vols. Oxford, 1906–58. |
| *AnalFranc* | *Analecta Franciscana.* Quaracchi and Florence, 1885–. |
| Argentré | Argentré, Charles Du Plessis d', ed. *Collectio iudiciorum de novis erroribus.* 3 vols. Paris, 1728. |
| Arquillière | Arquillière, Henri Xavier, ed. *Jacobus de Viterbo. De regimine christiano.* Paris, 1926. |
| Balić | Balić, Charles, ed. *J. Duns Scoti opera omnia.* Rome, 1950–. |
| Baronius | Baronius, Caesar. *Annales ecclesiastici.* 38 vols. Lucca, 1738–59. |
| Barth-Niesel | Barth, Peter, and Niesel, Wilhelm, eds. *Johannis Calvini opera selecta.* 5 vols. Munich, 1926–36. |
| *Bek.* | *Die Bekenntnisschriften der evangelisch-lutherischen Kirche.* 2d ed. Göttingen, 1952. |
| Beltrán | Beltrán de Heredia, Vincente, ed. *Domingo Báñez y las controversias sobre la gracia: Textos y documentos.* Madrid, 1968. |
| *BezTract* | *Theodori Bezae Vezelii . . . Tractationes theologicae.* 2d ed. 3 vols. in 1. Geneva, 1582. |
| *BFP* | *Bibliotheca Fratrum Polonorum quos Unitarios vocant.* 8 vols. Amsterdam, 1656–92. |
| *BFS* | *Bibliotheca Franciscana scholastica medii aevi.* Quaracchi, 1903–. |
| *Bibl.Mar.* | *Bibliotheca Mariana Medii Aevi.* Šibenik, 1931–. |
| *Bibl.Thom.* | *Bibliothèque Thomiste.* Le Saulchoir, 1921–. |
| Birch | Birch, T. Bruce, ed. *The "De Sacramento Altaris" of William of Ockham.* Burlington, Iowa, 1930. |
| Böhmer | Böhmer, Heinrich, ed. *Urkunden zur Geschichte des Bauernkrieges und der Wiedertäufer.* 2d ed. Berlin, 1933. |
| Borgnet | Borgnet, Auguste, ed. *B. Alberti Magni . . . Opera omnia.* 37 vols. Paris, 1890–99. |
| *BPIR* | *Bibliothek des königlichen preussischen historischen Instituts in Rom.* Tübingen and Rome, 1905–. |
| *BPP* | *Biblioteka pisarzów polskich.* Wrocław, 1962–. |
| Brampton | Brampton, C. Kenneth, ed. *The Defensor Minor of Marsilius of Padua.* Birmingham, 1922. |
| *BRN* | *Bibliotheca Reformatoria Neederlandica.* 10 vols. The Hague, 1903–14. |

| | |
|---|---|
| Bruni | Bruni, Gerardo, ed. *Incerti auctoris impugnationes contra Aegidium Romanum contradicentem Thomae super Primum Sententiarum.* Vatican City, 1942. |
| Brunschvicg | Brunschvicg, Léon C., ed. Blaise Pascal. *Oeuvres complètes.* 14 vols. Paris, 1904–14. |
| Bufano | Bufano, Antonietta, ed. *Opere Latine di Francesco Petrarca.* 2 vols. Turin, 1975. |
| CB | *Concilium Basiliense: Studien und Quellen zur Geschichte des Concils von Basel.* 8 vols. Basel, 1896–1936. |
| CCath | *Corpus Catholicorum.* Münster, 1919–. |
| CCSL | *Corpus christianorum. Series latina.* Turnhout, Belgium, 1953–. |
| Charland | Charland, Thomas M., ed. *Artes praedicandi: Contribution à l'histoire de la rhétorique au moyen âge.* Paris and Ottawa, 1936. |
| ChristRest | *Christianismi Restitutio.* Nuremberg, 1790. |
| Coll.Lac. | *Collectio Lacensis sive Acta et decreta sacrorum conciliorum recentiorum.* Rome, 1964. |
| Com. | *Comenium.* Prague, 1900–. |
| Combes | Combes, André, ed. *Ioannis Carlerii de Gerson "De mystica theologia."* Lugano, 1958. |
| Cotta | Cotta, Johann Friedrich, ed. Johann Gerhard. *Loci theologici.* 20 vols. Tübingen, 1762–89. |
| Coville | Coville, Alfred, ed. *Le traité de la ruine de l'église de Nicolas de Clamanges et la traduction française de 1564.* Paris, 1936. |
| CR | *Corpus Reformatorum.* Berlin and Leipzig, 1834–. |
| CSEL | *Corpus scriptorum ecclesiasticorum latinorum.* Vienna, 1866–. |
| CT | *Concilium Tridentinum: Diariorum, Actorum, Epistolarum, Tractatuum nova Collectio.* Freiburg, 1901–. |
| Davis | Davis, Charles T., ed. Ubertino de Casale. *Arbor vitae crucifixae Jesu.* Reprint ed. Turin, 1961. |
| Davy | Davy, Marie Madeleine, ed. *Guillelmi a Sancto Theodorico Epistola ad fratres de Monte Dei.* Paris, 1940. |
| de Groot | de Groot, Pieter, ed. *Hugonis Grotii Opera omnia theologica.* 3 vols. in 4. London, 1679. |
| Delorme | Delorme, Ferdinandus M., ed. Vitalis de Furno. *Quodlibeta tria.* Rome, 1947. |
| Denifle-Châtelain | Denifle, Heinrich, and Châtelain, Emile, eds. *Chartularium universitatis Parisiensis.* 4 vols. Paris, 1889–97. |
| Denzinger-Schönmetzer | Denzinger, Heinrich, and Schönmetzer, Adolf, eds. *Enchiridion symbolorum definitionum et declarationum de rebus fidei et morum.* 32d ed. Barcelona, 1963. |
| Döllinger | Döllinger, Johann Joseph Ignaz von, ed. *Quaestio domini Joannis Palomar . . . cui pariendum est.* In: *Beiträge zur politischen, kirchlichen und Cultur-Geschichte der sechs letzten Jahrhunderte,* 2:414–41. Regensburg, 1863. |
| Dotti | Dotti, Ugo, ed. *Epistole di Francesco Petrarca.* Turin, 1978. |
| DRTA | *Deutsche Reichstagsakten.* Munich, 1867–. |
| Du Pin | Du Pin, Louis-Ellies, ed. *Joannis Gersonii . . . opera omnia.* 5 vols. Antwerp, 1706. |
| Dykmans | Dykmans, Marc, ed. *Les sermons de Jean XXII sur la vision béatifique.* Rome, 1973. |
| Ed.Leon. | *S. Thomae Aquinatis opera omnia, iussu Leonis XIII edita.* Rome, 1882–. |

| | |
|---|---|
| Emmen | Emmen, Aquilinus, ed. *Petri de Candia, O.F.M. (Alexandri V Papae Pisani) Tractatus de immaculata Deiparae conceptione.* Quaracchi, 1955. |
| ERL | *English Recusant Literature, 1558–1640.* 394 vols. Menston, England, 1968–79. |
| Faber | Faber Stapulensis, Jacobus, ed. *Nicolai Cusae Cardinalis Opera.* 3 vols. Paris, 1514. Reprint ed. Frankfurt, 1962. |
| Fèvre | Fèvre, Justinus, ed. *Roberti Bellarmini . . . opera omnia.* 12 vols. Paris, 1870–74. |
| Finke | Finke, Heinrich, ed. *Acta Concilii constanciensis.* 4 vols. Münster, 1896–1928. |
| FIP | *Franciscan Institute Publications.* Saint Bonaventure, N.Y., 1951–. |
| OPh | *Guillelmi de Ockham Opera Philosophica.* |
| OTh | *Guillelmi de Ockham Opera Theologica.* |
| Txt | *Text Series.* |
| Flajšhans | Flajšhans, V., and Komínková, Maria, eds. *Spisy M. Jana Husi.* 3 vols. Prague, 1903–7. |
| FRA | *Fontes rerum Austraicarum.* Vienna, 1849–. |
| Friedberg | Friedberg, Emil Albert, ed. *Corpus Iuris Canonici.* 2 vols. Leipzig, 1879–81. |
| Galeota | Galeota, Gustavo, ed. *Bellarmino contra Baio a Lovanio.* Rome, 1966. |
| Gardner | Gardner, W. H., ed. *Poems of Gerard Manley Hopkins.* 3d ed. New York and London, 1961. |
| Gerberon | Gerberon, G., ed. Michel Baius. *Opera.* Cologne, 1696. |
| Glorieux | Glorieux, Palémon Jean, ed. Jean Gerson. *Oeuvres complètes.* 10 vols. Paris, 1960–73. |
| Goldast | Goldast, Melchior, ed. *Monarchia S. romani imperii: sive tractatus de jurisdictione imperiali et pontificia.* 3 vols. Frankfurt, 1611–14. |
| Goodspeed | Goodspeed, E. J., ed. *Die ältesten Apologeten.* Gottingen, 1915. |
| Graesse | Graesse, Th., ed. Jacob of Voragine. *Legenda aurea.* 2d ed. Regensburg, 1891. |
| Grisar | Grisar, Hartmann, ed. *Jacobi Lainez . . . Disputationes Tridentinae.* 2 vols. Innsbruck, 1886. |
| Hardt | Hardt, Hermann von der, ed. *Magnum oecumenicum Constantiense Concilium.* 7 vols. Frankfurt and Leipzig, 1697–1742. |
| Harvey | Harvey, W. W., ed. *Sancti Irenaei . . . Adversus Haereses.* 2 vols. Cambridge, 1857. |
| Heidelberg | *Nicolai de Cusa Opera omnia iussu et auctoritate Academiae Litterarum Heidelbergensis ad codicum fidem edita.* Leipzig, 1932–. |
| Heimpel | Heimpel, Hermann, ed. Dietrich of Nieheim. *Circa convocationem generalium conciliorum. Sitzungsberichte der Heidelberger Akademie der Wissenschaften: Philosophisch-historische Klasse* (1929–30), pp. 30–61. |
| Herrison | Herrison, Hendrick Jansz, ed. Menno Simons. *Opera omnia theologica.* Amsterdam, 1681. |
| Hocedez | Hocedez, Edgar, ed. *Aegidii Romani "Theoremata de esse et essentia."* Louvain, 1930. |
| Hödl | Hödl, Ludwig, ed. John of Paris. *De confessionibus audiendis (Quaestio disputata Parisius de potestate papae).* Munich, 1962. |
| Hoffmann | Hoffmann, Fritz, ed. *Die Schriften des Oxforder Kanzlers Iohannes Lutterell: Texte zur Theologie des vierzehnten Jahrhunderts.* Leipzig, 1959. |

| | |
|---|---|
| Hrabák | Hrabák, Josef, ed. *Jan Hus: Knížky o svatokupectví*. Prague, 1954. |
| Koch-Riedl | Koch, Joseph, and Riedl, John O., eds. *Giles of Rome. Errores philosophorum*. Milwaukee, 1944. |
| Kotter | Kotter, Bonifatius, ed. *Die Schriften des Johannes von Damaskus*. Berlin, 1969–. |
| KRA | *Kirchenrechtliche Abhandlungen*. Stuttgart, 1902–. |
| Krämer | Krämer, Werner. *Konsens und Rezeption: Verfassungsprinzipien der Kirche im Basler Konziliarismus*. Münster, 1980. |
| Kuyper | Kuyper, Abraham, ed. *Joannis a Lasco opera*. 2 vols. Amsterdam, 1866. |
| Ladner | Ladner, Pascal. "Johannes von Segovias Stellung zur Präsidentenfrage des Basler Konzils." *Zeitschrift für schweizerische Kirchengeschichte* 62 (1968): 1–113. |
| LB | *Erasmi opera omnia*, ed. Jean Leclerc. 10 vols. Leiden, 1703–6. |
| Leclercq-Rochais | Leclercq, Jean, and Rochais, Henri, eds. *Sancti Bernardi Opera*. Rome, 1957–. |
| Lo Grasso | Lo Grasso, Joannes B., ed. *Ecclesia et status: Fontes selecti historiae juris publici ecclesiastici*. 2d ed. Rome, 1952. |
| Lyons | *Opuscula omnia reverendi D. Thomae de Vio*. Lyons, 1585. |
| Maccarrone | Maccarrone, Michele, ed. "Una questione inedita dell' Olivi sull' infallibilità del papa." *Rivista di storia della Chiesa in Italia* 3 (1949): 309–43. |
| Mandonnet | Mandonnet, Pierre, ed. *S. Thomae Aquinatis . . . Scriptum super libros Sententiarum Magistri Petri Lombardi*. 4 vols. Paris, 1929–47. |
| Mansi | Mansi, J. D., ed. *Sacrorum conciliorum nova et amplissima collectio*. Florence, 1759–98. |
| Martène-Durand | Martène, Edmond, and Durand, Ursin, eds. *Veterum scriptorum et monumentorum historicorum, dogmaticorum, moralium amplissima collectio*. 9 vols. Paris, 1724–33. |
| Matteini | Matteini, Nevio, ed. *Il più antico oppositore politico di Dante: Guido Vernani da Rimini. Testo critico del "De Reprobatione Monarchiae."* Padua, 1958. |
| MBP | *Maxima Bibliotheca veterum Patrum et antiquorum scriptorum ecclesiasticorum*. Lyons, 1677–1707. |
| MC | *Monumenta conciliorum generalium saeculi XV*. 4 vols. Vienna and Basel, 1857–1936. |
| Meihuizen | Meihuizen, H. W., ed. *Menno Simons. Dat Fundament des Christelycken Leers*. The Hague, 1967. |
| Meneghin | Meneghin, Vittorino, ed. *Scritti inediti di Fra Alvaro Pais*. Lisbon, 1969. |
| MGH | *Monumenta Germaniae Historica*. Berlin, 1826–. |
| QGMA | *Quellen zur Geistesgeschichte des Mittelalters*. |
| Sch | *Schriften des Reichsinstituts für altere deutsche Geschichtskunde*. |
| St | *Staatsschriften des späteren Mittelalters*. |
| Miller | Miller, Perry, et al., eds. *The Works of Jonathan Edwards*. New Haven, 1957–. |
| Mirbt-Aland | Mirbt, Carl, and Aland, Kurt, eds. *Quellen zur Geschichte des Papsttums und des römischen Katholizismus*. 6th ed. Tübingen, 1967. |
| Moule | Moule, Handley Carr Glyn, ed. *Bishop Ridley on the Lord's Supper*. London, 1895. |
| Moxon | Moxon, R. S., ed. *Vincent of Lérins. Commonitorium*. Cambridge, 1915. |

MPPR                    *Monumenta politica et philosophica [humanistica] rariora.* Turin,
                        1959–.
Müller                  Müller, Ernst Friedrich Karl, ed. *Die Bekenntnisschriften der re-*
                        *formierten Kirche.* Leipzig, 1903.
Mylius                  Mylius, Arnoldus, ed. *Ruardi Tapperi . . . opera.* Cologne, 1582.
Niemeyer                Niemeyer, Hermann Agathon, ed. *Collectio confessionum in eccle-*
                        *siis reformatis publicatarum.* Leipzig, 1840.
Niesel                  Niesel, Wilhelm, ed. *Bekenntnisschriften und Kirchenordnungen*
                        *der nach Gottes Wort reformierten Kirche.* Munich, [1938].
Nolan                   Nolan, Kieran. *The Immortality of the Soul and the Resurrection*
                        *of the Body according to Giles of Rome.* Rome, 1967.
Oakley                  Oakley, Francis. *The Political Thought of Pierre d'Ailly.* New Ha-
                        ven, 1964.
Oberman-Courtenay       Oberman, Heiko Augustinus, and Courtenay, William J., with
                        Zerfoss, Daniel E., eds. Gabriel Biel. *Canonis misse expositio.* 4
                        vols. Wiesbaden, 1963–67.
Oberman-Zerfoss         Oberman, Heiko Augustinus, and Zerfoss, Daniel E., with Cour-
                        tenay, William J., eds. *"Defensorium obedientiae apostolicae" et*
                        *alia documenta.* Cambridge, Mass., 1968.
Opettex                 *Opuscula et textus historiam ecclesiae eiusque vitam atque doctri-*
                        *nam illustrantia: Series scholastica.* Münster, 1926–.
Palacký                 Palacký, František, ed. *Documenta Mag. Joannis Hus.* Prague, 1869.
Parker                  Parker, Thomas Henry Lewis, ed. *Iohannis Calvini Commentarius*
                        *in Epistolam Pauli ad Romanos.* Leiden, 1981.
Petrů                   Petrů, Eduard, ed. Petr Chelčický. *Drobné spisy.* Prague, 1966.
Pez                     Pez, Bernhard, ed. *Thesaurus anecdotorum novissimus.* 6 vols.
                        Augsburg, 1721–29.
PG                      *Patrologia graeca.* Paris, 1857–66.
PL                      *Patrologia latina.* Paris, 1878–90.
Plitt-Kolde             Plitt, Gustav Leopold, and Kolde, Theodor, eds. *Die Loci com*
                        *munes Philip Melanchthons in ihrer Urgestalt.* 4th ed. Leipzig
                        and Erlangen, 1925.
Pohl                    Pohl, Michael Joseph, ed. *Thomae Hermeken a Kempis . . . Opera*
                        *omnia.* 7 vols. Freiburg, 1902–22.
Pram.                   *Sbírka pramenů českého hnutí náboženského ve XIV. a XV. století.*
                        Prague, 1903–.
Preuss                  Preuss, Edward, ed. Martin Chemnitz. *Examen Concilii Tridentini.*
                        Berlin, 1861.
Previté-Orton           Previté-Orton, Charles William, ed. *The Defensor pacis of Marsilius*
                        *of Padua.* Cambridge, 1928.
PS                      The Parker Society for the Publication of the Works of the Fathers
                        and Early Writers of the Reformed English Church. *Publications.*
                        55 vols. Cambridge, 1841–55.
QFRG                    *Quellen und Forschungen zur Reformationsgeschichte.* Gütersloh,
                        1911–.
QMR                     *Quellen zur Geistesgeschichte des Mittelalters und der Renaissance.*
                        4 vols. Leipzig and Berlin, 1928–36.
Quaracchi               *Doctoris seraphici S. Bonaventurae . . . opera omnia.* Quaracchi,
                        1882–1902.
Rabeneck                Rabeneck, Johannes, ed. Luis de Molina. *Liberi arbitrii cum gratiae*
                        *donis . . . concordia.* Oña-Madrid, 1953.
Rembert                 Rembert, Karl. *Die Wiedertäufer im Herzogtum Jülich.* Berlin,
                        1899.

Reuter      Reuter, Quirinus, ed. *D. Zachariae Ursini . . . opera theologica.* 3 vols. Heidelberg, 1612.

Ricci      Ricci, Pier Giorgio, ed. Dante Alighieri. *De Monarchia.* Verona, 1965.

Roche      Roche, Evan, ed. *The "De primo principio" of John Duns Scotus.* Saint Bonaventure, N.Y., 1949.

Rossi-Bosco      Rossi, Vittorio, and Bosco, Umberto, eds. Francesco Petrarca. *Le Familiari.* 4 vols. Florence, 1933–42.

Ryba      Ryba, Bohumil, ed. *Betlemské texty.* Prague, 1951.

Ryšánek      Ryšánek, Fr., et al., eds. *Spisy Mistra Jana Husi.* Prague, 1959–.

SA      *Studia Anselmiana.* Rome, 1933–.

Savile      Savile, Henry, ed. Thomas Bradwardine. *De causa Dei contra Pelagium.* London, 1618. Reprint ed. Frankfurt, 1964.

SC      *Sources chrétiennes.* Paris, 1940–.

Schaff      Schaff, P., ed. *Creeds of Christendom.* 6th ed. New York, 1919.

Schard      Schard, Simon. *De iurisdictione . . . imperiali ac potestate ecclesiastica.* Basel, 1566.

Schlüsselburg      Schlüsselburg, Conradus, ed. *Haereticorum catalogus.* 13 vols. in 8. Frankfurt, 1597–1601.

Schmaus      Schmaus, Michael, ed. Thomas von Sutton. *Quodlibeta.* Munich, 1969.

Schmitt      Schmitt, F. S., ed. *Sancti Anselmi opera omnia.* Seckau, Rome, Edinburgh, 1938–61.

Schmitz      Schmitz, Hermann Joseph, ed. *Die Bussbücher und die Bussdisciplin der Kirche: Die Bussbücher und das kanonische Bussverfahren.* 2 vols. Düsseldorf, 1883–98.

Scholz      Scholz, Richard, ed. Giles of Rome. *De ecclesiastica potestate.* Weimar, 1929.

Schneemann      Schneemann, Gerhard, ed. *Controversiarum de divinae gratiae liberique arbitrii Concordia initia et progressus.* Freiburg, 1881.

Schuler-Schultess      Schuler, Melchior, and Schultess, Johannes, eds. *Huldreich Zwinglis Werke.* 8 vols. Zurich, 1829–42.

Sedlák      Sedlák, Jan, ed. *Táborské traktáty eucharistické.* Brno, 1918.

Sikes      Sikes, Jeffrey Garrett, et al., eds. *Guillelmi de Ockham opera politica.* 3 vols. Manchester, 1940–63.

Smolinsky      Smolinsky, Heribert. *Domenico de' Domenichi und seine Schrift "De potestate pape et termino eius."* Münster, 1976.

ST      *Studi e testi.* Rome, 1900–.

Stegmüller      Stegmüller, Friedrich, ed. *Neue Molinaschriften.* Vol. 1 of *Geschichte des Molinismus.* Münster, 1935.

Stella      Stella, P. T., ed. *Petrus de Palude. "Tractatus de potestate papae."* Zurich, 1966.

Strasbourg      *Martini Buceri auspiciis opera ordinis theologorum Evangelicorum Argentinensis edita.* Gütersloh and Leiden, 1955–.

Stupperich      Stupperich, Robert, ed. *Martin Bucers deutsche Schriften.* Gütersloh, 1960–.

Sylvester      Sylvester, Richard S., et al., eds. *The Complete Works of St. Thomas More.* New Haven, 1963–.

Thes.Salm.      *Theses Salmurienses: Syntagma thesium theologicarum in academia Salmuriensi variis temporibus disputatarum.* 2 vols. Saumur, 1641.

Thompson      Thompson, Craig R., ed. Erasmus. *Inquisitio de fide.* New Haven, 1950.

Thomson      Thomson, Samuel Harrison, ed. *Magistri Johannis Hus Tractatus de Ecclesia.* Cambridge, 1956.

van Eijl       van Eijl, Édouard, ed. "Les censures des Universités d'Alcalá et de Salamanque et la censure di pape Pie V contre Michel Baius (1565–67)." *Revue d'histoire ecclésiastique* 48 (1953): 719–76.

Vivès       Vivès, L., ed. Francisco de Suárez. *Opera.* 28 vols. Paris, 1856–61.

Vooght       Vooght, Paul de. *Jacobellus de Stříbro († 1429), premier théologien du hussitisme.* Louvain, 1972.

WA       *D. Martin Luthers Werke.* Weimar, 1883–.

Br.       *Briefe.*

DB       *Deutsche Bibel.*

Ti.       *Tischreden.*

Wackernagel       Wackernagel, Carl Eduard Philipp, ed. *Das deutsche Kirchenlied von der ältesten Zeit bis zu Anfang des XVII. Jahrhunderts.* 5 vols. Leipzig, 1864–77.

Wadding       Wadding, Luke, et al., eds. John Duns Scotus. *Opera omnia.* Reprint ed. 26 vols. Paris, 1891–95.

Walch       Walch, Christian Wilhelm Franz, ed. *Monimenta medii aevi ex bibliotheca regia Hanoverana.* 2 vols. Göttingen, 1757–64.

Walter       Walter, Johannes von, ed. Desiderius Erasmus. *De libero arbitrio Diatribe sive collatio.* 2d ed. Leipzig, 1935.

Walther       Walther, Carl Ferdinand Wilhelm, ed. Johann Wilhelm Baier. *Compendium theologiae positivae.* 3 vols. Saint Louis, 1879.

Werbeck-Hofmann       Werbeck, Wifrid, and Hofmann, Udo, eds. *Gabrielis Biel Collectorium circa quattuor libros Sententiarum.* 4 vols. Tübingen, 1973–.

WLW       *Wyclif's Latin Works.* 35 vols. London, 1883–1914.

Xiberta       Xiberta y Roqueta, Bartolomé Maria. *Guiu Terrena, carmelita de Perpinyà.* Barcelona, 1932.

Ypma       Ypma, Eelcko, ed. *Jacobi de Viterbio O.E.S.A. Disputationes de quolibet.* 4 vols. Würzburg, 1968–75.

Zumkeller       Zumkeller, Adolar, ed. "Ein 'Sermo Magistralis' des Augustinus von Rom, OESA, zur Verteidigung der Immakulata." In *Studia Scholastico-Scotica* 4:117–37. Rome, 1968.

# Reformation
# Defined

During the four centuries from the deaths of Thomas Aquinas and Bonaventure in 1274 to the births of Johann Sebastian Bach and George Frederick Handel in 1685, Western Christianity experienced fundamental and far-reaching changes in the interpretation—indeed, in the very definition—of church and dogma. Most of the changes were connected, in one way or another, with the Reformation of the sixteenth century, which is, therefore, usually the subject of scholarly study and theological discussion by itself. That century, from Luther's posting of the *Ninety-Five Theses* in 1517 to the outbreak of the Thirty Years' War in 1618, was, in politics and society no less than in theology and church doctrine, a major turning point in the history of the West.

Whatever validity there may be to such a concentration on the sixteenth century, however, the place of the Reformation in the history of the development of Christian doctrine becomes clear only in the context of that total history. Since it is to the conflicts of the sixteenth century that most Christian denominations in the West, not least Roman Catholicism itself, must trace the origins of their present doctrinal positions, it is certainly understandable, and probably inevitable, that readers who stand in one or another of the doctrinal traditions coming out of the period of the Reformation will have a special interest in the portions of this volume, and of the next, that deal with their own "church fathers." But those portions of these two volumes, and for that matter these two

1

volumes as such, are only a part of a total history
going back to the fathers of the entire church catholic;
and it is within the total history that the "church
fathers" of a particular confession or denomination
are to be understood (as, in most instances, they themselves wanted to be understood). There will be, and
there should be, books on the doctrine and the history
of the various denominations, as well as books of
"comparative symbolics," which draw the lines of
contrast and affinity between the several confessions;
some of these books will appear in the bibliography
of this volume. But in this book it would be a mistake
and a source of disappointment for a reader to move
with inordinate haste to the individual chapters or
paragraphs where the familiar names and issues of
those denominations may be expected to appear; for
some of them will not appear at all, and others will
receive attention only as they belong to the history
of the development of doctrine within the Christian
tradition as a whole.

Therefore the center of this narrative, in chapters
3 through 6, will continue the practice of previous
volumes in being organized on the basis of doctrines
and of doctrinal emphases, even though the preponderance of one or another doctrine in one or another
denomination means that the theologians and the
confessional writings of that denomination will pre-
dominate in the chapter—Lutheran in chapter 3, Reformed in chapter 4, Roman Catholic in chapter 5,
Radical in chapter 6. Yet in each such chapter, sources
from other denominational traditions than the pre-
dominant one will be prominent, because no one denomination had a monopoly on the doctrine: a
Reformed theologian will provide the epigraph for
the presentation of the "Lutheran" doctrine of justi-
See p. 139 below fication by faith. Organization on the basis of doctrines rather than of denominations or confessions
means, moreover, that the doctrine of a communion
such as the Church of England—Lutheran in its intellectual origins, Catholic in its polity, Reformed in
its official confessional statements, Radical in its Puritan outcome, and, according to the old saw, "Pelagian in its pulpit, but Augustinian in its prayer
book"—is not concentrated in any one chapter, but

scattered over several. For our attention continues to be directed to Christian doctrine, defined at the very outset of this work as "what the church of Jesus Christ believes, teaches, and confesses on the basis of the word of God."

See vol.1:1

Although there has been substantial documentation for that definition throughout the previous periods of the history of doctrine, it truly came into its own in the period covered by the present volume. Marsilius of Padua and Alvaro Pelayo were on opposite sides of the fourteenth-century controversy over the doctrine of papal authority and of its relation to the temporal powers; but when Marsilius spoke of "the catholic faith" as "one, not many . . . to be believed and confessed by all the faithful," his words found an exact parallel in Alvaro's formula, "the obedience, the faith and fidelity, the confession of the heart and mouth . . . of the holy catholic and orthodox church." Alvaro also invoked a distinction between "faith" defined as "what is believed by all the faithful" and "faith" defined as "that by which one believes [fides qua creditur]," and he defined "the unity of faith" as "the unity of doctrine." "The truth of the faith," Gerson explained in 1413, on the basis of Romans 10:10, "does not consist solely in believing with the heart, but it also consists in confessing with the mouth," as well as in condemning "false doctrine"; or, as he said elsewhere on the basis of the same text, it consisted in "openly confessing, defending, testifying, and preaching." His younger contemporary, Thomas à Kempis, likewise spoke of believing, confessing, and preaching, and sometimes of believing, adoring, and confessing—a formula echoed in the sixteenth century by Philip Melanchthon when, on the basis of the Shema of Deuteronomy 6:4 and in an explanation of the Nicene Creed, he defined "adoration" as "confession."

Writing in his official capacity as the author of the *Augsburg Confession* and of the *Apology of the Augsburg Confession*, Melanchthon recurred frequently to the theme of "the confession of doctrine," since "no faith is firm which does not show itself in confession." The *Augsburg Confession* was "a confession of the doctrine of our pastors and preachers and of our own faith, setting forth how and in what manner, on the

Mars.Pad.*Def.pac.*2.18.8 (Previté-Orton 310)

Alv.Pel.*Ep.*15.5 (Meneghin 144);Alv.Pel.*Planc.eccl.*1.60 (1560:65r)

Alv.Pel.*Planc.eccl.*1.63 (1560: 74v)

Gers.*Rép.cr.* (Glorieux 7:216–17)

Gers.*Mat.fid.*1 (Glorieux 6: 155);Gers.*Serm.*237 (Glorieux 5:420)

Thos.Kemp.*Vit.Chr.*2.1.15 (Pohl 5:295);Thos.Kemp.*Serm. nov.*20 (Pohl 6:179)
Thos.Kemp.*Vit.Chr.*1.1.11 (Pohl 5:25)

Mel.*Explic.symb.Nic.* (CR 23: 358)

Apol.Conf.Aug.4.193 (Bek.198)

Apol.Conf.Aug.4.385 (Bek.232)

basis of the divine and holy Scripture, these things are preached, taught, maintained, and communi-

Conf.Aug.pr.8 (Bek.45–46)

cated." Other sixteenth-century confessions—Reformed, Roman Catholic, and Lutheran—all took up the theme. The *Scots Confession* of 1560 opened its

Conf.Scot.1 (Niesel 84);Calv.
Rom.14:22 (Parker 303);Calv.
Ep.du.1 (Barth-Niesel 1:294)

first article with the declaration: "We confess and acknowledge. . . . We confess and believe." The first draft of the decree on justification at the Council of

CTrid.Decr.just.I.1;2 (CT 5:
385)

Trent employed the similar formula, "We firmly believe and simply confess," while the final draft of its decree on original sin had: "The holy, ecumenical, and general Council of Trent . . . ordains, confesses, and declares. . . . This holy synod confesses and be-

CTrid.5.Decr.1 (Alberigo-
Jedin 665–67)
Form.Conc.Epit.Sum.1 (Bek.
767)

lieves." And the Lutheran *Formula of Concord* of 1577 began its introduction with the words, "We believe, teach, and confess," invoking the same words in all but two of the affirmative sections of its subsequent articles. The very use of the title "confession" for most of the statements of Christian doctrine in the sixteenth century is evidence for the centrality of the idea.

Confessing was essential to the church because, with believing and teaching, it belonged to Christian doctrine. As an early session of the Council of Trent was reminded, reform of the structure or the morals of the church without reformulation of the doctrine of the church would not meet the objections and demands of the Protestant Reformers, for whom the doctrine was

Bonuc.ap.CTrid.Act.22.i.1547
(CT 4:572)

primary. Although some of his accents, even here, reveal that he was a Radical Reformer, for whom "reformation of church and dogma" actually meant "re-for-

See p. 306 below

mation of church and dogma," the Anabaptist theologian Balthasar Hubmaier was speaking for all the Reformers when he wrote: "A Christian life must begin first of all with doctrine, from which faith flows. . . . It is in the public confession of his faith that a man makes his first entrance and beginning into the holy, catholic, Christian church, apart from which there is

Hub.Lr.pr. (QFRG 29:307)

no salvation." Or, in the axiom of the German-Swiss Reformer, Henrich Bullinger, "Doctrine is the most

Blngr.Coen. (1558:3r)

important thing, which stands out above all others." In varying degrees, the Protestant Reformers tended to mean by "doctrine" a body of received "articles of

Conf.Belg.9 (Schaff 3:393);
Conf.Helv.post.11 (Niesel
238);Form.Conc.S.D.Sum.4
(Bek.834)

faith," as contained in the so-called three ecumenical creeds: the Apostles', the Nicene, and the Athanasian.

Apol.Conf.Aug.pr.11 (*Bek.*143)

Also in varying degrees, they could, with Melanchthon, make it a point "to stick as closely as possible to
traditional doctrinal formulas," so much so that, in the
conflict with Servetus, Protestant theology was more
directly, and more tragically, involved than was Roman
Catholic theology in the defense of Nicene and Chal-

See pp. 322–31 below

cedonian orthodoxy.

Because for Roman Catholic theology any "reformation" of established orthodox doctrine could mean
only "reaffirmation," the need to "stick closely to
traditional doctrinal formulas" was even more pronounced for its "defenders of the faith," who were
able to find the consensus of orthodox Christian antiquity for their opposition to Luther's denial of free

See pp. 258–60, 287–88 below
See pp. 258, 298–99 below

will, but endeavored to find it as well for the term
"transubstantiation." In this they sought to follow
the precedent of a thinker like Gerson, who had declared his intention "not to say anything other than
what others have said, although perhaps to say it in

Gers. *Vit.spir.*3 (Glorieux 3:
143);Gers.*Theol.myst.*1.pr.
(Combes 6)

another way [non quidem alia dicturus quam alii,
quamquam forte aliter]." Sometimes, however, this
defensive assertion of the desire to avoid novelty could
give way to a recognition that there had been authentic
development, if not downright change, in the church's
understanding of the meaning of the original deposit
of revelation. Such a recognition was made possible
by "the great distinction . . . between the articles of

Wic.*Luth.art.* (*CCath* 18:71)

faith and the good practices of the church." For example, "in accordance with the diversity of the times"
the church had modified its stand on poverty; for it
was God "who changes the times" and therefore the

Henr.Lang.*Cons.pac.*15 (Hardt
2:47)

meaning of the evangelical imperative of poverty. Even
the command in the institution of the Eucharist,

Matt.26:27

"Drink of it, all of you," was susceptible of alteration

See pp. 122–25 below

by the authority of the church, as was the decree of

Acts 15:29

the "apostolic council" in Jerusalem prohibiting the

See p. 276 below

eating of "things strangled." The possibility of some
analogous development in the very articles of faith
and doctrine was much more problematical; but when
it was acknowledged, it was frequently, though not
necessarily, identified with the view that not all authentic tradition was contained in Scripture and that
therefore the church had the power and authority to

Jac.Vit.*Reg.chr.*2.10
(Arquillière 292–93)

promulgate teachings, for example, on the doctrine

See pp. 43–44 below

See pp. 276–77 below

See vol. 1:3

Seeberg (1953) 1:7

about the Virgin Mary, without explicit scriptural warrant. Even by the end of the period being covered here, the status of that view of tradition apart from Scripture as an independent source of revelation was still ambiguous within the official doctrine of the Roman Catholic Church, whatever individual theologians may have held.

The distinction between what individual theologians held and what was believed, taught, and confessed by the church or churches was itself rendered increasingly ambiguous by the schism of the fourteenth and fifteenth centuries and above all by the Reformation of the sixteenth. But the very proliferation of documents called "confessions" shows, paradoxically, that the distinction was, if anything, becoming more important than ever. It likewise becomes more important for the structure of our narrative and for our selection of source material in this work. It has been above all in the treatment of the Reformation by the histories of dogma that what we have called "the danger of exaggerating the significance of the idiosyncratic thought of individual theologians at the expense of the common faith of the church" has manifested itself. For example, after insisting in its introduction that "not the clergy or the theologians . . . , but the Christian community is its subject," one such history, also in five volumes, devoted its entire fourth volume to the theology of Luther as an individual thinker, reserving even the doctrine of the particular "Christian community" and confession that came out of Luther's Reformation for a portion of its fifth volume. In spite of an all but irresistible attraction, the theology of a religious genius like Martin Luther (or Augustine or Thomas Aquinas) merits attention in a history of the development of Christian doctrine as "what the church of Jesus Christ believes, teaches, and confesses on the basis of the word of God" only because of its all but inestimable importance for that development, not because of its intrinsic appeal.

For each succeeding century in the periods to be discussed in volumes 4 and 5 of this work, the surviving amount of source material is substantially greater than it was for the preceding century, until, finally, there are certainly more pages of theology available from any one decade of the nineteenth or the twentieth century than from all of the second century. The increasing availability of texts from the later Middle Ages has illumined the ideas of individual thinkers from the fourteenth and fifteenth centuries, for example, William of Ockham, whose place in the history of political theory, of logic and metaphysics, and of doctrinal theology has been undergoing fundamental reassessment as the first critical edition of his works nears completion. For our present purposes in this work, however, Ockham provides substantial documentation for the presence of "doctrinal pluralism in the later Middle Ages" in such areas of doctrine See pp. 35, 53 below as predestination and the sacraments, as well as for the growing attention being given in the fourteenth and fifteenth centuries to the doctrine of the church. His political thought, like that of earlier Christian See vol.1:40–41;vol.2:143–44, 210–11;vol.3:51–52,300 thinkers, bears upon the history of doctrine chiefly because it provided the context for much of his teaching See p. 108 below about the nature of the church. For the same reason, even the political and social upheavals of the peasants, knights, and cities in the sixteenth century, to which so much of the best of present-day Reformation scholarship, both Eastern and Western, has been devoting itself, belong here only as they affected See pp. 313–22 below such ecclesiological issues as apostolic continuity.

Thus also the theme of "Nationalism and European Pauck (1939) 286–303 Christianity" in this period must be left for consideration elsewhere. When the Council of Constance was "divided into four nations, with many divisions *Serm.conc.Const.*23.ii.1416 (Finke 2:430–31) in each of these"; or when the Dominican Johannes Stojković of Ragusa (Dubrovnik) lamented, "with all the feeling and love in my heart," the separation of Joh.Rag.*Utraq.* (Mansi 29:712) the Hussite Czechs from the other Slavs; or when Luther, after his confrontation with the Thomist scholar Cardinal Cajetan (Tommaso de Vio), remarked, "He is an Italian, and that is what he re- Luth.*Ep.*18.x.1518 (*WA BR* 1: 209) mains"; or when, in what was almost certainly the most tragicomic episode at the Council of Trent, and one with ethnic overtones, Dionysius de Zanettinis, bishop of Chironissa and Milopotamos, nicknamed "the little Greek [Grechetto]," became involved in a match of shouting and beard-pulling in which he called

ap.CTrid.*Act*.17.vii.1546 (*CT* 5:348)

See pp. 98–110 below

See vol.3:154–56, 305–7 below
See pp. 21–22, 63–68 below
See pp. 313–22 below

See pp. 306–11 below

See pp. 176–77, 196–98 below
See vol.1:297–98;vol.3:80–95

Calv.*Praed.* (*CR* 36:266)

See pp. 125–26 below
See pp. 263–64 below

a fellow bishop "either an ignoramus or a scoundrel"—these and other such incidents, significant though they may be for the history both of nationalism and of European Christianity, cannot form part of this history of the development of doctrine. All personal and theological preferences aside, therefore, the criterion of selectivity on the basis of pertinence to the development of church doctrine rather than of theology will make Nicholas of Cusa more central than William of Ockham in ecclesiology, the mysticism of Gerson (like that of Bernard of Clairvaux and Bonaventure) more germane to the narrative than that of Meister Eckhart, and the radicalism of Menno Simons more relevant than that of Thomas Müntzer.

That same criterion has determined, again despite personal and theological preferences, the role of Renaissance thought in the story. Instead of receiving consideration in a discrete chapter or more, which it would unquestionably merit in any comprehensive intellectual history of these four centuries, humanism will be represented here principally by its achievements in the area of "sacred philology." The insistence of humanistic scholars on an understanding of the biblical text based upon a fresh reading of the Hebrew and Greek originals, even if such an understanding did not conform to some purported dogmatic consensus of the tradition, acted as a catalyst in the reconsideration of the doctrine of authority during the age of the Reformation. On the other hand, the revival of patristic learning, already in the fifteenth century and then even more in the sixteenth, provided much of the content for the discussion of several doctrines at issue: the real presence in the Eucharist, whose pluralistic history became evident through research in the texts of the fathers; predestination, whose place in the writings of Augustine, as published by Erasmus and other humanistic scholars, emboldened John Calvin to assert that "Augustine is completely on our side" on the question; and, perhaps above all, authority, where Augustine's consideration of the relation between Scripture and the church set the terms for the developments in the fifteenth century and for the debates in the sixteenth. It was also, at least in part, the antithesis between two ways of reading Au-

See pp. 140–41 below

gustine that underlay the dispute between the leading theologian of the Reformation and the leading scholar of the Renaissance over the freedom of the will. For, in an epigram that may be an exaggeration but is not a total distortion, "the Reformation, inwardly considered, was just the ultimate triumph of Augustine's doctrine of grace over Augustine's doctrine of the church."

Warfield (1956) 322

As it is the centrality of church doctrine rather than of theology that will shape the treatment here of both of the two centuries preceding the Reformation and of the century of the Reformation itself, so it will also determine the place in this narrative of the century that followed the Reformation. Like the thirteenth century, to which it bears certain analogies, the seventeenth century, as "the age of orthodoxy," must, in any "study in the history of theology," command serious scholarly attention. Precisely because it was an "age of orthodoxy," however, the attention it warrants in a study in the history of church doctrine must be quite different. For "orthodoxy" here meant the systematization of a doctrine that had already been promulgated in the confessional and dogmatic definitions of the sixteenth century, the clarification of the inner relation of doctrines to one another and of their outer relation to philosophy, and the documentation of their validity on the basis of Scripture and tradition. It did not mean primarily a development of doctrine, the very concept of which was anathema to most of the champions of each of the versions of "confessional dogmatics." Yet the forthcoming "crisis of orthodoxy East and West," which was to dominate much of church doctrine during the eighteenth century, would take the form it did because of the form of that orthodoxy in the seventeenth century.

See vol.3:268–307

Pelikan (1950) 49–75

# 1

# Doctrinal Pluralism in the Later Middle Ages

See vol. 3:270–84

Mandonnet (1923) 4

Oberman (1978) 80

Corp. Jur. Can.: Decr. Grat. 3.2
(Friedberg 1:1314–52)
Guil. Oc. Corp. 5 (Birch 182–
84); Vit. Furn. Quodlib. 2.3
(Delorme 62–66)

Matt. 26:26

Nicol. Cus. Ep. 2 (Faber 2–II:7r)

Although the century of Thomas Aquinas and Bonaventure had truly achieved a "reintegration of the catholic tradition," it would be a mistake to assume that this was "already universally accepted in the intellectual world" of the later Middle Ages. On the contrary, there was a "pregnant plurality of fourteenth-century thought" which was recognized by thinkers at the time and which continued into the fifteenth century and well beyond.

A brief recital of at least some specific instances of doctrinal pluralism that were explicitly acknowledged in the fourteenth and fifteenth centuries will confirm this impression. As will become evident in greater detail later, the doctrine of the Eucharist and the doctrine of Mary were especially fertile ground for diversity. Citing for support the admission of canon law that there was "a variety of opinions" in antiquity about the Eucharist, William of Ockham in the first half of the fourteenth century stressed the continuing variety of his own time. A century or so later, in a defense of the practice of withholding the chalice from the laity in the administration of Holy Communion, Nicholas of Cusa was willing to admit that "the church today has a different interpretation of the commandment in the Gospel ['Drink of it, all of you'] from the one it once had," but he argued that "the truth of the sacraments still stands," although "at diverse times one or another practice" had obtained. In support of his contention that there could be some variety of teaching on the Eucharist,

10

Guil.Oc.*Corp*.36 (Birch 444)

Petr.Aur.*Tract*.5 (*BFS* 3:71)
Henr.Lang.*Concept*.1.4 (1516:
2r);Henr.Lang.*Cons.pac*.18
(Hardt 2:57); Gers.*Joh.Mont*.
(Glorieux 10:17)

Gabr.Bl.*Fest.Mar*.1 (1499:A2v)

See p. 50 below

All.*Trin*.2;1 (Du Pin 1:627;
622)
See vol.3:112–14

Gabr.Bl.*Fest.Mar*.7 (1499:Dlv)
Gr.Arim.*Sent*.2.30–33.1.2
(1522–II:112r)

Brad.*Caus*.1.34 (Savile 300)
See vol.1:98–99, 123–32;vol.2:
279–80;vol.3:216–47

Nicol.Cus.*Ult*. (Heidelberg 4:
100)

Ant.P.*Conf*.1.1.11 (1490:11r)

Joh.Brev.*Tract*.1.3 (Du Pin 1:
829)

Joh.Brev.*Tract*.2.3 (Du Pin 1:
875)
Joh.Brev.*Tract*.3.1 (Du Pin 1:
883)

All.*Recom*. (Du Pin 1:603–4)
Matt.16:18

Ockham referred to divergent opinions among the church fathers about the bodily assumption of the Virgin. The opinions were considerably more divergent when it came to her immaculate conception, as one of his contemporaries had to grant and as continued to be evident through the latter part of the fourteenth century and into the middle of the fifteenth century, despite the formulation of the doctrine of the immaculate conception adopted by the Council of Basel in 1439.

Nor were the controversies confined to these two doctrines. On so central a dogma as the Trinity, there were, in addition to the teachings that had been settled in Scripture and the creeds, other issues that could best be "left to the disputation of the learned," whose opposition to one another was not to be a matter of concern. Anselm's ideas about original sin had a certain prima facie authority, and there were theologians who accepted them; but there were others who preferred an alternative definition. On the relation of the will of God to the commission of evil there were likewise discordant theories, but theologians endeavored to harmonize them. In this period, as in most others during the history of the church, the details of eschatology "have led to various opinions, so that everyone has an abundance of his own interpretations and no one agrees with anyone else." The casuistry of penance was notorious for producing differences of opinion. Underlying these and other variations were more fundamental divergences over the very definition of the nature and the locus of authority. "On this," asserted one expositor, "there are diverse opinions," going on to specify that this diversity extended to such problems as the kind of jurisdiction that Peter and his successors received from Christ as well as the possibility of heresy on the part of the pope. "A great prolixity" characterized the exegeses of the words of Christ, "You are Peter, and on this rock I will build my church."

It would not be difficult to multiply quotations from the writers of this period in documentation of its recognition of doctrinal pluralism. That is not to say, however, that the pluralism did not constitute a serious problem. Voicing anxieties that were, no doubt,

Eph.4:5

Gers.*Cur.st*.2 (Glorieux 3:239);
Gers.*Nupt*. (Glorieux 6:208–9)

Gers.*Lull*. (Glorieux 10:122)
Gers.*Ex.doct*.pr. (Glorieux 9:
458)
Chel.*St.vr*.1.14 (*Com*.22:44–
46)
Univ.Par.*Avis.conc*.33 (Finke 1:
143);Joh.Brev.*Tract*.1.1 (Du
Pin 1:811–12)
Joh.Pal.*Quaest.par*. (Döllinger
418)
Aug.*Bapt*.2.6 (*CSEL* 51:182)

See p. 68 below

Nicol.Cus.*Conc.cath*.1.5
(Heidelberg 14:48)

Nicol.Cus.*Ep*.1 (Faber 2–II:3r)

Guil.Oc.*Corp*.36 (Birch 440)

Gers.*Cons*.4.4 (Glorieux 9:
237–38)

widespread in the church, especially under the shadow
of schism, one of the outstanding churchmen of the
fifteenth century, Jean Gerson, asked: "If there is 'one
Lord, one faith,' and one law, and if, moreover, the
truth is common to all and comes from the Holy
Spirit, regardless of who expresses it, what will be the
outcome of this violent controversy between various
classes and orders of Christians, when a theologian is
defended, cherished, and preferred by one group but
not by another?" Elsewhere he warned against "a confusion of idioms and languages that are mutually un-
intelligible, as at the tower of Babel," and he equated
"varying doctrines" with "false prophecies." The same
anxiety was expressed (albeit with radically different
operative conclusions) by one of his polar opposites,
as well as by his colleagues at Paris and by others.
Not all of his contemporaries were quite that concerned. Drawing an object lesson from Augustine's
reinterpretation of Cyprian's teaching on the relation
between the holiness of the church and its unity, Nicholas of Cusa declared for a variety of opinions, so
long as they did not jeopardize the fraternal unity of
the church; for the faith was one, as Christ the creating
Logos was one, but the great variety of creatures par-
ticipating in the creating Logos all found their fulfillment in him. Therefore unity was not the same as
uniformity.

Throughout the period being covered by this volume—and perhaps even more during the period to be
covered by the next volume—there would continue
to be tension between the theologian who warned
church officials not to be precipitate in condemning
doctrinal pluralism and the church official who warned
theologians not to exalt their private and often ignorant opinions over the mind of the church. Yet such
tension would also help to produce some of the most
important doctrinal developments of the period, as
well as to set the stage for the Renaissance and the
Reformation. To examine the doctrinal pluralism of
the later Middle Ages and the specific developments
that came out of it, we shall rehearse the doctrines
whose history is recounted in the central chapters of
volume 3 of this work, using the titles of those chapters as subtitles here.

## Beyond the Augustinian Synthesis

See vol.1:330–31

The growth of medieval theology can be seen as a series of "Augustinian syntheses," in each of which one or another aspect of the world view associated with the name of Augustine had been dominant, in combination with particular ways of reading the Bible and the fathers of the church. The Augustinian syntheses of Bonaventure and of Thomas Aquinas, sometimes mutually complementary and sometimes mutually exclusive, both sought to preserve the substance of the doctrines of God and man, grace and the church, as these had come down from the fathers, and above all from Augustine, but to do so in a way that took account of the new challenges and new opportunities of the thirteenth century. Yet these syntheses did not even come near to exhausting all the possibilities of Augustinianism; nor, in the judgment of many, did Thomas satisfy all the doctrinal needs of the church. In fact, the fourteenth century witnessed a struggle between the Augustinian synthesis represented by Thomas's *Summa* and the other species of Augustinianism claiming to be more faithful to the tradition of Augustine and to the gospel. According to a legend widely held among Franciscans as a "moral certainty," the year in which Aquinas and Bonaventure both died, 1274, was also the year in which the creator of the most formidable of these other systems, John Duns Scotus, was born; and although his birthdate must probably be set in 1265 rather than in 1274, the intuition of the legend about his place in late medieval theology is correct.

Balić (1965) 8

The theological discussions of the period sometimes dealt with issues that did not directly involve the belief, teaching, and confession of the church. Thus one of Thomas's most influential critics took up the question whether a monk who died and then was resurrected would be obliged to return to the same religious order of which he had been a member: the answer was that while "on the basis solely of the contract of obligation" such a monk had been freed of his vows, he did have the duty to enter the religious life again, though not necessarily in the same community. That question was still agitating debate a hundred years later. Another critic attacked Thomas's surmise that

Aeg.Rom.*Quodlib*.5.26 (1646: 342–43)
Hs.*Sent*.4.38.8 (Flajšhans 2: 683)

Guil. Mar. *Var.sent. Thom.* 17
(*Opettex* 21:17)

Ramb. Bol. *Apol.ver.* 15 (*ST* 108: 179)

CVien. (1311–12)*Decr.* 1
(Alberigo-Jedin 360–61)

Oliv. *Post.Joh.* (*ALKGMA* 3: 491)
Ub. Cas. *Sanct.ap.* (*ALKGMA* 2:402)

Rich. S. Laur. *Laud. Mar.* 5.2
(Borgnet 36:281–83);Ps. Alb. M. *Mar.* 19 (Borgnet 37:42–44)

Ps. Alb. M. *Mar.* 98–110
(Borgnet 37:159–66)

See p. 25 below

Thos. Aq. *S. T.* 1.25.6 ad 3 (*Ed. Leon.* 4:299)

Guil. Mar. *Var.sent. Thom.* 7
(*Opettex* 21:13)
*Corr. "Quare"* 50 (*Bibl. Thom.* 9:220–22)
All. *Fals.proph.* 2 (Du Pin 1: 571–73;577); *Corr. "Quare"* 23 (*Bibl. Thom.* 9:104)

See vol. 3:296
Robt. Orf. *Corr.* 23 (*Bibl. Thom.* 31:105–6);Thos. Sut. *Quodlib.* 4. 11 (Schmaus 558–63)
See vol. 3:290–91
Joh. Par. *Corr. "Circa"* 6 (*SA* 12: 45);Robt. Orf. *Corr.* 6 (*Bibl. Thom.* 31:52)
Ramb. Bol. *Apol.ver.* 6 (*ST* 108: 46–109)
Jac. Mis. *Utraq.* 1.45;2.12
(Hardt 3:521;549);Joh. Rok. ap. Laur. Reich. *Diurn.* 4.iii. 1433
(*MC* 1:319)
Chel. *St.vr.* 1.75–76 (*Com.* 22: 177–80)
Thos. Aq. *S. T.* 3.76.2 (*Ed. Leon.* 12:180–82)

the body of Christ after his resurrection had been able to digest food, although it had not used this ability, but Thomas's pupil rejected the attack as "dangerous and contrary to the faith." For their part, the Franciscans, too, were charged with christological aberration, as when Peter John Olivi, a leader of the Spiritual Franciscans, was condemned posthumously for teaching that Christ was still alive when the lance pierced his side. Olivi's exposition of John 19:33 had explicitly asserted that the piercing took place "after the death of Christ," and his defenders vigorously denied that he had ever taught otherwise. It was a matter of considerable interest to determine what the color of the Virgin Mary's hair was: the answer was that it was either red or black, more likely the latter. She was also conversant with each of the seven liberal arts, including astronomy, as well as with theology, as summarized in the *Sentences* of Peter Lombard.

While even behind many of these seemingly idle inquiries there stood one or another passage from Augustine's works, much of the time it was the very content of the Augustinian tradition that all parties to the debates believed to be at stake. Thus the belief in divine omnipotence, which for the followers of Duns Scotus and of Ockham was fundamental to the definition of salvation itself, appeared to be in question when Thomas said that "given the things which actually exist, the universe cannot be better"; for this seemed to contradict the hope that God not only could, but would, make a better universe after the Last Judgment. Thomas's views about the superiority of intellect over will, and then particularly about the will of the angels who fell, called for examination, because his champions had to show that his theories about the fall were consistent with Augustine's teachings about creation and sin. Similarly, they had to validate his conclusion that the creation of the world ex nihilo was not demonstrable by reason alone but depended on the authority of faith; in some of their apologies this was the longest chapter of all. Followers of John Hus, the Czech reformer, condemned Aquinas, along with his teacher, Albertus Magnus; but when they found Thomas apparently approving, or at any rate not condemning, the practice of administering the

Nicol.Dr.*Utraq*.3;7 (Hardt 3: 606–7;630);Jac.Mis.*Corp*.5 (Hardt 3:917–18);Jac.Mis. *Com.parv*.(Ryba 154–56);Joh. Rok.*Utraq*. (Mansi 30:275–76)

Andr.Brd.*Utraq*.5 (Hardt 3: 403);Joh.Rag.*Utraq*. (Mansi 29:827;797;803)

Henr.Mrl.*Immac*.173 (*FIP Txt* 10:68);Joh.Vit.*Def.BVM*.5 (Alva 183)

Joh.Pol.*Immac*.1.2.6 (*Bibl. Mar*.1:15); Henr.Lang. *Concept*.3.10 (1516:12v);Henr. Wrl.*Immac*.107 (*FIP Txt* 10: 38)

Robt.Orf.*Corr*.72 (*Bibl.Thom*. 31:274)

Guil.Mar.*Var.sent.Thom*.41 (*Opettex* 21:25) Guil.Oc.*Op.XC.dier*.23;5 (Sikes 2:472–76;1:356–59) Guil.Oc.*Op.XC.dier*.9 (Sikes 2:391;404);Guil.Oc.*Jn*.11 (Sikes 3:59) ap.Ramb.Bol.*Apol.ver*.11 (*ST* 108:137,141)

Wyc.*Euch*.5 (*WLW* 16:139–40)

*Impug.Aeg*.2 (Bruni 11)

Henr.Wrl.*Immac*.174 (*FIP Txt* 10:69)

See vol.3:280

Wm.Mar.*Corr.Thom*.117 (*Bibl. Thom*.9:427) Robt.Orf.*Corr*.117 (*Bibl. Thom*.31:343);*Impug.Aeg*.15 (Bruni 40–41)

Robt.Orf.*Repr.Aeg*.43 (*Bibl. Thom*.38:121)

chalice as well as the host to the laity in Holy Communion, they quoted him with such frequency that their opponents were obliged to reassert their own claims to him. On other hotly contested points of the time, too, the Thomist position itself became a contested point. For example, "the holy doctor Thomas in many diverse passages flatly contradicts himself" on the immaculate conception of the Virgin Mary; it was possible to line up many such contradictions from his writings, and therefore even to quote him as a partisan of the immaculate conception. Again, because his exegesis of the locus classicus on the poverty of the church, Matthew 10:9, classified the alternative views of the fathers without taking a definitive position, it was possible for the advocates of extreme poverty either to condemn him for making it permissive rather than compulsory or to quote him in extenso against the more moderate view.

Such quotations were "for the sake of those who accept the statements of Thomas." His detractors continued to cite the condemnation of some of his teachings by the bishop of Paris in 1277 as proof of his unreliability; but his canonization in 1323 and the official withdrawal of the condemnation two years later assured him a place among the church's theologians. A careful examination of his teachings would show that he did not contradict himself, at any rate not in his authentic writings. By the fifteenth century, therefore, even those who diverged most from Thomas tried to put the best construction on his teaching, often by urging that in the *Summa* he retracted and corrected certain of the positions that he had taken in the *Sentences* and that "if he were alive today, he would retract what had to be retracted even more quickly and promptly." The classic case of his having issued such a retraction was his rejection in the *Summa* of the appropriateness of using a plural to call the Father and the Son "spirators" of the Holy Spirit in the Trinity, even though he himself had used it in the *Sentences*. His critics still attacked his doctrine of "spiration," and his followers defended him against the attacks, using his change of language as evidence for the conformity of his trinitarian doctrine to that of Augustine. Even those who were willing to go on

Hs.*Sent*.1.11.4 (Flajšhans 2:
88–89)

See vol.2:189

Hs.*Sent*.1.9.4 (Flajšhans 2:84)

*Impug.Aeg*.36;30 (Bruni 86;
76–77)

Ramb.Bol.*Apol.ver*.3 (*ST* 108:
28)

Wm.Mar.*Corr.Thom*.82 (*Bibl.
Thom*.9:331–32)

*Corr.*"*Quare*" 82 (*Bibl.Thom.*
9:333–34)

Joh.Par.*Corr.*"*Circa*" 1 (*SA* 12:
5)

1 John 4:10

See vol.1:302

Aug.*Grat.Christ*.1.26.27
(*CSEL* 42:147–48

Gr.Arim.*Sent*.2.29.1.2 (1522–
II:110r)

Vall.*Enc.Thos.Aq.* (*MPPR* 6:
349–51);Vall.*Annot*.1 Cor. 9:13
(*MPPR* 5:865)

See vol.3:285–86
Thos.Aq.*S.T.*1.1.8 (*Ed.Leon*.4:
22)
Aeg.Rom.*Res.mort*.4 (Nolan
124;129)
Barth.Bon.*Assump*.2 (*Opettex*
9b:67)

saying, as he was not, that "the Father is one spirator and the Son is another" did affirm with him the Augustinian tenet that the Father and the Son were only "one principle" in the Trinity.

Thus it was "impossible to base an argument against the position [of Thomas] on the words of [Augustine]" about the Trinity, for Thomas's position left "Augustine's reasoning" intact. "In attempting to attack Friar Thomas," therefore, "they attack with him such great doctors of the church as Augustine" and others. On the basis of his assertion that a sinful act of the will always proceeded from a defect in the intellect, Thomas came under criticism for seeming to agree with the heresy of Pelagius. The response to such criticism was to point out that this represented a misreading of Pelagius, who had taught that the human will was capable of meritorious deeds without the grace of God, needing only the instruction of the law, as well as a misreading of the teaching of Thomas, who had taught nothing of the kind. Turning the tables on their adversaries, the supporters of Thomas charged that his critics were the ones who were crypto-Pelagian in their views of nature and grace. The exclusive definition of the New Testament, "In this is love, not that we loved God but that he loved us," had served Augustine as proof that "we could not have the capacity to love him unless we had received it from him in his loving us first." A leading Augustinian of the fourteenth century quoted these words of Augustine, following them with the words of Aquinas on the need for grace, in the hope that "my opponent at least will not deny the doctrine of Saint Thomas," which was in fact the doctrine of Augustine, while a leading Augustinian humanist of the fifteenth century, in his parodistic *Encomium of Saint Thomas Aquinas*, objected to the effort of some latter-day Thomists to elevate him above Augustine. Thomas's formula in summary of Augustine, "Grace does not abolish nature, but completes it," proved useful even to his opponents when they wanted to formulate the doctrine of the resurrection or the doctrine of the bodily assumption of the Virgin Mary.

Even this brief review should have made clear that "it is against the evidence of history to range the thirteenth-century [or fourteenth-century] masters into two opposite groups: Augustinians and Aristotelians, as if they pledged themselves to follow exclusively either St Augustine or Aristotle"; for "St Augustine was the recognized Master of all, not of the so-called Augustinians alone," and of the "Aristotelian" Thomas Aquinas no less than of any of his "Augustinian" detractors. Nonetheless it is historically accurate to see in the fourteenth and fifteenth centuries a vigorous effort to go beyond—or behind—the Augustinian syntheses of the earlier period, including the Thomistic version, to Augustine himself. It had long been customary to quote Augustine for the definition of "seminal forms" as the primordial realities from which, in turn, the particular realities of the empirical world were produced; that practice continued in this period, but for at least some of those who quoted him that was enough to settle the matter. A sampling of tributes from across the spectrum of fifteenth-century thought will suggest his special standing. For Pierre D'Ailly, Augustine was "the truthful doctor," the "syndic" who was authorized to speak on behalf of all the doctors of the catholic church. Thomas à Kempis made a practice of calling him "prelate [praesul]." Wycliffe appealed from what was supposed to be Thomas's teaching to what he knew to be Augustine's. John Hus referred to Augustine as "the most outstanding interpreter of Scripture," who was more entitled to the name "successor of the apostles" than all of the cardinals and most of the popes, and anti-Hussite authors agreed, at least with his praise of Augustine. Nicholas of Cusa cited Augustine as "the most prudent among the preachers of the truth," as both "saintly and most learned."

In this sense everyone was an "Augustinian." Yet as there were some men who were "Augustinians" in the special sense that they belonged to a religious order governed by the so-called *Rule* of Augustine, so also some men (in the case of such as James of Viterbo, Gregory of Rimini, Girolamo Seripando, and Martin Luther, the same men) were "Augustinians" in the special sense that they sought to reaffirm the distinctive teachings of the "doctor of grace" against what they believed to be the virulent Pelagianism and

Callus (1946) 4

Thos.Aq.*Sent*.2.18.1.2 (Mandonnet 2:454)
Jac.Vit.*Quodlib*.2.5 (Ypma 2: 59);Vit.Furn.*Quodlib*.3.5.3 (Delorme 140–42)

All.*Curs.Bibl.* (Du Pin 1:617); All.*Serm*.21 (1490:C3v) Thos.Kemp.*Tr.tabern*.1 (Pohl 1:14–15);Thos.Kemp.*Inc.* (Pohl 3:44),*Serm.conc.Const.* 28.viii.1415 (Finke 2:416) Wyc.*Euch* 5 (WLW 16:156)

Hs.*Eccl*.9e,15d (Thomson 62; 121)

Joh.Rag.*Utraq.* (Mansi 29: 821–22) Nicol.Cus.*Ep*.2 (Faber 2–II: 5r);Robt.Bas.*Form.praed*.10 (Charland 246) Nicol.Cus.*Serm*.1.pr. (Heidelberg 16:2)

Trapp (1956) 146–274

Semi-Pelagianism of their own time. The two most influential spokesmen of "Augustinianism" in this latter sense during the first half of the fourteenth century were Thomas Bradwardine and Gregory of Rimini. As is not surprising in an author whose chief theological work bore the title *The Cause of God, against Pelagius*, Bradwardine sought to align himself unequivocally on Augustine's side in the conflict over grace. He marshaled an array of quotations on the priority of grace from Augustine's books, not only from the books specifically directed against Pelagius but from other treatises also, as well as from the *Sentences* of Prosper of Aquitaine. He saw Augustine as one who had "uniquely imitated the apostle" Paul by moving from a hostility toward the doctrine of divine grace to a position as "a herald of grace and a magnificent and vigorous champion of grace." Although some theologians disagreed about the proper view of grace, "the catholic doctrine" was preferable to all other views, and "on this issue who among all authors after Holy Scripture is more reliable than Augustine?" For Augustine had clearly grasped the paradox of the gospel: "When we act we are the ones who act, but He acts so that we may act." Although it sometimes seemed that "almost the whole world is running after [Pelagius] and inclining to his errors," the consensus of "the holy church of God" was on the side of Augustine.

Gregory of Rimini, too, saw "many of the moderns . . . inclining to an error of Pelagius that has been condemned," and against them he, too, cited the consensus of "the doctrine of the saints and the definitions of the church." For his interpretation of Augustine, Gregory, like Bradwardine, drew upon Augustine's "books, sermons, and epistles written against the errors of Pelagius" and upon the critique of Cassian's Semi-Pelagianism by Prosper of Aquitaine. The Pauline formula, "It is not of him that wills, nor of him that runs, but of God who shows mercy," which was "the most often quoted scriptural passage" in Bradwardine's treatise and which Lorenzo Valla used in criticism of Boethius to clinch his argument against free will, appeared in Gregory's *Sentences* as part of Augustine's catalogue of chief passages from the apos-

Brad.*Caus.*1.23 (Savile 239)
See vol.1:327
Brad.*Caus.*3.10 (Savile 683)

Brad.*Caus.*1.35 (Savile 311)

Brad.*Caus.*2.31 (Savile 606)

Brad.*Caus.*2.20 (Savile 549)

Brad.*Caus.*2.31 (Savile 602; 604)

Gr.Arim.*Sent.*2.26–28.1.1 (1522–II:92v–93r)

Gr.Arim.*Sent.*2.26–28.1.1 (1522–II:95v)

See vol.1:318–31
Gr.Arim.*Sent.*2.29.1.1 (1522–II:104v–105r)
Rom. 9:16 (Vulg.)
Oberman (1958) 16

Vall.*Lib.arb.* (*MPPR* 5:1008–9);Vall.*Volup.*3.11 (*MPPR* 5:978)

Aug.*Ep.*186.37 (*CSEL* 57:75)

Gr.Arim.*Sent*.2.29.1.2 (1522–II:109r)

Gr.Arim.*Sent*.2.29.1.2 (1522–II:107r;110r)

See vol.1:339

Prosp.*Auct*.8 (*PL* 51:209)

Brad.*Caus*.1.1 (Savile 19)

See vol.1:308

See vol.1:327–31

See vol.3:26–30
See pp. 8–9 above

See pp. 33–34, 57 below

tle Paul that had been used to refute Pelagius; for, he added, "Augustine explains that this was not said because there is no willing or running in man, but because he cannot do anything unless [God] has mercy on him." He was careful, moreover, to disengage the doctrinal question of the catholic position from the historical question of what may or may not have been the intended position of Pelagius. Gregory was also echoing both Augustine and Prosper when he declared that "except for the passages of Scripture, the entire argumentation of the councils and of the saints against Pelagius . . . is based on this, that the saints prayed" for forgiveness, that is, on the principle that "the rule of prayer should lay down the rule of faith."

Significantly, this brand of Augustinianism concentrated almost exclusively on the anti-Pelagian pole of his thought and largely overlooked the anti-Donatist pole. When Bradwardine mentioned the Donatists at the beginning of his book, he did not even refer to their doctrine of church and sacraments. Such a separation between the two poles of Augustine's thought had also been characteristic of the corpus of Augustine's own writings. The "Augustinian synthesis" that had resolved the conflicts during the century following his death and that had gone on to shape medieval doctrine set its repetition of the anti-Pelagian Augustine's doctrine of the sovereignty of grace into the context of the anti-Donatist Augustine's doctrine of the unity of the catholic church and the objectivity of sacramental grace. Although the two would not become completely unraveled until the Reformation, we may perhaps see the beginnings of the process here, also because at this same time the distinction between the "absolute" and the "ordered" will of God was being applied to the doctrine of the sacraments in such a way as to appear to make the efficacy of the means of grace dependent upon the arbitrary decree of God rather than upon any grace inherent in the sacraments themselves.

Yet we would be gravely abridging our account of the efforts during these two centuries to go beyond the Augustinian synthesis of the immediate past if we did not pay attention also to the search for an Augustine who could once more inspire and legitimate

See vol.1:27–41

See pp. 77–78, 140 below

Bouwsma (1975) 3–60

Levi (1933) 65–66

Pet.*Sen.*15.7 (Dotti 836–38)
Pet.*Fam.*4.1 (Rossi-Bosco 1: 153–61);Pet.*Secr.*2 (Bufano 1: 104)

Pet.*Secr.*1 (Bufano 1:68)
Pet.*Secr.*3 (Bufano 1:186)

Rom.1:25
Pet.*Secr.*3 (Bufano 1:232)

Pet.*Secr.*2 (Bufano 1:130)

Pet.*Secr.*2 (Bufano 1:138)
Pet.*Secr.*1 (Bufano 1:94)

Pet.*Secr.*1 (Bufano 1:56)

Aug.*Civ.*22.27–28 (*CCSL* 48: 854–56)
Vall.*Annot.*John 21 (*MPPR* 5: 846)

Pet.*Ign.*4 (Bufano 2:1122–24)

a synthesis of Christianity with classical thought. For one of "the two faces of humanism" was its preoccupation with Augustine, and eventually with many other Christian fathers, Greek as well as Latin. Indeed, one of the seminal works of the Italian Renaissance, Petrarch's autobiographical *My Secret* of 1342–43, consists of three dialogues between the author and Augustine. Whether we take it as an expression of "the modern desire for pleasure and for earthly happiness in search of self-justification" or as a statement of "the vacillating faith, the weakness, and the internal contradictions of Petrarch" or as "a sincere document from the beginning of Petrarch's conversion and a proof of the profound influence exerted on him by Saint Augustine," *My Secret* is in any case part of an effort to disengage Augustine from the scholasticism that claimed him as a founder and to claim him as a resource for Christian humanism. This Augustine was preeminently the Augustine of the *Confessions.*

Petrarch received the *Confessions* from one Augustinian and eventually presented it to another shortly before his death, and he gave credit to a passage from this book, "which I always have in my hands," for the fundamental transformation in his life. Whenever he would read it, he said, "it seems to me that I am reading not someone else's history, but the history of my own pilgrimage." In passages filled with echoes from the *Confessions,* Petrarch represented Augustine as denouncing him for loving creature more than Creator and for yearning after literary glory and earthly immortality. He was pursuing a quasi-monastic regimen of solitude and study, but all for the sake of personal ambition. There was nothing, Augustine warned him, that was more inimical to the true knowledge of God than self-gratification; but for this warning Augustine cited the authority of Plato, by whose thought his own early works had been shaped. Throughout the dialogues he urged the author to pay attention to the best in the classical philosophers, above all Plato and Cicero. Augustine's positive treatment of the thought of Plato, about which later Renaissance thinkers were more critical, served Petrarch as a justification for asserting that Plato would have become a Christian if he had been granted the opportunity—

Pet.*Ign*.4 (Bufano 2:1114)
Aug.*Conf*.3.4.7;8.7.17 (*CSEL* 33:48–49;184–85)
Pet.*Ign*.4 (Bufano 2:1108);Pet.*Fam*.2.9.10 (Rossi-Bosco 1:92)

Pet.*Ign*.4 (Bufano 2:1062–64)
Aug.*Trin*.13.4.7 (*CCSL* 50:390–91)

Pet.*Ign*.4 (Bufano 2:1126)

Trinkaus (1970) 1:14

See vol.3:304–6

Alv.Pel.*Ep*.2.23 (Meneghin 25)

Vit.Furn.*Quodlib*.1,2 (Delorme 5);Guid.Vern.*Repr. mon*.3 (Matteini 114);Gabr.Bl. *Can.miss*.45.Z (Oberman-Courtenay 2:191)

Ambr.Trav.*Ep*.10.29;10.39 (Martène-Durand 3:340;355)

All.*Tract*.2.3.6 (1490:Dlv)
Aug.*Conf*.2.6.13–14 (*CSEL* 33:39–40)

Gers.*Myst.theol.prac*.8 (Combes 180)

Gers.*Magn*.7 (Glorieux 8:305)

Ex.3:14

See vol.1:54
Aug.*Trin*.8.3.4 (*CCSL* 50:271–73)
Gers.*Myst.theol.prac*.12 (Combes 211–12)

Gen.1:26
Aug.*Trin*.14.19.25 (*CCSL* 50:456)

a claim for which he was able to cite support from other church fathers as well. Augustine's tribute to Cicero in the *Confessions* became a justification for Petrarch's willingness to make the same claim for him. Augustine had not, however, spoken of Aristotle in this fashion, but had attacked his kind of philosophy. This made it all the more deplorable that theologians should be preferring Aristotelian philosophy to the authority of Augustine.

From Petrarch's treatment of the authority of Augustine it is clear that "more important to him than the strict letter of Augustinian orthodoxy was the paradigmatic quality of the Saint's own experience of wandering, ambivalence, psychic division and ultimate resolution of his conflict and salvation through the aid of divine grace." Nor was he the only thinker in the fourteenth and fifteenth centuries to take Augustine, especially as he had revealed himself in the *Confessions*, as a paradigm for the inner life. An Augustinian subjectivism had repeatedly appeared in medieval thought and literature, and its influence had become more prominent through the influence of Franciscan spirituality. But now the names of Augustine and Francis not only continued to be linked with those of other masters of the spiritual life; the Augustinian impulse also manifested itself in a deepened emphasis on the place of experience in the apprehension of Christian truth. While still serving as a source for conventional theological proof texts, the *Confessions* also became the object of increasing literary attention and the foundation for a theology of experience. For Augustine's analysis of the hidden but profound motivations of sin had shown him to be "the most penetrating investigator of human thought processes," even though there were elements of mystical teaching on which Dionysius the Areopagite was even more helpful. In his application of the passage, "I am who I am," to the understanding of God as absolute good and pure being, Augustine had charted the way through an experiential to a metaphysical knowledge of the divine essence. The theme of the second part of Augustine's *On the Trinity*, the discovery that the words, "Let us make man in our image," implied an image of God that was trinitarian, was combined with the critical introspection of his *Confessions* to create a mystical theology—a theology that could be quite orthodox in its doctrine, but that could also become a threat to doctrinal orthodoxy.

As will become increasingly evident throughout these first two chapters, there was no important doctrinal issue in the fourteenth and fifteenth centuries that was unaffected by the study of Augustine, and on many of the issues his influence was decisive. The question of the immaculate conception of Mary was made necessary because of Augustine's definition of original sin and of its transmission through the propagation of the human race, but the form in which the question was eventually to be resolved also came from Augustine, who had ascribed to Mary an "abundance of grace for overcoming sin in every particular." The debates over the nature of the church, notably the reexamination of the relation between the spiritual realm and the political realm, took their start from "the great doctor of the church, Augustine, [who] in his book *The City of God* describes two cities," and the polemic against the medieval view of the spiritual and the political likewise became a polemic against him. When schism and scandal made it imperative to reopen the matter of "the wicked priest" and of the relation between the subjective state of the minister and the objective state of the sacraments, the focus had to be Augustine's resolution of that relation, as he had formulated it against the Donatists. And as the problem of the relative authority of the church and the Bible grew more insistent in the fifteenth and sixteenth centuries, the various alternative theories sought to come to terms with Augustine's declaration that he would not have believed the gospel if he had not been persuaded by the authority of the catholic church. In each of these issues there was a conscious effort to get beyond the Augustinian synthesis (or the several Augustinian syntheses) to the authentic teaching of Augustine himself.

### The Plan of Salvation

One issue on which Augustine had not spoken definitively, although he had managed to encompass most of its principal themes within his thought, was the

See pp. 63–68 below

See vol.1:314
Aug.*Nat.et grat*.36.42 (*CSEL* 60:263–64)

All.*Recom.* (Du Pin 1:603)

Chel.*St.vr.*1.40–41;1.69 (*Com.* 22:118–23;171)

See vol.1:309–11

See vol.1:303
See pp. 125–26, 263–64 below
Aug.*Ep.fund.*5 (*CSEL* 25:197)

See vol.1:258

doctrine of redemption and the plan of salvation. To the extent that any formulation could be called "definitive" for this doctrine in the Latin West, it would be the understanding of the work of Christ set forth by Anselm of Canterbury, which had both systematized the doctrinal development preceding him and shaped the development after him. How profoundly Anselm's formulation did in fact continue to determine late medieval soteriology can be gauged from the self-evident way in which the central ideas of his treatises on the atonement—the conflicting claims of justice and mercy in God, the need for rendering satisfaction to the offended honor of God, and the "necessary" sufficiency of the death of Christ the God-man as the price of this satisfaction—were employed throughout the fourteenth and fifteenth centuries. Yet beneath this consensus there were profound differences, unreconciled and perhaps even irreconcilable, about the redemptive significance of the life and teachings, the suffering and death, and the resurrection and ascension of Jesus Christ. Moreover, most of the authors who can be cited in support of the consensus simultaneously manifested one or more of the differences.

See vol.3:106–57

Writing a political tract early in the fourteenth century, Dante Alighieri directly paraphrased Anselm: "If there had not been a satisfaction for sin through the death of Christ, we would still be 'by nature children of wrath.'" One of Dante's severest critics, who found little else in that tract to approve, did nevertheless agree that "for the preservation of justice" Christ had "rendered plenary satisfaction to God for the entire human race," and he quoted Anselm as the authority for this view. Also early in the fourteenth century, Ubertino of Casale depicted a conflict between mercy and justice in the "divine consistory" of the Trinity; it was resolved when God became man, because "no one could render satisfaction for the whole human race except God, and no one owed it to God except man." His contemporary and Franciscan confrere, Cardinal Vital du Four, citing Anselm, argued that "in some sense the death of Christ is necessary even for God, to whom satisfaction needs to be rendered." A generation or so later, Gregory of Rimini

Dant.*Mon*.2.11.2 (Ricci 215)

Eph.2:3

Guid.Vern.*Repr.mon*.2 (Matteini 108–9)

Ub.Cas.*Arb.vit*.1.7;1.8 (Davis 22;27)

Vit.Furn.*Quodlib*.2.5 (Delorme 72–74)

also took up the question of the difference between mercy and justice in God, concluding that it lay in the distinction between those works of God in which he manifested himself as judge and those in which he manifested himself as one who takes pity. In one of his earliest works, composed about 1370, John Wycliffe, on the basis of Anselm's *Why God Became Man*, declared that without the incarnation "the satisfaction for the sin of the first man would not have been adequate" and that therefore the one who made satisfaction had to be of the same species as the one who had offended the honor of God. At the turn of the century, Wycliffe's most famous disciple, John Hus, also quoted Anselm on the satisfaction wrought by the suffering and death of Christ, and later on took this to mean that "no one can render satisfaction for himself, except through the principal satisfaction made by the Lord Jesus Christ," whose suffering had made penitential satisfaction possible.

In the first few years of the fifteenth century, Jean de Gerson was preaching about a "satisfaction rendered to justice, which has now been satisfied," and shortly before the end of his life he was still speaking, in connection with the "satisfaction" in the sacrifice of the Mass, about the sufficiency of the suffering of Christ. Peter Chelčický, a radical Hussite, wrote in the 1440s that by "dying in a human way" Christ had "achieved the forgiveness of sins for the world" from God and had "rendered satisfaction to God the Father." Also in 1440, Cardinal Nicholas of Cusa ascribed to the "voluntary and altogether innocent . . . death on the cross of Christ the man" the power to bring about both "the satisfaction and the cleansing" of human sin; but he had been speaking the same way in his sermons for the previous decade or so, and in his *Sifting of the Koran* of 1461 he interpreted the words of the prophet Isaiah, "He has borne our griefs," to mean that "the death of the Only-begotten, who was beloved of God more than all others, rendered abundant satisfaction." Thomas à Kempis, who is best remembered for other aspects of his doctrine of the work of Christ, could also say that through the cross Christ had "redeemed us and rendered satisfaction to God the Father for our sins." Near the end of the

Gr.Arim.*Sent.*1.8.2.2 (1522–I: 71v)

Wyc.*Ben.inc.*6;13 (*WLW* 7:88; 231);Wyc.*Serm.*3.24 (*WLW* 11: 187);Wyc.*Serm.*4.23;3.34 (*WLW* 13:197–98;293)

Hs.*Sent.*3.20.5 (Flajšhans 2: 447)

Hs.*Sent.*4.15.3 (Flajšhans 2: 594)

Gers.*Serm.*212 (Glorieux 5:65)

Gers.*Magn.*9 (Glorieux 8:416)

Chel.*St.vr.*1.17 (*Com.*22:50); Chel.*Post.*37 (*Com.*16:112)

Nicol.Cus.*Doct.ign.*3.6 (Heidelberg 1:137)

Nicol.Cus.*Serm.*1.3;3.1;17.1 (Heidelberg 16:18;45;270–72)

Isa.53:4

Nicol.Cus.*Alchor.*2.17 (Faber 1:140r–v)

See pp. 36–37 below

Thos.Kemp.*Serm.Dom.*23;26 (Pohl 3:195;233–34);Thos. Kemp.*Orat.*1 (Pohl 3:336)

fifteenth century Gabriel Biel took Anselm's treatise as his authority for teaching that when mankind "was not able to satisfy the divine justice . . . , the Father of mercies gave his Son, who . . . assumed a human nature, innocent and pure, . . . and by offering it to justice rendered satisfaction"; thus God the judge had, through the passion of Christ, himself brought "a condign satisfaction, or rather satispassion." And God had accepted "this sacrifice of Christ, namely, his death, as a satisfaction for our sin."

As in the Reformation period, so already in the late medieval period with which we are dealing here, the Anselmic metaphor of Christ's death as an act of satisfaction coexisted, often in the same theologians, with other ideas that contrasted with it or even contradicted it or that at the very least gave it a special coloration. The most important such idea in the fourteenth and fifteenth centuries was the widespread emphasis on the sovereign will of God. What has been said of Pierre D'Ailly can be said of many of his predecessors and contemporaries: "The basic tenet of his thought as of Ockham's, is the unity, freedom, and omnipotence of God." It was the explicit starting point of theological treatises on a variety of themes, and the implicit presupposition of others. One theologian opened both an essay on the relation of soul and body and a full-scale dissertation on the relation between church and state with the declaration of God's free and almighty will, a theme that would recur throughout his writings and throughout his life. As the primary efficient cause, itself uncaused and uncausable, God was, in the language of Duns Scotus, "necessary of himself," a being characterized by "intelligence and will." The statement of Augustine, that "the will of God is the first and the highest cause of all bodily appearances and motions," was treated as axiomatic: "The will of God," Bradwardine affirmed, "is the efficient cause of anything whatever that is done." Therefore the will of God was, quite literally, infinitely "greater in its freedom than our will."

In such a context, each of the usual themes of Anselm's doctrine received a distinctive emphasis and content. For if, as Anselm's critics both ancient and modern have charged, he seemed to subject God to

Gabr.Bl.*Fest.Chr*.11 (1499:E4r)

Gabr.Bl.*Sanct*.28 (1499:II5v–6r)

Gabr.Bl.*Can.miss*.72.1 (Oberman-Courtenay 3:192)

See pp. 160–65 below

Oakley (1964) 22

Wyc.*Comp.hom*.1 (*WLW* 3:9); Wyc.*Civ.dom*.1.1 (*WLW* 4:7) Wyc.*Ben.inc*.5 (*WLW* 7:75–76);Wyc.*Serm*.2.37 (*WLW* 9:272) Dns.Scot.*Prim.princ*.3.5 (Roche 50)

Dns.Scot.*Prim.princ*.4.4 (Roche 80) Aug.*Trin*.3.4.9 (*CCSL* 50:136)

Aeg.Rom.*Ren.pap*.4 (1554:3v)

Brad.*Caus*.1.9 (Savile 190)

Vit.Furn.*Rer.princ*.3.3.1.23 (Wadding 4:300)

his own justice and law as though these were independent entities, the stress on the freedom of God now led to the principle: "The will of God is the norm and the ground [regula et origo] of justice." Hence a human act was intrinsically good not in and of itself, but only by virtue of its having been defined as good by the free and sovereign will of God. The mercy of God was also an expression of that immutable will and completely subordinate to it: "God does not begin loving or hating someone at a certain point. . . . Neither prayers nor any merits, whether good or bad, can turn or change the divine will in the least, either this way or that; but whatever is to be saved or damned, rewarded or punished, in whatever degree, this he willed from eternity to be saved or damned." With this definition of mercy, Anselm's image of a dispute between justice and mercy within the councils of the Trinity (elaborated and dramatized in some later versions of the theory, sometimes with the additional factor of participation by the Virgin Mary) was really no longer necessary; for God willed whatever he wanted to will, and both justice and mercy were names for the expression of that will as it was perceived.

Not only justice and mercy, however, but the central Anselmic doctrine of satisfaction itself was "relativized" under the impact of this primary stress on the divine will. "How much did that merit [of Christ's death] avail for sufficiency [in the atonement]?" Duns Scotus asked, and he answered his own question: "Just as everything else, other than God, is good for the reason that it has been willed by God, and not the other way around, so also that merit had as much goodness as it was accepted to have." Therefore it was not, as Anselm had argued, "necessary" that mankind be saved through the suffering of Christ. Mankind could have perished, or a sinless man might have saved it, or each person might have been granted the grace to merit salvation individually—any of these, depending on what the will of God decreed. "But if we want to rescue Anselm," Scotus continued, "we can say that all of his reasonings proceed on the presupposition of the divine ordinance which ordained that man should be redeemed this way. . . . By his fore-

Dns.Scot.Rep.Par.4.14.1.8
(Wadding 24:205)

Gers.Vit.spir.1 (Glorieux 3:
123–24);Gers.Magn.9
(Glorieux 8:380)

Brad.Caus.1.23 (Savile 240);
Wyc.Serm.3.44 (WLW 11:381);
Aeg.Rom.Quodlib.1.2 (1646:6)

Ub.Cas.Arb.vit.1.7 (Davis 22);
Nicol.Cus.Serm.17.1
(Heidelberg 16:270–72)

Pannenberg (1954) 137

Dns.Scot.Ox.3.19.q.un.7
(Wadding 14:718)

See vol.3:141

Dns.Scot.*Ox.q.un*.10
(Wadding 14:738)

Dns.Scot.*Ox*.4.4.7.4 (Wadding
16:480)

Thos.Sut.*Quodlib*.3.18
(Schmaus 459)

Dns.Scot.*Ox*.3.13.4.9
(Wadding 14:463)
See p. 49 below
Dns.Scot.*Quaest.* (*BFS* 3:16–
17)

Dns.Scot.*Rep.Par*.3.7.4.4
(Wadding 23:303)
Rup.*Matt*.13 (*PL* 168:1628);
Hon.Aug.*Oct.quaest*.2 (*PL*
172:1187)

Matt.18:11;Gal.4:4–5;1 Tim.1:
15

Vit.Furn.*Quodlib*.2.12.2
(Delorme 88);Ps.Ans.*Concept.
BVM* (*PL* 159:309–10)

Gabr.Bl.*Fest.Chr*.2 (1499:A5v–
A6r)
Nicol.Cus.*Doct.ign*.3.5
(Heidelberg 1:134)

1 Cor.15:45–49
Nicol.Cus.*Conc.cath*.1.3
(Heidelberg 14:39)
Lovejoy (1955) 277–95
Wyc.*Serm*.4.47 (*WLW* 13:383);
Hs.*Sent*.2.31.3 (Flajšhans 2:
321);Gers.*Serm*.236 (Glorieux
5:419);Gers.*Magn*.10
(Glorieux 8:468–69)

Capelle (1946) 230–32

ordination God willed not to accept man for redemption except through the death of his Son." Although he tried to protect this idea of "acceptation" from the accusation that it was completely arbitrary, Scotus consistently maintained that there was nothing "necessary" about the death of Christ on the cross as the means of human redemption. At most, as another theologian put it, it could be called "the most appropriate [convenientissimus]" means.

If the incarnation and the cross were not "necessary," that could imply a diminution of the importance of Christ. For Scotus, however, quite the opposite was the case. He took it as an operating principle that "in paying homage to Christ I would rather go too far than not far enough to give him the praise that is due him." This "maximalism," which he applied also to the Virgin Mary within the limits set by the authority of the church and of Scripture, led Scotus to the position that since the incarnation of the Logos was supreme among the acts of God, it would be demeaning to the glory of Christ to maintain that the incarnation was caused by the fall of Adam. For "if the fall were the cause of the predestination of Christ, it would follow that the supreme work of God was merely a reaction to something else [occasionatum tantum]." This led ineluctably to the question, raised already in the twelfth century, whether there would have been an incarnation even if there had been no fall. It was possible to cite passages from the New Testament that seemed to say quite unambiguously "that if man had not sinned, the Son of God would not have been incarnate." On the other hand, that appeared to make redemption from sin the sole cause of the incarnation, when in fact God had by this means exalted human nature above all creatures. By becoming man, the Logos had become "the center of existence for human nature" and, as the second Adam, the key to the meaning of the first Adam. To attribute all of this to the sin of Adam was to posit what has been called "the paradox of the fortunate fall," which in this period was usually traced to Gregory the Great (although its origins are even earlier, perhaps in the work of Ambrose of Milan). Jean Gerson may be taken as a spokesman for a centrist position. Although he insisted that "the purpose of the incarnation was not the perfection of the universe nor the return of creatures to God, . . . but the only or at least the principal purpose was the cleansing of our flesh," he did concede that even without the fall God would have found the supreme way of revealing his love in Christ. But on this issue, as on all issues relating to the plan of salvation, everyone had to confess that "if God wanted to, he could" redeem any way he chose, for the will of God remained free, sovereign, and omnipotent.

Gers.*Serm*.252 (Glorieux 5: 601);Gers.*Magn*.11 (Glorieux 8:489)

The will of God articulated itself most comprehensively in divine predestination, of which the plan of salvation was an integral part, Christ himself having been "predestined to be the Son of God in power." In the fourteenth and fifteenth centuries, as in the fifth and sixth centuries, again in the ninth, and yet again in the sixteenth and seventeenth, the doctrine of predestination became a test case of Augustinianism. Notions of the relation between nature and grace that appeared excessively optimistic were "inclining to an error of Pelagius that has been condemned," and the antidote was a reassertion of Augustinian predestinarianism. Important as the quest for the authentic Augustine was in the renewed focus on the doctrine of predestination, however, the special form of that doctrine during this period, which in some theologians produced the anomaly of a predestinarian Semi-Pelagianism, is attributable to the further development of the doctrine of the divine will.

Gers.*Cant*.5 (Glorieux 8:615)
Wyc.*Serm*.1.32 (*WLW* 8:219); Gers.*Magn*.9 (Glorieux 8:410–11)

Rom.1:4(Vulg.)

See vol.1:318–28;vol.3:80–95

See pp. 224–28, 379–80 below

Gr.Arim.*Sent*.2.26–28.1.1 (1522–II:93r)

See p. 35 below

Scotus based his own doctrine of predestination on an understanding of the divine will as proceeding "not by diverse acts, but by a single act, yet in diverse manners [diversimode]": "first, he wills an end, and in this his action is perfect and his will blessed; secondly, he wills those things that are immediately ordained to that [end], namely, by predestinating the elect . . . ; thirdly, he wills those things that are necessary for the attainment of that end, namely, the benefits of grace." With Augustine, he quoted the doxology of Romans 11:33 as a warning against prying into the mysteries of God, but he added, significantly: "Let each choose that opinion that pleases him most, just as long as the freedom of God is

Dns.Scot.*Ox*.3.32.q.un.6 (Wadding 15:433)

See vol.3:276

Dns.Scot.Ox.1.41.q.un.13
(Wadding 10:699)

Dns.Scot.Prim.princ.4.4
(Roche 82)

Dns.Scot.Ox.1.40.q.un.2
(Wadding 10:680)

Dns.Scot.Ox.1.40.q.un.3
(Wadding 10:681)

See vol.3:272–74

Thos.Aq.Sent.1.38.5
(Mandonnet 1:907–15)

Brad.Caus.3.27 (Savile 713)
Guil.Mar.Corr.Thom.3 (Bibl.
Thom.9:18)

Robt.Orf.Corr.3 (Bibl.Thom.
31:38–39)

Corr."Quare" 3;78 (Bibl.
Thom.9:22;325–26)

Thos.Sut.Quodlib.2.5
(Schmaus 203)

Joh.Par.Corr.3 (SA 12:22)

Aeg.Rom.Praed.2 (1525:25)

Aeg.Rom.Cog.ang.10 (1503:
103v);Aeg.Rom.Quodlib.1.10
(1646:21–23)

Aeg.Rom.Quodlib.6.1 (1646:
351);Ramb.Bol.Apol.ver.3 (ST
108:25)

Schwamm (1934) 1

safeguarded without any injustice, as well as everything else about God that needs to be safeguarded." To safeguard the freedom of God, he argued that God, as first cause, caused events contingently and without necessity, and that therefore such causing was free. Thus God also predestined contingently, since it lay in his freedom not to have predestined, and God was not the captive of his own action but remained free. The denial of the freedom of God was attributable to the tendency of the human mind to treat "an act of the divine will as something in the past," when in fact whatever was eternal was in the present; so it was with the divine will, so that "in the 'now' of eternity God can will freely whatever he wills, in such a way as though his will were not determined in any way [ad nihil]."

As it had with his predecessors, this line of reasoning led Scotus into the problem of the foreknowledge of God, specifically the divine knowledge of future contingents. Thomas's explanation, that such terms as "contingency" and "necessity" pertained only to "lower," not to "higher," causes, became controversial in the fourteenth century. It was attacked as "containing a manifest error, indeed many errors"; and his defenders reaffirmed that God knew future contingents from eternity insofar as they were all in the present to him, rejecting the explanation of Bonaventure and others, that God had the "ideas [rationes]" of these contingent events before him, as well as the closely related explanation of such thinkers as Thomas Sutton that God perceived the "causes" of these events. Scotus's contemporary, Giles of Rome, took it as a basic principle that both "divine foreknowledge and future contingents stand, and neither of them abolishes the other." This led him into a consideration of whether the angels could have foreknowledge of future contingents, at least by conjecture. He came to the conclusion that the way God knew the future must be the same way as the way he knew the present. It is in the context of these investigations of the matter by the contemporaries and near-contemporaries of Scotus that we can assess the judgment that "he was the first to formulate clearly the source and the means of knowing future contingents," as well as the judgment that "Scotus attains the dimension of a new formulation of the question."

Pannenberg (1954) 118

In the light of what has been said already regarding his views about intellect and will, we can see that it was consistent with his general approach to the question when Scotus made the divine will central to his definition of predestination. "Predestination properly understood," he defined, "refers to an act of the divine will, namely, to the ordering of the election of some intellectual or rational creature to grace and glory through the divine will," adding however that in a derivative sense "it could also be understood as referring to an act of the intellect that accompanies this election." In the phrase "ordering to grace and glory," moreover, "glory" was the essential element and "grace" the means by which this end was to be attained. By shifting the emphasis from the divine intellect to the divine will, Scotus could also put the matter of foreknowledge in its place; for "the necessity of foreknowledge or of the foreknown as foreknown" was indeed a "necessity of immutability," but this did not make it a matter of "absolute determination," since such determination would pertain to the will of God, not to the knowledge or foreknowledge of his intellect. If foreknowledge by the divine intellect could not serve as the basis of predestination by the divine will, that meant that "there is in the one who is predestinated no basis for predestination somehow prior to the predestination." As for reprobation, on the other hand, there was "some sort of basis [aliqua causa]" in the one who was foreknown as damned, but this, too, must be formulated in such a way as not to render God "passive" in the act of reprobation, which, insofar as it was an action of God, was a free act of the divine will, no less than was the act of predestination to glory.

Dns.Scot. Ox.1.40.q.un.2
(Wadding 10:680)

Dns.Scot. Ox.3.7.3.2 (Wadding
14:349);Dns.Scot. Rep.Par.3.7.
4.2 (Wadding 23:301)

Dns.Scot. Quodlib.16.17
(Wadding 26:200)

Dns.Scot. Ox.1.41.q.un.11
(Wadding 10:697)

Other leading theologians of the period also concentrated their attention on the term "plan" in the phrase "plan of salvation" and made the doctrines of predestination and reprobation the focus of their soteriology (as well as of their ecclesiology). Such champions of Augustine as Thomas Bradwardine and Gregory of Rimini were willing, in opposition to the neo-Pelagianism they discerned around them, to fol-

Aug.*Enchir.*26.100 (*CCSL* 46: 103)

Gr.Arim.*Sent.*1.40–41.1.2 (1522–I:160r)

Gr.Arim.*Sent.*1.38.2.3 (1522–I:153r)

Gr.Arim.*Sent.*2.29.1.1 (1522–II:103v)

Gr.Arim.*Sent.*1.40–41.1.2 (1522–I:158v)

Brad.*Caus.*1.45 (Savile 421–22)

See vol.1:297
Aug.*Praed.sanct.*10.19 (*PL* 44: 974)

Aug.*Persev.*14.35 (*PL* 45:1014)

Brad.*Caus.*2.14 (Savile 515)
Aug.*Trin.*15.13.22 (*CCSL* 50: 495)

Ecclus.23:20

Brad.*Caus.*1.23 (Savile 237)

Brad.*Caus.*1.45 (Savile 425)
Aug.*Pelag.*2.7.15;4.6.16
(*CSEL* 60:475–78;538–40);
Aug.*Retract.*1.22.3 (*CSEL* 36: 107–8)
Mal.1:2–3;Rom.9:13

low their master all the way. In his *Enchiridion* and elsewhere, Augustine had quite overtly asserted a predestination to punishment no less than a predestination to grace. Quoting the *Enchiridion*, together with Romans 9:18, Gregory of Rimini declared: "Just as God has predestinated from eternity those whom he willed to, not on account of any future merits, so also he has condemned from eternity those whom he willed to, not on account of their future demerits." As omniscient, God did of course know both the merits and the demerits, but he did not base his predestination to either salvation or condemnation upon his knowledge. This knowledge, moreover, which extended to future contingents, did not abolish their contingency. Distinguishing between the "general assistance" of God, which extended to all actions of all creatures, and the "special assistance" granted only to some, "which is commonly called the assistance of grace," he used a catena of quotations from Augustine to make the point that this latter kind of divine assistance was the effect of predestination.

Bradwardine, too, identified the divine assistance of grace, together with justification, merit, perseverance to the end, and eternal blessedness, all as effects of predestination; and he took all of these to be implied in Augustine's definition of predestination as "the preparation of grace." Elsewhere Augustine had expanded this definition to read "the foreknowledge and the preparation of God's kindnesses." Reflecting this and other such passages from Augustine, Bradwardine sometimes made predestination and the foreknowledge of God identical: "To arrange his future works in his infallible and immutable foreknowledge is nothing other than to predestinate." Another passage from Augustine served as the basis for teaching, on the authority of the biblical statement that "before the universe was created it was known to him," that the divine foreknowledge of things was the cause of their coming into being. Bradwardine's treatment of Esau and Jacob as types of predestination to salvation and reprobation owed its inspiration to Augustine's exegesis of the biblical words, "Jacob have I loved, but Esau have I hated." All of this was directed against the neo-Pelagians and was intended to reinforce "the main motif of his doctrine of predestination: predestination does not happen on account of human works, but on account of the gracious will of God," together with its corollary and "the leitmotif in Bradwardine's doctrine of God: the absolute sovereignty of God."

Oberman (1958) 115

Oberman (1958) 75

The reformatory preaching of John Wycliffe makes it clear that the philosophical theology of a Duns Scotus and the radical Augustinianism of a Bradwardine or a Gregory of Rimini were not the only possible grounds for the doctrine of predestination, for Wycliffe put his version of the doctrine into the service of his program of church reform. This he did most explicitly by defining the church as the congregation of the predestined rather than the institution governed by the pope—a definition that stemmed from Augustine and that was taken over by Hus as well as by the Reformers of the sixteenth century. Behind this definition of the church lay the insistence that God himself was the first cause and the only cause of predestination to salvation as well as of damnation, with man playing a purely "passive" part in both. To an extent that appeared to lay his doctrine open to the charge of pagan fatalism, Wycliffe was willing to use the term "necessity" to describe the involvement of God in everything that happened, although he also asserted that no one could belong to the family of God unless he did so of his own free will. He admitted that he had changed his position on certain issues in the doctrine of predestination. Thus even the sin of Adam could be called "necessary" because it served as the occasion for the exaltation of the human race in Christ. Emphasizing that no one could know who was predestined to salvation and who was foredoomed, he nevertheless emphasized equally the existential obligation of the faithful to hope that they belonged to the company of the predestined, even though they could be deceived in that hope. Although God called both the predestined and the foredoomed, and the death of Christ benefited both, bringing salvation to the former and a mitigation of punishment to the latter, it was nevertheless only for the predestined that Christ had come into the world, only to them that Christ had addressed his message, and only from them that God accepted intercessory prayer. For

Wyc.*Serm.*4.5;4.18 (*WLW* 13: 42–46;148)

Wyc.*Serm.*4.4 (*WLW* 13:40)

See vol.3:303

See pp. 75–76, 173–74 below

Wyc.*Serm.*1.52 (*WLW* 8:347)

ap.Wyc.*Dial.*22–23 (*WLW* 5: 45–46)

Wyc.*Serm.*1.42 (*WLW* 8:282); Hs.*Eccl.*6B (Thomson 41)

Wyc.*Serm.*4.36 (*WLW* 13:305)

Wyc.*Serm.*1.54 (*WLW* 8:357)

Wyc.*Serm.*1.35 (*WLW* 8:236)

Wyc.*Serm.*2.50 (*WLW* 9:361)

Wyc.*Serm.*3.23 (*WLW* 11:182); Wyc.*Serm.*2.17 (*WLW* 9:124); Hs.*Sent.*1.40.4 (Flajšhans 2: 165–66) Wyc.*Serm.*1.34;1.52 (*WLW* 8: 228–29;343–44)

Wyc.*Serm.*2.24 (*WLW* 9:173–74) Wyc.*Serm.*4.10;4.11 (*WLW* 13:82–84;90–91)

Wyc.*Serm.*1.29 (*WLW* 8:193) Wyc.*Serm.*4.9 (*WLW* 13:76)

the truly predestined could not be damned, regardless of how much they had sinned, and the reprobate could not be saved.

Wyc.*Civ.dom*.1.2 (*WLW* 4:15)

By introducing (or reintroducing) such deterministic-sounding ideas as necessity, foreordination, and double predestination, these theologians of the fourteenth century were all also obliged to deal with the question of free will. To the question, "How can freedom coexist with necessity?" Duns Scotus replied: "One should not seek a reason for things for which no reason can be given." The freedom of the will was axiomatic, in spite of the antinomy between it and the divine will. It was no less axiomatic for the "Augustinians." Gregory of Rimini, replying to the charge that his emphasis on the need for grace implied a negation of free will, drew upon his distinction between the "general assistance" and the "special assistance" of God to assert that neither of them deprived man of his freedom, and went on to explain, on the basis of Augustine, that even in Adam free will had needed divine assistance to perform the good. Augustine was likewise the source for the argument by Wycliffe's disciple, John Hus, that the foreknowledge of God did not do away with either contingency or the free will of man. In addition to Augustine, Anselm provided definitions of free will that made it possible for these theologians to put forth such arguments even in a predestinarian system.

Dns.Scot.*Quodlib*.16.9 (Wadding 26:194)

See p. 62 below

Gr.Arim.*Sent*.2.26–28.1.3 (1522–II:100r)

Aug.*Corrept*.11.31 (*PL* 44:935)
Gr.Arim.*Sent*.2.29.1.1 (1522–II:103v)

Aug.*Civ*.5.9 (*CCSL* 47:136–40)
Hs.*Sent*.1.38.3 (Flajšhans 2:161)
Ans.*Lib.arb*.1 (Schmitt 1:208); Ans.*Conc*.3 (Schmitt 2:251–52)

Dns.Scot.*Quodlib*.16.8 (Wadding 26:194);Gr.Arim. *Sent*.2.23–25.1.1 (1522–II:91r)

Significantly, however, when Anselm defined free will in such a way as to include both human reason and the human will, the voluntarism of this period required the explanation that "among the powers of the soul, only the will is free by its own freedom and essentiality." The voluntaristic presupposition applied, and preeminently so, to the doctrine of God, making possible a distinction within the will of God that could also safeguard the freedom of the will of man. Thomas Aquinas had distinguished between the "absolute power" of God, according to which "God can do other things than those he has foreknown and preordained to do," and his "ordinate power," by which he did only what he had foreknown and preordained. "For God does things because he so wills; yet he is able to do so, not because he so wills, but because

Ans.*Lib.arb*.3 (Schmitt 1:212)

Jac.Vit.*Quodlib*.1.7.3 (Ypma 1:107)

Thos.Aq.*S.T.*1.1.25.5.ad 1
(*Ed.Leon.* 4:297);Wyc.*Serm.*1.
34 (*WLW* 8:231–32)

Guid.Vern.*Repr.mon.*2
(Matteini 102–3)

Petr.Lomb.*Sent.*1.46.1;1.45.1
(*Spic.Bon.*1–II:312–13;306);
Thos.Aq.*Sent.*1.46.1;1.45.1.ad
4 (Mandonnet 1:1050;1038)
Gabr.Bl.*Can.miss.*68.C-F
(Oberman-Courtenay 3:120–
23);Gabr.Bl.*Fest.Chr.*4 (1499:
B3v)

See p. 237 below

1 Tim.2:4

Brad.*Caus.*1.39 (Savile 356–
57);Vall.*Lib.arb.* (*MPPR* 5:
1009)

Thos.Sut.*Quodlib.*1.18
(Schmaus 127,129);Gers.*Myst.
theol.prac.*1 (Combes 129);
Barth.Pis.*Quad.*5 (1498:B2v)

Hs.*Sent.*1.46.3 (Flajšhans 2:
178)

Wyc.*Serm.*1.34 (*WLW* 8:231)

1 Tim.2:1

he is such in his nature." But that distinction was eventually applied to the will of God itself, issuing in a series of distinctions: between his "absolute will" and his "ordinate will"; between his "antecedent will," which was not always fulfilled, and his "consequent will," which was; and between "the will of his good pleasure [voluntas beneplaciti]," which it was impossible for any creature to resist, and "the will of his self-disclosure [voluntas signi]," which "is not always carried out, especially that which pertains to commands, prohibitions, and counsels."

By means of such distinctions, that perpetual crux of interpretation for Augustine and his predestinarian followers, the statement that God "desires all men to be saved and to come to the knowledge of the truth," could now be fitted into the schema of how the will of God operated. Augustine's explanation of the passage may still have been satisfactory to some; but the use of the passage by others to oppose what they regarded as an arbitrary doctrine of predestination, unworthy of either God or man, made it obligatory for the advocates of predestination to find a more satisfying resolution of the contradiction between the will of God as expressed in this passage and the will of God as executed in predestination and reprobation. And so it was one thing to say, "God desires all men to be saved," but quite another if one were to say, "God desires [i.e., decides] that all men are to be saved"; "for the first proposition is true according to the antecedent will of God, but the second is false, because it suggests that all men have fulfilled the commandments and consequently will be saved." Although according to the absolute power of God it was possible for all men to attain the beatitude of eternal life, "nevertheless it is contrary to the ordinate will of God that all men attain beatitude, and in the same way it is made impossible for anyone who has been foreknown as damned to attain beatitude, just as it is impossible for the number of those in the church triumphant to be increased." The context of the words from 1 Timothy 2:4 was the admonition "that supplications, prayers, intercessions, and thanksgivings be made for all men," but that admonition, too, had to be explained. The "simple people" who did pray

Brad.*Caus*.1.25 (Savile 250)

Aug.*Civ*.21.24 (*CCSL* 48:789–90)

Brad.*Caus*.1.23 (Savile 242)

for all men believed that they could change the will of God by their prayers; for this they were forgiven, because of their ignorance and their good intentions. For as Augustine had said, the church prayed for all men but was heard only for those who had been predestined.

See vol.3:106–7

The combination of predestination with voluntarism, and therefore the articulation of a doctrine that managed to appear simultaneously deterministic and Pelagian, found expression in the thought of William of Ockham and his followers. Ockham's treatise *Predestination and the Foreknowledge of God*, like Anselm's *Why God Became Man* two centuries or so earlier, was a philosophical treatment of church doctrine, relevant here for its dogmatic import rather than for its logical analysis; for, like Anselm, Ockham took

Guil.Oc.*Praed*.1;2.1;2.2 (*FIP OPh* 2:517–18;520;522)

as his starting point and as his norm the sayings of the fathers and the authority of the faith. "The entire difficulty in this subject" of predestination lay in the contradiction between the infallibility of the divine foreknowledge, whether this pertained to salvation and reprobation or to purely temporal matters, and

Guil.Oc.*Praed*.5 (*FIP OPh* 2:539)

a human free will that could, if it was truly free, negate that foreknowledge. The terms "predestination" and "reprobation" did not refer to realities that were dis-

Guil.Oc.*Praed*.1 (*FIP OPh* 2:514)

tinct and separate unto themselves, but to the God who granted eternal life or who imposed damnation. But this must not be taken to imply, as it was being taken, that the God who predestinated imposed a necessity on the one whom he predestinated; for "the created will does not follow the divine ordinance or determination necessarily, but freely and contin-

Guil.Oc.*Praed*.1 (*FIP OPh* 2:519)

Guil.Oc.*Praed*.4 (*FIP OPh* 2:537)

gently, and yet it does not follow from this that 'therefore the divine will can be hindered.'" Consequently it was valid to conclude that both in the predestined and in the damned there was a "cause" of their ultimate destiny—not indeed in the sense of "one thing having another thing as its effect," since in that sense God himself was the true "cause," but in the sense of

Guil.Oc.*Praed*.1 (*FIP OPh* 2:519)

a thing that had "priority . . . with respect to an inference" about the person.

Although among scholastic theologians these issues of predestination, contingency, and grace may have occupied a prominent, perhaps a dominant, place in the presentation of the doctrine of salvation, even a predestinarian theologian like Wycliffe was obliged to acknowledge that the "primary" component of salvation lay elsewhere, namely, in "coming to Christ through imitation," which was to be followed by the hearing of the words of Christ and by obedience to them in deeds. "For who will be saved unless he has imitated Christ in his virtue?" he added, concluding that "only he who is virtuous will be saved by faith, and no Christian can be virtuous unless he has imitated this leader." The imitation of Christ was the true rule of life, which would bring salvation to all who followed it (meaning, of course, the predestined). The example of Christ was the most familiar and the most reliable of all, and "every action of Christ is an instruction to us." What Christ had done in his deeds, he also taught in his words. Whether or not this principle also applied to his attitude toward owning property, and how, was a matter of widespread controversy. Frequently, but by no means consistently, such statements about the primacy of the imitation of Christ as the means for attaining salvation had as their context a more comprehensive summary of the saving work of Christ: imitation stood as the middle member of three such means, the first being the memory of the passion of Christ as the divine-human satisfaction for sin and the third being the veneration of Christ or the resistance of future temptation.

The imitation of Christ's example and the obedience to his teachings had, of course, been seen from the beginning as a component of salvation. Abelard's alleged overemphasis on it served to warn later thought, but that did not deter even his severest critics from making much of this theme. During the fourteenth and fifteenth centuries, however, the devotion to Christ as man and the imitation of his example became more intense, partly through the devotion to Francis of Assisi, and churchmen who otherwise might disagree joined in the assertion that "the sum of the Christian religion is the imitation of him whom we worship" and that "the entire Christian life consists in following Christ." The most widely read devotional handbook of the time—in fact, one of the most widely read books of all time—was the *Imitation of Christ*, which ap-

Wyc.*Serm.*1.59 (*WLW* 8:385–86)

Wyc.*Serm.*4.38 (*WLW* 13:315)

Wyc.*Serm.*3.15 (*WLW* 11:117)
Wyc.*Serm.*4.33;4.49;1.23 (*WLW* 13:284;13:394;8:158)
Wyc.*Civ.dom.*1.17 (*WLW* 4:122)
Ub.Cas.*Tr.scel.* (*AFH* 10:158);
Ub.Cas.*Arb.vit.*2.1 (Davis 81);
Wyc.*Serm.*1.23 (*WLW* 8:159)
See pp. 87–91 below

Wyc.*Serm.*4.41;4.45 (*WLW* 13:342;368)

See vol.1:142–46

See vol.3:127–29

See vol.3:147–51

Ub.Cas.*Arb.vit.*5.6 (Davis 447–49);Barth.Pis.*Quad.*34;17 (1498:K8r–K8v;E8r–E8v)

Alv.Pel.*Ep.*26.6;26.10 (Meneghin 174;181)
Hs.*Post.ad.*142 (Ryšánek 13:527);Gers.*Serm.*208 (Glorieux 5:17–18)

peared at the beginning of the fifteenth century and is usually attributed to Thomas à Kempis.

Here the contemplation of Christ and of his suffering stood in opposition to speculation about predestination, about why one person should be saved and another not. Instead of speculating about lofty and heavenly matters, the believer should find his peace in the passion of Christ. This meant that one was not to trust in one's own merits but only in the merits of the cross of Christ, "through whom the forgiveness of sins is granted, from whom there flow the riches of merits, with whom is the reward of the righteous." Thus the imitation of Christ was not a substitute for redemption through his cross and the infusion of merit, and yet the primary emphasis lay on following the example of Christ in his passion, as this was made possible by the forgiveness of sins. Contemplation of the passion and conformity to the entire life of Christ constituted the source of the greatest solace, and the contemplation of his death was the source of a "spiritual and inner life, filled with grace and virtue." Following Christ as he took up his cross meant interposing his suffering and death between oneself and the judgment of God, but it also meant holding forth before oneself the image of the crucified Christ and taking up his cross.

Sometimes, this imperative of Christ to imitate him was accompanied by the warning: "The time for my coming is near. See to it that I find you prepared. Behold, I have predicted this to you." The sense of living in the last times was widespread in these centuries. To be sure, ever since the transformation of the apocalyptic vision in the early church, the component elements of that vision had remained present in Scripture and in the creeds of the church. They may have seemed more or less quiescent for long periods, but repeatedly they had erupted when a historical crisis found a prophet to sound the alarm and issue the ancient summons: "Repent, for the kingdom of heaven is at hand." For some medieval believers (though perhaps not, it would seem from the sources, for as many of them as modern writers often suppose), one such apocalyptic moment had been the end of the first Christian millennium. Such a reawakening of the

Thos.Kemp.*Im.Chr.*3.58 (Pohl 2:256–57)
Thos.Kemp.*Im.Chr.*2.1 (Pohl 2:61)

Thos.Kemp.*Vit.Chr.*1.2.18 (Pohl 5:116)

Thos.Kemp.*Vit.Chr.*1.1.24 (Pohl 5:52)
Thos.Kemp.*Disc.cl.*13 (Pohl 2:309–11);Thos.Kemp.*Spir.ex.*4 (Pohl 2:339)

Thos.Kemp.*Mort.vit.* (Pohl 2:385)
Thos.Kemp.*Vit.Chr.*1.2.30 (Pohl 5:188)
Thos.Kemp.*Im.Chr.*1.25 (Pohl 2:54)
Thos.Kemp.*Cant.*20 (Pohl 4:268–72);Gers.*Ep.*83 (Glorieux 2:331–33)

Thos.Kemp.*Soliloq.*11 (Pohl 1:244)
Henr.Lang.*Tel.*34 (Pez 1–II:545–46);Petr.Lut.*Lig.frat.*1 (*BPIR* 10:44–45)

See vol.1:123–32

Matt.3:2

apocalyptic vision in the tenth century—or in the fourteenth and fifteenth—would not of itself belong to the history of the development of Christian doctrine, since, strictly speaking, the doctrine of the last things had always been on the books and apocalypticism was merely the application of the doctrine to a particular epoch. What made late medieval apocalypticism important doctrinally was the growing belief in this period that "the man of sin, the son of perdition," the Antichrist whose coming was to be the principal sign of the end, was not some emperor (Nero or Frederick II) nor some false prophet (Arius or Mohammed), but the visible head of Christendom himself. This growing belief will concern us in the next chapter, as part of the fifteenth-century debate over the catholicity of the church and the apostolicity of the papacy.

2 Thess.2:3(Vulg.)

See p. 109 below

## The Communication of Grace

To no area of Christian doctrine had the medieval development added more than it did to the communication of grace through the saints (especially through—and to—the Virgin Mary) and through the sacraments (especially through the Eucharist). Yet it is indicative of the doctrinal pluralism of the fourteenth and fifteenth centuries that these two media of communicating grace, and particularly the first, should have predominated in the controversies and in the constructive developments of the period. Both of these doctrines, moreover, involved the determination of what was authentically Augustinian teaching.

During the twelfth and thirteenth centuries the devotion to Mary had expressed itself in a vast body of literature, theological as well as poetic; yet the doctrinal outcome of the development had been anything but conclusive. Bernard of Clairvaux, celebrated as the most ardent of the devotees of the Virgin and as one who was privy to her innermost secrets, had left unresolved the problem of how her unique holiness was to be squared with the universality of original sin. When Thomas Aquinas and Bonaventure died in 1274, the problem was still not much nearer to being settled; and the legend that Duns Scotus was born in that year, historically inaccurate though it was, may

See vol.3:160–74
Chauc.Cant.15.497–98;Ub.
Cas.Sanct.ap. (ALKGMA 2:
403);Henr.Lang.Concept.1.3
(1516:1v);Thos.Kemp.Serm.
nov.25 (Pohl 6:237)

See vol.3:171

See p. 13 above

perhaps be seen as the expression of his historic contribution to the doctrine of Mary, for it was he "who fired France for Mary without spot." The dogma that was eventually to become official in 1854 had not yet taken shape when the period covered by the present volume of this work began, but by the time this period was over there was very little of substance to be added. Taking their lead from Scotus rather than primarily from their earlier master, Bonaventure, Franciscan theologians became the champions of the new Mariology, while many Dominicans, partly in defense of their master Thomas Aquinas, opposed it, although they, too, accepted it by the conclusion of this period, explaining that it was necessary to go beyond Thomas, as well as beyond Bernard and Bonaventure, in this matter.

As even a sampling will suggest, the traditional themes of patristic and medieval Mariology continued to figure prominently in this period: the ancient parallelism of Eve and Mary (which permitted the inversion "Eva/Ave"); the conciliar definition of Mary as Theotokos; and the identification of Mary (as well as of the church) as the "woman clothed with the sun" in Revelation 12:1. Among her many titles—such as "the venerable mother of Jesus, Queen of heaven, Ruler of the world"—"Queen of mercies" seemed to hold a special place because of its emphasis on her care for mankind. Like their predecessors, the writers of this period considered the relation of virginity and maternity in Mary, concluding that her divine maternity was an even greater good than her perfect virginity. The Ave Maria, which ranked alongside the Lord's Prayer itself as the holiest among all prayers, continued to serve as a text for an exposition of her prerogatives. Among these prerogatives as enumerated in the Ave Maria, the phrase "full of grace" pointed to the quality that set her apart even from the greatest of the other saints; she was, in fact, set apart from all angels as well as from all humanity. Although Stephen had also been called "full of grace" in Acts 6:8, Mary had possessed this fullness "in the supreme state possible for a mortal," perhaps already during her lifetime but certainly at its end. On the other hand, it was also necessary to stress that the fullness of grace pred-

Hpk.*Pms*.44 (Gardner 84)

Ambr.Cath.*Immac*.2 (1542: 52); Ambr.Cath.ap.CTrid. Act.16.xii.1546 (*CT* 5:720)

See vol.3:68–74;160–74
Aug.Rom.*Serm.mag*.6 (Zumkeller 131);Gabr.Bl.*Fest. Mar*.1;13 (1499:A1v.–A2r;G2v) Hs.*Sent*.3.4.5 (Flajšhans 2: 404);Ub.Cas.*Arb.vit*.1.11 (Davis 68)
Nicol.Cus.*Serm*.6.1;8,13–15 (Heidelberg 16:106;144–74; 252–60);Jac.Mis.*Zjev*.12:1 (*Pram*.18:453)
Thos.Kemp.*Vit.Chr*.1.2,25 (Pohl 5:153);Thos.Kemp.*Serm. Dom*.6;7 (Pohl 3:96;104–5)

Ps.Alb.M.*Mar*.162 (Borgnet 37:237)

Aeg.Rom.*Quodlib*.6.18 (1646: 413,415);Gers.*Magn*.4 (Glorieux 8:222)Ps.Alb.M. *Mar*.142 (Borgnet 37:201) Thos.Kemp.*Epit.mon*.5 (Pohl 4:147–48)
Joh.Rup.Serm.8 (*FIP Txt* 12: 17)

Luke 1:28(Vulg.)
Gers.*Magn*.11 (Glorieux 8: 480);Thos.Kemp.*Tr.tabern*.2 (Pohl 1:37,42);Thos.Kemp. *Serm.frat*.4 (Pohl 1:101–2) Vall.*Volup*.3.18–19 (*MPPR* 5: 984)

Gabr.Bl.*Sanct*.6 (1499:BB4r); Gabr.Bl.*Fest.Mar*.21 (1499: L2v);Wyc.*Serm*.2.11 (*WLW* 9: 76)

icated of Christ in such passages as John 1:14 set him apart also from his mother, since hers was a grace that had to be received before it was given to others while his grace was his own, and "without measure," by virtue of his divine nature.

The absolute necessity for a qualitative distinction between Christ and Mary served as a restraint on a tendency that had already become visible in the attribution to her of the title "mediatrix," which during this period found an eloquent spokesman in Thomas à Kempis. He called Mary "the expiator of all the sins I have committed" and "my only hope"; it was through her mediation that all mercy was granted, and through her intercession that all prayers were heard. Although Christ in his final hours of need had not sought her solace, mortals were to do so. Therefore, he said, "do not seek only Jesus," but "Jesus at your right hand and Mary at your left." Various titles, prerogatives, functions, and scriptural passages that had originally belonged to Christ were now by extension being "transferred" to Mary. One of the most important proof texts in the early debates over the Trinity had been Proverbs 8:22–31, whose designation of personified Wisdom as supreme among God's creatures had been a crux for orthodox doctrine; but now this passage was a reference to Mary, who was the crown of creation. Transposing the words of John 3:16, a thirteenth-century theologian could say: "Mary so loved the world, that is, sinners, that she gave her only Son for the salvation of the world." The words of Matthew 20:28 about Christ's giving his life for the redemption of many pertained also to Mary as, for that matter, christological proof texts such as Philippians 2:5–11, Hebrews 1: 1–2, and even Matthew 11:27, pertained to Francis.

Nor was it only the function of Christ that Mary took over, but after his ascension into heaven "the Virgin remains on earth, and, together with the Holy Spirit as Comforter and Teacher, she herself becomes the comforter and teacher of the disciples." She had been the teacher of Joseph about the details of the incarnation; and at the crucifixion, when all the disciples wavered in their faith, she alone had been "the total church and the total faith of the Christian church."

Barth.Pis.*Quad*.56 (1498:R4r); Ps.Alb.M.*Mar*.34;164 (Borgnet 37:71–74;241);Gers.*Magn*.5 (Glorieux 8:246)

John 3:34(Vulg.)
Ub.Cas.*Arb.vit*.1.7 (Davis 128);Jac.Vit.*Quodlib*.2.18 (Ypma 1:193)

See vol.3:165–68

Thos.Kemp.*Soliloq*.23;24 (Pohl 1:322;326)
Thos.Kemp.*Vit.Chr*.1.2.26 (Pohl 5:165)
Thos.Kemp.*Orat*.7 (Pohl 3:356)
Thos.Kemp.*Disc.cl*.14 (Pohl 2:312–13);Thos.Kemp.*Serm. Dom*.9;10 (Pohl 3:116;128)
Thos.Kemp.*Vit.Chr*.1.2.27 (Pohl 5:168–69)
Thos.Kemp.*Vall.lil*.33 (Pohl 4:127)
Thos.Kemp.*Disc.cl*.8 (Pohl 2:297);Thos.Kemp.*Spir.ex*.3 (Pohl 2:335);Thos.Kemp.*Serm. nov*.21;22 (Pohl 6:204;217)
Gers.*Magn*.11 (Glorieux 8:486)

See vol.1:191–97

Nicol.Cus.*Serm*.9.1 (Heidelberg 16:176);Gabr.Bl. *Fest.Mar*. 12 (1499:F7v)

Rich.S.Laur.*Laud.Mar*.4.19.6 (Borgnet 36:225)

Gabr.Bl.*Fest.Mar*.4 (1499:B4r)

See vol.1:255–58
Ang.Clar.*Ep*.4.2 (*ALKGMA* 1:558)
Barth.Pis.*Conform*.13.2.2 (*AnalFranc* 5:21)

Gabr.Bl.*Fest.Mar*.4 (1499:B4r)

Gers.*Magn*.12 (Glorieux 8:527)
All.*Leg*. (Du Pin 1:666);Ub. Cas.*Arb.vit*.4.27 (Davis 343); Joh.Brev.*Tract*.1.3;3.2 (Du Pin 1:832;888);Thos.Kemp.*Vit. Chr*.1.2.26 (Pohl 5:159)

Joel 2:28

Acts 2:17
Gers.*Serm*.247;249 (Glorieux
5:523–24;553)
Ps.Alb.M.*Mar*.119 (Borgnet
37:173–74)
Hs.*Post.ad*.30 (Ryšánek 13:
125);Gers.*Magn*.9 (Glorieux 8:
382–84)
Joh.Rup.*Serm*.8 (*FIP Txt* 12:
23)
Ps.Alb.M.*Mar*.79 (Borgnet 37:
136);Gers.*Magn*.2;6;9;11
(Glorieux 8:191;277;413;481);
Thos.Kemp.*Serm.Dom*.34
(Pohl 3:303);Gabr.Bl.*Fest.Mar*.
5.2 (1499:C4v)
Gers.*Magn*.12 (Glorieux 8:
528–29)
Nicol.Cus.*Serm*.12.1
(Heidelberg 16:243–44);Ub.
Cas.*Arb.vit*.4.29 (Davis 351–
52);Thos.Kemp.*Vit.Chr*.2.1.6
(Pohl 5:252–53);Wyc.*Serm*.1.
25 (*WLW* 8:166)
Ub.Cas.*Arb.vit*.4.34 (Davis
367)

Rich.S.Laur.*Laud.Mar*.10.18
(Borgnet 36:497)


1 Cor.14:34;1 Tim.2:12
Gers.*Ex.doct*.2.2 (Glorieux 9:
467–68)




Gers.*Magn*.11;3 (Glorieux 8:
505;215)




Thos.Wal.*Comp.serm*.3
(Charland 354)



Rich.S.Laur.*Laud.Mar*.2.1.17
(Borgnet 36:38)



Gabr.Bl.*Fest.Mar*.5.1 (1499:
C2r–C2v);Gers.*Magn*.4
(Glorieux 8:233–35)

Ub.Cas.*Arb.vit*.3.6 (Davis
168–69)

Gers.*Vit.spir*.3 (Glorieux 3:
147–48)

Gers.*Magn*.11 (Glorieux 8:
486)

The promise, "Your sons and your daughters shall prophesy," fulfilled at Pentecost, meant that Mary had joined with the apostles in prophesying. Therefore she could be said to have obtained the apostolate, too, indeed to have exceeded all the apostles, prophets, and philosophers in her knowledge. As "the teacher of the truth," she had revealed to the evangelists, specifically to Luke, those parts of the Gospel history that only she knew. She also acted as a "consultant" for the compilation of the Apostles' Creed. For Christ had "undoubtedly" made a special appearance to her after the resurrection, not mentioned in the New Testament, before appearing to anyone else. "Being totally filled with the Holy Spirit," she thus served as the teacher of the apostles and of the entire church. In fact, Mary was "the repository of all the books of the Old Testament and of the Gospels, all of which she knew completely." Since the New Testament forbade women to speak in the church or to teach and have authority over men, not even Mary was permitted to do so. When she revealed the facts of the life of Christ to the apostles and evangelists, she did not preach publicly and did not usurp the priestly character, but her position as mediatrix was "more eminent" than that of any apostle or any priest. Translating the name of Mary as "illuminator," a fourteenth-century manual of sacred rhetoric described her as the mediatrix who illuminated the eyes of the preacher to let him understand and interpret Scripture better.

Therefore "just as the Son is the Mediator between God and men, so also Our Lady is the mediatrix to the Son." But this meant that she was, "as the most blessed of all creatures, in conjunction with her Son, truly the mediatrix between all creatures and God, so that she is rightly called Queen of heaven, indeed, Queen of the world." For Christ had put all things into the hands of his mother, as he had received all things from his Father. Through the communication of properties between the two natures of Christ she had received "maternal authority over God," with the result that God was subject to her as a son is subject to his mother. It was not going too far, therefore, to say that Mary was to be "adored" and to salute her

Gers.*Serm.*230;215;248
(Glorieux 5:325;124;542)

Ps.Alb.M.*Mar.*162 (Borgnet
37:237)

as "the goddess of love, of love not impure but divine." The reason cited for not calling her "goddess of goddesses" was that this epithet might seem to exclude sinners and demons from her authority. At least two writers of this period, citing an otherwise unknown source identified only as "Dionysius," went so far as to declare that if the authority of the faith had not prohibited it, the Virgin would be "adored

Ub.Cas.*Arb.vit.*4.38 (Davis
398);Nicol.Cus.*Serm.*9.1
(Heidelberg 16:187)

Thos.Kemp.*Cant.*91 (Pohl 4:
378)

as God because of the magnitude of her glory." So transcendent had that glory become that not only was her mother Anna being invoked as "advocate," but Mary as the mediatrix between Christ the Mediator and mankind was herself being addressed through a mediator, her husband Joseph, who was asked to "render thy spouse, the most blessed Virgin, propitious to us, and obtain from her that we, unworthy though we are, may be adopted as her beloved chil-

Ub.Cas.*Arb.vit.*2.6 (Davis
125)

Joh.D.*F.o.* 4.16 (Kotter 2:208)
Henr.Wrl.*Immac.*177 (*FIP Txt*
10:71–72)

Ub.Cas.*Tr.scel.*(*AFH* 10:124);
Ub.Cas.*Arb.vit.*2.5 (Davis
443)

dren." To the possible objection that such a stress on Mary would "do injury to the Son" the response was a quotation from John of Damascus that "honor to the Mother redounds to the Son."

For many of these proponents of an exalted doctrine of Mary she also served, with her Son, as the supreme example of total poverty. So complete was her renunciation of worldly possessions that she had immediately distributed to the poor the gifts brought by the Magi. "As having nothing, and yet possessing

Ub.Cas.*Arb.vit.*2.5(Davis 103)

2 Cor.6:10
Ps.Alb.M.*Mar.*71 (Borgnet 37:
127–28)

Barth.Pis.*Quad.*51 (1498:P6v–
P7v)

everything," she gave up the usufruct of the riches she had through her Son, preferring to share his poverty just as she also shared his suffering. In the devotional and Lenten literature of this period, and eventually also in its doctrinal reflection, it became a concern "to contemplate above all the sorrow of the heart of Mary and to emphasize its union in distress

Colasanti (1959) 63
Thos.Kemp.*Cant.*21 (Pohl 4:
272)

with the heart of Christ." The Stabat Mater, which probably arose around the beginning of this period, is only the best-known example of the devotional literature dealing with the lamentation of the Virgin, as is the Pietà of its portrayal in the graphic arts. In their

Ub.Cas.*Arb.vit.*4.25 (Davis
336)

Ub.Cas.*Arb.vit.*1.7 (Davis 25);
Gers.*Consid.Jos.* (Glorieux 7:
79)

doctrine of Mary, these depictions, whether artistic or theological, manifested a counterpoint between her role as mediatrix, as the one who understood without wavering the mission of her Son and the meaning of his cross, and her purely human doubt and grief as

Ub.Cas.*Arb.vit.*4.12 (Davis 318);Ps.Brd.Clr.*Pass.Chr.* (*PL* 182:1134–42);*Serm.conc.Const.* (Finke 2:532–34)

Luke 9:51;22:44
See vol.1:243–56

See pp. 19–22 above

Gabr.Bl.*Fest.Mar.*11 (1499: F6r);Ub.Cas.*Arb.vit.*4.33;4.38 (Davis 362;397–402)
Joh.Rup.*Serm.*15 (*FIP Txt* 12:52);Vit.Furn.*Quodlib.*2.12.2 (Delorme 86)
Nicol.Cus.*Serm.*8.1 (Heidelberg 16:166);Thos. Kemp.*Cant.*28;84 (Pohl 4:293;373)
Vall.*Volup.*3.29 (*MPPR* 5:995–96)
Barth.Bon *Assump.*3 (*Opettex*) 9b:78);Ub.Cas.*Arb.vit.*4.41 (Davis 406)
Thos.Kemp.*Soliloq.*23 (Pohl 1:319),Thos.Kemp.*Serm.nov.*24 (Pohl 6:227)
See vol.3:172–73

Guil.Oc.*Corp.*36 (Birch 444); Gr.Arim.*Sent.*2.30–33.2.1 (1522–II:114v);Gabr.Bl.*Fest. Mar.*11 (1499:E8v);Nicol.Cus. *Serm.*8.1 (Heidelberg 16:160) Nicol.Cus.*Doct.ign.*3.8 (Heidelberg 1:142);Nicol.Cus. *Serm.*8.1 (Heidelberg 16:161–62)
Barth.Bon.*Assump.*1 (*Opettex* 9b:42;61)

Barth.Bon.*Assump.*2 (*Opettex* 9b:68)
Wyc.*Apost.*16 (*WLW* 12:221–22);Wyc.*Serm.*4.48 (*WLW* 13:389);Hs.*Sanct.*33.1 (Flajšhans 3:132)

Gabr.Bl.*Fest.Mar.*11 (1499: F5v)

Henr.Lang.*Concept.*3.9 (1516: 12v)

Petr.Aur.*Tract.*6 (*BFS* 3:92)

she contemplated her tragic loss—a counterpoint that had, ever since the New Testament, been characteristic of devotional and theological consideration of the sufferings of Christ himself. The stress upon the experiences of Mary drew upon, and contributed to, the new subjectivity associated with Franciscan devotion and with the growing attention to the Augustine of the *Confessions.*

Frequently the transcendent glory of Mary already "in this world [in via]" appeared as a corollary of her transcendent glory "in the world to come [in patria]" after she had been assumed into heaven at the end of her earthly life. It was fitting that the mediatrix between God and man should share not only in her Son's crucifixion but also in his glory. She was enthroned in heaven far above all the other saints, above the several hierarchies of angels, indeed above all creation, for she led them all into the glories of heaven. She was exalted higher than the heavens, having all the world under her feet, and for the sake of her Son she was clothed with all reverence and honor. Two questions that had attended the doctrine of the assumption still remained unanswered: the question of her death and possible resurrection, and the related question of whether she had been assumed in body as well as soul. Theologians of quite varying positions agreed that she had in fact died before being assumed, while the chronological precedence of the resurrection of Christ before that of any of the saints made a belief in her resurrection difficult in spite of the attractiveness of the idea. Those who held to the resurrection of Mary did so in order to affirm that her assumption was also in the body. Others, less inclined to speculate, preferred to leave the matter open. The stock argument from silence, that if Mary had not been assumed also according to the body she would have left the relics of her body on earth as lesser saints had, continued to be used to support an assumption according to both body and soul (as it would be in the official definition of the doctrine of the assumption in 1950).

There was, of course, one other problem with the assumption: Scripture did not say anything about it. But then, Scripture did not say anything about many other details of the life of Mary, which were nevertheless the proper subject of Marian doctrine and devotion. There was, for example, no reference in Scripture to an annunciation of her birth; but since there had been annunciations of the births of such "lesser saints" as John the Baptist, Isaac, and Samson (and even, according to some, of Thomas Aquinas), it appeared to follow that there could have been a special revelation to her parents also. Nor did the New Testament provide any information about whether or not Mary had been present at the institution of the Lord's Supper and whether or not she had received communion. The Bible was also silent about the later life of the Virgin, after she was commended to the care of the disciple John. Thus the doctrine of Mary was an especially perplexing instance of the relation between explicit scriptural teaching and nonscriptural tradition. For in many of these details of Mariology where Scripture said nothing either way, one was dealing, Gerson acknowledged, "more with a kind of conjectural probability than with the necessity of faith . . . , more with what could have happened than with what did happen." Here it was necessary to avoid "temerity" and to acknowledge that one was proceeding on the basis of "probable opinion" or "pious belief." Others were less cautious, positing a progressive revelation of divine truths about Mary through successive periods of church history and setting it down as a hermeneutical axiom that Scripture was to be interpreted in such a way as to redound to her perfection, so that from the title "Mother of God" it was possible for the church to "infer all holiness, all honor, all prerogatives" for Mary.

On the other hand, the assumption did have a place in the church's calendar, which had been sufficient grounds for Bernard to affirm it despite the lack of explicit biblical evidence, just as, conversely, the absence of a feast of the immaculate conception had been a reason not to assert it as a doctrine. There were still those in this period who recognized that "the feast of the nativity of Our Lady was established long after that of her assumption," and that the feast of her conception was an even more recent novelty, as were Trinity Sunday and various local commemorations of saints. At the beginning of the fourteenth century, the

Ps.Ans.*Concept.BVM* (*PL* 159: 303)
Ps.Alb.M.*Mar.*125 (Borgnet 37:178)
Luke 1:5–20;Gen.18:9–15; Judg.13:2–24
ap.Vall.*Enc.Thos.Aq.* (*MPPR* 6:348)
Nicol.Cus.*Serm.*9.1 (Heidelberg 16:180)

Andr.Brd.*Utraq.*2 (Hardt 3: 394);Jac.Mis.*Utraq.*1.2 (Hardt 3:431);Gers.*Magn.*9 (Glorieux 8:380–81);Ps.Alb.M.*Mar.*38 (Borgnet 37:77)

Gers.*Magn.*6 (Glorieux 8:284)

John 19:25–27

See pp. 120–22 below

Gers.*Serm.*232 (Glorieux 5: 344);Gers.*Ep.*56 (Glorieux 2: 269);Gers.*Magn.*9 (Glorieux 8: 380);Gers.*Jos.*pr. (Glorieux 4: 33)
Henr.Lang.*Concept.*3.7 (1516: 11r)

Ub.Cas.*Arb.vit.*1.8 (Davis 33); Dns.Scot.*Quaest.* (*BFS* 3:16–17);Henr.Wrl.*Immac.*186 (*BFS* 3:16–17)

Petr.Aur.*Tract.*6 (*BFS* 3:92)

See vol.3:171–72,300

Gers.*Consid.Jos.* (Glorieux 7: 71);Gers.*Serm.*232 (Glorieux 5:361)

All.*Serm.*12 (1490:Z1r–Z1v); Gabr.*Fest.Chr.*39 (1499:V3v); Robt.Bas.*Form.praed.*29 (Charland 267)

Petr. Aur. *Reper.* 8 (*BFS* 3:150)

Petr. Aur. *Tract.* 5 (*BFS* 3:73–74)

See p. 50 below
Sixt. IV. *Cum.praeex.* (*Corp.Jur. Can.:Extrav.* 3.12.1: Friedberg 2:1285)
Sixt. IV. *Grav.* (*Corp.Jur.Can.: Extrav.* 3.12.1: Friedberg 2:1285)

Petr. Verb. *Brd.* (1490:E6r–E6v)

Ps. Ans. *Concept.BVM* (*PL* 159:301–3)

Henr. Wrl. *Immac.* 167 (*FIP Txt* 10:64); Joh. Vit. *Concept.* 3 (Du Pin 3:1344)
Henr. Lang. *Concept.* 1.8; 3.12 (1516:4v;13r–13v)

Gr. Arim. *Sent.* 2.30–33.2.3 (1522–II:115v); Aeg. Rom. *Quodlib.* 6.20 (1646:418–20)

Petr. Cand. *Immac.* 2.C.16 (Emmen 101); Aug. Rom. *Serm. mag.* 21 (Zumkeller 136); Joh. Pol. *Immac.* 1.1.a.18 (*Bibl.Mar.* 1:11–12); Dom. Domen. *Pot.pap.* 1 ad 2 (Smolinsky 84)

See vol. 1:314
Aug. *Nat.et grat.* 36.42 (*CSEL* 60:263–64)
Joh. Pol. *Immac.* 1.2.a.2 (*Bibl. Mar.* 1:14); Petr. Cand. *Immac.* 2.B.3 (Emmen 84); Henr. Wrl. *Immac.* 69–71; 162 (*FIP Txt* 10:19–20;63); Petr. Aur. *Tract.* 4;5 (*BFS* 3:57–58;75–76)
Dns. Scot. *Quaest.* (*BFS* 3:13); Gualt. Cast. *Assump.* 1.17 (*Opettex* 9b:32–33)

Joh. Vit. *Concept.* 2–3 (Du Pin 3:1341–44); Gers. *Ep.* 80 (Glorieux 2:325)

Aug. *Jul.* 5.15.52 (*PL* 44:813)

best a supporter of the immaculate conception could do was to argue that "even though the church of Rome does not celebrate the conception . . . , it does not disapprove of the celebration," but he also pointed out that "all the churches of England and France do celebrate the feast of the conception." The Council of Basel (by then in schism from the pope) declared for such a feast on 18 December 1439, and Rome eventually conformed itself to this practice in 1477 and confirmed it in 1483; but long before it had done so formally, its permission of the celebration was being taken as approval. A pseudonymous treatise bearing the name of Anselm went so far as to maintain that the feast was in fact a very ancient one, which its enemies had abolished for a time and which now was being restored. But if the absence of such a feast had meant to Bernard that the doctrine of the immaculate conception was uncertain at best, the institution (or restoration) of the feast must mean that the doctrine was firm. Those who still resisted the doctrine were urged to observe the commemoration nevertheless; they had no recourse but to argue, in the face of the liturgical change, that the feast commemorated not her conception, but the sanctification that followed closely after it.

The strictures of Bernard—not only the liturgical ones but especially the substantive ones—continued to provide the basis for the case against the immaculate conception, both for its opponents themselves and for its proponents in their enumeration of objections to which they must respond. Ranged on the other side were various authorities, most notably the statement of Augustine identifying Mary as the exception to the rule about universal sinfulness. This statement, coming as it did from the one who had definitively formulated the doctrine of original sin, appeared to clinch the argument for the immaculate conception. It had become customary already in the thirteenth century to put the two passages from Bernard and from Augustine into juxtaposition and then, depending on the viewpoint, to explain one of them on the basis of the other. Thus Gregory of Rimini, citing other passages from Augustine that made Christ the only exception to the universality of original sin, explained that in

Gr.Arim.*Sent*.2.30–33.2.1–3
(1522–II:114r–115r)
Joh.Rup.*Serm*.16;25 (*FIP Txt*
12:57;92)

Petr.Aur.*Reper*.8 (*BFS* 3:142–
43)

Matt.6:12
Gabr.Bl.*Can.miss*.72.K
(Oberman-Courtenay 3:193)

Henr.Lang.*Concept*.2.8 (1516:
7r)

Gabr.Bl.*Fest.Mar.* (1499)

Gabr.Bl.*Can.miss*.32.A-F
(Oberman-Courtenay 1:328–
34)

Gabr.Bl.*Can.miss*.80.C
(Oberman-Courtenay 4:3)

Petr.Verb.*Brd.* (1490:E6r–E8r);
Henr.Wrl.*Immac*.20–22;164
(*FIP Txt* 10:5–6;63–64)

Henr.Lang.*Concept*.3.3;3.5
(1516:9r;10v)

See vol.3:171,300
Brd.Clr.*Ep*.174.9 (Leclercq-
Rochais 7:392)
Petr.Aur.*Tract.* (*BFS* 3:94);
Petr.Aur.*Reper*.8 (*BFS* 3:153);
Joh.Neap.*Immac*.1 ad 4 (*Bibl.
Mar*.1:89)

Petr.Cell.*Ep*.2.172 (*PL* 202:
623)

Guil.War.*Quaest.* (*BFS* 3:3,9)
Henr.Lang.*Concept*.1.4;1.6
(1516:2r;3r)

Thos.Sut.*Quodlib*.3.15
(Schmaus 441)

2 Cor.5:14

Gr.Arim.*Sent*.2.30–33.2.1
(1522–II:114v)
See vol.1:289–90

the passage under discussion he must have been referring only to actual sin, from which everyone, including Bernard, agreed that Mary was free. But this
explanation could not satisfy those who interpreted
Augustine's phrase "overcoming sin in every particular [ad vincendum omni ex parte peccatum]" as comprehending both actual and original sin, so that she
alone among all the saints did not have to pray the
words of the Lord's Prayer: "Forgive us our debts."

The controversial letter of Bernard to the canons
of Lyons was all the more troublesome because of his
standing as "bearer of the flame" for the Virgin. For
example, all but one of the *Sermons on the Festivals
of the Glorious Virgin Mary* of Gabriel Biel, a vigorous supporter of the immaculate conception, included at least one quotation from Bernard, just as
his exposition of the doxology to Mary in the Mass
quoted Bernard in every paragraph; and it was to
Bernard that he turned for the doctrine of her mediation. In the face of such eminent authority, a head-
on refutation of Bernard's letter, point by point, was
a difficult tactic, but there were some who undertook
it. Others found an extenuation in the large number
of patristic and medieval doctors who had shared Bernard's ideas, or they argued that both of the conditions stipulated by Bernard for accepting the doctrine
(a feast of Mary's conception and a pronouncement
by the see of Rome) had now been met. There even
arose a legend not long after his death that Bernard
had a black mark placed on his breast by God as
punishment for "writing what ought not to be written
about the conception of Our Lady." The legend was
used to discredit his doctrine of Mary generally, although that did seem to be going too far.

The most formidable argument that Bernard of
Clairvaux and Thomas Aquinas, as well as their later
followers, had directed against the immaculate conception of Mary was the charge that if she was born
without original sin, she did not need redemption—
which would detract from "the dignity of Christ as
the Universal Savior of all." If Christ died for those
who were dead, then his having died for the Virgin
necessarily implied that she, too, had been dead in
original sin. On the basis especially of Psalm 51:5,

Augustine had declared the universal need of all mankind for the redemption wrought by Christ. If Mary
was to be included, did that universal statement apply
to her? To this specific objection it was possible to
reply that she was exempt from other universal statements of Scripture, such as "Every human being is a
liar." But the fundamental reply to this entire line of
reasoning was "the great invention of Scotus, [who]
was to use this precise argument to *defend* the doctrine
under discussion." On the basis precisely of "the excellence of her Son as Redeemer," Scotus insisted that
the most perfect of Redeemers must have had "the
most perfect possible degree of mediation with respect
to one creature," and that the most fitting candidate
for this honor was his mother. The most perfect
method of redemption was to preserve rather than to
rescue her from original sin. As in the case of others
"the rescuing grace of redemption does away with
original sin," so in the case of Mary "preserving grace
does not do away with original sin, but prevents [it]."
In this sense it was even possible to assert that "Mary
needed Christ as Redeemer more than anyone did,"
for "she needed the suffering of Christ, not on account
of the sin that was present in her, but on account of
the sin that would have been present if that very Son
of hers had not preserved her through faith." She was
immaculately conceived because what nature had not
given to her, the special grace of God had accomplished in her. Despite the reductio ad absurdum that
then the most perfect method of all would have been
to preserve everyone from original sin, it was in her
case alone that this method of redemption by preservation was adjudged "the most fitting [decentissi-
mum]," and therefore her "restoration was not an act
of supplying what had been lost, but an act of increasing what [she] already had."

A basic reason for the difference between Mary and
all mankind was that there was never any actual sin
in her—an exemption from the universal rule that
everyone had to grant, regardless of views about
whether or not she had been conceived in original sin.
The paradox of that exemption evoked from Pierre
D'Ailly such an affirmation as this, addressed to Mary:
"It was not by thy righteousness, but by divine grace

Petr.Aur.*Tract*.6 (*BFS* 3:79);
Gers.*Ep*.79 (Glorieux 2:324)

Henr.Wrl.*Immac*.37 (*FIP Txt*
10:10)
Ps.116:11

Oberman (1963) 289

Dns.Scot.*Quaest.* (*BFS* 3:14);
Henr.Wrl.*Immac*.89 (*FIP Txt*
10:29)

Balić (1941) 84

Dns.Scot.*Quaest.* (*BFS* 3:19)

Guil.Wai.*Quaest.* (*BFS* 3:3,10)

Barth.Pis.*Quad*.37 (1498:L7v)

Gr.Arim.*Sent*.2.30–33.2.1
(1522–II:114v)

Petr.Aur.*Tract*.4 (*BFS* 3:54–55)

Gers.*Magn*.9 (Glorieux 8:427)

ap.Petr.Aur.*Reper*.8 (*BFS* 3:
141);Gr.Arim.*Sent*.2.30–33.2.3
(1522–II:115r)

that thou didst merit to be the only one without the woe of venial and mortal guilt, and, as is devoutly believed, without the woe of original guilt as well." His disciple Gerson took the affirmation the rest of the way, paraphrasing the Apostles' Creed in Middle French: "I believe that in the sacrament of baptism God grants, to every creature who is worthy of receiving it, pardon from original sin, in which every person born of a mother has been conceived, with the sole exceptions of our Savior Jesus Christ and his glorious Virgin Mother." This did not, he explained elsewhere, put her on the same level as Christ. In the case of Christ sinlessness was "by right," in the case of Mary it was "by privilege." Another paradox, and one that had been noted already by Bernard, appeared in the Gospel account of the annunciation, in which the angel had saluted Mary as "full of grace" and thus presumably not in need of further grace, but had gone on to explain to her, "The Holy Spirit will come upon you." It could well be asked whether or not the Virgin required sanctification, or more precisely, when she had received it. One way to resolve the paradox was to say that Mary, "as she was full of grace, was also confirmed in grace."

The paradox—or ambiguity—thus took the form of asserting in one and the same paragraph that she had been sanctified in the womb "and from then on [ex tunc] she abided in the purity of virtue," and yet also that "in the very moment of her consent, with the conception of the Savior, she was made firm, that is confirmed in good, so that for the rest of her life [de caetero] she could not sin." The theory of her having been sanctified in the womb entailed other difficulties, too. For one thing, there was no explicit testimony about it in the canonical Scriptures, only in the tradition of the church; but this stricture applied also to other chapters in the doctrine of Mary. More seriously, it did nothing to mark the Virgin as unique. There was explicit scriptural testimony that the prophet Jeremiah had been sanctified in the womb, and of John the Baptist it was possible to say that he "was 'full of grace' . . . , for he was not born 'a child of wrath,' even though he was conceived as such, but was sanctified in the sixth month." In addition to Jeremiah

All. *Tract.* 12 (1490:M4r); Gabr.
Bl. *Fest. Mar.* 7 (1499:D3r)

Gers. *Br.int.* (Glorieux 7:208)

Gers. *Ep.* 56 (Glorieux 2:266)

Aug. Rom. *Serm. mag.* 25
(Zumkeller 137); Henr. Wrl.
*Immac.* 65 (*FIP Txt* 10:17)
Brd. Clr. *Laud. Mar.* 4.3
(Leclercq-Rochais 4:49–50)
Rich. S. Laur. *Laud. Mar.* 12.2.5
(Borgnet 36:639–40)
Luke 1:28 (Vulg.)

Luke 1:35

Barth. Pis. *Quad.* 38 (1498:M2r)

Rich. S. Laur. *Laud. Mar.* 4.28.1
(Borgnet 36:251)

Ub. Cas. *Arb. vit.* 1.6 (Davis 18)

Jer. 1:5

Luke 1:28 (Vulg.)
Eph. 2:3
Nicol. Cus. *Serm.* 5.2
(Heidelberg 16:83); Wyc. *Serm.*
2.14 (*WLW* 9:97)

Gers.*Consid.Jos.* (Glorieux 7:
67);Gers.*Serm.*232 (Glorieux
5:349)
Hs.*Sanct.*2.3 (Flajšhans 3:6);
Hs.*Sent.*3.3.4 (Flajšhans 2:
399–400)

Joh.Rup.*Serm.*25 (*FIP Txt* 12:
91–92)

Ub.Cas.*Arb.vit.*4.34 (Davis
367)

Nicol.Cus.*Serm.*8.1
(Heidelberg 16:164);Rich.S.
Laur.*Laud.Mar.*4.28.1
(Borgnet 36:251)

See p. 27 above

Dns.Scot.*Quaest.* (*BFS* 3:16–
17)

Henr.Lang.*Concept.*3.11
(1516:13r)

Petr.Cand.*Immac.*2.B.1
(Emmen 76–77);Henr.Wrl.
*Immac.*91;178 (*FIP Txt* 10:31;
72)

Petr.Aur.*Tract.*1 (*BFS* 3:34)

Gr.Arim.*Sent.*2.30–33.2.1
(1522–II:114r)
Henr.Wrl.*Immac.*240 (*FIP Txt*
10:101–2)

and John the Baptist, Joseph, the husband of Mary, was also the recipient of this special prerogative. From these cases one could infer her sanctification in the womb by means of an a fortiori argument, but even then the difference between Mary and these other saints was simply one of degree rather than of kind, in that she had received "a more ample measure of grace" than they, "as great a measure of the Holy Spirit as anyone in this life could receive without being hypostatically united to God," as only the human nature of Jesus had been. Even if the difference took the form of asserting that Mary "not only never sinned, but was incapable of sinning," that was, in the eyes of many, insufficient without a more complete answer to the question of how and why it was so, unless also in her conception and birth she had been unique and set apart from the rest of humanity.

As in his teaching about the incarnation itself, so in his teaching about Mary, Duns Scotus considered that question on the basis of a theological method of "maximalism." It was possible for God either to preserve her from original sin altogether or to rescue her from it within an instant of her conception or to purify her of it at the end of a period of time. "Which of these three . . . it was that was done," he continued, "God knows. But if it does not contradict the authority of Scripture or the authority of the church, it seems preferable to attribute greater rather than lesser excellence to Mary." Or, as a later thinker put it, "I would rather err on the side of superabundance by attributing some prerogative to her than on the side of inadequacy by taking away from her some excellence that she had." Another component of this method was the oft-repeated formula: "Whatever was both possible and eminently fitting for God to do, that he did [potuit, decuit, fecit]." The defenders of the formula conceded that it seemed to be indispensable to the doctrine of the immaculate conception, and its critics objected that the issue was "not whether it was possible for her to be conceived without [original] sin, but whether in fact she was conceived without it." It could, and did, lead to such "superfluous" extremes as the theory that from the beginning of creation God had set aside a special portion of "prime matter" to be present in Mary at the time of the conception of the flesh of Christ, or the theory that Mary, being free of original sin, was also free of all its possible consequences, including physical weariness. Even some who favored the doctrine itself warned that there were certain gifts and privileges, as for example a total knowledge of the future, that Christ could have given his mother, but did not. Nevertheless, the method prevailed, and by the sixteenth century even the heirs of Thomas Aquinas were using it to substantiate the immaculate conception.

The thirty-sixth session of the Council of Basel decreed that the immaculate conception was a "pious doctrine, in conformity with the worship of the church, the catholic faith, right reason, and Holy Scripture." It prescribed that the doctrine be "approved, held, and professed by all catholics," and it forbade any preaching or teaching contrary to it. By the time of this session, however, Basel was itself under a cloud because of its statements and actions on the relation of the authority of the pope to that of a general council. Therefore the decree on the immaculate conception proved not to be canonically binding. Nevertheless, defenders of the immaculate conception in the fifteenth century made use of this decree to assert that while there may have been a time when it was permissible to question the immaculate conception, the church had now spoken out definitively on the question, and it was "foolish and impudent" to continue to oppose it. With or without the authority of Basel, the doctrine had become the generally accepted one in Western Christendom, believed by the faithful and taught by the doctors, long before it was finally and formally confessed by Pope Pius IX in the bull *Ineffabilis Deus* of 8 December 1854.

The other principal constituent element in the communication of grace, the doctrine of sacraments, also continued to be in flux during the fourteenth and fifteenth centuries. The medieval definition, or rather definitions, of sacrament, sometimes accompanied by an apposite quotation from Augustine, were still standard. Scotus defined it as "a sensible sign, which, by divine institution, efficaciously signifies the grace of God or the gratuitous action of God and is appointed

Joh.Vit.*Concept.*1 (Du Pin 3: 1336)

Gers.*Joh.Mont.* (Glorieux 10: 16–17)

Gers.*Ep.*56 (Glorieux 2:267–68)

Ambr.Cath.*Immac.* (1542:69)

Hug.*Man.*17.ix.1439 (*CB* 6: 589)

See p. 45 above

CBas. (1431–39).36 (Mansi 29: 183)

See p. 73 below

Gabr.Fl.*Fest.Mar.*1 (1499:A2v); Joh.Rag.*Auct.conc.*3 (*DRTA* 15:212)

See vol.3:206–10

Dns.Scot.*Ox*.4.1.2.9 (Wadding 16:109);Joh.Par.*Pot*.12 (Leclercq 208)
Robt.Orf.*Corr*.60 (*Bibl.Thom*. 31:223);Hs.*Coll*.12 (Ryšánek 7:86);Ub.Cas.*Arb.vit*.4.36 (Davis 376)

Dom.Domen.*Pot.pap*.1.con.3 (Smolinsky 75)

Hs.*Sent*.4.3.11 (Flajšhans 2: 531–32)
See vol.3:211–12
Mars.Pad.*Def.min*.15.9 (Brampton 51–52);Thos.Sut. *Quodlib*.3.19 (Schmaus 461); Aeg. Rom.*Eccl.pot*.2.12 (Scholz 106–7); Ub.Cas.*Sanct.ap*. (*ALKGMA* 2:390)

Wyc.*Euch*.5 (*WLW* 16:158)
Gl.ord.Eph.5:32 (*PL* 114:599)

Guil.Mar.Corr.*Thom*.60 (*Bibl. Thom*.9:243)

Robt.Orf.*Corr*.60 (*Bibl.Thom*. 31:223)

Corr.*"Quare"* 60 (*Bibl.Thom*. 9:245)

Joh.Par.Corr.57 (*SA* 12:279–80)

Ub.Cas.*Arb.vit*.2.6 (Davis 123)
Gers.*Consid.Jos*. (Glorieux 7: 63–64);Gers.*Cant*.5 (Glorieux 8:615);Gers.*Desp*.1 (Glorieux 7:11);Gers.*Nupt*. (Glorieux 6: 197)

for the salvation of a man who is still in this present life." Other definitions included "a sign of something sacred" and "the visible form of an invisible grace." As in earlier times, the validation of a sacrament by the institution of Christ was ambiguous in the case of several sacraments. From the Gospel accounts it was not clear, for example, just when Christ had instituted baptism, which had been practiced by John even before the public ministry of Jesus began. The most glaring ambiguity continued to be the institution of matrimony, in which there appeared to be "nothing that is essentially spiritual." Thomas Aquinas had taught that before the coming of Christ it had not been a sacrament, not even among the people of Israel. Like many other statements of Thomas, that became a matter of controversy in the next generation. Wycliffe was by no means the only one who could say in the area of sacramental theology: "It does not follow that if Thomas asserts this, it ought to be preached to the people." Quoting the *Glossa Ordinaria*, the opponents of Thomas asserted that already in the Garden of Eden the spiritual union of Christ and the church was the sacramental meaning of matrimony. His defenders replied with a classification of the various divinely instituted functions of matrimony both in the law of nature and in the law of grace. Among these functions the specifically sacramental one was not instituted until the passion of Christ, from which all the sacraments were derived. Another reply was to say that the words of the gloss referred strictly to matrimony in the state of innocence before the fall, and that therefore matrimony among the people of Israel had been only a prefiguring of the sacrament. Consistent with this emphasis on the state of innocence was the idea that the marriage of Mary and Joseph was "the most genuine of marriages" despite its not having been consummated, and that it was "a great sacrament, signifying the union of God and the church."

The rule that a sacrament had to have been instituted by Christ raised problems not only for those sacraments, like baptism and matrimony, that had preceded his passion, but also for those that appeared to have come into force only after his ascension. "Neither the angels nor the apostles nor the church, much less a member of the church, could institute sacraments," Biel defined, but immediately he had to add that "an exception is confirmation, which is not recorded as having been handed down by Christ according to the matter and form that are used in conferring it"; hence it was to be "believed without ambiguity, on the basis of the verbal tradition of the apostles handed down

Gabr.Bl.*Fest.Chr.*13 (1499:
F3v);Gabr.Bl.*Can.miss.*14.E
(Oberman-Courtenay 1:117)
Dom.Domen.*Pot.pap.*ad 14
(Smolinsky 119)

to the church, that he instituted it this way." Beyond the status of confirmation as a discrete sacrament there was the need to determine who possessed the authority to certify as a sacrament some sign or action that could not explicitly be traced to the historical institution of Christ as set down in the Gospel: the church as the body of Christ, or tradition as the on-going revelation of Christ, or the pope as the vicar of

Guil.Oc.*Ben.*3.3 (Sikes 3:230–
31);Wyc.*Serm.*3.16 (*WLW* 11:
125);Joh.Rag.*Utraq.* (Mansi
29:735)
Dns.Scot.*Rep.Par.*4.14.4.14
(Wadding 24:224)

Christ. It was agreed by theologians of different positions that, as sovereign even over his own means of grace, which were efficacious because of his "covenant [pactum]," Christ was not bound to the sacraments

Jac.Vit.*Reg.chr.*2.2 (Arquillière
168–69);Aeg.Rom.*Eccl.pot.*3.9
(Scholz 193)

he had instituted; but he had not communicated that sovereignty to anyone in the church, not even to the pope. That limitation also forbade the church or the

Joh.Par.*Pot.*10 (Leclercq 195)

pope "to institute new sacraments."

Of all seven sacraments, the sacrament of penance and the sacrament of holy orders were the ones that became problematical for the life of the church during

See pp. 91–98, 128–31 below

See vol.3:185,204

the later Middle Ages. But it was in keeping with the theological development of the Middle Ages that among the sacraments the Eucharist continued to hold the primary position, giving meaning and definition to all the others. The Eucharist was "the sacrament

Nicol.Cus.*Ep.*2 (Faber 2–II:6r)

of each of the other sacraments"; for if the body of Christ were not present in the Eucharist, none of the other sacraments would count for anything and all

Dns.Scot.*Rep.Par.*4.8.1.3
(Wadding 24:9–10)

devotion in the church would cease to exist. "The institution of this venerable sacrament" was supreme

Ub.Cas.*Arb.vit.*4.5 (Davis
283)

among all the works of Christ. While he was present in baptism by his power, he was present in the Eu-charist not only by his power but by his very "sub-

Jac.Mis.*Utraq.*1.2 (Hardt 3:
421–22)

stance." And so, the question of why there was no reference to the Eucharist in the creeds (even though there was mention of "one baptism for the forgiveness of sins" in the Nicene Creed), was answered by quoting the phrase "the communion of holy things [communio sanctorum]" in the Apostles' Creed: although the phrase could also mean "the communion of saints," it included the means by which saints came into being and therefore could be rendered "the communion of the sacraments." The continuing prominence of the Eucharist in this period may be seen from the way "all the great thinkers of the thirteenth century [and beyond] make a tentative effort at the elucidation of the eucharistic dogma"; in fact, "in Czech intellectual history at the end of the fourteenth and in the fifteenth century, the Eucharist occupies first place."

Gers.*Magn.*9 (Glorieux 8:414); Jac.Mis.*Zjev.*12:4 (*Pram.*18: 459)

Maglione (1941) 5

Sedlák (1918) 1

Not only among those, such as the more radical of the Czechs, who denied the real presence, but even among those who submitted themselves to church dogma, there continued to be a "variety of opinions" about eucharistic teaching, all the more so because certain questions had been left undecided by the councils as well as by Scripture and the fathers. Ockham's classification of theories about the conversion of the sacramental bread into the body of Christ listed three alternatives, only the second of which was considered orthodox: that the same substance that had been bread was now the flesh of Christ; that the substance of the bread ceased to exist and the substance of the body of Christ began to exist there under the accidents of the bread; and that the substance of the bread remained, together with the body of Christ in the same place. Even this roster did not exhaust the possibilities. Moreover, as Ockham himself noted, "catholics who agree in accepting this second opinion hold diverse opinions about the manner" of the presence. Thus, despite the reiteration of warnings against "curious and useless investigation of this profound sacrament" and despite the rejection of bizarre theories about the Sacrament, the expositors of Christian doctrine in this period could not leave the problem alone.

Guil.Oc.*Corp.*1 (Birch 164)

Guil.Oc.*Sacr.alt.*pr. (Birch 2); Guil.Oc.*Corp.*21 (Birch 274–76)

Guil.Oc.*Corp.*5 (Birch 182) Thos.Kemp.*Im.Chr.*4.18 (Pohl 2:136);Gers.*Magn.*9 (Glorieux 8:395);Guil.Oc.*Corp.*pr. (Birch 158)

Guil.Oc.*Ben.*3.10 (Sikes 3:240)

The belief, shared even by Hussite theologians, that there existed a "faith of the total catholic and universal church on the truth of this question" made it necessary to consult the recent and the distant past as a guide to correct eucharistic doctrine. A rehearsal of the preceding medieval development of the doctrine, in the ninth and in the eleventh century, served as a way of

Jac.Mis.*Corp.*2 (Hardt 3:885); Hier.Prag.ap.Fill.*Gest.conc. Const.*5.vii.1416 (Finke 2:61)

Radb.*Corp*.7 (*CCCM* 16:37–40)

Jac.Mis.*Corp*.3;9 (Hardt 3:892–93;903–4);Jac.Mis.*Com. parv.* (Ryba 156)
Jac.Mis.*Rem.*1;2 (Vooght 321–23;337–38)
See vol.3:187
*Corp.Jur.Can:Decr.Grat.*3.2.42 (Friedberg 1:1328–29)
Turr.*Vot.avis.* (Mansi 30:601)

Hs.*Corp.*2.1–2 (Flajšhans 1–II:10–11);Hs.*Sent.*4.12.3 (Flajšhans 2:577);Chel.*Repl.*30 (Petrů 197)

Joh.Par.*Corp.* (1686:95–96);
Guil.Oc.*Jn.*40 (Sikes 3:145);
Guil.Oc.*Corp.*21 (Birch 278);
Wyc.*Serm.*2.48;2.61;3.51
(*WLW* 9:349–50;9:454–55;11:446–47);Wyc.*Euch.*1;2;5;7;9
(*WLW* 16:25–26;30–32;117;125;225;279);Wyc.*Apost.*5;6;9;16 (*WLW* 12:68;79;108;229)
Joh.Rag.*Utraq.* (Mansi 29:848–49);Joh.Rag.ap.Laur.
Reich.*Diurn.*11.ii.1433 (*MC* 1:308);Gabr.Bl.*Can.miss.*80.N
(Oberman-Courtenay 4:16–18)

See pp. 199–200, 258 below

Aug.*Ev.Joh.*80.3 (*CCSL* 36:529)

See pp. 179–80, 190 below
Petr.Lomb.*Sent.*4.3.1
(Quaracchi 4:61)
Aeg.Rom.*Ren.pap.*16.1 (1554:22r);Gabr.Bl.*Can.miss.*48.C
(Oberman-Courtenay 2:233)

Petr.Lomb.*Sent.*4.9.1
(Quaracchi 4:199)
Aug.*Ev.Joh.*25.12 (*CCSL* 36:254)

Thos.Kemp.*Im.Chr.*4.10 (Pohl 2:118–19);Wyc.*Serm.*2.61
(*WLW* 9:455)

Gabr.Bl.*Can.miss.*29.E
(Oberman-Courtenay 1:292–93);Gabr.Bl.*Fest.Chr.*19 (1499:H8r)
Alv.Pel.*Ep.*9.5 (Meneghin 51–52)

discussing it in the fourteenth and fifteenth. One of those Hussite theologians quoted Paschasius Radbertus's formula of "the two modes of the natural body of Christ" as well as other passages from his works to prove his own substantial orthodoxy on the real presence. He also quoted Berengar's recantation of 1059, which had been incorporated into canon law, so that Berengar had become, rather ironically, a spokesman for eucharistic orthodoxy, as well as for the authority of a council to restrain heretics. Other Hussite theologians, including Hus himself, likewise made use of Berengar's confession to dissociate themselves from his heresy and to justify their views. Berengar's declaration seems to have been a good place to begin a proposed reconstruction of the church's teachings about the Lord's Supper; for the three eucharistic reinterpretations from the fourteenth century with which we shall be dealing—those of John of Paris, William of Ockham, and John Wycliffe—all called upon "the confession of Berengar" as an authority, as did their fifteenth-century opponents, who were defending transubstantiation. And in the sixteenth century Berengar would become once more an issue in the new debates over the eucharistic presence.

Looming above and behind these more recent medieval authorities were the church fathers, especially Augustine. The Augustinian formula, "The word is added to the element, and it becomes a sacrament, tantamount to a visible word," which was to play an important part in the sacramental thought of many of the Protestant Reformers of the sixteenth century, appeared in the *Sentences* of Peter Lombard, whence it passed, not only into the commentaries on the *Sentences* but into other works as well. Perhaps the most disquieting of Augustine's statements, also quoted in the *Sentences,* "Why are you preparing your teeth and your stomach? Believe, and you have already eaten," could simply serve to establish a distinction between the "spiritual eating" of faith and the "sacramental eating" of Holy Communion. In this way it provided a basis for resolving the pastoral problem of a communicant who was physically unable to ingest the consecrated elements. But its depreciation of "sacramental eating" in favor of "spiritual eating" could also

Chel.*Repl*.25 (Petrů 180)

Wyc.*Apost*.16 (*WLW* 12:220)

Andr.Brd.*Utraq*.4 (Hardt 3:
399);Gers.*Utraq*. (Glorieux 10:
57;67);Joh.Rag.*Utraq*. (Mansi
29:815;867)

Jac.Mis.*Rem*.2 (Vooght 328)

Dns.Scot.*Ox*.4.8.1.3 (Wadding
17:7–8)

ap.Joh.Par.*Corp*. (1686:109)

Příb.*Tract*.5 (Sedlák 74);Gers.
*Magn*.9 (Glorieux 8:395)
Wyc.*Serm*.1.13 (*WLW* 8:90–
92);Wyc.*Euch*.3;9 (*WLW* 16:
62–63;316–18);Chel.*Repl*.12
(Petrů 152)
Andr.Brd.*Orig.Hs*. (*FRA* 6:
335;339);Příb.*Tract*.1 (Sedlák
58–59);Joh.Rag.*Bas.conc*.41
(*MC* 1:82)
ap.Joh.Rag.*Bob*.155 (*MC* 1.
269);Laur.Reich.*Diurn*.21.i.
1433 (*MC* 1:294)
Jac.Mis.*Zjev*.13:12 (*Pram*.18:
545);Jac.Mis.*Corp*.6–7 (Hardt
3:917–21);Jac.Mis.*Ven.sacr*.13
(Vooght 401–2)

Gers.*Sup*. (Glorieux 10:141)

Dns.Scot.*Quodlib*.20.13
(Wadding 26:313)
Dns.Scot.*Quodlib*.20.2
(Wadding 26:298);Ub.Cas.*Arb.
vit*.4.5 (Davis 291–92)

Aeg.Rom.*Ren.pap*.20 (1554:
26v)

mean that "only he eats in reality [v pravdě] who believes in Christ," thus apparently making the reality of the presence a corollary of faith rather than an objective fact. It could even become a defense of the practice of withholding the chalice from the laity, on the grounds that true believers did not need to receive the Sacrament under both kinds; for if they believed, they had already received the body of Christ (and, presumably, his blood).

As the medieval "rule of faith" about the real presence had in considerable measure been a corollary of the "rule of prayer" expressed in private devotion and public liturgy, so by reciprocity the doctrine stimulated further devotional and liturgical development. "Practically all the devotion of the church," as Duns Scotus noted, "is related [in ordine] to this Sacrament," whose adoration in turn was one of the strongest proofs of the real presence, since such worship, if addressed to a mere symbol of the body of Christ, would be idolatrous. That is precisely what such worship was, according to critics of the medieval doctrine. Their opposition to this "idolatry" provoked accusations of atrocities committed against the Sacrament and against images of the saints, as well as theological defenses of the practice of adoring the eucharistic host on the grounds of the inseparable union between the Sacrament and the person of the God-man. Even a supporter of the doctrine of transubstantiation and adoration had to warn against various superstitious abuses of the sacrifice of the Mass being encouraged by overzealous preachers. But that did not detract from the sacrificial significance of the Mass, nor even from the practice of applying the sacrifice to some particular intention. As a sacrifice, the Mass benefited not only the priest who offered it but the entire church, on behalf of which he did so. The relation of this sacrifice to the sacrifice on Calvary continued to be a vexing issue. For everyone had to agree that "no sacrifice succeeded, or could succeed, the offering of Christ," the only true sacrifice and the only true priest. But, as two fourteenth-century writers asserted, "this sacrifice was offered once and for all [semel] as the price [of redemption], but it is continually recalled [recolitur iugiter] in the church through the mystery

Jac.Vit.*Reg.chr.*1.5 (Arquillière
136);Alv.Pel.*Planc.eccl.*1.63
(1560:77v)

that is consecrated and offered by the ministry of the
priests."

As we have noted earlier, however, it was above all
the nature of the eucharistic presence that continued,
despite the dogma of transubstantiation, to demand
further consideration by individual theologians. Evidently transubstantiation had been less of a solution,
and had achieved less of a settlement, than the self-
evidential language of the decree at the Fourth Lateran

CLater.(1215)*Const.*1
(Alberigo-Jedin 230)
Inn.III.*Sacr.alt.*4.7 (PL 217:
860–61)

Council suggested. In spite of that decree and the
sponsorship of so towering a figure as Pope Innocent
III, transubstantiation continued to evoke sharp disagreement. It had always run the risk of being taken
as a rationalistic "explanation" that somehow made
the doctrine of the real presence more plausible. As
the terms "substance" and "accident" came to acquire
increasingly technical significance in the vocabulary
of philosophy and then of theology, the way was open
to philosophical changes that would, in turn, affect
the eucharistic theory of one or another theologian.
But, as on so many other questions, "it is with Scotus
that the important change comes, because with Scotus
the doctrine of transubstantiation comes to be more a
question of the authority of the post-apostolic Church

McCue (1968) 403
Dns.Scot.*Ox.*4.11.1.2
(Wadding 17:319)

than of the understanding of the eucharist." The definition of Scotus, that transubstantiation was "the complete change of one substance into another substance,"

Aeg.Rom.*Corp.*3;47 (1481:2v;
38r);Aeg.Rom.*Quodlib.*4.6
(1646:212);Thos.Sut.*Quodlib.*
4.8 (Schmaus 546);Vit.Furn.
*Rer.princ.*3.1.3 (Wadding 4:
290);Guil.Oc.*Sacr.alt.*pr.
(Birch 2–4);Wyc.*Euch.*2
(*WLW* 16:48)

was, to be sure, present almost verbatim in many other
theologians of the fourteenth century, even though in
some cases the definition served the theologian, as it
had Scotus, as a foil for his own idiosyncratic reconstruction. These private theological proposals are, as
such, important here only insofar as they serve to document the continuing distinction between transub-

See vol.3:204

stantiation and the doctrine of "the true and real
existence of the body of Christ, [which] . . . can be
safeguarded in another way" than through the use of

Joh.Par.*Corp.* (1686:85)

transubstantiation. For, as Lorenzo Valla was to observe, the eucharistic miracle was no more difficult to
believe than the miracle of the incarnation, but for some
reason it was still causing "disquiet" even to those for

Vall.*Euch.* (*MPPR* 6:67);Vall.
*Volup.*3.25 (*MPPR* 5:990)

whom the incarnation was beyond question.

What most of them had in common was a concern
with the state of the eucharistic elements, bread and

Petr.Lomb.*Sent.*4.12.1
(Quaracchi 4:267)

Joh.Par.*Corp.* (1686:96–97)

See vol.2:88–89
Joh.Par.*Corp.* (1686:86–87)

Joh.Par.*Corp.* (1686:102–3)

Vit.Furn.*Quodlib.*2.9
(Delorme 79–80);Wyc.*Euch.*7
(*WLW* 16:221–22,228–30)

Joh.Lutt.*Guil.Oc.*34
(Hoffmann 79)

Buescher (1950) 156

Guil.Oc.*Corp.*12 (Birch 218);
Guil.Oc.*Sacr.alt.*3 (Birch 96)

Guil.Oc.*Corp.*40 (Birch 476)

Guil.Oc.*Corp.*6 (Birch 188);
Guil.Oc.*Sacr.alt.*3 (Birch 150)

Guil.Oc.*Corp.*31;41 (Birch
370–72;500)

Guil.Oc.*Sacr.alt.*3 (Birch 156)

Guil.Oc.*Corp.*31 (Birch 372)

Maglione (1941) 72

wine, after the change into the body and blood of Christ. Thus John of Paris argued, on the basis of Peter Lombard, that the authority of the faith did not make it obligatory to deny that the substance of the bread remained. He drew an analogy between the substance of the bread and the human nature of Christ, which according to the orthodox doctrine had its being only in his hypostasis and yet was not annihilated through the hypostatic union; and he was willing to use "impanation" as a term for describing the relation between the body of Christ and the bread. To his various opponents, all of this was no better than saying "that the substance of the bread truly remains and that it is truly bread and the body of Christ." William of Ockham was also accused of favoring the idea "that the substance of the bread is truly annihilated in the Sacrament of the Altar." Applying to the eucharistic presence his emphasis "upon the will of God, which, *de potentia absoluta,* can accomplish everything which does not involve a contradiction," he sometimes interpreted transubstantiation on the basis of God's power to separate substance and accident and as a way for faith to be meritorious by believing something without the evidence of experience or reason. The presence of the body of Christ in the Sacrament must not be thought of as "circumscribed by place," and therefore it was necessary to distinguish precisely between a change into the substance of the body and a change into "the quantity of the body of Christ." For while "that quantity which is, or was, substance" did not remain after the change of bread into the body of Christ, the "quantity" of color, taste, and mass did remain. This distinction between substance and quantity was a way of "easily preserving the whole truth about the Sacrament of the Eucharist." Whether or not the charges of eucharistic heresy against John of Paris and William of Ockham were valid, it is clear from the thought of Giles of Rome that it was possible even for an orthodox theologian to propose "a new concept . . . of 'body' . . . more harmonious with the faith" than at least some versions of transubstantiation seemed to be. He sought to avoid the notion of the annihilation of the substance of the bread in the sacramental change by suggesting that it remained po-

Aeg.Rom.*Corp*.34;40 (1481:
23v;29v);Henr.Gnt.*Quodlib*.9.
9;11.1.4 (1613–II:97r–98v;
194r)

Dns.Scot.*Quodlib*.10.21
(Wadding 25:430)

Wyc.*Civ.dom*.1.36 (*WLW* 4:
260)
Wyc.*Euch*.2;7 (*WLW* 16:52;
199)

Wyc.*Ben.inc*.11 (*WLW* 7:190–
91)
Wyc.*Serm*.3.58 (*WLW* 11:507);
Wyc.*Euch*.7 (*WLW* 16:216)
Wyc.*Euch*.5 (*WLW* 16:148)

Wyc.*Serm*.3.51 (*WLW* 11:445)
Wyc.*Euch*.8;9 (*WLW* 16:271;
303)
Wyc.*Euch*.1 (*WLW* 16:15)
Wyc.*Euch*.7 (*WLW* 16:230–31)

Wyc.*Serm*.2.61;4.42 (*WLW* 9:
463;13:351);Wyc.*Euch*.4
(*WLW* 16:87)
Wyc.*Euch*.4 (*WLW* 16:83–84)

Wyc.*Euch*.5 (*WLW* 16:123)

Wyc.*Serm*.2.61 (*WLW* 9:453)
Wyc.*Serm*.3.54 (*WLW* 11:471)
Wyc.*Euch*.5 (*WLW* 16:121)

Joh.Z.*Tract*. (Sedlák 4)

Joh.Z.*Tract*. (Sedlák 19–20)

Příb.*Tract*.3 (Sedlák 62–63)

Chel.*Repl*.10 (Petrů 149)

Chel.*Repl*.17 (Petrů 163)

Jac.Mis.*Rem*.1;3 (Vooght 319;
347)
Jac.Mis.*Ven.sacr*.4 (Vooght
392)

tentially in the matter of the body of Christ, a suggestion that Scotus found unacceptable, though not heretical.

It is even more clear from the thought of John Wycliffe how the idea of the "remanence" of the bread could also lead a theologian from the defense of transubstantiation to its total repudiation. Originally he had been able to say that "the priest confects the body of Christ, that is, he brings it about by his ministration that the body of Christ exists under the accidents through the sacred words"; eventually, however, he found this explanation untenable. Substance and accident could not be separated, and therefore the substance of the bread remained. In fact, "substance" and "accident" were not scriptural terms; nor was it proper to speak of a "conversion" of the elements. What was in the Eucharist was "the body of Christ in the nature of the bread, since what is there is the nature of the bread and not the nature of the body of Christ, as it is in heaven." It was in heaven according to its dimensions, in the host "according to its power [virtualiter]," where it was "present hidden." As long as the continuance of the bread as bread was affirmed, Wycliffe did not insist on any specific theory of the presence, but spoke of it as being "in some manner or other [quodammodo]." He did insist that the words of consecration, though figurative, were unique, not merely one blessing among others. Thus the body and blood were in the Sacrament "truly and really, but figuratively" or "spiritually and really" or "in a sign but not without being there really and truly." Among Wycliffe's Hussite disciples, the more radical followed him in his emphasis upon the remanence of the bread, as well as upon its unique quality as distinct from any other bread; but this dual insistence, which conservatives denounced as ambiguous, seemed to verge on depressing the Eucharist into "nothing more than a mere symbol [jedině púhé znamenie]," with no presence of the "true and substantial body of Christ" at all, but only of his "graces." The more moderate, however, having begun by teaching a Wycliffite doctrine of remanence and "spiritual" presence, eventually broke with the idea of "figurative language" in the Eucharist and even with the doctrine of remanence

Jac.Mis.*Corp*.5 (Hardt 3:913–14)
Jac.Mis.*Corp*.10 (Hardt 3:925–27)

itself, and sought to reinterpret Wycliffe in the same sense. More than the other views of the Sacrament with which we have been concerned, the Hussite theories presaged the fate of the doctrine of the Lord's Supper in the last two centuries of the period covered by this volume; for in the later Reformation, as in the Hussite Reformation, various doctrines of the sacraments would become principles of definition for various churches, which would find themselves divided most sharply by that which, they all agreed, had been intended to express the unity of believers with Christ and with one another.

## The One True Faith

Joh.Par.*Pot*.3 (Leclercq 181); Jac.Vit.*Reg.chr*.2.5 (Arquillière 212);Joh.Rag.*Utraq*. (Mansi 29:713)

Jac.Vit.*Reg.chr*.1.3 (Arquillière 111–12);Alv.Pel.*Planc.eccl*.1.63 (1560:76r);Joh.Pal.*Quaest.par*. (Döllinger 435)

Aeg.Rom.*Err.phil.conc*. (Koch-Riedl 66);Nicol.Cus. *Pac.fid*.4 (Heidelberg 7:11) Guil.Oc.*Jn*.5 (Sikes 3:46);Seg. *Sept.not*.1–2 (Krämer 430–31)

Joh.Brev.*Tract*.1.3 (Du Pin 1:829)

Gers.*Mat.fid*.6 (Glorieux 6:158),Gers.*Nupt*. (Glorieux 6:206) Gers.*Ex.doct*.pr (Glorieux 9:458) ap.Joh.Pal.*Quaest.par*. (Döllinger 418);Seg.*Eccl*.1.21 (Krämer 402)

Barth.Pis.*Quad*.27 (1498:J1v)

All.*Trin*. (Du Pin 1:627) Ang.Clar.*Alv.Pel*.16 (*AFH* 39:99);Nicol.Cus.*Conc.cath*.1.5 (Heidelberg 14:49)

Guil.Oc.*Corp*.36 (Birch 440)

The gravest peril to the oneness of "the one true faith" in the fourteenth and fifteenth centuries came from the loss of oneness in the "one true church," for the two were perceived as inseparable. The deepening concern over the unity of the church was likewise a desire to preserve—or to restore—"the unity of faith, by which is understood the unity of doctrine." This was the true and catholic faith, which was one and the same everywhere. To be a catholic meant to have explicit as well as implicit faith: implicit faith in the universal authority of Scripture and the church, but also explicit faith in the truths of Scripture and church confessed in the Apostles' Creed. As regards these truths of faith, no deviation or "variety of doctrines" was permissible, even though it may have been permissible before the church formulated its article of faith on a particular question, as it had been necessary in the period of the Old Testament to know and confess some articles only implicitly. But it was necessary to distinguish between these doctrines and other theological opinions, which were not clearly taught as explicit catholic truth and on which there could be various positions; for such a "variety of opinions" did not threaten the unity of the church and of its doctrine. Therefore the bishops of the church must not condemn this kind of "variety," even though it was their duty to reject deviation from explicit catholic doctrine.

It was, according to Duns Scotus, the task of theologians to treat both church doctrine and theological opinion, "to expound Scripture and to explicate the

Dns.Scot.Ox.3.24.q.un.16
(Wadding 15:46)

Dns.Scot.Quodlib.7.10
(Wadding 25:291)

Dns.Scot.Ord.pr.204 (Balić 1:
138)
Dns.Scot.Ord.pr.123 (Balić 1:
87)

All.Pot.eccl.3.1 (Du Pin 2:950)
Joh.Brev.Tract.1.3 (Du Pin 1:
840);Gers.Union.eccl.
(Glorieux 6:15)
Gers.Ex.doct.2.5 (Glorieux 9:
472)

Chel.Boj.(Petrů 97);Hs.Coll.88
(Ryšánek 7:517)

Ub.Cas.Declar. (ALKGMA 3:
178)

Ub.Cas.Rot.16;23 (ALKGMA
3:118;127)
Ub.Cas.Sanct.vest. (ALKGMA
3:72;75)

Eben.Consid.9 (DRTA 15:
829);Thdrc.Nm.Int.pac. (Finke
3:125)

Henr.Lang.Concept.1.7 (1516:
3v);Gers.Cons.4.4 (Glorieux 9:
237–38)

Univ.Par.Avis.conc.3;21 (Finke
1:133;139);Vall.Prof.rel.
(MPPR 6:288–89)
Thdrc.Nm.Mod. (QMR 3:
116);Guil.Oc.Op.XC.dier.71
(Sikes 2:596)

Robt.Orf.Repr.Aeg.1 (Bibl.
Thom.38:34)

Ramb.Bol.Apol.ver.6.1 (ST
108:50)

Seg.Gl.Eug.4 ap.Seg.Hist.conc.
Bas.18.42 (MC 3:1165)
Joh.Brev.Tract.1.3 (Du Pin 1:
834–35)

conclusions" drawn from it, which included consideration not only of the conclusions that were "necessary" but also of such as were merely "possible"; thus he could maintain that "our theology does not in fact deal with anything except the things that are contained in Scripture and with the things that can be drawn [elici] from these," the latter being "contained there potentially [virtualiter]." Therefore it was essential that the "disputation [of theologians] not be inhibited," especially in the deliberations of a general church council, since it was primarily to them, rather than to the prelates of the church, that this twofold task was entrusted, and the theologians deserved support rather than ridicule and criticism. A frequent target of such criticism was the allegedly excessive erudition of many, which caused them to neglect the one true faith of simple believers in favor of learned disputations. Spiritual Franciscans claimed to be following Francis in exalting prayer over study as the occupation of the theologian, and they denounced an excessively academic attention to philosophical theology, above all when it preferred pagan writers to the Bible. On the other hand, Henry Heinbuche of Langenstein, who was hailed as "second to none in our time in holiness of life as well as in knowledge," criticized those (including certain Franciscans) who had not been properly educated in Scripture and the fathers and who took it upon themselves to criticize a theologian of the stature of Bernard. Such theological ignorance, which seemed to some to have become epidemic, was, of course, particularly appalling when found in a pope.

The basic truth of theology consisted in the articles of faith. These were to be believed and taken on faith, but that did not imply that they were not also to become the object of "knowledge [scientia]," since that was what made theology a "science." The term "article of faith" could refer to a particular catholic truth stated explicitly in the creed or added to the creed by the authority of the church over the course of centuries; or it could refer to "the sum total of all catholic truth," which was complete and integral already and brooked no addition by anyone. The articles of faith included those truths that were expressly

Guil.Oc.*Dial*.2.5 (Goldast 2: 415–16);Ps.Alb.M.*Mar*.132 (Borgnet 37:187);Henr.Oyt. *Ver.cath*.3 (*Opettex* 16:10–11); Joh.Brev.*Tract*.1.3;3.4 (Du Pin 1:831;900–1)

taught in Scripture and such truths as could be necessarily inferred from Scripture: on this everyone agreed, but not on the question whether there were also some articles of faith not contained in Scripture but transmitted apart from Scripture through authentic tradition. In addition to the articles of faith of whatever sort, however, there were teachings that the

Gers.*Ex.doct*.1.1 (Glorieux 9: 459–60) Gabr.Bl.*Fest.Mar*.11 (1499: F6v)

church permitted as belonging to "the piety of faith" but did not require, as, for example, various pious beliefs about the Virgin Mary. Even among the articles of faith, not all were of equal importance with the fundamental doctrines of the Trinity and the person of Christ. A "catholic truth," by Ockham's defini-

Guil.Oc.*Ben*.2.2 (Sikes 3:214–15);Guil.Oc.*Dial*.2.2 (Goldast 2:411–12)

tion, was one "held to be catholic by all Christian and catholic peoples"; conversely, a heresy was "something contrary to divine Scripture or to the doctrine

Guil.Oc.*Op.XC.dier*.124;82 (Sikes 2:847;643);Guil.Oc.*Jn*. 34 (Sikes 3:130) Turr.*Aug.Rom*. (Mansi 30: 1008–9) See vol.3:18 Hs.*Sent*.4.13.5 (Flajšhans 2: 586–87);Hs.*Svat*.1 (Hrabák 21) Chel.*St.vr*.1.5 (*Com*.22:15)

of the universal church" if it was held pertinaciously. This was a definition of heresy in which most concurred, including John Hus, who, following a medieval designation, included simony as a heresy. Among Hus's followers, Chelčický complained that true faith was now being called heresy and vice versa, while Jakoubek ze Stříbra, whom Chelčický regarded as a

Chel.*Crk*. (Petrů 104)

heretic, set himself against heretical innovation by re-

Jac.Mis.*Purg*. (Walch 1–III:3)

taining the doctrine of purgatory, but likewise claimed to be battling innovation when he opposed the prac-

Jac.Mis.*Utraq*.1.30 (Hardt 3: 490–91)

tice of withholding the chalice from the laity. Other critics of the papacy, too, had recourse to the standard argument against innovation, charging that the pope's assertion of "plenitude of power" over divine and human law and the pope's claim to have the unilateral

Mars.Pad.*Def.pac*.2.25.20 (Previté-Orton 397);Joh.Par. *Pot*. (Leclercq 250);Dom. Domen.*Pot.pap*.1.con.3 (Smolinsky 70–71)

right to declare someone a heretic were "effrontery" and "novelty."

But to be "catholic," a theologian had the task not only of setting forth the articles of faith and of refuting heresies, but also of dealing theologically with those divine truths "that were also known by the philoso-

Dns.Scot.*Prim.princ*.4.10 (Roche 142) Dns.Scot.*Prim.princ*.3 (Roche 38)

phers as well" and of "demonstrating by reason what he [already] holds by an utterly certain faith." Thomas's performance of this task required defense against those who alleged that by classifying creation ex nihilo as an article of faith and not of proof, he had conceded

See vol.3:290–91

too much to the proponents of the doctrine of the eternity of the world; he had, in fact, according to

Corr. "Quare" 6 (Bibl.Thom.9: 37–38)

Ramb.Bol.Apol.ver.6.2 (ST 108:60)

Ramb.Bol.Apol.ver.6.3 (ST 108:109)
Ramb.Bol.Apol.ver.6.2 (ST 108:76);Robt.Orf.Corr.6 (Bibl. Thom.31:52–53)

Gers.Lull. (Glorieux 10:122); Gers.Cur.st.1 (Glorieux 3:231– 32)

Gers.Magn.7;9 (Glorieux 8: 314;392)

See vol.3:261
Nicol.Cus.Dir.spec.4 (Heidelberg 13:8);Nicol.Cus. Apol. (Heidelberg 2:8)
Dns.Scot.Quodlib.1.4 (Wadding 25:9);Dns.Scot.Prim. princ.4.9 (Roche 122,124)
Petr.Aur.Sent.1.1.6.56 (FIP Txt 3:348)
Robt.Orf.Repr.Aeg.11 (Bibl. Thom.38:66)

Dns.Scot.Prim.princ.4.9 (Roche 122,124)
Dns.Scot.Ord.1.42.6–9 (Balić 6:342–43)

Dns.Scot.Quodlib.7.3 (Wadding 25:284);Dns.Scot. Prim.princ.4.9 (Roche 130)
Dns.Scot.Rep.Par.pr.2.4 (Wadding 22:34–35)

Dns.Scot.Quodlib.7.23 (Wadding 25:302)

Gilson (1955) 463

his defenders, "destroyed the sophistic arguments [of these proponents] more effectively" than his critics ever would have. Rambert of Bologna, who had been Thomas's pupil, wrote his *Apology for the Truth* in support of the Thomistic position not only on the eternity of the world but on the total enterprise of relating faith and reason; Thomas had "shown that the things that faith says are not impossible, but he never says that these are demonstrations" that such things were true by reason. This assertion Rambert directed chiefly against those of Thomas's critics who maintained that no article of faith was capable of proof. As a later thinker observed, Thomas had avoided attempting to prove those things that were knowable only by faith, or using "sophistic and invalid" proofs even for those things that were capable of demonstration.

This latter reference was a criticism of Anselm's ontological argument for the existence of God; but the definition underlying that argument, that God was "that than which nothing greater can be thought," was, as Nicholas of Cusa pointed out, one that "all theologians" on both sides of the several controversies of the time accepted—Duns Scotus and Peter Aureoli, as well as Giles of Rome and his Thomistic opponent Robert of Orford (to name only a few). And while Scotus, speaking as a philosopher, did propound his own version of the ontological argument, he also insisted, speaking "in a strictly theological way," that the omnipotence of God, as the catholic faith understood it, was not subject to proof "on the basis of what is known naturally." Although there was, therefore, only "one knowledge of God," not two, there was at the same time an antinomy between theology and philosophy, because certain conclusions could not be either proved or disproved by a philosophical way of knowing. Thus the debates over "God and the ways of knowing" during the fourteenth and fifteenth centuries had "manifold philosophical consequences," but they also affected the course of doctrinal history. For during these same centuries, when there was occurring a shift of emphasis from the primacy of intellect (as this had been expounded by Thomas Aquinas) to the primacy of will (as this had been maintained by Au-

Gers.*Cant*.3 (Glorieux 8:601)

Gers.*Mont.cont*.4 (Glorieux 7:18)

Isa.7:9

See vol.3:258–59

Guil.Mar.*Corr.Thom*.6 (*Bibl. Thom*.9:32)

Ramb.Bol.*Apol.ver*.6.1 (*ST* 108:57–58;47);All.*Tract*.2.3.8 (1490:D2r)

Robt.Orf.*Corr*.6 (*Bibl.Thom* 31:50)

Gers.*Magn*.9 (Glorieux 8:387)

Gers.*Lull*. (Glorieux 10:123)
Gers.*Serm*.213 (Glorieux 5:92–93),Nicol.Cus.*Doct.ign*.3.11 (Heidelberg 1:151–52)

All.*Leg*. (Du Pin 1:664)

Gers.*Theol.myst*.1.5 (Combes 14)

See vol.1:344–49

See vol.2:254–70

See vol.3:144–57;303–7

gustine and Bonaventure), there was a related shift from a form of Christian reflection that "seeks, through reasons based on the true faith, to understand the nature of God" to a form that "holds principally to the love of God . . . without lofty inquiry," although in many thinkers of the time (including the author of the words just quoted) both forms were present.

During the twelfth and thirteenth centuries, the biblical justification for the first of these two forms of Christian reflection, the method of reason, had been the words of the prophet Isaiah: "Unless you believe, you will not understand." Those words continued to provide such justification during the fourteenth and fifteenth centuries. Because the passage was serving the critics of Thomas Aquinas as a proof text for their objections to his thought, his disciples, in order to specify the limits of the understanding that was possible in this present life, paraphrased it to say: "Unless you believe, you will not understand in any way; but if you do believe, you will understand in some way, although not perfectly." The corollary to this specification of limits for temporal understanding was an interpretation of the promise to mean that those who had had faith during this life would receive full understanding and vision in the life to come. The passage ruled out any effort to "understand in order that we may believe" or to convince unbelievers of the rational plausibility of the faith; rather, it was directed to those who "philosophize on the basis of religion as a presupposition." But it was necessary to carry the promise of Isaiah 7:9 further, by applying it not only to the "mental grasp" of truth about God, but also to that grasp which "clings" to God in love and desire. The worthy adherents of the faith were those who were willing to move through faith to this species of understanding as well, the understanding that took the form of "mystical theology."

Like the mysticism of Pseudo-Dionysius the Areopagite, which was the fountainhead for much of this thought, or the mysticism of Simeon the New Theologian and Gregory Palamas, or the mysticism of Bernard of Clairvaux and Bonaventure, this "mystical theology" in the fourteenth and fifteenth centuries may lay claim to our attention here only to the extent that it shaped the development of church doctrine. During these two centuries, much of it existed side by side with official church doctrine, neither shaping it nor (in the judgment of its critics) being shaped by it in any decisive way. Whether or not it is accurate, with some scholars, to see in the late medieval mystics a source for the more radical versions of Reformation theology, it is certainly accurate to identify them as one of the objects of the conciliar and confessional anathemas of the Reformation period, and therefore as one of the occasions for the doctrinal formulations adopted both by Roman Catholicism and by conservative Protestantism in the sixteenth century. Despite its considerable historical importance and great intrinsic interest, therefore, late medieval mysticism will figure in our narrative, in this and in later chapters, chiefly on this rather narrow basis. For that reason, Gerson and Nicholas of Cusa, as theologians and cardinals of the church who were concerned, explicitly and quite self-consciously, with the relation between mystical theology and church theology, must figure more prominently in this account than will some others, who would in turn overshadow them in any history of mysticism as such.

Taking as models Gregory the Great and Bernard of Clairvaux, Gerson set up as an ideal the theologian who was "ambidextrous," equally able to practice either the contemplative or the active life—and able to engage in either "affective" or "speculative" theology. But just as he preferred the contemplative to the active life, so also he urged that "scholastics . . . pay diligent attention to the writings of mystical theology." The forms of church doctrine had dealt more with "understanding [intelligentia]" than with "feeling [affectus]," which was the seat of mystical theology. Or, as Nicholas of Cusa put it, one must "leave everything behind and even transcend one's intellect," going "beyond all sense, reason, and intellect to mystical vision." While it was dangerous for devotion to exist without knowledge, as it did in certain heretical sects, it was also necessary to point out that speculative theology could serve an immoral purpose much more easily than mystical theology could. Because simple believers were sometimes more devout than

Wm.S.Th.*Ep.frat*.12 (Davy 74–75)
Gers.*Mont.cont*.3;27 (Glorieux 7:17;36);Gers.*Myst.theol.prac*.9 (Combes 188)

Gers.*Ep*.57 (Glorieux 2:275)

Gers.*Theol.myst*.1.8 (Combes 19)
Gers.*Theol.myst*.4.21 (Combes 51–52)
Gers.*Myst.theol.prac*.8 (Combes 172–73)

Nicol.Cus.*Poss*.17;15 (Heidelberg 11–II:22;19)

Gers.*Theol.myst*.1.8 (Combes 20)

Gers.*Theol.myst*.4.32 (Combes 82);Gers.*Magn*.7 (Glorieux 8: 302–4)

Thos.Aq.S.T.2.2.82.3 ad 3
(Ed.Leon.9:190)

Gers.Schol.myst.9 (Combes
229);Gers.Mont.cont.8
(Glorieux 7:21)

Gers.Theol.myst.4.30 (Combes
76–77)
Gers.Theol.myst.4.29 (Combes
73–74)

Gers.Theol.myst.4.30 (Combes
78)

Gers.Cant.1 (Glorieux 8:579)

Gers.Glor.1.8 (Glorieux 8:543)

Gers.Cant.pr. (Glorieux 8:576)

Gers.Magn.7 (Glorieux 8:307);
Gers.Schol.myst.8 (Combes
228)
Gers.Ex.doct. (Glorieux 9:
474);Gers.Magn.3 (Glorieux 8:
208)

Gers.Magn.1 (Glorieux 8:173–
74)

Gers.Ep.55;Ep.58 (Glorieux 2:
263;277)

Gers.Ex.doct. (Glorieux 9:475)
Gers.Cur.st.1 (Glorieux 3:231);
Gers.Serm.207;247 (Glorieux
5:8;523)

Gers.Magn.7 (Glorieux 8:295)

See vol.3:101–2

Gers.Glor.3.5 (Glorieux 8:553)

scholars were, as Thomas Aquinas had observed, they also "penetrate to mystical theology in a more rapid and more sublime manner than do those who are learned in scholastic or discursive theology." For mystical theology "does not have need of the sort of school that may be called 'the school of the intellect,' but is acquired in the school of feeling," in which one learned to practice the moral virtues and the sort of theology that was conducive to mystical purification and illumination. The object of speculative theology was the True, the object of mystical theology was the Good. Thus while speculative theology sought an intellectual "knowledge about [scientia]," mystical theology sought an experiential "knowledge of [notitia]." In this it showed that it stood more in the tradition of Augustine than in that of Aristotle.

The "doctrinal explanation" of scholastic and speculative theology could not do justice to mystical theology, because the ecstatic love that "consists in the experiential perception of the union of the soul, with God as its supreme object and goal, can in no way be communicated [tradi] through doctrine." Still it was essential to remember that there was a "doctrinal tradition of mystical theology" and that in its doctrinal content it was "not divergent or separate from scholastic theology." The "doctrine of mystical theology" and the "experience of doctrine" must be held together, despite the distinctions between them. Doctrine needed to have experience as its "companion." In addition to Gregory the Great and Bernard, therefore, Bonaventure was outstanding among theologians, "the wisest in intellect and at the same time the most devout in feeling," and for that reason he was an especially reliable guide. He combined a solidity in doctrinal theology with a profundity in devotional theology, not mingling the former with extraneous philosophical ideas nor the latter with alien notions. It was above all in *The Journey of the Mind to God* that he stood out from other theologians and other mystics (and, for that matter, from other Franciscans). By contrast, John Scotus Erigena had brought upon himself the accusation of pantheism because he had not been sufficiently careful in his language about the relation of God to the world of creatures. Nor had he been the only one, or the last one, to fall into such a trap. Gerson accused various mystical writers of the fourteenth century of blurring the distinction between Creator and creature in their language about the mystical union between the soul and God.

For a vulnerable point of mystical theology was its doctrine of "deification." This doctrine had long been a prominent feature of orthodox teaching, especially in the East, and was central to the mystical theology of Dionysius the Areopagite. Drawing upon that source, as well as upon indigenous Western Christian writers, Latin theology, too, went on speaking of salvation as deification. According to one pseudonymous writing of this period, for example, the union between the Virgin Mary and her Son was so close that the angels could adore her "deified flesh" in him, and Gerson found it natural to describe the repose of the soul in the love of Christ as "a peace that deifies." But this did not mean that when the rational spirit was transported into God, it was "altogether deified" and reabsorbed into the "idea" of itself that had existed eternally in the mind of God, losing its identity and its very creatureliness. Nicholas of Cusa defined the divine sonship conferred in salvation as "deification," which was a "participation in the power of God" that transformed the mind and permitted it to share in God's own perception of truth. This transformation did not obliterate human creatureliness. Rather it meant that "we shall then be in another manner what we now are in our own manner." Through deification, then, God and creatures would become "one" in such a way that "all things are what they are" and would be united in the oneness of God. Believers would "become God" and yet would "preserve the reality of their own being," and thus God would be "all in all" through Christ. Contrary to a mysticism that was in danger of heresy, the "mystical theology" that was at the same time churchly and orthodox took the favorite proof text for deification, the words of the psalm, "You are gods," to mean a change that was not ontological but "participative and assimilative."

The basis for a false doctrine of union with God and "deification" was, according to Gerson, a mis-

See vol.1:344–46;vol.2:10–16

Hon.Aug.Oct.quaest.2 (PL 172:1187);Barth.Pis.Quad.51 (1498:P4r)

Ps.Brd.Clr.Laud.Virg. (PL 182:1147)

Gers.Theol.myst.5.35 (Combes 94)

Gers.Theol.myst.8.41 (Combes 105–6)

Nicol.Cus.Fil.1 (Heidelberg 4: 39–40)

Nicol.Cus.Fil.2 (Heidelberg 4: 42)

Nicol.Cus.Fil.3 (Heidelberg 4: 51–52)

Nicol.Cus.Doct.ign.3.12 (Heidelberg 1:161)

See vol.2:260

Ps.82:6;John 10:34

Gers.Ep.13 (Glorieux 2:57,60)

reading of Dionysius. He had not taught "a cessation of all intellectual activity," but an elevation into "the better power of our mind and reason," which recognized that the truth of God transcended all categories of understanding and speech and was in that sense "ineffable." Nor was this negative or "apophatic" emphasis of Dionysius to become a basis for an agnosticism that would say "nothing is known about God unless all his properties are known." To know God, according to Dionysius, was to know him both through negation (by knowing that he was not like any of the creatures used to symbolize him) and through "excellence" (by knowing that he was the infinite perfection of qualities known imperfectly in creatures); for transcendence, the quality by which God was "above [super]" all things, was an affirmation as well as a negation. It was the special achievement of Nicholas of Cusa to have brought this "apophatic" dimension of "Dionysius, that great theologian," into conformity with "the one true faith" of the church, by means of his doctrine of "learned ignorance." In true Dionysian fashion, he spoke of God as transcending all concepts, and of the Trinity as transcending all number. God was at one and the same time the object of understanding and the one who transcended all understanding: that was the meaning of "learned ignorance" and of the ineffable name that God revealed to Moses from the burning bush. It was a theological assumption of this period that even if man had not sinned he could not have known God by purely natural means; for "by nature God is known only to himself." But Cusanus recognized with special clarity, on the basis of his reading of the Pseudo-Dionysius, that abstract and "spiritual" language about God was no less figurative and "symbolic," and hence no more literal or accurate, than concrete and physical metaphors were. Combining Augustine's formula that "we know what God is not rather than what he is" with Anselm's formula that "God is better than can be thought," he found the most appropriate formula by adapting the language of Dionysius: "The name of God is not 'the best,' but 'beyond the best [superoptimus].'" In God "maximum" and "minimum" coincided, for he was "the

Gers.*Ep*.55 (Glorieux 2:261–62)

Gers.*Cant*.2 (Glorieux 8:592–93);Gers.*Schol.myst*.11 (Combes 230–31)

Dion.Ar.*Myst*.2 (PG 3:1025)

Gers.*Magn*.7 (Glorieux 8:312–13);Nicol.Cus.*Doct.ign*.1.26 (Heidelberg 1:54)

Gers.*Glor*.1.6 (Glorieux 8:542)

Nicol.Cus.*Dir.spec*.14 (Heidelberg 13:29) Nicol.Cus.*Poss*.40 (Heidelberg 11–II:48);Nicol.Cus.*Doct.ign*.1.19 (Heidelberg 1:38);Nicol.Cus.*Vis*.17 (Faber 1:108ı) Nicol.Cus.*Apol* (Heidelberg 2:11–12);Nicol.Cus.*Doct.ign*.1.1 (Heidelberg 1:6)

Ex.3:14 Nicol.Cus.*Gen*.4 (Heidelberg 4:120)

Aeg.Rom.*Quodlib*.3.2 (1646:130;133) Dns.Scot.*Ord.pr*.152 (Balić 1:102–3)

Nicol.Cus.*Quaer*.1 (Heidelberg 4:17);Nicol.Cus.*Apol*. (Heidelberg 2:10;24)

Aug.*Ps*.85.8 (CCSL 39:1186)

Dion.Ar.*Div.nom*.2.3 (PG 3:640);Dion.Ar.*Myst*.1.1 (PG 3:997) Nicol.Cus.*Serm*.20.1 (Heidelberg 16:304) Nicol.Cus.*Doct.ign*.1.4 (Heidelberg 1:11)

Nicol.Cus.*Vis.*9–10;11 (Faber
1:103v;104v)

Nicol.Cus.*Poss.*11 (Heidelberg
11–II:14);Nicol.Cus.*Dir.spec.*2
(Heidelberg 1:11)

Aug.*Bapt.*2.4–5 (*CSEL* 51:
179–81)

coincidence of opposites." In this sense it did not matter what names one used for God, so long as one used "negative theology" or "learned ignorance" to protect any such name from distortion.

The effort of these theologians in the fourteenth and fifteenth centuries to accommodate the language of Dionysian mysticism about "deification" and "negative knowledge" to the common faith of the church was an especially poignant example of the doctrinal pluralism of the period. Everyone went on speaking about the one true faith as in some sense still "one," despite the variety of opinions about one article of faith after another. Yet doctrinal pluralism there had always been, and far more of it than the official position of bishops and theologians was willing to acknowledge. What had managed to hold the pluralism within bounds was Augustine's elevation of the catholic unity of the church as the context not only for moral reform but for theological difference: Augustine diverged from Cyprian in basic teaching, but shared with him the commitment to the unity of the catholic church, within which their divergence was tolerable. But doctrinal pluralism came to grief in the fifteenth century—and to tragedy in the sixteenth century—when this presupposition of catholic unity itself lost its credibility.

# 2

# One, Holy, Catholic, and Apostolic?

Bon.VIII.*Un.sanct.* (Lo Grasso 211)

Hs.*Eccl.*1.A (Thomson 1)

Bon.VIII.*Un.sanct.* (Lo Grasso 213)

Hs.*Eccl.*1.B (Thomson 2)
Gers.*Pot.eccl.*12 (Glorieux 6:237–38)

Gers.*Nov.pos.* (Glorieux 6:147)
Gers.*Serm.*210 (Glorieux 5:43)

Thdrc.Nm.*Mod.* (*QMR* 3:6)
Gers.*Serm.*209 (Glorieux 5:37)

Gers.*Petr.Lun.*1.1;1.3 (Glorieux 6:265)

In 1302 Pope Boniface VIII opened his most famous bull, *Unam Sanctam,* with the words: "By the requirement of the faith we are obliged to believe and hold one, holy, catholic, and indeed apostolic church"; in 1413 John Hus, the Czech Reformer, opened his most famous treatise, *The Church,* with the words: "Every pilgrim ought faithfully to believe the holy, catholic church." But Boniface was referring to the church whose visible head was "the Roman pontiff, [to whom] every human creature must be subject to be saved," as his closing words declared, while Hus was referring to "the totality of all who have been predestined," as he went on to explain a few paragraphs later. And Hus's nemesis at the Council of Constance, Gerson, while certainly no partisan of Pope Boniface, quoted the formula of the Nicene Creed, from which both Boniface and Hus were also quoting, as proof against Hus and Wycliffe that a church council had the right to condemn not only doctrinal aberrations, but also such errors as pertained to the moral implications of the faith. In a sermon delivered at Constance a few months before the execution of Hus, Gerson gave a brief definition of each of the attributes of the church enumerated in the Nicene Creed (which he called the Apostles' Creed, whereas one of his contemporaries attributed the phrase to the Athanasian Creed). He quoted the article of the creed again in another sermon at Constance as well as elsewhere, with the teachings of Hus in mind as a deviation from the true faith concerning the church.

The claims enunciated by Boniface VIII provoked a new and deeper study, on all sides, of the creedal formula, "one, holy, catholic, and apostolic." For Henry of Cremona this and other pronouncements

Henr.Crem.*Pot.pap.* (*KRA* 8:460);Aeg.Per.*Infid.* (*BPIR* 10:108–9);Petr.Pal.*Pot.pap.*1.2.A.1;2.pr. (Stella 125;203);Turr.*Auct.*1.89 (1563:50v)

were proof that Boniface had been "sent from God, as one who refused to give His glory and honor to another," and for Alvaro de Pelayo *Unam Sanctam* served as the basis for an exposition of the doctrine of the church, which he set in opposition to that of

Alv.Pel.*Planc.eccl.*1.60 (1560:65r–66r)
Alv.Pel.*Ep.*13.23 (Meneghin 109)

"the new heresiarch," Marsilius of Padua. Marsilius

Mars.Pad.*Def.pac.*2.20.8 (Previté-Orton 323)

had branded the teaching of Boniface as "erroneous . . . and [filled with] every conceivable falsehood." Dietrich of Nieheim attacked Boniface for failing to distinguish between the "apostolic church," of which the pope of Rome was the head, and the "catholic church" throughout the world, of which only Christ was the head: it was outside this catholic church, not outside the Roman church, that there was no salva-

Thdrc.Nm.*Mod.* (*QMR* 3:6–7)

tion. William of Ockham, who "probably influenced

Tierney (1972) 197
Guil.Oc.*Op.XC.dier.*80 (Sikes 2:639)

late medieval ecclesiology more than any other one man," cited the creedal formula in a dispute over the infallibility of the pope. But the formula was not only an effective weapon in the wars between various ecclesiastical factions, or between supporters of the ab-

Zab.*Schism.* (Schard 692);
Nicol.Cus.*Conc.cath.*3.41 (Heidelberg 14:461–62)

solute claims of the papacy and defenders of the independent rights of the empire. It also provided a convenient outline for organizing the issues of doctrine and of policy that were in controversy, most of which "could be reduced to four, namely, to those four that are listed in the creed where it is said: 'and

Jac.Vit.*Reg.chr.*1.2 (Arquillière 105)

in one, holy, catholic, and apostolic church.'"

Although the consideration of the church had of course never been altogether absent from the doctrinal discussions of previous periods, the first few years of the fourteenth century did witness a sudden upsurge of interest in the problems of ecclesiology: besides the *Unam Sanctam* of Boniface VIII in 1302, there were the treatises *Christian Government* by James of Viterbo in 1301–2, *The Power of the Church* by Giles of Rome also in 1301–2 (which provided some of the basis for *Unam Sanctam*), and *Royal and Papal Power* by John of Paris in 1302–3. "In early scholasticism there is seldom a discussion of any question connected

Landgraf (1952) 1–I:30

with the doctrine of the church," and there had been

Joh.Pal.*Quaest.par.* (Döllinger 421–23)

Dant.*Mon.*3.3.9 (Ricci 227–28);Guil.Oc.*Op.XC.dier.*8;37; 96 (Sikes 2:380;515;734–35); Guil.Oc.*Brev.*2.12 (*MGH Sch* 8:75–79); Guib.Tour.*Scand.* (*AFH* 24:36);Mars.Pad.*Def. pac.*2.26.2 (Previté-Orton 398)

See vol.3:300

Brd.Clr.*Cons.*4.3.6 (Leclercq-Rochais 3:453)

Heimpel (1932) 111
Grégoire (1965) 330;
Arquillière (1926) 10

Jac.Vit.*Reg.chr.*pr. (Arquillière 86–87)

Joh.Rag.*Utraq.* (Mansi 29: 727–28);Seg.*Mod.*78 (Ladner 60)

Krämer (1980) 69

no set of "questions" on the church in the *Summa Theologica* of Thomas Aquinas, although one could, of course, compile his ecclesiological statements from various of his writings; there was no special section on it in the *Sentences* of Peter Lombard, nor in the hundreds of commentaries on the *Sentences.* The definitions of the nature of the church had come more regularly from canon lawyers than from theologians— a circumstance that controversialists of this period such as Dante and William of Ockham deplored, frequently quoting the warning of Bernard of Clairvaux to Pope Eugenius that in his undue preoccupation with litigation he was in danger of becoming the successor of the emperor Constantine rather than of the apostle Peter. For although "one cannot say, as is often said, that the conception of the church in the High Middle Ages was developed only in a juridical way and not in a theological way—for example, in Thomas—one can assert that the definition worked out by the Middle Ages . . . was too weak for times of crisis like that of the schism." Therefore James of Viterbo, in "the first treatise on the church," explained that "the confession of faith is chiefly concerned with two matters, Christ as the King and Head and the church as his kingdom and body," but these two matters had not received equal attention from the doctors of the church, until "in our own time, and not without a reasonable cause, it is appropriate for the teachers of sacred doctrine to speak especially about" the doctrine of the church.

Once it had become part of the doctrinal discussion at the beginning of the fourteenth century, the church became, especially in the fifteenth century, a primary issue, or the primary issue, "the first and the most universal principal of doctrine and of the science of faith," upon which all other doctrines depended. So it was that at the Council of Basel "both the theologians of the council and the leaders of the Czechs found themselves compelled to discuss the concept of the church as the basis for all the items on the program." From the vast bibliography of primary texts devoted to the doctrine of the church during the fifteenth century, the titles of four may supply the headings under which to examine the discussions of the four attributes of the church stated in the Nicene Creed; as it happens, the chronological order of these texts corresponds to the order of the attributes in the creed.

## The Unity of the Church

Gers.*Unit.eccl.* (Glorieux 6: 136–45)

Gers.*Unit.eccl.* (Glorieux 6: 136–37)

Jean Gerson wrote a tract entitled *The Unity of the Church* in 1409. In it he maintained that the unity of the church "always abides," but he also taught that "this unity needs to be accomplished . . . through union." Two writers in the previous century had distinguished between three kinds of unity in the church; a "unity of totality," composed of individual believers as its parts; a "unity of conformity," by which the members of the church were conformed to one another through the gifts of grace that they shared; and

Jac.Vit.*Reg.chr.*1.3 (Arquillière 109–11);Alv.Pel.*Planc.eccl.*1.63 (1560:74r–74v)

Ang.Clar.*Alv.Pel.*90 (*AFH* 39: 131–32)

Matt.16:19

Guil.Oc.*Ben.*1.8 (Sikes 3:191)

a "unity of attribution," because of the common goal and common ground of the church provided by Christ, its head. The church was one, and the variety of religious orders and observances did not hinder that unity. Similarly, even when Ockham denied that the pope possessed the sole authority to bind and to loose, as promised to Peter, he went on to explain that since the authority belonged to all believers they all together constituted the one church.

All.*Serm.*19 (1490:B5v);Gers.*Mod.hab.* (Glorieux 6:29);Ambr.Trav.*Or.Sig.* (Mansi 30: 973)
Gers.*Union.eccl.* (Glorieux 6: 7;9)

All of this became problematical by the end of the fourteenth century as a consequence of the schism between Rome and Avignon. Although we cannot discuss here the general effects of the schism on the moral and political situation of European society or on the life and institutions of the church, it did of course raise fundamental questions for doctrine as well; for as one advocate of a council said in 1441, "the cause of this schism does not lie principally in law but in fact and in the diversity of doctrine with regard to

Eben.*Consid.*1 (*DRTA* 15:801)
Fill.*Gest.conc.Const.*pr. (Finke 2:13);Gers.*Mod.hab.* (Glorieux 6:30–31);All.*Ep.Jo.XXIII.*1 (Du Pin 2:880)
*Avis.Sig.* (Finke 3:73); All. *Emend.eccl.*1 (Du Pin 2:905); Seg.*Eccl.*(Krämer 398)
Henr.Lang.*Cons.pac.*2 (Hardt 2:3–4)
Joh.Rag.*Ep.*13.ii.1437 (*CB* 1: 380)
Gers.*Serm.*214;225;239 (Glorieux 5:115;258;455);Gers. *Mat.schism.* (Glorieux 6:72– 73);Gers.*Prop.Ang.* (Glorieux 6:128)

the faith." There appeared to be no historical precedent, in the West at any rate, for such a schism. The very orthodoxy of "the entire catholic faith" was in jeopardy, and mass apostasy had become a genuine threat; on the other hand, a reunion of the church could effect mass conversion of Muslims to Christianity. The schism was, as Gerson said over and over, like an "incurable cancer" that had infected the body of Christ, or, as one of his contemporaries called it,

Joh.Var.*Ep.Ben.XIII* (Du Pin 2:849)
Nicol.Cus.*Conc.cath*.2.19 (Heidelberg 14:205)
Joach.*Apoc*.int. (1527:22v)
All.*Serm*.2 (1490:S5v)

Gr.XII.*Mod.* (Finke 1:51)

Tok.*Neutr*.3.A (*DRTA* 16:561)

Seg.*Gl.Eug*.6 ap.Seg.*Hist.conc. Bas*.18.44 (*MC* 3:1173)

Thdrc.Nm.*Mod.* (*QMR* 3:5; 32);Thdrc.Nm.*Int.pac.* (Finke 3:128)

Zab.*Schism.* (Schard 688);Turr. *Vot.avis.* (Mansi 30:603)

Alv.Pel.*Planc.eccl*.1.12 (1560: 3r)

Seg. *Neutr*.2.4 (*DRTA* 14:377)

*Serm.conc.Const*.11.iii.1415 (Finke 2:404);Gers.*Serm*.210 (Glorieux 5:44)

Gers.*Serm*.209 (Glorieux 5:38)

Gers.*Union.eccl.* (Glorieux 6: 1–21)

Gers.*Unit.eccl.* (Glorieux 6: 140)

Gers.*Serm*.212 (Glorieux 5:86)

Ben.XIII.*Ep*.7.vii.1411 (Finke 1:43);Zab.*Ben.XIII* (Finke 2: 473–75)

"the cruelest plague that God could visit upon the world." The "not inappropriate" idea of Joachim of Fiore, that the church was an image of the divine Trinity, had now been grimly fulfilled when there were three claimants to the papal throne, so that all three had to join in summoning a council on the assumption that one of them possessed the legitimate authority to do so. Thus a refusal to choose among the claimants appeared to some to be the only way to promote the unity of the church. It was, to some, even worse when, after the relocation of the Council of Basel to Ferrara in 1438, there were not two heads with one body but, now, two bodies. It had become more than a rhetorical question to ask, "Which is that church that knows a single origin [and hence a visible unity]?" or to ask, "How can we know and be certain who the vicar of Christ is when there are two or even three men contending over the holy vicariate of Christ?" The massive fact of the schism made any attempt to define the church and its unity difficult without making the situation worse. Those who clung to the authority of the pope over council maintained that the schism only reinforced the necessity of locating the true church "on the basis of the apostolic see through the succession of bishops," ambiguous though that basis had become. But in the face of the divisions that had appeared, which threatened to undermine obedience to the church as such, the partisans of council over pope found it imperative to define the unity of the church primarily as its bond with "its one head, Christ," and only "secondarily" as its union with the pope as "the vicar of Christ," as well as to stress that "the unity of the church presupposes a moral unity."

Gerson, however, wrote not only his *The Unity of the Church* of 1409, but also an earlier appeal in 1391, entitled *The Union of the Church*, and he spent a large part of his life working for the reunion of Latin Christendom. Even in *The Unity of the Church*, moreover, he could speak of "the quest for the unity of the church with one undoubted vicar of Christ," and he quoted with approval the statement of Benedict XIII that he was willing to resign from the papacy or even to offer his life "to obtain the union of the church."

Evidently, then, the church was already one in some sense, but in another sense it needed to work and pray in order to become one. In a work of 1410, called *The Ways of Uniting and Reforming the Church in a Universal Council,* Dietrich of Nieheim asked: "Why is it necessary to work for the union of the universal church if that church is and always has been undivided, unified, and untouched by schism?" Two other works from about the same time dealt with that question by arguing that while the true church could not be destroyed by any schism, it was essential "to work for the union of the church" even by avoiding both parties in the schism for the sake of restoring unity, and to go on working toward union even after the scandal of "triple schism [triscisma]" had been removed. Therefore the Council of Basel, two decades or so later, could appeal to the Hussites: "Let us work as hard as we can to become one!"

Ben. XIII. *Ep.* 18. vii. 1415 (Finke 3:440–41)

Thdrc. Nm. *Mod.* (*QMR* 3:11)

Zab. *Schism.* (Schard 700)

Car. Mal. *fr.* (Finke 1:29)

ap. Joh. Rag. *Boh.* 71 (*MC* 1:136)

For it was not only the schism between the two popes at Rome and Avignon that was dividing the supposedly one and indivisible church during the fifteenth century, but there were at least two other schisms that joined it in making a "mockery" of the church and of its pretensions to unity: the Hussite revolt and the separation between East and West. The chairman at the Council of Basel, in turn, accused the Hussites of showing partiality toward the Greeks, and other critics also found affinities between them. When the Hussites demanded that the council invite representatives of the East, the council fathers responded that they had already intended to do so, but the Greeks in Constantinople objected to a guilt by association that linked their name with that of the Czechs. But in the minds of various Western churchmen, the schism within their own church and the schisms with the Czechs and the Greeks were closely connected. The Hussites, they believed, were finding a pretext in the East-West schism for persisting in their own separation from the Holy See; and, speaking to the Byzantine emperor, the ambassadors of the Western church declared: "With what yearning, with what fervor, our church has sought and still seeks peace and the union of the churches! . . . By our agreement in one place, we can restore peace to all of Christendom and to

*Serm. conc. Const.* xii. 1414 (Finke 2:387); Joh. Rag. *Miss. CP* (Mansi 31:265); Gers. *Prop. Ang.* (Glorieux 6:128); Eben. *Or. Bas.* 1 (*DRTA* 17:23); Jac. Parad. *Sept. stat.* (Goldast 2:1572) Jul. Ces. ap. Laur. Reich. *Diurn.* 28. i. 1433 (*MC* 1:297) ap. Joh. Rag. *Graec.* (*CB* 1:357–58); Henr. Kalt. *Err. Amed.* 6 (Krämer 436–37)

Stoeck. *Ep.* 3 (*CB* 1:64) ap. Joh. Rag. *Boh.* 149 (*MC* 1:255)

ap. Joh. Rag. *Miss. CP* (Mansi 31:251)

Turr. *Auct.* 1. 32 (1563:22r)

ap. Joh. Rag. *Miss. CP* (Mansi
31:266);Stoeck. *Ep.*18 (*CB* 1:
86);Joh. Pal. *Quaest.par.*
(Döllinger 428–29)

See p. 53 above

Henr. Kalt. *Lib.praedic.* (Mansi
29:1049)

Matt. 16:18

Hs. *Eccl.*7.B-C (Thomson 45);
Hs. *Post.ad.*73 (Ryšánek 13:
294)
Wyc. *Eccl.*17 (*WLW* 5:408–9);
Wyc. *Civ.dom.*1.39;1.43 (*WLW*
4:287–88;358)

Chel. *St.vr.*2.51 (*Com.*22:346)

Chel. *Crk.* (Petrů 99);Chel.
*Post.*9;13;13;51 (*Com.*14:117;
175;186;297)

Hs. *Sent.*4.21.3 (Flajshans 2:
624)

Hs. *Eccl.*5. G (Thomson 36)

Hs. *Eccl.*3. E (Thomson 15);
Wyc. *Serm.*2.54 (*WLW* 9:399)

Nicol. Cus. *Ep.*6 (Faber 2–II:
15v–16r)

Nicol. Cus. *Conc.cath.*1.4
(Heidelberg 14:44)

Gers. *Ep.*35 (Glorieux 2:164)

both churches; but without it, our own church is torn asunder, as you can see, and yours will undoubtedly not find peace either."

Despite the prominence of the doctrine of the Eucharist in the theology of the Hussites, they would probably have agreed with one of their opponents who said that "the entire schism between us" dealt with the relation between the commandment of Christ and the commandment of the church, especially as this was manifest in the denial of the chalice to the laity. Underlying this issue, in turn, was the question of the nature of the church and of its unity, as well as of its authority. For Hus defined the "church" spoken of in the words of Christ to Peter, "I will build my church," not as the church of Rome, but as "the gathering of the predestined." The definition itself, whose immediate source was Wycliffe, had come from Augustine and had been in use throughout the Middle Ages; but now it became a means for discriminating between "a physical understanding of the church" characteristic of the papal doctrine and an understanding of "the holy church as the bride of Christ, the congregation of the elect of God," which was the only accurate definition of the church. It meant that the predestined continued to belong to the true church in spite of "a temporary exclusion from the church," and therefore that membership in the true church was ultimately unknown even to its members. Thus it was one thing to be "in the church [in ecclesia]" by virtue of external affiliation, quite another thing to be "of the church [de ecclesia]" as a true and elect member.

To the adversaries of the Hussites, such distinctions between two churches and two kinds of membership, "as though you were of the second kind even though you are not of the first," seemed to be a heretical denial of the "one church" confessed in the creed, even though it was correct to identify "this body of the church," with which Christ existed in cosmic harmony, as "consisting only of the predestined." It was an error for Hus to declare "that only the church containing the predestined and morally upright is the universal church to which obedience is due, and not the Roman [church], for which 'teacher of others' is a misnomer." For while it was true that the predestinate were the ones who made the church "the true body of Christ," the Hussite definition would destroy all certainty about the church and with it all ability to function in the church. That accusation appeared to be borne out by such statements as that of Wycliffe, that since the elect were known to God alone, a body made up of human beings did not have the right to elect a pope and only "God could choose such a leader," as he had in the case of the apostle Matthias. The Hussite theologian John of Rokycana, concerned as he was for the church and its unity, recognized this functional "risk" in the simple definition of the church as consisting exclusively of the predestinate, and hence he added another definition: the church was "a mixture of the predestinate and the reprobate, or more precisely, the church of the predestinate, with which the reprobate and doomed are mixed." In response, John of Ragusa, who objected to the Hussite definition on functional as well as on doctrinal grounds, found this an improvement, though still far from adequate.

Much older and deeper than the Hussite schism, or even than the schism between Rome and Avignon within the West, was the schism separating East and West. The same councils that considered the other two schisms also gave attention to the East-West schism—the Council of Constance in 1418, but above all the Council of Basel-Ferrara-Florence. To be sure, there were some in the West to whom the separation from the East was so unimportant that they could declare that "from the nativity of Christ until the year 1316 there has been no schism in the church of God," but such total indifference was quite uncommon. More significant were the repeated declarations that a reconciliation with the Greek church was prerequisite to a settlement of other issues troubling the West; or the recognition by Ambrose Traversari that in spite of the "very great difficulty" of the matter, the Greeks deserved the utmost in understanding and patience; or the admission of Nicholas of Clamanges around the turn of the century that "our pride and avarice" were responsible for the schism with the Greeks; or the warning of Gerson at about the same time that even a resolution of the problem of papal authority would not be sufficient to heal the breach between the West-

Joh.Rag.*Utraq.* (Mansi 29:777);Turr.*Aug.Rom.* (Mansi 30:1011–15;1020)

Wyc.*Serm.*4.22 (*WLW* 13:193–94)
Acts 1:24–26
Joh.Rok.*Ep.*22.viii.1432 ap.
Joh.Rag.*Boh.*138 (*MC* 1:241)

Joh.Rok.*Sanct.com.*3.2 (Krämer 366–68)

Joh.Rag.*Eccl.*1.1.2 (Krämer 372)

Fill.*Gest.conc.Const.*25.ii.1418 (Finke 2:164–66)

See vol.2:270–80

Tel.*Vet.Nov.* (Du Pin 2:154)

Sig.*Ep.*v.1411 (Finke 1:392–93);Joh.Rag.*Bas.conc.*18 (*MC* 1:31)

Ambr.Trav.*Ep.*1.13 (Martène-Durand 3:22–25)

Nicol.Cl.*Ruin.eccl.*42 (Coville 148)

Gers.*Sub.schism.* (Glorieux 6:
22)
Gers.*Serm.*221 (Glorieux 5:
210)

Gers.*Serm.*212 (Glorieux 5:88)
Gers.*Conc.un.obed.* (Glorieux
6:52);Gers.*Stat.eccl.* (Glorieux
6:35);All.*Inst.ut.* (Finke 3:65);
All.*Mat.*1 (Oakley 253;264)
All.*Emend.eccl.*1 (Du Pin 2:
906);All.*Mat.*3 (Oakley 321)
ap.Joh.Rag.*Graec.* (CB 1:338;
354)
Joh.Rag.*Ep.*13.ii.1437 (CB 1:
378)

Nicol.Cus.*Conc.cath.*2.20
(Heidelberg 14:232);All.*Serm.*
19 (1490:B5v)

See pp. 312–13 below
Seg.*Gl.Eug.*9 ap.Seg.*Hist.conc.*
*Bas.*18.47 (MC 3:1192–93)

Mars.Pad.*Def.min.*12.4
(Brampton 36)

Joh.Rag.*Bas.conc.*50 (MC 1:
97);Joh.Rag.*Graec.* (CB 1:337)

Ambr.Trav.*Ep.*1.13 (Martène-
Durand 3:25)

Ambr.Trav.*Ep.*12.12 (Martène-
Durand 3:404)
Ambr.Trav.*Ep.*19.36 (Martène-
Durand 3:636)

Ambr.Trav.*Vers.Man.Cal.*pr.
(PG 152:13–14)

Ambr.Trav.*Ep.*3.13 (Martène-
Durand 3:68–69)

Ambr.Trav.*Ep.*1.15 (Martène-
Durand 3:31)

Ambr.Trav.*Ep.*15.10;12.9
(Martène-Durand 3:508;402)
Ambr.Trav.*Ep.*15.10 (Martène-
Durand 3:509)

Ambr.Trav.*Ep.*15.6;15.3
(Martène-Durand 3:503;495)

ern and Eastern churches. Recognizing how much the West owed to the learning and piety of the East, he lamented that "now nobody cares" and he interpreted the split as a cautionary tale of how unilateral action by one party in any schism could only make the alienation worse. The Turkish threat to Constantinople gave further urgency to the efforts at reunion and even provoked the suggestion that a union council meet there, which was, of course, politically impossible. The fall of the city in 1453 evoked from at least one Western observer, who had been reflecting on the reduction of Christendom to its Western branch, a profound examination of the ultimate sources of religious difference. The reform councils of the fifteenth century, even though they did not go along with the extreme suggestion made in the preceding century that there could not be a truly ecumenical council without the participation of the Greeks, did acknowledge that Eastern participation would represent "progress and improvement" for such a council.

The negotiations with the Greeks had as one of their important byproducts the production of Latin translations of various Greek fathers, particularly at the hands of the humanist and Camaldolese monk Ambrose Traversari. He combined an interest in the Greek fathers with a desire for better understanding with the Greek church, and he recognized that a good grasp of the fathers would be essential for the upcoming negotiations. For the Greeks were bringing with them a contingent of scholars as well as many books. Therefore he used the preface to one of his translations to address the pope with an appeal for the reunion of East and West. The ignorance of Greek among the Latins was one of the reasons for their failure to understand the conditions that had been laid down for negotiation. It was essential, he told the pope, to study and translate the fathers, "the Greeks no less than the Latins." His own study led him, for the first time, to read the *Ecclesiastical History* of Eusebius in Greek, which "fascinated me so much that it is hard to believe." The treatises of Athanasius he found difficult to put down. After reading Gregory of Nyssa on the Song of Songs, he was ready to say that this was "a greater work than Augustine on Genesis." Although

Ambr.Trav.*Ep*.12.7 (Martène-Durand 3:399)

Ambr.Trav.*Ep*.12.47 (Martène-Durand 3:436)
Ambr.Trav.*Vers.Pall*.pr. (Martène-Durand 3:694);
Ambr.Trav.*Ep*.16.2 (Martène-Durand 3:526)

Ambr.Trav.*Ep*.15.3 (Martène-Durand 3:495)

Ambr.Trav.*Ep*.16.22 (Martène-Durand 3:551)
Ambr.Trav.*Ep*.15.11 (Martène-Durand 3:512)

Ambr.Trav.*Vers.Man.Cal*.pr. (*PG* 152:13–14)

Alv.Pel.*Ep*.10.4;13.5 (Meneghin 56;103)
Petr.Pal.*Pot.pap*.1.1.3.2;2.3.3 (Stella 118;247)
Ang.Clar.*Ep.excus.* (*ALKGMA* 1:523)
See vol.2:260–61;266–67;176–79
Gers.*Theol.myst*.3.18 (Combes 42)
Ub.Cas.*Arb.vit*.4.36 (Davis 377)
Gers.*Utraq.* (Glorieux 10:65); Hs.*Sent*.4.11.7 (Flajšhans 2:575)

See vol.2:183–98;275–78
Ub.Cas.*Arb.vit*.1.3 (Davis 10)
Dns.Scot.*Ord*.1.11.1.9 (Balić 5:2–3)

Petr.Lomb.*Sent*.1.11.4 (*Spic. Bon.*1–II:119–20)
Mars.Pad.*Def.min*.12.4 (Brampton 37)

Joh.Brev.*Tract*.1.3 (Du Pin 1:834)

See vol.3:279–80
Robt.Orf.*Repr.Aeg*.39 (*Bibl. Thom.* 38:107)
See pp. 15–16 above
Thos.Sut.*Quodlib*.4.2 (Schmaus 506);Jac.Vit. *Quodlib*.3.8 (Ypma 3:128;134)

See vol.2:193–94

John 15:26

he translated some of Gregory of Nazianzus to pay off a debt, he was especially interested in his trinitarian works because of their importance for the debates with the Greeks. His translations of the martyrological *Life of Chrysostom* by Palladius and of Chrysostom's *Sermons on Matthew* were accompanied by deepening appreciation for Chrysostom and his teaching. But perhaps his most influential translation was that of Dionysius the Areopagite, which he undertook "not only with pleasure, but with the greatest delight" and which he completed despite the "extreme difficulty of this work." He was speaking for many of his Latin contemporaries in the fifteenth century when he contrasted the "wisdom and eloquence" of these Greek fathers with the present parlous state of the Greek church.

Western theologians, even radical theologians, continued nevertheless to speak of "Greek fornication" and "heresy" and to declare: "The Eastern church is schismatic and void." Although they did attack such distinctive Eastern teachings as the identity of the divine light with the essence of God, or the validity of confirmation when administered by a simple priest rather than by a bishop, or the legitimacy of the use of unleavened bread ("azymes") in the Eucharist, the most prominent doctrinal aberration of the Greek church was still its denial of the Filioque, which some were willing to label "impious blasphemy against God the Son." Duns Scotus and others suggested, on the basis of Peter Lombard, that the difference between Greeks and Latins over this matter was more verbal than substantial; and even when the denial of the Filioque was branded as heresy, this could be accompanied by the observation that it had not been heresy (for example, in the orthodox Greek church fathers) until its explicit condemnation by the Latin church. Aquinas's criticism of the Greek doctrine had itself been subjected to a criticism against which it had to be defended, and his assertion that the doctrine of Filioque was necessary to distinguish the Spirit from the Son was likewise reaffirmed in reply to criticism. As in the earlier stages of the controversy, Western theologians went on taking such passages as the words of Christ about the temporal mission of the Spirit,

All.*Serm*.11 (1490:Y4r–Y4v); Gr.Arim.*Sent*.1.14–16 (1522–I: 83v);Wyc.*Serm*.1.30 (*WLW* 8: 201)

"whom I shall send to you from the Father," to be a proof of the eternal procession of the Spirit from the Son as well as from the Father.

The stubborn and embarrassing reality of these three schisms, especially when combined with the doctrinal pluralism that was increasingly obvious within the "one true faith" of the church, made it obligatory for Western ecclesiology to clarify both the nature and the locus of the church's unity with greater precision and subtlety than may have been necessary earlier. To

Jac.Vit.*Reg.chr*.1.3 (Arquillière 107);Petr.Pal.*Pot.pap*.1.2.B.5 (Stella 137)

say that the church was "one . . . through the three virtues of faith, hope, and love," was necessary, but it was not sufficient, in face of the state of each virtue under the conditions of the time. It was a somewhat more fruitful line of thought to specify that "the catholic church is one, not on the basis of a unity of human beings, who are many, but on the basis of a unity of faith and a union of intention and confirmation of

Conr.Meg.*Guil.Oc*.8 (*BPIR* 10:375)

good morals serving the one faith"; for such a definition appeared to combine the subjective multiplicity of the individuals in the church with the objective unity of the faith. Its distinction between "unity" and "union," moreover, could be developed into the principle that "unity excludes multiplicity, while union

Jac.Vit.*Reg.chr*.1.3 (Arquillière 107);Alv.Pel.*Planc eccl*.1.63 (1560:73v)

Nicol.Cus.*Ep*.1 (Faber 2–II: 3v);Turr.*Aug.Rom*. (Mansi 30: 986)
Nicol.Cus.*Conc.cath*.1.1 (Heidelberg 14:79)

Nicol.Cus.*Doct.ign*.3.12 (Heidelberg 1:162)

consists in multiplicity," so that the oneness of the church "is more properly called 'union' than 'unity.'" Therefore the church was marked by "a varied participation in unity," a polyphonic harmony of many rather than a monophonic singleness of melody. In this it mirrored the union of the two natures, divine and human, in the single hypostasis of Christ. There were, as Gerson put it, "fluid" as well as "permanent"

Gers.*Prop.Ang*. (Glorieux 6: 132)

Gers.*Auct.conc*.9.2;9.4 (Glorieux 6:119)

Gers.*Ep*.49 (Glorieux 2:233)

1 Cor.12:11

Gers.*Auct.conc*.1.4 (Glorieux 6:114)

Gers.*Prop.Ang*. (Glorieux 6: 132)

elements in the continuity of the church, but until the consummation of history there would continue to be a community or an individual charged with responsibility for governing and teaching the church. "Although the Christian religion is one," therefore, "it is distinguished by a multiple and beautiful variety," which was the result of the activity of the Spirit. Or, in an epigram, "the Christian church is one in multiplicity [multipliciter una]."

In Gerson's distinction of "fluid" and "permanent" elements, "the pope comes and goes, but the papacy continues." When a pope died, the papal

Gers. *Vit.spir.*3 (Glorieux 3: 155)

Aug. Tr. *Dup.pot.* (*KRA* 8:494)

Jac. Vit. *Reg.chr.*1.3 (Arquillière 117)

Henr. Crem. *Pot.pap.* (*KRA* 8: 469)

Eph. 4:5–6

Alv. Pel. *Ep.*12.5;13.7 (Meneghin 94–95;105)

Jac. Vit. *Reg.chr.*2.5 (Arquillière 205)

Joh. Par. *Pot.*18 (Leclercq 230)

Joh. Par. *Conf.*7 (Hödl 46)

Joh. Par. *Pot.*3 (Leclercq 180)

Joh. Par. *Pot.*6 (Leclercq 186)

All. *Ext.schism.* (Du Pin 2:112)

Gers. *Aufer.*4 (Glorieux 3:296)
Matt. 16:19
Aug. *Bapt.*3.17.22 (*CSEL* 51: 213)
Gers. *Pot.eccl.* (Glorieux 6: 217);Joh. Rag. *Auct.conc.*3 (*DRTA* 15:210);Seg. *Prop.sec.* ap. Seg. *Hist.conc.Bas.*17.13 (*MC* 3:593)

office would abide, and with it the unity of the church. The precise connection between the papacy and the unity of the church had nevertheless been a point of controversy already in the fourteenth century. The champions of papal prerogative had contended that the church could not be one unless all the other apostles had received their authority solely through the mediation of Peter, and that apart from this unity of the church in Peter there was no grace and no forgiveness of sins. If the church was only one body, it must have only one head, who was Christ, and the pope governed it "in Christ's place." As there was "one faith, one baptism, one God," so also there must be "his one vicar over the earth, who . . . is in some way my father and god on earth. . . . I shall not separate from him, because outside the church there is no place where Christ is." Because Christ had withdrawn his physical presence from the world and from the church, he had entrusted to Peter and his successors "the universal governance of the church." To a critic of papal theocracy, such claims, valid though they were within certain limits, had seemed excessive. The church was "one mystical body, not in Peter or in Linus, but in Christ, who alone is the head of the church in the complete and proper sense." But that was not grounds for denying, as some did, that the papacy had any divinely given authority. Precisely because "the church, which requires a unity of faith for its own unity, could be divided by a diversity of opinions," it needed some one member to preserve its unity; that one member was "Peter and his successor"— not, however, as "lord [dominus]," but only as "administrator [dispensator]." The fifteenth-century advocates of conciliar authority went even further in limiting the claim of the pope to guarantee the unity of the church. "The unity of the church," one of them asserted, "does not necessarily depend upon, or originate from, the unity of the pope." For it was the Holy Spirit, as the Spirit of Christ, who granted life and unity to the church. The power of the keys was given, as Augustine had said, "to unity," which meant, to the general council as a representative of the church's unity, and not to the pope as such.

Joh.Par.*Pot*.18 (Leclercq 231)

See p. 70 above

All.*Mat*.1 (Oakley 262);Gers. *Pot.eccl*.9 (Glorieux 6:226–27)

See vol.2:168

Seg.*Mod*.88 (Ladner 63)

Kantorowicz (1957) 203

Guil.Oc.*Op.XC.dier*.93 (Sikes 2:680)

See vol.3:42–43
Guil.Oc.*Pot.pap*.1.2;1.10 (Sikes 1:17;1:41–42)
Inn.IV.*Ep.Fred.II* (Lo Grasso 195)

Aeg.Rom.*Eccl.pot*.1.4 (Scholz 12);Petr.Pal.*Pot.pap*.2.2 (Stella 223)

Much of the consideration of the unity of the church, including the discussions of schism, had become necessary "because of certain prominent men who, for the sake of the unity of the ecclesiastical hierarchy, strive to show that the pope has both swords," that of the church and that of the state. The new interest in the doctrine of the church at the beginning of the fourteenth century, signified by the sudden appearance of several treatises on the subject, had been stimulated by disputes over the relation between church and state. In the discussions of the unity of the church a century later, theologians were similarly concerned to show that the "one faith" of the "one church" implied one ruler, namely, the pope, by contrast with the civil and temporal realm, where there could and should be many rulers. For the history of political thought, therefore, these two centuries occupy a special place, as the time when the theoretical examination of the nature of the "state" (or "temporal power," as it was often called then) came into its own once more as a philosophical inquiry. As in earlier discussions of the relations between church and state, our attention to this development here must be confined to the direct implications of the controversies for ecclesiology as such, in spite of the complex interaction between church doctrine and political theory that ironically resulted when the church was "considered in a twofold manner, namely, as the mystical body of Christ and as a kind of political body."

The spectrum of political doctrine had as its counterpart a range of doctrines about the church. When "the Church was interpreted as a polity like any other secular corporation. . . . as a means to exalt the position of the emperor-like pope," this was an expression of the definition of the church as the visible kingdom of God on earth. Even a critic of this doctrine had to teach that "the church is the kingdom of Christ," for this term, together with the cognate term "city [civitas]," had firmly established itself in the Augustinian vocabulary of Western theology. But what that critic rejected was an interpretation of the notion of "kingdom," enunciated for example by a thirteenth-century pope, on the basis of which "the church 'has been set over the nations and over the king-

Jer.1:10

Jac.Vit.*Reg.chr.*1.1 (Arquillière 89)
Jac.Vit.*Reg.chr.*1.1 (Arquillière 94);Alv.Pel.*Planc.eccl.*1.62 (1560:69r)

Jac.Vit.*Reg.chr.*1.1 (Arquillière 95)
Jac.Vit.*Reg.chr.*2.5 (Arquillière 207)
Jac.Vit.*Reg.chr.*2.3 (Arquillière 182)

Jac.Vit.*Quodlib.*1.17 (Ypma 1: 210–11)

Aug.Tr.*Dup.pot.* (*KRA* 8:500)

Matt.28:18

Henr.Crem.*Pot.pap.* (*KRA* 8: 459–60)

Aeg.Per.*Infid.* (*BPIR* 10:106)

Matt.16:19
Jac.Vit.*Reg.chr.*2.5 (Arquillière 214–16)

Alv.Pel.*Planc.eccl.*1.52 (1560: 43v);Conr.Meg.*Trans.imp.*24 (*BPIR* 10:327)

Ptol.Luc.*Det.comp.*6 (*MGH Jur.*5:16–17)
Isa.45:22
Ptol.Luc.*Det.comp.*15 (*MGH Jur.*5:33)

doms.'" According to such an interpretation, the definition of the church as a kingdom was "the most correct, the truest, and the most fitting" definition for it, and it was "more proper" to refer to it as a kingdom than to use any of the other possible terms. Thence it followed that "just as the church is called the kingdom of Christ, so it may truly be called the kingdom of his vicar, that is, of the supreme pontiff, who is truly called a king and is one." Not only was he "the king of all spiritual kings" and "the pastor of pastors," but he was "the king both of secular and of spiritual kings." For "because Christ is both king and priest, therefore his vicar has both royal and priestly power, and it is through him that royal power is instituted, ordered, sanctified, and blessed," although it was specified that he possessed the latter "according to primary authority, not according to immediate execution."

The specification about "immediate execution" was an effort to set the moderate view apart from the extreme papalist position. One treatise espousing such an extreme position opened with the declaration of Christ just before his ascension: "All authority in heaven and on earth has been given to me." These words stood as a refutation of those "who say that the pope does not have jurisdiction over temporal matters throughout the world," for they proved that "the lord pope has not only authority, but total authority [plenitudo potestatis] . . . , full jurisdiction also in temporal matters." By his closing words on earth Christ had created a chain of command: all authority had been given to him, and he in turn gave to Peter "the keys of the kingdom of heaven, and whatever you bind on earth shall be bound in heaven, and whatever you loose on earth shall be loosed in heaven." On the basis of this unqualified language, it was clear that "this royal authority has been given in a special and principal way to Saint Peter, and in him to every one of his successors, indeed, to the total church." The authority to bind and loose meant that "total jurisdiction has been granted to the vicar of Christ" and that "the imperial dominion is dependent on the pope," in whose hands, as God's vicegerent, were "all the ends of the earth." Although Christ had spoken

Matt.18:18

Guil.Crem.*Rep.err.* (*BPIR* 10:
25–26)

Jac.Vit.*Reg.chr.*ep.ded.
(Arquillière 85);Aeg.Rom.*Ren.
pap.*25 (1554:33v)
See vol.3:136–37
Opic.Can.*Spir.imp.* (*BPIR* 10:
93);Henr.Crem.*Pot.pap.* (*KRA*
8:461)
Aeg.Rom.*Eccl.pot.*1.5 (Scholz
15)
Aeg.Per.*Infid.* (*BPIR* 10:116)
Gen.14:18–20
Petr.Lut.*Pont.emin.* (*BPIR* 10:
31–32)

Thdrc.Nm.*Mod.* (*QMR* 3:22)

John 18:36 (Vulg.)

Jac.Vit.*Reg.chr.*2.10
(Arquillière 290–91);Aeg.Per.
*Infid.* (*BPIR* 10:116–17);Ptol.
Luc.*Det.comp.*28 (*MGH Jur.*
5:58);Alv.Pel.*Planc.eccl.*1.37
(1560:12r)

Mars.Pad.*Def.pac.*2.4.4
(Previté-Orton 130)

Guil.Oc.*Imp.et pont.*5 (*BPIR*
10:459);Guil.Oc.*Brev.*2.16
(*MGH Schr* 8:87–90)

Dant.*Mon.*3.8.8 (Ricci 250);
Thdrc.Nm.*Mod.* (*QMR* 3:46);
Seg.*Diff.pot.*7 (Krämer 422)

All.*Reg.* (Du Pin 1:676–77);
Guil.Oc.*Pot.pap.*1.13 (Sikes 1:
56–57)

Matt.28:19–20

Mars.Pad.*Def.min.*11.2
(Brampton 31–32);Guil.Oc.
*Brev.*5.2 (*MGH Schr* 8:169–70)

See p. 116 below
Mars.Pad.*Def.pac.*2.28.22
(Previté-Orton 455)

1 Pet.2:9

similar words also to the other apostles, Peter was the only one whom Christ had designated as his vicar and as the head of the church. Peter had authority over all the other apostles, and as Peter's successor the pope had authority over all other bishops as well as over all other kings. The pope, and specifically Boniface VIII, was "the holy prince of the pastors and kings of the earth." Melchizedek, as a type of Christ, had possessed both "royal dominion" and "priestly dominion," which were joined together in his person. In this way Melchizedek "was in the same position as the pope," while Abraham, who offered sacrifice to Melchizedek, represented the kings of the earth in their obedience to the pope.

There was another saying of Christ that pertained to the relation between the spiritual and the temporal realms, a saying addressed not to Peter as his vicar or to the other apostles, but to "the vicar of the emperor" himself: "My kingdom," Christ said to Pontius Pilate, "does not belong to this world [non est de mundo hoc]." Although the supporters of papal authority in temporal matters explained this as applying to the exercise of power rather than to its possession, it was clear that when the doctrine of the church, and of the relation between church and state, took this as a proof text and drew radical conclusions from it, ecclesiology looked quite different. For then Christ was saying: "I have not come to rule by a temporal regime or dominion, as the kings of the world rule." The words to Peter about binding and loosing were not intended to be "without exceptions," but meant that Peter had received the spiritual authority necessary for governing the faithful in the church, not political authority over kings. Christ did not have temporal dominion according to his humanity, but according to his divinity. The great commission of Christ to his apostles before his ascension made them his "successors," but only according to his human nature, and therefore did not confer on them the "total authority" to which their "successors" now laid claim; everyone on all sides agreed that there were limits to the authority that Christ had conferred on Peter. And Melchizedek, as king and priest, was a prefiguration either of Christ alone in his priestly kingship or of all believers as a

Wyc.*Civ.dom*.1.11 (*WLW* 4: 75)

Mars.Pad.*Def.pac*.2.4.13 (Previté-Orton 142);Guil.Oc. *Brev*.2.6 (*MGH Schr* 8:64); Guil.Oc.*Imp.et pont*.7 (*BPIR* 10:461–62)

Matt.20:26

Joh.Par.*Pot*.8 (Leclercq 190)

Joh.Par.*Pot*.10 (Leclercq 199)

Joh.Par.*Pot*.1 (Leclercq 178)

Joh.Par.*Pot*.18 (Leclercq 229)

All.*Domin.* (Du Pin 1:643); All.*Indoct.* (Du Pin 1:653)

Joh.Par.*Pot*.10 (Leclercq 198)

Monahan (1974) xxix

See pp. 273–74 below

"royal priesthood," but in any event not of the pope as king of kings. In sum, "Christ, as King of kings and Lord of lords, did not turn over to [the apostles] the authority to carry on the secular judging of princes, nor did he confer on them any coercive power of enforcement; rather, he explicitly forbade them this when he said: 'It shall not be so among you.'"

A less radical ecclesiology could also take the words, "My kingdom does not belong to this world," as its starting point, but go on from them to the position that both church and state came from God and not one of them from the other. For the authority of the spiritual realm came from divine revelation, while that of the secular and temporal realm was "derived from the natural law and from that of the nations." The kind of justice necessary for the proper ordering of the temporal realm was attainable apart from Christ and without the supernatural virtues that could come only from grace. While all dominion, also in the temporal realm, came by the gift of Christ, it did not follow from this that saving grace was necessary for ruling. Hence it was a misrepresentation of the nature and mission of the church to claim that the pope had jurisdiction in temporal matters by some divine right, through the authority conferred on Peter by Christ. Instead of "ordering all things ultimately under a single head or in a single line of development," this ecclesiology "locates the unity outside this world, in God Himself" and gives "to the spheres of the temporal and spiritual, positions of hierarchical equality rather than of subordination and superiority to one another."

A concern for unity was no less at work in such a distinction between the spiritual and the temporal realms than in those doctrines that put the two realms together under the single kingship of the pope. Papalists and monarchists, conciliarists and Hussites—all were committed to the unity of the church both as a given and as a goal. As the "defenders of the faith" in the sixteenth century were to remind the Protestants again, the Augustinian definition of the church, upon which they all drew in one way or another, made unity the fundamental attribute of the church, to which even the holiness of the church was subordinate; for holiness was true of the church in the mind of God and in the eschatological light of eternity, but unity constituted the condition within which the church and its members strove toward an ever greater measure of empirical holiness. It was the breakdown of this Augustinian solution to the paradox of grace and perfection as applied to the church that made the schism of the fourteenth century and the reform movement of the fifteenth century the major crisis they were for the doctrine of the church as one, holy, catholic, and apostolic.

## The Holy Church

Wyc.*Eccl.*16 (*WLW* 5:377–78);
*Serm.conc.Const.*21.ii.1417
(Finke 2:487)
Dan.9:27
Matt.24:15

Chel.*Crk.* (Petrů 99)

Chel.*Crk.* (Petrů 100–101)
Chel.*Post.*9;13;14;51 (*Com.*14·117;175;186;297)

Chel.*Post.*42 (*Com.*16:180)

The scandal of a divided church served to aggravate the widespread sense of outrage over violations of the church's holiness, and it reminded at least some observers of the "abomination of desolation" predicted by the prophet Daniel and by Christ himself. Early in the third decade of the fifteenth century Peter Chelčický wrote a book with the title *The Holy Church,* whose opening paragraph affirmed the Hussite insistence on the church as the company of the predestinated, because "it is only with these words that we may speak of a 'holy' church" without any explanations or additions; for "in the saints, the righteousness commanded by God and predestination go together, and if a predestinated person keeps the righteousness commanded by God, he is then a member of the holy church." He returned to this definition in his later sermons, as he also protested against the equation of "apostolic" with "Roman" in the definition of the church.

All.*Serm.*2 (1490:S5v);All.*Inst. ut.* (Finke 3:64)

Sig.ap.Jac.Cerr.*Lib.gest.*1.i.
1415 (Finke 2:203)

The recognition that unity and holiness were inseparable was by no means an exclusively Hussite emphasis. According to the Emperor Sigismund, who convoked it, the very council that condemned Hus was to have the purpose of achieving both unity and holiness, as well as the defense of true doctrine, since "there cannot be true union without reformation, nor true reformation without union," and "minor matters" like the case of John Hus would not be allowed to interfere with this purpose. A later council, at which the Hussites were once more an issue, had the task, according to Sigismund, of "changing morals for the better and bringing the whole people to the way of

Sig.*Ep*.7.vii.1431 ap.Joh.Rag.
*Bas.conc*.47 (*MC* 1:89)

Eug.IV.*Ep*.vii.1434 (*CB* 1:330)

Joh.Pal.*Dial*. (*CB* 1:183)

Aeg.Carl.*Pun*. (Mansi 29:915)

Seg.*Eccl*.1.28 (Krämer 411)

Jac.Parad.*Sept.stat*. (Goldast 2: 1575)

See vol.1:156

Chel.*St.vr*.27 (*Com*.22:80);Jac. Vit.*Reg.chr*.1.5 (Arquillière 129)
Seg.*Eccl*.1.24–26 (Krämer 405– 8)

Joh.Rag.*Utraq*. (Mansi 29:779)

ap.Henr.Lang.*Cons.pac*.16 (Hardt 2:48)

Gers.*Serm*.212 (Glorieux 5:74)

Alv.Pel.*Ep*.13.31 (Meneghin 129)

Jac.Parad.*Sept.stat*. (Goldast 2: 1570)
Brd.Clr.*Cant*.33 (Leclercq-Rochais 1:243–44)
All.*Serm*.14 (1490:Alr);All. *Mat*.3 (Oakley 315)

unity"; for the pope himself acknowledged that the whole church, from head to foot, desperately needed reformation, and, as one of the participants put it, "without [reformation], the other . . . goals either cannot be attained or cannot endure." One of the accusations against the Hussites at this council was that they had permitted their zeal for the holiness of the church and their offense at the public sins in the church to carry them to the point of violating its unity. A schism on moral grounds had the tendency to go on spawning ever new schisms, for even the new sect would not be pure enough for some, who would separate themselves yet again in their quest for a truly holy church. Still, even the restoration of unity under one pope had not achieved true reform, one observer lamented in 1449. It was the attribute "holy" that had been the most prominent of the four classic attributes of the church in the ancient creeds, and theologians as far apart as Peter Chelčický and James of Viterbo were in agreement that this required a separation from sin and from all impurity. Among the many senses in which the church was holy, one of the most important to its defenders against heresy and schism in the fifteenth century was that "it cannot err in those things that are necessary for salvation, because at the time in which it would err in these things it would no longer be holy."

In at least some of the senses of the word, it was becoming increasingly difficult to call the church holy. Those who asked, "[If] church is built upon a solid rock. . . . How is it that you say it needs reformation?" were in the minority, at least among thoughtful churchmen, whose questions were rather: "Has not the entire state of the church become somehow brutal and monstrous?" or "Which shepherd today would give his life for his sheep? In fact, which shepherd has not been transformed into a wolf that devours their souls?" or "If [the pope] is unable or unwilling to reform his own curia, which he has under his wings, why is there any reason to believe that he can reform the church, which is so widely scattered?" Quoting the lamentations of Bernard over the corruption of the church, they would add the dismal comment: "And since then the church has

See vol.3:232;301
Thdrc.Nm.*Invect.*14 (Hardt 2:
310);Henr.Lang.*Cons.pac.*18
(Hardt 2:56–57);Joh.Var.*Ep.
Ben.XIII* (Du Pin 2:850);
Nicol.Cl.*Ruin.eccl.*12 (Coville
122)

Ub.Cas.*Arb.vit.*4.36 (Davis
379)


Nicol.Cus.*Conc.cath.*2.26–27
(Heidelberg 14:250–55)


Mars.Pad.*Def.pac.*2.24.11
(Previté-Orton 374);*Wyc.
Serm.*1.40 (*WLW* 8:266)

Oberman (1966) 9

Trinkaus-Oberman (1974)

Ub.Cas.*Sanct.vest.* (*ALKGMA*
3:52–72);Ub.Cas.*Decr.*5–7
(*ALKGMA* 3:132–33)

Barth.Pis.*Conform.*6.2.1;16.2.
pr. (*Anal.Franc.* 4:139;5:100)

Joh.XXII.*Cum.inter* (Argentré
3:295–96)

gone from bad to worse." Bernard's denunciation of the church as a "den of thieves" likewise found many echoes in this period. Except for a saving remnant, "whom the Spirit of Jesus has preserved for seed," the whole church was in a condition of deformation and in need of reformation. A departure from the form of the church's life that the fathers had handed down was responsible for the "excess and abuse" that had brought about the deformation. Or, as the more negative critics put it, "because the governance of the church is so infected, the entire mystical body of Christ is sick."

Yet it bears repeating that "to endow a medieval preacher or doctor with the title of Forerunner [of the Reformation], on the grounds that he assailed ecclesiastical abuses or called for reform, violates both the medieval *and* the Reformation understanding of the word 'reformation.'" Such polemical statements belong more naturally to the "pursuit of holiness" in the fourteenth and fifteenth centuries, which involved both the quest for personal sanctity and the inquiry after the nature and the locus of the holiness of the church. One avenue of this inquiry was the controversy over the definition of apostolic poverty. Much of the controversy within the Franciscan order—for example, about the distinction between use and ownership in the attitude toward property—pertains to the history of spirituality or of social ethics or even of economics rather than to the history of Christian doctrine. But it did become a doctrinal controversy when it took up the identification of apostolic poverty as true Christian perfection and therefore as the most pertinent index to the holiness of the church, as embodied in "conformity" to the exemplary and absolute poverty of Christ, his mother Mary, and the apostles. As an element of ecclesiology, the poverty contest went far beyond the confines of the Order of Friars Minor, whether Spiritual or Conventual or Observant, when Pope John XXII, in a series of pronouncements, not only denounced the "Spiritual" Franciscans in favor of the moderate faction, but supported his decision about the order with the teaching that Christ and the apostles had not practiced the absolute poverty inculcated by the Franciscans, and that they had not intended to make poverty permanently binding on the church.

According to the Spiritual Franciscan Ubertino of Casale, who wrote before John XXII, "the enemies of the perfection of the church" were undermining "the glory of poverty" and "the foundation of the church itself" with such a teaching, which amounted to a "falsification of the poverty of Jesus and his dear mother." The injunction that Christ gave to the twelve apostles, "Take no gold, nor silver," which had evoked from Francis the resolve to "do this with all my heart," had not been temporary but permanent in its force. There was a distinction between what was necessary for salvation and what was necessary for the "evangelical perfection" that Francis had taught, which consisted in "the utter purity" of "extreme poverty." The distinction meant that in "the present state of the church" the pope and other prelates did not have the obligation to follow this extreme poverty, but that the Franciscans must "unwaveringly hold to their primary poverty, as instituted by the Blessed Francis, and leave it to the other members of the church, according to their requirements, to abound in wealth." For his part, Francis had "imitated Christ perfectly" and had "wanted nothing of ecclesiastical authority," many of whose incumbents had spurned his "newfangled doctrine" about poverty in the church. Although it was a slander to attribute to the Franciscans the position that "only those who follow the spirit of poverty and of the Gospel are true priests," the relaxation of the Franciscan rule of absolute poverty did amount to a betrayal of perfection and a perversion of the doctrine of Christ. Hence the appeal, "Let us return to the beloved poverty of the apostolic estate," was a call to that poverty which was not only the "foundation" of the Franciscan order, but ultimately "the foundation of the church itself," a foundation and "perfect conjunction" with God that had been obliterated in the centuries after Christ, until the coming of Francis.

The declarations of Pope John XXII in opposition to the Spiritual Franciscans were labeled "heresy" by two of the most influential and provocative thinkers in the first half of the fourteenth century, William of Ockham and Marsilius of Padua (although "the influ-

Ub.Cas.Arb.vit.3.9 (Davis 200;184)
Matt.10:9
Thos.Cel. Vit.prim. (Anal. Franc.10:25)
Ub.Cas.Tr.scel. (AFH 10:125); Ub.Cas.Arb.vit.3.9 (Davis 185);Bonagr.Paup. (AFH 22: 491–93)
Ub.Cas.Arb.vit.5.3 (Davis 432);Ang.Clar.Alv.Pel.39 (AFH 39:107)
Ub.Cas.Arb.vit.5.5 (Davis 444)

Ub.Cas.Tr.scel. (AFH 10:169–70)

Ub.Cas.Declar. (ALKGMA 3: 170)

Ub.Cas.Arb.vit.5.3 (Davis 423;426)

ap.Ub.Cas.Sanct.ap. (ALKGMA 2:410–11)
Ub.Cas.Declar. (ALKGMA 3: 165–66);Ub.Cas.Sanct.vest. (ALKGMA 3:85);Ang.Clar. Alv.Pel.100 (AFH 39:139)

Ub.Cas.Arb.vit.3.9 (Davis 192)

Ub.Cas.Tr.scel. (AFH 10:137)
Ub.Cas.Arb.vit.3.9 (Davis 200);Ang.Clar.Alv.Pel.118 (AFH 39:148)

Barth.Pis.Quad.40 (1498:M7v)
Barth.Pis.Conform.9.2.4 (Anal.Franc.4:379)

Guil.Oc.Op.XC.dier.9 (Sikes 2:384);Mars.Pad.Def.pac.2.14. 8 (Previté-Orton 248–49)

Oberman (1963) 324
Guil.Oc.*Op.XC.dier.*106
(Sikes 2:776)
Guil.Oc.*Op.XC.dier.*6 (Sikes
1:366)

Matt.19:21

Guil.Oc.*Op.XC.dier.*78 (Sikes
2:636)

Guil.Oc.*Op.XC.dier.*23 (Sikes
2:468–69)
Guil.Oc.*Ben.*1.5 (Sikes 3:183–
84)

Guil.Oc.*Op.XC.dier.*100
(Sikes 2:751)
Acts 3:6
Guil.Oc.*Op.XC.dier.*9 (Sikes
2:386–87)
Guil.Oc.*Op.XC.dier.*11;5
(Sikes 2:410;1:352)
Guil.Oc.*Ben.*1.15 (Sikes 3:
207);Bonagr.*Paup.* (*AFH* 22:
323)

Guil.Oc.*Op.XC.dier.*93 (Sikes
2:686–87)
Mars.Pad.*Def.pac.*2.13 22
(Previté-Orton 237)
Mars.Pad.*Def.pac.*2.13.33
(Previté-Orton 238)

Mars.Pad.*Def.pac.*2.14.14
(Previté-Orton 251 52)

Mars.Pad.*Def.min.*3.5
(Brampton 7)

Wyc.*Serm.*1.4 (*WLW* 8:273)

Henr.Lang.*Tel.*18 (Pez 1–II:
528–29)

Gers.*Nupt.* (Glorieux 6:201–2)

Thos.Aq.*S.T.*2.2.185.6 ad 1
(*Ed.Leon.*10:479)

Matt.10:9
Wm.Mar.*Corr.Thom.*72 (*Bibl.
Thom.*9:296)
*Corr."Quare"* 72 (*Bibl.Thom.*
9:297);Åll.*Serm.*20 (1490:Clr)
Gabr.Bl.*Can.miss.*70.T
(Oberman-Courtenay 3:173)

ence of the anticlerical" Marsilius "on such church-dedicated men" as Ockham "is still largely over-rated"). While the possession of worldly goods did not of itself make someone "imperfect" and while it was necessary that at least some Christians go on owning them, the words of Christ to the rich young man, "If you would be perfect, go, sell what you possess," laid down the definition of "perfection" for all who would strive after it in the church. For "that poverty is to be regarded as specifically evangelical which is distinctively taught in the Gospel and enjoined on those who want to follow the doctrine of the Gospel perfectly." True perfection consisted in "being an imitator of Christ" and of the apostles in their poverty. There had been a difference between the apostles and other Christians in their adherence to the strict rule of poverty, but for the apostles the norm was: "I have no silver and gold." They were to conform their poverty to the example of the total poverty of Christ himself, who as God possessed all things but as man renounced them. Therefore Peter and his successors could not claim to be vicars of Christ in his dominion over temporal possessions and the temporal realm, for this dominion pertained to his divine nature. On the basis of these ideas of poverty as perfection and of Christ according to his human nature as "having observed the highest form of meritorious poverty," Marsilius went on to denounce "the successors of Christ and of the apostles" who laid claim to lands and cities. He even suggested that Christ had "forbidden to the apostles and to their successors any dominion over temporal goods."

Recognizing that such a campaign to "unburden" the church and the clergy of their wealth in order to restore the holiness of evangelical poverty could simply be a screen for the "audacity" of anticlerical lay officials and princes in despoiling church possessions, more moderate thinkers sought to redefine the question. One of the accusations against Thomas Aquinas had been that he had failed to interpret the words, "Take no gold" as a command. Apologists for Thomas declared that, if this was a command, it pertained only to the mission in the Gospel story and that it did not apply "to all believers"; but the accusation also en-

Corr."Sciendum" 71;96 (Bibl.
Thom.31:271;323)
Corr."Quare" 71 (Bibl.Thom.
9:294–95);Andr.Per.Ed.Bav.
(BPIR 10:65–66)
Hs.Svat.7 (Hrabák 67)
Matt.10:9

Joh.Pal.Dial. (CB 1:188)

All.Pot.eccl. (Du Pin 2:926)
Gers.Pot.eccl.12 (Glorieux 6:
239)

Gers.Nupt. (Glorieux 6:194)
Petr.Pal.Pot.pap.1.1.3.2 (Stella
114–20)
ap.Jac.Cerr.Lib.gest.4.xii.1414
(Finke 2:194)

Chel.Post.13 (Com.14:177)

Chel.St.vr.1.24 (Com.22:70);
Civ.Prag.Ep.xi.1431 ap.Joh.
Rag.Boh.80 (MC 1:158)

Wyc.Serm.4.16;2.6 (WLW 13:
132;9:37–38)

Jac.Mis.Zjev.8:12 (Pram.18:
329)

Dant.Mon.3.10.4 (Ricci 257);
Vall.Don.Const.43 (MGH
QGMA 10:108)
Guil.Oc.Brev.6.3 (MGH Schr
8:205)

Guil.Oc.Pot.pap.1.12 (Sikes 1:
53)

Aeg.Per.Infid. (BPIR 10:128)

abled some of them to point out the ambiguity of poverty as evidence of holiness and to argue that authentic perfection could coexist either with poverty or with riches. Poverty in and of itself was not necessarily a virtue and was not the same as perfection. The Hussites extended also to the secular clergy the application of the prohibition "Take no gold," but this met with opposition from various of their opponents. Between the absolute prohibition of church property by Wycliffe and Hus and the absolute claim to property as a divine right by the papal theocrats, "the church holds to the catholic middle way," that the ownership of property was not inconsistent with holiness but that it was not a corollary of Christ's commission to Peter. Churchmen were not bound to treat possessions the same way the apostles did. In fact, the temporal wealth accumulated by "doctors of theology" in the early church had been a consequence of their sound theology.

The most notable instance of such wealth (and the most notorious object of "murmuring" about it) was the Donation of Constantine, which can serve as a useful index to different attitudes toward the relation between the wealth of the church and the holiness of the church. Chelčický ridiculed the notion that "the church of Christ achieved a state of perfection only in that moment in which it accepted worldly power from Caesar." Constantine had "wanted to be more subtle than Christ," but proved to be a "devil" who seduced the church by corrupting it with riches and power. His fellow Hussite Jakoubek agreed that the Donation had been the work of the devil, but added that Constantine had done it "with good intentions." Dante maintained that Constantine had no right to make such a donation in the first place, nor the church to accept it, while Ockham cited the Donation, if indeed it was authentic, as proof that the emperor did not have his authority and possessions from the pope, but vice versa. At the opposite end of the political spectrum, Giles of Perugia used the Donation to prove that the pope did indeed have legitimate claim to his authority and possessions, and Conrad of Megenberg went even further to argue that Constantine before his baptism "was not emperor in the full sense of the

Conr.Meg.*Trans.imp*.21 (*BPIR* 10:316)

Jac.Vit.*Reg.chr*.2.10;2.5 (Arquillière 305;221)

All.*Pot.eccl*.pr. (Du Pin 2:926)

All.*Mat*.1 (Oakley 259)

All.*Serm*.1 (1490:S4r)

Gers.*Pot.eccl*.12 (Glorieux 6: 237)

Gers.*Conc.un.obed*. (Glorieux 5:54–55)
Joh.Schel.*Avis*.12 (*CB* 8:111–12)
Nicol.Cus.*Conc.cath*.3.2 (Heidelberg 14:328–29);Ambr. Trav.*Or.Bas*. (Mansi 29:1255)

Vall.*Don.Const*.1.27;4.36 (*MGH QGMA* 10:85;97)

Gers.*Vit.spir*.3 (Glorieux 3: 150)

All.*Indoct*. (Du Pin 1:649)

See pp. 75–76 above

Hs.*Eccl*.14.H (Thomson 109); Wyc.*Eccl*.1 (*WLW* 5:19)

Gers.*Ep*.35 (Glorieux 2:163)

word [abusivus erat imperator], because he reigned outside the church," but that his conversion and baptism (and the Donation) changed that. But for other champions of papal rights it was necessary to insist that Constantine did "obtain the empire justly, according to human right," in order to protect his right to cede this empire to the pope. Those who held to "the catholic middle way" praised the Donation of Constantine as an act inspired by God himself, and Constantine himself as the fulfillment of biblical prophecy. The Donation did not prove that what the emperor had was originally the property of the pope; it did prove that temporal possessions did not eo ipso corrupt the holiness of the church, and that the pope should share his wealth with the church. In a special category of fifteenth-century thinkers were those who questioned the authenticity of the Donation on the scholarly and historical grounds that "Constantine would never have made the gift" and therefore this "history is not history."

The proponents of "the catholic middle way" believed themselves to be defending the integrity of the state as well as the holiness of the church, especially against those "heretics" who seemed to be teaching that no one could properly hold office in either church or state unless he himself were righteous and holy. In opposition to Wycliffe and Hus, their principle was that in both church and state even "an unrighteous man can have the right to govern." As far as the political question was concerned, this polemical characterization appears to have been more accurate for Wycliffe than for Hus, but our interest here is in the ecclesiology. Both Wycliffe and Hus based their ecclesiology on the definition of the church as the number of the predestined, which was in turn the presupposition for the stipulation that the pope deserved the title "vicar of Christ" only "if he were a faithful minister, predestined to the glory of the head [of the church], Jesus Christ." The Council of Constance condemned this teaching, and Gerson included it among the "articles contained either formally or implicitly in the treatise of John Hus of Prague, which he entitled *The Church*, following the errors of John Wycliffe"; such a view would deprive the believer of

Gers.*Pot.eccl.*1 (Glorieux 6: 212)

Henr.Kalt.*Lib.praedic.* (Mansi 29:977);Petr.Lut.*Lig.frat.*7 (*BPIR* 10:59–63);Alv.Pel. *Planc.eccl.*1.54 (1560:48r);Turr. *Aug.Rom.* (Mansi 30:1031–33)

Henr.Kalt.*Lib.praedic.* (Mansi 29:977)

See pp. 107–9 below

Oberman (1963) 222

See vol.3:29–30;197;212–13

See vol.1:309–11

Aeg.Rom.*Eccl.pot.*1.2 (Scholz 7)

Aeg.Rom.*Ren.pap.*10.7 (1554: 15v–16r)

Alv.Pel.*Planc.eccl.*1.9 (1560: 2v);Alv.Pel.*Ep.*1.19;10.6;10.13; 11.11;13.10 (Meneghin 11–12; 57;62–65;77;107)

Corp.Jur.Can.:*Decr.Grat.*2.1.1. 77 (Friedberg 1:384)

Guil.Oc.*Corp.*2 (Birch 168)

any certainty about the ministry of the church. A generation later, Henry of Kalteisen, an anti-Hussite polemicist, insisted that "so long as a pope is faithful, even though in his morals he may be wicked, he can and should be called 'holy' or even 'most holy.'"

Significantly, he went right on to define the basis of this insistence: "Thus also the catholic church is called 'holy,' not on account of the holiness of all that are present in it, since many of them are sinners, but on account of its holy offices and on account of the holiness of the sacraments that are present in it." For the doctrinal issue in the disputes over the matter of a wicked pope was the holiness of the church itself, just as the doctrinal issue in the disputes over what to do if the pope were a heretic was the infallibility and indefectibility of the church. Thanks in part to the schism and in part to "the rising tide of Donatism" in the fourteenth and fifteenth centuries, the well-nigh universal acceptance of Augustine's doctrine that the sacraments were valid on objective grounds, quite apart from the virtue or wickedness of the minister or of the recipient, had begun to show significant cracks. Those who came to the support of papal authority were also explicit in their espousal of the traditional position on this question. "Holiness" was of two kinds, either of person or of status, and only the latter affected the sacraments. Even a priest ordained by a schismatic or heretical bishop did not have to receive reordination upon returning to catholic unity, provided the bishop himself had been validly consecrated and had followed the church's rite of ordination with the intention of conferring the holy orders of the church. Such statements would be easy to duplicate from other fourteenth-century papal protagonists, such as for example the Spiritual Franciscan Alvaro Pelayo.

They also appear, however, in those Spiritual Franciscan exponents of evangelical poverty who were unsparing in their attacks on the theocratic forms of the theory of papal authority. Thus William of Ockham, on the basis of a passage from canon law, rejected any difference between the Eucharist confected by a wicked priest and that consecrated by a good man. As an apologist for the Spiritual Franciscans and for their leader, Peter Olivi, Ubertino of Casale rejected the

Ub.Cas.*Sanct.ap.* (*ALKGMA* 2:412)

Ub.Cas.*Arb.vit.*3.3 (Davis 144)

Ub.Cas.*Arb.vit.*3.2 (Davis 138–39)

Ub.Cas.*Arb.vit.*4.5 (Davis 302–3)

Ub.Cas.*Arb.vit.*4.36 (Davis 375)

ap.Spinka (1966) 350

Wyc.*Civ.dom.*1.3 (*WLW* 4:24)

Wyc.*Serm.*1.4 (*WLW* 8:25)
Wyc.*Serm.*1.40 (*WLW* 8:268)

Wyc.*Serm.*1.51 (*WLW* 8:341)
Matt.16:18–19;John 20:21–23
Wyc.*Serm.*4.20 (*WLW* 13:175)
Wyc.*Serm.*3.3 (*WLW* 11:20)

Wyc.*Euch.*4 (*WLW* 16:113)

accusation that there was "any support" in Olivi for the "heresies" that would assert such a difference. Although Ubertino did not deny that there were wicked and "carnal" priests, in whom there was nothing left of the water of life, he assured the recipients of baptism and the other sacraments that a wicked priest could not jeopardize the validity of the sacraments, since Christ himself was in fact the minister, and therefore "the reality of the sacrament" was there. At the same time he counseled the faithful to avoid priests who were obviously in a state of mortal sin, even though "discipline is very defective today and intolerable evils are being tolerated," so that sometimes it was necessary "to receive the sacraments from a priest as long as he is being tolerated by the church." The catholic church would remain catholic even if there were only one believer left who adhered to it, even if the pope himself were a heretic or a schismatic.

The tendency of his contemporaries and of modern scholars to lump Hus together with Wycliffe "as a rebel against the established order" and as a neo-Donatist is understandable in the light of the extensive borrowings, many of them verbatim, from the English Reformer in the writings of the Czech Reformer, but in this instance they must be distinguished: Wycliffe did come to deny the validity of sacraments administered by a "wicked priest," but Hus did not follow him, although some of Hus's disciples did. In his treatise entitled *Civil Dominion,* Wycliffe made a point of noting that even if a minister were guilty of mortal sin, "God, in whose name he is ministering, supplies what will be of benefit to those who receive, just as though a righteous man were using" the power to minister. He stated the same in one of his earliest sermons, but qualified it in later sermons by saying that this was true "perhaps in some sense" or that wicked prelates and popes did not have the power of the keys, since the promises of Christ to the apostles did not apply to such prelates, "unless they follow the apostles in their morals." Christians must speak out against such clergy and avoid their ministrations, for there was a difference between "the moral goodness" of a host consecrated by a good priest and that of a host consecrated by an evil man. Chelčický, too,

Chel.*St.vr*.2.12;1.3 (*Com*.22:
257–58;11–12);Chel.*Post*.42
(*Com*.16:87)

Chel.*Crk*. (Petrů 100)

Thos.Aq.*S.T*.3.82.9 (*Ed.Leon*.
12:268)

Civ.Prag.*Ep*.xi.1431 ap.Joh.
Rag.*Boh*.80 (*MC* 1:162–63)

Hs.*Svat*.7 (Hrabák 72–73)

Hs.*Sanct*.66.2 (Flajšhans 3:
347)
Hs.*Eccl*.15.K (Thomson 129–
30)

Hs.*Sent*.4.13.3 (Flajšhans 2:
584);Hs.*Eccl*.10.M (Thomson
88)
Hs.*Sent*.4.5.3–4 (Flajšhans 2:
541–42)

Aug.*Ev.Joh*.46.6 (*CCSL* 36:
401)

Hs.*Eccl*.18.H (Thomson 163)

Wyc.*Eccl*.19 (*WLW* 5:443–45)

Hs.*Eccl*.5.G-H (Thomson 36–
38)

Jac.Mis.*Zjev*.11:2 (*Pram*.18:
409)

Jac.Mis.*Zjev*.17:4 (*Pram*.19:68)

Jac.Mis.*Zjev*.18:11–13 (*Pram*.
19:170)

See vol.3:212–13
*Serm.conc.Const*.23.ii.1416;10.
v.1416 (Finke 2:432–33;442–
44);Nicol.Cl.*Ruin.eccl*.15–17;
23 (Coville 124–25;130);Seg.
*Sim*.ap.Seg.*Hist.conc.Bas*.8.12
(*MC* 2:693–96);Seg.*Gabr*.2
(*DRTA* 14:353);Esc.*Avis*. (*CB*
1:218);Jul.Ces.*Sim*. (*CB* 8:
135–39)

held that sacraments "do not benefit" when received from the hands of those whose faith was dead, who drove souls "only to the devil."

Although Chelčický was joined by other Hussites in the insistence, for which it was possible to quote the authority of Thomas Aquinas, that it was a sin to receive the Sacrament from a priest whom one knew to be an open sinner, that does not make Hussitism "neo-Donatist." Hus himself forbade "giving tithes to or hearing Mass" from an unworthy priest, but immediately explained: "not that the Mass would not be holy." He emphasized, of course, that "every good Christian is a priest, but not every priest is a good Christian" and that a wicked priest was "a vicar of Antichrist." But he continued to teach the validity of the sacraments celebrated by any priest who had been properly ordained and who intended to confect the sacrament, since someone who was himself unclean could still cleanse another. He quoted with approval the warning of Augustine that those who preached Christ "for the sake of earthly gain" were nevertheless preaching Christ and "through them the voice of Christ is heard." Hus stayed close to Wycliffe's formulations in denying that ordination made even wicked priests a part of the church, but this did not cause him to deny the validity of their ordination. His enemies accused him of Donatism nonetheless, and among his followers it was especially Jakoubek ze Stříbra who took pains to dissociate his cause from any such implication. While making it clear that false believers, whether laymen or priests, did not belong to the true church, he was no less clear in declaring that "a person who is inwardly corrupt may hold a spiritual office and authority and may baptize and consecrate the body and blood of the Lord." The opposing view would be a source of doubt and confusion for both priest and people.

At one point Hus did go beyond the conventional Augustinian theory about validity: the perennial medieval dilemma of the status of the priest who had obtained his holy orders through simony. Simony was a problem that troubled Hus's opponents as well. Even those who called the Hussites "modern heretics" saw that "a virtuous and God-fearing man who does

Matt.Crac.*Squal.*11;9 (Walch
1–I:49;39);Ambr.Trav.*Ep.*1.14
(Martène-Durand 3:28);Joh.
Schel.*Avis.*1 (*CB* 8:110);Matt.
Mayn.*Avis.* 1 (*CB* 8:63)
*Serm.conc.Const.*18.vi.1416
(Finke 2:450)

Esc.*Can.poen.* (1491:6r)

Hs.*Svat.*2 (Hrabák 27)

Hs.*Sent.*1.A.inc.1.9.
(Flajšhans 2:7–8)
Hs.*Err.*6 (Ryba 52);Hs.*Svat.*7
(Hrabák 65)

Hs.*Svat.*9 (Hrabák 81)

See vol.3:18
Hs.*Sent.*4.13.5;4.25.4
(Flajšhans 2:587–88;640–44)

Chel.*Post.*8;37 (*Com.*14:103;
16:115);Chel.*St.vr.*2.27 (*Com.*
22:296)Joh.Rag.ap.Laur.Reich.
*Diurn.*7.ii.1433 (*MC* 1:304)

Gers.*Sim.* (Glorieux 6:171–7?)

Thos.Wal.*Comp.serm.*1
(Charland 329–30)

Gers.*Serm.*215 (Glorieux 5:
141)

Barth.Pis.*Quad.*22 (1498:G6v)

Gers.*Remem.agend.* (Glorieux
6:111);Gers.*Dial.spir.*
(Glorieux 7:168);Ant.P.*Conf.*1.
2.2 (1490:14v–15r);Esc.*Can.
poen.* (1491:8r)

Matt.15:14
Gers.*Aud.conf.*3;9 (Glorieux 8:
10;12)

See vol.3:210–11

Dns.Scot.*Ox.*4.14.1.14
(Wadding 18:37)

not want to commit simony can hardly obtain an ecclesiastical benefice," and that simoniacs brought judgment on themselves even when they confected valid sacraments. A bishop who knew about a simoniac and did nothing was an accessory after the fact. Convinced as he was that "there are very few priests who do not have a simoniacal ordination," Hus opposed all payment of surplice fees for any of the sacraments. Simony he defined as "the conscious intent to buy or to sell anything spiritual." Thus he included in his definition of the simoniac not only the priest who bought his ordination and the bishop who bribed his way into his office, but the layman who offered money in exchange for church services. Since the early Middle Ages simony had been a "heresy"; Hus appropriated this designation, as did Chelčický, who made a practice of calling it "the greatest heresy of all"—a practice that evoked the objections of John of Ragusa at the Council of Basel. An earlier anti-Hussite theologian, Gerson, also objected to an automatic identification of all simony as heresy and reassured believers concerned over the efficacy of a simoniac's ministrations that "Christ, the supreme pope, has supplied and goes on supplying what is lacking to the prelates in such cases."

Despite such reassurances about sacramental efficacy and objective validity, Gerson recognized that, among the sacraments, penance, like preaching, was a special case. It occupied a preeminent place as "the most important and almost the entire" spiritual resource for many believers; as one Franciscan theologian had pointed out, each of the three components of penance overcame the power of the devil in a special way. In the hands of a skillful and compassionate father confessor it was an instrument for restoring to the right path those who had strayed and for comforting the disconsolate, but if it was administered ineptly the entire process was corrupted. He would, Gerson said, rather postpone hearing confessions than be "a blind leader of the blind" who intimidated the penitents. Duns Scotus had emphasized that, necessary though they were, none of the usual three parts of the definition of penance—contrition, confession, and satisfaction—constituted its essence, since they

Dns.Scot.Ox.4.16.1.7
(Wadding 18:421)

Gers.Ep.31 (Glorieux 2:134;
141)

Gers.Vit.spir.4 (Glorieux 3:
177)

Gers.Aufer.13 (Glorieux 3:304)

Vit.Furn.Quodlib.3.12.1
(Delorme 187–88)

Jac.Vit.Quodlib.1.18 (Ypma 1:
216)
Dns.Scot.Ox.4.14.4.5
(Wadding 18:155);Dns.Scot.
Rep.Par.4.14.4.6 (Wadding 24:
221)
Mars.Pad.Def.pac.2.6.7
(Previté-Orton 165)

Gers.Mir.am. (Glorieux 7:198–
99)

Aug.Ev.Joh.46.6 (CCSL 36:
402);Aug.Bapt.4.11.17 (CSEL
51:241)

Matt.23:2–3

Aeg.Carl.Pun. (Mansi 29:901);
Henr.Kalt.Lib.praedic. (Mansi
29:1053–55;1061);Joh.Rag.
Auct.conc.3 (DRTA15:208);
Turr.Auct.1.87 (1563:49v–50r)

See p. 273 below

Conf.Aug.8.2 (Bek.62)

Gers.Serm.249 (Glorieux 5:
547–49)
Gers.Serm.249 (Glorieux 5:
558);All.Indoct. (Du Pin 1:
653);Esc.Gub.conc.6.1 (Hardt
6:250);Dom.Domen.Pot.pap.2.
4;2 ad 4 (Smolinsky 114;159–
60)
Gers.Magn.9 (Glorieux 8:419);
Alv.Pel.Ep.11.11 (Meneghin
77)

were human actions; rather, the sacrament of penance consisted in "sacramental absolution." The form of this absolution, in the formula "I absolve you of your sins in the name of the Father and of the Son and of the Holy Spirit," was, Gerson repeated, absolute rather than conditional. But if, as he also acknowledged, "the majority of those who hear confession are liable to suspension or irregularity and excommunication" for various sins such as simony and concubinage, this did constitute a pastoral and an administrative problem. The Scotist reminder, that it was on account of the will and the ordinance of God that penance as well as any other sacrament removed guilt, only intensified the concern about whether or not a simoniac or schismatic priest conformed to that ordinance. Scotus had denied any objective validity to an absolution pronounced by a layman, but that possibility continued to elicit interest among radical thinkers.

The fundamental response to the challenge of neo-Donatism was twofold: a call for reform, to bring the empirical reality of the church more closely into line with the creedal confession of its holiness; but meanwhile a reaffirmation of the essential correctness of the Augustinian doctrine that "holy baptism, the Mass, and the other sacraments do not lose their power because of the wicked life of the ministers." Augustine had quoted against Donatism the words of Jesus: "The scribes and the Pharisees sit on Moses' seat; so practice and observe whatever they tell you, but not what they do; for they preach, but do not practice." These words went on serving that purpose in the fifteenth century (as well as in the sixteenth, when the critics of the Reformation used them to argue that separation from the church was wrong even if the church was corrupt and when the Protestant Reformers cited them to exonerate themselves of the charge of neo-Donatism). Further biblical proof came from the case of Judas Iscariot. Gerson warned the clergy against standing in the "apostolic succession" of Judas, but he also used that warning as an occasion to point out that Judas had not been deposed from his office as soon as his crime of theft came to light; in fact, Christ had even shared his food with him on the night he was betrayed. The sacraments of a wicked priest continued

Gers.*Pot.eccl.*2 (Glorieux 6: 213)

Aug.Tr.*Dup.pot.* (*KRA* 8:490); Aug.Rom.*Ren.pap.*10.1 (1554: 11v)

Ges.*Aufer.*16 (Glorieux 3:307–8)

Gers.*Mod.hab.* (Glorieux 6:31)

Eph.5:27

Tok.*Eccl.*conc.2 (Krämer 364)

Alv.Pel.*Ep.*13.18 (Meneghin 117)

Nicol.Cus.*Ep.*1 (Faber 2–II:4r)

Nicol.Cus.*Conc.cath.*1.5 (Heidelberg 14:50)

Nicol.Cus.*Ep.*3 (Faber 2–II: 13r)

Nicol.Cus.*Ep.*1 (Faber 2–II: 3v)

to be valid because of his "character"—which meant not his moral qualities (as the word "character" would imply today), but the indelible and unrepeatable stamp that baptism, confirmation, and ordination conferred, regardless of moral qualities.

Therefore "the foundation of ecclesiastical authority is not the holiness" of the minister, and "neither schism nor heresy nor any other vice prevents the administration of the sacraments from having its efficacy." The sacraments were holy on account of the institution and the promise of Christ, the church was holy on account of the institution and the promise of Christ: "On account of her many secret faults, and especially on account of her public and scandalous sins, the church of Christ can be called spotted and wrinkled, and yet out of reverence for Christ, whose spouse she is, she may, indeed must, be called catholic, holy, and immaculate as regards her form." And the church would deserve to be called holy even if there were only one person left in the world who was holy. If, moreover, a believer was in doubt about the holiness of this or that prelate or pope, it was, according to Nicholas of Cusa, safer to obey the church despite the ambiguity than to refuse to obey at all. For the Holy Spirit conveyed grace even through a false priest, since it was not the human minister, but Christ, who carried on this ministry of the church through the Holy Spirit. The "common priesthood" of the church as a whole could not err, even though individual priests could and obviously did.

Underlying this restatement of the Augustinian definition of the holiness of the church in Nicholas of Cusa was not only the standard reminder that God alone knew who was a true and holy member of the church but also a more subtle epistemology. "In this world of sense experience," he argued, "it is necessary to draw a conjecture on the basis of sensible signs about the church of Christ itself. Therefore this conjectural church is the true church in this world of sense, on the basis of the limited knowledge of this world." He went on, moreover, to declare that "by a judgment of this conjectural sort, this church of Christ is regarded as holy, even though evil and false men are intermingled under its sacred signs." Just as

the apostle Paul himself had confessed, "I of myself
serve the law of God with my mind, but with my
flesh I serve the law of sin," and yet remained a member of the church, so the church itself had the right
to the name "immaculate" even though in fact "the
community is sometimes called all good, and sometimes all bad." Augustine had repeatedly compared
the church to the net in Christ's parable, which held
both good and bad fish until the Last Judgment. Such
comparisons continued to show that the evil and the
good were intermingled "not only in one ocean . . .
but even in one net." Sometimes the evil members of
the church could even be useful to the church and to
its real members, as teachers and interpreters of the
Scriptures.

In any event, it was more tolerable to have wicked
priests in the church, so long as they had been properly ordained, than to have none at all. And those,
for the time being, seemed to be the only two alternatives. Even in the fifteenth century there was an
increasing number for whom neither of these alternatives was any longer acceptable, as Chelčický's *The
Holy Church* made quite clear, and in the sixteenth
century both the number of the dissidents and the
intensity of their insistence on the holiness of the
church was to make this issue central to the program
of the Reformation.

### Catholic Concordance

Despite some occasional statements about how the
church would endure and be holy even if there were
only one true believer left, the universality of the
church in time and in space was in fact constitutive
of ecclesiology in the fifteenth century. Nicholas of
Cusa (Nicolaus Cusanus), who attended the Council
of Basel, devoted his book *Catholic Concordance* of
1432–33 to this universality. It was in many ways the
most profound exposition of catholicity in medieval
theology; for although it is an accurate generalization
to say that "the idea of world harmony . . . is an idea
which was ever present to the mind of the Middle
Ages," including for example the harmony among the
angels, his was the first system of thought to make
"catholic concordance" a theme that ran through the

Rom.7:25

Nicol.Cus.*Conc.cath.*1.4
(Heidelberg 14:48)

Matt.13.47–50
Aug.*Civ.*18.49 (*CCSL* 48:647)
Aug.*Petil.*3.2.3 (*CSEL* 52:164)

Guil.Oc.*Ben.*7.1 (Sikes 3:304)

Aeg.Carl.*Pun.* (Mansi 29:891)

Gers.*Or.priv.* (Glorieux 10:
136)

Petr.Brun.*Act.conc.Bas.*26.iii.
1432 (*CB* 2:71)

Spitzer (1963) 35
Aeg.Rom.*Eccl.pot.*3.3 (Scholz
160)

Nicol.Cus.*Conc.cath*.2.32
(Heidelberg 14:276)
Nicol.Cus.*Conc.cath*.2.34
(Heidelberg 14:290)

Nicol.Cus.*Doct.ign*.3.12
(Heidelberg 1:158)

Nicol.Cus.*Conc.cath*.1.12
(Heidelberg 14:71)

See vol.1:334

Aug.*Parm*.3.4.24 (*CSEL* 51:
131)

Nicol.Cus.*Conc.cath*.1.13
(Heidelberg 14:73)

See vol.2:167
Hinc.R.*Opusc.Hinc.L*.20 (*PL*
126:360)

Nicol.Cus.*Conc.cath*.2.1
(Heidelberg 14:94)

Jac.Vit.*Reg.chr*.1.4 (Arquillière
122–24);Alv.Pel.*Planc.eccl*.1.63
(1560:75v–76r)

Aeg.Rom.*Eccl.pot*.2.6;2.13
(Scholz 65–67;117)

life of the church, the unfolding of human history, the structure of the universe, and the very nature of God. Specifically, the church's own existence was dependent on "concordance," and it was through "concordance" that "the church is called 'catholic' in conformity with Christ." Or, as he said in a later work, "so long as we are here on earth as pilgrims, the truth of our faith cannot consist in anything else but the Spirit of Christ, . . . so that there might be diversity in concordance in the one Jesus." There would appear to be no significant question in the doctrine of the catholicity of the church that he did not treat, or at least touch, in his *Catholic Concordance*.

"The true church," according to Cusanus, "is that which is catholic." This meant that it was diffused widely, and would be diffused throughout the world before the end of time. As Augustine had said that "the [universal] judgment of the whole [Christian] world is reliable," so the author of *Catholic Concordance* found a "solid refuge in all doubts" in "the catholic church of the true faith, which is not confined" to any one place, by contrast with "some sort of sect of schismatics or heretics." The catholicity of the church and of its faith implied, moreover, that it was diffused throughout history as well as throughout the world. "Our faith of today," he said, "is in concordance with that faith which was spread through the world in those times"; therefore it was "necessarily true, because the unchangeable faith is one." From the definition of catholic tradition by Hincmar of Reims in the ninth century Nicholas quoted the requirement that "all Christian doctrine and any constitution or tradition ought to be such that it is in consensus with the universal church." The twofold definition of catholicity as universality "through the entire world" and as universality "from the beginning of the world to its end" belonged to many other discussions of ecclesiology in this period, in some of which catholicity became the ground for asserting that the church would not be truly catholic unless it had universal preeminence over all other powers on earth. Although the common usage of the word "catholic" brought to mind the prelates and clergy, it was actually a reference to "the universal congregation of the faith-

Gers.*Ep*.49 (Glorieux 2:234)

Aeg.Rom.*Eccl.pot*.2.7 (Scholz 72)

See vol.1:333

Gr.Arim.*Sent*.2.30–33.1.2 (1522–II:111v)

John 14:6

Nicol.Cus.*Conc.cath*.2.34 (Heidelberg 14:290)

Seg.*Mod*.46 (Ladner 49);Seg. *Gl.Eug*.2 ap.Seg.*Hist.conc.Bas*. 18.40 (*MC* 3:1155–56) Joh.Brev.*Tract*.2.1 (Du Pin 1: 851–58)

Nicol.Cus.*Conc.cath*.2.18 (Heidelberg 14:190–91)

Nicol.Cus.*Conc.cath*.2.4 (Heidelberg 14:105–6) Alv.Pel.*Planc.eccl*.1.16 (1560: 4v);All.*Mat*.2 (Oakley 308)

See pp. 122–25 below

Nicol.Cus.*Conc.cath*.2.26 (Heidelberg 14:252–53)

Jac.Mis.*Utraq*.1.29 (Hardt 3: 490)

Chel.*St.vr*.2.15 (*Com*.22:270) Guil.Oc.*Op.XC.dier*.124 (Sikes 2:854);All.*Indoct*. (Du Pin 1:661);Gers.*Schism*. (Glorieux 6:47) Nicol.Cus.*Conc.cath*.1.17 (Heidelberg 14:89–90);Joh. Rag.*Eccl*.1.2.8 (Krämer 379)

Nicol.Cus.*Conc.cath*.2.18 (Heidelberg 14:190–91)

Nicol.Cus.*Conc.cath*.2.34 (Heidelberg 14:291–92)

ful." The church was catholic on account of the sacrament of baptism, which was universal in its effects, bringing together all generations and all classes. As the canon of Vincent of Lérins had prescribed, true doctrine was that which "the catholic church, diffused everywhere, has always understood" to be true.

As such, true catholic doctrine could never go wrong, for Christ, who was the way and the truth, had promised to abide with his catholic church forever through the successors of the apostles. Indeed, if the church were ever to err, it would no longer be one, holy, catholic, or apostolic. "The indefectibility of the church" and its infallibility as the true and catholic church were the consequence of "the assistance of Christ until the consummation of the age." If the decision of a church council proceeded from the concordance of those present, that was a sign that the Holy Spirit was the author of such concordance; and "the greater the measure of concordance, the more infallible the judgment." For the universal church had the guarantee that it could not err in matters of faith. Therefore the Hussites were mistaken in making lay communion under both kinds compulsory, for this amounted to an accusation that the majority of priests and bishops for many centuries had erred in so fundamental a matter of faith as the Eucharist. The Hussites, of course, were not averse to making precisely that accusation, "that such a church [consisting of the pope, the cardinals, and the bishops] can sin and err," and that church councils (especially those that had condemned Hus and his followers) had erred. Others, too, pointed out that the guarantee of infallibility applied only to matters of faith, not to matters of fact. More controversial was the question of the locus of infallibility and the "degrees" of infallibility. For the promise of infallibility pertained "to the church as a whole, not to any particular member," not even to the pope.

The political implication of this qualified promise was that, while there was no record of any universal council of the church ever having erred in faith and doctrine, "this privilege does not extend to all provincial synods, not even to Roman pontiffs." The authority of church councils, and the relation of their authority to that of the pope, was indeed an issue of politics, both ecclesiastical and secular, in the fifteenth century, as a series of reform councils and their "conciliarist" advocates sought to deal with schism and scandal in the church: Pisa, 1409; Constance, 1414–18; Basel-Ferrara-Florence, 1431–49. In its intellectual and scholarly "foundations," moreover, conciliar theory proceeded from the presuppositions and by the methods of canon law rather than by those of doctrinal theology; when theologians dealt with the matter, as they often did, the authorities they cited, even Augustine and other church fathers, tended to come as much from Gratian as from Peter Lombard. Nevertheless, it was also an issue of doctrine, both in its own right as an essential part of the doctrine of the church and because of its bearing on doctrinal authority in general. Except perhaps for such theologians as Wycliffe and Hus, there was general agreement on the doctrine that the universal church was indefectible and infallible. But was this true of "a general council, to the extent that it relies on Holy Scripture," and was it true of a pope?

"A universal council . . . represents the universal church": this was the fundamental premise that determined the answer. The catholicity of the church expressed and manifested itself in the form of the general council, so that the Council of Constance "ascribed to itself this representation of the universal church," and both the Council of Constance and the Council of Basel introduced some of their decrees with the formula: "The most holy and sacred general council, legitimately gathered in the Holy Spirit, representing the universal church." Although the conclusions he drew from it for church and state were highly controversial and, in the eyes of many, heretical, the definition of a general council in the *Defender of the Peace* of Marsilius of Padua would have met with acceptance even from his adversaries: "A general council of Christians . . . or of those to whom this authority has been granted by the universal community [universitas] of faithful Christians," with representatives of all the provinces and notable communities of the Christian world. To him this implied necessarily "that no council can or should be

---

**Marginal notes (left column):**

Tierney (1955)

Nicol.Cus.*Conc.cath*.2.17;2.20 (Heidelberg 14:180;219)

All.*Pot.eccl*.3.4 (Du Pin 2:958) Nicol.Cus.*Conc.cath*.2.17 (Heidelberg 14:180);Esc.*Gub. conc*.9.1 (Hardt 6:299–302); Seg.*Gl.Eug*.5 ap.Seg.*Hist.conc. Bas*.18.43 (*MC* 3:1171)

Joh.Rag.*Auct.conc*.3 (*DRTA* 15:206–7);Jac.Cerr.*Lib.gest*.3. vi.1416 (Finke 2.298)

Fr.Per.*Bav*. (*BPIR* 10:84);Alv. Pel.*Ep*.13.12 (Meneghin 109)

Mars.Pad.*Def.pac*.2.20.2 (Previté-Orton 319)

Mars. Pad. *Def.min.* 12.4
(Brampton 36)

Mars. Pad. *Def.pac.* 2.19.2
(Previté-Orton 313)

Esc. *Gub.conc.* 3 (Hardt 6:185–86)
Thdrc. Nm. *Convoc.* (Heimpel 30)

Gers. *Pot.eccl.* 8 (Glorieux 6:225); Matt. Crac. *Squal.* 18
(Walch 1–I:79)

CConst. (1414–18) 39.
(Alberigo-Jedin 438–39)
Jac. Parad. *Sept.stat.* (Goldast 2:1574); Esc. *Avis.* (CB 1:215);
Petr. Brun. *Act.conc.Bas.* pr. (CB 2:2); Prael. Germ. *Ep.* 18.vii.1541
(CT 4:198)
Seg. *Gl.Eug.* 7 ap. Seg. *Hist.conc. Bas.* 18.45 (MC 3:1176); Paul. III. *Init.* (CT 4:229)

ap. Henr. Lang. *Cons.pac.* 12
(Hardt 2:24–25)

Ambr. Trav. *Ep.* 15.3 (Martène-Durand 3:497)

Ambr. Trav. *Ep.* 13.3 (Martène-Durand 3:448)
Ambr. Trav. *Ep.* 4.2;4.3
(Martène-Durand 3:86;87)
See vol. 1:262–63; vol. 2:24

Turr. *Auct.* 1.63–64 (1563:42v–43r); Joh. Pal. *Quaest.par.*
(Döllinger 420;427); Nicol. Cus. *Conc.cath.* 2.5 (Heidelberg 14:110)

Aug. *Bapt.* 2.3.4 (CSEL 51:178)

Gers. *Serm.* 241 (Glorieux 5:475); Nicol. Cus. *Conc.cath.* 2.5
(Heidelberg 14:111); Turr. *Auct.* 2.17 (1563:58r); Seg. *Gl.Eug.* 7
ap. Seg. *Hist.conc.Bas.* 18.45
(MC 3:1180–81)

called a general council unless the entire Greek church of the faithful has been duly called to it." If it was truly universal, such a general council had the right to claim for itself the special "direction and revelation of the Holy Spirit."

But although councils had "never been as necessary . . . nor as useful in the church of God at any time as they are now," it had been "a very long time since any general council was held in the Roman church." The long neglect of the general council as an instrument of church governance was "the worst of all plagues in the church" past and present. The Council of Constance sought to correct this by its decree of 9 October 1417, entitled *Frequens*, in which it called for regular councils; that decree was to be cited by the advocates of councils throughout the fifteenth and sixteenth centuries. But desuetude had led to confusion about the authority of a council; it could even lead some to argue that while a council was a necessary device in the primitive church because it had not yet acquired the panoply of laws and decrees prevailing in the modern church, the times had changed and the general council had lost its usefulness. As a result of this neglect, the historic conception of a council was largely unknown and needed to be reconstructed from the documents. Through the general renewal of historical interest during the fifteenth century, the study of the early ecumenical councils received new attention; for example, Ambrose Traversari studied a codex containing the *Acts* of those councils and made special note of a manuscript containing those of the First Council of Nicea as well as of one on the Council of Chalcedon and the Third Council of Constantinople. Thus the status of the so-called "robber synod" held at Ephesus in 449 could become the occasion for consideration of how even a synod convoked by an emperor, at which the representatives of the pope were present, could nevertheless turn out to be illegitimate. From the study of the history of councils it became evident that, as Augustine had put it, "plenary councils, gathered on behalf of the entire Christian world . . . are often corrected by those that follow them, when . . . something is discovered that had been unknown earlier." It was also evident, according to Ger-

Gers.*Mat.schism.* (Glorieux 6:
83)

son, that the general councils of the ancient church had not managed to gain universal assent from all the contending parties of their time, and consequently that such universal assent was not a reasonable expectation for the councils of the fifteenth century either.

A few years later, when the Council of Constance was in session, Gerson saw this judgment confirmed, and he drew upon the history of the early centuries for the observation that there had been times when only two or three theologians were in the right and the majority were in the wrong, but this "multitude was finally overcome by a very few catholics." That

Gers.*Jur.episc* 6 (Glorieux 6:
177)

did not, however, invalidate the authority of councils, but confirmed it; for "as long as the law of Christ stands, it is not possible for a general council, the universal church duly gathered in assembly, to err in

Gers.*Auct.conc.*5.1 (Glorieux
6:115)

determining the truths of the faith." Christ, as the ruler of the church, had promised the special assistance of the Holy Spirit in such matters as were beyond the reach of human investigation; in these matters the council could not err, though it might make mistakes in questions of fact, which were subject to in-

Gers.*Schism.* (Glorieux 6:47);
Gers.*Serm.*212 (Glorieux 5:89)

Seg.*Neutr.*1.1 (*DRTA* 14:369)

vestigation. For "if one cannot believe a general council, whom can one believe?" The determinations of a council in matters of faith and doctrine, which were the outcome of the special assistance of the Holy Spirit, were to carry "no less" an authority than that

Gers.*Sens.lit.* (Glorieux 3:336)

of the Apostles' Creed. It was likewise on the basis of what "we read as having happened in all the councils" that Nicholas of Cusa urged that "no conclusion,

Nicol.Cus.*Conc.cath.*2.15
(Heidelberg 14:171–72);Seg.
*Diff.*4 (*DRTA* 13:820–21)

above all in matters of faith, can be sure unless the votes are brought to the point of unanimity." The Council of Chalcedon in 451 was a prime example of how to attain such unanimity, and of how to assure

See vol.1:263–66
Nicol.Cus.*Conc.cath.*2.4
(Heidelberg 14:106)

eventual victory for the orthodox majority. Despite the instances when the majority of theologians at a particular moment had held a position contrary to what was to become the official teaching of the orthodox church, Cyprian's paraphrase of the apostle's ques-

Cypr.*Ep.*66.8 (*CSEL* 3:732)

Rom.3:3

tion, "What if some have departed from the faith?" was a statement of "the infallible rule that the majority

Nicol.Cus.*Conc.cath.*1.14
(Heidelberg 14:77–78)

always persist in the faith and in the truth of the law."

The history of ancient councils, however, raised an additional question, over which the various parties of the fifteenth century were in serious dispute: Who should convoke a general council? A related—but not identical—question was: Who had the authority to dissolve a general council? For the historical sources showed that the first eight ecumenical councils had been summoned and presided over by emperors, not by popes or other bishops. The defender of the prerogatives of the temporal arm in ecclesiastical business cited history to prove that "convoking or summoning a council . . . belongs solely to the authority of the secular magistrate." Conciliarists who refused to go that far did point out that the "general councils" about which the Book of Acts spoke "were convoked by the common consent of the church, not by the sole authority of Peter." All of this seemed to be in opposition to the position articulated already by Pope Gregory I, that "without the authority and the consent of the apostolic see, none of the matters transacted [by a council] have any binding force," which had led to the medieval assertion that "universal councils are especially convoked by the authority of the apostolic see," an assertion that continued to find support in the papal party at the councils themselves. The moderate conciliarists of the fifteenth century, in reaffirming the rights of the general council, tried to compromise by conceding that "as a rule [a council of] the universal church should be assembled by the authority of the pope," but that in special cases other believers could take it upon themselves to do so.

The schism had obviously turned into such a special case by the beginning of the fifteenth century. "For D'Ailly in 1380 it is beyond question that the general council he was demanding would, together with the (real) French pope, represent the universal church. . . . Altogether different is . . . the situation of the year 1410, when Dietrich is working toward a solution completely without the pope." The reason for the difference, as Dietrich of Nieheim himself formulated it, was that "when the issue is the deposition of the pope, the censure of the pope, and the limitation of his power, it does not in any way behoove him to be the one to convoke a general council." As an anonymous pronouncement circulated shortly before the Council of Basel put it, "When the pope or the car-

Esc. Gub. conc. 7 (Hardt 6:269–86)

Joh. Pal. Quaest. par. (Döllinger 419–20)

Car. Mal. Ep. 25.vii. 1415 (Finke 3:347);Nicol. Cus. Conc. cath. 2. 25 (Heidelberg 14:246–47); Seg. Mod. 124 (Ladner 79)

Mars. Pad. Def. pac. 2.21.7 (Previté-Orton 334)

All. Ext. schism. (Du Pin 2: 112);All. Serm. 2 (1490:T1r)

See vol. 1:354

Gr. M. Ep. 9.156 (MGH Ep. 2: 158)

Hinc. R. Opusc. Hinc. L. 20 (PL 126:362)
Joh. Maur. Prop. Const. (Mansi 28:33)

Gers. Auct. conc. 3.1 (Glorieux 6:115);Gers. Vit. spir. 3 (Glorieux 3:153–54)

Heimpel (1932) 126

Thdrc. Nm. Mod. (QMR 3:39); Lud. Pal. Resp. (Finke 1:243–44);Esc. Gub. conc. 7 (Hardt 6: 272–73) ap.Joh.Rag.*Bas.conc*.27 (*MC* 1:166)

Aeg.Rom.*Ren.pap*.24.1 (1554: 31r)

Aug.Tr.*Pot.coll.* (*KRA* 8:501); Alv.Pel.*Planc.eccl*.1.20 (1560: 4v)

Turr.*Auct*.2.8–9 (1563:56v–57r)

Joh.Pal.*Hist.* (Mansi 31:197–206)

Nicol.Cus.*Conc.cath*.2.17 (Heidelberg 14:180)
Gal.2:11
Nicol.Cus.*Conc.cath*.2.20 (Heidelberg 14:219);Seg.*Gabr.* 1 (*DRTA* 14:349);Seg.*Gl.Eug*.1 ap.Seg.*Hist.conc.Bas*.18.39 (Hardt 6:157);Jac.Parad.*Sept. stat.* (Goldast 2:1571);Esc. *Gub.conc*.1.2 (Hardt 6:157)
See vol.1:13

Zab.*Schism.* (Schard 703)

Vall.*Don.Const*.1.3 (*MGH QGMA* 10:58)

Thdrc.Nm.*Mod.* (*QMR* 3:87)

Oliv.*Ren.pap.* (*AFH* 11:356)

All.*Pot.eccl*.1.3;3.4 (Du Pin 2: 935;959)

Jul.Ces.*Disp.Bas.* (Mansi 30: 655)

Nicol.Cus.*Conc.cath*.2.15 (Heidelberg 14:170–71)

dinals refuse to promote the celebration of a general council at the stated time, or try to hinder it, they should be condemned as partisans of heresy." In the early fourteenth century there had been some discussion of where the authority of the papacy resided after a pope had died and before his successor had been chosen. The usual answer was that at least some of it devolved on the college of cardinals, but with the proviso that "the college cannot do everything that it can do while the pope is alive or that a living pope himself can do." Now it was not only the death of an individual pope, but the schism between two or even three claimants to the Holy See and thus the sickness unto death of the papacy itself, that had made the question of the relative authority of council and pope so urgent.

"But whether a universal council properly constituted, that is, one that represents the universal catholic church, is above the patriarchs and the Roman pontiff," wrote Cusanus, "I believe that there can be no doubt." If it was right for the apostle Paul to oppose the apostle Peter "to the face" when he was in error, it was even more right for a universal council to oppose the successor of the apostle Peter. Paul's opposition to Peter implied that "the plenitude of power is in the pope, but only if he is not in error; when he is in error, however, a council has to correct him." It likewise implied to Lorenzo Valla that a critical examination of the alleged Donation of Constantine was legitimate. Peter's guilt, moreover, had been "minimal" in comparison with that of "our popes" in the fifteenth century. Following the example of the apostle Paul, whose successors they were as teachers of the world, the cardinals of the church had the right to resist the pope, as even an early proponent of papal infallibility had conceded; this they would do by convoking a council. The power of the keys conferred upon Peter by Christ had been given to the church, not to Peter; hence "the church does not exist for the sake of the pope, but the pope for the sake of the church, and we do not say 'I believe in the pope' but 'in the holy catholic church.'" Although it was correct that the decisions of a council in matters of faith and doctrine required the ratification of the pope, it was

Nicol.Cus.*Conc.cath.*2.11
(Heidelberg 14:142)

Nicol.Cus.*Ep.*2 (Faber 2–II:
8v)

See vol.2:67–68;150–53
Nicol.Cus.*Conc.cath.*1.14
(Heidelberg 14:77);Seg.*Prop.
sec.*2 ap.Seg.*Hist.conc.Bas.*17.
12 (*MC* 3:590)
See p. 79 above

Zab.*Schism.* (Schard 700);Oliv.
*Ren.pap.*ad 5 (*AFH* 11:359)

All.*Leg.* (Du Pin 1:668–69)

All.*Pot.eccl.*3.1 (Du Pin 2:949)

Alv.Pel.*Planc.eccl.*1.54 (1560:
47v–48r)

Krämer (1980) 315

Franzen (1964) 69

Tierney (1972) 243

no less correct that for a papal epistle to receive the title and authority of an "apostolic epistle" required the ratification of a council. It was impossible for pope and council together to err in faith and doctrine, but a pope apart from a council was not infallible.

Yet Cusanus could assert that the assured way to infallibility was "to be in union with" the pope, although he also conceded that such popes as Liberius and Honorius I had been "seduced into schismatic error." The resolution of this anomaly lay in a distinction, similar to the one Gerson had drawn, between the pope and the papacy: "The pope is one thing," Francesco Zabarella, chairman at Constance, had said, "but the apostolic see is something else. . . . For the see cannot err." There was a related distinction to be drawn between the title of "supreme pontiff" and the title of "Roman pontiff," even though by divine ordinance the two were combined in one person; it was only because of the first of these that the church of Rome had the right to be called the head of all churches. The pope's third title was "head of the general council," which represented the universal church. Within this "threefold church [triplex ecclesia]," over which the pope presided, it was therefore necessary to make a distinction without making a separation. It was possible, however, to take this distinction between the universal church and the Roman church in such a way as to specify that, in another sense, "universal church" could mean "that church which has all other churches under it, and in this sense of the word only the Roman church has claim to the title 'universal church'"; on that basis the pope became "the supreme hierarch and the monarch of the entire church militant, the one to whom every soul must be subject."

This is only one illustration of "how heavily a spokesman and theoretician of papalism drew upon the conciliarists" for his argumentation, as well as of the paradox that the papacy "was in danger above all as a consequence of the papal theory and could be saved only through the conciliar theory." "Indeed, in this matter, there was a striking convergence" between the thought of the early proponents of papal infallibility and that of their opponents. The same argu-

Guid.Terr.*Quat*.Luke 11:52
(1631:373)

Guid.Terr.*Mag.infall.* (*Opettex*
2:16);Turr.*Auct.*1.9;1.60 (1563:
7v–8r;41v–42r)

Guid.Terr.*Mag.infall.* (*Opettex*
2:20)
Guid.Terr.*Quodlib.*4.11
(Xiberta 319–20);Petr.Pal.*Pot.
pap.*1.2.B.2 (Stella 128–29)

Guid.Terr.*Mag.infall.* (*Opettex*
2:16–17)

Xiberta (1932) 228

Guid.Terr.*Mag.infall.* (*Opettex*
2:21–27)

Inn.III.*Serm.div.*2 (*PL* 217:
656)
Guil.Oc.*Pot.pap.*1.9;1.10
(Sikes 1:39–40;42–43)
*Corp.Jur.:Decr.Grat.*40.6
(Friedberg 1:146)
Petr.Pal.*Pot.pap.*1.3.3 (Stella
195):Wyc.*Apost.*1 (*WLW* 12:
1);Henr.Lang.*Cons.pac.*13
(Hardt 2:29);Matt.Crac.*Squal.*
1.22 (Walch 1–I:93);Thdrc.
Nm.*Not.* (Finke 3:137);Joh.
Maur.*Prop.Const.* (Mansi 28:
32);Joh.Pal.*Quaest.par.*
(Döllinger 424–26);Dom.
Domen.*Pot.pap.*1 ad 6
(Smolinsky 93)

ments could, with adjustments, suit both cases. "In matters pertaining to faith and morals," wrote Guido Terrena, one of the first infallibilists, "the church has always been directed by the counsel of the Holy Spirit when it made its definitions." But from this he did not only draw the usual conclusion that "where the supreme pontiff with the college of the lord cardinals or with a general council are gathered together [congregantur] in the Lord's name and on behalf of his faith, there is Christ, who is the truth without error"; but in the very next sentence he was willing to change the plural "are" to a singular, declaring that "in the determination of the things that pertain to faith the pope is directed [dirigatur] by the Holy Spirit and the Holy Spirit speaks in him." On the basis of biblical and patristic statements about the indefectibility of the church he took the position that "the immutable and invariable authority of the catholic church . . . resides universally, after Christ, solely in the supreme pontiff and not in any private person." This did not, for example, give the pope the right to pronounce absolution on a sinner who was not penitent; but it did mean that "the lord pope, to whose authority it belongs to determine and declare the propositions that belong to the faith, cannot [non possit] err."

But if in such statements Guido Terrena "formulates splendidly the truths that five centuries later were defined by the Vatican Council" of 1870, he also had to deal, as would the Vatican Council of 1870, with the dilemma that would be raised if the pope himself should prove to be a heretic. Even Pope Innocent III, in whose pontificate the papacy had attained the summit of its power, temporal as well as spiritual, took it to be a necessary principle of faith that "only on account of a sin committed against the faith can I be judged by the church"; he was in fact accused of heresy by some critics, but nothing came of the charges. A famous passage in Gratian's compilation of canon law had taken up the contingency of a pope's being guilty of heresy, and in the fourteenth and fifteenth centuries it was this passage from Gratian, not the actual matter of papal infallibility, that set the grounds of discussion. A Franciscan champion of the papacy in the fourteenth century, who was sure that the see

Alv.Pel.*Planc.eccl.*1.55 (1560: 5v)

Alv.Pel.*Ep.*13.3 (Meneghin 97)

Alv.Pel.*Planc.eccl.*1.34 (1560: 6r);Conr.Meg.*Guil.Oc.*8 (*BPIR* 10:373);Fr.Per.*Bav.* (*BPIR* 10:81)

Joh.Par.*Pot.*13 (Leclercq 215)

Corp.Jur.:Decr.Grat.19.9 (Friedberg 1:64) Dant.*Inf.*11.8–9;Seg.*Gl.Eug.*4 ap.Seg.*Hist.conc.Bas.*18.42 (*MC* 3:1167);Turr.*Auct.*1.67 (1563:43v)

See vol.2:152–53 Rog.*Cath.Doct.*19.7 (*PS* 40: 181) Joh.Brev.*Tract.*3.2 (Du Pin 1: 885–86) See p. 342 below Joh.Par.*Pot.*19 (Leclercq 235); Esc.*Gub.conc.*1.2 (Hardt 6: 153) Hs.*Svat.*4 (Hrabák 34);Seg. *Mod.*76 (Ladner 59)

See pp. 87–88 above

Guil.Oc.*Brev.*3.15 (*MGH Sch* 8:137–40);Guil.Oc.*Op.XC. dier.* (Sikes 2:840)

Aug.*Trin.*1.8.17 (*CCSL* 50:50) Joh.XXII.*Serm.*15.xii.1331 (Dykmans 140)

Gers.*Joh.Mont.* (Glorieux 10: 12)

Guil.Oc.*Jn.*2 (Sikes 3:34–37)

of Peter had "never at any time deviated from the catholic faith," maintained that even the sin of heresy would not deprive the pope of his authority if he were willing to accept correction; but he acknowledged that if such a pope refused to accept correction and refused to step down, the college of cardinals did have the right to withdraw its allegiance from him and elect another pope, and that a general council had the right to condemn him as a heretic. Some were willing to go further: if cardinals and council were unable to remove the scandal, they were to invoke the intervention of the emperor.

The collection of canon law also contained the case of the alleged heresy of the fifth-century Pope Anastasius II, which continued to serve as the chief historical admonitory case on the subject, since it appears to have been only in the fifteenth century that the long-neglected details of the story of Pope Honorius began to emerge, although, once they had emerged, they provided ammunition also for Protestant attacks on papal infallibility. It was on the basis of the record of Anastasius and of several others that theologians spoke of "certain popes being found to be wicked and heretical and being rightly deposed." But among the several other popes in the catalogue of alleged heretics who had sat on the throne of Peter there was also John XXII. His actions, beginning in 1316, against the doctrine of poverty held by the Spiritual Franciscans became, for various champions of the Spiritual cause and above all for William of Ockham, proof that the pope was a heretic. This was confirmed when Pope John, in a sermon of 15 December 1331, espoused the belief that "the soul separated from the body [at death] does not have that vision of the Divinity which is its total reward according to Augustine, and it will not have [this vision] until the resurrection." Although he retracted these ideas in an official declaration three years later, he had meanwhile been condemned by theologians of unquestionable orthodoxy; and Ockham would not accept the explanation that John XXII had merely stated such opinions "as the teachings of others [recitando]," but insisted that the pope had meant them as his own.

The implications of canon law governing the case of a pope guilty of heresy permitted the classification of fifteenth-century ecclesiologists into three parties: those who held that the pope "cannot be reformed, judged, or condemned by a holy general council even on grounds of heresy"; those who approved of such condemnation, but only on the grounds of heresy; and those who extended the authority of the universal council over the pope to include "all matters touching the faith or the condition of the universal church." But that classification of alternative views did not include another interpretation of the papacy, which, taking off from the dual vision of "Angel Pope and Papal Antichrist," claimed to find in the pope a fulfillment of the New Testament prophecies of "the man of sin, the son of perdition" who was to come before the end of time. Langenstein believed that "there will not be any notable reformation of the church" until after the coming of Antichrist, and the eschatology of Nicholas of Cusa contained the vision of a persecution and general apostasy so complete that even the successor of Peter would fall before the power of "the satanic spirit of Antichrist"; then would follow the resurrection of the church. One result of the schism was that even those who would have been horrified at the thought of equating the papacy with Antichrist found themselves using the term for the other claimant to the throne of Peter, whom they regarded as illegitimate. But to Wycliffe and to Hus and his followers it was not the "antipope," but the pope himself who was the Antichrist. "Christ reigns, Antichrist will be destroyed" was their theme, which was to reappear in the polemics of the sixteenth-century Reformers.

So fundamental and powerful was the demand of catholicity, however, that even the obvious denial of it by the divisions of the Reformation could not be permitted to vitiate it. An apologist for Anglicanism entitled his apology *The Catholic Doctrine of the Church of England;* John Calvin devoted a large part of his *Institutes* to the theme of "the holy catholic church" as a means of grace; and the Lutheran theologian Martin Chemnitz, replying to the Council of Trent, took the canon of Vincent of Lérins, "that which has been believed always, everywhere, and by

Esc.*Gub.conc.*1.2 (Hardt 6: 142–46)

McGinn (1980) 155–73

2 Thess.2:3 (Vulg.)
Henr.Lang.*Tel.*22 (Pez 1–II: 532);Jac.Parad.*Sept.stat.* (Goldast 2:1574)

Nicol.Cus.*Ult.* (Heidelberg 4: 95)
Ub.Cas.*Arb.vit.*5,8 (Davis 464);Thdrc.Nm.*Invect.*6 (Hardt 2:301),Thdrc.Nm.*Mod.* (*QMR* 3:25)
Wyc *Serm* 2.9;4.22 (*WLW* 9: 66;13:195);Hs.*Eccl.*13.C (Thomson 103);Hs.*Sanct.*34.1; 34.12 (Flajšhans 3:137;146); Jac.Mis.*Zjev.*4:4 (*Pram.* 18: 196);Chel.*Boj.* (Petrů 40);Chel. *Post.*17;29;31 (*Com.*14:253; 407;428–29)
Civ.Prag.*Ep.*xi.1431 ap.Joh. Rag.*Boh.* (*MC* 1:153)

See pp. 172–73 below

Rog.*Cath.Doct.* (*PS* 40)

Calv.*Inst.*(1559)4.1.2 (Barth-Niesel 5:4)

See vol.1:333–39

Chem.*Exam.CTrid.*2.4.7
(Preuss 327)

all," as the basis for arguing that for a doctrine to be "catholic" and therefore "necessary," it must be able to claim the support of "either the word or the example of Christ and the apostles" as set down in Scripture.

### In Defense of Apostolic Obedience

As the controversies of the Reformation in the sixteenth century were to make clear once again, the first three attributes of the church in the creedal formula all finally came down to the fourth; for the fundamental issue in each of them was the nature and locus of authority in the church. Because the church was "built upon the foundation of the apostles and proph-

Eph.2:20

ets," the consideration of what made the church one or holy or catholic led to the question of what made it apostolic. Although it was intended to be one, "the

Thdrc.Nm.*Mod.* (QMR 3:91)

apostolic church itself" was now "wavering in schism"; unless the sin of simony were totally eradicated, the holiness of the church would be in jeopardy, and the

Thrdr.Nm.*Mod.* (QMR 3:109)

church "will not be apostolic, but apostatic"; "the apostles, as heralds of Christ," were "the founders of

Thos.Kemp.*Soliloq.*21 (Pohl 1:310)
Gers.*Petr.Lun.*1.8 (Glorieux 6:267)

the catholic faith," and therefore "the church is called 'catholic,' that is, universal and apostolic."

Unfortunately, exactly what it was that made the church apostolic and kept it so was no easier a question to answer than what made it one, holy, or catholic. In 1462 Gabriel Biel completed his treatise *In Defense of Apostolic Obedience*; in it he argued that obedience, which he defined elsewhere as the essence

Gabr.Bl.*Can.miss.*82.C
(Oberman-Courtenay 4:49)
Gabr.Bl.*Obed.apost.*1.6
(Oberman-Zerfoss 108)

of perfection in this life and of bliss in the life to come, should be more perfect now than it was in the Old Testament, a proposition that he identified with the rule that even those who doubted the justice of one or another papal act were "obligated for their

Gabr.Bl.*Obed.apost.*2.1
(Oberman-Zerfoss 154)

salvation to obey the apostolic see." Although such an identification was anything but the unanimous consensus of fifteenth-century ecclesiology, the idea of

Vall.*Prof.rel.* (MPPR 6:311)

speaking out "in defense of apostolic obedience" was. A Spanish theologian who defended church practice against the Hussites, John of Palomar, wrote a treatise

Joh.Pal.*Quaest.par.* (Döllinger 414–41)

under the title, *The Question of Who Is to Be Obeyed.* That was the fundamental issue involved in "apostolic obedience." Even if the answer to that question was

Tok.*Neutr*.3.F (*DRTA* 16:564)

Joh.Rag.*Auct.conc*.2 (*DRTA* 15:205)

Seg.*Gl.Eug*.3 ap.Seg.*Hist.conc.* *Bas*.18.41 (*MC* 3:1162–63)

See pp. 87–90 above
Oliv.*Ren.pap.* (*AFH* 11:351);
Aug.Clar.*Ep*.3.10 (*ALKGMA* 1:555);Ang.Clar.*Alv.Pol*.33;67; 166–71 (*AFH* 39:104;120;171–73)

Aeg.Rom.*Eccl.pot*.3.12 (Scholz 209)

Henr.Kalt.*Lib.praedic.* (Mansi 29:977)

Hs.*Err*.4 (Ryba 45–47);Wyc. *Civ.dom*.1.43 (*WLW* 4:384)

Hs.*Eccl*.19.E (Thomson 177–78)

2 Cor.11:13

Hs.*Post.ad*.87 (Ryšánek 13: 346);Chel.*Post*.1 (*Com*.14:5)

"the apostolic see," one had to add, now that the choice lay between Rome and Avignon: "Show me [which of them truly is] the Roman pontiff; and presto, there will be obedience!" The schism had undermined certainty about the credentials of the Roman pontiff, but it had also made ambiguous the very "question of who is to be obeyed," whether the "apostolic" pope or the "apostolic" council or some other "apostolic" authority, be it the "apostolic" Scripture alone or in conjunction with the "apostolic" tradition. All catholic theologians could agree on the obligation to obey the universal church, as the mother of all believers, but not on the specific structure of the church to which such obedience was due, especially if "he who held the apostolic see has separated himself from the unity of the church."

To John of Palomar, Gabriel Biel, and others of their view, the apostolic structure that was the proper object of "apostolic obedience" was the papacy. Two of the early spokesmen for the Spiritual Franciscans, the party whose troubles with Pope John XXII were to become such an important chapter in the struggles between the papacy and its critics, had defended the right of the pope to establish any new laws that did not contradict the faith and law of Christ, as well as the duty of obeying him "to the death." Another defender of papal power had urged at the conclusion of a treatise on *The Power of the Church:* "Fear the church and observe its commands!" and had gone on to explain what he meant: "The supreme pontiff . . . can be called 'the church,' . . . because his power is spiritual, heavenly, and divine, and is . . . without measure." Similarly, an anti-Hussite polemic of 1433 at Basel declared that the commandment of the pope was to be obeyed "even if it is really not founded on the letter of the law of God." To Hus, as to Wycliffe, such a notion of absolute obedience to superiors was an "error," and "apostolic obedience" meant obedience to the word of the apostles in Scripture, not to the command of their successors in office. The "false apostles" of whom the New Testament warned were those who spoke with a different voice from that of the genuine apostles and who deceived the souls of the believers, for the true successors of the apostles

Chel.*Post.*39 (*Com.*16:146)

CConst.(1414–18) *Act.*5
(Alberigo-Jedin 409–10)

Seg.*Neutr.*1.1;1.3 (*DRTA* 14:
369;379–80);Seg.*Mod.*136–37
(Ladner 84–85);Joh.Rag.*Bas.*
*conc.* 59 (*MC* 1:111)

Jac.Vit.*Reg.chr.*1.6 (Arquillière
138–40);Alv.Pel.*Planc.eccl.*1.63
(1560:78v)

Gers.*Pot.eccl.*1 (Glorieux 6:
211)

All.*Serm.*10;11 (1490:Y1v;Y3r)

Mars.Pad.*Def.pac.*2.26.13
(Previté-Orton 410)
Hs.*Eccl.*12.D;9.B (Thomson
98–99;58)

Hs.*Eccl.*2.D (Thomson 10);
Hs.*Coll.*82 (Ryšánek 7:475);
Jac.Mis.*Zjev.*21:14 (*Pram.*19:
392)

Joh.Rag.*Utraq.* (Mansi 29:782)

Hs.*Eccl.*18.C (Thomson 158)

Isid.Sev.*Orig.*7.9.1 (*PL* 82:
287)

were those who faithfully preached the word of God. Opposed to both these interpretations of "apostolic obedience" was the view expressed in the decree *Haec sancta,* promulgated by the Council of Constance on 6 April 1415, that obedience to the church meant above all obedience to the general council, while anyone who disobeyed the council, even the pope, was guilty of schism.

To be deserving of "apostolic obedience," the church must itself be "apostolic." What made it so? The three usual criteria of apostolicity were: that it be founded by the apostles, that it have been extended by the apostles throughout the world (since an apostle was one sent as a messenger), and that it be governed and administered by the apostles (through their legitimate successors). "The power of the church," as Gerson formulated it, was "the power that Christ granted in a supernatural and special way to his apostles and disciples and to their legitimate successors until the end of time." The stress was on "legitimate" successors because there were false successors, some of them in high places, who did "not feed the fire of charity, but the flame of cupidity." This warning from Cardinal D'Ailly took an even more polemical tone when it came from a Marsilius of Padua or a John Hus. Marsilius, attacking John XXII, spoke of his "diabolical writings, which he nevertheless calls 'apostolic,'" and Hus, contrasting the original apostles with their supposed successors, noted that "the apostles did not call themselves 'most holy popes,' 'heads of the universal church,' or 'universal pontiffs,' but since they had the Supreme Pontiff with them until the end of time, they called themselves 'servants of Christ.'" But Hus and his followers were in agreement with their opponent who said: "We confess the 'apostolic church' in the Nicene Creed for no other reason than that it is founded on the word and doctrine of the apostles," although Hus characteristically added "the life of the apostles" as part of the definition.

The use of the concept of apostolicity to legitimate the polity or the doctrine of the church did not exhaust the possible applications to which it could be put. If, as everyone had learned from Isidore of Seville, "apostle" meant one who had been sent by Christ to pro-

Mark 16:9

Nicol.Cus.*Serm*.12.1
(Heidelberg 16:243)

Thos.Kemp.*Orat*.15 (Pohl 3:
396)

Guil.Oc.*Op.XC.dier*.17 (Sikes
2:447)

See vol.3:232
Joh.Pal.*Civ.dom.* (Mansi 29:
1128–29)

Vall.*Prof.rel.* (*MPPR* 6:312–13)

Ang.Clar.*Alv.Pel*.158–63 (*AFH*
39:168–70)
Ub.Cas.*Sanct.vest.* (*ALKGMA*
3:87);Ub.Cas.*Rot*.1
(*ALKGMA* 3:94)

Ub.Cas.*Arb.vit*.5.3 (Davis
424;421–22)

Wyc.*Serm*.3.57 (*WLW* 11:501)

See pp. 106–8 above

Esc.*Gub.conc*.8.4 (Hardt 6:
297)

claim his message, and above all the message of his resurrection, the Gospel narrative made it clear that the "first" person whom Christ had sent after the resurrection was not one of the twelve but Mary Magdalene, who received from him an "apostolic mandate" to announce the message to the apostles and who therefore could be called "the apostle of the apostles [apostolorum apostola]." More common than such an occasional whimsy was the application of the term "apostolic" to monasticism, which was known as "the apostolic life," a term that medieval heretics had appropriated for their style of living in contrast to that of the catholic church. Underlying this usage was the belief, which "no one would deny" but which in fact some did, that monasticism had come down from the apostles themselves. The apostolic life of complete poverty had now experienced not only reform but renewal, through Francis of Assisi. Francis had been divinely inspired in composing his *Rule,* which came "completely from the Holy Spirit," without a word of Francis's own. "As though a new apostle," he had been given to the church as "the beginning of a new church," in which the work begun by the apostles would at last reach its consummation. The Franciscans appeared, in the eyes of their critics, to be claiming that those who followed him "exceeded the apostles" and that the church would be apostolic by its conformity to Francis rather than to the original apostles.

As the advocacy of papal supremacy and of papal infallibility by several Franciscans indicates, however, even they concentrated, in their understanding of what was "apostolic" in the church, on the universal equation of "apostolic" with "papal," and it was this equation that underlay discussions of apostolicity. "The apostolic or [seu] Roman church" was the common way of referring to that church of which the pope was the head, even when the very point being made was the distinction between this "apostolic or Roman" church as a "particular church" and the "catholic church" as the "church universal." Therefore also "the supreme ruler of the church is called 'the apostolic man [apostolicus]' . . . and the papal see is called 'the apostolic see' . . . and the papal dignity is called 'the apostolic office' . . . and the law of the pope [is called]

Alv.Pel.*Planc.eccl*.1.54 (1560:
48r–48v)

Thdrc.Nm.*Nem.un*.3 (1609:
297)

Hs.*Eccl*.15.H (Thomson 126)
Nicol.Cus.*Conc.cath*.2.13
(Heidelberg 14:154)

Joh.Brev.*Tract*.2.3 (Du Pin 1:
875)

Alv.Pel.*Planc.eccl*.1.63 (1560:
79r)

Mars.Pad.*Def.pac*.2.16.1
(Previté-Orton 273);Wyc.*Civ.
dom*.1.44 (*WLW* 4:418–19)

Thos.Aq.*Sent*.4.19.1.1.ad 3
(Mandonnet 4:975)

Jac.Vit.*Reg.chr*.2.5 (Arquillière
202)

Aeg.Rom.*Ren.pap*.24.1 (1554:
31r)
Petr.Pal.*Pot.pap*.1.1.1–2 (Stella
97–111)

Aug.Tr.*Dup.pot.* (*KRA* 8:489–
90)

Guil.Crem.*Rep.err.* (*BPIR* 10:
27)

Matt.28:19–20
Henr.Kalt.*Lib.praedic.* (Mansi
29:1007–8);Henr.Kalt. ap.
Laur.Reich.*Diurn*.21.ii.1433
(*MC* 1:315);Turr.*Auct*.1.22
(1536:15r)

Nicol.Cus.*Conc.cath*.2.13
(Heidelberg 14:150)

See vol.1:119,159
Cypr.*Unit.eccl*.4 (*CSEL* 3:212–
13)
Nicol.Cus.*Conc.cath*.1.6
(Heidelberg 14:56)

Turr.*Auct*.1.38 (1563:29r)

'the apostolic constitution.'" In opposition to such a restriction of the term to the pope, there were those who insisted that all the bishops were "sons or heirs of the apostles" and therefore "true vicars of the apostles," in fact, successors of Peter himself. But the usage of referring to Rome as "the apostolic see" was all but ineradicable.

The usage involved the disputed question of the relation between Peter and the other apostles in the plan and institution of Christ; for "although the church is called 'apostolic' from all the apostles, it is especially called so from the head of the apostles, Peter." In opposition to the view that all the apostles were equal, the defenders of papal prerogative maintained, on the basis of Thomas Aquinas and others, that while all the apostles had received "the power of the order [potestas ordinis]," which was their priestly authority to administer the sacraments, in equal measure, they had not received an equal "power of jurisdiction," which was the administrative authority to govern: Peter's jurisdiction extended over the church as a whole, while that of the other individual disciples applied to their particular dioceses. Although the disciples had received their power of jurisdiction immediately from Christ and not through Peter, nevertheless "after the ascension of Christ the apostles were subjected to Saint Peter." Some went so far as to say that the apostles had received from Peter the authorization to carry out their power of preaching and administering the sacraments. "Nor is it any problem that it was Christ who sent them into the whole world, for he did so without specific assignments [indistincte] and left the assignment to Peter."

Against this apparent isolation of Peter from the apostolic college came the insistence "that Peter did not receive any more power from Christ than the other apostles." The equivocal-sounding formulations of Cyprian about Peter and the apostles continued to be a way of warning against an exaggeration of Petrine primacy. As the relative authority of pope and council was engaging the attention of theologians and canon lawyers, the role of Peter in the original "apostolic councils" came in for careful scrutiny. "For in the first council held in Jerusalem, about which we read in the

Acts 15:25

Acts 15:28

All.*Serm*.2 (1490:T1r)

All.*Ext.schism.* (Du Pin 2:
112);All.*Mat*.2 (Oakley 306);
Jac.Parad.*Sept.stat.* (Goldast 2:
1570)

See vol.1:13,113

Gers.*Serm*.212;221 (Glorieux
5:72;209);Gers.*Prop.Ang.*
(Glorieux 6:133–34)

Zab.*Schism.* (Schard 702)

Nicol.Cus.*Conc.cath*.2.13
(Heidelberg 14:150)

See vol.1:352–53;vol.2:157–70

Matt.16:18–19 (Vulg.)

All.*Recom.* (Du Pin 1:603);
Jac.Vit.*Reg.chr*.1.6 (Arquillière
142–43)

Aeg.Rom.*Eccl.pot*.2.4 (Scholz
50);Hs.*Sanct*.22.8 (Flajšhans 3:
84);Nicol.Cus.*Ep*.1 (Faber 1–
II:3v);Mars.Pad.*Def.pac*.2.17.2
(Previté-Orton 289)

Laur.Reich.*Diurn*.10.i.1433
(*MC* 1:290);Nicol.Cus.*Serm*.4.
2 (Heidelberg 16:65)

Seg.*Eccl*.1.22 (Krämer 403)

All.*Recom.* (Du Pin 1:604)

Joh.Maur.*Super.* (Mansi 29:
527)

Acts of the Apostles, it was James who acted as spokesman in the presence of Peter. It does not say 'It has seemed good to Peter,' but 'It has seemed good to us in assembly'; and what follows is, 'It has seemed good to the Holy Spirit and to us.'" It was likewise not by the sole authority of Peter, but by "the common consent of the church" as a whole, of "the holy apostles and elders," that the council had been convoked. The issue in controversy at that council was the binding force of Old Testament law for Gentile Christians, the very issue over which Peter and Paul clashed. Therefore it was appropriate for James, not Peter, to state the council's verdict. In short, "even though Peter was the prince of the apostles, the plenitude of power did not reside in him alone, but as is clear in the passage that has been cited, Peter was a coruler at the council, as one member of the congregation."

An examination of the passages from the New Testament in which Peter received the primacy would reveal that "nothing was said to Peter that was not said also to the others." The locus classicus had long been the commission of Christ to Peter: "You are Peter [Petrus], and on this rock [petra] I will build my church, and the gates of hell shall not prevail against it. I will give you [tibi, sing.] the keys of the kingdom of heaven, and whatever you shall bind [ligaveris, sing.] on earth shall be bound in heaven, and whatever you loose [solveris, sing.] on earth shall be loosed in heaven." The identification of the "rock" in this passage had given rise to a "prolixity" of exegetical answers, as even a sampling of opinions from this period will bear out: a heterogeneous group of interpreters, on the basis of parallel use of the word "rock," made it a reference to Christ; again, it could be a reference to "faith," meaning the object of faith rather than faith as a personal virtue; or it could mean specifically "the faithful confession that Peter spoke"; hence it could even be a reference to "the divine Scripture and the sacred doctrine of Christ" as the foundation of the church; yet another solution was to accept the identification of Peter as the rock, but to connect it with Peter as preacher and missionary rather than with Peter as prelate; or it could apply to all the apostles as

Turr.*Auct.*1.52 (1563:38r)
Vall.*Annot.*Matt.16 (*MPPR* 5:816)
Matt.16:23
Vall.*Annot.*Mark 8:33 (*MPPR* 5:826)

"rocks," as Jerome had said, but to Peter "chiefly" and "especially"; still another answer was to skip the passage altogether in commenting on this chapter, but to linger over the following words to Peter, "Get behind me, Satan!"

Taken in any of these ways, the passage in question could not become a proof text for an ecclesiology that attributed the apostolicity of the church solely to its Petrine foundation. For two chapters later Christ had

Joh.Par.*Pot.*12 (Leclercq 209–10)

said to all the apostles: "Whatever you shall bind [alligaveritis, pl.] on earth shall be bound in heaven, and whatever you shall loose [solveritis, pl.] on earth shall

Matt.18:18 (Vulg.)

be loosed in heaven." Moreover, the confession was not Peter's alone, but was the response of all the apostles, and hence the commission was addressed to all

Seg.*Mod.*28–29 (Ladner 39)

John 21:17 (Vulg.)
Guil.Oc.*Dial.*3.4.10–11 (Goldast 2:857–58);Guil.Oc.*Imp.et pont.*6 (*BPIR* 10:460) Joh.Maur.*Super.* (Mansi 29:521);Jul.Ces.*Disp.Bas.* (Mansi 30:655)

Jac.Vit.*Reg.chr.*2.9 (Arquillière 268–72);Alv.Pel.*Planc.eccl.*1.51 (1560:41r)

Guil.Oc.*Pot.pap.*1.13 (Sikes 1:57);Petr.Pal.*Pot.pap.*1.2.B.5 (Stella 175)

of them as well. And while the command, "Feed [Pasce] my sheep," was spoken only to Peter, it gave him authority over individuals, but not over the universal church nor over the general council that represented the universal church. Besides, Christ had not entrusted to Peter or to all the apostles, much less to their successors, all His power, so that, for example, the pope did not have the right to institute sacraments or dispense anyone from the laws of God, or to perform the miracles that Peter had performed.

Although the equation of "Petrine" with apostolic and the relation of Peter to the other apostles justly received a major share of the discussion, there was also some consideration of the relation of Peter to Rome, and thus of the equation of "Petrine" with "Roman," but even more of the equation of "Roman"

Mars.Pad.*Def.pac.*2.16.16 (Previté-Orton 255);All.*Leg.* (Du Pin 1:668)

with "catholic." The New Testament did not in so many words locate Peter at Rome, although it was a widespread opinion that "Babylon" at the conclusion

1 Pet.5:13
Nicol.Cus.*Conc.cath.*2.34 (Heidelberg 14:297–98)
See vol.1:353

of his First Epistle was a code word for "Rome." As Gregory the Great had already observed, there were in fact two sees of Peter, since he had been at Antioch before coming to Rome. This meant that he had ruled as prince of the apostles already during his tenure as

Thdrc.Nm.*Mod.* (*QMR* 3:74–75)

bishop of Antioch, and hence that Petrine primacy was not tied inseparably to Rome. It meant also that the patriarch of Antioch could lay legitimate claim to succession from Peter, although Antioch had yielded

Nicol.Cus.*Conc.cath.*2.17 (Heidelberg 14:181)

its primacy to Rome. Even for those who distin-

Guil.Oc.*Imp.et pont*.25 (*BPIR* 10:478)

guished "the church of Avignon" from "the true Roman church," the residency of the popes at Avignon during most of the fourteenth century, although it was only a temporary necessity, had shown that it was possible to distinguish "Petrine" from "Roman," and therefore that it was wrong to argue the question of primacy on the basis of location; for while it was "to be believed that this most sacred see cannot be destroyed even as to its location, still, if Rome were to fall, the truth of the church would remain wherever the primacy and see of Peter would be," even if that had to be elsewhere.

Nicol.Cus.*Ep*.2 (Faber 2–II: 8v)

The episcopate of Peter at Antioch, and at Rome after that, could have even more far-reaching implications. Peter had the right to select any particular diocese and to be bishop wherever he pleased, but instead, as primate, he moved from one to another; "from that time, therefore, two episcopates come together in Peter and in his successors, that of the universal church and that of the particular Roman church." Hence it was absolutely necessary to distinguish between these two. The universal church could not err and could not fall, but the particular Roman church— to which it was customary to refer as "the apostolic church"—was only a part of the universal. The wicked were members of "the apostolic church" in this sense, but not of "the catholic church," which was the communion of saints. This equation of "Roman" with "apostolic," whose purpose it was to avoid the equation of "Roman" with "catholic," did not in most instances lead to the idea that it was Rome that was meant by the term "apostolic" in the Nicene Creed; but it did produce an identification, even by a critic, of "the apostles" with "the cardinals of the holy Roman church." Just as the other apostles had been "the members of Peter's household," so the cardinals were now in relation to the pope. Against this identification others directed the declaration that the bishops, not the cardinals, were the true successors of the apostles.

Petr.Pal.*Pot.pap*.1.3.3 (Stella 187)

All.*Pot.eccl*.1.1 (Du Pin 2:928–29)

Thdrc.Nm.*Mod.* (*QMR* 3:7–9)

Thdrc.Nm.*Mod.* (*QMR* 3:35)

Joh.Var.*Ep.card.* (Du Pin 2: 861);Aug.Tr.*Pot.coll.* (*KRA* 8: 505)

Henr.Kalt.*Lib.praedic.* (Mansi 29:1068–69)

Gers.*Repl.* (Glorieux 6:39); Thdrc.Nm.*Mod.* (*QMR* 3:67)

Thdrc.Nm.*Mod.* (*QMR* 3:1); Gers.*Conc.un.obed.* (Glorieux 6:55)

But some of the same writers could also use "apostolic church" in yet another sense, as a designation of "the primitive apostolic church." When, in response to the Hussites, it was said that "we honor the primitive church and the holy Roman church as

ap.Eben.*Diar.*25.vii.1434 (*MC* 1:742)

Vooght (1972) 190

See p. 90 above

Esc.*Gub.conc.*3 (Hardt 6:180)

Jac.Mis.*Zjev.*1:12;21:25 (*Pram.* 18:51;19:516)

All.*Serm.*12 (1490:Z2v)
Jac.Mis.*Zjev.*13:11 (*Pram.*18: 541)
Jac.Mis.*Corp.*7 (Hardt 3:922)
Guil.Oc.*Op.XC.dier.*11 (Sikes 2:417)
Henr.Kalt.*Lib.praedic.* (Mansi 29:984)
Jac.Mis.*Zjev.*21:14 (*Pram.*19: 394)
Eben.*Or.Bas.*3 (*DRTA* 17:25–26);Nicol.Cl.*Ruin.eccl.* (Coville 142)
Joh.Rok.*Utraq.* (Mansi 30: 300)

Gabr.Bl.*Can.miss.*57.0 (Oberman-Courtenay 2:407)

Vall.*Lib.arb.* (*MPPR* 5:999)

Jac.Mis.*Ven.sacr.*pr. (Vooght 388–89);Chel.*Post.*44 (*Com.*16: 203);Chel.*St.vr.*1.12 (*Com.*22: 34)

Petr.Pal.*Pot.pap.*2.2 (Stella 231)

Henr.Oyt.*Scrip.*1 (*Opettex* 12: 25)

See pp. 203–9 below

the mother and teacher of the catholic faith," that coordination of authorities stood in contrast to the disjunction between them that was characteristic not only of the Hussites but of various other reform movements as well, for all of whom "the opposition 'good/evil' is reinforced by the opposition 'ancient church/modern church.'" There was neither clarity nor consistency about the precise terminus ad quem of this primitive church. Those who regarded the conversion of the emperor Constantine and the Donation of Constantine as the fall of the church naturally drew the line there, while others could speak, a bit vaguely, of "that holy primitive church, which lasted more than two hundred years and a little bit after the times of Constantine and Pope Sylvester, in the time of Augustine and Jerome and of Pope Gregory the Great." The watchword, "We must look to the primitive church," with which a Hussite exposition of the Book of Revelation began and ended, had its counterpart in an anti-Hussite conciliarist's polemical comments about "such a great difference between the primitive church and the present church." The age of the primitive church had been a time when Christians abounded in virtue, when there was a deep devotion to the Eucharist, when the church practiced a community of goods, when the clergy were saintly, when even small children were well versed in the knowledge of Scripture, when the church lived in unity and peace rather than in schism, when doctrine and morals shone with the light of the Holy Spirit, when the fervor of genuine repentance made a resort to indulgences unnecessary, when "the imitators of the apostles" avoided the use of philosophy—all of this by way of contrast with "the modern church, which, if it does not want to fall into error, must conform itself in faith and works to the primitive church, which was filled with the Holy Spirit."

The norm of "the primitive apostolic church," to which everyone ascribed "the essence of perfection," included as its primary and decisive component the supreme, or even the sole, authority of the apostolic Scriptures. The full-scale articulation of the doctrine of Scripture, of its inspiration and inerrancy, was completed only in the period of the Reformation and then

See pp. 343–47, 351–52 below

Henr.Oyt.*Scrip*.1 (*Opettex* 12: 37–42)

See pp. 306–10 below

Doct.Prag.*Ep*.6.ii.1413 (Palacký 476) Hs.*Eccl*.16.B (Thomson 132–34)

Wyc.*Civ.dom*.1.44 (*WLW* 4: 409–10);Wyc.*Dial*.32 (*WLW* 5: 77);Hs.*Eccl*.8,F (Thomson 56)

Wyc.*Dial*.10 (*WLW* 5:19–20); Wyc.*Civ.dom*.1.44 (*WLW* 4: 416–18)

Gers.*Utraq.* (Glorieux 10:55)

Gers.*Sens.lit.* (Glorieux 3:334)

See pp. 59–60 above

See pp. 47, 49 above

Guil.Oc.*Jn*.15 (Sikes 3:72)

in the Protestant theologies that came out of the Reformation. Nevertheless, the struggle for the apostolicity of the church during the period under consideration here did necessarily concern itself with the doctrine of Scripture. Theology paid more attention to its authority than to its inspiration, although the latter was by no means absent from the discussion, and more to the relation of its (unquestionable) inerrancy to the (almost equally unquestioned) infallibility of the church than to the details of the process by which the Holy Spirit had protected the biblical writers from error even in geography, history, and science. Both the emphasis on the authority of the primitive church and the method of recovering it by means of careful biblical study received further impetus during the fifteenth century from the humanists.

Those who made the most of the authority of the primitive church were accused of "wanting to have Sacred Scripture alone [solam Scripturam sacram] as a judge," as well as of "wanting to interpret that Scripture according to their own ideas, without caring about the interpretation of the community of wise men in the church." Although the response of the accused was an effort to disavow the threat to the creedal and dogmatic tradition that seemed to be implicit in this position, it was quite clear that it was a position based on a sharp distinction between the word of God in "Scripture alone," which was the only authority deserving of total credence, and the word of "all the saints except for Christ," whether popes or church fathers or even apostles, apart from Scripture. The critics of this position agreed with its adherents that human reason and human custom were to be rejected if they conflicted with Scripture, but this was not the same as claiming "to want to follow and accept Scripture alone." The origins of these discussions lay in the fourteenth century. Duns Scotus had said that his theology dealt only with what was in Scripture and what could be drawn from Scripture, but one of the doctrines in the second of these categories was for him the immaculate conception of the Virgin Mary. Ockham had been more strict in enforcing the authority of "Sacred Scripture and the doctrine or assertion of the universal church" over that of the pope, as well as the superiority of Scripture to any church father, and sometimes even the uniqueness of the apostolic testimony in Scripture in comparison with canon law and with all the church fathers and all the universal church councils—indeed, in comparison with "the entire company of mortals." But his own view would seem to have been that "there are many catholic truths that neither are contained explicitly in Sacred Scripture nor can be inferred solely from its contents." Thereby he had made it possible or even imperative for the fifteenth century to appeal from his word to the word of God in Scripture, just as he had done in relation to earlier authorities. Others in the fifteenth century were speaking of "Sacred Scripture" as "superior to all the arts," whether Christian or pagan, and of the necessity to believe any particular statement in the Bible on the basis of the belief "that the entire Bible is true, and all the history written in it."

But this latter statement about belief in the Bible formed the introduction to a larger examination in which the principal controversial issue was whether "only those truths which are asserted explicitly in the canon of the Bible or which can be deduced solely from the contents of the Bible are catholic truths and should be believed as a condition for salvation" or whether there were also "many truths not found in Sacred Scripture, nor necessarily deducible from its content alone, [that] ought to be assented to as a condition for salvation." Both these views of "apostolic tradition" would have defined it as "that to which all must assent and from which none of the faithful may deviate," and, by contrast, would have defined "the unstable tradition of the children of this world" as that which was to be rejected. Both of them held, moreover, that the authority of Scripture stood "first and foremost" in the determination of articles of faith. Neither of them, on the other hand, was rejecting the authority of the church or proclaiming a doctrine of "Scripture alone," as certain heretics were seen to be doing. The question between the two views was whether the church, in exercising this doctrinal authority, had the right to promulgate as apostolic doctrines even some beliefs that could not find explicit warrant in what was "written in the Bible" or in what

Guil.Oc.*Corp.* (Birch 446–50)

Guil.Oc.*Brev.*1.8 (*MGH Sch* 8:48–49);Guil.Oc.*Dial.*3.3.4–5 (Goldast 2:821–23)
Guil.Oc.*Imp.et pont.*1 (*BPIR* 10:455)

Guil.Oc.*Dial.*1.2.2 (Goldast 2:412)

Gers.*Appell.* (Glorieux 6:285)

Thos.Kemp.*Doct.juv.*1 (Pohl 4:181–82)

Joh.Brev.*Tract.*1.1 (Du Pin 1:812)

Joh.Brev.*Tract.*1.3 (Du Pin 1:829–30)

Seg.*Prop.sec.* ap.Seg.*Hist.conc. Bas.*17.11 (*MC* 3:579)

Gers.*Nupt.* (Glorieux 6:196)

Gers.*Ex.doct.*2.1 (Glorieux 9:465);Gers.*Ver.cred.* (Glorieux 6:186)

was "deduced from this alone by an obvious conclusion," but that were rather purported to have "come down to us through the successive transmission of the apostles and others, as equivalent to the canonical Scripture" in authority and apostolic authenticity.

Gers.*Vit.spir.*2 (Glorieux 3: 137–38)

The proponents of this second definition of apostolic tradition were not, as a rule, arguing for the validity of later, new revelations to the church or to the pope, but for a second channel of apostolic revelation through which portions of the original message had been handed down apart from Scripture. "All the doctrinal institutions of the holy church," according to a fourteenth-century writer, "are derived either from the Scriptures of both Testaments . . . or from the apostolic tradition or from the ordinances of the fathers and the holy councils or from the approval of reasonable custom." This "either/or [vel/vel]" appeared to assume that there was an "apostolic tradition" that did not consist only in the valid method for interpreting Scripture and for drawing out what was implicit in it, but that was an independent source containing some genuinely apostolic teachings not available otherwise. When that same writer, therefore, admonished, "Let us understand the gospel of Christ, my brethren, as the holy Roman church, his spouse, declares and understands it," he seemed to be saying that the church had access to this second source, even though his words as they stood could be saying no more than that the catholic church was the only reliable interpreter of apostolic Scripture, a proposition on which every orthodox theologian would have agreed. The favorite patristic proof for an apostolic tradition outside Scripture came from Basil's treatise *On the Holy Spirit*, which had posited the existence of an "unwritten" teaching that proved the doctrine of the deity of the Holy Spirit. The incorporation of Basil's argument into Gratian's collection, where it served to validate extrascriptural canon law, made it available to the exponents of extrascriptural doctrinal tradition as well.

Alv.Pel.*Planc.eccl.*1.63 (1560: 77r)

Alv.Pel.*Ep.*11.30 (Meneghin 88)

Bas.*Spir.*27.66 (*SC* 17b:478–82)

Corp.Jur.Can.:*Decr.Grat.*1.11. 5 (Friedberg 1:24)

Henr.Oyt.*Ver.cath.*3 (*Opettex* 16:12–13)

But to the claim, "Look how many saving doctrines have been added . . . that Sacred Scripture does not contain," the proponents of the other view of tradition replied: "It does indeed contain them, according

Gers.*Ex.doct*.2.1 (Glorieux 9: 465)

Gers.*Ver.cred*. (Glorieux 6: 181–84)

Nicol.Cus.*Ep*.2 (Faber 1–II: 7r–7v)

Matt.16:18–19

Aeg.Carl.*Pun*. (Mansi 29:923)

Joh.Rag.ap.Laur.Reich.*Diurn*. 11.ii.1433 (*MC* 1:308);Henr. Oyt.*Scrip*.1 (*Opettex* 12:23)

Robt.Bas.*Form.praedic*.26 (Charland 264–65)

Matt.4:6

Joh.Pal.*Civ.dom*. (Mansi 29: 1111)

Henr.Oyt.*Ver.cath*.3 (*Opettex* 16:24)

Gers.*Auct.conc*.7.1 (Glorieux 6:118)

See pp. 14–15 above

to one or another of the degrees of catholic truth." These "degrees of catholic truth" included not only what was asserted in so many words by the Scriptures but also what had to be "concluded from this by a clear process of reasoning," even though it might not be explicitly stated. As for claims of nonscriptural tradition or of extrascriptural revelation, these were not normally binding on the church as a whole, unless they were validated "either by a miracle or by Sacred Scripture and especially by the church." The proper procedure for anyone in the church was to move "through the church to Scripture and to its understanding . . . , not through the authority of the Scriptures to the church." The prerogatives of "binding" and "loosing" granted to Peter through him to the church extended not only to absolution but to the determination of which books belonged in the canon and which did not. Thus the very Scripture whose "sole" authority was being pitted against that of the church depended for its authentication on the church. All Scripture with this authentication could claim equal inspiration by the Holy Spirit and therefore equal authority. Satan, in the temptation of Christ, had cited the authority of Scripture, but had interpreted it in a false way, thereby demonstrating the need to stick to that interpretation of Scripture which had been publicly and universally taught in the church. It was in this sense that apostolic authority consisted of both Scripture and church tradition, since no catholic truth was completely "outside" Scripture. And so if, in order to resolve the schism, there were a council "of both obediences," such a council could lay claim to apostolic authority for its interpretations of Scripture.

Those who espoused this more conservative view of the tradition as the authoritative interpretation of Scripture rather than as the continued expansion of scriptural revelation were, however, hard pressed to defend not only the developing Mariology of the time, which undeniably went beyond Scripture, but also a tradition that seemed not to supplement, but to contravene, the authority of Scripture, indeed of Christ himself: the denial of the chalice to the laity in Holy Communion. It had seemed obvious to such theologians as Thomas Aquinas and James of Viterbo that

Jac.Vit.*Quodlib*.3.26 (Ypma 3: 277–78)

Hs.*Ep*.95 (*Pram*.14:215)

Hs.*Ep*.141 (*Pram*.14:294–95)
Bartoš (1925) 9
Joh.Rag.*Utraq*. (Mansi 29: 761);Nicol.Cus.*Ep*.7 (Faber 2–I:19)

Joh.Rok.*Utraq*. (Mansi 30: 269)

Luke 14:16 (Vulg.)

Jac.Mis.*Salv*. (Ryba 116)

Jac.Mis.*Utraq*.1.28 (Hardt 3: 487)

Jac.Mis.*Utraq*.2.6 (Hardt 3: 540)

Matt.5:19

Nicol.Dr.*Utraq*.1 (Hardt 3: 594)

Civ.Prag.*Ep*.xi.1431 ap.Joh. Rag.*Boh*.80 (*MC* 1:164)
Joh.Rag.ap.Laur.Reich.*Diurn*. 3.iv.1433 (*MC* 1:337);Joh.Rag. *Utraq*. (Mansi 29:862)

Nicol.Cus.*Ep*.2 (Faber 2–II: 7v)

Gers.*Serm*.241 (Glorieux 5: 477)

the institution of Christ made the use of both the host and the chalice necessary for the perfection of the Sacrament. The charge that therefore the administration of the Eucharist under only one species violated the perfection of the Sacrament became an issue when John Hus, in the last months before his death, finally urged that "the communion of both species" be reestablished and that "not custom, but the example of Christ," be normative. Under the leadership of "the second founder of the Hussite movement," Jakoubek ze Stříbra, whom critics rightly identified as "the first to violate the universal practice of the church," i.e., communion under only one species, the Hussites set out to prove that "the communion of the divine Eucharist under both species, namely, bread and wine, is of great value and aid to salvation and is necessary for the entire people of believers, and it was commanded by our Lord and Savior." Christ himself was the "certain man" in the Gospel who had prepared a supper and invited guests to it; therefore those who accepted his invitation were obliged to receive the supper as he had instituted it, under both species.

Communion under only one species was "elevating the tradition and custom of modern prelates above the apostolic and evangelical tradition," indeed, above "the evangelical traditions instituted by the Lord Jesus" himself. If Christ had forbidden his followers to "relax one of the least of these commandments," how much more strictly must the church observe his commandments pertaining to this Sacrament and not alter them on the basis of some human tradition. The church had not received from Christ the power to repeal or modify his statutes. Advocates of communion under one species agreed that the fundamental issue was the authority of the church. Since the church was the body of Christ and was directed by his Spirit, it did have the right to change the mode of administering his Sacrament, just as it had the right to change it back again, which is what it eventually did do, though only temporarily, in the *Compacts* of the Council of Basel. Even when there was no warrant in the text of Scripture alone for such a change as the withholding of the chalice, the usage of the church and its tradition constituted sufficient grounds to justify the change. When communion under both species had been the usage of the church, reception under only one was wrong; now that the church prescribed one species, the original practice was wrong. For the undisputed fact of Christ's having instituted the Eucharist under both species did not constitute a "precept" in the strict sense, whose transgression brought guilt and damnation. What was a "precept" in this sense was the command to celebrate and to offer the sacrifice of the Mass, which must be under the species of both bread and wine, but this pertained only to those who did the celebrating and sacrificing, that is, to the priests.

Despite an occasional attempt to prove from New Testament references to "communion in the breaking of bread" in connection with "the doctrine of the apostles" that communion under only the species of the bread had been "apostolic practice and that of the primitive church," even the Council of Constance had already acknowledged that the faithful had received under both kinds in the primitive church, and the chief need was to explain that usage and to justify the subsequent change. Some suggested that the reception under both kinds in the early church had rested on an excessively literalistic reading of such statements as the words of Christ, "Unless you eat the flesh of the Son of man and drink his blood, you have no life in you," which caused "many to err by communicating under both sacramental species." Early Christian practice, in particular the recorded lives of the hermits who had gone for years without receiving Holy Communion, proved that the primitive church did not take such statements of Christ as precepts that must be obeyed. Yet the question had to be asked, "What moved the more recent church to change the pristine practice?" to which even an advocate of communion under one species replied that it had happened because "devotion decreased and diminished with the growth of evil" in the church. When the love of the church was at its peak, believers communicated often and under both species; when it was only warm, they received more rarely and by means of intinction; and now that it was merely tepid, they received even less often and under one species. Thus "the usage was commensurate with the love of the church."

Joh.Rag.Utraq. (Mansi 29:834)

Seg.Utraq.ap.Seg.Hist.conc.
Bas.12.29 (MC 2:1085–86)

Joh.Rag.Utraq. (Mansi 29:824–25)

Acts 2:42

Joh.Rag.Utraq. (Mansi 29:743)

CConst.(1414–18) Act.13
(Alberigo-Jedin 418–19)

John 6:53
Andr.Brd.Utraq.5 (Hardt 3:405)

Seg.Utraq.ap.Seg.Hist.conc.
Bas.12.37 (MC 2:1103–4)

Andr.Brd.ap.Jac.Mis.Utraq.2.18 (Hardt 3:556)

Nicol.Cus.Ep.3 (Faber 2–II:10v;13r)

Nicol.Dr.*Utraq*.2 (Hardt 3: 599)

Andr.Brd.*Utraq*.6 (Hardt 3: 405)
Leo M.*Ep*.43.5 (*PL* 54:279)

Jac.Mis.*Salv*. (Ryba 134–36)
Jac.Mis.*Utraq*.2.1;1.36 (Hardt 3:530;502)

Joh.Rok.*Utraq*. (Mansi 30: 300)

Nicol.Dr.*Utraq*.3 (Hardt 3: 601)

Civ.Prag.*Ep*.xi.1431 ap.Joh.
Rag.*Boh*.80 (*MC* 1:167)

Nicol.Cus.*Ep*.2 (Faber 2–II: 6v)

Gers.*Ver.cred*. (Glorieux 6: 182);Gers.*Vit.spir*.2 (Glorieux 3:138)

See vol.1:303

Aug.*Ep.fund*.5 (*CSEL* 25:197)

Gabr.Bl.*Obed.apost*.1
(Oberman-Zerfoss 74–76)

Henr.Oyt.*Ver.cath*. (*Opettex* 16:11–12)

All.*Reg*. (Du Pin 1:692);All.
*Leg*. (Du Pin 1:666);Seg.*Mod*.
77 (Ladner 60)
Guid.Terr.*Infall*. (*Opettex* 2: 17–18)

But if both species had been the norm in the primitive church, as Constance admitted, it should be so now, insisted the advocates of the restoration of the chalice. As for the argument that ancient heretics such as Nestorius and Pelagius had communicated under the two species, the answer, on the basis of "Augustine," was that "at one time those who ate the body of Christ under the form of the bread and did not drink his blood under the form of the wine were suspected of Manichean heresy." The primitive church was stronger and it observed the use of both species; therefore it was "appropriate to be conformed in matters of faith to the primitive church." In the administration of the Sacrament every priest was to follow the pattern of the primitive church, but those who denied the chalice to the laity were in effect hereticizing anyone who strove to imitate "what the holy apostles of our Lord Jesus Christ believed and taught." Fundamentally, then, the dispute came down to two basically divergent definitions of what made the church "apostolic." As an adversary of the Hussites accurately stated their position, "you say that first of all one must obey the commandment of Christ, and only then that of the church," while for him and for those who stood with him such a disjunction was unthinkable. The church was truly apostolic because of its undoubted succession from the apostles and its unbroken adherence to apostolic truth.

The classic formulation of this latter definition of the apostolicity of the church and of its relation to apostolic Scripture was the frequently quoted dictum of Augustine: "For my part, I should not believe the gospel except as moved by the authority of the catholic church." It appeared, for example, near the beginning of Gabriel Biel's *In Defense of Apostolic Obedience* as proof that "the truth that holy mother church defines or accepts as catholic is to be believed with the same veneration as if it were expressed in Holy Writ." It could be used to show that without the authority of the church Christians could not trust even the truths of Scripture. Critics of papal hegemony cited the formula to refute the equation of Rome with the universal church, while advocates of papal infallibility also found support in it, as did the ad-

Jul.Ces.*Disp.Bas.* (Mansi 30:
661);Joh.Rag.*Auct.conc.*5
(*DRTA* 15:217)

Andr.Brd.*Utraq.*13 (Hardt 3:
413);Joh.Rok.ap.Laur.Reich.
*Diurn.*10.iii.1433 (*MC* 1:322)

Nicol.Cus.*Ep.*2 (Faber 1–II:
7v);Joh.Rag.*Utraq.* (Mansi 29:
784;855)

Andr.Brd.*Orig.Hs.* (*FSA* 6:
345–46);Joh.Rag.*Utraq.*
(Mansi 29:713–14)

Gers.*Vit.spir.*2 (Glorieux 3:
139)

Gers.*Aufer.*12 (Glorieux 3:302)

Gers.*Sens.lit.* (Glorieux 3:335)

Gers.*Ver.cred.* (Glorieux 6:182)

Gers.*Utraq.* (Glorieux 10:58)

Gers.*Utraq.* (Glorieux 10:67)

Matt.28:20

Gers.*Ex.doct.*1.1 (Glorieux 9:
459)

vocates of conciliar supremacy. In the dispute over communion under both species, the defenders of one species as well as the defenders of two claimed to be proceeding on the basis of Augustine's principle. One of its most frequent applications was to the question of the canon, in opposition to the idea of "Scripture alone," as evidence that it was the church that had determined the content of the same Scripture now being quoted against it. From the determination of the canon it was a logical step to see in the formula also the authorization for the church to decide the right interpretation of Scripture.

These versions of the Augustinian axiom all found a voice in the thought of Jean Gerson, who managed, in the course of references to it spanning most of the first quarter of the fifteenth century, to sound practically all the variations on the theme of apostolicity with which we have been dealing here. In 1402 he cited the axiom as evidence of how much greater the authority of the primitive church was than that of pope or council or church now. In 1409 it was proof that the final appeal in all matters, whether of faith or of action, was to the church. In 1413–14 it stood as a refutation of the arbitrary right of the private interpretation of Scripture. In 1416 he was using it to argue for the mutual interdependence of church and Scripture, neither of which could gain credence without the other. In 1417 it served to validate the authority of the church to discriminate between those books of the New Testament that were authentically apostolic and those that were not, as well as to urge that individual theologians subject their private opinions to the public doctrine of the church. And in 1423 he found in it a paraphrase of the promise of Christ to be with his church, which therefore possessed "a not unequal authority" to that of the gospel. But by the first quarter of the sixteenth century there had arisen a new understanding of the gospel, and therefore of the church, and therefore of apostolicity, that was to compel the redefinition of all of these—and eventually of Christian doctrine itself.

# 3

# The Gospel as the Treasure of the Church

The two phenomena of the fourteenth and fifteenth centuries described in the preceding chapters—the pluralism of late medieval doctrine and the demand for the reformation of the church—came together in the life and teaching of Martin Luther and in the Reformation. Not since Augustine had the spiritual odyssey of one man and the spiritual exigency of Western Christendom coincided as they did now. It had not been his "will or intention" to elevate his own private theological concerns to the status of doctrinal issues affecting the entire church, and he long professed the conviction that what he had "discovered" was something that the best theologians of the church must have known all along. The eventual realization that such was not the case precipitated his theology into the public forum of the church, both through the condemnations of his teachings and through the incorporation of those teachings into official confessional statements during and after his own lifetime. It was the young Luther whose ideas were the beginning of the Reformation, and it is therefore the young Luther on whom most Reformation scholars properly concentrated when they "reversed the long-established order and interpreted the creeds and confessions of the Reformation in the light of the teaching of the Reformers, instead of adapting the dynamic faith of the Reformation to the doctrines of the creeds." What interests us in this history of church doctrine, however, is the "publica doctrina" of Luther's Reformation: set down in part by Luther himself and his

Luth.*Pr.op.lat.* (WA 54:180)

Luth.*Latom.* (WA 8.45)

Pauck (1961) 334

127

colleague Philip Melanchthon; formulated in part by
the confessional generation of Lutherans who followed them in the second half of the sixteenth century; but also articulated in part by other Protestants,
such as John Calvin and Heinrich Bullinger, who
shared with Luther many (though by no means all)
of the doctrinal emphases being described here.

At the heart of the church doctrine that came out
of Luther's Reformation was the axiom he enunciated
in 1517: "The true treasure of the church is the most
holy gospel of the glory and grace of God." As it
stood, the axiom echoed the language of theologians
East and West throughout the centuries, none of whom
would have questioned it. Yet all the decisive terms
in this axiom—such words as "church," "gospel," and
"grace"—came to mean something in the sixteenth
century that many of these theologians would not
quite have been able to recognize or acknowledge.
Luther himself admitted as much when, in explaining
it, he observed that "the gospel of God [as he had
learned to understand it] is something that is not very
well known to a large part of the church" and something that he had not learned from the scholastic theologians. Therefore his followers preferred to be called
"Evangelicals," even though they noted that "nowa-
days you call 'Lutherans' those who have the gospel
of Christ." The components of his "gospel of the
glory and grace of God" and the reasons that it alone
was for him "the true treasure of the church" made
Luther a Reformer of church and dogma and made
his Reformation an important chapter in the history
of Christian doctrine.

### Divine Justice and Human Righteousness

The immediate context for Luther's statements, indeed the specific occasion both for his own religious
struggle and for his theological attack on conditions
in the church, was, however, neither of the developments set forth in earlier chapters, neither doctrinal
pluralism nor ecclesiology as such, but "the failure of
confession," whether as an answer to his own quest
for certainty or as a sacrament of the church. "Without [penance] none of the sacraments is of any use to
sinners," as a twelfth-century theologian had said; on

Luth. *Disp.indulg.*62 (WA 1:
236)

Cont.*Just.* (CCath 7:29–30)

Luth. *Res.disp.indulg.*62 (WA 1:
616)

Luth. *Res.Lips.* (WA 2:414)

Buc. *Caen.* (Strasbourg 1:23)

Bgn. *Conjug.episc.* (1525:B5r;
G1r);Henr. VIII. *Coerc. Luth.*
(1523:A4v–B1r)

Bainton (1950) 54

See vol.3:210

See p. 95 above

CTrid.(1545–63) *Decr*.14.5
(Alberigo-Jedin 707);Grop.
*Enchir*.2 (1547):117r–117v);
Grop.*Cap.inst.* (1549:F6v–F7r)

CLater.(1215) *Const*.21
(Alberigo-Jedin 245)
*Corp.Jur.Can.:Decr.Greg.IX*.5
38.12 (Friedberg 2:887)

Matt.4:17(Vulg.)

Dns.Scot.*Ox*.4.16.1.7
(Wadding 18:421)

Gabr.B1.*Can.miss*.2.G
(Oberman-Courtenay 1:20–21)

Gabr.Bl.*Can.miss*.26.F
(Oberman-Courtenay 1:244)

Gabr.Bl.*Can.miss*.8.A;85.P
(Oberman-Courtenay
1:58–59;4:111)

the other hand, as a fifteenth-century theologian had seen, none of the sacraments was more vulnerable to the doubts about the priesthood and about sacramental validity that were an unavoidable consequence of the schism and corruption infecting the church. Yet now it was not so much the state of the priest as the state of the penitent that was the problem.

As the uses of its language in the sixteenth century suggest, the turning point in the medieval history of the doctrine of penance was the decree of the Fourth Lateran Council in 1215: "All believers of both sexes who have attained the age of discretion must faithfully confess their sins in person at least once a year to their own priest, and must make the effort to carry out the imposed penance according to their ability." This decree was incorporated into canon law, and it helped to shape the preaching and piety of the late Middle Ages (as well as such literary works as "The Pardoner's Tale" of Geoffrey Chaucer and Passus V of William Langland's *Piers Plowman,* whatever the status of the "pardon" in this scene may have been). As it evolved in the pastoral practice of the church and in doctrinal reflection on that practice, the sacrament of penance, often called simply "confession," had come to concentrate on the preparation and the attitude of the penitent as he stood before the tribunal of divine justice. The word "Repent [Μετανοεῖτε]," with which, according to the Gospels, the preaching of Jesus was inaugurated, was translated as "Do penance [Penitentiam agite]." Duns Scotus and his followers recognized that what made such "penance" a sacrament was not the penance of the sinner, whether understood as his penitent sense of contrition or as his penitential acts of confession and satisfaction, but the divine absolution pronounced by the priest. For there had to be the assurance that it was God who did the absolving. A corollary of this assurance was the recognition that the priest could not know what the judgment of God was about the apropriate penance for a particular sin. Nor, on the other hand, could the priest know whether or not the contrition and confession of the penitent were sincere; for that matter, the penitent himself did "not have a consciousness or sense" even of every mortal sin, as was proved by the prayer of

Ps.19:12(Vulg.)
Eccl.9:1(Vulg.)
Barth.Pis.*Quad*.2 (1498:A6v)

Gabr.Bl.*Can.miss*.31.C
(Oberman-Courtenay 1:315)

See pp. 33–34 above

Gabr.Bl.*Sent*.1.17.1.2.2.D
(Werbeck-Hofmann 1:416)

See pp. 17–19 above

Gabr.Bl.*Sent*.1.17.1.2.3.F
(Werbeck-Hofmann 1:417)

Oberman (1971) 119–41

Ast.*Can.paen*. (Schmitz 1:800)
Ps.100:4(Vulg.)

David, "Cleanse me from my secrets," and by the statement of Solomon, "A man does not know whether he is worthy of love or of hatred."

Before a God to whom all hearts were open, all desires known, and from whom no secrets were hid, the sinner did his penance and made his confession, "not so that [God] would change his judgment in response to our prayer, but so that by our prayer we might acquire the proper disposition and be made capable of obtaining what we request." For when God forgave sin, this did not signify a change in him, but in the sinner. God could, of course, by his "absolute will," forgive sins without human penance or prayer; but it was his ordinance that "no one can be beloved and acceptable to God for eternal life without having in himself a certain infused quality, which is charity or grace." As the polemic against "modern Pelagians" of the fourteenth and fifteenth centuries indicates, such an emphasis on the infused quality of charity or grace in the sinner as the indispensable presupposition of acceptability to God stood in need of defense against the charge that it was a relapse into "the error of Pelagius, who taught that God must necessarily give eternal life to someone who performs an act that is morally good, and that the necessity is not of his grace, but [of his justice], in such a way that if he did not grant it, he would be unjust." God was not subject to some superior authority, not even to his own justice, but his "absolute will" was sovereign. Yet he could, by his "ordered will," enter into a covenant by which he promised that "he would not deny his grace to those sinners who did whatever lay within their powers to do."

It was the ordered will of God that had established the sacrament of penance, together with all the other sacraments. By the ordinance of his sacramental covenant, God required that the sinner could not become acceptable to divine justice without the confession of his sins, in accordance with the word of the psalm, "Enter his gates by confession." Despite the emphasis on the objectivity of absolution as the essence of the sacrament, therefore, the subjective state of the penitent was, on the basis of the ordered will of God, decisive for each of the three components of the sacrament: contrition, confession, and satisfaction. John Fisher, who a decade or so later was to become a spokesman of the case against Luther, published in 1508 a sermonic exposition of the penitential psalms. In it he contrasted the "wholesome penance" of David and of Mary Magdalene (whom he identified with the "woman taken in adultery" of the Gospel pericope) with the penance of Judas, whose suicide was a "bitter and shameful kind of satisfaction" that was of no benefit to him "because he wanted hope and despaired of forgiveness." The ground of penance was, in those who had just begun living the Christian life, "a fear of punishment, which arises from self-love," but in those who had progressed it was "a love of God and of righteousness," becoming "a dislike of sin more because it is against God and righteousness than because it is a cause of punishment." Pastorally as well as theologically, however, this was bound to raise enormous difficulties, as the question of a prominent fifteenth-century penitential theologian suggests: "Is a confession valid if it has been made by someone who is not contrite, who does not sorrow sufficiently for his sins or does not intend to refrain from them in the future?" To clarify the question, he quoted, from Thomas Aquinas, the distinction between the two kinds of sorrow as, respectively, attrition, arising from self-love, and contrition, arising from love of God and of righteousness. But neither he nor other authorities on penance provided "ways of telling whether an individual's sorrow at a particular time is attrition or contrition by classifying his motivation."

For although the distinction was aimed at the sinner who was improperly or insufficiently contrite, it was Luther's experience that "no one is sure of the integrity of his own contrition," and that consequently there could be no assurance of forgiveness based on the quality or quantity of one's contrition, which could never be worthy or sufficient. Divine justice, the attribute of God by which he rewarded the obedient and punished the disobedient, was too absolute in its demands and too transcendent in its holiness to be satisfied by the works of attrition or even of contrition, or by any other human works of piety and morality. To be "holy" meant to be "separated" and set

Fish.*Pen.Ps*.1 (1508:A5r)

Fish.*Pen.Ps*.2 (1508:C6r)
Fish.*Unic.Magd.* (1519);Caj.
*Nov.Test.*12.2 (1530:M3r–M4v)
John 8:3–11

Fish.*Pen.Ps*.4 (1508:H1r)

Gabr.Bl.*Sent*.4.14.1.3.7.DD
(Werbeck-Hofmann 4–I:445)

Ant.P.*Conf*.1.2.5 (1490:17v)
Thos.Aq.*Sent*.4.17.2.2.ad 3
(Mandonnet 4:866–67)

Ant.P.*Conf*.1.2.5 (1490:19r);
Fish.*Pen.Ps*.2 (1508:C6r),Fish.
*Confut*.6 (1523:182)

Tentler (1977) 262

Luth.*Disp.indulg*.30 (WA 1:
234)

Luth.*Grnd.Urs*.14 (WA 7:385–
87)

Luth.*Ps.grad*.130:3 (WA 40–
III:344–37)

Luth. *Magn.*49 (WA 7:575)

Luth.*Jes.*6:2 (WA 31–II:48)

Luth. *Zn. Geb.*pr. (WA 16:399–400);Luth.*Gal.*(1535) 4:30 (WA 40–I:687)

Luth.*Oper.Ps.*9:9 (WA 5:301)

Luth.*Rom.*2:8 (WA 56:196)

Luth.*Latom.* (WA 8:104)

*Disp.Vinar.*12 (1563:211–12)

Luth.*Ps.90.*pr. (WA 40–III:486)

Luth.*Ps.90:*8 (WA 40–III:554)

Luth.*Ps.90:*2 (WA 40–III:513)

Luth.*Ps.90:*3 (WA 40–III:517)
Luth.*Pred.*9.iii.1522 (WA 10–III:1)

Luth.*Ps.90:*7 (WA 40–III:536)

See vol.1:52–54

Luth.*Konz.* (WA 50:590)

See vol.1:249–51

Isa.28:21(Vulg.)

apart from everything that was profane and sinful, and the holiness of God meant that "God alone is holy, but the whole people and whatever the people do are completely defiled." Before the judgment of God even so outstanding a saint as Bernard of Clairvaux had to acknowledge that his righteousness could not withstand the divine justice and that he could not have confidence in his own holiness. Indeed, "if [Christ] were to judge men in accordance with his justice and equity, who would be able to stand before his tribunal, regardless of how holy he might be?" Nor was it only Luther's individual experience of the justice of God that he claimed to be articulating here, but the experience of the psalmists and prophets of the Bible, as the exegetical provenance of these statements indicates.

In the language of the Bible, God's justice against sin was called "the wrath of God," or, as Luther called it, "the wrath of his severity." The wrath of God was an even graver consequence of sin than was the corruption of sin itself, bringing with it as it did the curse of God and the punishment of death. Nowhere in the Bible did Luther find the doctrine of the wrath of God more profoundly stated than in Psalm 90, traditionally ascribed to Moses, who was here "Moses at his most Mosaic, that is, a stern minister of death, God's wrath, and sin," and who in this psalm expressed "all that can possibly be said about man's tragic condition." Since God was eternal and omnipotent, "his fury or wrath toward self-satisfied sinners is also immeasurable and infinite." The psalm referred wrath directly to God the Creator, ascribing "both good and evil to the one God." Although death was a fate that man shared with all other creatures, human death was unique because it was a consequence of sin and of divine wrath. With the expositors of the Christian doctrine of God since the ancient church, Luther affirmed the metaphysical absoluteness of the divine nature, which could not die or suffer or be wrathful. But as he affirmed this in order to go on immediately to the declaration that, by the communication of properties, God in Christ had really suffered and died, so he also insisted that the wrath of God was real— the "alien work of God," to be sure, in the sense that

Apol.Conf.Aug.12.51 (Bek.261)

Luth.Gal.(1535) pr. (WA 40–I: 49)

"God's own proper work is to quicken and console," but only too real to the terrified conscience in the presence of divine justice.

Luth.Dtsch.Kat.1 (Bek.560); Luth.Gal.(1535) 3:6 (WA 40–I: 360);Bgn.Annot.1 Thess.1:8 (1524:51r);Bgn.Bed. (1525: B4r)

Yet the reality of the wrath of God was the supreme illustration of the principle that "the trust and faith of the heart alone make both God and an idol. If your faith and trust are right, then your God is the true God. . . . For these two belong together, faith and God." For "as one believes, so one has." Hence the conscience of the sinner, in the face of a justice that made absolute demands but that had rendered impossible the fulfillment of such demands, confronted a God who nevertheless commanded: "Attribute jus-

Luth.Serv.arb. (WA 18:677)

tice to me." As "the eternal and immutable judgment of God, whose accusation and assault you will not easily endure," this divine justice created "horrible

Luth.Gen.42:26–28 (WA 44: 503)

torments of the heart and fury of conscience." In these torments or "terrors of a conscience that feels God's wrath against our sins and looks for forgiveness of

Apol.Conf.Aug.4.142 (Bek.188)

sins and deliverance from sin," it was worse than useless to speak of doing whatever lay within one's powers to do, or to lay claim to a merit that supposedly

Apol.Conf.Aug.4.20 (Bek.163)

had been earned by such natural powers. Rather, one had to recognize that one was dealing with the hidden mystery of God, whose will was past all finding out and whose predestinating omnipotence was beyond all bargaining. God did not foreknow anything con-

Luth.Serv.arb. (WA 18:685)

tingently, but "by his unchangeable, eternal, and infallible will he foresees and proposes and accomplishes

Luth.Serv.arb. (WA 18:615) Luth.Dict.Ps.18:11 (WA 3: 124);Luth.Serv.arb. (WA 18: 685);Zw.Ver.fals.rel.3 (CR 90: 643);Zw.Gen.17:1 (CR 100:99)

everything." This was "God the hidden [absconditus] and transcendent," whose holiness and justice man could not know by his own natural powers. What is more, man in his fallen state could not know himself accurately either; nor could he adequately understand the demands of divine justice, much less satisfy them. Hence "through the law comes the

Rom.3:20 Luth.Gal.(1519) 4:27 (WA 2: 555)

knowledge of sin,' and for this reason also the disturbing of one's conscience." While men apart from this revelation attempted to measure the actions of God on the basis of human law and to require that God do what seemed right to them or stop being God, such a way of judging was nothing but a "doctrine of

Apol.Conf.Aug.4.288 (Bek.217)

reason"; for, quite the other way around, it was the function of divine law to declare what was right in

Apol.Conf.Aug.4.79 (Bek.176)

Apol.Conf.Aug.12.34 (Bek. 257–58)

Luth.Gal.(1535)3:19 (WA 40– I:485)

Luth.Gal.(1535) 2:16 (WA 40– I:231)

Luth.Latom. (WA 8:109);Zw. Ver.fals.rel.8 (CR 90:702)

See vol.3:143
Gabr.Bl.Can.miss.57.0
(Oberman-Courtenay 2:407)

Camp.Depr.stat.eccl.2 (CT 12: 10–11)

Coch.Luth.art.2 (CCath 18: 27)

the sight of God and thus to reveal the wrath of God against sin. Far from bringing confidence and assurance, the law brought only accusation and terror to the conscience, "the terrible and indescribable wrath of God," for the law was "the word that denounces sin." The law was indeed an illumination, but "a light that illumines and shows, not the grace of God or righteousness and life, but the wrath of God, sin, death, our damnation in the sight of God, and hell." Such an awareness of divine judgment, which brought knowledge of oneself through the revelation of the law of God, was the basis of authentic repentance.

This authentic repentance stood in contrast to "the fictitious penance of the scholastics, as it is taught to this hour." The public discussion of penance did not come, in the first instance, out of Luther's own struggle to discover the meaning of righteousness and justification, nor out of any other dogmatic concern of his, but from his attacks on usages associated with the third step of the sacrament of penance, the rendering of satisfaction and the use of indulgences as a means of doing so. Although the idea of satisfaction as the restoration of that which sin had taken away had been a part of the penitential practice and doctrine of the church since early centuries, it was recognized that there had been "little or no use of indulgences" during those centuries. Even when writing against Luther, the defenders of indulgences had to acknowledge that indulgences had been handled "scandalously and very foolishly," and also that they had been developed as a necessary expedient, "when the love and devotion for doing penance [through acts of penance and self-denial] grew increasingly cold," so that "through indulgences many of the people might be moved and prompted to repentance and sorrow . . . who would otherwise not have made confession or done penance." The "use of indulgences" eventually became an almost indispensable component of the church's disciplinary and pastoral program, through such devices as the promise of plenary indulgence attached to the preaching of the Crusades; as such, indulgences belong to the history of canon law and of church administration (and also, as the trilateral deal between the Holy See, Albrecht of Brandenburg, and the banking house of Fugger was to show, to the tangled history of church finances). Strictly speaking, there was not yet a mature "doctrine" of indulgences. In fact, the statement of such a doctrine to which collections of sources, whether Roman Catholic or Protestant, have continued to refer as the standard formulation was itself provoked by Luther and the Reformation and was issued as a bull by Pope Leo X on 9 November 1518; but each of its component doctrinal elements had long been a part of the church's official teaching.

In his bull the pope cited the danger that some might use an "ignorance of the doctrine of the Roman church regarding indulgences and their efficacy" as a pretext for opposing or denying what the church taught. The basis of indulgences was the familiar idea of the special authority of the pope as the successor of Peter and the vicar of Christ on earth, an authority conveyed in the words of Christ to Peter granting him the power to bind and loose. That power, although it had been a justification in the controversies between church and state for the pope to install and to depose temporal rulers, was conceded by a Marsilius of Padua to apply to the forgiveness of sin. If sin was to be "loosed" through the exercise of the authority of the church, there must be a method of coping with both of the consequences that the commission of sin entailed, defined by Anselm and others as the guilt incurred by sin and the punishment merited by sin. The sacrament of penance—in which "by virtue of contrition our sins are forgiven, by confession they are forgotten, but by satisfaction they are so cleanly done away with that no sign or token remains"—was the divinely instituted means of grace for dealing with the guilt.

But to deal with what Pope Leo called "the temporal punishment for actual sins that was owed in accordance with divine justice," the church had instituted indulgences. They were a way of remitting the temporal punishment by applying to the penitent "the superabundance of the merits of Christ and the saints," whose holy lives had earned divine merit far in excess of their own requirements. By its authority to bind and loose the church had the power to transfer, from this "treasure" of merits, the remission of tem-

Denzinger-Schönmetzer 356–57;Mirbt-Aland 503–4

Leo X.*Cum post.* (*Ed.Leon.*11: 469)

Matt.16:19
See pp. 82–83 above

Mars.Pad.*Def.pac.*2.6.3 (Previté-Orton 161)

Ans.*Cur d.h.*1.11 (Schmitt 2: 68–69)

Fish.*Pen.Ps.*2 (1508:C2r)

Gabr.Bl.*Can.miss.*58.L (Oberman-Courtenay 2:423–24)

poral punishment to the sinner. The temporal punishment included not only that endured "in this present life," but also that borne "in purgatory," and hence the bull spoke of an "indulgence both for the living and for the departed." This was in accordance with the doctrine formulated in the preceding century at the Council of Florence as part of the reconciliation of the Eastern and Western churches, that those penitents who had not been able to render proper satisfaction for their sins in the present life could be "cleansed by the punishments of purgatory after death." One way to mitigate those punishments of purgatory was by the granting of indulgences on behalf of the departed.

Luther's attack on indulgences, while occasioned by certain abuses and excesses associated with the selling of indulgences in 1517, was finally directed against the system of indulgences itself, not merely against a distortion of the system. The immediate target of his statement that "the true treasure of the church is the most holy gospel of the glory and grace of God" was the claim that there was a "treasure" of merits of Christ and the saints upon which the church was authorized to draw for the remission of punishments. He "did not know at the time" about the financial transactions underlying the indulgence traffic, and he expressed the wish that "indulgences be preached according to the spirit and intention of the pope," which would remove the abuse and misunderstanding. But what he did know was that "the pope cannot remit any guilt except by declaring and showing that it has been remitted by God," and that there was a conflict between "the bounty of indulgences" and "the need of true contrition." The summons of the inaugural preaching of Jesus, therefore, could not mean that the sinner should merely "do penance" by going through the steps of contrition, confession, and satisfaction (including indulgences), as prescribed by the law of the church. On the contrary, "when our Lord and Master Jesus Christ said, 'Repent,' he willed the entire life of believers to be one of repentance."

The component elements of the doctrine of indulgences all came in for revision or, eventually, for rejection. As his opponents were able to prove, Luther

See vol.2:279

CFlor.(1439)*Def.* (Alberigo-Jedin 527)

Luth.*Disp.indulg.*62 (WA 1:236)

Luth.*Disp.indulg.*58 (WA 1:236)
Luth.*Pr.op.lat.* (WA 54:180)

Luth.*Disp.indulg.*91 (WA 1:238)

Luth.*Disp.indulg.*6 (WA 1:233)

Luth.*Disp.indulg.*39 (WA 1:235)

Matt.4:17

Luth.*Disp.indulg.*1 (WA 1:233);Luth.*Thes.Antinom.*3.7 (WA 39–I:350);*Apol.Conf.Aug.* 12.132 (*Bek.*280);*Zw.Ver.fals. rel.*7;8 (CR 90:695;702–3)

See pp. 250–51 below

Zw. *Wort.* (CR 92:820–21);Zw.
*Bek.*3 (CR 93–II:239–40)

Luth.*Grnd.Urs.*37 (WA 7:450–51);Luth.*Res.disp.indulg.*15
(WA 1:234)

Clebsch (1964) 93

2 Macc. 12:43–45

Luth.*Feg.*1 (WA 30–II:369);
Frth.*Disp.purg.* (1531);Buc.*Ep.
apol.* (Strasbourg 1:107);Calv.
*Theol.Par.*17 (CR 35:28)

1 Cor. 3:15

Luth.*Feg.*4 (WA 30–II:378);
Frth.*Disp.purg.* (1531)

Apol.*Conf.Aug.*12.16;12.26
(*Bek.*255–56)

Luth.*Pr.op.lat.* (WA 54:180)

Luth.*Pr.op.lat.* (WA 54:184)

Luth.*Res.disp.indulg.*52 (WA 1:
603)

went on asserting for years after the indulgence conflict that he had "never denied the existence of a purgatory." But in 1530 he published his *Disavowal of Purgatory,* and shortly thereafter his English disciple, John Frith, issued his own *Disputation of Purgatory,* which "articulated Frith's full thought on the topic and presented a well-reasoned understanding of Luther's conception of justification by grace alone through faith." These treatises, on the basis of an examination of the proof texts for the idea of purgatory, came to the conclusion that the "cornerstone" among these, the account of the "sin offering" by which Judas Maccabaeus "made atonement for the dead, that they might be delivered from their sin," lacked authority because the book in which it appeared did not properly belong to the canon of Scripture, while others, such as the statement of the New Testament that a man "will be saved, but only as through fire," did not refer to purgatory at all, but to the fire of opposition through which the preaching of the gospel must pass here in this life; the weight of patristic exegesis in favor of purgatory could not decide the question. It was "clearly false and foreign to the Holy Scriptures as well as to the church fathers" to promise that "by the power of the keys, through indulgences, souls are delivered from purgatory." When he prepared the ninety-five theses on indulgences, Luther was certain, as he recalled later, "that in this case I should have a protector in the pope"; but, partly as a consequence of this controversy, he concluded that the "human right" by which he conceded jurisdiction to the pope, "unless it be founded on divine authority, is a diabolical lie."

It is evident from this autobiographical preface to his collected Latin writings, published the year before his death, that Luther came to the controversy over indulgences from his own personal struggles over the demands of divine justice, and that in his doctrinal development the public concern and the personal concern coalesced. Indulgences were not only scandalous but dangerous, because they tended "to take away from men the fear of God and through indulgences hand them over to the wrath of God," and all this in the name of remitting "the temporal punishment for

Leo X. *Cum post. (Ed.Leon.*11: 469)

Rom.1:17(Vulg.)

Luth.*Pr.op.lat.* (WA 54:185)

Luth.*Gal.*(1519) 2:21 (WA 2: 503)

Luth.*Pr.op.lat.* (WA 54:186)

Bgn.*Chr.gl.* (1527:33)

Rom.1:17(Vulg.)
Hab. 2:4

Aug.*Spir.et litt.*9.15 (CSEL 60: 167)

Rog.*Cath.Doct.*11.3 (PS 40: 115)
Oec.*Rom.*1:17 (1526:10v–11r)

See pp. 353–59 below

actual sins that was owed in accordance with divine justice." Inevitably, such manipulation appeared to Luther to be a trivialization of the divine justice whose awesome meaning he had been probing in Scripture. There he had pondered the enigmatic statement of the apostle Paul, that "the justice of God is revealed in" the gospel. Believing that this referred to "the active justice of God," which dispensed rewards and punishments, both temporal and eternal, in accordance with what the sinner deserved, Luther perceived such a "gospel" to be a condemnation, not a consolation: "Did God have to heap misery upon misery by the gospel, and by the gospel threaten us with his justice and wrath?"

He found an answer to his question in a "new definition of justice," when he concluded that the justice of God revealed in the gospel was "passive justice," with which God invested the sinner through faith in Christ, as the complete verse from Paul declared: "For the justice of God is revealed in [the gospel] from faith to faith, as it is written: 'The just lives from faith.'" For this definition he found some corroboration in Augustine, who had spoken of divine justice as "not that whereby he is himself just, but that with which he endows man when he justifies the ungodly." This rendering of the gospel was what Luther meant when, in his attack on the indulgence traffic, he identified "the most holy gospel of the glory and grace of God" as "the true treasure of the church." The message of the gospel was the doctrine of justification by faith.

## Justification by Faith

Although Luther's "discovery" of justification by faith took place in the struggle of his own conscience as it sought an answer to the question, "How do I obtain a God who is gracious to me?" the doctrine of justification by faith was to become one that "all churches reformed, with a sweet consent, applaud, and confess," including those churches that opposed Luther on many other points. Thus the seventeenth-century Reformed followers of John Calvin knew that they disagreed with the followers of Luther on many questions, but they recognized that all of them

*Conf.Aug.*20.8 (*Bek.*159);Mel.
*Annot.Rom.* (*CR* 15:445);Calv.
*Inst.*(1559) 3.11.1 (Barth-
Niesel 4:182)

Calv.*Sad.* (Barth-Niesel 1:469)

*Marb.Art.*5 (*WA* 30–III:179–
80);*Cons.Send.* (Niemeyer
554);*Bez.ap.Coll.Mont.Bell.*5
(1588:187);*Decl.Thor.*4.1
(Niemeyer 673)

Blngr.*Grat.just.* (1554)

Blngr.*Grat.just.*3.1. (1554:49v)

Blngr.*Dec.*3.9 (1552:155r)

See pp. 17–19 above

Luth.*Oper.Ps.*17:13 (*WA* 5:
485)

Luth.*Rom.*5:12 (*WA* 56:309–
10)

Luth.*Gal.*(1519) 2:16 (*WA* 2:
489);Luth.*Pr.Brent.Amos* (*WA*
30–II:650)

See vol.1:289–90

Ps.51:5

Luth.*Ps.51:*5 (*WA* 40–II:384)

*Conf.Aug.*2.3 (*Bek.*53)

See pp.225–26 below

agreed on this doctrine as the foundation of the entire
Reformation, in fact, the chief doctrine of Christianity and the chief point of difference separating
Protestantism from Roman Catholicism. Repeatedly,
the various efforts in the sixteenth and seventeenth
centuries to unite Lutheran and Reformed teachings
were able to affirm this doctrine as one that they
shared, diverge though they did on other doctrines.
It was a Swiss Reformed theologian, Heinrich Bullinger, who, in the title of a book published in 1554
and dedicated to the Lutheran king of Denmark,
managed to include all the constituents of this common confession more trenchantly than any one title
had: *The Grace of God that Justifies Us for the Sake
of Christ through Faith Alone, without Good Works,
while Faith Meanwhile Abounds in Good Works.* In
it he defended the Protestant doctrine against "writings that are not so much insulting as they are
wicked." For, as he said elsewhere, justification was
"the head and foundation . . . of evangelical and apostolic doctrine."

The presupposition for the doctrine of justification
was a vigorous reassertion of Augustinian anthropology. Joining himself to the criticism leveled by late
medieval Augustinianism against "the new Pelagians,"
Luther identified Pelagianism as the one perennial heresy of Christian history, which had never been fully
exterminated and which, under the patronage of the
church of Rome, had now become dominant. He used
his exposition of the Epistle to the Romans to rehearse
Augustine's polemic against Pelagius and the Pelagians,
and he noted three years later that Augustine had been
at his best as an interpreter of Paul when he was writing in opposition to the Pelagians. Commenting on
the most important proof text for Augustine's doctrine of original sin, "Behold, I was brought forth in
iniquity, and in sin did my mother conceive me," he
declared that he "did not yet know this teaching when
I had been a doctor of theology for many years," so
Pelagian were his theological professors. Hence it is
clear that in condemning "the Pelagians and others,
who deny that original sin is sin," those who spoke
for Luther had in mind the adherents of various
confessional camps who minimized the power of sin;

for "what is the difference between the Pelagians and

*Apol.Conf.Aug.*18.2 (*Bek.*311)

our opponents?"

That rhetorical question occurred in the introduction to a discussion of the doctrine of free will—an indication of how important the question of the freedom of the will had become, especially as a consequence of the exchanges between Luther and Erasmus. Luther accused Erasmus of reviving the Pelagian heresy, in fact of going even beyond it, in his willingness

Luth.*Serv.arb.* (*WA* 18:678; 664)

to ascribe freedom to the fallen will of man, and he declared that "the Pelagians alone would have prevailed against everyone if the conclusion of [Erasmus]

Luth.*Serv.arb.* (*WA* 18:675)
Eras.*Lib.arb.*1.b.2;4.17 (Walter 12–13;91)

were to stand." Erasmus claimed to have on his side the teaching of the church fathers over the centuries, in contrast to the unheard-of doctrine of Luther, whose

Eras.*Lib.arb.*1.b.2 (Walter 13)
Eras.*Lib.arb.*1.a.10 (Walter 9–10)

See pp. 32–33 above

only precedent lay in Manicheism (which Luther sought to repudiate) and in the teachings of Wycliffe (which Luther had made his own). Erasmus identified the difference between Pelagianism and orthodoxy as consisting in opposing views about whether or not man continued to require the grace of God to attain

Eras.*Lib.arb.*2.a.3 (Walter 21–22)

salvation. Putting himself on the side of those "who

Eras.*Lib.arb.*4.16 (Walter 90)

ascribed something to free will, but the most to grace," he noted that "those who are the furthest removed from the opinion of Pelagius attribute the most to grace, but almost nothing to free will, but they do not abolish it altogether," for they still left to the will

Eras.*Lib.arb.*2.a.12 (Walter 30)
Eras.*Aug.*pr. (Allen 2157)

a certain "striving and effort." Erasmus yielded to none in his admiration for Augustine, and he was able to present his own doctrine of free will as a version

Eras.*Lib.arb.*2.a.10 (Walter 27–28)

of the Augustinian doctrine, since Augustine had, with more or less success, attempted to posit the freedom

See vol.1:301–2

of the will after the fall.

The criticisms of Augustine's success in this attempt that were heard during and immediately after his own

See vol.1:320–23

lifetime had the intent of making free will and moral responsibility less ambiguous than he had left them, and the medieval discussions of Augustinianism had also usually been aimed at salvaging the freedom of

See vol.3:82–84

the will. At the hands of Luther, however, the uneasy combination of the Augustinian doctrine of sin and grace with a declaration of free will was resolved in the opposite direction. Luther accused the scholastics of treating Augustine's doctrine of "grace alone" as

Luth.*Disp.schol.theol.*1 (*WA* 1:224)

Luth.*Ep.Joh.*4:15 (*WA* 20:753)

Luth.*Ep.Joh.*5:4 (*WA* 20:776)

Luth.*Gen.*18:2–5 (*WA* 43:14)

Luth.*Disp.schol.theol.*8–11 (*WA* 1:224)

Luth.*Grnd.Urs.*36 (*WA* 7:455); Calv.*Nec.ref.* (*CR* 34:483); Calv.*Theol.Par.*2 (*CR* 35:9)

See vol.1:301

Aug.*Pelag.*1.2.5 (*CSEL* 60:425–26)

Luth.*Serv.arb.* (*WA* 18:636)

Luth.*Serv.arb.* (*WA* 18:752)

Luth.*Gen.*26:9 (*WA* 43:463); Form.*Conc.S.D.*2.44 (*Bek.*889)

Ec.*Enchir.*31 (*CCath* 34:313)

an exaggeration, and he charged that as a result "Augustine has to this day not been accepted by the church of Rome"; but he himself went on to criticize Augustine for having said so little about faith, although at other times he did see in Augustine something of a predecessor of his own doctrine of justification by faith. He opened his *Disputation against Scholastic Theology* with a spirited defense of Augustine, arguing (against the Manicheans) that the human will was not "evil by nature, that is, essentially evil," but then going on immediately to insist (against Scotus and Gabriel Biel) that it was "nevertheless innately and inevitably evil and corrupt" and therefore "not free to strive toward whatever is declared good." Augustine became the patron for the teaching of the Reformation that free will existed in name only, not in reality. Now Augustine had at times expressed himself this way, particularly against the Pelagians; but when they pressed him on the question and accused him of denying that man after the fall possessed free will, he reaffirmed his position that "free will did not perish in the sinner," since the sinner committed his sin by his own free will, not by external force, much less by divine necessity. Luther, on the other hand, was not afraid to maintain in his polemic against Erasmus that "we do everything by necessity and nothing by our free will, since the power of the free will is nothing and neither does the good nor is capable of it in the absence of grace," and he confined free will to "natural matters, such as eating, drinking, procreating, governing" and the like.

In later years, notably in his *Lectures on Genesis*, Luther apparently sensed the need to moderate this Manichean-sounding language, upon which his opponents had seized as proof that in seeking to avoid the extreme of Pelagianism he had "resuscitated the once-dead Manichean heresy" instead. The moderating of his language seems to have come none too soon. For in the *Lectures on Genesis* he also had occasion, in commenting on the creation story, to set forth his interpretation of the doctrine of the image of God, an interpretation whose potential implications were far-reaching. While he was engaged in his controversy with Erasmus, he was also preaching on

Genesis; there he contrasted the doctrine of the "image of the Trinity" as formulated by "our teachers ancient and modern," especially Augustine, with "the simple statements and way of speaking of Scripture," which explained the image of God on the basis of the parallel between the first Adam and Christ as the second Adam. That same contrast provided the basis for a fuller statement of the idea of the divine image in the later lectures. While here he did not "condemn or find fault with" the Augustinian and scholastic concepts that the image of God was an image of the Trinity, he did question their usefulness, "especially when they are subsequently spun out further, for there is also added a discussion concerning free will, which has its origin in that image." In this later exposition, as in the earlier sermons, he emphasized that Adam's state as one who was created in the divine image was no longer even intelligible to fallen man, who had no experience of it; much less was it correct to say that the image was still present, for "it was lost through sin in Paradise." Luther's "understanding of the image of God is this: that Adam had it in his being and that he not only knew God and believed that he was good, but that he also lived a life that was wholly godly; that is, he was without the fear of death or of any other danger, and was content with God's favor." All of that was lost and would be fully restored only after Judgment Day. In its place had come death and the fear of death, blasphemy, hatred toward God, and lust: "These and similar evils are the image of the devil, who stamped them on us."

The fateful introduction, here in Luther's *Genesis*, of the notion of an "image of the devil" in man in place of the "image of God," directed as it was against the peril that the doctrine of the image of God and of the freedom of the will as part of the content of that image would glorify human powers at the expense of grace and thus jeopardize the doctrine that the role of the human will in conversion was "purely passive," provided a follower of Luther in the next generation, Matthias Flacius, with the warrant to define original sin as "the image of the devil, contrary to the image of God." Because "the rational soul and especially its noblest substantial powers, namely, the intellect and

Luth.*Decl.Gen.*1:24–27 (*WA* 24:49)

Luth.*Gen.*1:26 (*WA* 42:49)

Luth.*Gen.*1:26 (*WA* 42:45–46); Mel.*Enarr.symb.Nic.* (*CR* 23: 255–56);Zw.*Klar.* (*CR* 88:344–45)

Luth.*Gen.*1:26 (*WA* 42:47–48)

Flac.ap.*Disp.Vinar.*6 (1563: 112)

Flac.*Essent.imag.*42 (1570:70)

Eras.*Hyp.*2 (*LB* 10:1454) Flac.ap.*Disp.Vinar.*7 (1563: 132;134)

Flac.*Clav.* (1628–II:637);Flac. ap.*Disp.Vinar.*3 (1563:60);Flac. *Essent.Imag.*58 (1570:93–94)

the will, which previously had been so brilliantly fashioned that they were the true image of God, . . . have now, by the deception of sin, been so completely inverted that they are the true and living image of Satan," original sin had become the "substance" of human nature, and, as "Scripture and Luther affirm," was not simply an "accident" that adhered to man but did not change his essential nature. For as a well-known Reformation hymn taught, "through Adam's fall the nature and substance of man is totally destroyed." In opposition to Anselm's definition of original sin as the lack of original righteousness, Flacius insisted that it was not merely privative but was a positive "acquisition of evil." Although the *Augsburg Confession*, as a brief summary of doctrine, had not explained this fully, "need and confession now require us to distinguish more accurately." Flacius sought to document his teaching with a catena of quotations from Luther, particularly of course from *The Bondage of the Will,* and to disengage it from the Manichean view of evil, as well as from the "Stoic view of predestination," on the grounds that these ancient errors had made sin a consequence of creation rather than of the fall.

So radical a version of Luther's doctrine of sin had become necessary, in Flacius's judgment, because, under the "corrupting" influence of philosophy, some who claimed to follow Luther had gravely compromised his doctrine. In the thought of Philip Melanchthon, who sometimes attacked the teaching of Erasmus but who also tried unsuccessfully to mediate between Erasmus and Luther on the freedom of the will, "the doctrine of the natural light [of reason] is the fundamental philosophical doctrine." Despite his earlier endorsement of Valla's denial of free will, therefore, he and his disciples eventually rejected Valla's position as "Manichean," seeking to set their view apart from both "the Pelagian and the Manichean blasphemies." The hardening of Pharoah's heart by God was "permissive, not causative." For in those who were converted there must be something that set them apart from those who refused to be converted. And in a formulation that was to become a focus of the controversy, Melanchthon identified three causes of such

Flac.*Clav.* (1628–II:639)
Flac.ap.*Disp.Vinar.*2;3 (1563: 33;50);Flac.*Essent.imag.*75 (1570:143)

Speng.*Ld.*71.1 (Wackernagel 3: 48)
See vol.3:112–13

Flac.*Clav.* (1628–II:636)

Flac.ap.*Disp.Vinar.*7 (1563: 135)

Flac.*Clav.* (1628–II:641–45); Flac.ap.*Disp.Vinar.*1;3 (1563: 24;49–50)
Flac.ap.*Disp.Vinar.*4;6 (1563: 75;114)

Flac.*Hist.* (1549:D3v)

Flac.*Clav.* (1628–II:660;636)

Flac.ap.*Disp.Vinar.*4 (1563:83)

Mel.*Enarr.Symb.Nic.* (CR 23: 206–7)

Mel.*Ep.*22.vi.1537 (CR 3:383)

Dilthey (1957) 171
Mel.*Loc.*(1521) (Plitt-Kolde 70)

Mel.*An.* (CR 13:158);Mel.*Loc.* (1535–41) (CR 21:373)
Strig.*Hum.vir.*1;3–4 (Schlüsselburg 5:52–53;60–66)
Ex.4:21
Mel.*Explic.Symb.Nic.* (CR 23: 392)

Mel.*Loc.*(1533) (CR 21:332)

Strig.ap.*Disp.Vinar.*5;13 (1563: 100;236);Pez.*Lib.arb.* (Schlüsselburg 5:102)

Pez.*Lib.arb.* (Schlüsselburg 5: 92)

Strig.ap.*Disp.Vinar.*2;4;6;11 (1563:38;82;115;199)

Strig.ap.*Disp.Vinar.*2 (1563:30; 45)
Strig.ap.*Disp.Vinar.*3;7 (1563: 52–53;134)
Strig.ap.*Disp.Vinar.*9 (1563: 169)
Strig.ap.*Disp.Vinar.*12 (1563: 219–20)
Strig.ap.*Disp.Vinar.*12 (1563: 215)
*Apol.conf.Aug.*18 (*Bek.*311–13)
Strig.*Hum.vir.*6 (Schlüsselburg 5:70–75)
Flac.ap.*Disp.Vinar.*10 (1563: 180)
Strig.*Disp.Vinar.*8 (1563:151)
See vol.1:325–27
Hes.*Confut.Syn.*1 (Schlüsselburg 5:330–31)
Strig.*Hum.vir.*5 (Schlüsselburg 5:66);Strig.ap.*Disp.Vinar.*2;3;4; 8;10 (1563: 40;71;151;175)

See vol.3:156
Brd.Clr.*Grat.*1.2 (Leclercq Rochais 3:166)
Strig.*Hum.vir.*2 (Schlüsselburg 5:55–56)

Strig.ap.*Disp.Vinar.*3 (1563:61)
Strig.*Decl.* (Schlüsselburg 5: 88–90)

Strig.ap.*Disp.Vinar.*1;2;4 (1563:22;37;74)
Strig.ap.*Disp.Vinar.*10 (1563: 183)
Strig.ap.*Disp.Vinar.*13 (1563: 234)
Ams.*Vict.* (Schlüsselburg 5: 548);Hes.*Anal.Vict.* (Schlüsselburg 5:516)
*Conf.sent.Wit.* (Schlüsselburg 5:528);Buc.*Ep.apol.* (Strasbourg 1:92);Strig.*Hum. vir.*5;8 (Schlüsselburg 5:69;86)

Strig.ap.*Disp.Vinar.*6 (1563: 119)

Strig.*Hum.vir.*7.10 (Schlüsselburg 5:81)

conversion: "the word, the Holy Spirit, and the human will assenting to the word of God rather than resisting it." The basis of this modification of Luther's doctrine was the contention that "the total image of God has not been destroyed and altogether abolished in the fall of man, as many falsely contend."

Melanchthon's pupils, particularly Victorinus Strigel, while uncomfortable with the harsh language of Luther's *Bondage of the Will*, also laid claim to Luther's teaching as expressed in "many passages" of his other writings and in his lectures at Wittenberg, and to Melanchthon's teaching as expressed not only in his private theological writings, which had received Luther's enthusiastic commendation, but in official confessions such as the *Apology of the Augsburg Confession*. Moreover, the Greek and Latin fathers also supported a doctrine of free will, and, despite Flacius's charges of "Pelagianism," it was not Pelagian to agree with them. Prosper of Aquitaine, whose interpretation of Augustine was "pleasing" also to the anti-Melanchthonians, was a prime authority for a doctrine that sought to preserve grace and free will simultaneously. The familiar axiom of Bernard, "Take away free will, and there is nothing that needs to be saved; take away grace, and there is nothing to save it," preserved them both in an "erudite" fashion. Flacius's doctrine, on the other hand, was "following the opinion of Manicheus." For man still did possess the "capacity" to respond to divine grace, and there still was a distinction between man, who could act "freely," and the other creatures, which could act only "naturally." Hence it was a mistake to make no distinction between man and the devil, to speak of the human response as "purely passive," or to use the favorite metaphor of opponents such as Amsdorf and Heshusius and to describe the human condition before conversion as that of "a stump or a stone"—an "insulting" term and one "filled with blasphemy." For if men were not able to assent to the word of God, they could not be held accountable for refusing to assent. "Grace abolishes merit," not in the sense that "we do not do anything at all," but in the sense that "we do not satisfy the law and are still far from perfection." Therefore free will remained the "substance" of hu-

man nature, namely, its intellect and will, while original sin was an "accident."

Confronted by a choice between a doctrine of creation in the image of God that implied free will as a
factor in conversion and a doctrine of the fall that
implied a replacement of the image of God by an
image of Satan, which had now become the "substance" of human nature, the confessional generation
of Lutherans, who laid claim to Luther's "continuing
position," strove to set forth "the doctrine in accordance with the analogy of the word of God . . . and
purged of all errors, whether Pelagian or Manichean."
Despite its superficial similarity to Luther's doctrine,
the denial of free will by Valla was in error, because
it obliterated all contingency and led to a "Stoic" fatalism. There was an "ambiguity" in such terms as
"substance" and "nature." But if the term "substance"
was meant in the technical Aristotelian sense, it was
unacceptable to speak of original sin as the "substance" of human nature; for Scripture "distinguishes
between original sin and the person or subject," and
"even after the fall, human nature is God's creature
and handiwork." Luther had spoken of original sin
as he had in order to indicate that even if one were
to commit no actual sins, his nature and person would
still be sinful. Through the fall "we have all sinned in
Adam and have lost the image and glory of God,"
and with it the freedom "to choose in spiritual matters." Yet the main concern of the doctrine was to
preserve Luther's insistence on the absolute need for
grace. Before conversion there were "only two efficient causes, namely, the Holy Spirit and the word of
God as the Holy Spirit's instrument whereby he effects conversion"; there was no third cause in the
human will. All of this was not divine "necessity or
coercion," as Strigel had charged, but it was divine
monergism.

It was this divine monergism that was at stake for
Luther not only in the controversy with Erasmus, but
in his disputes with scholasticism and in his biblical
commentaries. It had as its corollary the exclusion of
any notion of merit as the basis for man's relation to
God, and specifically the rejection of "the fictitious
distinction between merit of congruity and merit of

Strig.ap.*Disp.Vinar*.8 (1563: 144)

*Form.Conc.S.D*.1–2 (*Bek*.843–46)

Chyt.*Pecc.orig*.20 (Schlüsselburg 2:238)

*Form.Conc.S.D*.1.3 (*Bek*.846); Hutt.*Comp*.8.8 (1728:104–5)

Chem.*Loc*.7 (1604–I:426)
Chyt.*Pecc.orig*.20;pr. (Schlüsselburg 2:236;227)

Chyt.*Pecc.orig*.15 (Schlüsselburg 2:233)

*Form.Conc.S.D*.1.34 (*Bek*.855)

*Form.Conc.S.D*.1.5 (*Bek*.846–47)

Chem.*Loc*.8.3 (1604–I:566)

Hes.*Anal.Vict*. (Schlüsselburg 5:514)

*Form.Conc.Epit*.2.19 (*Bek*.781)
Strig.ap.*Disp.Vinar*.5;11 (1563: 93;203)

*Form.Conc.S.D*.2.60 (*Bek*.896)

Apol.Conf.Aug.4.19 (Bek.163);
Luth.Gal.(1535) 2:16 (WA 40–
II:223)

Gabr.Bl.Can.miss.59.N
(Oberman-Courtenay 2:440–
42)

Luth.Serv.arb. (WA 18:770);
Calv.Rom.3:27 (Parker 76)

Gabr.Bl.Can.miss.59.N
(Oberman-Courtenay 2:442)

Oberman(1963) 170

Luth.Gal.(1535) 2:16 (WA 40–
II:224)

Apol.Conf.Aug.4.108 (Bek.274)

Matt.5:11–12,46;6:4,6,18

Luth.Matt.5–7.conc. (WA 32:
542–44);Calv.Conc.acad.
(Barth-Niesel 1:6)
Luth.Serv.arb. (WA 18:693–
96);Bgn.Annot.Col.1:15 (1524:
34v);Mel.Comm.Rom. (CR 15:
541–42);Zw.Schl.20 (CR 89:
178–79);Calv.Nec.ref. (CR 34:
486–87);Hunn.Just. (1590:191–
93)

Luth.Latom. (WA 8:107–8)

Conf.Aug.15.3 (Bek.69–70)

Conf.Aug.26.2–4 (Bek.100–
101)

Luth.Gal.(1519) 2:21 (WA 2:
503)

Blngr.Sum.9.2 (1556:160v)
Apol.Conf.Aug.4.73 (Bek.174–
75);Mel.Comm.Rom. (CR 15:
504)

condignity": What a sinful man did for himself, insofar as he was able, was defined as merit of fitness or congruity ("meritum congrui" or "meritum de congruo"); what a just man, enabled by divine grace, did for himself or others was defined as merit of worthiness or condignity ("meritum condigni" or "meritum de condigno"). The idea of merit, whether of congruity or of condignity, was a relapse into Pelagianism, according to Luther. Biel had defined the merit of congruity as dependent "not on a debt of justice, but only on the generosity of the one who accepts it," that is, of God, or, as he said elsewhere, "not on the basis of a preceding pact, but of sheer generosity"; thus it was a "semi-merit," as a modern scholar has termed it. But for Luther "there is no 'congruity' or work performed before grace, but only wrath, sin, terror, and death." Justification was the very antithesis of merit, whether before grace or in a state of grace, and passages in the Scriptures that spoke of "reward," for example the Sermon on the Mount, were to be interpreted in the light of the principle that "grace and merit are mutually exclusive": Scripture used "rewards" as a means of admonishing and comforting the faithful with the knowledge that their obedience to the divine will was truly pleasing to God.

The principal antithesis of the doctrine of justification, for Luther as for "the simple and Pauline way" of speaking on which he claimed to base his doctrine, was that between salvation by grace through faith and salvation by good works. In the setting of the dispute over indulgences this stricture against works applied with special severity to "human traditions instituted to propitiate God, merit grace, and make satisfaction for sins," all of which were "opposed to the gospel and the doctrine of faith." The proliferation of these human requirements about works that were thought to earn the favor of God had "obscured the grace of Christ and the doctrine of faith." Yet the stricture was not confined to such human works but included all works, "even those of God's most holy law." To perform divinely commanded works on the supposition that God would grant salvation in exchange for them was to commit sin and to be alienated from God. The "exclusive particles" employed in the Pauline epistles,

Rom.3:28;Eph.2:9

Luth.*Rom*.3:27–28 (WA 56:264)

Luth.*Serv.arb*. (WA 18:772)

Strig.*Hum.vir*.7.1
(Schlüsselburg 5:75–76)
See p. 18 above
Rom.9:16(Vulg.)
Hes.*Confut.Syn*.9
(Schlüsselburg 5:348);Luth.
*Serv.arb*. (WA 18:716);Calv.
*Inst*.(1559)2.5.17 (Barth-Niesel
3:316–17);*Form.Conc.Epit*.2.6
(*Bek*.778)

*Conf.Aug*.20.1 (*Bek*.41)

Luth.*Gut.Werk*. (WA 6:275)

Luth.*Gut.Werk*.(WA 6:211)

Luth.*Gen*.12:4 (WA 42:452)

Luth.*Matt.5–7*.5:8 (WA 32:327–28)

phrases such as "apart from works of law" or "not because of works," defined the quest for justification: "never to stand still and never to rest in accomplishment; not to regard any works as if they had ended the search for righteousness, but to wait for this end as if it dwelt somewhere beyond one's reach." The righteousness of faith did not consist of any works whatever, but of the favor of God, without which even the most righteous of works were not righteous at all. Although the champions of the freedom of the will tried to buttress their position even with the favorite passage of the anti-Pelagians, "It is not of him that wills, nor of him that runs, but of God who shows mercy," there was "nothing that more vigorously opposes the fictitious cooperation [synergia] of man than this passage."

Such unconditional denials of the efficacy of works, including the good works of believers, in establishing the right relation between God and man were, almost inevitably, accompanied by the protestation: "Our teachers are falsely accused of forbidding good works." Luther's *Treatise on Good Works* was an exposition of the Decalogue, setting forth the specific good works enjoined by each commandment but closing with the insistence "that faith must be the foreman behind this work. Without faith no one is able to do this work. In fact, all works are entirely comprised in faith." For "if righteousness consists of faith, it is clear that faith fulfills all commandments and makes all its works righteous." Faith was not opposed to good works; on the contrary, it was only by the righteousness of faith that one could be set free from the anxiety of seeking to appease the wrath of God by works and could go on for the first time to perform good works, as the example of Abraham's faith made evident. The good works of faith were works for the benefit of "the neighbor," now that it was no longer necessary to perform them for one's own benefit or to gain the favor of God.

As a technical term for the establishment (or reestablishment) of the right relation between God and man, "justification" was largely confined to the Pauline epistles, and there principally to the epistles to the Romans and Galatians (on both of which Luther commented extensively and, in the case of Galatians, repeatedly). But the content of the doctrine of justification was, for Luther, the universal teaching of all the Scriptures, both of the Old Testament and of the New. Hence he praised the Gospel of John as a masterpiece in its exposition of the doctrine of justification and found it unique in its presentation of this doctrine side by side with the Trinity and the person of Christ, even though neither the term "justification," nor for that matter even the term "faith" as a noun, appeared there. But when Christ in that Gospel said, "He who believes has eternal life," this text was, according to Luther, "the cornerstone of our justification." For the issue was not one of terminology, but of the gospel message, whose doctrine of "justification" was synonymous with the gift of "eternal life," to which this text referred, and with "the forgiveness of sins." The principle that one was to regard nothing as the theology of Luther that could not be reduced to a simple corollary of the forgiveness of sins was undoubtedly an exaggeration, but it was an exaggeration that conformed to Luther's own estimate of the decisive place of forgiveness in all doctrine and, above all, in the doctrine of justification. The one thing that Scripture taught was that life was possible only "under the forgiveness of sin," without which the church and Christianity itself would fall. The testimony of Scripture and the personal experience of the believer joined to identify the forgiveness of sins as "the very voice of the gospel."

By defining justification as the forgiveness of sins, Luther emphasized even more sharply its gratuitous character. The scholastic doctrine of merit, whether "of congruity" or "of condignity," was guilty of "usurping the right that belongs to Christ alone. Only" he delivers from sin and grants righteousness and eternal life." The prayer of the psalmist for mercy and forgiveness was the negation of such merit or of any other claim that the sinner might seek to put forward; for it "disentangles him not only from his own righteousness but also from the wrath of God," placing the entire transaction between God and man outside the realm of human striving. Far from being merely the removal of sin in its guilt and power, the for-

Luth.*Ev.Joh.*6–8.6:53 (WA 33: 200)

Luth.*Ev.Joh.14–15.*pr. (WA 45: 468)

John 6:47

Luth.*Ev.Joh.*6–8.6:47 (WA 33: 161)

*Apol.Conf.Aug.*4.76 (*Bek.*175); *Form.Conc.Epit.*3.7 (*Bek.*783)

Billing (1952) 7

Luth.*Ps.grad.*130:3 (WA 40–III:348)

*Apol.Conf.Aug.*27.13 (*Bek.*381)

Luth.*Gal.*(1535) 2:16 (WA 40–I:236–38)

Luth.*Ps.51:*1 (WA 40–II:341–42)

giveness of sins was a positive force; "for where there is forgiveness of sins, there are also life and salvation." In explaining the fifth petition of the Lord's Prayer, "And forgive us our debts, as we forgive our debtors," Luther was therefore obliged to declare that forgiving others was a "condition" of being forgiven and at the same time to explain that God's forgiveness was "not on account of your forgiving, for God does it altogether freely, out of pure grace, because he has promised it, as the gospel teaches." Although the doctrine of the justification of the sinner was not present in so many words throughout the Scriptures, Luther was able to find it wherever the Scriptures spoke of forgiveness; and in so doing, he was following the precedent of the apostle Paul, who had quoted the words of the Psalms, "Blessed is the man to whom God has not imputed sin," to show that "David pronounces a blessing upon the man to whom God reckons righteousness apart from works."

These texts, together with the text, "God was in Christ, reconciling the world to himself, not imputing [non reputans] their trespasses to them," had given to justification and forgiveness a definition as the non-imputation of sin, a definition that was accepted as valid. But now, by extension this became the positive imputation of faith in Christ as righteousness: As Melanchthon said at the beginning of the Reformation, "all our righteousness is the gratuitous imputation of God." Luther developed this positive definition in extenso. In the doctrine of justification "these three things are joined together: faith, Christ, and acceptance or imputation." Christian righteousness was "a trust of the heart in God through Christ," on account of which "God overlooks sins. This is accomplished by imputation," when for the sake of Christ "God reckons imperfect righteousness as perfect righteousness and sin as not sin, even though it really is sin." He was able to say, quite indiscriminately, "for the sake of our faith in Christ or for the sake of Christ," because the antithesis between faith and works precluded the possibility of attributing to faith a merit that would earn justification. Or, as he said later in the same commentary, "This is the reason why our theology is certain: it snatches us away from ourselves

Luth.*Kl.Kat.*6.6 *(Bek.*520)

Matt.6:12

Luth.*Dtsch.Kat.*3.93–96 *(Bek.* 684–85)

Luth.*Rom.*4:7 *(WA* 56:284); Mel.*Comm.Rom.*(*CR*15:590)

Ps.31:1–2(Vulg.)

Rom.4:6–8

2 Cor.5:19(Vulg.)

Thos.Aq.*S.T.*2.1.113.2 ad 2 (*Ed.Leon.*7:329–30)

Mel.*Annot.Rom.* (*CR* 15:454)

*Conf.Aug.*4.3 *(Bek.*56)

Mel.*Thes.bacc.*10 (Plitt-Kolde 251)

Luth.*Gal.*(1535) 2:16 (*WA* 40–I:233)

Luth.*Gal.*(1535) 3:6 (*WA* 40–I: 367–68)

Luth.*Gal.*(1535) 3:6 (*WA* 40–I: 370)

and places us outside ourselves, so that we do not depend on our own strength, conscience, experience, person, or works, but depend on that which is outside ourselves, that is, on the promise and truth of God, which cannot deceive." Thus justification was both "through Christ" and "through faith," neither without the other. Imputation meant that "God averts his eyes from our sins, yes, even from our righteousness and virtues, and reckons us as righteous because of faith, which lays hold of his Son."

The apparent symmetry between "through faith" and "through Christ" as correlatives could, however, be deceptive, as became evident when it was necessary to specify just what was being imputed. Having asserted that "no one will be justified by any works whatever . . . , but by faith alone," Luther went on to explain that "we must live by alien righteousness," and that "those who know Christ . . . rely . . . on the life and righteousness of Christ alone." The concept of an alien righteousness, the righteousness of Christ, as imputed to the believer in the divine act of justification, meant that, to be quite precise, one would describe justification as taking place "on account of Christ" but only "through faith," with Christ as the ground and faith as the instrument. Although Luther himself was not always so utterly precise as that, those who systematically formulated his teaching explained that in the Epistle to the Romans "'justify' is used in a forensic fashion to mean 'to absolve a guilty man and pronounce him righteous,' and to do so on account of an alien righteousness, namely that of Christ, which is communicated to us through faith." And Luther himself, in the course of an academic disputation, did use the concept of the alien righteousness of Christ, a righteousness "outside ourselves," to prove that justification must be through faith alone, without works, since these could not take hold of such a righteousness.

He found a prophecy of this righteousness of Christ in a locus classicus of the Old Testament for justification, the words of Jeremiah: "The Lord is our righteousness," which stood as proof that the Christ who justified was true God. But this prophecy became, in the next generation, the basis for a conflict between

Luth.*Gal.*(1535) 4:6 (*WA* 40–I: 590)

Luth.*Rom.*5:2 (*WA* 56:299)

Luth.*Gen.*15:6 (*WA* 42:564)

Mel.*Comm.Rom.*(*CR* 15:515)

Luth.*Jes.*11:4 (*WA* 31–II:86)

Luth.*Jes.*11:9 (*WA* 31–II:88)

Apol.*Conf.Aug.*4.305 (*Bek.*219)

Luth.*Disp.just.*27–29 (*WA* 39–I:83)

Ec.*Ev.*Quas.1 (1530–I:92r)

Jer.23:6
Luth.*Gen.*35:6–7 (*WA* 44:184); Mel.*Enarr.Symb.Nic.* (*CR* 23: 223–24);Mel.*Explic.Symb.Nic.* (*CR* 23:367–68)

the forensic understanding of justification as the imputation of an alien righteousness and the identification of the righteousness granted in justification with that of the divine nature of Christ as "the Lord our righteousness." Andreas Osiander had published the articles of agreement coming out of the Marburg Colloquy of 1529, to show that on most major doctrines, and especially on justification, there was consensus among Protestant leaders; among these articles was the statement "that faith is our righteousness before God, for the sake of which God accounts and regards us as righteous, faithful, and holy," but that this was "for the sake of his Son, in whom we believe and thereby receive and participate in the righteousness, life, and all blessings of his Son." It was this second emphasis that Osiander took as his own, directing it against those who had misunderstood Luther's intent. Luther's equation of justification with the forgiveness of sins and with salvation became for Osiander, long before the conflict, another way of asserting that the content of justification was Christ the divine Lord himself; for "what is the forgiveness of sin? Is it not . . . God's Word and God himself?" Christ had thus become "our righteousness," as the apostle taught. It was in the light of these various biblical statements that he interpreted the words about faith being reckoned as righteousness: righteousness was the Lord himself, whose nature was love. Luther's language about righteousness "outside ourselves" was a figurative concession to simple believers. In sum, "If one asks what righteousness is, one must answer: Christ dwelling in us through faith is our righteousness according to his divinity, and the forgiveness of sins, which is not Christ himself, but is earned by Christ, is a preparation and cause of God's conferring on us his righteousness, which is God himself."

Although Osiander cited the authority of Luther's doctrine of justification for this emphasis, his opponents, despite their controversies on many other points, joined to oppose him: a Lutheran opponent such as Matthias Flacius contrasted quotations from Osiander's works with quotations from Luther's works; on the other hand, writing against Flacius, a disciple of Calvin was able to claim that, despite Lu-

See p. 139 above

Osndr.*Mar.*7 (1529:2v–3r)

Osndr.*Mit.* (1551:Zv)

Osndr.*Schatz.* (1525:B2v)

Osndr.*Schatz.* (1525:A4v)
1 Cor.1:30

Osndr.*Mit.* (1551.D3;J3;O2v)
Rom.4:3,5
1 John 4:8

Osndr.*Disp.* (1551:M4v)

Osndr.*Mel.* (1553:03)

Flac.*Gegn.*(1552)

ap.Calv.*West*.3 (*CR* 37:246);
ap.Calv.*Hes*. (*CR* 37:504)

Bez.*Flac*.22–25 (*BezTract* 2:
169)

Men.*Gerecht*. (1552)

Calv.*Inst*.(1559) 3.11.5 (Barth-
Niesel 4:186)

Calv.*Inst*.(1559) 3.11.6 (Barth-
Niesel 4:187);Mel.*Enarr.Rom*.
3:21 (*CR* 15:856–64)

Form.*Conc.S.D*.3.4 (*Bek*.914–
16)
Mel.*Explic.Symb.Nic*. (*CR* 23:
452)

See vol.3:141–43

See p. 164 below

Form.*Conc.S.D*.3.25 (*Bek*.922)
Chem.*Loc*.11 (1604–II:795);
Flac.*Clav*. (1628–I:493)
Jer.23:6

Form.*Conc.S.D*.3.17 (*Bek*.919);
Conf.*Helv.post*.15 (Niesel
245);*Conf.Remon*.18.3 (1622:
59–60)

theran attempts to associate Calvin with Osiander's teachings, "Calvin has detected, refuted, and condemned the illusions of [Osiander] more clearly and solidly than anyone else." The identification of the righteousness of justification with the righteousness of Christ according to his divine nature was a species of "alchemy," which made a metaphysical transformation of created human nature the basis of the new relation between God and man, "a mixture of substances by which God—transfusing himself into us, as it were—makes us part of himself." Osiander was guilty of defining the righteousness of justification as the essential divine righteousness of Christ as Son of God, rather than as the righteousness that came from his priestly act of expiation. The Lutheran *Formula of Concord* of 1577, speaking for most "teachers of the Augsburg Confession," defined Christ as "our righteousness, not according to the divine nature alone or according to the human nature alone, but according to both natures; as God and man he has by his perfect obedience redeemed us from our sins, justified and saved us." The "obedience" of Christ, "for the sake of which we are accepted," was "perfect" because, as several of the "teachers of the Augsburg Confession" came to understand it, it not only rendered passive satisfaction to the punitive justice of God (as Anselm had taught), but active satisfaction to the demands of the law for a perfectly righteous life. This righteousness of Christ was "imputed" to the believer through faith, and that was the meaning of the words in Jeremiah, "the Lord our righteousness." Thus Luther's "forensic" doctrine of imputation, as made precise by Melanchthon, gained dominance in the confessional interpretations of justification (whether Lutheran, Calvinist, or Arminian) over other ways of speaking that could also find a legitimate place within the full range of Reformation thought.

One of the grounds for the objection to Osiander's definition of the righteousness of justification as the essential righteousness of Christ "within us" was its apparent affinity with the scholastic definition of grace as an infused quality in man rather than as the favor of God, as Luther defined grace in his preface to Romans: "Grace actually means God's favor, or the

Luth. *Vor.N.T.* (*WA DB* 7·8);
Calv. *Rom.*4:16 (Parker 93);
Snds. *Serm.*15.6 (*PS* 41:297)

Luth. *Ps.51*:10 (*WA* 40–II:422)
John 1:16

Luth. *Ev.Joh.1–2.*1:16 (*WA* 46:
654)

Luth. *Grnd.Urs.*11 (*WA* 7:375–
77);Bgn. *Chr.gl.* (1527:73)

Luth. *Latom.* (*WA* 8:92)

Luth. *Latom.* (*WA* 8:106)

See vol. 3:114–16

Apol. *Conf.Aug.*4.380–81 (*Bek.*
231–32)

1 Cor.13:13

See vol.3:23–24

Thos. Aq. *S.T.*2.2.4 (*Ed.Leon.*8:
43–53)
Thos. Aq. *S.T.*2.1.55.1 ad 1
(*Ed.Leon.*6:349)

See vol.3:215–16

good will which in himself he bears toward us." He contrasted a definition of grace as "a quality hidden within the heart" with a definition of it as "the continuous and perpetual operation or action through which we are grasped and moved by the Spirit of God." The phrase "grace upon grace" in the Gospel of John distinguished between "two types of grace," the first of them being "the grace of Christ" as "the chief fountain of all grace" and the second being "that grace which we draw from Christ, which he distributes among us." Salvation and forgiveness came solely by the grace of Christ, and "all toil and effort to seek other ways leading to heaven are futile and vain." And so justification meant that mercy and grace were bestowed freely and out of pure mercy, without human effort or achievement. The locus of righteousness was not in the justified believer, but in the mercy of God. Divine grace, therefore, was even "a greater good than that health of righteousness which . . . comes from faith. . . . The grace of God is an outward good, the favor of God, the opposite of wrath." It was an Augustinian consensus that good works were pleasing to God only on account of grace and that therefore believers should place their confidence in the grace of God, but this was vitiated when grace was interpreted as a disposition within man rather than as the unmerited favor and forgiving mercy of God. It was also necessary to add that "whenever this is mentioned, faith should be added, since we take hold of God's mercy, reconciliation, and love toward us only by faith."

A faith that was capable of taking hold of grace and reconciliation in such a way likewise must be correctly defined and understood. As part of the Pauline triad of faith, hope, and love, faith had, at least since Augustine's treatise entitled *Faith, Hope, and Love*, received much of the attention it warranted in the setting of an analysis of the "theological virtues." In addition, "'faith' is sometimes the term for that which is believed," as in a phrase like "the one true faith." Now that it had become necessary to specify precisely what "justifying faith" was, these definitions, not incorrect in themselves, needed deepening and sharpening: "The faith that justifies is no mere historical knowledge,

Apol.Conf.Aug.4.48 (Bek.169);
Mel.Doct.Paul. (CR 11:38);
Zw.Bek. (CR 93–II:194)

Luth.Gal.(1535) 2:16 (WA 40–
I:228–29)

Calv.Rom.4:14 (Parker 91);
Blngr.Sum.6 int.;6.1 (1556:86r;
87r–88r)

Luth.Gal.(1535) 2:16 (WA 40–
I:228–29)

Luth.Kl.Kat.2.3–4 (Bek.511)
Luth.Gal.(1535) 2:21 (WA 40–
I:299);Bgn.Chr.gl. (1527:19–
20)

Luth.Latom. (WA 8:112)

Luth.Kirchpost. (WA 10–I–1:
469)

Apol.Conf.Aug.4.338 (Bek.226)

Luth.Gal.(1535) 3:6 (WA 40–I:
370)

Luth.Rom.4:7 (WA 56:272)
Hermann (1960) 1

but the firm acceptance of God's offer promising forgiveness of sins and justification." Luther set himself against scholastic theology with the simple antithesis: "Where they speak of love, we speak of faith." "Faith" here meant more than virtue or knowledge (though not less). It meant, above all, "a firm trust [fiducia]," for which "Christ is the object of faith, or rather not the object, but, so to speak, the one who is present in the faith itself." Thus faith was "a sort of knowledge or darkness that can see nothing." It was, then, believing "in" Christ; that included, as Luther's exposition of the Apostles' Creed showed, believing "that" the life, death, and resurrection of Christ were historically true—but above all that they were true "for me," a phrase that one was to "accept with a sure faith and apply to himself" without doubting.

At the same time it became necessary to protect these encomia of faith from the impression that they referred to faith as "believing in believing" or that the imputation of faith as righteousness took place apart from Christ as its object and content. In the very course of one of his most telling critiques of scholasticism Luther could warn his reader: "Observe, faith is not enough, but only that faith which hides under the wings of Christ and glories in his righteousness." In a sermon delivered at about the same time, he attacked those among recent scholastic thinkers who located the forgiveness of sins and justification in a sheer act of divine imputation. In opposition he stressed that "against this horrible, terrible interpretation and error, the holy apostle has the practice that he always connects faith to Jesus Christ." It was accurate to say that "faith justifies" or that "faith saves," but only in the sense that faith was the divinely created ability to appropriate the promise of grace in Christ. That was why Luther encountered no difficulty or confusion in teaching that justification was "for the sake of our faith in Christ or for the sake of Christ," since these two phrases meant exactly the same.

The doctrine of justification by faith implied that the justified sinner was, throughout his life, "righteous and a sinner at the same time [simul justus et peccator]," a formula that "contains the whole of the theology of Luther." Its most important biblical basis

Zw.*Klar.* (*CR* 88:351);Calv.
*Rom.*7:15 (Parker 149);Blngr.
*Dec.*3.8 (1552:138r)

was the seventh chapter of the Epistle to the Romans.
The Reformers could cite the precedent of Augustine,
who had previously applied this chapter to Paul the

Aug.*Retract.*2.27.2 (*CSEL* 36:
131–32);Aug.*Pelag.*1.10.18–1.
11.24 (*PL* 44:560–62)

Pharisee but eventually concluded that it must refer
to Paul the Christian, and thus to all Christians. As
he described himself here, "there is the one man Paul,
who recognizes himself to be in two different situa-
tions: under grace he is spiritual, but under the law

Luth.*Latom.* (*WA* 8:119)

carnal. It is one and the same Paul who is under both."
But because that by which the justified sinner could
be called "righteous" was not a righteousness of his

Luth.*Rom.*7:25 (*WA* 56:347)

own, but was "the righteousness of Christ," his confidence must be and remain in the cross. And because
that by which the justified could be called a "sinner"
was his own sin, also after baptism, it was unsatis-
factory to dismiss the "concupiscence" of the baptized
sinner as a "spark of sin [fomes peccati]," for the New

Apol.*Conf.Aug.*2.38–45 (*Bek.*
154–56)

Mel.*Comm.Rom.* (*CR* 15:652–
53);Mel.*Enarr.Rom.*7:22 (*CR*
15:942);Strig.*Hum.vir.*7.9
(Schlüsselburg 5:80);Flac.*Clav.*
(1628–I:153)

Testament called it "sin," and sin it truly was. This
paradox of "righteous and a sinner," which, together
with this interpretation of Romans 7, became a characteristic teaching of Luther's various disciples, became as well one of the distinguishing marks between
his doctrine of justification by faith and even those
Roman Catholic doctrines of justification that seemed

See pp. 283–84 below

to be the closest to his.

## The Theology of the Cross

Although Luther himself never wrote a full-length
exposition of his entire theology and, even when he
undertook "to confess [his] faith before God and all

Luth.*Ab.Chr.*3 (*WA* 26:499)

the world, point by point," did not present a system
so much as a series of statements, he did find a term
to characterize his system of thought. Contrasting the
theologian falsely so called, "who looks upon the invisible things of God as though they were clearly
perceptible in those things that have actually happened," with the authentic theologian, "who comprehends the visible and manifest things of God seen
through suffering and the cross," he labeled the first
system "a theology of glory" and the second "a the-

Luth.*Disp.Heid.*19–21 (*WA* 1:
354)
Ltmr.ap.Rdly.*Conf.Ltmr.*1 (*PS*
39:113)

ology of the cross," or, in the phrase of Hugh Latimer,
"that religion that has the cross annexed to it."
At the basis of the theology of the cross was the
proposition that "God can be found only in suffering

and the cross," so that "he who does not know Christ does not know God hidden in suffering." In a similar vein the early Melanchthon declared that "to know Christ is to know his benefits." The polemical target of both these propositions was a theological method that the authors attributed to scholasticism, which treated the truths of the Christian faith as objects of intellectual curiosity without reference to the cross and benefits of Christ. Specifically, the dogmas of the Trinity and the person of Christ were not an exercise in logical inquiry or metaphysical speculation. Luther ridiculed the scholastics for investigating the relation between the two natures of Christ and branded such investigation as "sophistic." "What difference does that make to me?" he continued. "That he is man and God by nature, that he has for his own self; but that he has exercised his office and poured out his love, becoming my Savior and Redeemer—that happens for my consolation and benefit." For, as Luther said in a sermon of 1525, Christ was not called "Christ" because he had two natures, but because of his office as Savior. And Melanchthon attacked the scholastics for "obscuring the glory and the benefits of Christ" despite the formal correctness of their doctrine about the person of Christ.

It is, however, a gross anachronism to conclude from these statements and from others like them "that in Luther's Reformation the old dogmatic Christianity was abolished" and that with the Reformation "the history of dogma comes to an end." On the contrary, it would be more accurate to see in Luther's Reformation a further stage in the development of "the old dogmatic Christianity," as the Anselmic doctrine of atonement through the satisfaction wrought by the suffering and death of Christ had represented an earlier stage of the development. Working within an Augustinian understanding of sin and grace, Anselm had taken as his starting point the Western reading of the settlement achieved at the Council of Chalcedon: Christ was "the God-man," who was not under the necessity of dying (since he was almighty) nor under the obligation of dying (since he was sinless), but who of his own free will had assumed human nature into the person of the Son of God, so that by his dying

Luth.Disp.Heid.21 (WA 1:362)

Mel.Loc.(1521) (Plitt-Kolde 63)

Luth.Kirchpost. (WA 10–I–1: 147)

Luth.Pred.2.Mos.17 (WA 16: 217–18)

Apol.Conf.Aug.4.3 (Bek.159)

Harnack(1931) 3:861

See vol.1:263–66

he might voluntarily achieve the satisfaction owed by humanity and make it available to his fellowmen (since he did not need it for himself). The communication of the satisfaction of Christ through the means of grace in the church had, however, raised an entire new set of problems, as the late medieval doctrines of salvation and the sacraments demonstrated. Despite some recurring debate over the doctrine of the person of Christ, however, the essential content of the Chalcedonian dogma had stood firm. What the medieval development of the doctrine of redemption required next was not an "abolition" of the "dogmatic Christianity" of Nicea and Chalcedon, but a closer scrutiny of how the "benefits" of redemption were to be appropriated—which was the scope of the passages quoted from Luther and Melanchthon.

Their distinctive account of the means of appropriating redemption, the doctrine of justification by faith, was, at least in the form it took in the theology of the Reformers, a doctrine for which it proved to be extremely difficult to document a continuous history in the ancient church, despite the claim that there was proof for it not only in the Scriptures but also in the church fathers, or, at any rate, that there were "traces [vestigia]" of it. Not only this particular answer to the question of justification, but even the very question of justification itself, was anything but a commonplace in patristic thought, Eastern or Western. This gave the opponents of the Reformation doctrine the opportunity to charge that it was an innovation and hence a violation of the doctrinal tradition. Yet it made sense only if it was seen as a development not only from Augustinian anthropology, as the Reformers sought to demonstrate, but from the dogma of the Trinity. The disengagement of the Reformation doctrine from any theory of "bare imputation" and the emphatic insistence that the only valid object of justifying faith was the person of Jesus Christ as the incarnate Son of God located this doctrine within the framework of trinitarian theology. Perhaps the most precise way of designating the place of the doctrine of the Trinity in the teaching of the Reformers would be to say that for them it remained a fundamental dogmatic presupposition; it was a doctrine they

See vol.3:141–43

See pp. 22–28 above

Mel.*Eccl.* (CR 23:622);Chem. *Exam.CTrid.*1.8.2 (Preuss 162–65)

*Apol.Conf.Aug.*4.29 (*Bek.*165); Blngr.*Dec.*3.9 (1552:158r) Mel.*Comm.Rom.* (CR 15:493; 525),Mel.*Enarr.Rom.* (CR 15: 803)

See p. 253 below

See p. 284 below

See p. 154 above

held in common with the medieval doctors, and hence it was not a direct polemical issue.

Initially, the same appeared to be true of the doctrine of the person of Christ. What the *Augsburg Confession* asserted about the two natures as "so inseparably united in one person that there is one Christ, true God and true man" met with the explicit approval of the appointed critics of the *Confession*, which was in turn acknowledged by its defenders. Sporadic efforts by various Roman Catholic opponents to locate heretical tendencies in the christology of Luther on the basis of some of his obiter dicta proved to be basically unsuccessful. Rather, it was the controversy between the two major parties of Protestantism, the Lutheran and the Reformed, over the real presence of the body and blood of Christ in the Lord's Supper that was responsible for the most detailed Western preoccupation with the intricacies of christology since the ancient church. The confessions of both sides affirmed their loyalty to the orthodox doctrine of the person of Christ as promulgated at the Councils of Ephesus and Chalcedon, while theologians on both sides (as well as on the Roman Catholic) appropriated the anti-Nestorian slogan of the Council of Ephesus in calling the Virgin Mary "Theotokos." Each side, moreover, professed to find in its opponents a parallel to one or the other of the heretical extremes condemned at those councils: Luther took the occasion of a historical examination of Ephesus to brand Ulrich Zwingli a "neo-Nestorian," and Calvin saw it as an unintended implication of the Lutheran doctrine of the real presence "that [Christ's] body was swallowed up by his divinity," which was the "Eutychian" heresy condemned at Chalcedon. The christological controversy went on for a century or so, between Reformed and Lutheran theologians and then among Lutheran theologians themselves.

What precipitated it was the contention, which seems to have been first advanced by Cornelius Hoen, that the ascension of Christ to the right hand of God precluded his bodily presence in the elements of the Eucharist, since it was to the "advantage" of his disciples and of the church in all ages that they should no longer have direct physical access to him. Johan-

*Conf.Aug.*3.2 (*Bek.*54)

*Apol.Conf.Aug.*3 (*Bek.*158)

*Coch.Phil.*1.2.6 (1534:C3r–C4v)

*Conf.Helv.post.*11 (Niesel 238);*Form.Conc.S.D.*8.46 (*Bek.* 1031)
Luth.*Ev.Joh.*14–15.14:16 (*WA* 45:558);Luth.*Magn.*ep.ded. (*WA* 7:545);Oec.*Mis.*5(1527: E2v);Zw.*Mar.* (*CR* 88:399); Blngr.*Dec.*4.6 (1552:235r); Blngr.*Sum.*6.5 (1556:93r); Blngr.*Conc.*1.22 (1561:96r); Bez.*Conf.*3.23 (*BezTract* 1:5); *Form.Conc.S.D.*8.24 (*Bek.* 1024);Diet.*Cat.*3 (1545:Q1v)

Luth.*Konz.* (*WA* 50:591); Andrs.ap.*Coll.Mont.Bell.*6 (1588:233)

Calv.*Inst.*(1559) 4.17.29 (Barth-Niesel 5:384)

See vol.1:259

Zw.*Bgn.* (*CR* 91:560);Zw. *Wort.* (*CR* 92:907–8)

John 16:7

Zw.*Gen.*21:8 (*CR* 100:132)

Ec.*Enchir.*29 (*CCath* 34:290)

Oec.*Dign.euch.*1 (1526:A2v)
Oec.*Ant.*13 (1526:C1r)
Zw.*Amic.exeg.*5 (*CR* 92:695–701)

Oec.*Ant.*11 (1526:B4v)
Oec.*Billic.* (1526:C4v)
Matt.28:20
Oec.*Corp.* (1526:D6v);Zw.*Wort.* (*CR* 92:917–21;951)

Oec.*Antisyn.*47 (1526:N1v)

Zw.*Unt.*2 (*CR* 91:818–19)

Heb.5:7
Cat.*Gen.*1.79 (Niesel 11)

Blngr.*Sum.*8.8 (1556:151v);
Blngr.*Nacht.*2 (1553:D3r)

Blngr.*Resp.Brent.* (1562:6v)

Cat.*Heid.*48 (Niesel 160)

Urs.*Ex.ver.doct.*5 (Reuter 1:843)

nes Oecolampadius, who was regarded as the modern originator of this idea, expanded on Hoen's exegesis. Attacking those "for whom it is not sufficient for the glory of Christ that his holy body is sitting at the right hand of the Father, as it is stated in the articles of the creed on the basis of the Scriptures," he set it forth as a universal consensus and "stable foundation" of sound doctrine that the resurrected body of Christ was in heaven. Here on earth Christ ruled his church with his Spirit and his grace, being "present in his power [virtute]" rather than "in his body." The promise that he would be present with his church until the end of the age did not mean that his body would be present, for "the body of Christ is not everywhere where Christ is." This did not amount to "taking Christ away" or making his body a phantasm, as defenders of the medieval doctrine charged. In sum, Christ was saying: "When you see me ascend up to heaven, you will see clearly that you have not eaten me literally and that I cannot be eaten literally." If the body of Christ was now in heaven, it could not be correct to speak of his corporeal presence in the Sacrament.

Whatever the right way of speaking about that presence might be among all the possible ways, it would not do to disregard the difference between it and the "corporeal presence" by which, in the days of his flesh, he could be said to have been in one or another place. As Bullinger put it, "the body of Christ is in heaven in a state of glory, not here below on earth in a state of corruptibility"; therefore "the body of Christ and his blood cannot be eaten or drunk bodily by the human mouth." For "the heaven into which our Lord was taken up is a certain place, not on this earth nor everywhere, but distinct from the earth, above this corruptible world." The presence of Christ with his church after the ascension was "according to his divinity, majesty, grace, and Spirit," but not according to his human nature which was at the right hand of God. The ascension of Christ was distinct from his sitting at the right hand of the Father, as the language of the Apostles' Creed made clear. Though "severed and removed" from this human nature by "the whole space between heaven and earth," the soul of the be-

Calv.*Inst.*(1559) 4.17.24
(Barth-Niesel 5:376);Calv.*Cn.*4
(Barth-Niesel 1:521);Las.*West.*
25 (Kuyper 1:304–5)

See vol.1:249–51

Bez.*Ep.theol.*60 (1575:269);
Zw.*Wort.* (CR 92:937;940)

John 3:13(var.)

Luth.*Wort.* (WA 23:147);
Andrs.ap.*Coll.Mont.Bell.*7
(1588:332);Grop.*Leyb.*1 (1556:
17r;30r)

Luth.*Wort.* (WA 23:133)

Luth.*Wort.* (WA 23:145)

See p. 202 below

Luth.*Wort.* (WA 23:149–51)

Luth.*Symb.* (WA 50:266–67)

Form.*Conc.S.D.*8.87 (Bek.
1046)

liever was also united with it and nourished by it in the Eucharist.

In response to this argumentation, as stated by Oecolampadius and Zwingli, Luther extrapolated from the orthodox doctrine of the "communication of properties" to ascribe the omnipresence of the divine nature of Christ to his entire glorified person, both divine and human. While his opponents interpreted the passage otherwise, Luther substantiated this use of the communication of properties from the very words of Christ: "No one has ascended into heaven but he who descended from heaven, the Son of man, who is in heaven." This meant that, already during his life on earth and certainly after his glorification, the body of Christ was in heaven and on earth at the same time, indeed, that it was present everywhere. For the phrase "the right hand of God" did not refer to a specific place, not even to a place in the sky, but to "the almighty power of God, which at one and the same time can be nowhere and yet must be everywhere." That almighty power and majesty was communicated to the human nature of Christ through the incarnation, so that, while retaining its essential properties, it shared in those of the divine nature, within the single concrete person of the incarnate Logos. From this it followed that even if Christ had not said, "This is my body," his body and blood must be present everywhere, including the bread and wine of the Eucharist. Although his critics retorted that such a construct seemed to be making the eucharistic presence only one instance of a general ubiquity of Christ's human nature and thus ran the risk of depressing the Sacrament into a corollary of this metaphysical a priori, Luther insisted that he was not basing his belief in the words "This is my body" on a rationalistic hypothesis, but on the word and promise of Christ.

The proper recognition of the relation between the divine and the human in the person of Christ was, for Luther and those who followed him, not a speculative theory, but the necessary basis for the doctrine of the work of Christ, for Christian "consolation," and hence for the theology of the cross. For at the very height of the disputes over the hypostatic union of the two natures in Christ and the communication of properties, Luther penned his theologically most typical—and historically most influential—statement of christological doctrine, in explanation of the Apostles' Creed: "I believe that Jesus Christ, true God, begotten of the Father from eternity, and also true man, born of the Virgin Mary, is my Lord, who has redeemed me, a lost and condemned creature, delivered me and freed me from all sins, from death, and from the power of the devil, not with silver and gold but with his holy and precious blood and with his innocent sufferings and death, in order that I may be his, live under him in his kingdom and serve him in everlasting righteousness, innocence, and blessedness, even as he is risen from the dead and lives and reigns to all eternity." In that sentence the doctrine of the person of Christ stood in apposition to the subject, but the doctrine of the work of Christ formed the predicate: Christ was what he was in order to do what he did.

This statement, moreover, contained no specific echoes from Anselm's version of the doctrine of the atonement, although such an echo of "satisfaction" did occur in the corresponding section of Luther's *Large Catechism.* Luther was quite capable of employing the language of Anselm to describe the transaction between Christ and the Father by which the justice of God was satisfied, and the mercy of God fulfilled, in the salvation of the human race. In an early set of lectures on the New Testament he could say of Christ: "He is the one who has made satisfaction, he is the one who is righteous, he is my defense, he is the one who died for me." And in a later set of lectures on the New Testament he could represent the Father as giving instruction to the Son to "pay and make satisfaction for" the sins of all men. His colleague, Johann Bugenhagen, spoke of the work of Christ as "rendering satisfaction to the law," and doing so "freely in our stead"; the use of such language seemed especially appropriate when it was set into polemical opposition to the notion of a satisfaction wrought by human acts of penance. Another colleague, Philip Melanchton, was even more explicit in his appropriation of such language. He acknowledged Anselm as an authority on the doctrine of atonement,

*Marginal references (left column):*

Luth.*Kl.Kat.*2.4 (*Bek.*511)

Luth.*Dtsch.Kat.*2.2.31 (*Bek.* 652)

Luth.*Rom.*2:15 (*WA* 56:204)

Luth.*Gal.*(1535) 3:13 (*WA* 40–I:441)

Bgn.*Annot.*Eph.2:14 (1524:9r)
Bgn.*Annot.*Col.2:13 (1524:42r)

Bgn.*Bed.* (1525:A2r);Bgn.*Sac.* (1525:A4r);Bgn.*Chr.gl.* (1527:13);Calv.*Nec.ref.*(*CR* 34:485–86)
Mel.*Disp.part.poen.*14 (*CR* 12:506);Mel.*Cat.puer.* (*CR* 23:189);Mel.*Comm.Rom.* (*CR* 15:663)

Mel.*Post.* (*CR* 24:579)
Mel.*Comm.Rom* (*CR* 15:623);
Mel.*Enarr.Rom.*5 (*CR* 15:917)

Mel.*Enarr.Symb.Nic.* (*CR* 23:
260);Mel.*Explic.Symb.Nic.*(*CR*
23:582);Mel.*Comm.Rom.*(*CR*
15:657)
Mel.*Annot.Rom.*10 (*CR* 15:
477)

Chem.*Loc.*11 (1604–II:793)

Hutt.*Comp.*12.7 (1728:186)

See pp. 23–28 above

Aulén (1969) 105

Luth.*Gal.*(1535)3:13 (*WA* 40–
I:441)

See vol.3:136

as well as on the definition of original sin, and he repeatedly stressed the need for the justice of God to be satisfied if the mercy of God was to grant the forgiveness of sins and salvation. Christ alone was "righteous before God," he alone had "made satisfaction to God." Melanchthon's pupil Martin Chemnitz, who helped to make Melanchthon's theology acceptable to later generations by bringing it into line with Luther's, followed him in teaching "that Christ rendered satisfaction for all sins, for their guilt and for their punishment, so that nothing remains for our sufferings or satisfactions to do in expiating sins," while a younger contemporary of Chemnitz taught that "the merit of Christ made satisfaction to divine justice."

But in Luther, and even in these later Lutherans, the repetition of this vocabulary did not necessarily imply an acceptance of Anselm's entire schema, any more than it had in the centuries immediately preceding Luther. In an exposition of his doctrine of the work of Christ on the cross that has been called "perhaps the passage which of all others most exactly sets forth the central points on which Luther's whole teaching depends," he stated his interpretation of what Christ had done on the cross and of how he had done it. After asserting, in the words quoted earlier, that the Father's instruction to Christ had been to "pay and make satisfaction for" the sins of all men, he went on to describe, in the language of a medieval Easter hymn with its roots in the Greek and Latin fathers, the "wondrous duel" between life and death, between Christ and the enemies to whom the human race was in thrall as the consequence of sin. Seeking to attack and conquer Christ as they had all men who had preceded him, the enemies were themselves conquered instead: "Thus in Christ all sin is conquered, killed, and buried, and righteousness remains the victor and the ruler eternally." Death, too, was "conquered and abolished," and the ancestral curse pronounced on Adam and Eve must yield to the blessing of Christ.

Despite his own use of terms and metaphors from Anselm's *Why God Became Man* both here and elsewhere, therefore, Luther accused scholasticism of having "completely obliterated" this "chief doctrine of the Christian faith" about the conquest of sin, death, and the devil through Christ the victor. It was, moreover, being "obscured once more" by the Radicals of his own time. Among these Radicals he presumably meant to include also those who were disagreeing with him over the doctrine of the relation between the divine and human natures in Christ; for he urged that "it was necessary that he who was to conquer these [enemies] in himself should be true God by nature," and therefore that the human nature of the crucified should, by the communication of properties, have received from the divine nature the majesty and power to prevail over the enemies of mankind. This christological doctrine and the theology of the cross were corollaries in his teaching, as were the doctrine of justification by grace through faith and the doctrine that the cross of Christ was the victory of God over the tyranny of sin, death, and the devil; "for it belongs exclusively to the divine power to destroy sin and abolish death, to create righteousness and grant life." Christ had clothed himself in the person of the sinner, had taken the law and the curse upon himself, and by what Luther, this time echoing Augustine, called a "fortunate exchange," had suffered death "for us"; "but because he was a divine and eternal person, it was impossible for death to hold him," and by his resurrection he broke the power of death.

Yet as it has been a common oversimplification to reduce Luther's theology of the cross to a version of the Anselmic theory of atonement through satisfaction, so it is also a form of reductionism to make the image of "Christus Victor" exclusive—something he himself did not do. Another point of divergence between his concept of the atonement and Anselm's was the greater emphasis he laid on the life of Jesus, and not only on his death and resurrection, as integral to the work of redemption. The law of God, which was one of the "enemies" over whom Christ the victor prevailed, was as well a divine demand that man had the obligation to fulfill but could not obey. In relation to the law in that sense Luther spoke of "Christ the fulfiller." Christ had assumed the penalties for sin incurred by man because of his disobedience to the

Luth. *Gal.*(1535) 3:13 (*WA* 40-I:441)

Luth. *Gal.*(1535) 3:13 (*WA* 40-I:442)

Aug. *Conf.*10,43.68–70 (*CSEL* 33:278–80)

Luth. *Gal.*(1519) 5:4 (*WA* 2:563)
Luth. *Gal.*(1519) 4:4–5 (*WA* 2:534)

Luth. *Gal.*(1519) 2:18 (*WA* 2: 497)

Luth. *Gal.*(1519) 3:20 (*WA* 2: 523)

Men. *Gerecht.* (1552:N2v); Hunn. *Just.* (1590:30–31)

Form. *Conc.S.D.*3.15 (*Bek.*918–19)

Form. *Conc.S.D.*3.58;56 (*Bek.* 933–35)

Luth. *Gal.*(1535) 5:8 (*WA* 40–II:43);Luth. *1 Pet.*4:1 (*WA* 12: 371);Luth. *Thes.Antimon.*5.50–51 (*WA* 39–I:356)

See vol. 3:147–48

Luth. *Stras.* (*WA* 15:396)

Luth. *Himm.Proph.*2 (*WA* 18: 196–97)

Luth. *Vor.N.T.* (*WA DB* 6:10)

Luth. *Matt.*5–7.7:24–27 (*WA* 32:535)

law. But he had also become obedient to the law in his life. He who did not need the law to tell him what he ought to do, and who by his perfection went beyond the imperatives of the law, for the sake of humanity obeyed the law. Luther could go so far as to declare that "the law was not put in our hands for us to fulfill it, but was put in the hands of Christ, who was to come, for him to fulfill it." This image of "Christ the fulfiller" eventually achieved systematic formulation in the distinction between the passive obedience of Christ, by which he suffered and died on the cross, and his active obedience, by which he met the demands of the law "from his holy birth to his death in the stead of us poor sinners"; therefore it was "the total obedience of Christ's total person" in both life and death that was "reckoned to us as righteousness."

The fulfillment of the law by his active and passive obedience was, of course, not the sole purpose of the human life of Jesus Christ, nor of his cross. For, as Luther had learned from Augustine, "Scripture presents Christ in two ways: first, as a gift . . . ; secondly, as an example for us to imitate." To "Christ the victor" and "Christ the fulfiller" must be added "Christ the example." Like Anselm and Bernard before him, Luther emphasized Christ as gift far more than Christ as example. As example, Christ was "comparable to other saints"; therefore this was "the least important aspect of Christ." An interpretation of the work of Christ that concentrated only on Christ as "an example and lawgiver," at the expense of Christ as "our treasure and the gift of God," was a betrayal of the gospel as the treasure of the church. The same stricture applied to an interpretation of the work of Christ that remained preoccupied with his moral teachings rather than with the cross. If he had to make a choice between an account of the miraculous deeds of Christ and an account of his teachings, Luther said in his preface to the New Testament, he would choose the teachings; therefore he preferred the Gospel of John to the Synoptics. The teaching of Christ in the Sermon on the Mount was "much different from any that [people] had been accustomed to hearing before." But "Christ the teacher," like "Christ the example,"

Luth.*Ev.Joh.*6–8.6:63 (*WA* 33:259)

was of no avail and could not "make you alive and spiritual" apart from faith in the Christ of the cross.

These conceptions of the work of Christ as satisfaction, victory, fulfillment of the law, example, and instruction belonged to the theology of the cross for the obvious reason that they described what Christ had done on the cross, as a summary of his entire life and teaching. Yet by the term "theology of the cross" Luther intended still more: "He deserves to be called a theologian," he said in his early specification of the theology of the cross, "who comprehends the visible and manifest things of God seen through suffering

Luth.*Disp.Heid.*20 (*WA* 1:362)

and the cross." In a more profound sense, then, the theology of the cross was an account of the very meaning of revelation as the simultaneous disclosing and hiding of "the visible and manifest things of God," which were not accessible through the direct ways of knowing by reason or experience, but only through the indirect way of the cross. Although God showed forth his gifts, including the gift of Christ, no one could know God through these gifts unless God em-

Luth.*Serv.arb.* (*WA* 18:782)

ployed another way as well; this was what was meant by comprehending the manifest things of God through the cross, in which God was both hidden and revealed.

Taken to its most radical consequences, such an interpretation of revelation and knowledge led to the following definition of faith: "It is the nature of faith that it presumes on the grace of God. . . . Faith does not require information, knowledge, or certainty, but a free surrender and a joyful bet on his unfelt, untried,

Luth.*Pred.*25.vii.1522 (*WA* 10–III:239)

and unknown goodness." Luther appears to have stood in a philosophical tradition that questioned, on logical grounds, the probative force of the Thomistic demonstrations of the existence of God. More importantly, however, he questioned, on theological grounds, the identification of any God "proved" in this way with the God and Father of the Lord Jesus Christ. Commenting on the principal proof text from

See vol.3:286–89

Rom.1:20

See vol.3:261

the New Testament that had been used to establish the demonstrability of the existence of God, he did put forth an observation like that of Anselm and other medieval thinkers, that "there must be that which is more sublime than everything else, which is higher

Luth.*Rom.*1:20 (*WA* 56:177)

Luth.*Serv.arb.* (*WA* 18:719)

Luth.*Gen.*45:3 (*WA* 44:591)

Luth.*Pred.*15.viii.1517 (*WA* 4: 647–48)

E.Seeberg (1929) 1:129
Luth.*Res.disp.indulg.*58 (*WA* 1: 614)
Luth.*Ps.147:*13 (*WA* 31–I:436)

Luth.*Gal.*(1535) 2:6 (*WA* 40–I: 173)

Luth.*Ab.Chr.* (*WA* 26:339)

See p. 154 above

Luth.*Wort.* (*WA* 23:151);*Apol. Conf.Aug.*4.67 (*Bek.*173)

Luth.*Gen.*26:9 (*WA* 43:460)

than all and helps all." Even in his opposition to the glorification of man's natural capacity in the thought of Erasmus, he ascribed to "natural reason" the recognition, even apart from Scripture, that God was almighty and his foreknowledge was infallible. But the "speculative questions about God" asked by philosophers, which did "arrive at some kind of knowing," led at best to a knowledge that was "merely objective" and that could not know whether or not "God cares." As he said in a sermon of 1517 on the Feast of the Assumption of the Blessed Virgin Mary, an "ascent to the knowledge of God" by these means was "dangerous" and produced "despair," for all it could discover of God was "the magnitude of his power, wisdom, and justice."

By contrast, "the theologian of the cross" was one whom he once defined, in "an extremely characteristic expression," as a theologian "who with the apostle knows only the crucified and hidden God." The true God wanted to "remain hidden and do everything behind his masks"; all of creation was such a "mask" of God, as were the offices and structures of human society. It was necessary to distinguish between God and his masks. God was "a supernatural, inscrutable being who exists at the same time in every seed, whole and entire, and yet also in all and above all and outside all created things. . . . Nothing is so small but God is still smaller, nothing so large but God is still larger." To grasp this God, who was everywhere and yet nowhere, faith was summoned to look not at his "masks," but at his revelation. It was one thing for God to be present, but quite another for God to be present "for you." He was present "for you" when he added his word and bound himself to it, saying, "It is here that you are to find me." And so "when you have the word, you can take hold and grasp him with certainty." God strictly forbade the speculative investigation of his divinity, which would remain hidden except in Christ, the Word of God, through whom "the unrevealed God" became "the revealed God," while yet remaining hidden. For the Christ in whom God was revealed was Christ crucified, about whom it was anything but obvious that he was the revealed God. To see the love of God in Christ was to see the

Col.2:3
Luth.*Gal.*(1535) 1:3 (*WA* 40–I: 79)

Luth.*Dtsch.Kat.*2.3.65 (*Bek.* 660)

Luth.*Dict.Ps.*75:8 (*WA* 3:516)

Bgn.*Annot.*Col.1:15 (1524:35r)

Bgn.*Annot.*Eph.1:13 (1524:3r)

Bgn.*Chr.gl.* (1527:128)
Mel.*Loc.*(1521) (Plitt-Kolde 141;161)

Mel.*Annot.Rom.* (*CR* 15:443)

Luth.*Kirchpost.*pr. (*WA* 10–I: 9)
*Form.Conc.S.D.*5.3 (*Bek.*952–53)

Mel.*Loc.*(1521) (Plitt-Kolde 144);Zw.*Klar.* (*CR* 88:374)
Luth.*Thes.Antinom.*3.34 (*WA* 39–I:351)

Luth.*Vor.N.T.* (*WA DB* 6:8)

one in whom "all the treasures of wisdom and knowledge are hidden." Or, as Luther summarized his doctrine of revelation in his *Large Catechism,* "we could never come to recognize the Father's favor and grace were it not for the Lord Christ, who is a mirror of the fatherly heart [of God], apart from whom we see nothing but a wrathful and terrible judge." Yet because even in Christ God was hidden as well as revealed, Luther went on to insist: "Neither could we know anything of Christ, had it not been revealed by the Holy Spirit" in the word of the gospel.

## The Centrality of the Gospel

The center of Luther's theology of the cross, as well as of his understanding of human history and experience, was the gospel of Jesus Christ. As he said in his early comments on the Book of Psalms, "the gospel imposes the cross and life upon us," which was, he continued, "a saving combination as long as this life endures." A coworker expressed Luther's teaching when he defined the gospel as "the knowledge of the grace and mercy of God through Christ," a message that announced "the forgiveness of all sins and the inheritance of eternal life" through Christ, who was the "mercy seat" of God. Another coworker put it more simply still: "The gospel is a promise"; for "the gospel teaches that Christ, the Son of God, has been given for us and is our righteousness before God." And one of Luther's own definitions read: "The gospel is a discourse about Christ, that he is the Son of God and became man for us, that he died and was raised, that he has been established as Lord over all things." Everyone acknowledged that the word "gospel" was not used in the same sense either in the New Testament or in the language of the church, as for example when it was applied to the first four books of the New Testament, some of whose content was not at all "gospel" according to these definitions. Therefore, although the content of these books of the New Testament was the life and deeds of Christ, "to know his works and the things that happened to him is not yet to know the true gospel, for you do not yet thereby know that he has overcome sin, death, and the devil."

Luth.*Gal.*(1535) 2:4–5 (*WA* 40–I:164)

Luth.*Gal.*(1535) 2:14 (*WA* 40–I:207)

Luth.*Gal.*(1535) 2:14 (*WA* 40–I:210)

Luth.*Ev.Joh.*1:17 (*WA* 46:663)

Luth.*Gal.*(1535) 2:17 (*WA* 40–I:250)

John 1:17

Luth.*Ev.Joh.1–2.*1:17 (*WA* 46:658)

Luth.*Dict.Ps.*85:8 (*WA* 4:9)

Luth.*Dav.* (*WA* 54:79)

See p. 235 below

In its strict sense as the good news of salvation through the victory of Christ, the gospel stood in the sharpest possible contrast to the law. Out of that contrast Luther shaped one of the most pervasive themes of his theology of the cross. "The truth of the gospel is this," he said, "that our righteousness comes by faith alone, without the works of the law," and therefore the only "real theologian" was one who "knows well how to distinguish the gospel from the law." "The knowledge of this topic, the distinction between the law and the gospel," he went on, "is necessary to the highest degree, for it contains a summary of all Christian doctrine." Everyone was to learn to make this distinction "not only in words but in feeling and in experience." He blamed his own confusion and doubt "for over thirty years" on his failure to make this distinction properly, and he found his scholastic opponents on the Roman Catholic side as well as his Radical opponents on the Protestant side guilty of confusing law and gospel. All of them "turn this upside down," as was inevitable, because they did not understand the doctrine of justification and in its place taught its "very opposite, namely, that Moses is Christ and Christ is Moses."

The use of Moses and Christ to represent the law and the gospel had a precedent in the New Testament itself, where "grace and truth" were the line of demarcation between what had come through Moses and what had come through Christ. The law, as the word of Moses directed to the outer life of men, was able to instruct and sanctify only the flesh, whereas the gospel, as the word of Christ directed to the inner life of men, was able to instruct and sanctify the spirit. It was the special ministry of Moses to proclaim the wrath of God in the law, and the death that was the consequence of man's disobedience. Thus Luther portrayed Christ as saying to Moses: "I will not preach as you, Moses, are obliged to preach. For you must proclaim the law. . . . Therefore your preaching produces only wretched people; it shows them their sins, on account of which they cannot keep the law." It was not surprising, therefore, that some of his contemporary critics were reminded of Marcion, the second-century heretic, whose "special and principal work," as described by his chief opponent, Tertullian, was "the separation of the law and the gospel," and who consequently and consistently rejected the authority of Moses and the Old Testament in favor of the sole authority of Christ and the New Testament.

Such a reading of Luther's distinction between law and gospel was, however, quite superficial, and it was altogether mistaken in its equation of that distinction with the distinction between the Old and the New Testament. It has been ingeniously suggested that if Luther had been a professor at a modern university, he would have to hold the chair of Old Testament, to which he devoted most of his classroom lectures, spending, for example, the final decade of his life on a lengthy exposition of the Book of Genesis. That exposition demonstrated, moreover, that, far from equating the Old Testament with law and the New Testament with gospel, he found the message of the gospel throughout the Scriptures. Moses at his best was a prophet who predicted the coming of Christ, presenting the "protevangelium" and the promise of Christ. Moses had predicted his own surrender of authority to Christ, as the prophet whom men were to heed. At the same time, Luther recognized that there were commands throughout the New Testament. This meant that there was gospel in the Old Testament and law in the New. The distinction between law and gospel was not a matter of biblical location or of chronology, but of "rightly dividing the word of truth."

Nor were law and gospel distinct as to origin: God was the author of both. When God gave the law through Moses on Sinai, he accompanied it with signs of his power and holiness, to reinforce it by the declaration of his sovereignty. Moses was the chosen spokesman of God, a man "full of faith" and wisdom, whose "law" in five books was given by none other than the Holy Spirit himself. This pertained not only to the moral law as contained in the Decalogue, but to the ceremonial law as embodied in the Levitical priesthood, which was the principal part of the law of Moses. Therefore the ceremonial law had carried the same authority as had the moral law within the law of Moses, so that the New Testament phrase

---

See vol.1:72–77

Mel.*Loc*.(1521) Plitt-Kolde 140)

See vol.1;6

Luth.*Gen.* (WA 42–44)

Gen.3:15
Luth.*Decl.Gen*.pr. (WA 24:11)

Luth.*Deut*.18:15 (WA 14:675)

Luth.*Deut*.18:15 (WA 14:678)

Luth.*Gal* (1535) 3:17 (WA 40–I:469);*Apol.Conf.Aug*.4.188 (*Bek*.197)

2 Tim.2:15

Luth.*Gal*.(1535) 3:19 (WA 40–I:483–84)

Luth.*Gen*.41:40 (WA 44:428)

Luth.*Gen*.30:14–16 (WA 43:672)

Luth.*Gen*.26:2–5 (WA 43:442)

Luth.*Serv.arb*. (*WA* 18:765);
Luth.*Gal*.(1535)2:16;3:21 (*WA* 40–I:217–18;510–11);Calv. *Rom*.3:20 (Parker 66–67)

Luth.*Himm.Proph*. (*WA* 18: 81);Luth.*Gen*.9:12–16 (*WA* 42: 374);Luth.*Thes.Antinom*.2.24 (*WA* 39–I:348)

Luth.*Thes.Antinom*.2.38 (*WA* 39–I:349)

Apol.*Conf.Aug*.4.5 (*Bek*.159); Mel.*Enarr.Symb.Nic*. (*CR* 23: 336–38)

Apol.*Conf.Aug*.4.257 (*Bek*. 210);Luth.*Thes.Antinom*.2.4–5 (*WA* 39–I:347)
Luth.*Thes.Antinom*.4.27 (*WA* 39–I:353)

Matt.22:37–40

Lev.18:5;Rom.10:5;Gal.3:12
Luth.*Gal*.(1535) 3:12 (*WA* 40–I:425)

Eras.*Lib.arb*.2.a.16 (Walter 35–36)

Luth.*Serv.arb*. (*WA* 18:677)

Luth.*Gal*.(1535) 2:16 (*WA* 40–I:223–36)

"the works of the law" pertained to both. Although both the law and the gospel had come by the revelation of God, there was this difference between them: the gospel could be known only through such revelation, while the law of Moses was, at least in principle, coextensive with the law of nature and was valid only insofar as it was the same as the law of nature. But since God was the source also of the natural law, this difference in the means of transmission was not a difference in ultimate origin and authorship. The Holy Spirit had revealed both the law and the gospel, and both were his truth; but his purposes in giving them, and therefore the effects that each was intended to have and did have, were completely different.

For, as Melanchthon's *Apology of the Augsburg Confession* summarized the Lutheran distinction, "all Scripture should be divided into these two chief doctrines, the law and the promises." It was the intention and function of the law, the *Apology* went on to declare, to be "the word that convicts of sin. For the law works wrath, it only accuses, it only terrifies consciences." This it did because no one could live up to its demands: not only a completely upright and moral life, but an upright heart, a motivation for life that loved God above all things and loved the neighbor perfectly. Hence it was in a tone of irony that both the Old and the New Testament said of the works of the law that "he who does them shall live by them," since no one could. To the argument of Erasmus that the presence of so many commands in both the Old and the New Testament implied an ability to obey them, Luther retorted: "Reason thinks that man is mocked by an impossible commandment, whereas I maintain that by this means man is admonished and awakened to see his own impotence." Once the penitent sinner had been awakened this way by the proclamation of the law to recognize his true condition before God, the law had performed its task and must yield to the promise of the gospel, which the sinner accepted by faith alone, without any merit or reliance on the works of the law. The forgiven sinner "died to the law," was no longer bound by it, no longer owed it obedience, and did not even know it any

Luth.*Gal.*(1535) 2:19 (*WA* 40–I:270)

longer. To be justified by faith alone meant to live by the gospel alone.

Did that mean that the law of God, including the Ten Commandments themselves, did not pertain to the state of grace at all? If this were Luther's position (as he sometimes seemed to be saying), then why, as

Luth.*Antinom.* (*WA* 50:470)

he himself asked his opponents, would he have taken the trouble to expound the Ten Commandments so

Luth.*Kl.Kat.*1(*Bek.*507–10); Luth.*Dtsch.Kat.*1 (*Bek.*560–645)

often and so carefully, putting them at the beginning of both his catechisms not only as an accusation of sin and as a means of arousing repentance but as a description and norm of the Christian life? Such questions arose more than once during Luther's own lifetime, and in the generation after his death they broke out more vigorously, in a series of disputes commonly grouped under the heading of "antinomian controversies." At issue were two connected but distinct problems in the Christian use of the law in relation to the gospel: the functions of the two as means for inducing repentance, particularly in believers; and the use of the law as a curb to "maintain external discipline" in society and as a mirror to disclose sin, but also as a rule to supply moral standards for Christians,

Form.*Conc.Epit.*6.1 (*Bek.*793)

the so-called "third use of the law." The various teachings that Luther and then his later followers denounced as antinomian had in common "the

Mel.*Enarr.Rom.*3:20 (*CR* 15: 853–55);Luth.*Thes.Antinom.*1. 24;2.10 (*WA* 39–I:346;348)

blasphemous [contention] that the law should be utterly removed from the church."

Exegesis and experience had combined in Luther to identify the law as the divinely appointed instrument for exhibiting the wrath of God and the sin of man, but a confession that spoke in his name could assert: "The gospel declares that all men are under sin and

Apol.*Conf.Aug.*4.62 (*Bek.*172) Mel.*Explic.Symb.Nic.* (*CR* 23: 442);Mel.*Comm.Rom.* (*CR* 15: 562);Mel.*Enarr.Rom.*1:1(*CR* 15:819)

are worthy of eternal wrath and death." Thus the gospel was "the preaching of repentance" as well as "of the promise." On the basis of such assertions the "antinomians" drew the conclusion "that one should first preach grace and then the revelation of wrath," while Luther insisted that one should follow the sequence of the Epistle to the Romans, proclaiming first the law to work repentance and then the gospel to

Luth.*Antinom.*(*WA* 50:474) Luth.*Thes.Antinom.*4.14 (*WA* 39–I:352)

grant consolation; opposition to the use of the law was tantamount to the abolition of repentance. The "gospel" that revealed sin and wrath was "gospel" in

Form.Conc.Epit.5.6 (Bek.791)

Aug.Ep.Joh.7.8 (PL 2033)

See pp. 154–55 above

Luth.Eis. (WA 51:441)

Luth.Thes.Antinom.4.37 (WA 39–I:354)

Luth.Thes.Antinom.5.14 (WA 39–I:355)

See pp. 212–16 below

Luth.Capt.Bab.pr. (WA 6:498)

the broader sense of "the total teaching of Christ," which included (in the precise sense) both "law" and "gospel." The second problem was subtler. Augustine's oft-quoted "short precept," "Love and do what you will," had already expressed the spontaneity of the life of love. Luther emphasized the spontaneity still more; at the same time, he went on using the law, particularly the Decalogue, as a guide to the will of God for human conduct. That paradox—either pole of which, when taken by itself, could, according to Luther, lead to distortion of the law, whether antinomian or legalistic—was for him a corollary of the paradox of his doctrine of justification. If man were still—or once again—Adam before the fall, the antinomian rejection of all preaching of the law would be correct. But because the believer was "righteous and a sinner at the same time," it was true both that "after justification good works follow spontaneously without the law" and that the justified, "to the extent that they are under death, must also still be under the law and sin." The clarification of the three uses of the law was to become an even more important issue in the theology and church doctrine of Reformed Protestantism.

The relation of the gospel to the law, while it was responsible for these far-reaching doctrinal definitions, was by no means the only connection to other ideas and teachings shaped by the centrality of the gospel. For although Luther's original break with Roman Catholic theology and practice was based on the charge that it represented a fundamental confusion between law and gospel, he soon learned that the break required him, in the name of the centrality of the gospel, to criticize and revise the meaning of "one, holy, catholic, and apostolic church" as well, and to call for a fundamental rethinking of the medieval conception of the seven sacraments. Having begun by conceding to the papacy an authority at least as a human institution, he came to deny it any authority whatever and to denounce it as Antichrist. Similarly, as he acknowledged in the same work, he had begun by denouncing abuses in the sacramental system while continuing to affirm its essential validity, but had now come to denounce the system itself as one by which the authentic sacraments "have been subjected to a miserable captivity." Before his career as Reformer was over, he had found it necessary to differentiate his views both of the church and of the sacraments no less from those of his fellow Reformers than from those of his Roman Catholic opponents. On some of the ecclesiological and sacramental issues he was obliged to say that although the pope was the Antichrist "seated in the temple of God," the church in which he was seated was still the temple of God. Despite the corruption of both faith and practice, the reality of the body of Christ was still with "the papists," just as communion under one kind, though a violation of Christ's ordinance, was still "truly the Sacrament."

Complicated or even contradictory though such a position seems to be, Luther felt able to boast that as a consequence of the Reformation "a seven-year-old child knows what the church is," namely, that confessed in the Apostles' Creed, "the holy catholic [or, as he preferred to say, 'Christian'] church, the communion of saints." This confession of the reality of the church as the communion of saints he set over against the institutionalism he attributed to Roman Catholic doctrine and over against the individualism he took to be implied in at least the more radical versions of Protestant doctrine. Both of these distortions of the nature of the church were basically the result of a distortion of the gospel. For the church was "the assembly of all believers, among whom the gospel is preached in its purity and the holy sacraments are administered according to the gospel." That definition, as it was formulated, was intended to be a maximum, distinguishing the Evangelical view from views of the church that added other institutional requirements such as liturgical uniformity or obedience to the papacy; but it acted as a minimum definition as well, denying a right to the name "church" where these two conditions did not obtain. Yet alongside such definitions Luther and his colleagues could also sometimes repeat the traditional Augustinian idea of a "church of the predestined," known only to God, which was present wherever there were, in the mystery of the divine will, those whom God had elected

Luth.*Capt.Bab*.pr. (*WA* 6:501)

2 Thess.2:4

Luth.*Br.Wink*.(*WA* 38:221)

Luth.*Br.Wink*.(*WA* 28:244)

Luth.*Schmal.Art*.12.2–3 (*Bek.* 459–60)

Luth.*Dtsch.Kat*.pr. (*Bek*.556); Zw.*Schl*.8 (*CR* 89:59)

Conf.*Aug*.7.1 (*Bek*.61)

Zw.*Can.miss*. (*CR* 89:570–71); Zw.*Ems*. (*CR* 90:252–55)

See pp. 75–76 above

to be members of his true church, even though now they might be among the enemies of visible Christendom. It was a definition of the church that would acquire special significance in Reformed theology, where the importance assigned to the doctrine of divine election had as its corollary that one must leave to God alone the knowledge of his church, for its foundation was his secret election. Therefore the church was indeed the communion of saints, but with the important proviso that "the church is hidden, and the saints are concealed."

What kept this doctrine of the church from skepticism and paralysis was the foundation of the church in the word of the gospel, which was the bridge between the "invisible" and the "visible" church (even though the use of these as technical terms was a later effort to formulate Luther's teaching). For "where the word is, there the church is," but "where the word is not, even though the titles and the office are present, there the church is not." Against the one who bore the title "successor of Peter" it was appropriate to quote the declaration of Peter: "We have a firmer prophetic word." The church was the daughter of the word, not the mother of the word, so that Luther could go so far as to declare: "If I were the only one in the entire world to adhere to the word, I alone would be the church." In reply to the warning that this stress on the hiddenness of the church would make a mockery of the command of Christ to "tell it to the church," Luther and his followers, citing that very command, insisted that they were "not dreaming about some Platonic republic," for in speaking of the church they were careful to "add its marks, the pure teaching of the gospel and the sacraments." The reality of the church, then, was principally functional rather than institutional. But if the church was not a Platonic republic, it was also not "the supreme outward monarchy of the whole world," a legal corporation among legal corporations. Such an external definition ignored the very power by which the church existed and for which it existed, the power of the gospel. This power had been replaced by the power of the sword; but the apostle had asserted that "the weapons of our warfare are not carnal," and therefore the battle against the

Mel.*Comm.Rom.* (CR 15:678)

See pp. 217–32 below

Zw.*Schl.*8 (CR 89:58);Blngr.*Sum.*6.11 (1556:99v–100r)

Luth.*Serv.arb.* (WA 18:652); Luth.*Ambr.Cath.*(WA 7:722); Calv.*Theol.Par.*18 (CR 35:30–31)

Luth.*Gen.*11:10 (WA 42:424)

Bgn.*Conjug.episc.*(1525:F8v)

2 Pet.1:19(Vulg.)

Luth.*Gen.*7:17–24 (WA 42:334)

Ec.*Enchir.*1 (CCath 34:33)

Matt.18:17

Mel.*Enarr.Rom.*9 (CR 15:975)

See p. 272 below

Apol.*Conf.Aug.*7.20 (Bek.238); Mel.*Eccl.* (CR 23:640);Zw.*Ems.* (CR 90:255)

Apol.*Conf.Aug.*7.23 (Bek.239)

See pp. 81–83 above

2 Cor.10:4 *Conf.Aug.*28.17 (Bek.123); Mel.*Pot.pap.*31 (Bek.481)

Bgn.*Off.* (1524:C2v)

Apol.*Conf.Aug.*7.24 (*Bek.*239–40)
Dan.11:36;2 Thess.2:4

Luth.*Himm.Proph.*1 (*WA* 18:66)

See pp. 313–22 below

Conf.*Aug.*21.2 (*Bek.*83b);Zw.*Schl.*17 (*CR* 89:103–11)

Buc.*Regn.Chr.*1.3 (Strasbourg 15:35);Zw.*Klar.* (*CR* 88:376–77)
Luth.*1.Pet.*2:9 (*WA* 12:316–17)

Luth.*Capt.Bab.* (*WA* 6:564)

Luth.*Sup.ann.* (*WA* 53:73–74)

Luth.*Inst.min.* (*WA* 12:190–91)

Luth.*Ep.*23.i.1541 (*WA Br* 9:317–18);Luth.*Ep.*19.i.1542 (*WA Br* 9:597–99)

Luth.*Bisch.* (*WA* 53:231);Calv.*Nec.ref.* (*CR* 34:523–24)

Luth.*Gal.*(1535) 6:5 (*WA* 40–II:154)

kingdom of Antichrist was to be fought "with the gospel, not with carnal weapons." Resorting to carnal weapons was itself one of the signs of that very kingdom of Antichrist, as foretold by the Scriptures.

Yet when the Reformation Radicals seemed to echo Luther's very words by coming out with the claim that they alone adhered to the word and that therefore they alone were the church, Luther accused them of supposing that they had "swallowed the Holy Spirit feathers and all." In opposition to the left wing of the Reformation, with its rejection of traditional criteria of catholic continuity, he became even more explicit than he had been before in his stress upon the office of the ministry, not as a clerical estate but as the appointed instrument for the proclamation of the word of God. The title of priest did not belong to the clerical estate in the church. In the most fundamental sense, only Christ was a true priest, for he was the sole Mediator between God and man. Derivatively, the title applied to all believers, whom Christ by baptism admitted to the priesthood. The ordained "priests, as we call them, are ministers chosen from among us. All that they do is done in our name; the priesthood is nothing but a ministry." The manner of its appointment, together with the notion of an unbroken succession of bishops going back to the apostles, did not matter very much to him. In an emergency he could counsel the Hussites that a community of believers had "both the right and the command to commit by common vote this office [of the ministry] to one or more, to be exercised in its stead," and he and his followers repeatedly approved or recommended the ordination of pastors and even the consecration of bishops in various lands and territories without attention to the canonical requirements, and even "without any chrism." But howsoever the minister may have been appointed, it was to him that God entrusted the task of preaching the word, and his ministry was "proper and well established" when through it he sought "the glory of God and the salvation of souls," rather than his own glory, as both the Roman Catholic priesthood and the Radical "fanatics" did. Therefore it was altogether consistent with Luther's own view of the ministry when the *Augsburg*

Conf.Aug.5.1 (Bek.58)

*Confession* put its article on the office of the ministry immediately after its article on the doctrine of justification, with the formula: "To obtain such [justifying] faith God instituted the office of the ministry."

In the *Augsburg Confession* and even more pronouncedly in the *Apology*, as well as in other writings, this stress on the office of the ministry and on catholicity as a mark of the church led Melanchthon to emphasize the continuity of the church's teaching, though not necessarily the alleged "orderly succession" of its institutional structure, with the "uncorrupted antiquity" of the church of the fathers. Luther had always valued such continuity with ancient doctrine, above all with the creeds of the ancient church, as "testimony that I stand with the true Christian church, which has maintained these symbols or confessions until now, and not with the false, vainglorious church, which is the worst enemy of the true church and has introduced all sorts of idolatry alongside these beautiful confessions." But he would not concede to the continuity with the fathers a normative status alongside the authority of that Scripture in whose name he was willing to withstand the fathers and councils. When Melanchthon, in the *Apology of the Augsburg Confession*, described it as his long-standing policy "to stick as closely as possible to traditional doctrinal formulas in order to foster the attainment of harmony," he might seem to be expressing nothing more than a similar appreciation of doctrinal continuity, especially because of the repeated insistence that the ancient creeds and councils had not "spawned new dogmas" but merely summarized Scripture. Yet at that very time he was also struggling with the relation of Luther's doctrine of the real presence to those "traditional doctrinal formulas."

For in the same year as the *Augsburg Confession*, Johannes Oecolampadius had published a *Dialogue* setting forth the patristic doctrine of the Eucharist. Contrary to Melanchthon's attempt to prove that a sound interpretation of Augustine and of other Greek and Latin church fathers, who "often believed more correctly than they wrote," would show them "not to be in contradiction with the received doctrine of the Lord's Supper," Oecolampadius maintained that

Mel.*Eccl.* (CR 23:597–98)
Mel.*Enarr.Symb.Nic.* (CR 23:220)

Luth.*Symb.* (WA 50:262)

Luth.ap.*Disp.Lips.* (WA 2:323)

Apol.*Conf.Aug.*pr.11 (Bek.143)

Mel.*Enarr.Symb.Nic.* (CR 23:200)

Oec.*Dial.* (1572[1530])

Mel.*Comm.Rom.* (CR 15:738)

Mel.*Coen.* (CR 23:745)

Oec.*Dial.*([1530]1572)

the idea of a merely spiritual presence of the body of Christ was the one that actually had the chief claim to continuity with the fathers. Two years later, Luther made the same claim for his own position on the real presence, acknowledging that it would be "dangerous" to teach such an idea if it were "a new article" of faith, but affirming that it was rather an article that had been "held from the beginning and throughout Christendom by common consent."

Luth.*Alb.Pr.* (WA 30–III:552)

Anyone who denied this was condemning the entire Christian church as heretical. In opposition to the Anabaptist rejection of infant baptism, Luther argued for the correctness of this practice from its continuity

Luth.*Wied.* (WA 28:167–68)

throughout Christian history, going so far as to declare: "We confess that under the papacy there is the correct Holy Scripture, correct baptism, the correct Sacrament of the Altar, the correct keys for the forgiveness of sins, the correct office of the ministry, the correct catechism, namely, the Our Father, the Ten Commandments, and the articles of the [Apos-

Luth.*Wied.* (WA 28:147)

tles'] Creed." He was able to take over a medieval eucharistic hymn celebrating the identity of the body

Luth.*Ld.*24 (WA 35:452–53)

in the Sacrament with the body born of Mary, adding stanzas of his own. The documentary evidence from the fathers as Oecolampadius the patristic scholar had assembled it, however, made that supposed "common consent" seem to Melanchthon to be considerably less secure. And when, on the other hand, some of the Reformation Radicals began attacking

See pp. 322–31 below

the dogmas of the Trinity and the two natures in Christ, he found the affirmation of the catholic consensus as a mark of the authentic church even more imperative. The declaration of loyalty to the Nicene

Conf.*Aug.*1.1 (*Bek.*50)

Creed in the *Augsburg Confession* and the incorporation of the Apostles' Creed, the Nicene Creed,

Lib.*Conc.* (*Bek.*21–30)

and the Athanasian Creed in the dogmatic corpus to which a pastor had to subscribe for ordination were all expressions of this commitment to the catholicity of the church's doctrine, despite the recognition that

Mel.*Eccl.* (CR 23:606)

even the Council of Nicea had been "incautious" on some points and that these creeds did not contain some of the doctrines (such as justification by faith)

See p. 157 above

that Luther had singled out as integral to the meaning of the gospel.

The substitution of a functional for an institutional definition of the nature of the church and the concern for catholicity in the teaching on the Eucharist both suggest how important the sacraments were for the doctrine of the church. The preaching of the gospel and the administration of the sacraments were con-stitutive of the church: it was through baptism that "we are first received into Christendom"; likewise, "the whole gospel and the article of the creed, 'I be-lieve in the holy Christian church, the forgiveness of sins,' are embodied in this Sacrament [the Eucharist] and offered to us through the word." When speaking about justification by faith alone, moreover, it was essential that the "alone" not be understood as ex-cluding the word of God and the sacraments, for these were the means by which faith was created. So inex-tricable a part of the doctrine of justification were the sacraments that when the Anabaptists rejected the or-thodox view of baptism or when Zwingli rejected the orthodox view of the Eucharist, Luther maintained that, to be consistent, they could not possibly stand correctly on the central question of justification or on any other doctrine, although he was willing to con-cede that one could be saved by hearing the word of God even from such a source. But the sacraments were so vital that whoever erred on them, "in even one point," was to be avoided.

They were vital not only because they belonged to the body of scriptural teaching (though also for that reason, of course), but because, properly understood, the sacraments were an epitome of the very gospel; without them no one could be a Christian. In one of the most widely disseminated of his early writings, *The Babylonian Captivity of the Church*, Luther ad-dressed himself to the question of the sacraments as such in more detail than he was to do even in those of his later works that were concerned with one or another of the individual sacraments. Noting, as oth-ers had before him, that in the New Testament the Latin word "sacramentum," as a translation of the Greek "μυστήριον," did not mean what the church had eventually come to mean by "sacrament" and that, according to the usage of the New Testament, Christ himself was the sacrament in a unique sense,

Conf.Aug.7.2 (Bek.61)
Luth.Dtsch.Kat.4.2 (Bek.691)

Luth.Dtsch.Kat.5.31 (Bek.713–14)

Apol.Conf.Aug.4.73 (Bek.175)

Luth.Wied. (WA 26:161–62)

Luth.Wort. (WA 23:127);Luth.Ab.Chr. (WA 26:317)

Luth.Wied. (WA 26:164)

Luth.Ab.Chr. (WA 26:341)

Luth.Dtsch.Kat.4.1 (Bek.691)

See p. 256 below

See vol.3:206–7; pp. 308–9 below

1 Tim.3:16
Luth.Capt.Bab. (WA 6:551)

Luth.*Capt.Bab.* (WA 6:502–7)

Luth.*Capt.Bab.* (WA 6:507)

Luth.*Capt.Bab.* (WA 6:512)

Luth.*Anb.* (WA 11:454)

Luth.*Capt.Bab.* (WA 6:560–61)

Luth.*Capt.Bab.* (WA 6:560–61)
Blngr.*Ggn.*5.A.6–5.B.6 (1551: 20–21);Blngr.*Dec.*5.6 (1552: 326r);Blngr.*Sum.*8.4 (1556: 144v)
Luth.*Pred.*10.iv.1531 (WA 34–I:300)
Luth.*Capt.Bab.* (WA 6:501; 572);Luth.*Dtsch.Kat.*4.74 (*Bek.*705–6);*Apol.Conf.Aug.* 12.41;13.4 (*Bek.*259;292); Chem.*Exam.CTrid.*2.7.1.1.4 (Preuss 426)

Luth.*Pred.*16.iii.1522 (WA 10–III:61–62)

Bgn.*Sac.* (1525:A4v)

Luth.*Hspost.* (WA 52:520)
Aug.*Ev.Joh.*80.3 (*CCSL* 36: 529)

See p. 54 above

he reviewed the seven sacraments of the medieval church and denounced the abuses to which they had been subjected in teaching and in practice, including the withholding of the chalice from the laity. "By far the most wicked abuse of all" in both teaching and practice was the notion that the sacraments availed because of human merit, and specifically that the Eucharist was "a good work and a sacrifice"; for this struck at the heart of the gospel message. In a treatise amplifying some of the issues raised in his *Babylonian Captivity,* Luther came out even more unequivocally against the medieval definition and numbering of the sacraments, and he urged that the two essentials in any sacrament were the word of God and the outward sign and hence that baptism and the Eucharist were the only true sacraments of the New Testament church. The church did not have the authority to institute new sacraments for which there was no explicit command and promise in Scripture. That ruled out the other so-called sacraments: confirmation, matrimony, ordination, and extreme unction. The rejection of the attempt to expand the number of sacraments from two to seven became standard in Protestant polemics, as Bullinger's repeated treatment of the subject shows. Penance (or, more properly, confession and absolution) was a special case. In the *Babylonian Captivity* as well as in later documents of Luther's Reformation, the technical status of penance as a sacrament remained ambiguous. Actually, the technical status was not very important, particularly because "sacrament" was an ecclesiastical term, not a biblical one. Sacrament or not, confession certainly was a means of grace, of which Luther could say: "I would long since have been overcome and strangled by the devil if [private] confession had not sustained me."

What gave confession such great and efficacious power was not its place in a total sacramental system, but its relation to the word of God in the gospel. It was an especially personalized form of the general absolution that was proclaimed, or at any rate should be, in every sermon. From Augustine had come the formula: "The word is added to the element, and it becomes a sacrament, indeed, a kind of visible word in itself." The first half of the formula became a widely

Zw.*Tf.* (*CR* 91:248);Luth.
*Schmal.Art.*3.5 (*Bek.*449–50);
Grop.*Leyb.*1 (1556:40v)

Apol.*Conf.Aug.*13.5 (*Bek.*449–
50)

See p. 190 below

Luth.*Kl.Kat.*4.1 (*Bek.*515)

Luth.*Kl.Kat.*6.8 (*Bek.*520);
Bgn.*Bed.* (1525:B4r)

Luth.*Schmal.Art.*3.4 (*Bek.*449)

Luth.*Ambr.Cath.* (*WA* 7:721)
Hier.*Hebr.nom.*Matt.B (*CCSL*
72:135)
Ec.*Ev.*1 Adv.3 (1530–I;5r)

Matt.21:1

Luth.*Kirchpost.*Ev.1 Adv. (*WA*
10–I–2:48)

used definition of the nature of a sacrament, while the term "visible word" served as a designation of sacrament not only for Luther and his colleagues, who tended to speak of word and sacrament coordinately, but even more appropriately for Calvin and his colleagues, in whose teachings an attention to this aspect of sacramental doctrine predominated over a concern with such questions as the nature of the eucharistic presence. For Luther, too, the word was the force that endowed a sacrament with its special status: baptism was "not merely water, but water used according to God's command and connected with God's word"; in the Eucharist it was "not the eating and drinking [that] in themselves produce [the effects of the Sacrament], but the words 'for you' and 'for the forgiveness of sins.'" Therefore he could include, in a list of the means by which the gospel was communicated, not only "the oral word" and the three sacraments of baptism, the Eucharist, and "the power of the keys" in absolution, but also "the mutual conversation and consolation of brethren," which was likewise a channel for the same word of God.

The designation of the word of God in the gospel as an "oral word" was not peculiar to this passage in the *Smalcald Articles,* but was a persistent theme. When he referred to the word of God in the gospel, Luther explained, he was "not speaking about the written gospel, but about the vocal one." On the basis of an etymology from Jerome, which Luther had in common with his enemy Johann Eck, he explained the biblical name "Bethphage" to mean "a house of the mouth, not a house of the pen," because Christ himself had not written but preached, and had not commanded his disciples to write but to preach, so that "the gospel might be brought out of dead Scripture and pens into the living voice and mouth." Thus while the Latin text of the *Augsburg Confession* made it the condition of church unity "to agree concerning the doctrine of the gospel and the administration of the sacraments," the equally authoritative German text declared that "it is sufficient for the true unity of the Christian church that the gospel be preached in conformity with a pure understanding of it and that the sacraments be administered in accordance with the

Conf.Aug.7.2 (Bek.61)

Conf.Aug.5.4 (Bek.58)

Luth.*Wort.* (WA 23:151)

Luth.*Worm.* (WA 7:877)

See vol.1:304–6

Luth.*Vor.N.T.*(WA DB 6:537);
Luth.*Capt.Bab.* (WA 6:118)

Luth.*Wort.* (WA 23:95–99);
Luth.*Ab.Chr.* (WA 26:403–7)

Luth.*Ab.Chr.* (WA 26:263)
Eras.*Lib.arb.*1.b.4 (Walter 14–15)

Luth.*Serv.arb.* (WA 18:655)

divine word"; presumably, one was to understand "doctrine" in the light of "preached," and vice versa. The constant objection to other Protestant theologians, from Zwingli to the Radicals, was that "they teach that the Holy Spirit comes to us through our own preparations, thoughts, and works, without the external word of the gospel." Omnipresent though God unquestionably was, he did not wish to be known or grasped apart from his word. Luther said at the Diet of Worms that his conscience was captive to the word of God.

Was this word of God identical with the Bible? Like the question of Augustine's doctrine of the Eucharist, this question has itself become a point of subsequent theological controversy, whose principal issue has been the doctrine of biblical inspiration developed by later generations of Luther's followers and then repudiated by still later generations, with both parties laying claim to the authority of the Reformer. Although the question is therefore an anachronism, both sides could find some support in his language. As we have noted, he did value the spoken word above the written word of Scripture. He could deal with various books of both the Old and the New Testament, above all the Epistle of James, in a fashion that was difficult to harmonize with a high doctrine of biblical inspiration and inerrancy. Above all, Luther could sometimes dwell upon the centrality and the authority of the gospel with an almost obsessive intensity, testing liturgical practice, ethical precept, and even theological dogma by this criterion rather than by the norm of conformity to the literal meaning of the biblical text.

Yet when pressed to authenticate his teaching in controversy over a theological doctrine, for example the real presence of the body and blood of Christ in the bread and wine of the Lord's Supper, it was the norm of conformity to the literal meaning of the biblical text that he invoked: "An uncertain text is as bad as no text at all. Now what kind of Supper can that be, in which there is no text or sure word of Scripture?" In reply to the view of Erasmus that the text of Scripture was unclear in meaning, he asked: "Then why did it have to be brought down to us by an act of God?" and he quoted the classic proof text, which

See pp. 343–47 below

2 Tim.3:16

Bgn.*Annot*.2. Tim.3 (1524: 109v)

See p. 208–10 below

*Conf.Aug.*pr.8 (*Bek*.45)

Ps.68:26

*Form.Conc.Sum.*3 (*Bek*.834)

Luth.*Konz.* (WA 50:629–30)

was to be the foundation of the later doctrine of the inspiration of the Bible: "All scripture is inspired of God." Yet one of the earliest of Lutheran commentaries on the Pauline epistles simply skipped over this passage in its exposition of the Second Epistle to Timothy. Unlike other Reformation confessions, the *Augsburg Confession* did not open with a statement of the authority and inspiration of Scripture, nor with a list of the canonical books of the Old and New Testaments, contenting itself with the statement that it was "setting forth how and in what manner, on the basis of the divine Holy Scriptures, these things are preached, taught, communicated, and embraced." Fifty years later it appeared necessary for the *Formula of Concord* to begin with the prolegomenon: "We pledge ourselves to the prophetic and apostolic writings of the Old and New Testaments as the pure and clear fountain of Israel, which is the only true norm according to which all teachers and teachings are to be judged and evaluated"; but even this thetical statement eschewed such questions as inspiration and canonicity.

In sum, "the word of God cannot be without the people of God, and the people of God cannot be without the word of God. Who would preach or listen to preaching if no people of God were there? And what could or would the people of God believe if the word of God were not present?" It was in the name and by the authority of the word of God that Luther became a Reformer, and it was to the power of the word of God that he attributed whatever good may have come out of all his teaching and preaching. Nevertheless, all the issues of his teaching were to acquire a different configuration when, also in the name of the authority of the word of God, others set about to reform the church and its doctrine in a way and to a degree that went far beyond his.

# 4

# The Word and the Will of God

The theology of Martin Luther was a theology of the word of God: the climax of his best-known hymn was the defiant line, "The word they still shall let remain." Yet he and his immediate followers seemed to manifest a striking lack of specificity, or even of interest, in some of the most crucial questions involved in the doctrine of the authority of the word. Subsequent generations of Lutheran theologians would repair these inadequacies, and in great detail. But even before they did, the issues raised by the problem of the authority of Scripture as the word of God had been the object of painstaking research in other Protestant groups. In contrast not only to Roman Catholicism, but eventually also to Lutheranism, they were to denominate themselves "Reformed in accordance with the word of God [nach Gottes Wort reformiert]." To be sure, the Lutheran *Formula of Concord* spoke of the *Augsburg Confession* as "the common confession of the reformed churches," which "distinguishes our reformed churches from the papacy and from other condemned sects and heresies," meaning by this latter designation the other Protestant groups, including the very ones that were later called "Reformed," to whom the Lutherans denied the right to appeal to the *Augsburg Confession* and against whom they insisted on the sole authority of the original and "unchanged [invariata]" text of the *Augsburg Confession*. Well before the Peace of Westphalia, which is sometimes identified as the first official document to embody the nomenclature that was to become stan-

Luth. *Lied.* 23 (WA 35:457)

*Form. Conc. Sum.* 5 (*Bek.* 835)

183

dard, the twenty-sixth session of the Synod of Dort, on 10 December 1618, stated its requirement that "those Remonstrants who demand acknowledgement as teachers in the Reformed Church demonstrate that they have not retreated from the doctrine of the Reformed churches," and the Remonstrants in reply attacked those who "want to appear to be the only ones who are the orthodox and pure Reformed." "Reformed" is a designation that, with varying degrees of accuracy, could be applied to a far wider and more international community of churches than the largely (though never quite exclusively) Germanic ones that identified themselves as Lutheran. Even the Church of England, which defied all efforts to categorize it confessionally, was in some sense a "Reformed" communion, as its *Thirty-Nine Articles* and its delegation at the Synod of Dort attest.

Whatever the specific circumstances of its adoption may have been, the designation "Reformed in accordance with the word of God" contained the implicit judgment that although the word of God had been affirmed also by Luther and his followers, it had not been permitted to carry out the Reformation as thoroughly as it should have. In principle there was no disagreement on the matter of authority. Calvin recognized that while in addressing Roman Catholics he would have to contend for the sole authority of the Bible, he was, in dealing with his Lutheran opponents such as Joachim Westphal, writing to "men who constantly cry out 'the word of God, the word of God'"; but he had, he went on to say, "better evidence than Westphal can produce from his party" for "the reverence which we feel for the word of God." Calvin's *Institutes of the Christian Religion* of 1536 had shown him to be "in all respects a true disciple of the early Reformers, especially Luther," as were many of the other fathers and founders of the Reformed churches. Zwingli expressed his admiration for Luther, calling him "a veritable Hercules," but claimed that he himself had "begun to preach the gospel of Christ" before he had ever heard of Luther, and to reject the corporeal presence in the Eucharist before he had heard of Carlstadt. Calling Luther "our theologian," Johannes Oecolampadius characterized his "outstanding

Syn.Dord.*Sess*.26 (*Act.Syn. Dord*.1:98)

Conf.Remon.pr. (1622:C1v)

See pp. 2–3 above

Calv.*West*.1 (CR 37:20)

Calv.*West*.2 (CR 37:108)

Pauck (1961) 64

Zw.*Amic.exeg*.6 (CR 92:722–24)

Zw.*Schl*.18 (CR 89:144–50)

Zw.*Subsid*. (CR 91:463–65)

Oec.*Conf.*1 (1521:15)

Oec.*Luth.* (1521:A2r)

Oec.*Mis.*4 (1527:D2r)
Oec.*Antisyn.*83 (1526:S7r)

Oec.*Bill.Ant.*9 (1526:B1v)

Buc.*Caen.* (Strasbourg 1:21)

Buc.*Regn.Chr.*1.4 (Strasbourg 15:40–41)
Calv.*Scand.* (Barth-Niesel 2:216)

Calv.*Nec.ref.* (CR 34:459)

Calv.*Serv.arb.* (CR 34:250)
Calv.*Inst.* (1559)4.3.4 (Barth-Niesel 5:46)

Calv.*West.*2 (CR 37:95)

Las.*Sac.*ded.;pr. (Kuyper 1:101;113)

Blngr.*Alb.* (1532:A4v;A7r)

Blngr.*Resp.Brent.* (1526:5r)

Blngr.*Resp.Brent.* (1526:5r);
Zw.*Amic.exeg.*pr. (CR 92:569);
Zw.*Wort.* (CR 92:817)

Blngr.*Resp.Brent.* (1526:49v)

Calv.*Nec.ref.* (CR 34:473)

Calv.*West.*2.pr. (CR 37:50)
Calv.*Scand.* (Barth-Niesel 2:215)

Calv.*West.*1;2;3 (CR 37:17;105;220)

Calv.*Nov.Pol.* (CR 37:349);
Calv.*Hes.* (CR 37:461–62)

Conf.*Aug.*10.1 (Bek.64)

erudition" as "purely Christian," and in defense of Luther declared that he "comes closer to the truth of the gospel than do his adversaries." Despite their later disagreement over the Eucharist, which he rejected as "something that Luther had tacked on" to the word of God and that was not therefore to be taken as the word of God, he went on expressing his admiration for "our faithful coworker and preacher of the inexpressible majesty and praise of God." Bucer urged his opponents to pay attention to Luther, although he admitted that the Reformation in Germany had been only partly successful. For his part, Calvin regarded Luther as "a great miracle of God," as one whom God himself had raised up "to light us into the way of salvation," indeed as "an apostle," or "at any rate an evangelist," who especially deserved credit for attacking the theory of transubstantiation. "By the achievement of one man in our own age," Jan Łaski wrote, "in the eyes of God undoubtedly a chosen instrument, I mean Martin Luther, this horrible monstrosity [of the Mass] has fallen headlong into ruin." Heinrich Bullinger, too, acknowledged that Luther was "a learned man" and a chosen "instrument" of God," whose "faithful and useful labors" commanded respect.

But he was still "a human being, one who could and did err," and it was wrong to elevate his views over those of "all of the most learned and orthodox antiquity." Although Calvin went on claiming that he was "still pursuing the same course in the present day" that Luther had pursued, he regretted that the "marvelous consensus" between Luther and other Protestants, including himself, on almost all points of doctrine—which he sometimes enumerated in great detail—had been marred by "some amount of dispute" on "the symbols" or sacraments. He regretted also that Luther had found so few genuine "imitators" in the generation that claimed to be his doctrinal legatees, and he took as the most faithful legatee of Luther's teaching Philip Melanchthon, whose memory he revered. Melanchthon, who had written the *Augsburg Confession* of 1530, had revised the original wording of Article X on the Eucharist (which had been acceptable to the champions of transubstantia-

Confut.Conf.Aug.10 (CCath 33:100–101)

Conf.Aug.Var.10 (CR 26:357)
Calv.West.1 (CR 37:19)
Calv.West.2;3 (CR 37:91;148)
Calv.West.3 (CR 37:230)
Urs.Ex.ver.doct.9 (Reuter 1:887–903);Blngr.Resp.Brent.(1562:3v);Las.West.2–5 (Kuyper 1:275–77);Bez.Ep.theol.1 (1575:8)

Las.West.10 (Kuyper 1:282)
Blngr.Alb. (1532:A7r–A7v);Blngr.Dec.5.7 (1552:343r)
Calv.West.2 (CR 37:83)

Calv.West.2 (CR 37:51)

Calv.Cn.5 (Barth-Niesel 1:527–29);Las.West.41 (Kuyper 1:338)

Oec.Mis.4 (1527:D2r)

Calv.West.2 (CR 37:100)
Bez.Coen.34 (BezTract 1:245)

See pp. 207–8 below

Zw.Klar. (CR 88:338–84)

Zw.Gen.12:1 (CR 100:68)

Snds.Serm.1.9 (PS 41:12)
Blngr.Sum.1.3;8.2 (1556:6v;140v)

tion) to read instead: "that with the bread and wine the body and blood of Christ are truly presented [exhibeantur] to those who eat the Lord's Supper." This version, the so-called *Variata*, Calvin accepted, finding "not a single word contrary to our doctrine" of the Lord's Supper in it and citing the intention of Melanchthon as the "author" in support. Ursinus, Bullinger, Łaski, and Beza likewise found nothing objectionable in the *Augsburg Confession*.

Luther had gone too far—and not far enough. He had gone too far in his attacks on Zwingli, through whom Łaski had been led to the gospel and whom Bullinger and Calvin honored as a "martyr" and a "faithful and vigorous teacher of the church." Those attacks had initially deterred Calvin from even reading Zwingli. Calvin went on criticizing Zwingli and Oecolampadius for failing to emphasize that though the bread and wine in the Eucharist were "signs," they were "the kind of signs with which reality" was joined; he criticized Luther, on the other hand, for continuing to speak, despite his rejection of transubstantiation, in such a way as to give the impression that he "intended to assert the sort of local presence that the papists dream about." Luther had not gone far enough in recognizing that this notion of presence was an addition to the word of God, which "without the word of God we cannot hold as the word of God." He had correctly denounced superstitious practices, but "because of the weakness of the time he nevertheless kept them" and did not go so far as to abolish them. One such was the practice of kneeling before the consecrated Host. Reformed teaching, therefore, put at the head of its agenda (and at the head of many of its doctrinal statements) the task of carrying "reform in accordance with the word of God" to its necessary consequences, with a consistency and a rigor that went considerably beyond Luther. *The Clarity and Certainty or Power of the Word of God* was the title of Ulrich Zwingli's first important book and a recurring theme. Because "the foundation of our religion is the written word, the scriptures of God, the undoubted records of the Holy Ghost," Reformed theology defined itself as a theology of "the word and the will of God [gottes wort und meinung]"; for "in this task of ours 'the word of God' means the language of God, the revelation of the will of God."

## Word and Spirit

The primacy of the word of God was fundamental to the doctrine of the Reformation and to "the whole substance of the Christian religion." When his Roman Catholic opponent appealed to the catholicity of the church, governed by the Holy Spirit, and to its consensus as the guarantee of divine truth, Calvin replied by agreeing that the church was governed by the Spirit, but he went on to insist that the Spirit had "bound it to the word"; for it would be "no less unreasonable to boast of the Spirit without the word than it would be absurd to bring forward the word itself without the Spirit." In Zwingli's succinct formula, "God teaches through his Spirit and through the letter that has been written by the inspiration of his Spirit and ordinance, and he says: 'Search the Scriptures.'" Like Abraham, "we are to believe every word of God." The church was universal throughout history, but it could be recognized only "in the word of God." Otherwise Christ and his word would be subject to the church, whose regulations were "commandments of men." It has been observed that "in reading Calvin one may soon come to think that his favorite descriptive word for the Spirit is 'Teacher,'" but that "if Calvin occasionally makes a statement which implies that the teaching of the Holy Spirit is apart from the word, then he is quick to correct himself." Thus, in a manner reminiscent of Augustine's early Neoplatonism, he could speak of the Holy Spirit as "that inner teacher," but later in the same work he bound the Spirit to the word and the word to the Spirit, and elsewhere he linked the preaching of the word and "the special revelation of the Spirit" as the cause of conversion in the elect.

In his earliest known theological writing Calvin explained "seeking the righteousness of God" as "clinging to the word of God" and despising "the trifles and dreams of men." The theme was to recur throughout his works; and just a year before his death, after the bruising controversies over the doctrine of the Trinity and the validity of orthodox dogmatic formulas, he was warning against "formulas that are re-

Blngr.*Dec.*1.1 (1552:1r)

Calv.*Nec.ref.* (*CR* 34:502);Zw. *Klar.*pr. (*CR* 88:339–41);Rdly. *Ep.*7 (*PS* 39:344)

Sad.*Genev.* (Barth-Niesel 1: 450)

Calv.*Sad.* (Barth-Niesel 1:465–66)

John 5:39

Zw.*Bek.*1 (*CR* 93–II:109)

Zw.*Gen.*16:13 (*CR* 100:97)

Calv.*Theol.Par.*18 (*CR* 35:30); Rdly.*Conf.Ltmr.*2.5 (*PS* 39: 122–23)

Las.*Hos.*2.1 (Kuyper 1:416)

Zw.*Speis.* (*CR* 88:107)

Forstman (1962)75

See vol.1:295

Calv.*Rom.*7:5 (Parker 140)

Calv.*Rom.*10:16 (Parker 234)

Calv.*Occ.prov.*13–14 (*CR* 37: 314–15)

Matt.5:10
Calv.*Conc.acad.* (Barth-Niesel 1:9–10)

See pp. 322–31 below

Calv.*Ep.Pol.* (CR 37:647)

Calv.*Br.admon.* (CR 37:637)

Calv.*Rom.*4:22 (Parker 98)

Calv.*Rom.*14:23 (Parker 304)
Lact.*Inst.*4.5 (*CSEL* 19:284–86)

Calv.*Rom.*10:2 (Parker 222)

Calv.*Rom.*1:16 (Parker 25)

Calv.*Rom.*10:8 (Parker 227)

Calv.*Rom.*14:11 (Parker 298)

Calv.*Rom.*10:14 (Parker 232)

See p. 52 above

See pp. 320–21 below

Oec.*Mis.*16 (1527:Q1r)
Oec.*Antisyn.*62;56 (1526:P7r; O6r)

mote from the usage of Scripture" and against any nonscriptural "speculation about the mysterious essence" of the Trinity. The theme of the word of God was, of course, dominant in the *Institutes,* but it could be heard perhaps even more resonantly in his *Commentary on Romans.* Abraham was justified by faith "because, relying on the word of God, he did not reject the grace that was promised"; conversely, when the apostle condemned whatever was not "of faith," he was rejecting "anything that does not have the support and approval of the word of God." Calvin made his own the statement of Lactantius that the only true religion was the one that was joined to the word of God. Its basis, therefore, was not secret revelation, but the ministry of the word of God. Within the limits prescribed by the word, and only there, could the human mind contemplate the "mysteries of heaven." The mysteries of God and his majesty could not be known or honored any other way than "when acknowledged from the word"; only at the end of the world would it be otherwise. The word of God, as "the normal mode" of communicating divine truth, was "required for a true knowledge of God"; nevertheless, it was this only according to "the ordinary dispensation of God," and the apostle "had no desire to prescribe a law to [God's] grace" by denying God permission to work outside this dispensation.

For this paradox, that man was bound to the word of God but that God was not bound by it, there had been parallels in the medieval doctrine of the sacraments, and it was to the reconsideration of the importance of the sacraments that Reformed teachers applied this paradox the most rigorously. (Applying it with equal rigor to the reconsideration of the importance of the preached and written word itself became the burden of the Radical Reformers.) As Oecolampadius already recognized, "it is true that I do not ascribe as much to the external word . . . as Luther," for "the external word does not bring me resurrection," nor was it "the object of faith." He spoke disparagingly about theories that seemed to make God captive to the word, the bread, the letter, and the sacraments, as the means by which he communicated himself, theories of "inverbation, impanation, inliteration, and insacramentation." Specifically this implied that "the word and the sacraments" were not, "as the presence of God, more miraculous" than any other instruments through which God elected to work; it implied likewise that "presence" must not be ascribed in a unique sense to the sacraments. For just as Christ was not locally present in the mouth or the voice of the preacher, so also he was not locally present in the bread of the sacrament. The presence in the one was no more, and no less, than the presence in the other: word and sacrament were symmetrical.

Therefore it followed, according to Calvin, that "believers have, outside the Lord's Supper, what they receive in the Supper itself." The sacraments were dependent on the word of God, apart from which they had no function, and it was an error to fasten upon them as though they were in themselves necessary for salvation. To obviate such errors, Zwingli expressed the wish "that the word 'sacrament' had never been accepted in German," though he went on using it. Since Christ had instituted the sacraments by means of the word and tied them to the word, it followed, according to Bullinger, that "the word of the Lord is more important than the sacraments," as the apostle attested when he described his mission as one of preaching the gospel, not of baptizing. This did not negate any presence of Christ in the church, and even in the Lord's Supper, but it did mean that there was a "spiritual, divine, and life-giving presence of Christ the Lord in the Supper and outside the Lord's Supper, by which he . . . proceeds to enter our hearts, not through empty symbols, but through his Spirit." These emphases of Calvin and of Bullinger were brought together in the *Zurich Consensus* of 1549, according to which "the sacraments are appendages [appendices] of the gospel." The preaching of the word of God was supreme and central in the church, and the sacraments were "attached as seals to the letter." The grace that was offered in the sacrament was the same grace that was offered in the word, although Calvin did concede that in the Lord's Supper "we have a more ample certainty and a fuller enjoyment" of this grace. As in the Old Testament the content and utility of circumcision had depended on the word of God, so it was with the sacraments of the New Testament as well.

The most trenchant formula for this understanding of the relation between word and sacrament was Augustine's terminology of "the visible word," which Luther and his associates had also employed alongside their language about the real presence, but which now became a favorite of Reformed teachers, because it "points to the determinative orientation of the sacrament: it is the word made visible." In his early *Short Treatise on the Holy Supper of the Lord* Calvin explained that God had added a visible sign to his word; in the first edition of the *Institutes* a reference to the idea of "visible word" was one of the very few explicit citations of Augustine; and in his later polemical writings on the subject he found in the concept of visible word, which "we have always confessed," a common ground with his opponents, but claimed to be more consistent than they in regarding the bread and wine of the Lord's Supper as nothing other than visible words. It was likewise in keeping with Augustine's sacramental theology to interpret the presence of Christ "everywhere" despite his "absence according to the flesh" as the presence of one "who is with us in his word," for this presence could apply only to the preaching of the gospel. As Oecolampadius had already insisted, it was with the "flesh and blood of his word" that Christ nourished the entire human race. Bullinger summarized the "similarity" of sacrament to word by explaining that "the word is spoken in the sacraments," but that "in the recitation of the words of the Lord in the Supper there is no power of calling him down or of transmuting" the elements into the body and blood of Christ. "Reciting" the words over the sacrament, and in an alien tongue at that, was "a horrible pollution of the sacraments of God," a kind of "magic."

There was no need to call Christ down from heaven or to transmute the elements in the sacrament, because the sacraments were "external things" and deserved to be honored as such, but could not bring comfort to the human heart. Only Christ "himself is our sacrament, even if all the external symbols that the church uses were to be removed." To him, and not to "anything else instead of him," all statements about the

Aug.*Ev.Joh.*80.3 (*CCSL* 36: 529)

See pp. 179–80 above
Las.*Sacr.* (Kuyper 1:134);Urs. *Expl.Cat.*2.78.2 (Reuter 1: 271);Bez.ap.*Coll.Mont.Bell.*5 (1588:167)

McLelland (1957)129

Calv.*Cn.*1 (Barth-Niesel 1: 504–5)

Calv.*Inst.* (1536)4 (Barth-Niesel 1:119)

Calv.*West.*1;3 (*CR* 37:19;181)

Calv.*West.*3 (*CR* 37:217)

Calv.*West.*3 (*CR* 37:172)

Oec.*Corp.* (1525:F2v)

Blngr.*Dec.*5.6 (1552:331v,327r, 329r)

Conf.*Ung.*33 (Müller 414)
Calv.*Inst.*(1559)4.17.15;4.17.39 (Barth-Niesel 5:360;403);Zw. *Tf.* (*CR* 91:247)

Oec.*Ev.Joh.*31 (1533:120r)

Oec.*Corp.* (1525:D2v,F5v)

Conf.Helv.post.21 (Niesel 264)

Calv.West.1 (CR 37:17)
Calv.Cn.2 (Barth-Niesel 1:507)

Blngr.Perf. (1551:19,24–25)

Calv.West.1 (CR 37:22)

Calv.Rom.4:11 (Parker 87)

Calv.West.1 (CR 37:24)
Aug.Ev.Joh.26.18 (CCSL 36: 268)

Blngr.Dec.5.7 (1552:336r)

Calv.West.1 (CR 37:17)

Ltmr.ap.Rdly.Conf.Ltmr.1 (PS 39:114–15);Las.Sacr. (Kuyper 1:136)

Calv.Ep.du.1 (Barth-Niesel 1: 299)

Buc.Caen. (Strasbourg 1:44–45;24;36);Calv.Inst.(1559)4.14.5–6 (Barth-Niesel 5:262–63)

Oec.Theob.Bill. (1526:F3v)
Calv.Inst.(1559)3.2.36 (Barth-Niesel 4:47)

Blngr.Ver.2 (1578:7v–8r)

Blngr.Sum.8.3 (1556:142v–143r);Blngr.Dec.5.7 (1552: 341v)

Calv.West.3 (CR 37:162)

sacraments were to be referred, and from him the entire power of the sacraments was derived; for "the Lord Jesus is the content and the substance of the sacraments." If he truly was the perfection of those who believed in him, it was false to require any other means of perfection; this did not exclude the "exercises" that he had instituted for his church as "guides" to him, but it did put them strictly into their proper place. It was, according to Calvin, "the summa of our doctrine" about the sacraments that attributing to dead creatures what properly belonged to God alone was depriving God of his due glory. Whatever benefit came from the sacraments was the action of God alone, and that "by his hidden and, as they say, 'intrinsic' power." The power of God in the sacraments was "hidden grace" not, as the doctrine of transubstantiation maintained, because the substance of the elements had been mysteriously changed into the body and blood of Christ under the forms of bread and wine, but because through them God accomplished his will in the elect and only in the elect, as Augustine had taught.

On the sacraments, therefore, it was imperative that sound doctrine deviate neither to the left nor to the right, by avoiding both the extreme of a "superstition" that exaggerated their value and the extreme of a "profane contempt" that depressed them "in a manner that is frigid or less splendid" than they merited. The tendency of some in the ancient church "to esteem the Sacraments but lightly, as to be empty and bare signs" had sometimes, for quite understandable reasons, caused the church fathers "in their fervour . . . to run too far the other way, and to give too much to the Sacraments." In addition to such terms for the sacraments as the "bond" uniting believers with Christ and with one another, the categories of "seal" and "sign" were especially well designed to avoid both extremes. Ultimately, of course, the blood of Christ, offered in the sacrifice of the cross, was the true "seal" of salvation, as was the Holy Spirit himself. But as "seals attached to the letter" of the word of God, the sacraments took their meaning from the word and yet were not extraneous to it. The concept of "sign" and "signification" was even more appropriate to them. It had been God's practice from the beginning to "add

Zw.Gen.9:17;15:8;17:10 (CR 100:59;88–89;106–7)
Aug.Doct.christ.1.2.2 (CCSL 32:7)
Oec.Resp.post. (1527:9–10);
Oec.Mis.11 (1527:K1r–K1v);
Blngr.Dec.5.6 (1552:322r)
Zw.Tf. (CR 91:218);Zw.Gen. 24:2–4 (CR 100:159);Blngr. Nacht.2 (1553:C4r)

Oec.Mis.15 (1527:P2v)
Oec.Antisyn.26 (1526:K3r);
Oec.Theob.Bill. (1526:D6v)
Calv.West.3;1 (CR 37:161;17)
Zw.Schl.18 (CR 89:121–22)

Cons.Tig.9 (Müller 161);Calv. West. (CR 37:20)

Blngr.Dec.5.6 (1552:323v);
Rog.Cath.Doct.25.4 (PS 40: 250)

Zw.Pecc.orig.3 (CR 92:392)

Blngr.Assert.orth. (1534:67r);
Blngr.Nacht. (1553:C7v)

Cran.Gard.1 (PS 15:11)
Bez.ap.Coll.Mont.Bell.3 (1588: 92)

Bez.Flac.14 (BezTract 2:146)

Calv.West.1.pr. (CR 37:7–8)

Calv.West.2 (CR 37:56)

Calv.Cn.2 (Barth-Niesel 1:509)

Calv.Opt.rat. (CR 37:518)

Calv.West.3 (CR 37:187);Zw. Bek.1 (CR 93–II:203–4)

external signs to his promises," as an accommodation to human weakness. Augustine's well-known distinction between "sign [signum]" and "reality [res]" in Book One of his *On Christian Doctrine* served as the basis for the discussion. In each of the sacraments that distinction between the sign and the reality signified by it was fundamental. Confusing the sign and the reality, as the common people did in their "simplicity" and as the "scholastic and papist" theologians did in their error, was what led to superstition; for if the Mass was a "sacrifice," how could it be a sign? At the other extreme was the replacement of the "distinction" between sign and reality by a "disjunction," which Reformed doctrine insisted was not what it had in mind either.

Although the use of the term "sign" for "sacrament" pertained to the definition of sacrament as such, and specifically also to baptism, most of the debate about it arose over its adequacy in application to the Lord's Supper. It was a "calumny," Reformed teachers replied to their critics, to charge them with maintaining that there was "no mystery" in the Supper, but only a "bare sign, nothing but bread and wine," a "bare token" that would be something like a painted fire, which gave neither light nor heat. Any such notion of a "bare representation, . . . as dead men are represented through statues or other images," was "manifest impiety." When they declared that there was "a true communication" of the body of Christ to believing communicants, this proved that they were not speaking only of "a bare and empty sign," and they were prepared to oppose any effort to reduce the Supper to this. The bread and wine were, rather, "visible signs, which represent the body and the blood to us and to which the name and title of the body and blood is attributed." Even "represent" was not an adequate term; it would be more accurate to say that they "present" the body and the blood. When God set forth a "sign," it was not empty, but had "reality and efficacy joined" to it. Thus the dove through which the Holy Spirit appeared at the baptism of Christ was certainly not the Holy Spirit, even though "the evangelist does not hesitate to call the dove 'the Holy Spirit'"; nor was it "a vain figure, but rather a sure

Calv.*Cn*.2 (Barth-Niesel 1:509)

Blngr.*Sum*.8.3 (1556:141v–
142r);Zw.*Unt*.1 (CR 91:793);
*Conf.Scot*.21 (Niesel 108)
Blngr.*Sum*.8.8 (1556:152v–
153r)

Zw.*Bek*.1 (CR 93–II:65–66)

Buc.*Ep.apol.* (Strasbourg 1:95)

Calv.*West*.1 (CR 37:31–32);
Calv.*Opt.rat.* (CR 37:519);Las.
*Sum.cont.* (Kuyper 1:478)

Calv.*West*.3 (CR 37:183)

Rdly.*Br.decl.* (Moule 106);
Rdly.*Conf.Ltmr*.1.5 (PS 39:
106,109)

Hub.*Unt.* (QFRG 29:290)

Calv.*West*.2 (CR 37:47)

sign of the presence of the Holy Spirit." And so, as
had been correctly taught since Christian antiquity,
"the sacrament is a sign of a holy thing, indeed, of a
holy thing that has been designated by the word of
God," yet not an "empty sign," but a genuine eating
of Christ himself by the believer.

Most of these protestations came in the course of
the eucharistic controversies between Reformed and
Lutheran theologians. Zwingli and Oecolampadius
identified the point of controversy as the issue whether
"the words [of institution] must be spoken over the
Supper because they cause something to happen."
Bucer, writing in 1530, spoke of those who "contend
that the body and blood of Christ are present and are
eaten corporeally," some of whom said that it took
place "under the appearance of bread," while others
said that it was "under the bread itself." Calvin sometimes maintained that the only issue between the two
eucharistic doctrines was over how the body and blood
of Christ were communicated, not over the reality of
the communication. That simplification of the issues
could be expanded in the course of the same polemical
exchange to include the question of whether "it is
necessary that the substance of the body" be eaten in
the Supper, as well as of whether unbelieving communicants received the true body. Nicholas Ridley
listed the issues as: transubstantiation, "any corporeal
and carnal presence of Christ's substance," the adoration of the Host, the definition the Mass as sacrifice,
and the reception of the true body by an evil communicant; but all five of these, he added, "chiefly hang
upon this one question, which is, what is the matter
of the Sacrament." In addition to these questions of
content, the controversies brought into the open some
fundamental disagreements between the two main
branches of classical Protestantism, despite their
agreement about the supreme and sole authority of
the Bible as [the] word of God, over the principles
governing the interpretation of that word, and particularly over the proper and improper use of figures of
speech in determining the meaning of the biblical text.

One after another, the expositors of the Reformed
view of the Lord's Supper formulated their underlying
hermeneutical principles. "Christ, who is recognized

by faith alone and worshiped by faith alone," had, according to Hoen, "withdrawn his corporeal presence from us"; hence the bread was a "sign" of his presence. "We must understand first of all," Zwingli argued in 1526, "that throughout the Bible there are to be found figures of speech, [which are] . . . to be understood in another sense"; and he proved it from Old Testament usage. In the following year Oecolampadius called it a "rule" that "in dealing with signs, sacraments, pictures, parables, and interpretations, one should and must, in accordance with the principle of signs or sacraments, understand the words figuratively, and not understand the language simply." Ursinus, too, spoke in 1564 of a hermeneutical "rule," as did Bullinger at about the same time, who called it a "universal rule for interpreting the sacraments," that "in the sacraments the signs receive the name of the things that are signified, yet without being transformed into them." "What words can be more plain, than to say, 'This is my body'?" Thomas Cranmer asked, and he answered: "Truth it is indeed, that the words be as plain as may be spoken; but that the sense is not so plain." To Calvin it was an "axiom" that "whenever sacraments are being dealt with, it is usual for the name of the things signified to be transferred by metonymy to the sign." Metonymy, he explained, was not the same as parable or allegory, but implied that God was representing himself "truly" by it. As Beza explained in his replies to Lutherans, the language of the sacrament involved several kinds of metonymy, including "the container for the contents" in the use of the word "cup" for that which it contained. The statement of Zwingli that the idea of a physical eating of Christ's body was "abhorrent to sense," or of Oecolampadius that "there is nothing in this sacrament that either is a miracle or surpasses human understanding," or even of Bullinger that "we do not need other witnesses here than our own senses, which do not sense or see or taste or feel anything but bread and wine," had, ever since Luther, led to the charge that this was a rationalistic hermeneutics. Like Zwingli, Calvin denied that it was dictated by philosophy, but he did hold that "the order of nature is part of theology" in the question of the presence, and he op-

Hn.*Ep.chr.* (*CR* 91:516–17)

Zw.*Unt.*3. (*CR* 91:842);Zw. *Ver.fals.rel.*18 (*CR* 90:796–99); Zw.*Subsid.* (*CR* 91:472);Zw. *Amic.exeg.* (*CR* 92:731–32)

Zw.*Gen.*17:10 (*CR* 100:105)

Oec.*Mis.*3 (1527:C1r) Urs.*Ex.ver.doct.*1 (Reuter 1: 811)

Blngr.*Sum.*8.8 (1556:151r); Blngr.*Dec.*5.9 (1552:368v)

Cran.*Gard.*3 (*PS* 15:103)

Calv.*West.*1 (*CR* 37:36)

Calv.*Hes.* (*CR* 37:472)

Bez.*Coen.*3 (*BezTract* 1:213); Bez.*Flac.*4;10 (*BezTract* 2:128– 29;141);Zw.*Ver.fals.rel.*18 (*CR* 90:799)

Zw.*Subsid.* (*CR* 91:490–91); Zw.*Amic.exeg.* (*CR* 92:594; 621)

Oec.*Corp.* (1525:A7r–A7v)

Blngr.*Dec.*5.6 (1552:332r) Luth.*Wort.* (*WA* 23:127);Luth. *Ab.Chr.* (*WA* 26:321) Zw.*Wort.* (*CR* 92:884–88;906– 7) Calv.*West.*2 (*CR* 37:78–79); Urs.*Expl.Cat.*78 (Reuter 1: 269) Calv.*West.*3 (*CR* 37:214)

posed whatever would give the impression that Christian doctrine involved any absurdity. It was not to some rationalistic a priori, but to "the rule of faith" that sound hermeneutics must conform.

The hermeneutical problem came to a focus on the interpretation of the sixth chapter of the Gospel of John, which contained the puzzling combination of Christ's words, "Unless you eat the flesh of the Son of man and drink his blood, you have no life in you," and his words a few verses later, "it is the spirit that gives life, the flesh is of no avail." Zwingli, whose liturgy for the Lord's Supper included the reading of John 6:47–63, quoted the two verses together, to prove that "whenever he speaks of eating his flesh and drinking his blood he simply means believing in the worth of that suffering which he bore for our sakes," no more and no less. Rejecting the effort to make of this chapter an equivalent of the words of institution recorded in the other three Gospels, as well as the contention that nothing was being said here about the sacraments at all, Oecolampadius argued that the flesh of Christ became food "by no other kind of eating than faith." For its clarification of that point as it pertained to the Lord's Supper, John 6 (which, everyone agreed, spoke about faith) became "the iron wall" of the Reformed position. Calling it rather a paper wall that had the color of iron, Luther also agreed that what Christ was describing "to the very end of the chapter" was faith; but from this he drew the conclusion that the Lord's Supper was not the subject of the chapter at all, so that "The flesh is of no avail" did not pertain to the body of Christ in the Supper. He even claimed to have proved his point so successfully that in his last book Zwingli did not use the passage. In fact the passage remained for Bullinger the key to the understanding of the accounts of the institution of the Eucharist in the Synoptic Gospels: the chapter must refer to the Lord's Supper. Calvin was, characteristically, somewhat more cautious. The words, "Unless you eat the flesh of the Son of man," did not refer to the Lord's Supper, and "The flesh is of no avail" could not be interpreted in such a way as to contradict the necessity "of eating the crucified flesh if it is to benefit us." But he and his colleagues

Calv.*Rom*.6:1 (Parker 119)

Calv.*West*.2;3 (CR 37:74;184)

John 6:53

John 6:63

Zw.*Act*. (CR 90:19–20)
Zw.*Ver.fals.rel*.7 (CR 90:698–99)

Zw.*Unt*.2 (CR 91:817);Zw.*Bek*. (CR 93–II:181–90)

Oec.*Ev.Joh*.32 (1533:120v)

Oec.*Theob.Bill*. (1526:G3v)

Oec.*Antisyn*.54 (1526:N8v);
Zw.*Ver.fals.rel*.18 (CR 90:776–81)
Oec.*Mis*.8 (1527:F4r)

Luth.*Wort*. (WA 23:167)

Luth.*Ab.Chr*. (WA 26:372)

Luth.*Ev.Joh*.6.51 (WA 33:182)
Luth.*Ev.Joh*.6.63 (WA 33:259–60)

Luth.*Krz.Bek*. (WA 54:152)
Blngr.*Coen*. (1558:13v)
Blngr.*Dec*.5.6 (1552:335r)

John 6:53
Calv.*Ev.Joh*.6:53 (CR 75:154)

Calv.*Ev.Joh*.6:63 (CR 75:159)

Calv.*West*.3 (*CR* 37:188;200);
Buc.*Ep.apol.* (Strasbourg 1:
97);Las.*Sacr.* (Kuyper 1:222);
Las.*Hos*.1.21 (Kuyper 1:411);
Urs.*Expl.Cat*.2.78.4 (Reuter 1:
275–76);Bez.*Ep.theol*.5 (1575:
55)

did use John 6 to explain the "eating" in the Lord's Supper as something other than "the physical eating by which these crude theologians dream of feeding themselves."

The classic exposition of the Gospel of John, which Luther and Calvin in their own commentaries on John quoted far more often than any other, was that of Augustine. His exegesis of John 6 and his application of his general theory of signs to the Eucharist, the two features of his sacramental theology that had turned out to be the most problematic for the development of

See vol.3:77–80,195–96,207–8

Bez.*Coen*.30 (*BezTract* 1:237)

eucharistic doctrine in the Middle Ages, now acquired new respectability as "the most genuine" supports for Reformed teaching. Augustine enjoyed the special advantage that his authority was universally acknowledged. Hence the defenders of the Lutheran doctrine of the real presence could not avoid "citing Augustine

Calv.*Hes.* (*CR* 37:501)

Calv.*West*.3 (*CR* 37:215)

as a patron or a witness," nor could they very well "dare to deprive him of the title 'theologian.'" There were passages in his writings that seemed to favor the

See vol.1:305

Lutheran position, as when he argued for the objectivity of the presence (on the basis of the test case of

See vol.3:196

Calv.*Bapt*.5.8.9 (*CSEL* 51:270)
Zw.*Bek*.1 (*CR* 93–II:95)
Las.*Sacr.* (Kuyper 1:119)
Calv.*West*.1 (*CR* 37:28);Bez.
*Conf*.4.50 (*BezTract* 1:31)
Aug.*Civ*.21.25 (*CCSL* 48:795)
Calv.*West*.3 (*CR* 37:155)

Judas) even when a communicant received the body and blood unworthily. But "Augustine does not share [Luther's] opinion," and elsewhere he had corrected himself, also with regard to Judas, "explaining more fully" that "anyone who is not in the body of Christ cannot be said to eat the body of Christ." He had also seemed to speak "in a haphazard way" about the Lord's Supper, thereby permitting himself to be used in support of mutually contradictory theories of the presence. But "this holy doctor is in fact consistent

Calv.*Hes.* (*CR* 37:503)

Blngr.*Resp.Brent.* (1562:49v);
Calv.*West*.2;3 (*CR* 37:60;149);
Zw.*Ver.fals.rel*.18 (*CR* 90:809–
10;814–15)

Calv.*West*.3 (*CR* 37:153–77)
Bez.*Coen*.10–28 (*BezTract* 1:
245–54)

throughout." That meant to the champions of the Reformed doctrine of sacraments that "Augustine is on our side and speaks out in suport of us against [the Lutheran doctrine]," as extensive reviews of proof texts from his works demonstrated. Beza assembled catenae of such proof texts from Augustine, and in one case he even printed the word "signifies" in capital letters

Bez.*Flac*.21 (*BezTract* 2:167–
68)

each time Augustine used it.

See pp. 54–55 above

Among such proof texts from Augustine, their clear favorite (which was still being quoted by defenders of transubstantiation against Reformed theology, to

Lat.*Def.Buc*.2 (*CCath.* 8:44)

prove that God was not bound to the sacraments) was

the commonplace from his *Exposition of the Gospel of John*, "Believe, and you have already eaten." Oecolampadius quoted it to show that the object of the believing about which Augustine was speaking was not the body of Christ substantially united with the bread, but the central mystery of the incarnation, passion, resurrection, and ascension of Christ; hence it must mean a spiritual eating that could not be confined to the act of outward eating. Zwingli saw Augustine's words as setting forth "the whole basis of the sacrament" and paraphrased them to mean that "when you partake of the two elements of bread and wine, all that you do is to confess publicly that you believe in the Lord Jesus Christ," since such believing meant, in Augustine's words, that "you have already eaten." Rejecting the views of his Lutheran opponent about the eating of the body of Christ as "Capernaitic," Calvin quoted the passage of Augustine in support. Bullinger cited it to reject the notion of a "corporeal presence," since the true way of eating Christ's body and blood was to believe in him; and in the *Second Helvetic Confession* of 1566 he used it to back up the view that "this spiritual eating and drinking takes place even apart from the Lord's Supper, whenever and wherever someone believes in Christ." Ursinus incorporated it into a florilegium of patristic texts on the nature of the presence. Beza quoted it to explain what he and his colleagues meant when they described Luther's doctrine as "Capernaitic." With some debt to one or more of these interpreters, Edwin Sandys, archbishop of York, quoted the formula to back up the principle that "he cannot be partaker of the body of Christ, which is no member of Christ's body."

In the light of an Augustine so interpreted, it was possible to understand the development of eucharistic faith and practice "since the times of the holy apostles, as it was greatly changed and as in the course of time it acquired quite another form." Tertullian was still sound in his doctrine of the Supper, for he had explained "my body" as "the figure of my body"; this was a reading of Tertullian's words that both Luther and Roman Catholic theologians rejected. Roman Catholics cited as "clear testimony for transubstantiation" the ambiguous formula of Irenaeus, that "the

Aug.*Ev.Joh*.25.12 (*CCSL* 36:354)

Oec.*Corp*. (1525:F5r)

Oec.*Mis*.9 (1527:H3r)

Zw.*Unt*.1 (*CR* 91:807–9)

Calv.*West*.3 (*CR* 37:154)

Blngr.*Dec*.5.9 (1552:373r);
Blngr.*Sum*.8.8 (1556:152r)

*Conf.Helv.post* 21 (Niesel 265)
Urs.*Fr.ver.doct*.8 (Reuter 1:884)

Bez.*Coen*.18 (*BezTract* 1:229)

Snds.*Serm*.4.21 (*PS* 41:88);
Cran.*Gard*.3 (*PS* 15:118)

Blngr.*Nacht*.1 (1553:B3r);Rdly.
*Br.decl*. (Moule 160–63)
Zw.*Amic.exeg*. (*CR* 92:739–40);Zw.*Wort*. (*CR* 92:972–73);
Blngr.*Or.err.miss*.3 (1528:B1r);
Calv.*Hes*. (*CR* 37:496);Bez.
*Coen*.3;9 (*BezTract* 1:214;223)
Tert.*Marc*.4.40.3 (*CCSL* 1:656)
Luth.*Wort*. (*WA* 23:217–29)
Fish.*Corp*.4.26 (1527:200v);
Grop.*Leyb*.1 (1556:60v–69r)

Grop.*Leyb*.1 (1556:58r);Fish.
*Corp*.4.32 (1527:192r–192v)
See vol.1:167

Iren.*Haer*.4.18.5 (Harvey 2: 207–8)

Eras.*Iren*.pr. (Allen 1738)

Conc.*Witt*.1 (*CR* 3:75)

Luth.*Wort*. (*WA* 23:229–37)

Calv.*Theol.Par*.5 (*CR* 35:15); Las.*Hos*.2.5 (Kuyper 1:439)

Calv.*West*.3 (*CR* 37:189);Las. *Sacr*. (Kuyper 1:120)

Calv.*Hes*. (*CR* 37:473);Las. *West*.29 (Kuyper 1:316–17)

Bez.*Flac*.15 (*BezTract* 2:156)

See pp. 176–77 above
Zw.*Wort*. (*CR* 92:970);Calv. *Hes*. (*CR* 37:490)
Blngr.*Or.err.miss*.5 (1528:C7r–D6v)
Las.*Coen*. (Kuyper 1:560–62)
Zw.*Bek*.1 (*CR* 93–II:81–85); Calv.*Hes*. (*CR* 37:490)

See vol.3:219–30

Oec.*Corp*. (1525:K1v–K2r); Calv.*West*.3 (*CR* 37:209)
Calv.*Hes*. (*CR* 37:490–91); Cran.*Gard*.3 (*PS* 15:196)
Las.*Hos*.18 (Kuyper 1:409); Blngr.*Dec*.5.6 (1552:334r);Urs. *Ex.ver.doct*.8 (Reuter 1:880)

Rdly.*Br.decl*. (Moule 142–43); Cran.*Gard*.3 (*PS* 15:173)

Blngr.*Coen*. (1558:8v)

Blngr.*Or.err.miss*.4 (1528:B5v–C5r)
Blngr.*Or.err.miss*.5 (1528:C7r–C7v)

Eucharist . . . consists of two realities, earthly and heavenly." That ambiguity—associated as it was with the church father whose very name, as Erasmus had pointed out in the preface to his edition of Irenaeus in 1526, meant "peacemaker"—suited it well to serve as the proposed compromise solution in the *Wittenberg Concord* of 1536, in which Luther, Melanchthon, and Bucer momentarily came together on a statement of the doctrine of the presence of the body and blood of Christ in the Lord's Supper. Luther had, in response to the "word-torturing" effort of Oecolampadius to claim the authority of Irenaeus for his version of the presence, subjected the formula to a close reading in favor of his own views. Nevertheless, Calvin and his associates were able to put Irenaeus to effective use in defending the Reformed doctrine not only against the condemnation of various Roman Catholic spokesmen, but also against the Lutherans' insistence that the presence of the body of Christ in the Supper was not "spiritual"; for, despite the collapse of the *Wittenberg Concord* itself, the Lutherans had continued to subscribe to the Irenaean formulation, although Reformed theologians noted Lutheran dissatisfaction over its ambiguity. On the basis of Oecolampadius's scholarly work on the patristic doctrine of the presence, and of Bullinger's researches into the evolution of the idea of transubstantiation, Reformed theology could appropriate Chrysostom, Cyril, Hilary, and Epiphanius, as well as Ambrose (despite his having been the one whose doctrine had rescued Augustine's doctrine in the course of the medieval development)—indeed, virtually every other orthodox church father except perhaps John of Damascus.

In the patristic era there had been no controversy about the Lord's Supper, and the turning point in the history of sacramental doctrine had clearly been at the end of that period. Since "what our Lord and Savior instituted was a Supper, not a Mass," its transformation by Gregory the Great into "the Mass, the monstrous fountainhead of all superstitions," was such a turning point, although it was a mistake to put "the whole blame" on him. After Gregory there was still no doctrine of transubstantiation. The case of Ra-

See vol.3:74–80

Trith.*Scrip.eccl.* (1512:66r)

Blngr.*Alb.* (1532:A3v–A4r)
Blngr.*Or.err.miss.*5 (1528:C7v–C8r)

See vol.3:186

Cran.*Gard.*1;3 (*PS* 15:14;77)

Blngr.*Conc.*2.2 (1561:118r)

Rdly.*Disp.Ox.* (*PS* 1:206)

See vol.3:186–202

Blngr.*Conc.*2.2 (1561:119v–120r)

Las.*West.*19 (Kuyper 1:291)

Cran.*Gard.*1 (*PS* 15:14)

See p. 54 above

Luth.*Ab.Chr.* (*WA* 26:442–43)

Zw.*Ver.fals.rel.*18 (*CR* 90:783–84);Zw.*Unt.*1 (*CR* 91:801–6);*Conf.Helv.post.*21 (Niesel 264)

See vol.3:198

Oec.*Corp.* (1525:E3r)

John 6:63

Oec.*Ev.Joh.*36 (1533:137v)
Calv.*Inst.*(1559)4.17.12 (Barth-Niesel 5:355);Calv.*Ep.du.*1 (Barth-Niesel 1:307);Calv.*West.*1;2;3 (*CR* 37:27;58;154);Cran.*Gard.*3 (*PS* 15:113);*Conf.Helv.post.*21 (Niesel 264)

tramnus, as described by the biographical compiler Trithemius at the end of the fifteenth century, was proof of this; for there was no documentation to show that his doctrine of the Eucharist had been condemned by the church. What had been condemned at Vercelli in 1050 was a book attributed to John the Scot. (It was, in fact, Ratramnus's book.) Under the name of "Bertram," that book became a force in the Reformation debates, especially in England, being printed in 1531 under the sponsorship of Oecolampadius, and translated into English in 1549. Bullinger praised "Bertram" as "pious and learned," and Nicholas Ridley accepted Oecolampadius's view as his own doctrine of the presence and as an accurate interpretation of "Bertram," who "was the first that pulled me by the ear, and that brought me from the common error of the Romish church."

But no incident in the medieval history of the doctrine of the Eucharist had made as much of an impact as the tragedy of Berengar, whose writings were known only from quotations in the works of his opponent Lanfranc and who had been "constrained to make a devilish recantation." Various reconsiderations of the doctrine of the eucharistic presence in the later Middle Ages had taken off from that recantation. Defending the doctrine of the real presence, Luther likewise defended both the treatment of Berengar by the pope and the concession extracted from him. Zwingli and Bullinger, on the other hand, condemned both. The phraseology of Berengar's confession, that "the bread and wine are the true body and blood of our Lord Jesus Christ . . . handled and broken by the hands of the priests and ground by the teeth of the faithful," indicated to what extremes a literal doctrine of the real presence might go, and it was against such crass conceptions of eating the flesh of Christ that the words, "The flesh is of no avail," were directed. Calvin found the phraseology "monstrous," quoting it over and over again for its shock value against those who shared Luther's view of the affair. When a Lutheran theologian also recoiled at the crudity of the formula but went on urging the necessity of the Lutheran view of the real presence, Calvin ridiculed the inconsistency of wanting to say that the true body of Christ was

Calv.*Hes.* (CR 37:469–70)

Calv.*West.*2;3 (CR 37:57;210)

See pp. 184–87 above

Calv.*West.*3 (CR 37:232);Zw.
*Amic.exeg.*6 (CR 92:711)
Zw.*Bek.*1 (CR 93–II:32);Zw.
*Wort.* (CR 92:861–62)

See p. 177 above

See vol.3:184–204

Oec.*Corp.* (1525:A2v);Oec.
*Antisyn.*6 (1526:H6v);Oec.
*Resp.post.* (1527:37);Blngr.*Or.
err.miss.*5 (1528:D6r);Blngr.
*Dec.*5.10 (1552:379r);Blngr.
*Resp.Brent.* (1562:86v)

Rdly.*Br.decl.* (Moule 119,158);
Cran.*Gard.*1 (PS 15:45);Las.
*Sacr.* (Kuyper 1:144)

Blngr.*Alb.* (1532:A4r)

*Form.Conc.S.D.*7.35 (*Bek.*983)
Bez.*Flac.*29–30 (*BezTract* 2:
195)

Calv.*Hes.* (CR 37:473);Calv.
*West.*3 (CR 37:225);Las.*West.*
11 (Kuyper 1:283);Zw.*Bek.*1
(CR 93–II:72–73)

Las.*Hos.*2.5 (Kuyer 1:442–43);
Bez.*Ep.theol.*8 (1575:77)

Zw.*Wort.* (CR 92:971–72);Urs.
*Ex.ver.doct.*5 (Reuter 1:847–
48)

eaten by the mouth but at the same time that it was not ground by the teeth. Or, to be consistent, anyone who regarded Berengar as a heretic ought to return to "the pope's camp."

Despite their admiration for Luther and their sense of having in common with Luther's followers most of the body of Christian doctrine, Reformed theologians were reluctantly compelled to acknowledge that on the doctrine of the Lord's Supper Lutheranism was "more friendly to the papists than to us," as the "papists" themselves admitted. That acknowledgment appears to have been more than a polemical device, for it recognized, as did Luther, that there was more continuity between the medieval eucharistic development and the Lutheran confessional position than there was between the latter and the Reformed teaching. Luther's acceptance of the real presence and rejection of transubstantiation made his position analogous to that of medieval theology before transubstantiation had become official; in short, Luther had, despite his polemics against Peter Lombard, retained the Lombard's eucharistic doctrine. Transubstantiation was the "fantastical invention" of Innocent III, "in his congregations with his monks and friars" at the Fourth Lateran Council. Luther had frequently attacked Innocent, but he could not find any theologian who agreed with him before Peter Lombard and Pope Innocent. The Lutheran theory that the body of Christ was present "in, with, and under" the bread of the Supper, which Reformed polemics repeatedly attacked, was not significantly better than the theory of transubstantiation that it claimed to oppose—if, indeed, there was any real difference between the two doctrines of presence. Nor had it proved to be any more effective than transubstantiation in preventing "artolatory," the idolatrous worship of the bread in the Lord's Supper. Although the doctrine of a substantial presence and the interpretation of the Lord's Supper as a sacrifice logically belonged together and those who defended the presence had difficulty refuting the sacrificial interpretation, there was the fortunate inconsistency of a real and profound difference: the Roman Catholics "attribute to their work [in the Mass] a part of the satisfaction for the living and the dead, which the Lutherans by constrast do not do, since they come to the Lord's Supper not to give something, but to receive grace." Otherwise, the Lutheran doctrine, which the Reformed came to call "consubstantiation," was as much a "materialistic theology" as was the Roman Catholic doctrine of transubstantiation. There were only two possibilities: "either transubstantiation or a trope." "The Ubiquitarians, both Lutheran and popish," were very much alike.

Rather than either of these, the doctrine that must always prevail in the church was that all the sayings of Scripture about "the presence of the Lord in the church and about eating him" were to be interpreted "not carnally or corporeally, but spiritually." "Spiritual eating" and the notion of a physical body were mutually exclusive. As a principle of interpretation, this pertained to biblical texts, but also to the vocabulary and usage that had developed in the liturgical and dogmatic tradition of the church. Each of the major themes of eucharistic faith and practice must have a meaning that conformed with this "summary . . . of the Christian faith," that is, with this principle of interpretation. Already in 1523 Zwingli was insisting that the most important of these themes was that of memorial. If it were to be legitimate to speak of "substance" at all, as both Calvin and Łaski were sometimes willing to do, it could only be when its meaning had been purged of "the crude notion about an eating of the flesh." If the traditional language about "presence" were to be acceptable, as it was to Reformed theologians, it must not be any natural or local presence, but a spiritual presence that conveyed the "efficacy and power" of the body of Christ. And if, in the light of these redefinitions, the church called the Sacrament "Holy Communion," this implied, according to 1 Corinthians 10:16, the "communion" of those who shared in it, rather than the "communication" or "distribution" of the actual body and blood; as Zwingli reminded him, Luther himself had interpreted the passage this way, but then had changed his interpretation. Nevertheless, since there was no communion without communication, it was "an execrable blasphemy" to deny that "a true communication of

---

Oec.*Mis*.6 (1527:F1r)

Urs.*Expl.Cat*.2.78.4 (Reuter 1: 279–82)

Calv.*West*.3 (*CR* 37:192)

Bez.*Coen*.3 (*BezTract* 1:217)

Rog.*Cath.Doct*.29 (*PS* 40:293)

Blngr.*Coen*. (1558:6r–6v)

Zw.*Ver.fals.rel*.18 (*CR* 90:787)

Zw.*Wort*. (*CR* 92:895)

Zw.*Schl*.18 (*CR* 89:137–39)

Calv.*Cn*.2 (Barth-Niesel 1: 510);*L,as West*.28 (Kuyper 1: 315)

Calv.*Opt.rat*. (*CR* 37:521);Zw. *Wort*. (*CR* 92:834)

Calv.*Ep.du*.1 (Barth-Niesel 1: 307);Bez.*ap.Coll.Mont.Bell*.3 (1588:75)

Zw.*Bgn*. (*CR* 91:569);Zw. *Amic.exeg*. (*CR* 92:637–40); Zw.*Subsid*. (*CR* 91:497–99); Zw.*Bek*.2 (*CR* 93–II:230–34); Oec.*Antisyn*.63 (1526:Q1r); Oec.*Theob.Bill*. (1526:F5v) Zw.*Amic.exeg*. (*CR* 92:749– 50);Zw.*Wort*. (*CR* 92:962–63)

Luth.*Serm.sacr*. (*WA* 2:74) Luth.*Himm.Proph*. (*WA* 18: 167)

Calv.*West*.3 (*CR* 37:192)

Jesus Christ is presented to us in the Supper," but it was "the rightful use of a communion granted to us from elsewhere."

As these redefinitions of the central terms of eucharistic doctrine indicate, it was alien to the Reformed way of teaching to draw ontological parallels between the Eucharist and the incarnation. Whether or not Reformed polemics was right in charging that the Lutheran theory of the ubiquity of the exalted human nature of Christ threatened to make the sacramental presence a mere corollary of this massive cosmic presence, it was a characteristic of Reformed theologians, and a characteristic not sufficiently grasped by Lutheran polemics, that in their attempts to specify just what the Reformed churches did teach about the Lord's Supper and how this differed from what other churches taught, they would recur to the doctrine of the Holy Spirit. Zwingli set "the indwelling Spirit" against "the body that is eaten physically," and already in the first edition of his *Institutes* Calvin enumerated the three "benefits" granted by God in word and sacrament: "First, the Lord teaches and instructs us by his word; secondly, he confirms by the sacraments; and finally, he illumines our minds with the light of his Holy Spirit and opens the entrance to our hearts with the word and the sacraments." Jan Łaski, who "in the understanding of the Sacrament of the Altar stood very close to John Calvin," began with an objective characterization of other positions and then presented as a third view the teaching that "refers [the sacramental union] to the work of the Holy Spirit, . . . who in any of Christ's institutions constantly bears witness to him and glorifies him." Theodore Beza, in a dispute with Lutherans, urged them not to go on ignoring the relation of the Holy Spirit to both baptism and the Lord's Supper. The confessions picked up this emphasis. To eat and drink the body and blood of Christ, said the *Heidelberg Catechism*, means "to be united more and more to his sacred body through the Holy Spirit, who dwells both in Christ and in us." Christ, in a mysterious manner, "accomplishes in us everything that he represents to us by these holy signs," according to the *Belgic Confession*, since "the operation of the Holy Spirit is

---

*Marginal references (left column, top to bottom):*

Calv. *Cn.*2 (Barth-Niesel 1:508)

Las. *Sacr.* (Kuyper 1:149);Las. *Coen.* (Kuyper 1:566–69)

Calv. *West.*2 (CR 37:66);Oec. *Corp.* (1525:G3r)

Zw. *Wort.* (CR 92:897)

Calv. *Inst.*(1536)4 (Barth-Niesel 1:121)

Bartel (1955) 172

Las. *Sum.cont.* (Kuyper 1:474)

Bez. ap. *Coll.Mont.Bell.*9 (1588:440–41)

Cat. *Heid.*76 (Niesel 167);Urs. *Expl.Cat.*76 (Reuter 1:263)

Conf.Belg.35 (Schaff 3:429–30)

secret and incomprehensible." The "spiritual eating" in the Supper did not mean, the *Second Helvetic Confession* explained, that "the food is changed into the Spirit," but rather that the body and blood of Christ "are communicated to us 'spiritually,' through the Holy Spirit, who applies to us and confers upon

Conf.Helv.post.21 (Niesel 264)

us" forgiveness of sins and life eternal. All three of these Reformed confessions happen to come from the 1560s, the decade of Calvin's death, but it would not be difficult to multiply passages from the later statements of the Reformed faith as well. To cite only one example, the *Westminster Shorter Catechism* of 1647 attributed the efficacy of the sacraments to "the working of his Spirit in them that by faith receive them," as it attributed the efficacy of "the reading, but especially the preaching, of the word" to "the Spirit of

West.Cat.(Shorter) 91;89
(Müller 650)

God." Here, too, the theme of "word and Spirit" demonstrated its centrality in Reformed doctrine. It remained to be seen, in the conflict with Anabaptism, what would happen to this theme when the subject under discussion shifted from the Lord's Supper to

See pp. 313–22 below

baptism.

## Obedience to the Word and Will of God

The controversy over the Lord's Supper brought out on both sides a detailed consideration of the authority, the inspiration, and the interpretation of the Bible. More pointedly than in his conflicts with the Roman Catholic view of the relation between the authority of Scripture and the authority of the church, Luther bore down on the inviolability of every single word of Scripture: as Zwingli parodied his words, "Is, is,

Zw.Bek.1 (CR 93–II:115)
Luth.Ab.Chr. (WA 26:418)

is: there it stands!" "The Holy Spirit," Luther insisted, "neither lies nor errs nor doubts." Similarly, the clarity of Scripture, which he had defended against

Luth.Serv.arb. (WA 18:653–58)

Erasmus, appeared to him to be forfeit if his opponents had their way about the use of "tropes" and the figurative interpretation of the eucharistic language of

Luth.Wort. (WA 23:215)

the New Testament.

In keeping with their view of word and Spirit, the interpreters of the Reformed understanding of the Lord's Supper were no less insistent on its congruence with the intention of the Holy Spirit in the word. The medieval theory of the real presence was based on a false definition of authority, being derived not from the plain and unglossed words of the evangelists but

Oec.*Dign.euch.*1 (1526:A3v)

from the determination of the church. There were variations in the text of these words from one evangelist to another, "but all four, no doubt, as they were all taught in one school, and inspired by one Spirit,

Rdly.*Br.decl.* (Moule 97)

taught one truth." It was the agreement between the two main branches of Protestantism on the sole authority of the Bible as inspired by one Spirit, over against the coordination of the authority of the Bible with the authority of the church, that made their disagreement over the Lord's Supper so ironic and so

Calv.*West.*3 (CR 37:183–84)

painful. To settle a disagreement over the Sacrament, it was not only the word of God in general, but specifically the institution of Christ in the Supper that

Calv.*Cn.*4 (Barth-Niesel 1:522)

stood as the authority. For the institution of any sacrament must, together with its intention, be decisive

Calv.*West.*1 (CR 37:16)

for the determination of its meaning and content. "In our doctrine" of the Supper, Calvin contended, "the stable authority of the word and the institution of the

Calv.*West.*2 (CR 37:89)

sacrament" were correlated. Since both sides believed beyond controversy that Christ, as the Son of God, was their sole and supreme Teacher, "in whose doctrine it is not permissible to change even a word or a syllable," they both had the obligation also to attend

Calv.*West.*3 (CR 37:184)

to his meaning in the institution of the Lord's Supper.

The reason for such an emphasis on the words of institution was not, as it had been in medieval teach-

See vol.3:200

ing, that they effected the eucharistic miracle of trans-

Calv.*Inst.*(1559)4.17.20 (Barth-Niesel 5:367)

forming bread and wine into the body and blood of Christ. Rather, it was that the Lord's Supper, according to the institution of Christ, was "in remembrance of me" and in remembrance of his sacred history. That divinely instituted remembrance of the body that had suffered for human salvation was more valuable than any presence of the body would be,

Oec.*Dign.euch.*1 (1526:A8v)

according to Oecolampadius; for even if it were, "as they say, 'present,' the flesh does not accomplish anything now that is not already conferred by the re-

Oec.*Resp.post.* (1527:26)

membrance which the Holy Spirit arouses." The theme of remembrance was especially prominent in Zwing-

Zw.*Art.LXVII.*18 (CR 88:460);Zw.*Schl.*18 (CR 89:111);Zw.*Ver.fals.rel.*18 (CR 90:807);Zw.*Tf.* (CR 91:297)

li's and in Bullinger's interpretations of the Lord's Supper: it was "a remembrance of the sacrifice" of

Zw.*Wort.* (CR 92:892)

Christ—not of his body, but of his death. Christ had

Blngr.*Nacht*.2 (1553:C6r–C6v)

Locher (1981) 222

Las.*Hos*.1.8 (Kuyper 1:402)

Blngr.*Dec*.5.9 (1522:361r);
Blngr.*Or.err.miss.* (1528:A6r–A6v)

Zw.*Act*.pr. (*CR* 91:14)

Zw.*Ord.* (*CR* 91:687–94)

Urs.*Fract.pan.* (Reuter 3:813–18);Zw.*Act*.pr. (*CR* 91:17);
Las.*Sacr.* (Kuyper 1:197);Bez.
*Ep.theol*.2 (1575:25)

Bez.*Ep.theol.* 24 (1575:143)

Blngr.*Nacht*.1 (1553:A5v)

Calv.*West*.3 (*CR* 37:184)

Calv.*West*.3 (*CR* 37.226–27);
Zw.*Can.miss.* (*CR* 89:588–89);
Zw.*Tf.* (*CR* 91:232–33)
Rdly.*Lam.* (*PS* 39:56–57)

Rdly.*Br.decl.* (Moule 126)

Calv.*West*.3 (*CR* 37:186–87)

Blngr.*Coen.* (1558:2v)

Blngr.*Coen.* (1558:4v)

instituted the Supper so that the mystery of his incarnation and crucifixion might not be forgotten in the church. And while it is important to note that "this 'remembrance' is not a merely intellectual process, and it does not awaken association with the past, but rather with the present," indeed, with past, present, and future, it did so by the action of the Holy Spirit when the faithful remembered Christ. Consequently, the best form for the celebration of the Lord's Supper was the simple one that the apostles had received from Christ and transmitted to all the nations. One early example of this "right Christian form" was Zwingli's liturgy of 1525, with "as little ceremony and ritual as possible." A "right form" included the breaking of the bread, as well as such practices as using wooden vessels, reclining during the Supper, and receiving the bread in the hand; but such matters of form were not to become an absolute requirement. This was not a simplistic primitivism, for it was based on the assumption that not only the original celebration by Christ and his apostles, but every celebration of the Supper, was Christ's. What bound the primitive celebration then to the remembrance of it now was the Spirit through the word.

Therefore Calvin's stress on the inviolability of "even a word or a syllable" in the institution of Christ as set down in the word of God was not equivalent to a concentration on "individual words and syllables" without attention to "the mind" that spoke through them. Nor did an emphasis on biblical inspiration carry with it, "as it were an infallible rule, that in doctrine and in the institution of the sacraments Christ used no figures, but all his words are to be strained to their literal [propre] significations." For while it was infallibly true that what Christ promised, that he also gave, it was wrong to apply his words in such a crude way as to maintain that there was no difference between bread and body. Central though the words of institution were, Bullinger urged that they must be related to other passages that spoke of the Supper if the entire mystery of the Sacrament was to be set forth. But immediately he went on to disavow any suggestion that the message of salvation itself was figurative in its language or in its interpretation. It was not an infallible rule, as the Lutherans claimed, that Christ had not used figurative language in the institution of the sacraments; so, on the other hand, it was not a "universal rule" that "is" must always be taken as "signifies." The first chapter of the Book of Genesis and the first chapter of the Gospel of John "are historical, without any ceremonies, and they will not tolerate my using the word 'sign,'" while the words of institution in the Lord's Supper "are expository [auslegende] words, and not simply historical ones"; therefore the Supper was not "mere history," but a sign and a "commandment."

Declaring his loyalty to the true intent of the words of institution, Calvin avowed: "For my part, I would rather perish a hundred times than to put one little word of Christ on the scales against the whole of philosophy. . . . For to us the authority of Christ is not only sacrosanct, but self-authenticating." Adherence to the institution of Christ in the Supper was part of a total obedience to the word and will of God, an obedience that was, as he affirmed in the closing sentence of his *Commentary on Romans,* "the purpose of the preaching of the gospel." To his Anabaptist critics on the Radical left he addressed the admonition to "desire to render obedience to the truth," while to those on the Roman Catholic right who used the specter of the Radicals to charge the Reformation with having fomented unrest he sent the message: "It is the will of our Master that his gospel be preached. Let us follow his command and follow wherever he calls. What the outcome will be, it is not up to us to inquire." To both groups, and to all others, he explained "the nature of faith" as obedience to the gospel. For according to Calvin the gospel could properly be called "the rule of life," to which the appropriate response was "obedience," which, both in Greek and in Latin, was a special form of "hearing" the word of God. "Obedience to the will of God," therefore, was a recurring phrase in this theology, where it was synonymous with obedience to the word of God.

If the gospel was "the rule of life," it was likewise true that "the principle of living right" was total dependence on the will of God; and "only then is the life of the Christian a composed one when it has the

Calv. *West.*3 (CR 37:199)

Oec. *Mis.*3 (1527:C4v–D1r)

Zw. *Wort.* (CR 92:888–89); Zw. *Bek.*1 (CR 93–II:61–65)

Calv. *West.*2 (CR 37:79)

Calv. *Rom.*16:26 (Parker 330)

Calv. *Anab.*pr. (CR 35:55)

Calv. *Nec.ref.* (CR 34:511)

Calv. *Rom.*1:5 (Parker 16)

Calv. *Rom.*2:21 (Parker 50)

Rom. 10:16–17

Calv. *Inst.*(1559)3.19.4;2.15.5 (Barth-Niesel 4:284–85;3:479)

Calv. *Rom.*14:5 (Parker 294)

Calv.*Rom*.14:8 (Parker 295–96)

Oec.*Rom*.pr. (1526:2r)

Calv.*Nec.ref.* (*CR* 34:474)

See pp. 228–29 below

Calv.*Astrol.* (*CR* 35:527)
Calv.*Harm.ev.*Matt.2:1 (*CR* 73:81–82)

Calv.*Rom*.11:36 (Parker 263)

Calv.*West.* (*CR* 37:79)

Calv.*Rom*.3:10 (Parker 63)

Rom.3:10

Calv.*Rom*.14:5 (Parker 294)

Calv.*Rom*.14:8 (Parker 295–96)

Calv.*Rom*.3:4 (Parker 57)

Calv.*Ep.du.*1 (Barth-Niesel 1: 324–25)

Calv.*Rom*.ded. (Parker 3)

Zw.*Klar.* (*CR* 88:353;358)
Zw.*Art.LXVII*.1 (*CR* 88:458);
Zw.*Schl.*1 (*CR* 89:21–26)

Zw.*Wort.* (*CR* 92:853)

Buc.*Ec.*1 (Strasbourg 1:239)

1 Pet.4:11

Buc.*Regn.Chr.*1.6 (Strasbourg 1:239)

2 Tim.3:16

will of God as its aim." For, as Oecolampadius had already put it in his own *Commentary on Romans*, "the aim of the entire Scripture is to vindicate the glory of God, so that God might reign in all, chiefly in the hearts of men." Obeying the word of God and aiming to follow the will of God meant seeking the glory of God, which, Calvin felt able to claim, was receiving a far loftier treatment in the Reformed churches than it had previously. Thus when, for example, he encountered the practice of divination through astrology, he denounced it as a derogation of the honor of God and an encroachment upon the majesty of God, since the proper study of the stars was "confined to the limits of nature." The honor and glory of God must be the supreme goal and purpose for the human race, from which nothing could be allowed to detract. The sacrosanct and self-authenticating authority of Christ constituted, for Christians, the strongest of all possible arguments, surpassing all purely human proofs. But that characterization of the argument from divine authority came in Calvin's exposition of the words of the apostle Paul, "As it is written." The corollary to the gospel as "the rule of life" and to dependence on the will of God as "the principle of living right" was what he termed "the primary axiom of the entire Christian philosophy": "God is truthful." An obedient listening to the truthful voice of God meant the acceptance of "the oracle that has been received from the holy mouth of the eternal God" in his word, which believers must hold in "veneration."

Therefore "the word of God is certain and powerful," Zwingli declared and went on to defend its clarity against those who asserted the authority of the church over it; it contained no contradictions. Martin Bucer, in the first chapter of his reply to Eck, explained that a priest deserved to be heard only if he "speaks the oracles of God"; "all doctrine," he said elsewhere, "must be derived from the Divine Scriptures, without anything being added or subtracted." And when Calvin took up the attacks of the theologians of the Sorbonne against him and the Reformed faith, he began his reply with an assertion of the authority of the word of God, citing the text, "All Scrip-

Calv.*Theol.Par*.pr. (*CR* 35:5–7)

Urs.*Loc.theol*.1 (Reuter 1:426–47)

Blngr.*Ggn*.1.A.1 (1551:2)

Blngr.*Sum*.1 (1556:1r–22r)

Conf.*Helv.post*.1 (Niesel 222–23)

Conf.*Remon*.1 (1622:1–8)

Conf.*Belg*.2–7 (Schaff 3:384–89)

Conf.*Helv.pr*.1 (Müller 101)

Conf.*Tetrap*.1 (Stupperich 3:42–45)

See pp. 343–47 below

ture is inspired by God." Ursinus inaugurated his lectures on systematic theology with the doctrine of the uniqueness and sole authority of Scripture. Likewise, when Bullinger took up the task of explaining the antitheses between the Reformed and the Roman Catholic churches, it was with the assertion: "The holy, biblical Scripture, because it is the word of God, has standing and credibility enough in and of itself" and did not need the authority of the church to establish it. The same topic formed the first chapter of his *Summa*. Nor was it only in his private writings that he assigned this priority to the authority and inspiration of the Bible. The *Second Helvetic Confession*, which he penned in the name of the churches, commenced the same way, with the equation of Scripture and the word of God, and included the famous explanation: "The preaching of the word of God is the word of God." Despite its opposition to Orthodox Calvinism on other counts, the *Remonstrant Confession* of 1621/22 opened with an article entitled: "Holy Scripture, its Authority, Perfection, and Perspicuity." Although the *Belgic Confession* did not make the authority and inspiration of Scripture its very first order of business, it did introduce the topic in its second article and continued with it to the end of the seventh article. In this the *Belgic Confession* and the *Second Helvetic Confession*, written at almost the same time, were following the precedent of the *First Helvetic Confession*, as well as of the *Tetrapolitan Confession*, which the Reformed cities had presented to the Diet of Augsburg in 1530 at the same time that the Lutherans presented theirs and which was based on the Lutheran confession; but the Lutheran *Augsburg Confession* did not begin with, nor even contain, any such article, and neither did the *Apology of the Augsburg Confession*.

Such assertions of the authority and inspiration of the Bible in Reformed theologians and church confessions were still, in most instances, far from the completely developed doctrine of inspiration that was, during the seventeenth century, to become characteristic of later theologians, and even of some confessions, among the Lutherans no less than among the Reformed. It has been suggested that "in only one

O.Ritschl (1908) 1:67

Prof.fid.Franc.pr. (Müller 657)

Calv.2 Tim.3:16 (CR 80:383)

Calv.Inst.(1559)4.8.9 (Barth-Niesel 5:141)

Blngr.Sum.1.2 (1556:5r)
Joh.D.F.o.4.17 (Kotter 2:209)
2 Tim.3:16

Blngr.Sum.1.6 (1556:13v);Calv.Rom.15:4 (Parker 306)

Conf.Helv.post.2 (Niesel 224)

Conf.Ung.4.27 (Müller 411);
Bez.Conf.4.27 (BezTract 1:22);Syn.Dord.Sess.6 (Act.Syn.Dord.1:21)

See vol.1:114

Blngr.Scrip.auth. (1538)
Blngr.Coch. (1544);Blngr.Antibib. (1544)

Calv.Inst.(1559)4.9.14 (Barth-Niesel 5:163)

See pp. 275–76 below

Calv.Ant.4 (CR 35:413)

single [Reformed confession] is inspiration characterized as a dictation by the Holy Spirit." That was the confession framed by the congregation of Reformed exiles in Frankfurt in 1554, whose preface included the statement that "the only foundation of this faith is that of Holy Writ, which the prophets and apostles have handed down to us in written form by the dictation of the Holy Spirit." Calvin did describe the prophets as "organs of the Holy Spirit," whose writings "are dictated by the Holy Spirit," and the apostles, by contrast with their successors, as "the sure and authentic amanuenses of the Holy Spirit." Bullinger spoke of "the biblical Scripture as certain, inerrant, and incontrovertible" and argued, as had Christian exegetes generally, that although the standard proof text for inspiration referred in the first instance to the Old Testament rather than to the New Testament, of which it was itself a part, its comprehensive statement, "All Scripture is inspired by God," included the New Testament as well as the Old.

The doctrine of the authority and inspiration of Scripture carried a number of implications. Since the Bible, though interpreted chiefly by those who had the requisite calling and training and who should therefore know Hebrew and Greek, was intended as the authority for the entire church, it followed that there must be reliable translations into vernacular languages. Another implication of the doctrine was the specification not alone of the predicate "inspired by God," but also of the subject "all Scripture." Bullinger devoted several treatises, one of them addressed to Henry VIII and two others in reply to Cochlaeus, to the question of the church's authority to determine the content of the biblical canon. While Calvin, in his *Institutes*, said that he would "prudently skip over what they teach on the power to approve Scripture," the action of the fourth session of the Council of Trent in fixing the precise canon of the Bible so as to include the apocryphal or "deuterocanonical" books of the Old Testament elicited from him some discussion of that "power," in which he laid claim to the "consensus of the ancient church" for not "promiscuously" incorporating these books in the biblical canon. For, as Bullinger acknowledged in the first of the sermons that formed his *Decades,* "the subject and the place [of the doctrine of biblical authority] now demand that we also collect and specifically enumerate those sacred books in which the very word of God is contained."

Therefore the Reformed confessions of faith in the sixteenth century, again by contrast with the Lutheran, frequently presented (sometimes, but not always, at the beginning) the roster of books that belonged to the canon; and the seventeenth-century *Westminster Confession,* summarizing the earlier confessions, introduced its roster with the formula, "Under the name of Holy Scripture, or the word of God written, are now contained all the books of the Old and New Testament, which are these," and concluded it with the formula, supported by such passages as 2 Timothy 3:16, "All which are given by inspiration of God, to be the rule of faith and life." By contrast, "the books commonly called apocrypha" were not inspired, did not belong in the biblical canon, and were not to be "made use of" in any way different from "other human writings." The *Thirty-Nine Articles* of the Church of England had treated them more positively, as books that "the church doth read for example of life and instruction of manners," but not "to establish any doctrine." Luther had similarly spoken of them as "useful to read," but not on a level with the genuinely canonical books. These differences of attitude were reflected in the very editions of the Bible; for "much Protestant (especially Calvinist) opinion disapproved of the Apocrypha, which are frequently absent from extant copies of Geneva Bibles [the English version of 1560], particularly those printed in Holland," and "in modern times the English Bible has more often been issued without than with the Apocrypha." At the Synod of Dort it was specified that, if the Apocrypha were included, the difference between them and the canonical books should be clearly indicated by a special typeface and separate pagination.

The criteria for the biblical canon and the jurisdiction of church or council to apply these criteria in determining (or, as Protestants preferred to see it, in recognizing) which books belonged to it were all part of the total issue of the relation between church and Scripture as authorities. "The difference between us and the papists," according to Calvin, "is that they do not think that the church can be 'the pillar of the truth' unless she presides over the word of God. We, on the other hand, assert that it is because she reverently subjects herself to the word of God that the truth is preserved by her and passed on to others by her hands." In the age from Adam to Moses, when there were no written books, it had therefore still been the case that "the word of God comes before the church," regardless of whether that word was written or oral, since "the preaching of the word of God is the word of God." The church was always the company of true believers, but true faith did not base itself on anything human, not even on the church and its traditions, but only on the clear word of God. It was a contradiction to affirm that the Scriptures were perfect in truth and free of all falsehood and then to claim that "the doctrine of the word of God in them should be sought and gathered not from their unanimous meaning, but from some sort of sense and consensus of the church." When Christ spoke to the disciples about still having much to say to them, he was not, as the advocates of tradition contended, promising further revelations to the church after the New Testament but referring to the content of his word to them. The revelation of Christ to the church was complete and perfect, and the prophets and apostles had deposited it fully in the books of Scripture, "which are correctly believed to be inspired by the Holy Spirit and which we truly call 'holy' and 'authentic.'"

1 Tim.3:15

Calv.*Scand.* (Barth-Niesel 2: 234–35)

Blngr.*Sum.*1.5 (1556:10r);Rog. *Cath.Doct.*19.4 (*PS* 40:173)

*Conf.Helv.post.*1 (Niesel 223)

Blngr.*Ver.*2 (1578:5v)

Las.*Hos.*2.5 (Kuyper 1:428)

John 16:12

Zw.*Speis.* (*CR* 88:135)

2 Tim.3:16

Blngr.*Perf.* (1551:35–38)

The fathers of the church had defeated heresy by citing the authority of Scripture, so that loyalty to them required a subjection to the same authority, with which they did not want their own writings to be equated. The epigram of Cyprian, "A custom without truth is nothing more than an ancient error," became an appropriate way of making the point that the truth of God in Scripture took precedence over the customs of the church, however ancient they might be. Those who were "abandoned by the word of God" would "flee for aid to antiquity," but genuine antiquity was, more often than not, on the side of the Reformed,

Blngr.*Assert.orth.* (1534:12r; 13r)

Blngr.*Sum.*1.8 (1556:18r)

Blngr.*Sum.*1.10 (1556:20v–21r)

Cypr.*Ep.*74.9 (*CSEL* 3:806)

Blngr.*Or.err.miss.*3 (1528:A7r–A7v);Blngr.*Dec.*5.9 (1552: 362r);Calv.*Admon.Paul.III.*22 (*CR* 35:268);Calv.*Scand.* (Barth-Niesel 2:233)

Calv.*Nec.ref.* (*CR* 34:523)
Buc.*Ep.apol.* (Strasbourg 1: 117)

Zw.*Apol.Arch.*31 (*CR* 88:290)

Calv.*Scand.* (Barth-Niesel 2: 231–32);Calv.*Nec.ref.* (*CR* 34: 497)

See pp. 196–98 above

Calv.*West.*3 (*CR* 3:207);Calv. *Rom.*1:2 (Parker 13)

ap.*Disp.Zof.*1;11 (1532:6v–7v; 135r)

See pp. 322–23 below

Blngr.*Sum.*1.10 (1556:19r)
Blngr.*Conc.*1.17 (1561:70r); Blngr.*Sum.*6.2 (1556:89r)

Blngr.*Conc.*1.5 (1561:16v)

Blngr.*Dec.*1.1 (1552:1r)

Calv.*Rom.*14:4 (Parker 293)

Calv.*Rom.*10:5 (Parker 224)

Las.*Hos.*2.5 (Kuyper 1:421)

Zw.*Schl.*5 (*CR* 89:32)

while their opponents labeled as "ancient" those traditions that "the recent greed of some has invented." When ecclesiastical antiquity did not support the Reformed, as in the question of celibacy, the most venerable antiquity of all was the apostolic authority of Scripture. When, on the other hand, antiquity was on their side, as they believed it to be in the question of the real presence over against the Lutheran as well as the Roman Catholic position, Reformed teachers defended themselves against the charge of doctrinal novelty by declaring "that we today do not teach anything else than what was accepted then without any controversy." The Radicals of the Reformation claimed to be carrying out more consistently the sole authority of Scripture, which theoretically they had in common with Lutheran and Reformed teachers. Against them (and, at the same time if possible, against other opponents) the Reformed defended orthodox antiquity, including the "homoousios" of the Nicene Creed. But the idea of a nonscriptural tradition was without foundation, and the genuine "apostolic tradition" was that embodied in the Apostles' Creed. Not everything Christ had said or done was contained in Scripture, but everything necessary was.

Because, in Bullinger's words, "the word of God" meant "the language of God, the revelation of the will of God," obedience to the word of God was also obedience to his will as disclosed in his law. It was the custom of Scripture to connect its statements about the power of God with statements about the will of God, and for the proper comprehension of what Scripture meant by "law" it was essential to observe that the term was used in a twofold way: to describe commandments, rewards, and punishments; but also to identify "the universal doctrine made known by Moses." In the former sense, the law was that from which Christ set sinners free and to which the gospel stood in contrast or even in opposition; it was a "malicious distortion" to treat "the entire doctrine of the word of God" as law, or to say "that the gospel is a law." But in the latter sense, the law was both a "universal doctrine" and a permanently valid one, which the coming of Christ had confirmed and reinforced and which stood in perfect harmony with the gospel both as its presupposition and as its consequence, since it was the two together, the law as well as the gospel, that represented the content of the word and will of God. This interpretation of the law of God and of its relation to the gospel was another manifestation of the simultaneous affinity and divergence between the Reformed and the Lutheran versions of the Protestant faith, although neither the affinity nor the divergence figured as prominently in the polemical exchanges between the two churches as did such doctrines as the Eucharist and predestination.

Yet the polemical exchanges did not utterly ignore the matter. One of the earliest documents in the exchange, Zwingli's treatise *On the Providence of God* of 1530, concentrated much of its attention on a criticism of Luther over the question of the "chief use of the law." According to Zwingli, the law was, in its essence, "the character, will, and nature of God," given to teach that the goal of life was the knowledge of God and fellowship with him. There were "certain people" (clearly a reference to Luther) who had "not spoken of the law circumspectly enough," because they had paid attention exclusively to the law as "it terrifies, damns, and passes sentence." On the contrary, "the law in reality does not do that at all, but rather sets forth the will and intention of God." Although he could define the gospel as the message, present already in the Old Testament, "that in Christ sins are forgiven," he could also say: "I call everything gospel which God reveals to men and demands from men"; and he concluded; "This also puts an end to the dispute about law and gospel." "The law," he said later in the same work, "is a gospel for the man who honors God." Christ had not only fulfilled the law; he had also renewed it. For Bullinger as well, there was "nothing changed" in the Decalogue with the coming of Christ, as could be seen from the way "Jesus inculcated it in the Gospel." Because "the law of God contains the most perfect doctrine both about faith in God and about all good works," the law was intended for the instruction of those who had been justified by faith, to tell them what they should follow and what they should avoid.

---

*Marginal references:*

Zw.*Prov.* (Schuler-Schultess 4: 102–5)

Zw.*Schl.*19;22 (CR 89:159–60; 232–33);Zw.*Ger.* (CR 89:481); Zw.*Ver.fals.rel.*9 (CR 90:707)

Zw.*Gen.*12.1 (CR 100:67–68)

Zw.*Ver.fals.rel.*7 (CR 90:691); Zw.*Val.Comp.* (CR 91:64–66)

Zw.*Schl.*16 (CR 89:79)

Zw.*Schl.*22 (CR 89:232)

Zw.*Ger.* (CR 89:496)

Blngr.*Dec.*3.8 (1552:139v– 140v)

Blngr.*Dec.*3.8 (1552:137v)

According to Bullinger, however, that was the second use of the law, for he saw "the chief and proper function of the law" as that of convincing sinners of their guilt and showing them that they were "the children of death." In his earliest known work, Calvin likewise developed the distinction between the law and the gospel in a manner quite reminiscent of Luther: the law commanded, threatened, and urged, but did not promise the kindness of God; the gospel did not impel or press, but taught the supreme kindness of God. Like Luther, he read the Epistle to the Romans as a statement of that "antithesis" between the two, between Moses and Christ. But his reading of Romans did not take the accusations of the law against trespasses as "the total function and use of the law, but only as a part." Some kind of law was universal throughout the human race, as the testimony of a heathen like Cicero demonstrated. It was wrong even to imagine that there had been an abrogation of the law, Calvin argued in the final edition of his *Commentary on Romans,* inasmuch as the Ten Commandments had been given by God for all time. Evidently, then, the apostle Paul in Romans was using the term "law" in two distinct senses, sometimes to mean the whole of divine revelation and sometimes to refer only to that which contained commands, rewards, and punishments. As Zwingli had pointed out, one could say both that "Christ is a law" and that "Christ is the end of the law." The law could be called a "yoke" in two senses: when it made salvation conditional on perfect obedience, it was an unbearable yoke and must be replaced by the gospel; but when "it bridles the desires of the flesh and provides a standard for leading godly and upright lives, it is right for the sons of God to submit their necks to this yoke," as the words of Christ about his "yoke" proved.

In the latter sense, the law was permanently binding, "because the will of God must stand forever." When the *Heidelberg Catechism* defined the new life of the Christian believer as "taking delight in living according to the will of God in all good works" and went on to define such works as "those only which are done from true faith, according to the law of God" as given in the Ten Commandments, this was a ped-

Blngr.*Dec.*3.8 (1552:136r);Bez. *Conf.*4.24 (*BezTract* 1:20)

Calv.*Conc.acad.* (Barth-Niesel 1:5);Urs.*Expl.Cat.*19.3 (Reuter 1:103)
Calv.*Rom.*10:8 (Parker 228)

Calv.*Rom.*10:5 (Parker 224–25)

Calv.*Rom.*5:20 (Parker 118)

Calv.*Rom.*2:14–15 (Parker 45–46)

Calv.*Rom.*7:3 (Parker 138)

Calv.*Rom.*10:5 (Parker 224)

Zw.*Schl.*16 (*CR* 89:82)

Matt.11:29–30

Calv.*Act.*15:10 (*CR* 76:350)
Calv.*Harm.ev.*Matt.11:29–30 (*CR* 73:321–22)

Calv.*Rom.*7:3 (Parker 138)

*Cat.Heid.*3.90–92 (Niesel 171–72)

Urs.*Expl.Cat.*91.5 (Reuter 1: 317)

Bez.*Ep.theol.*20 (1575:124)
Ord.*Zür.* (CR 91:699–800)
Calv.*Form.pr.* (Barth-Niesel 2: 19)

See p. 171 above

Luth.*Ld.*10 (*WA* 35:426–28)

See pp. 171–72 above

Urs.*Expl.Cat.*2.54.3;2.85.2 (Reuter 1:209–10;295–97)

Calv.*Sad.* (Barth-Niesel 1:467)

Calv.*Inst.*(1559)4.1.9 (Barth-Niesel 5:13)
Blngr.*Dec.*5.1 (1552:274r)
*Conf.Helv.pr.*14 (Müller 104);
*Conf.Helv.post.*17 (Niesel 251)

Buc.*Regn.Chr.*1.4 (Strasbourg 15:42)

Buc.*Regn.Chr.*1.8;2.12 (Strasbourg 15:70;122)

Bez.*Ep.theol.*74 (1575:307)

Bez.*Ep.theol.*24 (1575:145)

*Conf.Remon.*22.10;24 (1622: 69–70;73–76)

agogical expression of the Reformed insistence that "the obedience that is owed to God" must be an obedience to the word and to the will of God, and that "by far the most important use of the law among believers themselves" was as "the one and only norm and rule of all good works." The same insistence was embodied in the *Christian Order of Service at Zurich* of 1535 and in Calvin's *Form of Prayers* of 1545, both of which contained the Ten Commandments as a liturgical response. Yet Luther, too, had included the Ten Commandments in both of his catechisms, and had moreover expounded them as a standard for the Christian life, not only as a summons to repentance; and he, too, had versified the Ten Commandments and set them to music, though not as a regular part of the liturgy. Thus the difference between the Lutheran and the Reformed doctrine of the uses of the law is not as easy for historical research to define as it was for confessional polemics, in which Lutherans charged Calvinists with "legalism" and Calvinists claimed to see the antinomianism of some among Luther's disciples as already implicit in his own thought.

One general index to the difference is the role assigned to church discipline in the ecclesiologies of the two. Calvin (and with him Ursinus, the author of the *Heidelberg Catechism*) identified "three things on which the safety of the church is founded, viz., doctrine, discipline, and the sacraments," although in the *Institutes* he did not call discipline one of the identifying "notes" of the church; nor did Bullinger, either in his private writings or in the confessions to which he contributed, make it a specific mark. Bucer praised the Reformed churches of Hungary because they had "accepted the discipline of Christ in addition to his pure doctrine," and he put "the discipline of the church" alongside the teaching of the word and the administration of the sacraments as a "third" requirement. Beza used almost identical language in praising John Knox, but would not make the observance of the commandments a mark of the visible church. But several of the Reformed confessions, including the Arminian *Remonstrant Confession* issued in response to the Calvinism of the Synod of Dort, did include what the *Scots Confession* called "ecclesiastical discipline, uprightly

Conf.Scot.18;25 (Niesel 102; 114);Conf.Belg.29 (Schaff 3: 419–21);Conf.Ung.7 (Müller 428–29);Prof.fid.Franc.4 (Müller 664–65)

Conf.Boh.(1535)8 (Niemeyer 797)

Conf.Boh.(1575)11 (Niemeyer 836)

Blngr.Sum.4.4 (1556:52v);Calv. West.2 (CR 37:103)

Ex.20:4
Cat.Gen.143 (Niesel 17);Cat. Heid.92;96 (Niesel 171–73)
Aug.Hept.2.71 (PL 34:620–21)

Luth.Kl.Kat.1.1 (Bek.507–8)
Calv.Inst.(1539)3 (CR 29:379);
Urs.Expl.Cat.3.93 (Reuter 1: 326);Chem.Loc.12(1604–III: 74)
Urs.Apol.Cat.8 (Reuter 2:33);
Urs.Loc.theol.9.4 (Reuter 1: 681–82)
See vol.2:107

Calv.Theol.Par.16 (CR 35:27);
Bez.ap.Coll.Mont.Bell.9 (1588: 393;401);Episc.Inst.3.1.3 (1678–I:131)
Calv.Nec.ref. (CR 34:462);
Episc.Wad.2.2 (1678–II:133–36)

Blngr.Or.err.miss.4 (1528:C5r–C5v)

Blngr.Assert.orth. (1534:13v)
Conf.Helv.post.4 (Niesel 226–27);Zw.Ver.fals.rel.29 (CR 90: 900–906)

See vol.2:117–33

Zw.Wort. (CR 92:821–24)

administered, as God's word prescribeth," as the third such mark. It was indicative of the transition of the Hussite Unity of Bohemian Brethren from the Lutheran orientation of their *Confession* of 1535 to the Calvinist inspiration of their *Confession* of 1575 that the former had required the practice of church discipline and excommunication but had not made it a necessary mark of the church, but the latter specified it, together with the preaching of the word and the administration of the sacraments, as one of "the sure and infallible notes of the holy church."

There likewise developed a difference between Calvinists and Lutherans over the application of certain commandments of the Decalogue. In the polemics, the very numbering of the Ten Commandments became an issue, with the Reformed catechisms listing the prohibition of graven images as the second commandment, not merely as an explanation of the first, as the Lutherans and Roman Catholics, following Augustine, counted it in their catechisms; on both sides there was the recognition that the issue was in itself not one of great moment. But the anomaly that Calvinist iconoclasts could cite the authority of Eastern Orthodox iconodules on the division of the commandments suggests that it was the meaning and the applicability, not the numbering, of the commandments that was the real issue. Both Calvinists and Remonstrants pointed out that there had been a decree in the ancient church against the use of images in churches, and they attacked as sophistic ingenuity the view that condemned idolatry but sanctioned the worship of images. Although Bullinger asserted, in an early comparison of East and West on the Mass, that the Eastern churches were "less given over to superstitions" than the Western, he knew the history of the iconoclastic controversy; and when he came to write the *Second Helvetic Confession*, he made "idols, or images of Christ and of the saints" the topic of a special article, in which the principal arguments of the Byzantine defenders of images were refuted, briefly but firmly. This was, at least in part, an attack on Luther's more tolerant attitude toward the retention of images. In a brief tract entitled *A Treatise on the Worship of Images*, Bishop Nicholas Ridley, declaring

Rdly.*Imag*.3 (*PS* 39:94)

Rdly.*Imag*.1 (*PS* 39:84)

Bez.ap.*Coll.Mont.Bell*.9 (1588: 418)

Pauck (1928)65

Calv.*Inst*.(1539)8 (*CR* 29:88); Calv.*Occ.prov*.13–14 (*CR* 37: 314) Calv.*Inst*.(1559)3.23.7 (Barth-Niesel 4:401)

Cont.*Praed*. (*CCath*. 7:63); *Form.Conc.Ep*.11.19 (*Bek*.821); Cast.*Occ.prov*.pr. (*CR* 37:273); Milt.*Par.L*.3.114–34

that "there never was anything that made more division, or brought more mischief into the church, than the controversy of images" in the time of iconoclasm, summarized the Calvinist interpretation of the second commandment: "If by virtue of the second commandment, images were not lawful in the temple of the Jews, then by the same commandment they are not lawful in the churches of the Christians." Or, in the dramatic words of Theodore Beza against the Lutheran practice, "Our hope reposes in the true cross of our Lord Jesus Christ, not in that image. Therefore I must admit that I thoroughly detest the image of the crucifix . . . [and] cannot endure it."

The most characteristic difference between Lutheran and Calvinist views of obedience to the word and will of God, however, lay outside the area of church dogma, in what has been called, with reference to Bucer, his "Christocracy": the question of whether, and how, the law of God revealed in the Bible, as distinguished from the natural law accessible through reason, was to be obeyed in the political and social order. That difference, when combined with the Reformed doctrine of covenant and applied to the life of nations, was to be of far-reaching historical significance, for it decisively affected the political and social evolution of the lands that came under the sway of Calvinist churchmanship and preaching.

### The Eternal Will of God, Hidden and Revealed

Yet it was obvious from Scripture as well as from the experience of the church past and present that those who would respond with such "obedience of faith" to the proclamation of the word of God would never be more than a minority, and that most of the human race would never so much as have the opportunity to refuse the word. Therefore the most "awesome [horribile]" implication of the Reformed view of obedience to the word and will of God—and the one upon which its opponents, differ though they might among themselves otherwise, all fastened most often in their polemics—was the Calvinist doctrine of double predestination. The first edition of John Calvin's *Institutes* in 1536 referred to election in Christ before the creation of the world, along with redemption and

Calv.*Inst.*(1536)1 (Barth-Niesel
1:63)
Calv.*Inst.*(1536)2.4 (Barth-
Niesel 1:87)
Cat.*Heid.*54 (Niesel 162)

Urs.*Expl.Cat.*54.6 (Reuter 1:
211–12)

Art.*XXXIX.*17 (Schaff 3:497–
99)

Blngr.*Dec.*4.4 (1552:217r–219r)

Calv.*West.*2 (CR 37:118–19)

Bez.*Coll.Mont.Bell.* (1588:
329–62)

Toss.*Praed.*1;2;6 (1609:6;12;
39)

See pp. 140–45 above

reconciliation, as the foundation of "the architecture of Christian doctrine." This edition of the *Institutes* (and then the *Heidelberg Catechism*) also treated the idea of predestination in connection with the clarification of the definition of the church as "the people of God's elect," although Ursinus did explain the *Heidelberg Catechism* as saying that "the efficient cause of the difference [between the elect and the reprobate] is the election of God," which he identified as both election and reprobation; yet the *Institutes* of 1536 (and then the *Thirty-Nine Articles of the Church of England*) did not make explicit reference to the corollary idea of a predestination to damnation at all. Similarly, of the fifty sermons collected in 1552 into the *Decades* of Heinrich Bullinger, just one half of one sermon was devoted to predestination, in the context of the doctrines of creation and providence. With each subsequent edition of Calvin's *Institutes,* the amount of space devoted to predestination increased, as did the consideration specifically addressed to the problem of the "reprobate," those whom God had predestined to damnation. Yet as late as 1556, when this process had already gone almost as far as it ever would (the climax came in 1559, with the final edition of the *Institutes*), Calvin indignantly repudiated the accusation that his exposition of the certainty of salvation took predestination as its starting point.

In this as in other respects, Calvin and Calvinism represented themselves as championing the doctrine of the real Luther against the perversions of his doctrine by his later disciples. For example, after Reformed and Lutheran theologians had met in a colloquium at Montbéliard in March 1586, Theodore Beza drew upon Luther's *Bondage of the Will* for support in his response to the dispute over predestination. Likewise, in opposition to "the authors of the *Augsburg Confession*," who wanted to avoid the topic, Daniel Tossanus cited as authorities for it Augustine against the Pelagians and Luther against Erasmus. Especially during that controversy with Erasmus, Luther had allowed his affirmation of the sovereignty of divine grace to take the form of a theory of double predestination, but had pulled back from flatly asserting all that was implied in such a theory. In the immediate aftermath of the controversy, one of his closest associates, quoting the saying of Christ that God had "hidden these things from the wise and understanding," went on to quote the concluding words of the saying, "Yes, Father, for such was thy gracious will," as an answer to the question of "why God confounds the wise and . . . elects the simple." But the outcome of Luther's consideration of predestination was the admonition to keep silent about the question as a potential source of either despair or presumption. Such an admonition, while laudable for its reverence toward the mystery of the divine will, would, in Calvin's eyes, defraud the faithful of what Scripture had revealed, which was intended to be necessary and useful also when it spoke about predestination. The eternal will of God was a "secret will" or a "hidden counsel" or a "concealed judgment." But it was essential to maintain a distinction between the secret counsel of God and his revealed will and not to "bury election in the secret counsel of God." For God had decided to "communicate the secrets of his will" and had done so by his word, so that there was "a consensus between the hidden counsel of God and the outward voice of his doctrine"; God would judge the world according to the latter, but also in harmony with the former.

To this eternal will of God, hidden and revealed, the ultimate destiny of all must be referred. When the Book of Acts spoke about "the determinate counsel and foreknowledge of God" at work in the crucifixion, it subordinated the foreknowledge to the divine counsel or decree. By attributing not only the life and death of Christ but also the actions of his enemies to the hand and counsel of God, it made the divine will the cause of their damnation no less than of the salvation of the believers. The God of whom Peter spoke here in Acts was no mere spectator of the events, but their author. Basing the predestination of God on his foreknowledge of human virtue or merit would make the human condition, not the divine decree, the cause of salvation or of damnation. "Foreknowledge" referred to God's omniscience, for which past, present, and future were all the same; it extended to all creatures and all events, evil as well as good. "Predestina-

Matt. 11:25–26
Bgn.*Chr.gl.* (1527:173–74)

Mel.*Loc.*(1535) (*CR* 21:452)

Calv.*Inst.*(1539)8 (*CR* 29:863)
Calv.*Occ.prov.*7 (*CR* 37:302–4);Calv.*Rom.*8:33 (Parker 187)
Calv.*Occ.prov.*1 (*CR* 37:289)

Calv.*Rom.*11:34 (Parker 262)

Calv.*Rom.*8:33 (Parker 187)

Calv.*Inst.*(1539)8 (*CR* 29:862)

Calv.*Occ.prov.*7;11 (*CR* 37:302;310)

Acts 2:23

Calv.*Act.*2:23 (*CR* 76:38–40)

Acts 4:28
Calv.*Occ.prov.*4 (*CR* 37:301);
Calv.*Inst.*(1559)1.18.1 (Barth-Niesel 3:220);Urs.*Loc.theol.*6.2 (Reuter 1:572);Bez.*Cast.*2 (*Bez Tract* 1:359–60)
Calv.*Inst.*(1559)3.22.6 (Barth-Niesel 4:386)

tion," on the other hand, was defined as "the eternal decree of God by which he has decided within himself what he wills to happen to each individual human being." The distinction proved to be deceptive in its simplicity and clarity. The church fathers had defined the four key terms—"foreknowledge," "predestination," "election," and "providence"—in various ways. Moreover, the most important discussion of predestination in the New Testament, that of the Epistle to the Romans, did not observe the distinction, but used the verb "foreknow" to refer to the eternal predestinating will of God by which he determined whom he would adopt as his children.

In the treatment of these four terms, the relation between predestination and providence called for special attention. Calvin had spoken in the first edition of the *Institutes* about "those who have been elected by the eternal providence of God," and he had treated providence and predestination together as chapter 8 in the first expansion of his *Institutes,* the edition of 1539. The two topics remained linked, becoming chapter 14 in the editions of 1543–45 and 1550–54: "The Predestination and Providence of God." But when he came to the definitive edition of 1559, he made providence the theme of the concluding chapters of Book One, on the knowledge of God the Creator, but incorporated the discussion of predestination in Book Three, as part of the discourse on the appropriation of the grace of Christ through the action of the Holy Spirit. At almost the same time, Bullinger also separated "The Providence of God" as chapter 6 from "The Predestination of God and the Election of the Saints" as chapter 10 of the *Second Helvetic Confession.* The *Bremen Consensus* considered providence in its fifth article before continuing in its seventh with predestination and in its eighth with reprobation, while the *Westminster Confession* treated "God's Eternal Decree" as its third chapter and "Providence" as its fifth; the *Heidelberg Catechism* included an explicit question on providence, but referred to predestination only implicitly; the *Belgic Confession* contained in its thirteenth article a lengthy affirmation of the Christian doctrine of providence, against the Epicurean doctrine that God "leaves all

*Marginal references:*

Calv.*Inst.*(1539)8 (*CR* 29:864–65);Blngr.*Dec.*4.4 (1552:217r)

Calv.*Inst.*(1539)8 (*CR* 29:864)

Rom.8:29

Calv.*Rom.*8:29 (Parker 182)

Calv.*Inst.*(1536)4 (Barth-Niesel 1:86)

Calv.*Inst.*(1539)8 (*CR* 29:861–902)

Calv.*Inst.*(1543–45;1550–54)14 (*CR* 29:861–902)

Calv.*Inst.*(1559)1.16–18 (Barth-Niesel 3:187–227)

Calv.*Inst.*(1559)3.21–24 (Barth-Niesel 4:368–432) *Conf.Helv.post.*6 (Niesel 228–29)

*Conf.Helv.post.*10 (Niesel 234–35)

*Cons.Brem.*5 (Müller 753–55)

*Cons.Brem.*7–8 (Müller 756–62)

*West.Conf.*3 (Müller 549–53)

*West.Conf.*5 (Müller 554–56) *Cat.Heid.*27 (Niesel 155–56); Urs.*Loc.theol.*6 (Reuter 1:570–605) *Cat.Heid.*54 (Niesel 162)

things to chance," and, after interposing an article on the fall and original sin, went on to a much shorter statement of the doctrine of election, whose description of reprobation was that God "left others in their ruin and fall [trébuchement], into which they had hurled themselves." The separation of providence and predestination obviated a confusion of the two concepts that would have folded special predestination, which pertained only to angels and humans and was concerned with their ultimate destiny, into a general doctrine of divine providence, which God "condescends to extend even to the level" of the birds and other creatures. Providence and predestination were nevertheless "cognate" doctrines, for God employed his providential care over his entire creation in carrying out his eternal predestinating will. One difference was that predestination referred to "the ultimate goal" of God's will, while providence included "other intermediate goals" as well.

The will of God was the decisive factor. Calvin did not hesitate to make his own the axiom of Augustine that "the will of God is the necessity of things," but then went on to explain that what God had willed would happen "of necessity" while what God had foreseen would happen "truly"; thus he endeavored to disentangle foreknowledge, providence, and predestination from the all-encompassing determinism that might seem to be implicit in the Augustinian axiom. Again, after declaring that the will of God was "the cause of all the things that are," he immediately went on to explain that the will of God was "the highest rule of justice," so that "whatever he wills, by the very fact that he wills it, must be considered just"; thus he laid the central emphasis not on an abstract theory of causality, but on the concrete affirmation of the justice of God and of its claim on the obedience of man. But that claim required that divine causality be identified as sole and total in salvation and in damnation; "for when it is said that God hardens or shows mercy to whomever he wills, men are warned by this to seek no cause outside his will." The will of God was, moreover, to be spoken of in the singular, not as "the two wills" that Calvin's opponents professed to see in his teaching: God did not

*Conf.Belg.*13 (Schaff 3:396–98)

*Conf.Belg.*16 (Schaff 3:401)

*Calv.Inst.*(1559)3.23.4 (Barth-Niesel 4:398);*Tuss.Praed.*4 (1609:23)

*Calv.Harm.ev.*Matt.6:26 (*CR* 73:210)
*Zw.Ver.fals.rel.*24 (*CR* 90:842);
*Blngr.Dec.*4.4 (1552:217r)

*Calv.Rom.*8:28 (Parker 181)

*Bez.Praed.* (*BezTract* 3:402)

*Aug.Gen.ad. litt.*6.15.26 (*PL* 31:350)

*Calv.Inst.*(1559)3.23.8 (Barth-Niesel 4:402);*Bez.Cast.*1 (*Bez Tract* 1:351);*Bez.Praed.* (*Bez Tract* 3:408)

*Calv.Inst.*(1559)3.23.2 (Barth-Niesel 4:395–96)

*Rom.*9:18
*Calv.Inst.*(1559)3.22.11 (Barth-Niesel 4:393)

*Cast.Occ.prov.*7 (*CR* 37:278)

THE WORD AND THE WILL OF GOD

Calv.*Resp.neb*** 37:262)
Calv.*Inst.*(1559)1.18.3 (Barth-

Calv.*Inst.*(1559)3.22.4 (Barth-
Niesel 4:383);Calv.*Rom.*9:11–
14 (Parker 203–5);Rog.*Cath.*
*Doct.*17.5 (** 40:149)

Calv.*Inst.*(1539)8 (** 29:886)

Calv.*Rom.*9:23 (Parker 213)

Calv.*Rom.*11:7 (Parker 244–45)

Calv.*Inst.*(1559)3.23.1 (Barth-Niesel 4:393–94)

Bez.*Praed.* *BezTract* 3:406; 419–20)

have a "double will," nor did he by his secret plan decree a sin that he had forbidden in his law. The "single and simple" will of God, whose cause was nothing outside of God himself, was what distinguished the saved from the damned. Or, as he had said already in 1539, quoting Augustine, the reason that God did not save the damned was "that he did not want to, and why he did not want to, is his own business."

What set this doctrine of predestination apart from most others in the millennium between the official version of Augustine's doctrine promulgated by the Synod of Orange in 529 and the official version of Luther's doctrine set forth in the *Formula of Concord* of 1577 was the candid acknowledgment that "reprobation" could not be merely the absence of a positive election to salvation, but must itself be a positive act of the divine will predestinating to damnation. If some variation in "their own merit" was not, and could not be, the quality that distinguished those who were saved from those who were damned, "then how do the former differ from the latter?" Calvin asked. And he did not hesitate to answer his own question: "Who would not be able to see here that it is election alone that discriminates among them?" Therefore he inserted into the final edition of his *Institutes* the statement, apparently intended as a criticism of the Lutheran view of predestination as only election to salvation, that "election itself could not stand except as set over against reprobation," since it would be "highly absurd to say that others acquire by chance or obtain by their own effort what election alone confers on the few." It must follow that "those whom God passes over, he condemns, and this he does for no other reason than that he wills to exclude them from the inheritance that he predestines for his own children." Reprobation to damnation by the eternal will of God was an ineluctable corollary of election to salvation by the same eternal will of God; it was not based on God's foreknowledge of human conduct any more than salvation was.

The standard example of reprobation in the Bible was Pharaoh, whose heart God had "hardened, so that he will not let the people go." To forestall the

Ex.8:32

Aug.*Grat*.23.45 (*PL* 44:911)

Calv.*Inst*.(1539)2 (*CR* 39:353)

Ps.Aug.*Praed.et grat*.6–7 (*PL* 45:1668)

See vol.3:84

Luth.*Serv.arb*. (*WA* 18:711–14)

Luth.*Serv.arb*. (*WA* 18:722)

Blngr.*Dec*.3.10 (1552:166r–166v)

Blngr.*Sum*.3.1 (1556:35r)

Calv.*Rom*.9:17 (Parker 208)

Calv.*Inst*.(1539)2 (*CR* 29:354)
Bez.*Cast*.8–9 (*BezTract* 1:399–404)

most drastic implications of this text, Augustine had argued, from the counterbalancing verse which stated that "Pharaoh hardened his heart," that "thus it was both that God hardened him by his just judgment and that Pharaoh hardened himself by his own free will." So thorny did the question nevertheless remain that there was fathered on Augustine a milder interpretation (criticized by Calvin), according to which God's hardening of Pharaoh's heart was based on his foreknowledge of how Pharaoh would act by his own free will. There was similarly fathered on Jerome an entire work (now no longer extant) called *The Hardening of the Heart of Pharaoh* (whose authenticity was credited by some but questioned by others) with the purpose of avoiding the conclusion that God had from eternity determined to harden Pharaoh's heart and had done so by his own will and action quite apart from the free will and action of Pharaoh himself. But the Reformers asserted precisely that conclusion. Luther, writing against Erasmus, drew the implication that Pharaoh did not have a free will to obey the word and will of God communicated to him through Moses, but had disobeyed "of necessity" because God hardened his heart; the account of Pharaoh encompassed all the other passages of Scripture on the subject and contained irrefutable evidence about both the bondage of the human will and the omnipotent freedom of the divine will. "The withdrawal of grace," Bullinger defined on the basis of Pharaoh, "is hardening, and when we are left on our own we are hardened," adding elsewhere that all such passages in Scripture were a proof of the just judgment of God. It was indeed "just," Calvin insisted, but it was also "concealed": God had not merely "hardened [Pharaoh's heart] by not softening it," but he had "turned Pharaoh over to Satan to be confirmed in the obstinacy of his breast"—an exegesis by Calvin that Beza defended against its critics.

The case of Pharaoh also provided Calvin with the most incontrovertible refutation possible of the attempt by some "compromisers to dilute" the harsh but clear language of Scripture, which did not speak merely about "permission" by God, but also about "the action of divine wrath" when it used the term

Calv.*Rom.*9:18 (Parker 209)

Calv.*Occ.prov.*3 (CR 37:295–96)

Calv.*Inst.*(1559)1.18.1 (Barth-Niesel 3:219)

Calv.*Inst.*(1559)3.23.8 (Barth-Niesel 4:402)

Calv.*Inst.*(1559)3.23.7 (Barth-Niesel 4:401)

Rom.9:23

Calv.*Rom.*9:23 (Parker 214)

Calv.*Rom.*11:7 (Parker 245)

Dowey (1952)218–19

Calv.*Praed.* (CR 36:266)

Calv.*Inst.*(1559)3.22.8 (Barth-Niesel 4:389)

See vol.1:297; p. 31 above

Aug.*Enchir.*26.100 (CCSL 46:103)

Calv.*Occ.prov.*3 (CR 37:296–97)

Aug.*Corrept.* (PL 44:915–46)

"hardening." Calvin dismissed the distinction between divine action and divine permission as "frivolous" and demanded to know what the real difference between the two could be when applied to God. In spite of the rearrangement of the 1559 edition of his *Institutes*, by which the treatise on providence and the treatise on predestination were assigned to widely separated parts of the opus, the rejection of such a distinction between doing and permitting in God was added to the first, so that it appeared in both: the distinction was a "falsehood" and an "evasion" despite its claims of "moderation," and it pretended that "God did not establish the condition in which he wills the chief of his creatures to be." With unrelenting rigor, Calvin pressed his rejection of the notion of divine permission all the way to the point of attributing to God's active predestinating will even the fall of Adam into sin and the consequent verdict of eternal death on "so many peoples, together with their infant offspring." Thus even where the express statement of the text of Scripture confined itself to saying that God had "prepared beforehand for glory the vessels of mercy," he was constrained to add: "Undoubtedly both preparations [to glory and to perdition] depend on the hidden counsel of God." Those whom God blinded were not those who by their wickedness had merited it, but "those who were foreordained to damnation [reprobati] by God before the foundation of the world."

In his willingness to draw conclusions of such "radical, one might say reckless consistency" from the teaching of Scripture about the operation of the will of God in relation to sinful humanity, Calvin claimed that "Augustine is completely on our side," so that it would be possible to splice together statements from Augustine's writings into an entire volume about predestination that would say everything. The familiar language of Augustine about "the damnation of those whom he had justly predestined to punishment and the salvation of those whom he had kindly predestined to grace" came to Calvin's aid in his argument for the principle that the only possible doctrine of predestination was a doctrine of double predestination. Augustine's treatise, *Rebuke and Grace,* was a complete and

Calv.*Inst.*(1559)3.23.13 (Barth-Niesel 4:407)
Aug.*Persev.*14.37–16.40 (*PL* 45:1015–18)

Calv.*Inst.*(1559)3.23.13;3.21.4 (Barth-Niesel 4:407–8;4:373)
Aug.*Praed.sanct.* (*PL* 44:959–92)
Blngr.*Grat.just.*1.3 (1554:8v)

Calv.*Inst.*(1539)8 (*CR* 29:868)

Calv.*Inst.*(1559)3.22.8 (Barth-Niesel 4:389)

Cont.*Praed.* (*CCath* 7:58)

Blngr.*Sum.*3.3 (1556:40r)

Rog.*Cath.Doct.*9.1 (*PS* 40:96); Wic.*Luth.art.* (*CCath* 18:82)

Bez.*Cast.*13–14 (*BezTract* 1:413)

ap.Syn.Dord.*Sess.*99 (*Act.Syn.Dord.*1:238)
Syn.Dord.*Rej.err.*1.4 (Schaff 3:557)
Syn.Dord.*Rej.err.*2.3 (Schaff 3:563)

Conf.*Remon.*pr. (1622:A3r)

satisfying refutation of the charge that an emphasis on the totality of the divine initiative in predestination would destroy the moral imperative. Passages from another of his anti-Pelagian treatises, *The Gift of Perseverance,* written near the end of his life, were quoted in extenso to prove that predestination was a legitimate theme for Christian preaching; Augustine's *Predestination of the Saints* supported the doctrine of justification by faith alone. In response to the accusation that his doctrine of double predestination was a novelty in the history of Christian doctrine, Calvin therefore was able to cite the testimony of Augustine, and Augustine in turn "does not allow himself to be dissociated from the other fathers."

Beyond Augustine's explicit predestinarianism (which, as Calvin's opponents reminded him, had never been officially adopted by the church), Augustine's doctrine of sin and grace (which by contrast had become the public doctrine of "all of Christendom," that is to say, of Western Christendom) also necessarily entailed the doctrine of predestination, and of a double predestination at that. None of the Reformers, of course, openly espoused Pelagianism, since, as Protestants and Roman Catholics agreed, "all churches of God believe" the Augustinian doctrine. But as Beza put it in his response to Castellio, "Now I am dealing with Pelagius, and therefore I am sending you back to Augustine's school." Or, in the vivid language of the Synod of Dort during the following century, the Remonstrant opponents of double predestination were not only smuggling Pelagianism back into the church and "resembling Pelagius," but actually "summoning the Pelagian error back up out of hell." In response, the Remonstrants, in the preface of their *Confession,* objected to the exclusive canonization of "this one man Augustine," whose standing had become so great that "even among those who otherwise do not usually place a high estimate on the authority of councils and fathers" it was a sufficient refutation of any position for it "to seem to have even some affinity to that of Pelagius."

Reformed theology had special reason to stress its opposition to Pelagianism and its loyalty to the Augustinian doctrine of original sin. For in 1525 Zwingli

Zw.Tf. (CR 91:300;307)

Zw.Gen.4:7 (CR 100:33)

Zw.Pecc.orig.2 (CR 92:377)

Zw.Pecc.orig.1 (CR 92:372);
Zw.Ver.fals.rel.10 (CR 90:708)

Zw.Pecc.orig.2 (CR 92:384–88)

Rom.4:15

Zw.Gen.5:3 (CR 100:37–40);
Zw.Fid.rat.4 (CR 93–II:797);
Zw.Wort. (CR 92:827–28);Zw.
Bek.3 (CR 93–II:236)

Zür.Einleit. (Müller 8);Zw.
Schl.5 (CR 89:44);Zw.Tf. (CR
91:307–9)

Eph.2:3

Conf.Tetrap.3 (Stupperich
3:53)
Luth.Wort. (WA 23:69);Luth.
Ep.Joh.1:8 (WA 20:621);Luth.
Ab.Chr. (WA 26:503)
Blngr.Dec.3.10 (1552:169v–
170r)

Aug.Pecc.merit.3.8.15 (CSEL
60:141)

Calv.Inst.(1539)2 (CR 29:311)

See vol.1:318
Blngr.Dec.3.10 (1552:167r–
167v)
See vol.3:112–14
Calv.Inst.(1539)2 (CR 29:311);
Blngr.Dec.3.10 (1552:167r)

Blngr.Dec.3.10 (1552:167r)

had denounced "all the fables of the papists about 'hereditary sin.'" In a treatise of 1526, while espousing a doctrine of the bondage of the natural will, he had criticized as "careless" certain earlier doctrines of original sin. He took the position that original sin was not a personal guilt, but only guilt by metonymy, because "sin is connected with guilt"; of itself original sin did not cause damnation, at any rate not in the children of Christians. In his *Commentary on Genesis* of 1525–27 and in his personal *Confession of Faith* of 1530, moreover, he had explained his view that there was no transgression where there was no law, and hence no "sin in the strict sense of the term"; but he had gone on to specify that the sin of Adam, "which clings to us, is truly a sickness" and one that brought with it "the necessity of dying." A confession of the city of Zurich of 1523 had already spoke of sin as "the fracture caused by the fall and the weakness of the flesh," and the *Tetrapolitan Confession* of 1530, which had a more official character than Zwingli's *Confession of Faith*, described the human condition as that of being "by nature children of wrath and therefore unrighteous, so that we do not have the power to accomplish anything that is righteous or God-pleasing." Such statements as these could be cited to exonerate Zwingli from Luther's constant accusations that he denied the orthodox Augustinian doctrine of original sin.

In its statements of the Augustinian doctrine, the main body of Reformed teaching more than made up for whatever ambiguities there may have been in Zwingli's theology. Calvin referred to Augustine to make clear that although original sin was in one sense the sin of another, namely, of Adam, it was at the same time the sin of each person individually. Bullinger set his definitions of sin and grace into explicit opposition with those of Pelagius and his follower Celestius. Calvin and Bullinger were agreed that Anselm's definition of original sin as "the absence of righteousness" was inadequate, even though it did "comprehend the whole meaning of the term." Original sin was correctly defined as sin, because "first, it makes us liable to the wrath of God, and, second, because it produces works in us that Scripture calls 'works of the flesh.'" The image of God, in which Adam had been created, had made him "partaker of the wisdom, justice, and goodness of God." But that image was now "extinguished" and replaced by "guilt, unrighteousness, and unholiness." Grace, on the other hand, was to be defined as "the favor and gracious will, indeed, the very goodness and mercy of God, by which, without any merit of ours, . . . he loves us poor sinners and, as a Father, accepts us"; it was the subject of the "eternal decree" of God, by which he had decided to grant his grace to the world through Christ. But to Reformed theology, this Augustinian consensus of all the Reformers, that works were not a factor in salvation, must imply no less consistently that works were not a factor in damnation, either; the rejection of works and the exaltation of the grace and glory of God as supreme did not apply only to the reconciliation of man to God or to the means of grace and other instruments of salvation, but to the eternal will of God by which he had chosen some and condemned others. Not only, therefore, was "Augustine completely on our side" in the doctrines of sin and grace; but it must be the complete Augustine, the Augustine who wrote *The Predestination of the Saints* and *The Gift of Perseverance* no less than the Augustine who wrote *Original Sin*.

Sharing Augustine's complete doctrine meant also sharing the criticisms of that doctrine, particularly the rejection of it as fatalistic. To Castellio, "predestination" in Calvin's usage seemed interchangeable with "fate." By having sentenced the reprobate to eternal damnation before they were born, not to say before they had sinned, "that God of Calvin's" was forcing them to sin, so that he might be just in his condemnation. If God hardened their hearts simply because he willed to do so, it was vain of him to admonish them not to harden their own hearts. From the Roman Catholic side, too, Calvin's predestinarianism was equated with fatalism. Calvin made the rejoinder that despite the superficial similarities that his critics claimed to see, there was a total difference between fate and predestination: fate, as used by the Stoics, referred to a necessity that compelled even God to fit into a preestablished or-

---

Margin notes (left column):

Gal.5:19

Calv.*Psych.* (CR 33:181)

Blngr.*Sum.*3.3 (1556:38r); Blngr.*Dec.*3.10 (1552:169r)

Blngr.*Sum.*5.2 (1556:76r–76v)

Blngr.*Sum.*5.3 (1556:77r)

Calv.*Inst.*(1539)8 (CR 29:869)

Calv.*Rom.*11:6 (Parker 243–44)

Calv.*Praed.* (CR 36:266)

See vol.1:320–21

Cast.*Occ.prov.*pr. (CR 37:273)

Cast.*Occ.prov.*13–14 (CR 37:281)

Heb.3:8

Cast.*Occ.prov.*8–9 (CR 37:279)

Cont.*Praed.* (CCath 7:63)

der; predestination, as used by Scripture, was "the free counsel of God," by which he "moderates both the human race and the individual parts of the world in accordance with his immense wisdom and justice." Although he was reluctant to engage in logomachy, he would not accept the term "fate" for his doctrine, not only because of the apostle's warning against "novelties of terminology" but because it was both slanderous and mistaken to impute "that dogma" to the biblical view of providence and predestination. It was erroneous to take divine foreknowledge as "necessity" or "fatal necessity" or "Stoic necessity," for the "necessity of sinning" lay in "the fault of the will" of man, not in "compulsion" by God.

The burgeoning enthusiasm for astrology during the sixteenth century, in which, among many others, Pope Leo X and Philip Melanchthon had both been caught up (although Luther and Zwingli had not), provided Calvin in 1549, and some years later his pupil Beza, with an opportunity to clarify the entire problem of fate, necessity, and predestination, and for once to do so in a context other than the polemical defense of the doctrine of divine election. Calvin made it clear that he was not attacking "the true astrology [i.e., astronomy]," which he defined as "the knowledge of that natural order and arrangement to which God has subjected the stars and planets," but those "charlatans [trompeurs]" who claimed to be able to predict the course of a man's life on the basis of his date of birth. Like Luther, he based his opposition both on the rational grounds of the inherent absurdity and contradiction of astrological theories and on the theological grounds of the divine prohibition of such a "pollution" of the will and word of God. Specifically, alluding to the command to Abraham to try to count the stars, Calvin insisted that the divine promise of blessing to Abraham and his posterity was not dependent on the position of the heavenly bodies. The grace that God conferred on his children had nothing to do with the consideration of the planets, nor was it on this that "God has founded his eternal election." That would deserve to be called fatalism, but divine election would not; for it was based on the will and

Calv.*Occ.prov.*pr (CR 37:287)

1 Tim.6:20(Vulg.)

Calv.*Inst.*(1539)8 (CR 29:890)
Blngr.*Dec.*3.10;4.2 (1552:165v; 199v)
Bez.*Praed.* (*BezTract* 3:431)
Calv.*Serv.arb.*2 (CR 34:280)

Bez.*Ep.theol.*29 (1575:168–73)

Calv.*Astrol.* (CR 35:516)

Gen.1:14
Calv.*Astrol.* (CR 35:521–22)

Luth.*Dec.praec.* (WA 1:404)

Calv.*Astrol.* (CR 35:513)

Gen.15:5

Calv.*Astrol.* (CR 35:525)

Calv.*Astrol.* (CR 35:520)

Calv.*Inst.*(1559)1.16.3 (Barth-Niesel 3:192)

"secret plan" of a God and Father who was revealed in Christ, not on an impersonal conjunction of the stars.

Calv.*Resp.neb.* (*CR* 37:262)

Other criticisms of the Calvinist doctrine were also echoes of earlier attacks on Augustinianism, and the responses of Reformed spokesmen regularly drew upon those of their theological patron. To the objec-

Cont.*Praed.* (*CCath* 7:55)
Snds.*Serm.*10.22 (*PS* 41:190)
Toss.*Praed.*6 (1609:44)
Aug.*Persev.*21.56 (*PL* 45:1028)

tion that the doctrine of predestination would lead to moral laxity, they replied that "holiness is the end of our election" and quoted Augustine's *Gift of Perseverance* in support. To the charge that "the prayer of men is useless" if everything had already been decided by God, the answer was that prayer "has also been

Blngr.*Sum.*7.2 (1556:120r)

ap.Calv.*Occ.prov.*1 (*CR* 37:288)
ap.Calv.*Rom.*9:22 (Parker 212)
Calv.*Inst.*(1559)3.23.8 (Barth-Niesel 4:402);Bez.*Cast.*1 (*BezTract* 1:339–41)

incorporated into the plan and will of God." To the thought that "the purpose of creation is eternal judgment" and that therefore God was unjust in his arbitrary decision to save some and to damn others, it was necessary to oppose the axiom that the glory of God was equivalent with his justice, as well as the distinction between the justice by which God condemned the reprobate and the mercy by which he

Calv.*Rom.*9:14 (Parker 205)

saved the elect; Scripture made it manifest that God did sometimes deprive the reprobate of "the capacity to hear his word" and at other times used the preach-

Calv.*Inst.*(1539)8 (*CR* 29:885)

ing of that word to blind and harden them. And to the recurring taunt, "Who has disclosed the hidden will [of God] to Calvin? For if Calvin and his followers know it, it is not hidden, but if they do not know it, why do they make affirmations about something

Cast.*Occ.prov.*7 (*CR* 37:278)

Eph.3:10(Vulg.)

unknown?" the appropriate rejoinder was: "His will is one and simple in him, but it appears 'manifold' to us because, on account of the feebleness of our minds, we do not grasp how, in diverse ways, it wills and

Calv.*Inst.*(1559)1.18.3 (Barth-Niesel 3:224)

yet does not will something to take place."

Andrs.ap.*Coll.Mont.Bell.*10 (1588:543)

Yet the gravest of all objections was the question of consolation, hope, and the certainty of election—not, of course, its objective certainty, which, being grounded totally in the will of God, was an absolute and unchangeable decree; but its subjective certainty in the conscience of the anxious believer. Calvin insisted, as early as the first edition of his *Institutes*, that "to have trust is not to fluctuate, waver, be borne up and down, hesitate, remain in suspense, and despair, but to get a steady mind with an abiding cer-

Calv.*Inst.*(1536)1 (Barth-Niesel 1:59)

Calv.*Inst.*(1536)5 (Barth-Niesel 1:174)

Calv.*Inst.*(1539)8 (*CR* 29:879)
Calv.*Inst.*(1559)3.24.4 (Barth-Niesel 4:414)

See pp. 288–89 below

Eph.1:4

Rom.8:16

Calv.*Ant.*6.can.15 (*CR* 35:479)
Thos.Aq.*S.T.*2.1.112.5 (*Ed. Leon.*7:326–27)
Calv.*Rom.*8:33;38 (Parker 187; 191)

Blngr.*Dec.*4.4 (1552:217v);Bez. *Praed.* (*BezTract* 3:436)

Calv.*Inst.*(1539)8 (*CR* 29:880)
Calv.*Rom.*10:14–17 (Parker 231)
Calv.*Rom.*11:2 (Parker 241)

Calv.*Inst.*(1539)8 (*CR* 29:882)
Bez.*Praed.* (*BezTract* 3:412)

Calv.*Rom.*9.7 (Parker 200)
Calv.*Inst.*(1559)3.24.1 (Barth-Niesel 4:410)

Bez.ap.*Coll.Mont.Bell.*9 (1588:483)

Blngr.*Dec.*4.4 (1552:217r)

Conf.*Helv.post.*10 (Niesel 235)

tainty and a solid assurance." The knowledge and assurance that one's sins were forgiven must be clear and certain; otherwise there would be "no rest, no peace with God, no confidene or security" for the conscience. That insistence did not change with the increasing emphasis on predestination: from the first to the very last revision of the *Institutes* he continued to warn that "Satan has no more grievous or dangerous temptation to dishearten the faithful than when he disquiets them with doubt about their election." Against the statement of the Council of Trent about predestination, he stressed that all believers were to have a certainty of their election through the testimony of their adoption as children of God. Such a certainty did not depend, as Thomas Aquinas had taught, on a "special revelation" to the individual, but on "a sense that is common to all the faithful." That "sense" was well expressed in Bullinger's formula: "If you have communion with Christ, you have been predestined to life and you belong to the number of the elect."

To deal with questions about the certainty of election, it was essential "to begin with God's call, and to end with it." God's call was present wherever the word of God was preached, even though this "universal call of God" was not always successful; for there was both a universal call and a special call, and it was "a manifest error" to "substitute" the universal for the special. Ultimately, the call of God, whether universal or special, was subordinate to the secret election of God. Thus "the preaching of the gospel streams forth from the fountain of election," and not vice versa. Despite the admonition to begin and end with the call of God, therefore, the quest for certainty of election could not end in any "a posteriori judgment" or appeal to experience, important though experience was as part of the total plan of God; but, in Bullinger's formula, "the end of predestination or predetermination is Christ, the Son of God the Father." Or, as the same author put it in a church confession, "Let Christ therefore be the mirror in which we contemplate our predestination." That same metaphor of Christ as "mirror" enabled Calvin to specify that "we shall not find assurance of our election in ourselves,

Calv.*Inst.*(1539)8 (*CR* 29:880)

Aug.*Praed.sanct.*15.30 (*PL* 44:981);Aug.*Persev.*24.67 (*PL* 45:1033–34)

Rom.1:4

Calv.*Inst.*(1559)3.22.1 (Barth-Niesel 4:380)

Calv.*Ant.*6.can.15 (*CR* 35:479)

Bez.*Praed.* (*BezTract* 3:403)
Calv.*Scand.*pr. (Barth-Niesel 2:163)
Calv.*Astrol.* (*CR* 35:537)

Calv.*Rom.*9:14 (Parker 204)

Calv.*Inst.*(1559)3.21.1 (Barth-Niesel 4:370)

Calv.*Rom.*11:34 (Parker 261);
Calv.*Inst.*(1539)8 (*CR* 29:880)

Ecclus.3:21

See vol.2:31;vol.3:99,259

See pp. 209–10 above
Blngr.*Assert.orth.*pr.
(1534:A2v)

Blngr.*Sum.*3.1 (1556:34v)

Blngr.*Dec.*4.4 (1552:217r)
Calv.*Rom.*11:25;16:25 (Parker 256;328)

See p. 67 above
Calv.*Occ.prov.*7 (*CR* 37:304);
Calv.*Inst.*(1559)3.21.2;3.23.8
(Barth-Niesel 4:371;4:403)

Calv.*Occ.prov.*3 (*CR* 37:300);
Calv.*Rom.*11:33 (Parker 261)

Calv.*Rom.*9:22 (Parker 213)

and not even in God the Father" in himself, but only in "Christ the mirror." Augustine had identified the man Jesus as the most "illustrious instance of predestination," whom God had chosen purely by grace and not by foreknowledge of his sinlessness. Citing these "wise" statements, Calvin, too, called Christ, as the head of the church, "the clearest mirror of free election." He invoked the metaphor yet again when, in his *Antidote* to the Council of Trent, he argued that all believers could and should be certain of their election by looking at it "in Christ, as though in a mirror." Theodore Beza, on the other hand, called election and reprobation the "mirror" in which to view the glory of God. The contrary metaphor was that of the "labyrinth." A series of personal tragedies; a preoccupation with astrology; but most of all, a blasphemous curiosity about predestination—any of these could be a "labyrinth" from which there was no escape but Christ.

It was a fatal mistake, in investigating predestination, to "go beyond the oracles of God." The warning of Sirach, "Seek not what is too difficult for you, nor investigate what is beyond your power," was, despite the noncanonical standing of Ecclesiasticus, a caution that pertained to the two natures in Christ, to the fall and the origin of evil, and to the mystery of the will of God in predestination. In the face of "a mystery that is incomprehensible until the time of revelation," a healthier attitude was what Calvin, quoting Nicholas of Cusa, called "learned ignorance." The appropriate response to the mystery was neither to pry into "what the Lord has left hidden in secret," nor on the other hand to keep silent about "what he has brought into the open," but to pay attention to the word of God with awe and wonder. The justice of God in double predestination was a subject "to adore rather than to scrutinize." Thus Bullinger's correlation of "the word and the will of God," according to which "'the word of God' means the language of God, the revelation of the will of God," applied with special force to the Reformed doctrine of predestination. As a mildly Reformed confession put it, "that will of God is to be followed which we have expressly declared to us in the word

Art.XXXIX.17 (Schaff 3:498–99)

Rog.Cath.Doct.17.10 (PS 49:157–58)

of God"; this was true, a commentator on it explained, for all "our doings, but chiefly in the matter of predestination."

## The Will of God for the World

The fearful symmetry of salvation and reprobation in the doctrine of double predestination could easily lead its critics, and sometimes its exponents as well, to construct from it a system in which the eternal will of God, as contained in his decrees, became an all-encompassing (and all-explaining) first and only cause. But, as one scholar has warned, "Calvin's doctrine of the decrees, especially the decree of reprobation, cannot by a process of extrapolation be lifted out of its context and set above the doctrines of creation and redemption without being transmuted into a rationalistic metaphysic which would then change the nature

Dowey (1952)218

See pp.223–24 above

See pp. 221–22 above

of his entire theology." Calvin did reject a distinction between God's willing and God's permitting, he did defend himself against the charge that he was attributing to God two or more contrary wills, and he did insist on the unity of God's will. But in the very context of that insistence he could quote, as something with which "all godly and modest people" would agree,

Aug.Enchir.26.100 (CCSL 46:103)
Calv.Inst.(1559)1.18.3 (Barth-Niesel 3:225);Bez.Cast.2;7 (BezTract 1:374;392);Bez.Praed. (BezTract 3:409)

the words of Augustine in the Enchiridion, "that in a strange and ineffable fashion even that which is done against his will is not done without his will." There was then, a will of God for the world, "against" which (though not "without" which) sin was committed (though not permitted). In the formula of Ursinus,

Urs.Loc.theol.6.2 (Reuter 1:600)

"God does, and does not, will one and the same action." The elucidation of just what the will of God was for the world became an assignment for the two generations of Reformed theology following Calvin's death. It received confessional definition in the first half of the seventeenth century, but many of its implications had to await the doctrinal (and the political) history of later centuries for their full effect and classical formulation.

The most controversial attempt at such an elucidation within the Reformed communion was the one associated with the names of Jacob Arminius and Simon Episcopius, which eventually challenged openly the central affirmations of the Calvinistic doctrine it-

Episc.*Inst.*4.3.6 (1678–I:356–59);Episc.*Camer.*1 (1678–II:209)

Episc.*Inst.*4.2.20 (1678–I:306)

Conf.Remon.pr. (1622:C3v)

Conf.Remon.6.8 (1622:23)

Conf.Remon.6.1 (1622:19)

Conf.Remon.2.9 (1622:10)

Episc.*Inst.*4.2.17–18 (1678–I:299–303)

Conf.Remon.2.5 (1622:9)

Episc.*Inst.*4.2.22 (1678–I:311)
Remon.4 (Schaff 3:547);Conf.
Remon.17.6 (1622:27);*Sent.*
Remon.3.2 (*Act.Remon.*1:74)

Aug.*Ev.Joh.*49.24 (*CCSL* 36:431);Calv.*Ev.Joh.*11:43 (*CR* 75:269)

Conf.Remon.17.3 (1622:56)

self. Arminianism acquired its own confessional status in the *Remonstrance* of 1610 and then, after the Synod of Dort, in the *Remonstrant Confession* of 1621/22. Reiterating and developing many of the objections to predestinarianism that had already been current during Calvin's lifetime, the Arminian and Remonstrant protest focused on the problem of will: of the human will as responsible for conduct and therefore in some genuine sense free of "fatalistic necessity"; and of the divine will as addressed to all and therefore in some genuine sense universal, but also as free of sin and evil and free of coercion, since such freedom was "the perfection of the [divine] will." Calvin's "fictitious fate of predestination" was "hostile to religion" because it managed to undercut both the free will of God and the free will of man. Against "the iron and fatalistic necessity of the Stoics, Manicheans, and Predestinarians," as well as against the "blind chance" of the Epicureans, stood the biblical doctrine of "the providence of God in the world, which rules everything in a wise, holy, and just manner." The providence of God, which followed immediately upon creation and which extended also to the work of redemption, was universal in its scope, pertaining to "this entire universe and especially to man," as an expression of "the wisdom, justice, and equity of God." These divine attributes of wisdom, justice, and equity, as disclosed in providence, meant that God was free from "any internal necessity of his own nature or of any external power of some other force"; therefore it was Arminian and Remonstrant doctrine, no less than it was Calvinist doctrine, that God did foreknow future contingents and that he was free "to dispose for his creatures whatever he wills," death or life, command or prohibition.

It was likewise Remonstrant doctrine, no less than Calvinist, that the grace of God, defined as "undeserved and unmerited favor," was, as the *Remonstrance* put it, "the beginning, the progress, and the completion of all good." But that did not mean that grace was "irresistible." The analogy, drawn by Augustine and after him by Calvin, between God's call to faith and the summons to resurrection addressed by Christ, irresistibly, to a dead body, was fallacious.

Sent.Remon.3.8 (Act.Remon.1: 75)

Episc.Lib.arb.4 (1678–II:203)

Conf.Remon.17.7 (1622:57–58)

Calv.Inst.(1559)1.18.1 (Barth-Niesel 3:219)

Episc.Inst.4.2.21 (1678–I:308)

Conf.Remon.6.3 (1622:20)

Conf.Remon.2.9 (1622:11)

Conf.Remon.20.3 (1622:63)
Episc.Jud.2 (1678–I:437);
Episc.Quaest.33 (1678–II:31–32)

Episc.Inst.4.4.13 (1678–I:387)

Remon.conc. (Schaff 3:549)

Conf.Remon.2.2 (1622:9)

Conf.Remon.5.7 (1622:18)

Episc.Inst.4.5.5 (1678–I:410–12)

Conf.Remon.2.2 (1622:8–9)

Sent.Remon.3.9 (Act.Remon. 1:75)

Episc.Inst.4.5.7 (1678–I:414);
Episc.Camer.1 (1678–II:209)

For "those whom God calls to faith, he calls seriously"; if it were impossible to resist the grace of God, his offer of "a reward for Christian virtue" and his threat of punishment for immorality would both be vain. On the other hand, the distinction between what God willed and what God permitted, which Calvin had dismissed as a "falsehood" and an "evasion," was essential to prevent "the overthrow of all religion": divine permission did not imply that "it is not possible for anything but disobedience to follow," but rather that "man can be disobedient, yet only if he so wills." Therefore God permitted evil not because he willed it, but to leave man free. And, contrary to Calvin's theory, it was similarly "with the permission of God and in accordance with his just judgment," but by their own action, that the hearts of sinners were "hardened." Hardening, also in the case of the Jews, was a divine "declaration," not the initiative of a divine "action."

When Calvinist predestinarianism drew a closer and more direct link of causation between the eternal will of God and human action or human destiny, this was an attempt to "rise higher or to descend deeper" than the revelation of God's will allowed. "To know God truly" according to Scripture meant to "fulfill the will of God," but God could not rightly demand "subjection to an alien will" on man's part if there had been a decree of double predestination even preceding the fall. The doctrine of the will of God constituted the third and final section of the *Remonstrant Confession*, following upon sections dealing with the being of God and the works of God. Although "there is not in God a secret will that contradicts his will as revealed in the word," and therefore the notion of a twofold will of God for salvation and for reprobation, which seemed to be implicit in the Calvinist doctrine of double predestination, was, "among all dangerous errors, the most dangerous," there was quite another sense in which it was altogether proper to speak about a twofold will. For "the divine will contained in the covenant of grace . . . comprehends two principal parts: first, what God himself, through Jesus Christ his Son, has decided to do in us or on our behalf, so that we might become participants in the eternal salvation that has been offered through him; second, what he wills to be done by us through the mediation of his grace if we really want to attain eternal salvation." The difference between such a twofold will and the twofold will of double predestination was that it did not attribute self-contradiction to God, but total consistency. To the extent that it was legitimate to speak about the divine will under such a category as "decree," it must be on the basis of the way the divine decrees were carried out in the two basic divine actions of creation and redemption; even there, moreover, the words of Scripture about the "counsel" of God were not to be interpreted in a deterministic sense.

The will of God for the world disclosed in both of these divine actions was universal in its scope. Ever since the rejection of the dualism of Marcion in the ancient church, the unity of God had stood as a guarantee of the universality of this creating will, to which the opening affirmation of the Apostles' Creed bore witness. On this there was no controversy among the Reformation parties, despite repeated attempts by various of them to identify their opponents as neo-Marcionites for their position on one or another doctrine. But the universality of the will of God in salvation, as distinct from creation, did become a matter of controversy, as did the eternity of damnation. The *Remonstrance* of 1610 declared that Jesus Christ was "the Savior of the world," not only the Savior of the elect, and that he had "died for all men and for every man, so that he has obtained for them all, by his death on the cross, redemption and the forgiveness of sins," although only those who believed could share in this forgiveness. It was a "decree" of God that Christ should be "the propitiation for the sins of the whole world." As it had been a "universal evil that has come upon us from Adam," so it must be a "remedy for all" that had been granted by God in "his beloved Son, Jesus Christ, as the New and Second Adam," who "governs all things" in accordance with his will.

In this Arminian form, the assertion that the will of God for the world was a universal will for salvation did not truly come into its own as a church doctrine until the rise of Methodism in the eighteenth century. During the Reformation period, its principal signifi-

*Conf.Remon.*9.1 (1622:32)

*Conf.Remon.*2.6 (1622:10)

*Conf.Remon.*4.2–3 (1622:15–16)

Acts 4:27–28
Episc.*Inst.*4.4.15 (1678–I:396–97)

See vol.1:112

*Conf.Remon.*5.1 (1622:16)

Zw.*Wort.* (*CR* 92.941–42;958);
Herb.*Enchir.*13 (*CCath* 12:60);
Form.*Conc.Epit.*8.23 (*Bek.*809)

Episc.*Quaest.*62 (1678–II:67–68)

Remon.2 (Schaff 3:546);*Sent. Remon.*2.2–3 (*Act.Remon.*1:73–74)

1 John 2:2
*Sent.Remon.*1.5 (*Act.Remon.*1:71–72)

*Conf.Remon.*7.4 (1622:25)

*Conf.Remon.*8.8 (1622:30)

See vol.1:326–27

cance for official dogma lay in the antithetical formulations it evoked, particularly the *Canons* of the
Synod of Dort and the *Westminster Confession,* and in
the reactions of Puritanism to what it deemed to be the
incursions of Arminian doctrine into Anglican teaching. It was as a consequence of the Arminian challenge
that Reformed doctrine on the issues in controversy
took the form at Dort of the five "heads of doctrine"
that came to be identified, rightly or wrongly, as the
distinctive emphases of orthodox Calvinist teaching,
which the Remonstrants believed themselves obliged
to reject openly. In that sense it is correct to draw the
parallel that "the Canons of Dort have for Calvinism
the same significance which the Formula of Concord
has for Lutheranism," but only with the prior stipulation that none of the Reformed confessions "has the
same commanding position as the Augsburg Confession in the Lutheran Church."

The parallel between the *Canons* of Dort and the
*Formula of Concord* may be misleading for another
reason as well. Although the Lutheran confession,
too, was put forth as a "restatement" of the *Augsburg
Confession* only on those points of doctrine over which
there had been controversy within Lutheranism, it
had managed to deal with a far larger range of doctrines than did its Calvinist counterpart, which confined itself to "divine predestination and the heads [of
doctrine] immediately connected with it," viz., unconditional predestination, limited atonement, total
depravity, the irresistibility of grace, and the final perseverance of the saints. On each of these, the Synod
of Dort affirmed its allegiance to normative Reformed
teaching, as promulgated in the *Belgic Confession,* to
whose authority the several national delegations to
the synod subscribed, and in the *Heidelberg Catechism,* which was endorsed as "a very accurate compendium of orthodox Christian doctrine." The
language of the *Heidelberg Catechism* had been far
less explicit on some of these doctrines than that of
the later Calvin and of still later Calvinism, but the
Remonstrants criticized it for confining the doctrine
of providence to temporal matters. The *Belgic Confession* had dealt with the doctrines at somewhat greater
length, although it, too, had stopped short of an un-

Episc. *Quaest.*53 (1678–II:57–58)

Schaff (1919)515

Schaff (1919)357

*Form. Conc.S.D.*pr. (*Bek.*829)

Syn. Dord.*Can.*pr. (Schaff 3:551)

Syn. Dord.*Sess.*144–46 (*Act. Syn.Dord.*1:348–49)

Syn. Dord.*Sess.*148 (*Act.Syn. Dord.*1:366)

*Cat.Heid.*54 (Niesel 162)

See p. 220 above

*Consid.Cat.Heyd.*27 (*Act. Remon.*1:109)

*Conf.Belg.*16 (Schaff 3:401)

*Consid.Conf.Belg.*16 (*Act. Remon.*1:92–93)

1 Tim.2:1–4

See pp. 34–35 above

*Calv.Rom.*ded. (Parker 2–3)

*Buc.Rom.*9:17 (1562:455–60)
*Urs.Loc.theol.*6.2 (Reuter 1:586–87)

See pp. 223–24 above

*Bez.Praed.* (*BezTract* 3:407);
*Toss.Praed.*2 (1609:17)

*Calv.Occ.prov.*13–14 (*CR* 37:314)

*Calv.1 Tim.*2:4 (*CR* 80.268–69);*Calv.Occ.prov.*1 (*CR* 37:292)

*Calv.Inst.*(1539)8 (*CR* 29:888)

*Bez.Cast.*13–14 (*BezTract* 1:419)

John 3:16

John 17:9
*Bez.ap.Coll.Mont.Bell.*10 (1588:544–45)

ambiguous doctrine of double predestination, and, as the Remonstrants pointed out, its words "could be, and have been, construed in diverse ways."

There had also been diverse ways of construing the admonition of the apostle Paul to pray for kings and rulers because of "God our Savior, who desires all men to be saved and to come to the knowledge of the truth." This passage had always been a conundrum to Augustinian doctrines of predestination and the will of God. Martin Bucer, to whose exegesis of the Pauline epistles Calvin acknowledged his indebtedness, followed Augustine's explanation that the saving will of God of which the passage spoke pertained not to individuals, but to classes of men. Ursinus, too, interpreted the passage to refer to "all classes" rather than to all individuals; but, unlike Calvin, he and other orthodox Reformed theologians found the distinction between "will" and "permission" in God, if properly understood, a useful one for such an interpretation. It was essential, according to Calvin, not to superimpose 1 Timothy 2:1–4 on the doctrine of predestination, but rather to read it in the light of "the term 'election,' [which] occurs so often in Scripture." Then it would be evident that "the apostle's meaning here is simply that no nation of the earth and no class of society is excluded from salvation." By any other interpretation, this command to pray for pagan kings and emperors, "an almost hopeless group of men," would be "absurd" on the face of it. There must be, Beza argued, a proper "order of causes" in the interpretation of this passage, just as the term "world" in the passage, "God so loved the world," must refer only to the elect, since Christ explained later in the same Gospel that he was not praying for the "world."

Faced now, in the Remonstrant challenge, with what it believed to be just such an effort to subordinate the doctrine of election to the teaching of a universal will of God for the salvation of the world, the Synod of Dort restored the order between election and redemption as Calvin had taught it. "This was," Dort affirmed, "the sovereign counsel and most gracious will and purpose of God the Father, that the quickening and saving efficacy of the most precious death of his Son should extend to all the elect," and to them alone; for "it was the will of God that Christ . . . should effectually redeem . . . all those, and those only, who were from eternity chosen to salvation, and given to him by the Father." The Remonstrant proposition, "Jesus Christ the Savior died for each and for all," was, as one Calvinist theologian put it to the synod, "ambiguous because of its incompleteness": "If you add, 'believers,' the proposition will be clear and true; but if you add 'people,' it remains ambiguous." Repeatedly the synod gave its attention to the question, "Whether the will of the Father in giving the Son over to death, and of the Son in undergoing death, was to grant salvation to each and to all." A lengthy *Confession*, submitted by a French Reformed theologian who could not attend, effectively framed the synod's answer to that question, arguing that since Christ interceded for those whom he had reconciled, and since he had declared on the very night of his betrayal, "I am not praying for the world but for those whom thou has given me" it necessarily followed that "Christ has not reconciled the world," but only the elect.

To ward off the standard Remonstrant objection that such a doctrine of limited atonement was in fact a limitation of the power and sufficiency of Christ, who, as Savior of the whole world, had died for each and for all, the synod introduced its statement about the limitation of the will of God for salvation with a summary of the Anselmic doctrine of redemption as satisfaction. "God is not only supremely merciful, he is also supremely just," it began. Therefore nothing other than the death of Christ, being "of infinite worth and value," could avail as "the only and most perfect sacrifice and satisfaction for sins." The message of that perfect satisfaction was anything but limited in its audience. The promise of the gospel and the call to repentance and faith must be announced and published wherever God sent the gospel, "promiscuously and without discrimination." But that did not mean that all who heard it would believe, for many would perish in unbelief; yet this was not due to "any defect or insufficiency in the sacrifice offered by Christ on the cross, but to their own fault." Nor did it mean, moreover, that the will of God for the world had failed

Syn.Dord.*Can*.2.8 (Schaff 3:562)

*Remon*.2 (Schaff 3:546)

ap.Syn.Dord.*Sess*.99 (*Act.Syn. Dord*.1:247–48)

Syn.Dord.*Sess*.72 (*Act.Syn. Dord*.1:230)

John 17:9

ap.Syn.Dord.*Sess*.143 (*Act.Syn. Dord*.1:343)

*Remon*.2 (Schaff 3:546)

Syn.Dord.*Can*.2.1 (Schaff 3:561)

Syn.Dord.*Can*.2.3 (Schaff 3:561)

Syn.Dord.*Can*.2.5 (Schaff 3:561)

Syn.Dord.*Can*.2.6 (Schaff 3:561)

of its intended result, as though human unbelief could frustrate the divine will. Therefore the sacrifice of Christ, although of infinite worth and sufficiency, was not for the world, but only for the predestined.

It was on the basis of this teaching about the will of God for salvation that the doctrine of predestination was to be understood. "We are to judge the will of God," the Synod of Dort affirmed, "from his word." From the word of God it was evident that the ground of divine election was not in anything human, neither in human holiness nor in human faith, present or foreknown, but that these human virtues were the results of election. Hence the only ground and "sole cause of this gratuitous election" was "the good pleasure of God." The answer of the synod to the topic discussed, for example, at its sixty-seventh session, whether election was "single or multiple," was clear and unequivocal: "This election is not multiple." Although that statement as it stood referred only to the election to salvation, the same set of *Canons* also spoke in the singular of a "decree" when it identified the difference between the elect and the reprobate: "That some here below are endowed by God with faith, and that others are not thus endowed, proceeds from his eternal decree." The contrary opinion, "that God did not decree, by his just will alone, to leave anyone in the fall of Adam and in the common condition of sin and damnation," was condemned. So was the teaching that "the will of God for the salvation of believers" was the full content of the decree of election.

The "five heads of doctrine" of the Synod of Dort fixed the orthodox Reformed understanding of the will of God for the world in a form that was to become normative. Thus when, in the next century and in another continent, Jonathan Edwards took up the topic of "universal redemption," it was with a brief comment on "the controversy between the Remonstrants and anti-Remonstrants [or, as the manuscript of the work had it, 'Calvinists and Arminians']" that he began. When he undertook to discuss such issues as freedom and foreknowledge, his discussion assumed the form of a point-by-point refutation of the Arminian positions on these issues, as expounded "by some of the greatest Arminians, by Episcopius in par-

Syn.Dord.*Can*.2.8 (Schaff 3: 562)

Syn.Dord.*Can*.1.17 (Schaff 3: 556)

Syn.Dord.*Can*.1.9 (Schaff 3: 553–54)

Syn.Dord.*Can*.1.10 (Schaff 3: 554)

Syn.Dord.*Sess*.67 (*Act.Syn. Dord*.1:237)
Syn.Dord.*Can*.1.8 (Schaff 3: 553)

Syn.Dord.*Can*.1.6 (Schaff 3: 552)

Syn.Dord.*Rej.err*.1.8 (Schaff 3: 558)

Syn.Dord.*Rej.err*.1.1 (Schaff 3: 556)

Edw.*Orig.Sn*.2.4.1 (Miller 3: 322)

Edw.Fr.Wll.3.2 (Miller 1:288)
Edw.Fr.Wll.2.9 (Miller 1:218–19)

P.Miller (1956)98

Grop.Enchir.2 (1547:36v);Mrl.
Pecc.orig.3 (CT 12:556)

Edw.Rel.Aff.2 (Miller 2:169)

Syn.Dord.Can.pr. (Schaff 3:551)

Syn.Dord.Can.1.17 (Schaff 3:556);Bez.ap.Coll.Mont.Bell.9;10 (1588:459–60;498–99)

Conf.Remon.9.1 (1622:32)

Conf.Helv.post.10 (Niesel 235)
Calv.Inst.(1559)3.22.1 (Barth-Niesel 4:380)

ticular" and by a treatise to which Edwards referred throughout, entitled *Discourse on the Five Points*, which were the same "five heads of doctrine" taken up in the *Remonstrance* and in the *Canons* of the Synod of Dort. To do so, however, Edwards "went back, not to what the first generation of New Englanders had held, but to Calvin"; he "became, therefore, the first consistent and authentic Calvinist in New England."

"What the first generation of New Englanders had held," together with their Puritan colleagues in old England, was a system that came to be called "covenant theology" or "federal theology." Yet it is important to remember that the theme of "covenant" was one that Roman Catholic theologians also found useful; and, before it became the watchword of a theology that was somehow set against Calvinism, "the covenant of grace, and God's declared ends in the appointment and constitution of things in that covenant" was, for orthodox Calvinism as it was to be again for Edwards, an authentic way of describing the will of God for the world, a way that took its place within the context of the doctrine of election in the total body of Reformed teaching. In the preface to its *Canons*, the Synod of Dort doxologized: "Blessed forever be the Lord, who . . . has given witness to the entire world that he does not forget his covenant." The vindication of the will of God expressed in the doctrine of double predestination was proof—not to the elect alone, but "to the entire world"—of his faithfulness in keeping his covenant. The synod also drew upon the idea of the covenant to deal with the question of how, in the light of this doctrine of predestination, parents were to regard the will of God for their children: "The children of the faithful are holy, not indeed by nature, but through the blessing of the covenant of grace, in which they together with their parents are comprehended." The Remonstrant party made use of the theme in its own doctrine of the will of God, which it called "the will of God that is comprehended in the covenant of grace."

Just as Christ was "the mirror in which we contemplate our predestination" and "the clearest mirror of free election," so the mirror of the will of God in

Calv.*Rom.*9:11 (Parker 201–2)

Deut.10:14–15;Matt.11:21

Syn.Dord.*Rej.err.*1.9 (Schaff 3: 558)

Zw.*Gen.*17:2 (*CR* 100:102)

Buc.*Regn.Chr.*1.5;2.5 (Strasbourg 15:58–59;104–5)

Calv.*Rom.*9:4 (Parker 196)

Calv.*Nec.ref.* (*CR* 34:481)

See vol.1:23

Mel.*Com.Rom.*9–11 (*CR* 15: 677–702);Mel.*Enarr.Rom.*9–11 (*CR* 15:974–98) Calv.*Rom.*9–11 (Parker 191–263)

Bez.*Praed.* (*BezTract* 3:416)

the covenant was the history of his dealings with the people of Israel. "As the blessing of the covenant separates the people of Israel from all other nations," Calvin formulated the analogy between election and covenant, "so also the election of God makes a distinction between men in that nation, while he predestines some to salvation and others to eternal damnation"; there was no need to seek a "higher cause" than the goodness and the severity of the will of God. Taking up the analogy, the Synod of Dort cited the language of "choosing" in Old and New Testament as proof that the will of God, not the superior virtue of a nation, was the basis of that separation of the people of Israel from all other nations. Zwingli pointed out that "to give a covenant" was a peculiarly Hebrew way of speaking; Bucer pointed out that the covenant with Israel, though given at one specific moment, also had to be renewed; Calvin pointed out that because the covenant had been given once and for all while the promises of God were scattered throughout the Scriptures, it was necessary to refer all the promises to the covenant as "their only head, in the same way as the special help, by which God declares his love to believers, flows from the one and only fountain of election." The promises of the Old Testament, but also its prayers and petitions, took their start from the covenant of God with the patriarchs. The most important discussion of the covenant with Israel in the New Testament was that of the apostle Paul in Romans 9–11, on the basis of which the church had repeatedly sought to make sense of the relation between the various covenants of God. Yet it is indicative of the relative importance of the covenant in Reformation systems that Melanchthon did not explicitly refer to the covenant in either of his commentaries on Romans 9–11, while Calvin made it a central subject of his exposition, especially of chapter 9, and even Beza dealt with it en passant in his exegesis of that chapter.

In addition to the considerations of the subject occasioned by this exegesis, Reformed theology addressed the meaning of covenant in numerous special ways. Bullinger, for example, composed a treatise in 1534, *On the Single and Eternal Testament or Cov-*

Blngr. Test. (1534)
Urs.Loc.theol.1.1 (Reuter 1: 427–28)

Matt.26:28;Mark 14:24;Luke 22:20;1 Cor.11:25

Blngr. Test. (1534:43r–44v)
Zw. Tf. (CR 91:499–502);Zw. Subsid. (CR 91:499–502);Zw. Hub.2 (CR 91:634–40)

Urs.Ex.ver.doct.1 (Reuter 1: 809)

Oec.Dign.euch.1 (1526:B1r)
Blngr. Test. (1534:4v)

Blngr.Dec.5.6 (1552:325v)
ap.Eus.H.e.5.23–25 (GCS 9: 488–98)

See pp. 197–98 above

Blngr. Or.err.miss.3 (1528:A8r)

Blngr.Nacht.1 (1553:C1r)

Heb.9:16–17(Vulg.)

Urs.Expl.Cat.18.2 (Reuter 1: 98–99)

Urs.Expl.Cat.18.2.2 (Reuter 1: 99)

Blngr. Test. (1534:25v)
Blngr.Dec.3.8 (1552:136r)
Blngr. Test. (1534:17v)

Blngr.Sum.1.2 (1556:4v)

*enant of God,* and Zacharias Ursinus opened his systematic theology with an explanation of the covenant; it became a recurring theme in their other writings as well as in their systematics. The reference to the covenant in all four versions of the words of institution of the Lord's Supper, spoken in the setting of a celebration of the Jewish Passover, the festival of the covenant with Israel, made it possible to ground the defense of the Reformed doctrine of the sacraments, of baptism and especially of the Lord's Supper, in "the nature of the signs of the covenant," in opposition to theories that put exclusive emphasis on the presence. God, who "deigned to call the mystery of divine unity and fellowship by a human title," had accommodated himself to the human practice of confirming a covenant with "signs of good faith," by attaching his own "signs of faith and truth, I mean the sacraments," to his "eternal covenant." The well-known letter of Irenaeus to Pope Victor I must be quoted alongside his formula about the Eucharist, for in the letter he had shown that "the Eucharist is nothing else than a symbol of the covenant of unity, faith, and doctrine." The distortion of the Eucharist into a sacrifice of propitiation was a violation of the divine institution of Christ, who had ordained it to be "a testament, covenant, and legacy." Christ was the only sacrifice of propitiation. Hence the doctrine of the atonement was quite amenable to treatment under the rubric of covenant or testament, as the usage of the Epistle to the Hebrews showed. Therefore, in the formula of Ursinus, "the doctrine of the covenant of God is intimately connected with the doctrine of the Mediator." He went on to adapt the Anselmic doctrine of the Mediator to the doctrine of the covenant: "This covenant cannot take place without a mediator, for we could not make satisfaction for ourselves."

Christ was the one and only Mediator, and there "was only one method of true salvation"; therefore there was "only one covenant, and only one church of all the saints before and after Christ," both of the Old Testament and of the New. Scripture, all of which was related "to this one goal," was "one Book of the Covenant, whether before or after the birth of Christ our Lord." Thus the covenant was "one in substance,

Urs.*Expl.Cat.*18.2.3 (Reuter 1:
99)

Rom.4:16

Calv.*Rom.*4:3 (Parker 81)

Blngr.*Sum.*2.8 (1556:31r)

Blngr.*Test.* (1534:29v–30r)
Calv.*Rom.*8:15;9:4 (Parker
169;196–97)

Calv.*Rom.*8:15 (Parker 169)

Ps.72:5

Calv.*Rom.*9:3 (Parker 194)

Calv.*Rom.*11:1 (Parker 240)
Blngr.*Test.* (1564:6v–7r)

Calv.*Inst.*(1559)3.21.7 (Barth-
Niesel 4:378)

Jer.31:33
Blngr.*Sum.*2.8 (1556:31r)

Blngr.*Dec.*2.6 (1552:121r)

Urs.*Expl.Cat.*18.2.4 (Reuter 1:
101);Blngr.*Test.* (1534:35r–35v)

Blngr.*Test.* (1534:16r)

Blngr.*Dec.*3.6 (1552:121v)

Blngr.*Test.* (1534:38r)

Blngr.*Test.* (1534:20v)

although twofold in circumstances." Abraham, as the
father of believers, believed not merely in any one
statement of God to him, but in "the entire covenant
of salvation and grace of adoption." That covenant of
salvation had been begun in Adam, extended in Noah,
illumined in Abraham, and deposited in written form
through Moses, through whom it was "renewed" and
"expounded more fully." The "law" that Moses had
written down, moreover, contained the covenant of
grace. When the apostle Paul set the law of Moses
into opposition with the gospel, he emphasized only
the distinctive function of the law, its commands and
prohibitions, not the covenant of grace that was also
embodied in it. This covenant of God, given to the
people of Israel through Moses, was "in perpetuity,"
as long as sun and moon should shine; "thus the abolition of the covenant would be more strange than
the destruction of the whole world." It was absurd
even to suggest that human unfaithfulness could ever
undo the eternal covenant between God and Israel.
The covenant proved that salvation was by grace alone.
At the same time, the covenant with Israel was prime
evidence that when God established a covenant he did
not automatically confer with it "the Spirit of regeneration that would enable them to persevere in the
covenant to the very end." That was why there also
had to be the "new covenant" that had been predicted
by Jeremiah. Christ had been the "consummation" of
the covenant, for in him it had appeared "most ex-
cellently, purely, and clearly of all." The "new covenant" in him differed from the old covenant in various
respects, notably in its "amplitude," because "in the
new [covenant] the church is distributed throughout
all the nations" of the world.

Because it summarized "the entire content of piety"
practiced by "the saints of all epochs" through "the
succession of times," "covenant" became a historical
category for describing the will of God for the world
"in time," complementary to (and sometimes in tension with) the "eternal predestination" by the will of
God in the decrees. The histories narrated in Scripture
were "living paradigms of the covenant." Eventually
the "decrees" and the "covenant" would form separate
chapters of Christian doctrine, as in the *Westminster*

*Confession* of 1647. After declaring that "God from
all eternity did . . . ordain whatsoever comes to pass,"
so that "by the decree of God . . . some men and
angels are predestined unto everlasting life, and others

West.Conf.3 (Müller 549–50)

foreordained to everlasting death," the confession went
on to speak of "a voluntary condescension on God's
part, which he hath been pleased to express by way
of covenant," first a "covenant of works" in creation

West.Conf.7 (Müller 558)

and then "the covenant of grace" after the fall. In that
configuration, the indigenous Reformed idea of covenant had already evolved into a full-blown "federal
theology." But the covenant had been functioning
throughout Reformed theology from the beginning
as a counterbalance to predestination, encompassing
as it did both the special call of God and the universal

Calv.Inst.(1539)8 (CR 29:882)

call of God, both the particularity of the covenant
with the nation of Israel as a prime instance of election

Calv.Rom.9:11 (Parker 201–2)
Urs.Expl.Cat.18.2.4 (Reuter 1: 101)

by grace alone and the universality of a will of God
that was "distributed throughout all the nations." It
had the additional advantage of being a relation between God and the "nation"—first the nation of Is-

Calv.Rom.11:16 (Parker 250)

rael, but then also the Gentiles, "not as individuals"

Calv.Rom.11:21 (Parker 252)

but as "the body of the Gentiles." In combination
with the distinctive Reformed understanding of the
application of the law of God, as proclaimed by the

See p. 217 above

church, not only to individuals, but to society, the
motif of covenant moved far beyond the narrow confines of church doctrine, in which it had a subordinate
though significant place, into the area of social and
political history, in which it became a basis for an-
nouncing the word and will of God to the world and
of eliciting obedience to the will and word of God
not only from the church but from the state as well.

# 5 The Definition of Roman Catholic Particularity

See pp. 98–110 above

See vol.2:280–95

Han.*Conc.*12 (*CT* 12:98–99)

Clicht.*Oec.*pr. (1526:2v);Naus.
*Misc.*5.3 (*CT* 12:398);Tap.
*Orat.*4.2 (Mylius 2:343)
1 Cor.11:19(Vulg.);Acts 20:29;
2 Thess.2:11
See vol.3:18

Fish.*Confut.*29 (1523:462)

Ab.Chrys.ap.CTrid.*Act.*16.v.
1547 (*CT* 6–II:90);Arch.ap.
CTrid.*Act.*25.v.1547 (*CT* 6–I:
158)

See p. 128 above

The Protestant Reformation of the sixteenth century made a decisive contribution to the development of the doctrine of the Catholicity of the church, over which the fifteenth century had been contending. For just as it was the confrontation with the Latin church and with Protestantism that evoked "the definition of Eastern particularity" in doctrine, so also it was because of the Reformation that in the West the doctrine of Catholicity, and the Catholicity of doctrine, came to be defined, and hence also to be circumscribed, with a particularity that had not been deemed necessary before. As they watched the Reformation advance from one heterodox deviation to another, its adversaries could "discern the complete fulfillment of the prediction[s] of the divinely inspired Paul" about the rise of "heresies"; and they followed their predecessors, patristic and scholastic, in accepting or even welcoming the opportunity that such "heresies" provided for clarifying orthodoxy. In the process of defining Catholic particularity, doctrinal emphases that had previously been able to coexist as parts of a comprehensive (or undifferentiated) Catholic tradition now became the themes of opposing and mutually exclusive systems, only one of which eventually took the name "Catholic" as its own.

That paradox of a "Catholic particularity" found its identification in the use of the name "Roman Catholic," problematic though the name remained. We are employing it here, sometimes a bit anachronistically, as we have employed the names "Evangelical" and

See pp.183–84 above

See vol.1:333;vol.3:14–15
Aug.Alf.Witt.Abg.(CCath 11:
29–30)

Ambr.Cath.Apol.ver.2.6
(CCath 27:127)

Ambr.Cath.Consid.1 (1547:7v)

Mor.Tyn.9 (Sylvester 8:1028)

See vol.2:230

Aug.Alf.Babst.stl. (1520:A2v)

Aug.Alf.Babst.stl. (1520:B1r)

Aug.Alf.Babst.stl. (1520:B4v)

Han.Conc.7;5 (CT 12:93;91);
Camp.Depr.stat.eccl.pr. (CT
12:6)

Fabr.Praep.4 (CT 4:10)

Diet.Phim.2 (1532:D3r)
Henr.VIII.Coerc.Luth. (1523:
A2r)

Coch.Aeq.dis. (CCath 17:6–
7);Aleand.Conv.conc. (CT 12:
120)

Schatz.Scrut.1 (CCath 5:23)

Wic.Ret.Luth. (1538:A2r)
Ambr.Cath.Apol.ver.pr.
(CCath 27:10);Ambr.Cath.
Excus.disp.3 (1521:17r)
Ambr.Cath.Consid.1 (1547:6r–
6v);Mrtr.ap.CTrid.Act. 3.
iii.1547 (CT 5:1004);Tap.Orat.
1.9–10 (Mylius 2:329–30)

"Reformed" in earlier chapters, and are capitalizing the word "Catholic" as we have the other two: everyone claimed to be "catholic" and "evangelical" and (eventually) "reformed," but now each of these became a denominational label. The name "Roman Catholic" conjoined the universality of the church "over the entire world," which had long been the content of the term "Catholic," with the specificity of "only one single see"; thus "we may say . . . that when we now speak of 'the Roman Church,' this should be understood as referring to 'the Catholic Church,'" since it was only here that "those who are rightly called 'Catholic' and 'ecclesiastical' are present." Only in "the common, known Catholic Church" were "the truth of doctrine and holiness of grace" available. Adapting the classification of John of Damascus to a changing situation, an early opponent of Luther enumerated five groups laying claim to the name Christian: "Greeks, Russians, Bohemians, Mohammedans, and the congregation under Saint Peter and his successor," but only "under Saint Peter and his successor is there no distinction between Bohemian or Greek or Latin or any other language," and therefore the authentic Catholicity that brought with it the supernatural grace of God.

While there had been heresies and schisms before, it soon became clear that the Protestant Reformation represented a threat that was in many ways unprecedented; unprecedented also was the sheer range of doctrines in dispute. The prime mover here was the "heresiarch" Luther. Although he had said some sensible things at the beginning, he "steadily deteriorated" and became "the first to break the bond of peace and unity" that the church in Germany had enjoyed in its inner life and in its relations with the rest of Christendom. Despite the recognition that the doctrinal pluralism inherited from the late Middle Ages was leading to sectarianism quite apart from any of the effects of the Reformation, "the whole business depends on one man, namely, the author of the schism": Luther himself had become the chief issue, "Martin the heretic, Martin the schismatic, Martin the prince of utter pride and temerity"; and he remained so also after his death. Because Luther had come first

See pp. 184–87 above

Coch.*Luth.art*.2 (*CCath* 18:20)
Ec.*Imag*.pr.;14 (1522:A2r; C2v)

Ec.*Enchir*.16 (*CCath* 34:194–95)

Coch.*Aeq.dis*. (*CCath* 17:23)

Bonuc.ap.CTrid.*Act*.22.i.1547 (*CT* 4:572)

Coch.*Aeq.dis*. (*CCath* 17:18)

Lain.*Disp.Trid*.1.3.14 (Grisar 1:20)

Fish.*Sac*.ep.ded. (*CCath* 9:5); Wic.*Luth.art*. (*CCath* 18:98)

and continued to receive the loyalty of so many Protestant leaders, the responses to his attacks, together with the counterattacks on him, occupied a dominant place in the polemical literature. Eventually others came in for attack as well, but even then he was part of the issue, as when Cochlaeus acknowledged that he had "often defended the teaching of the church . . . against other heretics" or when Eck, after having lumped Luther with the Protestant iconoclasts, later commended him for his defense of images against the radicals.

One reason for the difference between the Reformation of the sixteenth century and the reform movements of the Middle Ages was the concentration of the Protestant Reformers on doctrine, and hence the attention of the church's apologists to what one of them called "the reformation of doctrine," by which, he hastened to explain, he did not mean "that the pope should forsake the old doctrine and teach and approve your new kind of doctrine." As was pointed out in an early session of the Council of Trent, the primary concern of the Protestant Reformers was the "wrong teaching" in the church, from which the "wrong conduct" proceeded. The response to that concern included the explanation that it had been specifically "for the sake of doctrine" that various reforms, such as the requirement that bishops be resident in their dioceses, were going forward, as well as the refusal to permit the isolation of any one doctrine from the total corpus of church teaching; for although there were different levels of importance among doctrines, "it will not do to deny one article and to affirm the others, but rather it is necessary to affirm every one of the doctrines, or in any case not to dissent completely from any of them." Of course, much of the discussion did focus on one or another individual doctrine, and we shall in many instances be drawing upon the treatises devoted to one doctrine in addition to those that considered all the principal doctrines seriatim. We shall be considering these doctrines in the chronological order in which they came onto the agenda of the debates until 1530, principally by the initiative of Luther, but we shall carry those debates beyond the form they took initially.

## Defenders of the Faith

The most eminent of the literary apologists to write against the Reformation was certainly Desiderius Erasmus, the greatest scholar of the age. But the most conspicuous apologist was, almost as certainly, King Henry VIII of England, who in 1521 published his *Assertion of the Seven Sacraments* against Luther's *Babylonian Captivity.* For this treatise, Pope Leo X on 11 October 1521 bestowed on Henry the title "Defender of the Faith," as the king himself and his defender, John Fisher, reminded Luther in 1523 and as various observers were to go on recalling, with irony or with praise, long after England's break with Rome. With or without such a title, the defense of the faith was an assignment that many took up, for it was "right and proper to begin with the faith."

To be true to its task, the defense of the faith must entail a refusal to defend the indefensible, for the evils that had befallen the church were well deserved. "I frankly acknowledge," wrote the Flemish humanist and polemicist Josse Clichtove, "that there are very many missteps" in such areas of church life as fasting, penance, celibacy, and monasticism; and it was the duty of church officials to clean up such abuses. There was "superstition," "immoderate ambition among monks," excessive "credulity" in the cult of the saints, "crass ignorance" about Scripture, and need for instruction of the people (and by a better-educated clergy). By "boldly passing judgment" on such abuses, the Reformation had performed a useful service, but its demand for "pure doctrine and uncorrupted morals" was no justification for "overthrowing all the authority of all the ages of history." The removal of an abuse must not involve removal of "the substance of the matter" that had been subject to abuse.

Despite the distinction between doctrine and practice that underlay these discussions of abuses, there were certain practices so inseparable from their doctrinal implications that a change in practice now, while permissible on dogmatic grounds, would amount to a doctrinal concession. Clerical celibacy was one such, communion under one kind another. Notwithstanding the differences of East and West on celibacy and the undeniable differences between the ancient and the

Henr.VIII.*Coerc.Luth.* (1523: title p.);Fish.*Confut.pr.* (1523:9)
Pg.*Mosc.* (1543:11r);Guidic. *Eccl.emend.*3 (*CT* 12:241); Snds.*Serm.*3.5 (*PS* 41:57)

Herb.*Enchir.*1 (*CCath* 12:16)

Coch.*Aeq.dis.* (*CCath* 17:11)

Sad.*Orat.* (*CT* 12:1098–10) Clicht.*Improb.Luth.*7 (1533: 34r);Clicht.*Hom.*46;45 (1535: 396–408;395–96)

Aleand.*Conv.conc.*1 (*CT* 12: 121);Naus.*Misc.*2 (*CT* 12:372) Camp.*Depr.stat.eccl.*1 (*CT* 12:7) Clicht.*Ven.sanct.*1.7 (1523: 16v);Clicht.*Annun.*9 (1519:29r) Caj.*Ref.eccl.*3 (*CT* 12:35–36); Ambr.Cath.*Sac.* (1537:17); Ambr.Cath.*Consid.*4 (1547: 104v–106r)

Lat.*Resp.Buc.* (*CCath* 8:11); Lat.*Def.Buc.*1 (*CCath* 8:32)

Coch.*Aeq.dis.* (*CCath* 17:27); Wic.*Luth.art.* (*CCath* 18:66)

Wic.*Luth.art.* (*CCath* 18:71)

Coch.*Obsc.vir.*3 (*CCath* 15: 11–13);Latom.*Conf.secr.* (1525: E7v)

Caj.*Opusc.aur.*3 (1511:F3r–F5v);Wic.*Luth.art.* (*CCath* 18:75)
Clicht.*Improb.Luth.*13 (1533:55v);Herb.*Enchir.*35 (*CCath* 12:120–22);Ambr.Cath.*Comm.* 1 Cor.7:26 (1566:167)
Luth.*1 Cor.*7 (*WA* 12:92–142);Zw.*Supplic.Hug.* (*CR* 88:204–5);Bgn.*Conjug.episc.* (1525:A5v);Buc.*Regn.Chr.*2.46 (Strasbourg 15:231–34);Hub.*Rech.*18 (*QFRG* 29:479–80)
Zw.*Apol.Arch.*63 (*CR* 88:320)
Clicht.*Improb.Luth.*8 (1533:35r)
Caj.*Utraq.*1 (Lyons 3:293);Lat.*Def.Buc.*2 (*CCath* 8:52–53)

Sal.ap.CTrid.*Act.*9.iii.1547 (*CT* 5:1013);Pgn.ap.CTrid.*Act.*30.ix.1551 (*CT* 7–I:175)
Schatz.*Scrut.*8 (*CCath* 5:107–8);Lat.*Def.Buc.*2 (*CCath* 8:38)
Ec.*Ev.*1 Adv.2 (1530–I:3r)

Lat.*Resp.Buc.* (*CCath* 8:6);Lat.*Def.Buc.*2 (*CCath* 8:47–50)

Henr.VIII.*Assert.* (1521:A4v);Ec.*Enchir.*29 (*CCath* 34:299);Lat.*Def.Buc.*2 (*CCath* 8:52–53)

Henr.VIII.*Assert.* (1521:D2v)

Caj.*Resp.Luth.*4(Lyons 1:127);Ambr.Cath.*Excus.disp.*4 (1521:81v);Fish.*Confut.*17 (1523:306)

Clicht.*Improb.Luth.*14 (1533:58r–63r)

Matt.4:17(Vulg.)

See p. 136 above

Luth.*Disp.indulg.*1 (*WA* 1:233)
Ambr.Cath.*Apol.ver.*4.3 (*CCath* 27:261–63);Fish.*Confut.*21 (1423:329)

Wic.*Luth.art.* (*CCath* 18:70)

Coch.*Luth.art.*2 (*CCath* 18:26–27)

modern church on monastic discipline, what the apostle Paul said in 1 Corinthians 7 about the superiority of virginity still stood, for all the efforts of the Reformers to circumvent it. On the other hand, 1 Corinthians 10–11 was an arsenal of passages in defense of communion under both kinds. They not only "seemed or appeared" to prove it, they were "firm" proof. And so it was necessary to maintain that these passages "pertained only to the practice of that church and time" rather than to the practice of the church in Jerusalem or of the present time, and that the consensus of Western Christendom in support of the present practice demonstrated its continuity with the primitive church. That had been "a blessed time" in church history and yet an "undeveloped" time before it had been "taught by the fathers to understand that both kinds are appropriate for the priests and that the laity can be content with the bread alone." From the logic of the Protestant arguments it was also becoming manifest that a denial of the legitimacy of communion under one kind would lead to a denial of the real presence itself.

The Protestant arguments were raising accusations against the Catholic faith, as well as heretical alternatives to it, that called for response and defense; before the arguments were over, no article of faith had been left unscathed. It all began with Luther's *Ninety-Five Theses*, which seemed to be aimed at depriving the pope of his power and the people of their consolation. Against this attack it was necessary to defend the doctrine of purgatory, the doctrine of the "treasury of merits," and the practice of praying for the faithful departed; these belonged together as parts of the penitential system, which it was the duty of Roman Catholics to accept. In opposition to the very first of the theses, according to which the command, "Do penance," was a mistranslation and did not refer to the sacrament of penance but to lifelong repentance, the defenders of the faith argued for the correctness of the translation and of its application. Although they conceded that the system was liable to corruption and had been invented to compensate for the decline in Christian devotion, the opponents of the Reformation retorted that indulgences were, for that very reason, needed now more than ever.

Caj.*Indulg*.1 (Lyons 1:90)
Pg.*Cont*.9 (1541–I:189v)

Ambr.Cath.*Apol.ver*.4.3
(*CCath* 27:262)

Wic.*Pus*. (1534:C4v;D1r);Wic.
*Luth.art.* (*CCath* 18:89)

Luth.*Serm.poen.* (*WA* 1:322)

Ps.19:12
Ambr.Cath.*Apol.ver*.4.8
(*CCath* 27:281);Ambr.Cath.
*Excus.disp*.4 (1521:76r–77r);
Latom.*Conf.secr.* (1525:B7v)

Wic.*Pus*. (1534:A3v)

See p. 161 above
Cont.*Confut*.5 (*CCath* 7:11–
13);*Confut.Conf.Aug*.12
(*CCath* 33:106–9)

See vol.3:129–44

Cypr.*Ep*.43.5 (*CSEL* 3:594);
Cypr.*Laps*.14;34 (*CSEL* 3:247;
262)

Wic.*Pus*. (1534:E2v)

Wic.*Luth.art.* (*CCath* 18:90);
Grop.*Cap.inst.* (1549:E2r–E2v)

Pg.*Cont*.9 (1541–I:201v–202r)

Caj.*Indulg*.5 (Lyons 1:103–5)

Mor.*Luth*.1.15 (Sylvester 5:
256)
Ambr.Cath.*Apol.ver*.4.12
(*CCath* 27:299–303);Ambr.
Cath.*Excus.disp*.4 (1521:92v;
102r)
Fish.*Confut.int*.4;37 (1523:20;
617–35);Castr.*Haer*.12;8 (1571:
888;578)

See pp. 136–37 above

There had admittedly been a historical development of the penitential system but not of its essential
content, which was "immutable," although the
"manner and time" for performing contrition,
confession, and satisfaction were subject to the decrees, and to the dispensations, of the church. The
system had been in force for more than a thousand
years and must not be overthrown now, simply because of the abuses that had crept into its administration. Luther's opposition to compulsory auricular
confession on the grounds that, according to the
psalm, no sinner "can discern his errors" was a misunderstanding of that biblical verse and of the sacrament of penance. His insistence on "conversion"
as part of genuine repentance was "not invented by
the Lutherans, but has been here" all along. The
unanimous accusation of all the Reformers that penitential "satisfaction" for the damage caused by sin
detracted from the genuine "satisfaction" of the cross
(even though the metaphor of satisfaction by Christ
was derived, at least in part, from the disciplinary
satisfaction of the church) had completely missed the
mark. On the basis of Cyprian's frequent use of such
terms as "righteous satisfaction" for the act of rep-
aration performed by the penitent sinner, Georg
Witzel, who had returned from Lutheranism to Roman Catholicism after the issuance of the *Augsburg
Confession*, recognized that "this word is very controversial," but put the question to Luther: "Did not
Cyprian believe in the satisfaction of Christ? Whose
bishop and martyr was he, then?" Cyprian had
"graphically" described the Protestant theory of satisfaction and had no less graphically denounced it.

Perhaps the gravest doctrinal threat in the Reformation's attack on indulgences was its eventual damage to the idea of purgatory. Luther had, Thomas
More charged, "done away" not only with indulgences but with purgatory itself. Opponents like More
recognized this more clearly than Luther, especially
the contradiction between his continued acceptance
of purgatory and his doctrine of the sole authority of
Scripture. When he eventually did reject purgatory,
they were in a position to remind him of his earlier
protestations of loyal adherence to it and to call him

back to his original Roman Catholic orthodoxy. They were obliged to acknowledge, however, that even those who "assent to the ecclesiastical tradition about the punishments of purgatory" were hard put to provide "a definition or even description" of it. Perhaps the best statements on it were still those in Augustine's *City of God* and in his *Enchiridion*.

Neither the attacks of the various Protestants on the various scholastics nor the Protestant effort to enlist the support of Augustine could be permitted to stand. It was understandable that, as a Dominican, Ambrosius Catharinus would rally to the Thomist cause, but he also had high praise for the Franciscan Bonaventure, specifically for *The Journey of the Mind to God*. More germane to the issues of the Reformation was the supposition of its continuity with the orthodox leaders of reform movements inside the Roman Catholic Church of the fifteenth century, not only with John Hus the condemned heretic but also with Gerson the revered cardinal. Luther's opponents turned his quotations of Gerson against him, and they cited Gerson as a defender of the faith against the heresies of the time and as an orthodox authority on such questions as the doctrine of images, the doctrine of Mary, and the mystical theology of Dionysius the Areopagite. Therefore Luther had no right to claim Gerson, whose "protesting" had not been heretical, as that of the "Protestants" was becoming. Gerson's mentor, Pierre D'Ailly, and Nicholas of Cusa had also been Roman Catholic reformers, not Protestant schismatics. The campaign to reclaim Augustine as a spokesman for the "royal" middle way of the Catholic position, "declining neither to the right nor to the left," consisted in an exposition of his views on such controverted issues as the doctrine of grace and the relation of church and Scripture. But it was no less necessary to resist the attempt of Protestants to make him a patron "for their own deviation rather than for the Catholic" faith. As an Augustinian, Luther ought to emulate his example. Instead, he was "quoting Augustine, but lacerating the words of Augustine." For "Augustine, of all ancient theologians easily the principal one . . . , who according to the consensus of all Catholics shines among the lights of the church as the

Wic.*Purg.* (1545:A2r)

Wic.*Purg.* (1545:B8r;C4v)
See vol.1:355
Wic.*Purg.* (1545:B8r;C4v)

Henr.VIII.*Assert.* (1521:C3v–C4r)

Latom.*Ling.*2 (1517:26–27)

Ambr.Cath.*Apol.ver.*1.7 (*CCath* 27:45–46;49–50); Ambr.Cath.*Consid.*1 (1547:18r)

Ambr.Cath.*Apol.ver.*1.8 (*CCath* 27:71)

Luth.*Dtsch.Kat.*4.50 (*Bek.*701); Luth.*Schmal.Art.*pr. (*Bek.*410)

Wic.*Luth.art.* (*CCath* 18:66)

Clicht.*Oec.*1.1 (1526:6v)

Ec.*Imag.*18 (1522:D1v);Clicht. *Annun.*5 (1519:19r);Ec.*Dion. Ar.*pr.1 (1590:8r)

Ambr.Cath.*Apol.ver.*1.8;1.1 (*CCath* 27:56,70;13)

Ec.*Ps.*20.pr.;7 (*CCath* 13:8; 48);Ec.*Ev.*5 Lent.4 (1530–I:125v)

Clicht.*Eluc.eccl.*1 (1517:68v)

See pp. 263–64 below
Coch.*Obsc.vir.*7 (*CCath* 15:30)

Wic.*Aug.* (1539:A3v)
Henr.VIII.*Assert.* (1521:A4v)

Ec.*Rit.*22 (1519:B2r)

Lat.*Def.Buc.*4 (*CCath* 8:98);
Wic.*Hag.* (1541:195r–196r)

very brightest star for so many centuries— he condemns your position and supports mine."

The Protestant identification of Augustine as the
principal ancestor for the distinctive doctrines of the
Reformation was visible in the first commentary on
a New Testament book that Luther published (although it was not the first that he delivered), his *Lectures on Galatians* issued in 1519, where he took
Augustine's *Nature and Grace* as testimony to his
own basic view that in the usage of Scripture "the
'righteous' are not wholly perfect in themselves, but

Luth.*Gal.*(1519)2:17 (*WA* 2:
495)

God accounts them righteous and forgives them because of their faith in his Son Jesus Christ." At other
times he was less confident that he had Augustine on

See pp. 139–41 above

his side. His opponents saw it as characteristically
Augustinian to emphasize the Pauline doctrine of the

1 Cor.13:13

supremacy of love over faith as "the greatest" among

Fish.*Confut.*1 (1523:63)

the triad of faith, hope, and love. Augustine had quoted
these very words of Paul, together with many others
in praise of love, as the climax of one of the most

Aug.*Grat.*17.33–36 (*PL* 44:
901–3)

important of his anti-Pelagian works (the very portion
of his total output that seemed most to favor the Protestant cause). The words of Paul about "the love of

Rom.5:5

God poured into our hearts through the Holy Spirit"
may well have been Augustine's favorite passage from
Scripture, quoted over and over, also in the treatises
against Pelagianism.

Hence it was necessary, in the name of the true
Augustine, to point out to the Reformers that "you

Herb.*Enchir.*2 (*CCath* 12:21)

will never find it said about faith that it is 'the bond

Col.3:1(Vulg.)

of perfection'" as it was said about love. Love "does

Pg.*Cont.*2 (1541–I:70r)

not permit anything to be preferred to it," not even

Ec.*Ev.*9 Pent.3 (1530–II:138r)

faith. It was a mark of these "newfangled Christians"
to speak of "faith alone," and in so doing to ignore

Wic.*Cred.* (1535)
Fish.*Confut.*10 (1523:220);Pg.
*Cont.*2 (1541–I:49v);Grop.
*Enchir.*2 (1547:136r)

the variety of meanings the word "faith" had in Scripture, where it did not refer only to "trust." Luther
went so far as to insert the word "alone" into his
translation of Romans 3:28, making it read: "that man
is justified without the works of the law, through faith

Luth.*DB* (1522) Rom.3:28
(*WA DB* 7:38)

alone." While he defended the insertion on the grounds
that "it conveys the sense of the text" and was more

Luth.*Dol.* (*WA* 30–II:636–37)

idiomatic German, his critics attacked him for "lacerating and falsifying" not only the biblical text but

Ec.*Enchir.*5 (*CCath* 34:97–98);
Coch.*Luth.art.*2 (*CCath* 18:
10)

the biblical doctrine. Sometimes they interpreted his

Coch.*Luth.art.*2 (*CCath* 18:8–9)

Herb.*Enchir.*4 (*CCath* 12:27–31)

See p. 146 above
Ambr.Cath.*Apol.ver.*1.1 (*CCath* 27:12)

Schatz.*Scrut.*2 (*CCath* 5:38)

Caj.*Ev.*Luke 18:14 (1530:125r)

Wic.*Hom.orth.*Quinq.Ep. (1546:138v–139r)

Gal.5:6

Oberman (1963) 176
Diet.*Phim.*7 (1532:X4r)

Dried.*Cap.*4 (1534:254–63)

Grop.*Enchir.*2 (1547:132r–147v)

Grop.*Enchir.*2 (1547:137r)

formula of "by faith alone" as though it implied the exclusion of the sacraments (or even of Christ himself) from the process of salvation, but usually it was the relation of faith to good works that was seen, and correctly, as the real issue. Taking up the constant boast of the Reformers about being authentically "Pauline" by contrast with the scholastic theologians, the critics countered this alleged Paulinism with the argument that "it is not the intention of Saint Paul, in his repeated praise of faith, to set it forth as though the entire hope of salvation rested on it alone."

What the Protestant Reformation had done with its doctrine of justification by faith alone, as the debates at the Council of Trent were to make clear, was to bring into the open some of the unresolved questions about justification in late medieval theology. In much of medieval theology, going back to Augustine, the doctrine of justification was not the primary focus for the presentation of the mode and content of salvation. The use of the term "justify" in the New Testament meant that anyone undertaking to expound the epistles of Paul as well as other passages was obliged to address himself to the issue. But just as love was more central to the Augustinian system than faith, so also justification by faith did not become a chapter title on its own; and even when it did, the "faith" was seen as "faith formed by love [fides charitate formata]." It has been noted that "Biel has a remarkable doctrine of justification," in which, "seen from different vantage points," justification could be described as by grace alone or by works alone, without any sense of contradiction. When writing against the Reformers, "those who stand for the Catholic side" sometimes manifested no less remarkable conceptions of justification.

One of the most significant of these was that developed by Johann Gropper. Into the chapter of his *Enchiridion* devoted to the doctrine of penance he inserted a lengthy excursus dealing with the doctrine of justification. Summarizing the message of the New Testament as comprehending two parts, "the promise of the free forgiveness of sins" and "inner renewal," he set himself against the suggestion that the first of these was caused by the second, as well as against the

Grop.*Enchir.*2 (1547:133r)

Grop.*Enchir.*2 (1547:141v)

Grop.*Enchir.*2 (1547:137v–138r)

Grop.*Antididag.*8 (1547:33r–35r)

Grop.*Buc.* (1545:11r)

Grop.*Enchir.*2 (1547:143v–144r)

Sad.*Genev.* (Barth-Niesel 1:446)

Cont.*Just.* (CCath 7:34)

suggestion that "the imputed righteousness of God" should be distinguished from "the righteousness of a good conscience, which comes by faith." It was dangerous to use the word "justification" only for the imputation of righteousness, not for the renewal. Faith was said to justify "not in the sense that it is the cause of justification, but because there is nothing else with which we receive the mercy and grace of God that renews us," and hence it could properly be called a "formal cause."

In his *Antididagma* he elaborated this into a threefold sense of justification: the first—involving the forgiveness of sins through the imputation of the righteousness of Christ, reconciliation with God, the renewal of the Holy Spirit, and the gift of eternal life—was that by which "enemies of God" were transformed into "friends of God," and it "is undoubtedly accomplished solely by the grace and mercy of God, through faith, which takes hold of these gifts"; the second, by which those who had received these gifts retained them and matured in them, was "not through faith alone but also through works," as James 2:24 taught; the third "consists in this, that we obtain forgiveness for our daily transgressions" throughout this life. There was one justification through baptism, but another through penance. As he said in the *Enchiridion,* "a man is not justified in such a way that, having once been justified as in a moment, he no longer stands in need of any other justification. On the contrary, one who has been justified by grace . . . henceforth needs a continuous and perpetual justification" until death.

Similarly, Cardinal Sadoleto, addressing the Reformed congregation at Geneva, could say: "We obtain this blessing of complete and perpetual salvation by faith alone in God and in Jesus Christ"; but immediately he went on to make clear that by "faith alone" he did not mean "a mere credulity and confidence in God . . . to the exclusion of love." Cardinal Contarini, in his *Epistle on Justification* of 1541, concluded that "those who say that we are justified by works speak the truth, and those who say that we are not justified by works, but through faith, also speak the truth." For there were in the usage of Scripture two "modes" of justification, and "a twofold righteousness," the believer's own and the imputed righteousness of Christ. When it came to the ground of reliance and hope, "we must depend, as on something solid that will surely sustain us, on the righteousness of Christ conferred upon us, not on the holiness and grace that inheres in us." But it was no less true that "the faith that justifies is faith formed by love," without which there was no genuine justification. Underlying this seeming contradiction was the effort to hold together two passages that the Reformers had difficulty harmonizing, the words of Romans 3:28 that justification was by faith without works and the words of James 2:24 that justification was by works and not by faith alone. In view of the Reformers' insistence on the sole authority of Scripture, the words of James could not have been more effective "if he had seen Luther and his followers with the very eyes of his body."

Sometimes in the polemics it was not simply the means of salvation but its meaning that was at issue. Witzel and others reproached the Reformers for "making the forgiveness of sins too easy" and for an overemphasis on forgiveness, which manifested itself especially in the Lutheran concentration on forgiveness as the principal purpose of the Eucharist. Contarini defined justification as "the spiritual birth by which we become 'participants of the divine nature,'" which he equated with grace. Gropper used the same biblical formula in his reply to Bucer, and at the Council of Trent the theme of salvation as deification, not merely forgiveness, would be sounded several times. When Sadoleto, attacking Calvin, employed the patristic leitmotiv that God had become man in order that man might become God, he touched a sensitive point. For while Zwingli could speak of salvation as "transformation into God" and Calvin or even Beza did not shrink from the formula "participants of the divine nature," the notion that "the restoration of the human race" would mean "the absorption of corporeal nature by the spiritual essence of God," which had been seen as the promise of this formula, represented a christological and a sacramental theory that Reformed theology found unacceptable.

---

Marginal notes (left column):

Cont.*Just.* (*CCath* 7:29);Cont. *Confut.*1 (*CCath* 7:2)

Cont.*Just.* (*CCath* 7:29)

See p. 181 above

Ambr.Cath.*Apol.ver.*1.10;4.11 (*CCath* 27:79;285);Herb. *Enchir.*4 (*CCath* 12:30)

Ambr.Cath.*Comm.*James 2:20 (1566:530–31);Grop.*Enchir.*2 (1547:142r;145v–146r)

See vol.1:141–55

See pp. 147–49 above

Wic.*Ret.Luth.* (1538:A8v)

Wic.*Luth.art.* (*CCath* 18:98); Lain.ap.CTrid. *Act.*17.ii.1547 (*CT* 5:934)

Wic.*Euch.*10 (1534.P2₁–P3v)

2 Pet.1:4
Cont.*Confut.* (*CCath* 7:1–2); Cont.*Praed.* (*CCath* 7:47–48); Caj.*Ev.*John 10:34 (1530:179v) Grop.*Buc.* (1545:9v);Grop. *Enchir.*2 (1547:132v–133r) Stl.ap.CTrid.*Act.*13.i.1547 (*CT* 5:812);Salm.ap.CTrid.*Act.*23. vi.1546 (*CT* 5:266);CTrid. *Decr.just.*I.7 (*CT* 5:386)

See vol.1:155,206

Sad.*Genev.* (Barth-Niesel 1:445)
Zw.*Schl.*13 (*CR* 89:72–73) Calv.*Nob.Pol.* (*CR* 37:351); Calv.*Rom.*5:2 (Parker 104); Bez.*Ep.theol.*7 (1575:65–66)

Calv.*West.*3 (*CR* 37:168);Zw. *Amic.exeg.*5 (*CR* 92:681–82)

See p. 178 above

Henr.VIII.*Assert.* (1521:F4r)
Henr.VIII.*Assert.* (1521:K2r)
Henr.VIII.*Assert.* (1521:C1v)

Blngr.*Dec*.5.9 (1552:369r)

Mor.*Luth*.2.15 (Sylvester 5: 528)

CTrid.*Act*.17.i.1547 (*CT* 5: 835–39)

Henr.VIII.*Assert.* (1521:J4r)

Clicht.*Oec*.pr. (1526:2v);Pg.
*Cont*.4 (1541–I:135v)

Zw.*Amic.exeg.*ep.ded. (*CR* 92: 563)

Henr.VIII.*Assert.* (1521:C2r)

*Confut.Conf.Aug*.13 (*CCath* 33:110–11);Mor.*Luth*.1.12
(Sylvester 5:214);Fish.*Def*.12.8
(1525:99v);Fabr.*Praep*.13 (*CT* 4:12);Diet.*Cat*. (1545:Q5v)

See p. 179 above

Clicht.*Hom*.33 (1535:294–95)

Diet.*Cat*.4 (1545:R8r–S4r)
Clicht.*Improb.Luth*.10 (1533: 42v–45r);Herb.*Enchir*.19–20
(*CCath* 12:76–78)

Despite repeated objections that it was a slander, the Roman Catholic suspicion that the idea of justification by faith "alone" was aimed at the sacramental system itself, since "faith is enough, without the sacrament," and that it would lead to "the subversion of the sacraments," was repeatedly confirmed when Protestants would counterpose "faith alone, which is the spiritual eating" of the body and blood of Christ, to "any work of ours, including the bodily eating of the body of Christ." Such attacks began with Luther's treatise of 1520, *The Babylonian Captivity of the Church*, which Thomas More called a "fount of confusion" especially on the doctrine of the sacraments, and which was to be the most important single source at Trent for the catalogue of "the errors of the heretics" regarding the sacraments. It was, according to Henry VIII, the import of the treatise that "those who come over to [Luther] from the Catholic Church will be set free from the use and the faith of the sacraments." Such suspicions found corroboration when, as the Protestant movement developed, those elements of Catholic sacramental teaching to which Luther had continued to maintain adherence, particularly the real presence in the Lord's Supper as well as the doctrine of baptismal regeneration and the practice of infant baptism, came increasingly into question.

King Henry's *Assertion of the Seven Sacraments*, together with most of the other definitions of Catholic sacramental teaching against the Reformers, objected to the reduction in the number of the sacraments from seven to two. About the inclusion of baptism and the Eucharist in any list of "sacraments" there was no serious controversy, and at least some of the Reformers were willing to include confession. Much of the Roman Catholic case for the inclusion of confirmation, matrimony, holy orders, and extreme unction came down to the question of the authority of the church, on the basis of a tradition that was at least partly oral, to define sacraments for which "the Gospel does not make mention of a specific institution." Confirmation and extreme unction were sometimes described separately, but frequently received a single explanation, especially because the defenders of the

Clicht.*Improb.Luth*.10 (1533: 43r)

Lain.*Disp.Trid*.1.3.25 (Grisar 1:38);Grop.*Enchir*.2 (1547: 193r);Grop.*Buc.* (1545:15v)
Eph.5:32(Vulg.);see vol.3:212

Grop.*Cap.inst.* (1549:E5r)

Wic.*Euch*.1 (1534:A4r)
Herb.*Enchir*.43 (CCath 12: 152–53)
Fish.*Def*.12.16–17 (1525:102r–103r)
See p. 51 above
Grop.*Enchir*.2 (1547:179r)

See vol. 3:212–13

Ec.*Enchir*.7;35 (CCath 34:107–17;365–68)

Grop.*Buc.* (1545:12v)

Fish.*Confut*.1 (1523:86);Grop. *Leyb*.2 (1556:262r)

Fish.*Corp*.2.29 (1527:93r)
See vol.1:146–47,168–69; vol.3:136–37,188–90
Luth.*Capt.Bab.* (WA 6:513);
Zw.*Schl*.18 (CR 89:111–57);
Zw.*Can,mass.* (CR 89.583–87)
Schatz.*Scrut*.6 (CCath 5:86–96);Herb.*Enchir.*16 (CCath 12: 66–70)

Coch.*Aeq.dis.* (CCath 17:31–32)
Luth.*Capt.Bab.* (WA 6:518);
Buc.*Caen.* (Strasbourg 1:24)
Henr.VIII.*Assert.* (1521:F3r–53v)

Schatz.*Scrut*.6 (CCath 5:95);
Fish.*Confut*.15 (1523:267–68);
Fish.*Def*.6.1;8.4 (1525:58r;71r)

Wic.*Euch*.8;1 (1534:J1r;B1r)

Cat.*Heid*.2.80 (Niesel 168–69)

Heb.10:10

Mal.1:11
Ec.*Enchir*.17 (CCath 34:207; 199);Fish.*Corp*.2.17 (1527: 74v);Diet.*Phim*.9 (1532:Z2r–Z4r);*Confut.Conf.Aug*.24 (CCath 33:162–71)

sacramental system admitted that there was for confirmation "no express command in particular" in the sayings of Christ in the Gospels. The defense was that such sacraments, though "promulgated" by the apostles, had been "instituted" by Christ. For matrimony, they cited the standard proof text in which it was called "a great sacrament," although some writers acknowledged that the word "sacramentum" in the Bible "is never used for what in church usage" was called a "sacrament." Again there was no express institution of it as a sacrament in the Gospels; but it did confer grace, and that set it apart from the marriage of non-Christians. The sacramental status of holy orders was inseparably bound up with the larger question of the institution of the church and of its structures by Christ himself.

Although all the sacraments had been instituted by Christ for the church, some of them (baptism, the Eucharist, absolution, and ordination) were "absolutely necessary." Among these, the Eucharist was unique, for it was "confected before it is administered," and after having been confected it remained beyond the original celebration of the sacrifice of the Mass. It was the sacrificial definition of the Mass to which all the Reformers in their attacks, and their opponents in their defenses, devoted their chief attention. The benefit of the Eucharist as communion depended on the preparation of the communicant; as sacrifice, however, it benefited not only the participants but all those for whom it was offered, whether living or dead. Describing it as a testament and a promise, as Luther and Bucer had, was inadequate. It was a testament, to be sure, but because the New Testament was superior to the Old, "the most holy Sacrament of the Eucharist" must be "both a testament and a sacrifice for us." Where there was an altar, there must be a sacrifice. To the principal objection against the sacrificial interpretation, the reply was that Christ had indeed "offered a perfect sacrifice once and for all," but that this same "pure offering" was to be sacrificed "in every place": "There is no other sacrifice than the body of Christ, repeated everywhere in the Mass." To deny this was to "contradict all of Sacred Scripture and the church."

Aug.Alf.*Witt.Abg.* (CCath 11: 26)

Clicht.*Ven.sanct.*2.16 (1523: 88v–89r)

Coch.*Luth.art.*2 (CCath 18: 16)

Fish.*Def.*4.8 (1525:40c)
Henr.VIII.*Assert.* (1521:E3v);
Pg.*Cont.*4 (1541–I:139r)

Henr.VIII.*Assert.* (1521:E3r–E3v)

Ambr.Cath.*Excus.disp.*2 (1521: 6r–6v)
Ec.*Ev.*Maund.Thu.1 (1530–I: 133v)
Clicht.*Eluc.eccl.*1 (1517:44r)
Clicht.*Oec.*1.1 (1526:5r);Wic.*Euch.*7 (1534:H1r–H1v);Mor.*Tyn.*6 (Sylvester 8:661);Grop.*Leyb.* (1556:245r–247r)
Lat.*Def.Buc.*2 (CCath 8:44);
Grop.*Leyb.*1 (1556:174v–1786v)
Caj.*Euch.*5 (Lyons 2:143–44);
Wic.*Euch.*6 (1534:G2v)

Luth.*Capt.Bab.* (WA 6:512);
Luth.*Anb.* (WA 11:441)

See p. 140 above

Clicht.*Improb.Luth.*1 (1533: 3r–3v)

Cont.*Confut.*4 (CCath 7:7)

Tap.*Orat.*6.5 (Mylius 2:355–56)

Ambr.Cath.*Apol.ver.*1.9 (CCath 27:74–75);Schatz.*Scrut.*1 (CCath 5:9)
Dried.*Concord.*2.3 (1537:191);
Dried.*Lib.chr.*1 (1540–I:73–74)
Cont.*Praed.* (CCath 7:58–59)
Dried.*Grat.lib.arb.*1 (1537–I: 17–18)

Because the sacrifice and the real presence were corollaries, some, as early as 1524, discerned in the rejection of the first a softening of belief in the second in favor of a theory of mere "sign." Another corollary was the veneration of the consecrated Host, a worship paid to Christ himself. "Without the Mass," therefore, "one cannot have the Sacrament of the body and blood of Christ; for to consecrate or transform is nothing other than to celebrate Mass, and the transformation is the principal part of the Mass." Belief in the transformation was ancient, although the term "transubstantiation," defined at the Fourth Lateran Council, was a relatively recent invention. Nor did it depend on a particular philosophical theory, "for the church does not believe it because [the scholastics] dispute this way, but because the church has believed this from the beginning." Transubstantiation, as part of the rule of faith, was not, as Luther charged, a creation of "the Thomistic church" that belonged only in the lecture hall; it belonged also in the pulpit and was a statement of the rule of prayer. Therefore the confession of Berengar did deserve to stand as a confession of the Catholic doctrine. On the other hand, "Believe, and you have already eaten" meant no more than the Catholic doctrine that God was not bound to the sacraments. It was wrong to set "spiritual eating" and sacramental eating in opposition.

The rejection of the sacrificial view of the Eucharist was part of the larger campaign against neo-Pelagianism, a campaign that found its classic exposition in Luther's *Bondage of the Will* of 1525 against Erasmus. The defenders of the faith repeated the arguments of Erasmus against Luther, sometimes from firsthand study of both writers, but also sometimes without having read Luther's treatise; but they found it necessary to go beyond Erasmus and to criticize Luther's contradictory ideas about free will. The Reformers were "accusing the entire doctrine of the scholastics, in fact, the entire church" of the Pelagian error, "as though it were destroying the grace of Christ by preserving free will." This so-called Augustinianism was based on a misunderstanding of Augustine and of his place in Catholic doctrine. He had contended not only against Pelagius but also against the Manicheans, to

Eras.*Hyp*.2 (*LB* 10:1523)
Ec.*Rit*.3 (1519:A3r);Henr.
VIII.*Coerc.Luth*. (1523:A4r);
Fish.*Confut*.36 (1523:652)

whom the Protestant denial of free will, "rebounding from Pelagius," was manifesting a strong family resemblance. Even against the Pelagian heresy, moreover, Augustine had affirmed the cooperation of divine grace and free will in the baptized, although there

Wic.*Luth.art*. (*CCath* 18:84)

were some who said that he had been "driven to plain

Pg.*Cont*.1 (1541–I:45r–45v)

absurdities" in his opposition to Pelagius. At the same time, it was important for Roman Catholic theology

Cont.*Praed*. (*CCath* 7:44;51)

not to "turn away into the heresy of Pelagius" in its opposition to Reformation teachings.

Anyone who claimed to be Augustinian, indeed, "anyone who is Christian confesses freely, on the basis of Romans 5, the hereditary sin [that comes] from

Wic.*Luth.art*. (*CCath* 18:82)
Cont.*Praed*. (*CCath* 7:49)
Coch.*Luth.art*. (*CCath* 18:34
Luke 10:30
Schatz.*Scrut*.1 (*CCath* 5:18–19)
Isa.40:3
Ec.*Ev*.4 Adv.2 (1530–I:21v)
Matt.11:30
Ambr.Cath.*Apol.ver*.5 (*CCath* 27:273)

Adam upon and into all men." The freedom of the will had been "corrupted," reason "diseased," and the will itself "weakened"—"half dead," as the Gospel said, but not utterly destroyed. Otherwise, the summons to "prepare the way of the Lord" would be a mockery, as would the promise of Christ that his yoke was easy and his burden light. Moral accountability and guilt would both be invalidated if there were not

Clicht.*Improb.Luth*. (1533:6r–6v)

enough freedom of the will to make a person responsible. When such a person was ready for grace, it did not coerce his free will but "inclined, influenced, and

Schatz.*Scrut*.5 (*CCath* 5:84)

drew the will to consent." There was no antithesis between grace and free will, nor between grace and merit. Scripture repeatedly held out the prospect of

Ec.*Enchir*.5 (*CCath* 34:86–88)
Clicht.*Improb.Luth*.3 (1533:13r);Cont.*Confut*.2 (*CCath* 7:4)
See pp. 145–46 above

"rewards," to the discomfiture of the Protestant Reformers, who had similar difficulty with the innumerable passages that spoke of "merit." The biblical way of speaking, "in the pages of both Testaments," was to comprehend both grace and merit, both gift and reward, as "saintly and Catholic" theologians had

Schatz.*Scrut*.1 (*CCath* 5:13–14)
See p. 130 above

always done. For, in the scholastic axiom that was repeated over and over against the Reformers, God

Herb.*Enchir*.38 (CCath 12:132);Ec.*Ev*.Adv.2 (1530–I:21v)
Clicht.*Improb.Luth*.1 (1533:3r–3v);Ambr.Cath.*Consid*.2 (1547:46v)

would not deny his grace to those who did what lay within their powers to do.

As it was articulated in Luther's *Bondage of the Will*, the Protestant doctrine of predestination early became the object of Roman Catholic attention, provoking the

Herb.*Enchir*.44 (*CCath* 12:153)

warning that "the predestination of God does not impose any coercive necessity." Then when Zwingli, quoting the text, "As many as were ordained to eternal

Acts 13:48

life believed," drew the conclusion, "Therefore those

Zw.*Fid.rat.* (CR 93–II:800–801)

Ec.*Rep.art.Zw.*6 (1530:D3v–D4r)

Caj.*Nov.Test.*2.1 (1530:C4v)

Clicht.*Improb.Luth.*2 (1533:7v)

See pp. 254–55 above

Cont.*Praed.* (CCath 7:44–45)
Dried.*Concord.*2.3 (1537:200;207–9);Wic.*Ret.Luth.* (1538:D5r)
Cont.*Praed.* (CCath 7:63)
Clicht.*Improb.Luth.*2 (1533:11v);Dried.*Concord.*1.2;1.2;2.3 (1537:57;197);Cont.*Praed.* (CCath 7:55,61)
Rom.11:33

Rom.8:29–30

Schatz.*Scrut.*2 (CCath 5:28)

Caj.*Mos.*Ex.10:1 (1539:191)
Dried.*Concord.*2.3;1.1 (1537:239;11–12)

Ambr.Cath.*Comm.*Rom.9:18 (1566:93)
*Confut.Conf.Aug.*18 (CCath 33:116–19)

Luth.*Dol.* (WA 30–II:643)

*Apol.Conf.Aug.*21.14 (Bek.319);Mel.*Torg.Art.* (Bek.83b);
*Conf.Aug.*21 (Bek.83b–83c)
*Conf.Helv.post.*4 (Niesel 226–27);see pp. 216–17 above
Ec.*Imag.* (1522);Grop.*Enchir.*4 (1547:259v);Castr.*Haer.*8 (1571:71–78)

See vol.3:174–84
Zw.*Ver.fals.rel.*23 (CR 90:839–41)
Coch.*Luth.art.*2 (CCath 18:28–30)

who believe are ordained to eternal life," Eck warned him that such an inversion was not permissible, logically or theologically: not all who believed were predestined. Because the Catholic tradition was characterized by "plurality" and "ambiguity" in its treatment of predestination and reprobation, Luther's thought was perhaps "not to be condemned out of hand on this point." But after Calvin had worked out his mature doctrine of double predestination, Contarini, who was not without sympathy for Protestant teaching, expressed his alarm that there were some, "quite well versed in the writings of Saint Augustine," who were "setting forth to the people extremely difficult and intricate dogmas." It was wrong to set Augustine in opposition to the other church fathers this way, for such a doctrine of predestination was fatalism. To the critics of this doctrine, the way of reverence was to stand in silent awe before the "depth" of the mystery of predestination, and, rather than treating predestination in isolation, to observe the "golden chain" of the Epistle to the Romans: "Those whom he predestined he also called; and those whom he called he also justified; and those whom he justified he also glorified." The hardening of the heart of Pharaoh "is not a positive act of God," but a negative divine response to the free action of Pharaoh, who was himself "the cause of his ruin and rebellion" and who had aggravated his own situation before God took action against him. In such a view, which avoided Manicheism and Pelagianism, lay the "royal road" of the Catholic faith.

In 1530 Luther and Melanchthon set forth, more systematically than before, the Reformation's critique of the cult of the saints on two grounds: there was "not a single word of God commanding" their invocation; and this cult "transfers to the saints honor belonging to Christ alone" by making them mediators and propitiators. The Reformed sharpened this critique to include the use of images, calling forth a defense based on earlier Eastern and Western apologies. Clichtove's treatise, *The Veneration of the Saints*, though written some years earlier, stated the orthodox doctrine developed in the Middle Ages with such balance and care that, despite Protestant attacks, it continued to serve as a model. Through a proper in-

Clicht. *Ven.sanct.*2.15 (1523: 83v–87v)

Clicht. *Ven.sanct.*2.7 (1523:61v)
Clicht. *Ven.sanct.*2.5;1.7 (1523: 57v;16v)

See vol.3:178–79
Clicht. *Ven.sanct.*2.7 (1523: 64r);Diet.*Phim.*6 (1532:S4r)
Aug.*Civ.*8.27;22.10 (*CCSL* 47: 248–49;48:828)

Clicht. *Ven.sanct.*2.1 (1523: 49v–50r);Lat.*Def.Buc.*3 (*CCath* 8:65–66)

Clicht. *Ven.sanct.*2.4 (1523:54v)

Grop.*Cap.inst.* (1549:C6v)
Ec.*Enchir.*15 (*CCath* 34:186);
Cont.*Confut.*6 (*CCath* 7:13–14);Diet.*Phim.*6 (1532:S4r–T1r);Pg.*Cont.*13 (1541–II:51r)

Dict.*Phim.*6 (1532:Q3r)

2 Macc.15:12–16;12:42

Clicht.*Improb.Luth.*14 (1533: 61v);Ec.*Enchir.*15 (*CCath* 34: 175);Pg.*Cont.*13 (1541–II:53r)

Aug.Alf.*Witt.Abg.* (*CCath* 11: 26);Ambr.Cath.*Consid.*2 (1547:66r)

Zw.*Ec.*1.3 (*CR* 92:188)
Zw.*Bek.*3 (*CR* 93–II:236);
Hub.*Rech.*9–10 (*QFRG* 29: 470–72)
Zw.*Mar.* (*CR* 88:401–5);Hub.
*Ent.* (*QFRG* 29:273)
Henr.VIII.*Assert.* (1521:R3r);
Dried.*Eccl.scrip.*4.3 (1533:501; 303);Clicht.*Hom.*12 (1535: 107–8);Diet.*Phim.*6 (1532: O2r);Castr.*Haer.*10 (1571:632)
Clicht.*Eluc.eccl.*4 (1517:210v–211r)

Clicht.*Eluc.eccl.*1 (1517:48v)
Clicht.*Hom.*9 (1535:78)
Diet.*Salv.Reg.*9 (1526:C3v–D1r)
Aug.Alf.*Salv.Reg.* (*CCath* 11: 74–77)
See p. 308 below

Diet.*Salv.Reg.*8 (1526:C2v–C3r)

Grop.*Cap.inst.* (1549:C3r)
Diet.*Salv.Reg.*ep.ded. (1526: A2r)
Diet.*Salv.Reg.* (1526);Aug.Alf.
*Salv.Reg.* (*CCath* 11)

vocation of the saints, he urged in response to the substantive critique, the glory of God was not diminished but magnified. For the "ultimate and supreme" attention of Christian devotion was to God, but the invocation of the saints was an aid to it. It was essential to avoid both extremes: the notion that the saints conferred grace and could rescue souls from hell, but also the hoary objection that the veneration of the saints was idolatrous. From Augustine's *City of God* came the explanation of the fundamental difference between the cult of the saints and the pagan practices to which Protestant critics were comparing it. The "adoration" paid to the Creator pertained to him alone, the "adoration" of saints was that appropriate to God's "creatures"; strictly speaking, "the church does not adore the saints . . . but honors them." Christ was the only "Mediator of redemption," but the saints were "mediators of intercession." To the other Protestant objection it was possible to cite the "express" testimony of 2 Maccabees, disputed though its canonicity was, and to argue from this: "Now if the Jews believed this firmly and without hesitation . . . , should not Christians do so [even more] in the light of the law of the gospel?"

The Virgin Mary was a unique case on both sides. Although Roman Catholic polemics accused the Reformers of blaspheming her, they had continued to call her "the highest of creatures next to her Son" and the "Mother of God," and to assert her perpetual virginity. Nevertheless, it was necessary to point out that they had no right to such views on the basis of their doctrine of "sola Scriptura" and to emphasize the distinctively Roman Catholic view of her. She was "the habitation of the entire Trinity," the one through whom, by the incarnation of the Son of God, "the world is said to be saved," and from whom "we have received the fullness of grace." She was properly called "mediatrix," for in a special way she interceded with God on behalf of the church. As Erasmus too was at pains to point out, prayer to her did not conflict with prayer to God; nor did it mean that "we ascribe to her the merit of our salvation, for here is Jesus, your Son." At least two tractates against "Luther and his party" took the form of commentaries on the Salve Regina, which,

Diet.*Salv.Reg.*3 (1526:B3r)

Clicht.*Annun.*1 (1519:5r–7v)

Clicht.*Eluc.eccl.*2 (1517:88r)
Aug.Alf.*Salv.Reg.* (*CCath.* 11:61)
Ambr.Cath.*Apol.ver.*1.4
(*CCath* 27:32);Caj.*Concept.*2
(Lyons 2:138)
Clicht.*Annun.*9 (1519:31v)
Ambr.Cath.*Immac.*2 (1542:56)

Mor.*Her.*1.25 (Sylvester 6:151);Eras.*Hyp.*1 (*LB* 10:1318)

Mor.*Her.*4.16 (Sylvester 6:419)

though only some centuries old, was more ancient than the Protestant doctrine. The annunciation was "the first mystery" of redemption, and her resurrection immediately after her death was taken for granted, as was her voluntary poverty. Her immaculate conception, while still problematical, enjoyed wide support by now and was eventually affirmed even by those who had had reservations about it. As part of the total Christian tradition, the doctrine of Mary, too, belonged to "this faith [as] taught by Christ, preached by his apostles," and confessed by the orthodox and Catholic fathers.

## The Gospel and the Catholic Church

See p. 110 above
Dried.*Eccl.scrip.*4 (1533:503);
Ems.*Ven.Luth.* (*CCath* 4:50)

Pol.*Henr.VIII.*1;2 (1536:17r;31v)

At every stage and on every issue of the defense of the Roman Catholic faith against the Reformers, and more pointedly after the issuance of the *Augsburg Confession* in 1530, it became evident to all that, just as in the fifteenth century, there was one issue implicit within all the other issues: the doctrine of authority. To the erstwhile "Defender of the Faith" against Luther, Cardinal Pole could now put the question: "What validity does the practice of the church have for you?" Having listed the three topics of his defense against Bucer—the Eucharist, the saints, and celibacy—another writer continued: "To these a fourth has been added in my epistle, namely, the authority of the church, which is so necessary in this dispute that without it you cannot assert anything that is sure and firm." With it, however, "whatever there is of disagreement and controversy between us could be easily settled."

Lat.*Def.Buc.*2 (*CCath* 8:37)

Pg.*Cont.*3 (1541–I:113r)

Pach.ap.CTrid.*Act.*11.x.1546
(*CT* 5:491)

Therefore the problem of authority had disturbed the church more than the doctrine of justification. As the Protestants should remember,the condemnation of Pelagianism, which they were citing against Rome, had been accomplished through the authority of Rome.

Dried.*Grat.lib.arb.*1 (1537–I:60)

Matt.18:17

Writing against Luther, Clichtove quoted the words of Christ about "listening to the church" as a warrant also for those institutions and observances of the church that lacked explicit documentation in the Gospels, such as for example the canonical hours; writing against Oecolampadius, he described it as "the peculiarity of heretics" that they always attacked the Apostolic See and its loyal adherents. For the New

Clicht.*Improb.Luth.*5;6 (1533:20v–21r;28v)
Clicht.*Improb.Luth.*9 (1533:41v);Ec.*Enchir.*32 (*CCath* 34:340)
Clicht.*Oec.*1.3 (1526:13v);
Aug.Alf.*Malag.* (1520:E2r);
Dried.*Lib.chr.*1.2 (1540–I:47–48)

Matt. 15:9
Zw. Schl. 16 (CR 89:86–90); Zw. Apol. Arch. 1 (CR 88:271); Conf. Aug. 26.22; 27.37 (Bek. 104; 116)

Ambr. Cath. Sac. (1537:25)

Testament aspersions on "the commandments of men" did not, as Zwingli and others assumed, refer to "the commandments of prelates" as such, but only to those that were "perverse and opposed to the law of God." When the Reformers happened to be right in their doctrine, they "have this from the church and from its Scripture," for it was "the church that has defended this truth in times past" against the heretics; those

Wic. Luth. art. (CCath 18:100–1); Latom. Conf. secr. ep. ded. (1525:A5v)

Diet. Phim. 3 (1532:H2r)

who rejected the authority of the church were not entitled to its truth. The only "infallible judge" was the Roman Catholic Church. Therefore although the

Ambr. Cath. Consid. 3 (1547: 89r–89v)

Wic. Cat. eccl. 4.9 (1535:H2v)

Protestants seemed to accept all the articles of the creed, they had rejected the article, "I believe one, holy, catholic, and apostolic church," upon which "the entire creed depends."

See vol. 1:303

Theologically the most succinct, and rhetorically the most effective, formulation of the doctrine of authority was Augustine's fundamental principle: "For my part, I should not believe the gospel except as

Aug. Ep. fund. 5 (CSEL 25:197)

moved by the authority of the Catholic Church." It had been a gauge of various theories of authority in

See pp. 125–26 above

the later Middle Ages, and now it became so again.

Luth. Res. Lips. 12 (WA 2:429–32)
Luth. Beid. gest. (WA 26:575–78)

Luth. Menschlehr. (WA 10 II: 89); Luth. Henr. (WA 10–II: 216–18)

Zw. Apol. Arch. 36 (CR 88:293)

Zw. Val. Comp. (CR 91:70–71)

Luther interpreted these words of Augustine as supportive of his position against Rome, although he could also reply to their use by asking: "Even if Augustine used these words, who gave him authority that we must believe what he says?" Zwingli reacted to the formula in a similar vein, although he did not accept the Roman Catholic interpretation of it. Protestant spokesmen insisted that Augustine was not teaching

Mel. Eccl. (CR 23:605;595); Blngr. Sum. 1.4 (1556:9r–9v); Urs. Loc. theol. 1.3 (Reuter 1: 435)

"that the authority of the church is greater than that of the word of God, or that the church can repeal articles [of faith] laid down in the word of God"; rather, he meant to assign to the early church the authority to distinguish authentic from inauthentic

Art. Ratis. 1. A (CR 4:350)

Scripture.

Rdly. Conf. Ltmr. 2.7 (PS 39: 128)

But "that same vehement saying of St Augustine . . . was wont to trouble many men." Also after Leipzig, Eck quoted it to prove that "Scripture is not

Ec. Enchir. 1 (CCath 34:27–28)
Ambr. Cath. Excus. disp. 3 (1521: 29v)

Luth. Capt. Bab. (WA 2:561)

authentic without the authority of the church." Thus it vested in the church the power to recognize the books of the canon, as Luther admitted; but Roman Catholic theologians argued that this power belonged, according to Augustine's dictum, to the church

Dried.*Grat.lib.arb*.1 (1537–I: 19);Dried.*Eccl.scrip*.4 (1534: 563)

Diet.*Phim*.2;3 (1532:E3v;H3r–H3v)

See p. 211 above

Grop.*Antididag*.2 (1547:21r); Ambr.Cath.*Clav*.2 (1543:215; 29)
Tap.*Orat*.3.3 (Mylius 2:336); Grop.*Leyb*.1 (1556:38r)

Ambr.Cath.*Consid*.2;3 (1547: 37v–38r;90r)
Henr.VIII.*Assert*. (1521:R2r–R2v)

Luth.*Henr*. (WA 10–II:216–18)

Mor.*Luth*.2.21 (Sylvester 5: 598–610)

Mor.*Her*.1.30 (Sylvester 6:181)

Mor.*Tyn*.7 (Sylvester 8:676–77)

Wic.*Ret.Luth*. (1538:B3r)

Lat.*Def.Buc*.3;5 (CCath 8:62; 101–2);Mor.*Her*.1.25 (Sylvester 6:148–49)

Fish.*Sac*.3.21 (CCath 9:67)

Matt.4:17(Vulg.)

Grop.*Enchir*.2 (1547:124r–124v)
Ambr.Cath.*Apol.ver*.4.3 (CCath 27:262)

throughout Christian history. The question of that power was itself a complex one, in the light of the Protestant doctrine of the sole authority, rather than merely the primary authority, of Scripture, as Johann Dietenberger pointed out when he used the words of Augustine to prove that "credibility comes to the Scriptures from the universal authority of the church," not from some intrinsic self-authenticating force within the books themselves. But the interpretation of Scripture, not only its identification, was the import of the saying of Augustine, as the sorry spectacle of the eucharistic controversy was making clear. Yet because "the heretics do not observe this rule," they were interpreting Scripture wrongly and denying some of the Scriptures that the church had included in its canon. In his attack on Luther's *Babylonian Captivity* Henry VIII pressed this point, eliciting a detailed reply from Luther, to which Thomas More replied in even more detail. Beyond being able to know "which was the true Gospel" as distinct from some "pseudo-Gospel" that did not belong in the New Testament, "the church also has from God the power of distinguishing the true meaning of Scripture from the false." From this "it follows that the church cannot err in the sacraments and in necessary articles of faith." In his later writings More again cited Luther's acceptance of the Augustinian formula, "Luther's own words against Luther's own heresies," to prove the validity of the "traditions of the apostles," unwritten as well as written.

The Protestant effort "to cleanse the church with paper" seemed to be "the basic foundation of all your assertions," for Protestants based upon it "the entire force of your argument, by which you dissent from the true Catholic Church." The error in this view of authority was the substitution of the exclusive principle, "Nothing is to be admitted beyond Holy Writ," for the orthodox principle, "Nothing is to be received contrary to the Scriptures." Thus in the penitential system, it was true that the command "Do penance" did not specify the details of the sacrament; these had been left to the church, whose legislation, documented for example in Ambrose, was binding on believers. What the principle of "sola Scriptura" did was

Eras.*Hyp*.1;2 (*LB* 10:1326; 1414);Tap.*Orat*.3.2 (Mylius 2: 336);Ambr.Cath.*Consid*.2 (1547:36v)

Lat.*Def.Buc*.5 (*CCath* 8;104)

Herb.*Enchir*.9;10 (*CCath* 12: 44;49)

2 Cor.3:6

John 16:13
Diet.*Phim*.1;2;3 (1532:B3r; E3r;H4r)
Zw.*Wort*. (*CR* 92:856–57);
Blngr.*Dec*.5.1 (1552:275r);
Ec.*Ev*.Pres.1 (1530–1:26r);
Fish.*Corp*.1.27 (1527:46r);
Fish.*Confut*.pr. (1523:43);Mor.
*Tyn*.3 (Sylvester 8:266)

Wic.*Ret.Luth*. (1538:A6r)

Ec.*Enchir*.4 (*CCath* 34:81–82)

Ambr.Cath.*Clav*.2 (1543:216–17);Grop.*Buc*. (1545:8r);Grop.
*Cap.inst*. (1549:H7r)

Eras.*Hyp* 1 (*LB* 10:1302)

Lat.*Def.Buc*.5 (*CCath* 8:111)

Williams (1962) 511

Luth.*Wied*. (*WA* 26:155)

Ec.*Enchir*.39;3 (*CCath* 34:408; 75)

Latom.*Conf.secr*. (1525:B5v)

Ambr.Cath.*Consid*.2 (1547: 45r–45v)

Ec.*Rep.art.Zw*.1(1530:C1v);
Coch.*Luth.art* 1 (*CCath* 18:6)
Wic.*Pus*. (1534:F1v)

to substitute the private judgment and arbitrary subjective authority of the individual for that of the church, and thus to "change the entire meaning of Scripture in accordance with your own opinion." Yet "apart from the Catholic Church" there could not be any "living and efficacious propagation of the word," but only the tyranny of "the letter that kills and deceives." Christ had directed his disciples not only to Scripture but to "the Spirit of truth" who would guide the church. It had been the universal experience of the orthodox church that heretics—for example, as Zwingli and Bullinger admitted, the Arians—"arose out of Holy Scripture, badly understood." Thus "each one who reads Scripture takes it to be the way he is—the Catholic as Catholic, others as something else."

When the Reformation had grown from one man to an entire movement, becoming more heterogeneous and more radical in the process, the futility of "sola Scriptura" as a means of combating false doctrine was ever more obvious: "Who is to be the judge among them? Who will ever harmonize all of this? Will it be Scripture—or the church?" It was a false alternative, for the two belonged together; and "if Sacred Scripture is the clearest possible" authority, how was it that some who accepted it were denying the real presence while others were still affirming it? It was by "drawing upon patriarchal precedent" in Scripture that some Radicals were advocating and practicing polygamy. On the other hand, since they had to admit that infant baptism, though apostolic, was not expressly taught in Scripture, the more conservative among the Reformers, "defending themselves against the Anabaptists, are pulling back from their base" of holding to the sole authority of Scripture. Such inconsistency in the face of a radical biblicism that was threatening those elements of the dogmatic consensus to which they wanted to retain their loyalty put them into the position of violating their own principle of authority. Although "they often speak scandalously about it," they wanted to keep the dogma of the Trinity, which was indeed a statement of biblical teaching but did not appear in the very words of any one biblical passage; the same was true of atonement as "satisfaction."

At the same time, in an area of doctrine in which most or all of the Reformers had forsaken the Catholic dogmatic consensus, their definition of authority did not prevent them from "distorting with an alien meaning" the passages of Scripture that spoke of free will. The very translation of the Bible had provided opportunities for such distortions, as in the addition of the word "alone" to the locus classicus on justification or in the addition of the word "only" to make Romans 3:20 read, "Through the law comes only knowledge of sin"—a rendering that was attacked as false and that Luther deleted from the final edition of his German Bible. Such "laceration and distortion of Scripture" was evidence that "the interpretation of the holy fathers" was to be preferred to an exegesis that ignored the tradition. Therefore it followed "that all such as so construe the Scripture that they would make the Scripture seem to be contrary to the faith of Christ's church, do damnably construe it, contrary to the teaching of God and his Holy Spirit." The experience of the Reformers themselves was proving that their idea of "the perspicuity of Scripture" was a delusion, and that orthodox authority was to be found in "the concord between Holy Scripture, the church, and the councils."

Nowhere did the Reformation view of authority seem to its critics to be more vulnerable than on the canon of Scripture. The orthodox Catholic answer to the canon was that of Augustine, as adapted by Gratian: those books "that the Apostolic See has accepted and that others have received from it" had the right to be called "canonical Scriptures of the Catholic churches." Although the Reformers, as More complained, "say they believe nothing else but" the canonical Scriptures, they "bring into question" the canonicity of those parts of Scripture that contradicted Protestant teaching, specifically, the Books of Maccabees and the Epistle of James. Before the Reformation controversy, Clichtove was citing 2 Maccabees as "Holy Scripture" in support of prayers for the dead; after the eruption of the controversy, he defended the use of such deuterocanonical books within the church, though not in disputation with the Jews, who did not acknowledge them. Their canonicity, de-

Clicht.*Improb.Luth*.1 (1533: 4v)

Rom.3:28

Luth.*DB* (1522) Rom.3:20 (*WA DB* 7:38) Wic.*Luth.art.* (*CCath* 18:84)

Luth.*DB* (1546) Rom.3:20 (*WA DB* 7:39)

Ec.*Ev*.2.Adv.5;1.Lent.3 (1530–I:13v–14r;95v)

Mor.*Tyn*.1 (Sylvester 8:133–34)

Lat.*Def.Buc*.5 (*CCath* 8:105)

Ec.*Enchir*.2 (*CCath* 34:47)

Grop.*Cap.inst.* (1549:H2r); Ambr.Cath.*Clav*.1 (1543:13–15) Aug.*Doct.christ*.2.8.12 (*CCSL* 32:39) Corp.*Jur.Can.:Decr.Grat*.1.19.6 (Friedberg 1:61–62)

Caj.*Pont*.14 (*CCath* 10:97); Aug.Alf.*Witt.Abg.*(*CCath* 11:30)

Mor.*Tyn*.2 (Sylvester 8:156)

Clicht.*Eluc.eccl*.3 (1517:139r)

Clicht.*Ven.sanct*.2.12 (1523: 75v–76r);Serip.*Lib.Scrip*.1 (*CT* 12:487)

Dried.*Eccl.script*.1 (1533:15)
Wic.*Purg.* (1545:D2r–D2v);
Herb.*Enchir*.48 (*CCath* 12:
163);Ambr.Cath.*Clav*.2 (1543:
31);Aug.Alf.*Salv.Reg.* (*CCath*
11:69–70);Ec.*Enchir*.25
(*CCath* 34:261–62)
Clvs.*Libr.can*.2 (*CT* 12:474)

Ambr.Cath.*Excus.disp*.3 (1521:
29v–30v);Pg.*Cont*.10 (1541–II:
7v–8r)


James 5:14(Vulg.)
Henr.VIII.*Assert*. (1521:T3r–
U1r)
Mor.*Luth*.1.19 (Sylvester 5:
290)


Latom.*Ling*.2 (1517:32)


Herb.*Enchir*.4 (*CCath* 12:30)

Ambr.Cath.*Apol.ver*.1.10
(*CCath* 27:79)
Ambr.Cath.*Apol.ver*.4.110
(*CCath* 27:285)

Diet.*Phim*.ep.ded. (1532:A2v)


Fish.*Sac*.ep.ded. (*CCath* 9:5)

Eras.*Pseudev.* (*LB* 10:1578)


Lat.*Def.Buc*.4 (*CCath* 8:79)


ap.Calv.*Scand.* (Barth-Niesel
2:221)
Henr.VIII.*Coerc.Luth.* (1523:
A4r);Herb.*Enchir*.46 (*CCath*
12:157)
Coch.*Obsc.vir*.4 (*CCath* 15:
21)

Serip.*Sacr*.1 (*CT* 12:752)

Fish.*Confut*.16 (1523:288)
Greb.*Prot.* (*CR* 90:371);Hub.
*Gespr.Zw*.1;2 (*QFRG* 29:180;
186);Menn.*Gell.Fab*.3
(Herrison 272)
Ec.*Rep.art.Zw*.6;7 (1530:E1r;
E3r)

fended also in general volumes of isagogics, became a standard component in the Roman Catholic defense of purgatory, the invocation of saints, and the doctrine of Mary, but their status remained ambiguous. The dispute about the canonicity of the Epistle of James arose in connection with two polemical topics: the sacramental status of extreme unction, for which the command that "the presbyters of the church should pray over [the sick person], anointing him with oil in the name of the Lord," was the principal biblical proof; and the apparent contradiction between its version of justification and that of the Pauline epistles. Coming to its defense, Roman Catholic polemicists, while admitting that it had achieved canonical status only "gradually," argued that if James should be rejected because of the contradiction, one could with equal right "reject Paul and other ecclesiastical writers, since the church has by its tradition handed down both" Paul and James. The proper method was to note the distinction between them, as the great Catholic theologians like Thomas Aquinas had done; for "the Holy Spirit is not a liar, either in Paul or in James."

Such a willingness, when there was a conflict with a cherished notion, to surrender "at will" portions of the very biblical canon in the name of which the notion had been advanced in the first place illustrated for the defenders of the faith how closely interrelated the several articles of faith were. As Erasmus complained, "Confession has been abrogated, but now there are many who do not confess even to God." Rejection of one component of Catholic truth would lead to "another, and yet another from that, once the window . . . has been opened." Sometimes these theological versions of the "domino theory" could spin themselves out in curious ways: the Reformers were charged with taking positions that, consistently carried out, would lead to atheism; the politically conservative Lutheran Reformers were said to be fomenting sedition and revolution or even fostering pacifism; and the doctrine of the universal priesthood was accused, by some but not by all, of implying the ordination of women. Not only would it have been more consistent, as the Anabaptists also observed, if Zwingli, who maintained that "on baptism all the

Zw.*Tf.* (CR 91:216;258)

Zw.*Tf.* (CR 91:228–29)

Herb.*Enchir.*50 (CCath 12:170)
Coch.*Luth.art.*3 (CCath 18:43);Coch.*Phil.*2.19 (1534:F1r)

Wic.*Luth.art.* (CCath 18:98)

Herb.*Enchir.*23 (CCath 12:80)

See p. 179 above

Conf.*Helv.post.*14 (Niesel 242)

Ambr.Cath.*Consid.*1 (1547:20v–21r)

Caj.*Miss.sac.*2 (Lyons 3:286);
Fish.*Corp.*1.31;3.17 (1527:50r;138r);Diet.*Phim.*2;3 (1532:D4v–E1r;F3v)

Las.*Hos.*2.5 (Kuyper 1:433)

Lat.*Def.Buc.*5 (CCath 8:1560)

Ec.*Enchir.*1 (CCath 34:22);
Wic.*Luth.art.* (CCath 18:95–96)

Herb.*Enchir.*17 (CCath 12:72)

Ec.*Enchir.*29 (CCath 34:299);
Fish.*Confut.*1.pr. (1523:D3r–D3v)

Fon.ap.CTrid.*Act.*22.ix.1551 (CT 7–II:180)

Sad.*Genev.* (Barth-Niesel 1:454);Fabr.*Praep.*68 (CT 4:21)

Ec.*Enchir.*4 (CCath 34:81–82)

theologians since the time of the apostles have been in error," had permanently rejected infant baptism, instead of returning to it; but "the synagogue of the Lutherans, [which] seems to be calling everything into doubt," also was reviving the ancient heresy of advocating rebaptism. And so "Luther has stirred up and caused the sect of the Anabaptists," which was proof that, once there was a single error, innumerable others would follow. Additional evidence came from the differences on auricular confession, which the Lutherans continued to support but the Reformed had gone on to reject. In a book published shortly after Luther's death, Ambrosius Catharinus accused him of "an incredible inconstancy in doctrine" and of having "steadily gone from bad to worse."

The most frequently cited evidence for this progressive radicalization of Reformation teaching came from the development of the Protestant doctrine of the Eucharist. Although some Protestants objected to a taxonomy solely on this basis, Roman Catholic writers went on pointing out to the Reformed that there were some who completely rejected the Mass and some who kept parts of it, while "Luther himself is said still to approve almost the entire structure of the ancient ceremony." To the Lutherans, meanwhile, they maintained that those who were now denying the sacraments were all legitimate children of Luther, regardless of how "repugnant" they now were to his official heirs. The deterioration of eucharistic orthodoxy had moved from the denial of the sacrificial nature of the Mass to the denial of the real presence, or at any rate to a theory of consubstantiation in place of transubstantiation. Another diagnosis was to trace the change in Oecolampadius from his restoration of the chalice to the laity in July 1524 to his rejection of the real presence less than a year later, until he became, among all the Reformers, "the most fanatical enemy of this most holy Sacrament." Because truth was always one and falsehood was varied and multiform, the rise of these sects was evidence that the truth was not with any of them, but with the Catholic Church. It was evidence also that "there must be some other judge than Scripture, namely, the church," to determine whose doctrine of the Eucharist was correct.

Dried.*Eccl.scrip*.4 (1533:599)

Ems.*Ven.Lut.* (*CCath* 4:84)
Ambr.Cath.*Apol.ver.*ded.
(*CCath* 27:3)
Ec.*Ps.*20.pr.;2;3 (*CCath* 13:6;
12;21–22)

Pol.*Henr.VIII.*2 (1536:37r)

Ec.*Ev.*Trin.3 (1530–II:87r);F.c.
*Eleg.* (1544:A2v;B3v)
Henr.VIII.*Coerc.Luth.* (1523:
A4v);Ambr.Cath.*Consid.*
(1547:35r)
Ec.*Enchir.*39 (*CCath* 34:405)

Ec.*Dial.*2.3 (1517:B4r)
Ec.*Rit.*2 (1519:A2v);Aug.Alf.
*Witt.Abg.* (*CCath* 11:36)
Ambr.Cath.*Excus.disp.*4 (1521:
81r)

Wic.*Luth.art.* (*CCath* 18:94)
Eras.*Pseudev.* (LB 10:1582);
Wic.*Ret.Luth.* (1538:C2v);Sad.
*Genev.* (Barth-Niesel 1:450);
Tap.*Orat.*1.6 (Mylius 2:328)

Ec.*Rit.*3 (1519:A3v)

Aug.Alf.*Malag.* (1520:E2r);
Clicht.*Oec.*1.3 (1526:13v)
See pp. 109, 172 above
Aug.Alf.*Malag.* (1520:E4r);Pg.
*Cont.*12 (1541–II:24r)

Naus.*Misc.*5.1 (*CT* 12:392–96)
Ambr.Cath.*Comm.*2 Thess.2:
3–4 (1566:384);Herb.*Enchir.*13
(*CCath* 12:59–60)
Ambr.Cath.*Consid.*1;2 (1547:
6v;34r)

Calv.*Nec.ref.* (*CR* 34:522–24);
Mel.*Pot.pap.*7 (Bek.472)

The church had made this determination for its teaching and practice in its tradition. Defying the principle that "it is safer to follow the old than to make up something new," the Reformers were propagating "new dogmas." Although Eck could, in contrasting "the church" with "the innovators," sometimes be referring only to the differences between the Vulgate and modern translations of the Bible, his more general usage and that of his colleagues was to attack the "novelty-mongers" for ignoring the masterpieces of the Christian tradition in favor of "what the damnable and accursed heretics have written." Luther's error was a recrudescence of Hus and Wycliffe, as Eck had proved at Leipzig and went on charging in his later polemics; for the Hussites had become proverbial for their heretical opinions, and "the perverse dogmas of Luther" were identical with those opinions, making him the "patron" of the Hussites. Thus there was nothing truly new in the Reformation, and yet at the same time it was guilty of introducing "new error" into Christian doctrine. As Erasmus and others put it, the choice lay between a tradition of fifteen centuries and one of a decade or so. And the root cause of the division and apostasy was the resolve of the Protestants, in their obedience to what they took to be the word and will and God and the gospel, "to be constrained by the authority of no sacred council, no supreme pontiff, no holy doctor, no university"—in short, by none of the authoritative voices of the Catholic Church.

Among these voices of Catholic authority, it was the supreme pontiff, the pope, whom the Protestants, in keeping with the propensity of "all heretics" for opposing the Apostolic See, had attacked with special fervor, identifying him as the Antichrist of biblical prophecy, just as the Hussite heretics had before them. In addition to acknowledging that there had been "abuses" in the papacy and then labeling Protestantism as the real Antichrist, the defenders of the faith recalled Luther's own earlier obeisance to Leo X and, under the pressure of the contention that the claims of the papacy were utterly devoid of biblical legitimacy, undertook to rehearse the standard exegetical proofs for the divine authority of the papacy, many

See vol.2:157–70;vol.1:352–55;
vol.3:46–48;pp.115–16 above

Cont.*Pot.pont.* (*CCath* 7:42)

See vol.2:159

John 21:15–17

Eras.*Adnot.*John 21 (*LB* 6:418)
Aug.Alf.*Babst.stl.* (1520:B4v);
Fish.*Confut.*25 (1523:411)
Caj.*Pont.*11 (*CCath* 10:62);
Caj.*Ev.*John 21:16 (1530:211v)

Aug.Alf.*Babst.stl.* (1520:A3v)

Pg.*Cont.*16 (1541–II:105r)
Pol.*Henr.VIII.*1 (1536:18r);
Pol.*Sum.pont.*5 (1569:10r–13r);
Pol.*Conc.*23;28 (1562:12r;15r)

Luke 22:32(Vulg.)

Caj.*Resp.Luth.*5(Lyons 1:128);
Fish.*Confut.*23 (1523:410)
Caj.*Ev.*Luke 22:32 (1530:
131r);Herb.*Enchir.*31 (*CCath*
12:108–9)
Aug.Alf.*Babst.stl.* (1520:A4v)

Caj.*Pont.*3 (*CCath* 10:21)
Matt.16:22
Aug.Alf.*Babst.stl.* (1520:A4r)
See vol.1:13

Ec.*Enchir.*3 (*CCath* 34:68)

Caj.*Pont.*3 (*CCath* 10:21)

Ec.*Enchir.*3 (*CCath* 34:68)
See pp. 107–9 above

John 3:18(Vulg.)
Caj.*Pont.*13 (*CCath* 10:83)

of which had developed in the course of the East-West schism. There were, to be sure, arguments from reason as well, "even if there were no passage in the Sacred Page," simply on the basis of the providence of God for the governance and unity of his church. Yet the question was finally to be decided from the words of Christ to Peter in the Gospels, principally from the three standard passages: Matthew 16:18–19; Luke 22:32; and John 21:17.

Christ's charge to Peter, "Feed my sheep," which, as even Erasmus agreed, meant in Greek, "You shall govern my sheep," was not simply "imperative" but "constitutive"; it meant: "You, and none other as an equal with you, shall protect my sheep . . . , to prevent them from being poisoned by any heresy against the faith, against the Holy Scripture, against the seven sacraments." No one who was a "sheep of Christ" could be exempt from the authority of Peter and his successors. And so, as Cardinal Pole insisted repeatedly, these words made Peter the vicar of Christ. Christ's statement to Peter, "I have prayed for you, so that your faith will not defect," was "universal" in its validity but unique in being addressed solely to Peter; yet it pertained not to the "person" of Peter or a later pope, but to the "office," which would abide even when the person died. The crucial test, of course, was not death but defection, whether by Peter or a pope. Peter had "erred" when he forbade Christ to go up to Jerusalem to die, he had "become a heretic" when he denied his Lord, and he had been reproved by Paul for his Judaizing. "Nevertheless, he does not stop being the rock" on which Christ built his church; nor did Paul's reproof imply that they were "equals" in "government and power" but only in "the office of the apostolate," which they did share. As for the classic problem of the defection of a pope, Cardinal Cajetan took the position that a pope who fell into heresy would eo ipso stop being pope, for by losing the true faith he would have forfeited his claim to be the successor of Peter, before the divine forum if not before "the ecclesiastical forum."

As it had especially since the later Middle Ages, the biblical legitimation for the papacy came principally from the declaration of Christ, "You are Peter, and

Matt.16:18

Ambr.Cath.*Clav*.2 (1543:113)
Ambr.Cath.*Apol.ver*.2.1
(*CCath* 27:93)
Wic.*Hag.* (1541:247a;109v);
Lain.*Disp.Trid*.2.2.56 (Grisar
1:76–77)

Caj.*Pont*.1 (*CCath* 10:1–2);
Caj.*Apol.* (1513:6r)

Pol.*Henr.VIII*.2 (1536:45r)

Cont.*Pot.pont.* (*CCath* 7:37–
39)
Ambr.Cath.*Apol.ver*.2.13
(*CCath* 27:149)
See p. 116 above
Aug.Alf.*Babst.stl.* (1520:C2r)

Ec.*Enchir.*3 (*CCath* 34:57)
Caj.*Pont*.13 (*CCath* 10:81)
Iren.*Haer*.3.3.1–3 (Harvey 2:
8–12)
Fish.*Corp*.4.21 (1527:191v)
See p. 198 above
Coch.*Luth.art*.2 (*CCath* 18:
32)
Pol.*Sum.pont*.20 (1569:58v)
See vol.1:159
Luth.*Def.Ec.jud.* (WA 2:636–
37);Calv.*Nec.ref.* (CR 34:522)

Caj.*Pont*.5;6 (*CCath* 10:41;
45);Lain.*Disp.Trid*.2.3.60;2.3.
66 (Grisar 1:80–81;90)

John 21:17

John 10:27

Caj.*Pont*.11 (*CCath* 10:64)

Mor.*Tyn*.9 (Sylvester 8:1012)

Ec.*Resp.art.Zw*.6 (1530:D2r)
Guidic.*Eccl.emend*.2 (CT 12:
236;234)
See p. 75 above

on this rock I will build my church." Although Luther's hermeneutical law of the single sense of Scripture led him to apply it only to Peter, it provided "irrefutable proof" that Christ had conferred the primacy not only on Peter but (according to "many Latin" writers) through him on Clement and all the subsequent popes. The church of Rome was different from all the other churches in this: its head was "the same as the head of the Catholic Church." And Peter was different from all the other apostles in this: he alone had confessed Christ as the Son of God; and while the power to forgive sin and to bind and loose had been conferred on all, the "feeding" of the Christian flock and the "confirming of the dogmas that pertain to the Christian faith" belonged solely to Peter and his successors, which made the pope "the vicar of Christ." He remained this also if he moved from Rome, although it was "fitting and proper" that he be there; the "new lie" that Peter had never been at Rome, as well as the objection that not Rome but Jerusalem had the real primacy, did not merit serious attention. The list of Roman bishops in Irenaeus—now available, but only gradually, in Erasmus's editio princeps of 1526— was evidence for the antiquity and the unique orthodoxy of the Roman see. But the Protestant attempt to exploit the variants in Cyprian's *On the Unity of the Church* for polemical advantage could not stand up to a careful explication of the text: Although Cyprian was speaking of the apostles as "equals," he also said that "the unity of the church has its origins from one, namely, Peter."

Although the "sheep" whom Peter was commanded to "feed" were the elect of whom Christ said, "My sheep hear my voice, and I know them," his rule over the church was not confined to the elect. The shepherds whom Christ appointed were not hidden, but known to all; hence it was appropriate to ask the Protestants "whether the flock of sheep over which Christ set the known shepherds was his flock and his church or not." If they replied in the affirmative, as they must, then it followed that it was mistaken to define the church as only the company of the elect, which had been "the error of the Wycliffites and Hussites." Otherwise, what concrete entity could Chris⸗

Matt.18:17
Eras.*Hyp*.1 (*LB* 10:1298–99);
Ec.*Enchir*.1 (*CCath* 34:33)
Clicht.*Hom*.18 (1535:157)
Herb.*Enchir*.8 (*CCath* 12:42–43)

Diet.*Cat*.1.9 (1545:F4r)

Fish.*Sac*.1.21 (*CCath* 9:20)

1 Tim.3:15

Eph.5:27

Ec.*Rep.art.Zw*.6 (1530:E1r)

Mor.*Tyn*.8 (Sylvester 8:836)
Lat.*Def.Buc*.5 (*CCath* 8:139);
Grop.*Enchir*.1 (1547:20v)

Coch.*Phil*.4.63 (1534:T2r–T2v)

Luth.*Antinom*. (*WA* 50:477);
Luth.*Wied*. (*WA* 26:147)
Coch.*Luth.art*.2 (*CCath* 18:31)

Tap.*Orat*.2.2 (Mylius 2:333)
Wic.*Luth.art*. (*CCath* 18:110)
Ec.*Enchir*.1 (*CCath* 34:19)

Lat.*Def.Buc*.2 (*CCath* 8:57)
Coch.*Aeq.dis*. (*CCath* 17:18)

Ambr.Cath.*Excus.disp*.3 (1521:21r)

Grop.*Enchir*.2 (1547:107r)
Ambr.Cath.*Apol.ver*.4.3
(*CCath* 27:262)
Herb.*Enchir*.28 (*CCath* 12:100)
Fish.*Confut*.27 (1523:437–38);
Fish.*Corp*.6.26 (1527:277r)
Fish.*Corp*.1.20;3.5 (1527:35v;
121v–123v)
Ec.*Enchir*.34 (*CCath* 34:360–61)
Aug.Alf.*Malag*. (1520:E4v);
Ems.*Ven.Lut*. (*CCath* 4:71);
Ambr.Cath.*Excus.disp*.3 (1521:15r)

1 Pet. 2:9
Caj.*Nov.Test*.3.1 (1530:E2v–E3v);Fish.*Sac*.1.19;2.1;3.19
(*CCath* 9:18;21;65);Juv.ap.
CTrid.*Act*.12.xii.1551 (*CT* 7-II:433)
Schatz.*Scrut*.7 (*CCath* 5:96–105)

have had in mind when he commanded, "Tell it to the church"? As the mystical body of Christ, governed by the Holy Spirit, the Catholic Church was nevertheless "publicly known," not "hidden." Of course it was not a building made of stone; but it was the visible, institutional, hierarchical church that was called "the pillar of truth." The promise of indefectibility did not pertain only to a church that was empirically "without spot," which for that matter was not present among the Protestants either, but to "this church on earth, which is still engaged in warfare." Any other "church" was nothing more than a Platonic idea and a chimera. Against the Radicals Luther made such statements as: "A thousand years ago you and I did not exist, yet the church was preserved without us"; this was an appeal to the institutional and even papal church, not to the "hidden" church of the elect. Thus the Reformers had to admit that the church was one and that it had existed before they ever came along, although now they were opposing its institutions.

"Or [did they mean to claim] that it was not the few who had seceded from the many, but the many from the few, that is, the Catholics from the Lutherans?" Any such presumptuous claim was "the ancient error of the Donatists." It was of a piece with the Protestant habit of putting asunder what God had joined together: the sacrifice of the heart and "the highest sacrifice of God" in the Mass; the fraternal confession of believers to one another and sacramental confession to a priest; spiritual repentance and the penitential system; praying in the Holy Spirit and "outward worship" and "ceremonies"; adoration of Christ "in spirit and in truth" and adoration of Christ in the Sacrament; "the church of the Spirit" and "the physical church"; "the faith of Christ" and "the decretal epistles" of canon law. While conceding the Protestant point that in the New Testament the word "priest" did not refer to the apostles as such but either to Christ or to every believer, those who were defending "the evangelical priesthood" of the Roman Catholic Church against the Reformers interpreted the universal priesthood of all believers as that "by which a man offers himself completely as a sacrifice

Herb.*Enchir.*15 (*CCath* 12:65);
Fish.*Sac.*2.48;3.14 (*CCath* 9:
49;61);Schatz.*Scrut.*7 (*CCath*
5:99);Steph.Sest.ap.CTrid.*Act.*
22.xii.1551 (*CT* 7–I:425)

Holl (1948) 322

See. p. 175 above
Wic.*Luth.art.* (*CCath* 18:106);
Coch.*Obsc.vir.*4 (*CCath* 15:
18);Fish.*Confut.*13 (1523:239)

Lat.*Def.Buc.*5 (*CCath* 8:123)

Caj.*Pont.*2 (*CCath* 10:5)

Dried.*Lib.chr.*3 (1540–II:69–
72)

Coch.*Phil.*4.19;4.21(1534:
Q1v–Q2r)
Apol.*Conf.Aug.*7.1–8 (*Bek.*
233–35);*Conf.Helv.post.*18
(Niesel 258)

Matt.23:2–3

See pp. 96–97 above

Aug.Alf.*Babst.stl.* (1520:C2v–
C3r);Cap.ap.CTrid.*Act.*22.i.
1547 (*CT* 5:850)
Ambr.Cath.*Apol.ver.*2.17
(*CCath* 27:159);Caj.*Pont.*13
(*CCath* 10:86)
Lat.*Def.Buc.*5 (*CCath* 8:133);
Ambr.Cath.*Clav.*2 (1543:208–
9)
Ems.*Ven.Lut.* (*CCath* 4:74);
Fish.*Sac.*2.14 (*CCath* 9:28);Pg.
*Cont.*11 (1541–II:15v)

Herb.*Enchir.*33 (*CCath* 12:
115–16);Pg.*Cont.*3 (1541–I:
127r)

See vol.1:311–12
Tap.*Orat.*2.8 (Mylius 2:335);
Grop.*Cap.inst.* (1549:A4r)
Lat.*Def.Buc.*2 (*CCath* 8:57)

Ambr.Cath.*Comm.*1 Cor.1;
Eph.4 (1566:134;310)

to God" rather than, as Luther did, "the mutual and fraternal support, assistance, and intercession" of Christians for one another. They denounced Luther's advice to the Hussites that in an emergency the members of a congregation, being "priests," should designate one of their number as their minister.

Above all, they were intent on defending the Catholic doctrine of the priesthood against "the insanity of the Donatists." To apply Matthew 16:18 to Peter as an individual, not to the papacy, was a repetition of the Donatist heresy that "ecclesiastical authority does not reside in wicked ministers," which was a failure to distinguish the sacraments of the church, even those confected by such ministers, from the "false sacraments that are in the temples of idols." Against this "same old defense of the heretics" and Donatists, they taught that "the church is holy, even though the wicked also are present in it . . . , not on the basis of a holiness of life or a probity of morals, but from the dignity of the office" of the priesthood and the sacraments. Such a statement could find almost verbatim parallels in the confessions of the Lutheran and Reformed churches, which likewise quoted the familiar admonition of Christ to obey the Pharisees who sat in the seat of Moses as evidence that God made use of the ministry of evil men. That same passage became the Roman Catholic proof text in response to the complaint that clergy were living in sin as well as in support of the idea that the authority of Peter was not affected by his fall. In opposition to the Protestants it proved the authority of prelates in the church, and it served as the basis for a further elaboration of the traditional argument from Old Testament priesthood and sacrifice to New: "If Christ wanted such great honor paid to the seat of Moses . . . , how much more should those be listened to and observed who sit in the seat of Christ!"

This reassertion of the Augustinian case against Donatism took its inspiration from Augustine's conviction that the unity of the church—its "universality, antiquity, and consensus"—must be paramount. In 1 Corinthians Paul had warned against schism, in Ephesians against "heretical deserters," and Augustine had warned against those who accepted the authority of

Diet.*Phim*.1 (1532:C2r)

Pol.*Disc.pac.* (1555:B3r)

Caj.*Summul*.E (1530:G8v–
H1v);Grop.*Buc.* (1545:11v)
Aug.Alf.*Babst.stl.* (1520:A2r);
Ambr.Cath.*Consid*.3 (1547:
74r)

Lat.*Def.Buc*.2 (*CCath* 8:54–
55)

Pg.*Mosc.* (1543:2r;9r)

See pp. 178–81, 215–16 above

Pg.*Cont*.3 (1541–I:114r)

Lat.*Def.Buc*.5 (*CCath* 8:136)

Grop.*Buc.* (1545:17v–18r)

Fish.*Confut*.pr. (1523:44)

Luth.ap.*Disp.Lips.* (*WA* 2:275)
Coch.*Luth.art*.2 (*CCath* 18:7);
Ambr.Cath.*Consid*.1 (1547:8r)

Köstlin (1897) 1:208

Scripture but violated unity. Now, with the growing "internal disorders of Christendom," it was incumbent on all parties to recognize that, evil as the abuses in the church were, they were not nearly so dangerous as schism and heresy. If no other argument for communion under one kind availed, there still remained the question of whether the restoration of the chalice was worth the price of schism. Dogmatically there were "very few points" at issue between the Russian Orthodox Church and the West, yet it would "totally perish, chiefly because it has strayed from the unity of the church." Thus to the Protestant emphasis on word and sacraments as marks of the church, correct though it was, it was necessary to add the mark of unity; for "it was not from these marks . . . but from unity itself, which is indivisible, that the church has been . . . transmitted to us from its first origins," and Christ had instituted the hierarchy to preserve unity. Diversity was one thing, schism quite another, and Luther was "the author of schism." As Augustine had said and as Luther had once agreed, there was no graver sin than sectarianism, which could not be justified even by the supposed centrality of the gospel. Augustine himself had confessed that he would not have believed the gospel if he had not been moved by the authority of the Catholic Church.

### From Pluralism to Definition

By closing ranks as they did in defense and in counterattack, the Roman Catholic theologians of the first half of the sixteenth century sometimes gave the impression of greater doctrinal homogeneity than they possessed, but the need to come together on definitions of the church's teaching in many (though by no means in all) of the controverted areas brought their differences into the open. The Roman Catholic Church in the middle of the century reacted to the Reformation with a series of definitions on the principal doctrines in controversy, but was obliged to decide which of the various alternatives it would define. It moved from pluralism to definition on several fronts, but chiefly on the two sets of issues identified by some later theologians as the "formal" and "material" principles of the Reformation: the nature and locus of authority; and the doctrine of justification, with its presuppositions in the doctrine of original sin. This it did at the Council of Trent, which met in a series of thirty-five sessions, intermittently between 1545 and 1563.

In his "Bull of Convocation" of 22 May 1542, Pope Paul III prescribed the usual three subjects for its agenda: "whatever pertains to the purity and truth of the Christian religion; whatever pertains to the restoration of good morals and the correction of evil morals; whatever pertains to the peace, unity, and harmony of Christians among themselves, whether princes or people." In each case, these three issues likewise reflected at least three distinct though related needs: to meet the Protestant Reformers on their own grounds; to harmonize contradictions within the patristic and medieval traditions; and to resolve the differences among the defenders of the Roman Catholic faith themselves. Although the third of these threatened periodically to take over the deliberations of the council, it was repeatedly necessary to insist that the first was the real occasion for the council, and the other two an obstacle to addressing the first. That insistence made itself heard especially in the debates on the sacraments: "It is enough for the council," one of the papal legates prescribed, "that it condemn heresies, where there is still much to be done, but not that it decide all scholastic disputes."

Like other sixteenth-century statements of faith, the definition of Roman Catholic particularity at Trent opened with a statement on the problem of authority, specifically with a definition of the biblical canon. Protestant polemics had reopened the question, which philological scholarship had complicated still further. In addition, there remained the discomfiting presence, within the received ecclesiastical tradition, of a "double canon" of the Old Testament, with Jerome and Augustine ranged on opposite sides. The Council of Florence had, on 4 February 1441, adopted an official list of canonical books, which therefore carried presumptive authority; but because of the confused state of the text of the decrees of that council, it was not quite obvious that its legislation on the canon of Scripture was binding, although the most detailed diary of the

*Margin notes:*

Guidic.*Eccl.emend.*4 (*CT* 12:243)

Paul.III.*Init.* (*CT* 4:230)

Cresc.ap.CTrid.*Act.*21.ix.1551 (*CT* 7–I:143)

See pp. 182,210 above

Pasch.ap.CTrid.*Act.*7.vii.1546 (*CT* 305–6)

See p. 310 below

Clvs.*Libr.can.*2 (*CT* 12:472–74)

CFlor.(1438–45)11.*Decr.Copt.* (Alberigo-Jedin 572)

ap.Mass.*Diar.*III.26.ii.1546 (*CT* 1:495–96)

Cerv.*Ep.*27.ii.1546 (*CT* 10:399–400)

Mass.*Diar.*III.12.ii.1546 (*CT* 1:478)

Sevrl.*Comm.*15.ii.1546 (*CT* 1: 32)

CTrid.4.*Decr.*1 (Alberigo-Jedin 663–64)

Council of Trent did report that "everyone agreed that [the list of canonical books] adopted at the Council of Florence should be simply accepted." Accepted it was, not "simply," but only after "many voiced their opinions, without observing any particular order." When the vote came, it was unanimous to approve all the books contained in the canon defined at Florence, namely, the longer canon that included the "deutero-canonical" books such as Maccabees and Ecclesiasticus.

For most of the Reformers, the question of the canon, insofar as it was a doctrinal issue of authority rather than a historical issue of authorship (although the two were, of course, closely tied), was part of the doctrine of "sola Scriptura," much as the right of the church to fix the canon appeared to contradict that doctrine. For the defenders of the Roman Catholic faith, before the Council of Trent and at the council, "sola Scriptura" was likewise the dogmatic point in contention, also in the debates over the canon; and the council's catalogue of the biblical books to be included was set, both syntactically and dogmatically, in the context of an assertion, against "sola Scriptura," of the authority of "written books and unwritten traditions," both of which had somehow come "from the mouth of Christ" or been inspired by the Holy Spirit. Neither the critics of this decree nor its champions always noted with sufficient care, however, that it was to "the apostolic tradition" that the council finally ascribed such authority. There were some who urged a clarification of the notion of "apostolic tradition," on the grounds that, for example, the command to abstain "from things strangled," which clearly had scriptural warrant as an apostolic tradition decreed by an apostolic council, was no less clearly "obsolete" now, having been "abrogated through desuetude" as the faith of the church had grown and developed; the church, moreover, had abolished it "by its own authority." Others lumped together indiscriminately the definition of two wills in Christ by the Third Council of Constantinople in 681 and the "tradition" that "Saint Anne is the mother of the Virgin Mary."

Above all, the disputes over "sola Scriptura" in the sixteenth century, like earlier debates, had forced con-

CTrid.4.*Decr.*1 (Alberigo-Jedin 663)

ap.Mass.*Diar.*III.17.ii.1546 (*CT* 1:481)

Acts 15:29

ap.Sevrl.*Comm.*26.ii.1546 (*CT* 1:33)
Lain.*Disp.Trid.*1.2.10 (Grisar 1:12);Ambr.Cath.*Consid.*2 (1547:37r);Pol.*Conc.*54 (1562: 29r–30r)
Fish.*Confut.*16 (1523:271)

See vol.2:62–75

Jaj.*Trad.eccl.*2 (*CT* 12:524)

See pp. 120–22 above

Ang.Pasch.*Trad*.1 (*CT* 12:525)

ap.CTrid.*Act*.22.iii.1546 (*CT* 5:31)
Brd.Clr.*Praec.et disp*.9.19 (Leclercq-Rochais 3:266)

Lain.*Disp.Trid*.1.4.38 (Grisar 1:55);Diet.*Phim.* (1532:B1r)

ap.Sevrl.*Comm*.5.iv.1546 (*CT* 1:45)

CTrid.4.*Decr*.1 (Alberigo-Jedin 663)

CTrid.*Act*.8.ix.1551 (*CT* 7–I: 114)
Vauch.ap.CTrid.*Act*.1.xii.1546 (*CT* 5:679)

Pol.ap.Sevrl.*Comm*.14.vi.1546 (*CT* 1:75)
ap.CTrid.*Act*.31.v.1546 (*CT* 5: 172);Mrl.*Pecc.orig*.1 (*CT* 12: 554);Card.leg.*Ep*.19.v.1546 (*CT* 10:492–93)

See pp. 225–27 above

*Lib.Ratis*.4 (*CR* 4:194–98)

sideration of the question: Was all revelation contained in Scripture, and what was the status of so-called traditions that were nonbiblical and postbiblical, but not antibiblical? Or, in the formulation of one bishop at Trent, "If you believe the divine Scripture that was written by the hands of the evangelists and apostles, why do you not believe the divine voice that was transmitted by the mouth of the church?" A draft decree submitted to the council included the sentence: "This truth of the gospel is contained partly [partim] in written books, partly [partim] in unwritten traditions." Quoting formulas such as that of Bernard, it prescribed that the two should be regarded with "an equal feeling of respect [par pietatis affectus]." Although it may well have represented the majority view, the formula "partly/partly" evoked sharp reaction. It was "ungodly," one bishop declared, to put Scripture and nonscriptural tradition on the same level. The substitution of the phrase "written books *and* unwritten traditions" for "partly/partly" made the final text more generally acceptable, also because it kept the reference to "an equal feeling of piety and reverence"; but this "and" could be taken as synonymous with "partly/partly," or it could mean that the truth of the gospel was completely contained in Scripture as this was made explicit in subsequent tradition. With this decree the council also defined its own method of proceeding, which would be, as stated in a later session, to draw its teaching "from Sacred Scripture, the apostolic traditions, the holy and approved councils, the constitutions and authorities of the supreme pontiffs and holy fathers, and the consensus of the Catholic Church"—all of these if possible, fewer if need be.

On the doctrine of original sin, too, there was much in the sixteenth century that remained unresolved. The church fathers had written extensively about it but had not produced a binding definition; earlier councils, principally regional rather than ecumenical, had issued decrees dealing with it, but these were not wholly definitive; and there appeared to be a widespread consensus on the orthodoxy of the Augustinian doctrine, set down in official documents from the Roman Catholic and the Protestant side, but this had

Grop.*Buc.* (1545:8r–9v)

See vol.1:279–92

See pp. 313–22 below

See vol.1:290–92;316–18

Aug.*Serm.*115.4 (*PL* 38:657);
Serip.CTrid.*Act.*28.v.1546
(*CT* 5:169);Serip.*Pecc.orig.*6
(*CT* 12:548);Ambr.Cath.
*Consid.*2 (1547:43r)

Coch.*Patr.parv.*1.4 (*CT* 12:
171–74)

See pp. 139–41, 224–27 above

See pp. 17–19 above

Mrl.*Pecc.orig.*5 (*CT* 12:558)

*Confut.Conf.Aug.*2 (*CCath* 33:
80–81)

Thos.Aq.*S.T.*3.27.3.resp. (*Ed.
Leon.* 11:292)

See pp. 154–55 above

Fish.*Confut.*2 (1523:123)
Ambr.Cath.*Consid.*2 (1547:
45v–46r)
Leo X.*Ex.Dom.*2–3
(Denzinger-Schönmetzer 358)

Bert.ap.CTrid.*Act.*4.vi.1546
(*CT* 5:184)

Aug.*Pecc.merit.*4 (*PL* 44:153)

Serip.*Concup.*1 (*CT* 12:550–
51);Pol.ap.Sevrl.*Comm.*14.vi.
1546 (*CT* 1:76)
Serip.*Pecc.orig.*4 (*CT* 12:544);
Dried.*Grat.lib.arb.*1 (1537–I:
153)
Rom.6:6;7:24
Mrl.*Pecc.orig.*12 (*CT* 12:563);
Grop.*Enchir.*2 (1547:40v)
CTrid.*Decr.min.*vi.1546 (*CT*
12:568);CTrid.*Act.*7.vi.1546
(*CT* 5:197)

ap.CTrid.*Act.*7.vi.1546 (*CT* 5:
197)

been insufficient to prevent wide divergence. The relation of this doctrine to tradition, problematical in Augustine's own time, had surfaced again in Reformation debates: the Anabaptist denial of infant baptism, the practice from which the doctrine of original sin had developed, was based on the charge that the New Testament knew nothing of it, while the defense of infant baptism was based on the claim that there was an "apostolic tradition," albeit an unwritten one, to support it. Without tradition the doctrine would be forfeit, but by a fortunate inconsistency the Reformers had kept it—not only kept it, but accused their opponents of being the ones to betray Augustinian anthropology. This was an echo of the Augustinians of the two preceding centuries, who were still being cited in the sixteenth century.

As part of their attack on "neo-Pelagianism" the Reformers made a point of calling the concupiscence that remained after baptism "sin," in contrast to the scholastic terminology, according to which it was a "spark [fomes]." Such terminology was inadequate because the justified believer was not only righteous but a sinner at the same time. Yet in the light of the Catholic doctrine of baptismal grace this "remaining spark cannot be sin," and the teaching of the Reformers had been condemned repeatedly, above all by the papal bull against Luther. Through these channels it came into the discussions at Trent. One of the council fathers said that the "spark" was not "that through which we are subject to the hatred and wrath of God, but that which inclines us toward sin." But Seripando, the general of the Augustinians, insisted, on the basis of his order's eponym, that concupiscence was "the root of all sins" and "the reason for sin," also in the baptized and regenerate, and that this truly was subject to divine displeasure. Undeniably it was sin "in some sense," for Paul had sometimes called it that, although "the body of sin" or "the body of death" was more precise. These ideas of Seripando were put into successive draft decrees, which also affirmed the scholastic formula that original sin remained in the baptized "materially but not formally," although there was some objection to the formula on the grounds that the council was summoned to articulate "the mind

Mart.ap.CTrid.*Act*.8.vi.1546
(*CT* 5:207)

ap.CTrid.*Act*.9.vi.1546 (*CT* 5:
212–13)

Eph.4:14

See pp. 225–26 above

Coch.*Phil*.2.14 (1534:E2r)

CTrid.5.*Decr*.1 (Alberigo-
Jedin 665–67)

Pol.ap.CTrid.*Act*.21.vi.1546
(*CT* 5:257);Cas.ap.CTrid.*Act*.
20.vii.1546 (*CT* 5:365);Sarac.
ap.CTrid.*Act*.9.xi.1546 (*CT* 5:
643)

Patav.*Just*.pr. (*CT* 12:603)
Cerv.ap.CTrid.*Act*.21.vi.1546
(*CT* 5:257)
Pach.ap.Sevrl.*Comm*.21.vi.
1546 (*CT* 1:83)

of the Catholic Church," not the opinions of the scholastic doctors.

The eventual form of the decree, as adopted by the fifth session of the council on 17 June 1546, presented itself as a recital, in five anathemas, of the Augustinian doctrine of original sin, "which the Catholic Church scattered throughout the world has always taught," over against the "winds of doctrine" of the age, whether Semi-Pelagian or Manichean, Lutheran or Anabaptist. The sin of Adam consisted in the loss of "the holiness and righteousness in which he had been created," and, being "transmitted by propagation, not by imitation," it had involved the entire human race in death and captivity to the devil: this the council defined against various kinds of Pelagianism, including what it took to be Zwingli's doctrine. The only "remedy" for sin was "the merit of the one Mediator, our Lord Jesus Christ, who has reconciled us to God by his blood." In opposition to Anabaptism, the council defended the baptism of infants as appropriate and necessary because they had inherited original sin from Adam through their parents. And in opposition to Luther, it rejected the idea that through baptism "the guilt of original sin" was not removed but was only "not imputed." "This holy synod confesses and believes," the decree added, "that the concupiscence or the spark [fomes] remains also in those who have been baptized," but despite the use of the term "sin" for it in the New Testament the Catholic Church had never understood it to be sin in the strict sense of that word.

As the condemnation of Luther's teaching about the continuance of original sin in the regenerate had shown, the doctrine of original sin was closely tied to the doctrine of justification. The development of the two doctrines, however, had not been uniform; for despite the assertion that the doctrine of justification had been "defined long since by the fathers," it had in fact "not been decided on in the councils" and therefore needed to be handled differently. Yet now that the Reformation had raised the question of justification in a new and vigorous way, it behooved the defenders of the faith to speak out on it in formulas that were consistent with what had been "defined long since by the fathers." Although it was an "intricate

Card.leg.*Ep*.21.vi.1546 (*CT*
10:530)
Sarr.ap.CTrid.*Act*.28.ix.1546
(*CT* 5:435)
Lip.ap.CTrid.*Act*.1.x.1546
(*CT* 5:457);Rov.ap.CTrid.*Act*.
2.x.1546 (*CT* 5:462);Pach.ap.
CTrid.*Act*.11.x.1546 (*CT* 5:
491)

CTrid.*Decr.just*.II.pr. (*CT* 5:
420);Coch.*Phil*.3.6 (1534:H1v)

Serip.ap.CTrid.*Act*.13.vii.
1546;8.x.1546;26.–27.xi.1546
(*CT* 5:333;486;668);Serip.*Just*.
1.2 (*CT* 12:614–15);Grop.
*Enchir*.2 (1547:132r)
Steph.Sest.ap.CTrid.*Act*.25.x.
1546 (*CT* 5:609)
CTrid.*Decr.just*.II.7 (*CT* 5:
423)

and difficult" problem, it was likewise the one issue on which, "as far as dogma is concerned, the importance of this council depends," the principal point of difference with the Protestants. Or, as the second draft of the decree on justification said in its opening words (which some found to be exaggerated), "at the present time there is nothing more vexing and disturbing to the church of God than the novel, perverse, and erroneous doctrine of some men about justification." There was also a recognition, voiced most explicitly by Seripando and his fellow Augustinians, that justification differed from some other doctrines because of its "practical" rather than "speculative" character, so that it was appropriate to speak of it "as each has experienced it" and the true "experts" on it were those who had known themselves to be sinners and who had learned through experience what it meant to be justified by a forgiving God—David, Paul, and Augustine (and, they might have added but did not, Martin Luther). The doctrines of justification propounded by the Reformers had revealed the pluralism of views about justification present among those who claimed to share the Roman Catholic tradition; although that pluralism was voiced throughout the debates at Trent, the council fathers sought in their definition to respond to the Reformation without involving themselves in the disputes of several schools of theology within Roman Catholicism.

ap.CTrid.*Act*.28.viii.1546 (*CT*
5:418–19)

The debates over justification were the main item on the agenda of the council during the entire second half of 1546. Heeding the admonition voiced at the outset that "they should apply themselves to this doctrine of justification with diligence, since otherwise there will be no decision," the council formulated "this decree after a great deal of discussion," as the primate of Ireland said when it was almost finished; or, as the minutes for 7 December 1546 put it, "and so, with praise to Almighty God, the preface and five chapters on justification were settled and approved today," although "three doubtful ones remain to be decided." It soon became evident that it would be premature to formulate even a preliminary draft decree before extensive debate. By the time a definitive text achieved acceptance, there had been numerous

Bert.ap.CTrid.*Act*.21.vi.1546
(*CT* 5:259);Serip.ap.
CTrid.*Act*.21.vi.1546 (*CT* 5:
260)

Vauch.ap.CTrid.*Act*.7.xii.1546
(*CT* 5:643)

CTrid.*Act*.7.xii.1546 (*CT* 5:
693)
Pasch.ap.CTrid.*Act*.21.vi.1546
(*CT* 5:259);CTrid.*Act*.30.vi.
1546 (*CT* 5:283)

draft decrees, at least five official ones and several individual efforts, especially by Seripando. No other decree of this council, and few decrees of any council before or since, received such meticulous care. The evolution of the decree also led to a structural clarification, which seems to have originated with the second of Seripando's proposed drafts on 26 August 1546 and then was employed in the council's own second draft of 23 September, whereby the positive content of the decree was set off in "chapters," followed by the polemical condemnations in "canons," whose purpose it was that all believers "might know not only what they are to hold and follow, but also what they are to avoid and flee."

Although there had not been, strictly speaking, a conciliar dogma of justification, that did not preclude an appeal to "the perpetual consensus of the Catholic Church." At the very beginning of the discussion of justification, one of the questions posed was that of the biblical, conciliar, patristic, and traditional authorities for the doctrine. The appeal to "perpetual consensus" ran through successive formulations of the decree. The canon of Vincent of Lérins ("a golden book"), defining the consensus of antiquity as the criterion of Christian orthodoxy, was the norm. Therefore even the doctrine of Thomas Aquinas, despite the position of honor and authority he enjoyed at Trent, must yield to "the teaching of the ancient fathers," which more adequately expressed "the consensus of the church." Alongside the Vincentian canon stood the other ancient principle, that "the rule of prayer should lay down the rule of faith." As this principle had enabled Augustine and his followers to lay claim to the patristic tradition for the doctrine of original sin despite the absence of explicit testimony on the subject, so now various participants at Trent cited the "tradition" of the church's prayers as an authority on justification. In those prayers it was not through works but through the righteousness of Christ that believers sought liberation; therefore, Seripando urged, the council should put itself on the side of the patristic—that is, the Augustinian—tradition, and he warned that failure to do so would bring upon it the "ignominy" of using the absence of an explicit dogma

Serip.*Decr.just.form.alt.* (*CT* 5: 828–33)

CTrid.*Decr.just.*II (*CT* 5:426–27);Cerv.ap.CTrid.*Act.*23.ix. 1546 (*CT* 5:420)

CTrid.6.*Decr.*1.16 (Alberigo-Jedin 678)

CTrid.6.*Decr.*1.8 (Alberigo-Jedin 674)

ap.CTrid.*Act.*22.vi.1546 (*CT* 5:261)
CTrid.*Act.*17.xii.1546 (*CT* 5: 724);CTrid.*Decr.just.*II.pr.,7; IV.7 (*CT* 4:421,423;696)
Grop.*Leyb.*I (1536:33v–34v)
See vol.1:333
Rov.ap.CTrid.*Act.*2.x.1546 (*CT* 5:464)

Cerv.ap.CTrid.*Act.*21.xii.1546 (*CT* 5:734)

See vol.1:339
Prosp.*Auct.*8 (*PL* 51:209)

ap.CTrid.*Act.*22.vi.1546 (*CT* 5:262)

Serip.ap.CTrid.Act.26.–27.xi.
1546 (CT 5:670–71)

See p. 101 above
ap.CTrid.Act.13.i.1547 (CT 5:
800–802)

Mont.ap.CTrid.Act.15.i.1547
(CT 5:833–34)

CTrid.6.Decr.1.7 (Alberigo-
Jedin 673)
Nav.ap.CTrid.Act.19.x.1546
(CT 5:55–56);Patav.ap.CTrid.
Act.22.vi.1546 (CT 5:263);
Patav.Just.3 (CT 12:606)
Lain.ap.CTrid.Act.26.x.1546
(CT 5:621)

CTrid.6.Can.33 (Alberigo-
Jedin 681)

Sal.ap.CTrid.Act.17.viii.1546
(CT 5:414)

ap.CTrid.Act.5.i.1547 (CT 5:
759)

CTrid.6.Can.1 (Alberigo-Jedin
679)

See p. 255 above

Laur.ap.CTrid.Act.22.–28.vi.
1546 (CT 5:279)
Thos.Aq.S.T.2.1.113.2 (Ed.
Leon.7:329–30)

Pasch.ap.CTrid.Act.7.vii.1546
(CT 5:303)

as an excuse for silence on the question of justification. When the final decree on justification was adopted, various bishops urged that, despite the abuse of the title by the Council of Constance, it include the claim of "representing the universal church." As the chairman explained at a later session, the reason for avoiding this claim was to prevent the establishment of a bad precedent.

That final decree affirmed its assent to the consensus of the universal church by seeking to ground the doctrine of justification in the plan of salvation through Christ, who had "merited justification for us by his most holy passion on the wood of the cross and rendered satisfaction for us to God the Father." "Passion and satisfaction" in the Anselmic formula stood as the presupposition for the doctrine of justification. Taking up a point that had been made in the debates, the closing canon of the final decree rejected out of hand any accusation that the doctrine of justification it was promulgating took anything away from the glory of God or the merits of Christ; and the opening canon—which, after earlier objections that condemnation of Pelagianism was "superfluous," received virtually unanimous approbation because by it "the heresy of the Pelagians is strangled"—anathematized anyone "who says that man can be justified before God by his own works, whether done by his own natural powers or through the teaching of the law, without divine grace through Jesus Christ." But "salvation" was not to be reduced to the forgiveness of sins, as it had appeared to be in Luther's system. Despite the report, in a summary of the discussions at Trent about the definition of justification, that "all the theologians" present had agreed that "being justified is tantamount to having sins remitted by God through grace," this was to be taken in the light of the principle, derived from Thomas, that "the remission of guilt cannot be understood unless the infusion of grace be present" also. Bishop Musso of Bitonto went so far as to separate the remission of sins through Christ, which took place first, from justification, which was not based on "the righteousness of Christ imputed to us, but on our own righteousness, when each of us through the passion of Christ acquires his own righ-

Muss.ap.CTrid.*Act*.9.vii.1546
(*CT* 5:317);Sevrl.*Comm*.9.vii.
1546 (*CT* 1:88)

CTrid.*Decr.just*.IV.8 (*CT* 5:
700)

CTrid.6.*Decr*.1.7 (Alberigo-
Jedin 673)
CTrid.*Decr.just*.I.5;II.7;III.8
(*CT* 5:386;424;636)

ap.CTrid.*Act*.22 vi 1546 (*CT*
5:261)

Card.leg.ap.CTrid.*Act*.30.vi.
1546 (*CT* 5:281)

CTrid.*Decr.just*.I.pr. (*CT* 5:
385)

Cast.*Haer*.3 (1571:170)

Cost.ap.CTrid.*Act*.22.vii.1546
(*CT* 5:369)

ap.CTrid.*Act*.vii.1546 (*CT* 5:
392)

Lain.ap.CTrid.*Act*.26.x.1546
(*CT* 5:625)

teousness." The seventh chapter of the final form of the decree (which was identical with the eighth chapter of the fourth draft) stipulated that justification was "not only the remission of sins, but also the sanctification and renewal of the inner man through the voluntary acceptance of the grace and gifts" of God; each of the drafts had contained some such stipulation.

First among the desiderata formulated by the theological commission as discussions began was the definition of "what justification is both as to the meaning of the term and as to its content." To aid in clarifying such a definition, the legates of the pope at the council proposed a threefold division of the question: "how someone who is an unbeliever becomes a believer"; "how someone who is already justified can . . . preserve his justification"; and "how if, after justification, someone falls away by sinning, he is to rise again." That division, incorporated into the preface of the first draft of the decree, facilitated the discussion in various ways. For example, this made it possible to distinguish between the justification of adults (for which, contrary to the teaching of the Reformers about the bondage of the will, free consent was necessary) and the justification of infants (for which only baptism was necessary); otherwise, the theologians warned, it would seem that the stress on the role of the will in justification applied also to infants. Hence "it would not be inappropriate to acknowledge," said a vigorous defender of free will, that "infants are saved on account of the righteousness of Christ that is imputed to them," as they were condemned on account of the unrighteousness of Adam that had been imputed to them. But the distinction among the several "states" and meanings of justification likewise helped to precipitate a lengthy controversy over the two closely connected notions of "twofold righteousness [duplex justitia]" and of the imputation of the righteousness of Christ to the believer in justification. The first version of the decree on justification condemned the teaching that "justification is only the imputation" of the righteousness of Christ, together with the teaching that "the righteousness that is granted in justification is only the righteousness of Christ" merited on the

CTrid.*Decr.just.*I.4;6 (*CT* 5:386)

Luth.*Ep.Joh.*2:18(*WA* 20:669)

See pp. 253–55 above

Serip.ap.CTrid.*Act.*8.x.1546 (*CT* 5:486)

Clvs.ap.CTrid.*Act.*8.x.1546 (*CT* 5:486)

Mir.ap.CTrid.*Act.*27.ix.1546 (*CT* 5:432)

Jer.23:6

Mir.ap.CTrid.*Act.*18.x.1546 (*CT* 5:550)

Lain.ap.CTrid.*Act.*26.x.1546 (*CT* 5:617)
Cons.ap.CTrid.*Act.*16.x.1546 (*CT* 5:542)
See pp. 154–55 above

Lun.ap.CTrid.*Act.*15.x.1546 (*CT* 5:524)

2 Cor.5:19

Isa.53:4–6

Lain.ap.CTrid.*Act.*26.x.1546 (*CT* 5:612–29);Mir.ap.CTrid. *Act.*18.x.1546 (*CT* 5:551)

Serip.ap.CTrid.*Act.*26.–27.xi. 1546 (*CT* 5:668)

CTrid.*Decr.just.*IV.*Can.*10;V. *Can.*10 (*CT* 5:714;777);CTrid. *Act.*5.i.1547 (*CT* 5:759)

cross rather than a "righteousness that is in [the believer] himself," although it was of course through Christ and from God. Luther distinguished sharply between "two kinds of righteousness, mine and Christ's." There had also developed a Roman Catholic version of the distinction, in response to the Reformation. At Trent its champion was Seripando, who saw the question as "whether we who are justified . . . are to be judged before the divine tribunal on the basis of only one righteousness, namely, the righteousness of our works proceeding from the grace of God that is in us, or of a twofold righteousness, namely our own . . . and the righteousness of Christ, with the passion, merit, and satisfaction of Christ completing the imperfection of our own righteousness." One respondent urged that the righteousness of God, that of Christ, and that of the believer "are one and the same"; another, after declaring at one session that "there are two righteousnesses, one of them perfect, which is Christ's and is granted to us, the other imperfect, which is our own," went on three weeks later to assert that, according to the biblical formula about "the Lord our righteousness," "we are not righteous in actuality [formaliter] through the righteousness that is in Christ, but through that which is in us," which shared in Christ and in his righteousness.

The formula of a double righteousness was unacceptable; for the entire complex of imputation and double righteousness was, according to Diego Laínez in a lengthy and influential critique, a "novelty" whose first inventor was Luther. It would undercut the structure of satisfactions, indulgences, and purgatory. Luther's concept that the justified sinner could be "righteous and unrighteous at the same time" was "extremely false"; nor could biblical language about "not imputing their trespasses" to sinners or about imputing those trespasses to Christ on the cross be inverted to say that the righteousness of Christ was imputed to believers. In spite of Seripando's defense and his effort to document the patristic evidence for it, the theory of twofold righteousness failed of support and did not find its way into the council's decrees. What did appear, however, after several alternatives had been reviewed, was a canon anathe-

CTrid.6.*Can*.10 (Alberigo-Jedin 679)

matizing both the idea "that men are justified without the righteousness of Christ, by which he merited for us," and the teaching (attributed to Luther) that the righteousness of Christ alone could make them "actually [formaliter] righteous."

ap.CTrid.*Act*.22.vi.1546 (*CT* 5:261)

In addition to calling for a definition of justification, the initial questions posed by the theologians also asked: "What are the causes of justification?" and "In what sense is it to be understood that man is justified through faith?" The precise meaning of

Caj.*Ev*.Luke 7:47 (1530:101v); Dried.*Concord*.1.2 (1537:39) Grop.*Antididag*.9 (1547:35v–36v)

Grop.*Enchir*.2 (1547:141v)

"cause" when applied to justification or predestination had been a problem in earlier responses to the Reformers. Gropper, who gave careful attention to this question, also warned against carrying it into the pulpit. At Regensburg in 1541, under Gropper's leadership, Protestant and Roman Catholic spokesmen had been able to agree that the "formula of speaking" of the Reformers, that "we are justified by faith alone," was not unacceptable, but only with the understanding that "it is the firm and sound doctrine that the sinner is justified through a faith that is living and

*Lib.Ratis*.5 (*CR* 4:198–201)
Cerv.ap.CTrid.*Act*.28.xii.1546 (*CT* 5:742);Pasch.ap.CTrid. *Act*.7.vii.1546(*CT* 5:304)

active." Because "the apostle very often uses this mode of speaking, that we are justified through faith, as a guide and way to righteousness," the council fathers were concerned to identify which of the "causes" of justification faith was—which of the four traditional Aristotelian causes or, in at least one case, which of

Pinar.ap.CTrid.*Act*.26.vi.1546 (*CT* 5:277)
CTrid.*Decr.just*.IV.8 (*CT* 5:700–701)

ten causes. In response to the effort of the fourth draft of the decree to resolve this problem, Seripando reminded his colleagues that neither the Scriptures nor "the ancient fathers of the Catholic Church" had so much as mentioned this system of causes, and that it was "philosophy that creates these difficulties for us when we seek to talk about divine mysteries on the basis of its rules"; but if the decree was to speak of the passion of Christ as the "meritorious cause" or of baptism as the "instrumental cause," it was appro-

Serip.ap.CTrid.*Act*.28.xii.1546 (*CT* 5:743);Dried.*Concord*.2.3 (1537:184)
CTrid.*Decr.just*.V.7 (*CT* 5:763; 776)
CTrid.6.*Decr*.1.7 (Alberigo-Jedin 673–74)

priate to add that the effect of these "causes" was "applied to us through faith." But with a slight revision in the fifth draft, the definition of the causes of justification received official approval.

The role of faith as a "cause" of justification depended for its clarification on a greater precision in the definition of faith itself. The New Testament "makes

Wic.*Cred*.pr. (1535:A2r–A2v)

Wic.*Cred.* (1535:D2r)

Caj.*Nov.Test.*5.4 (1530:G8v)

Wic.*Cred.* (1535:A4v)

Rov.ap.CTrid.*Act.*6.vii.1546
(*CT* 5:292)

CTrid.*Decr.just.*I.12;20 (*CT* 5:
388;391)

CTrid.6.*Decr.*1.6 (Alberigo-
Jedin 672)
Bert.ap.CTrid.*Act.*8.vii.1546
(*CT* 5:309–10)

1 Cor.13:2

Gal.5:6

Cas.ap.CTrid.*Act.*10.xii.1546
(*CT* 5:699)
Hier.Syr.ap.CTrid.*Act.*9.vii.
1546 (*CT* 5:320)
Laur.ap.CTrid.*Act.*23.vi.1546
(*CT* 5:264);Castr.*Haer.*7
(1571:502)

Crz.ap.CTrid.*Act.*21.vii.1546
(*CT* 5:366)

ap.CTrid.*Act.*17.xii.1546 (*CT*
5:724–25)

CTrid.6.*Decr.*1.8 (Alberigo-
Jedin 674)
CTrid.*Decr.just.*I.12;II.*Can.*6;
III.*Can.*8;IV.*Can.*8 (*CT* 5:
387–88;426;640;714)

CTrid.6.*Can.*9;12 (Alberigo-
Jedin 679)

Stl.ap.CTrid.*Act.*13.i.1547 (*CT*
5:814–15)
ap.CTrid.*Act.*31.xii.1546 (*CT*
5:750)
James 2:24
CTrid.6.*Decr.*1.10 (Alberigo-
Jedin 675)
Serip.ap.CTrid.*Act.*13.vii.1546;
13.xii.1546 (*CT* 5:336;370)

a practice of adding [in its definition of faith] what it was that the apostles believed" as true; the theological tradition had treated it as a "theological virtue," hence as "faith formed by love"; and the Reformers, above all Luther, had defined it chiefly as "trust [fiducia]," which his critics had to concede was sometimes the correct meaning. When one spoke of "justification by faith," therefore, it mattered a great deal which one, or more, of these definitions dominated. Quoting the Athanasian Creed, the first draft of the decree on justification went on to define "the faith that God requires" as "evangelical faith, by which we believe certainly the doctrine that has been handed down by Christ in his own teachings, through the apostles, and through the church." The final draft, too, described faith as "believing to be true what has been divinely revealed and promised." In a classification of the several meanings of the word, "historical faith [fides historica]" came first, followed by the "miraculous faith" that could move mountains, and finally by "Christian evangelical faith," which justified because it was, as Paul called it, "faith working through love." This faith working through love, moreover, was "not only trust, as the Lutherans say," but was "the beginning and foundation of the entire spiritual edifice," comprehending all the other virtues and being inseparable from them. For it was "not by faith alone," but "more by hope and love than by faith" that those who were justified took hold of the righteousness of Christ. Justification was attributed to faith because it was faith that "disposed" one toward justification. Or, as the final decree stated, "faith is the beginning of human salvation, the foundation and the root of all justification"; but it also followed the precedent of earlier drafts and appended a canon condemning anyone who "says that the sinner is justified by faith alone, as though nothing else were required to cooperate," and another condemning the definition of faith as nothing but trust. In condemning the idea of faith alone, "we are not rejecting faith, but are rather confirming it by means of love." The decree included, after some discussion, the statement of the Epistle of James that "a man is justified by works and not by faith alone," to prove that justifying faith was faith active in love and works.

Dz.Luc.ap.CTrid.*Act*.12.viii.
1546 (*CT* 5:330)

Patav.*Just*.4 (*CT* 12:606–7);
Dried.*Concord*.1.2 (1537:44)

CTrid.*Decr.just*.I.15(*CT* 5:389)

Steph.Sest.ap.CTrid.*Act*.25.x.
1546 (*CT* 5:610)
Aug.*Ep*.186.3 (*PL* 33:820)
Scrip.ap.CTrid.*Act*.23.vii.1546
(*CT* 5:373)
CTrid.6.*Decr*.1.16 (Alberigo
Jedin 677–78)

See vol.3:156;p. 144 above
Brd.Clr.*Grat*.1.2 (Leclercq-
Rochais 3:166)

Steph.Sest.ap.CTrid.*Act*.25.x.
1546 (*CT* 5:610)

Dried.*Lib.chr*.1.1 (1510 1:33)

CTrid.*Decr.just*.IV.11;*Can*.20
(*CT* 5:706;715)
CTrid.*Act*.6.i.1547 (*CT* 5:761)
Pach.ap.CTrid.*Act*.11.x.1546
(*CT* 5:492);Fon.ap.CTrid.*Act*.
12.x.1546 (*CT* 5:495);Scrip.ap.
CTrid.*Act*.9.x.1546;26.–27.xi.
1546;31.xii.1546 (*CT* 5:489;
666;751)

CTrid.6.*Can*.20;21 (Alberigo-
Jedin 680)

Not, of course, to diminish the role of divine grace, but to safeguard the role of human works springing from grace, the council found it necessary to urge both; for "grace and free will operate in such a way that all works are completely God's and completely our own," as Bishop Juan Bernal Díaz de Luco put it. Patavinus was not speaking only for himself, nor only for his fellow Augustinians, when he insisted that it was a consensus of all theologians that works without grace did not justify. The first draft of the decree pronounced an anathema upon anyone who would say anything of the sort: It was fitting to speak of "merit" and of "reward," as Scripture regularly did, but this was because the works of the justified were performed "with grace as the leader and the will as the partner." The ground and "principal cause of the merits of the righteous" was not the moral perfection of their works, but the promise of God, which was infallible. Quoting Augustine, one could refer to them as "gratuitous merits," since they were, at one and the same time, bestowed as a gift and earned as a reward, neither of these without the other. Or, quoting the well-known words of Bernard, one could declare: "I am confirming the legitimacy of merits; for 'take away free will, and there is nothing that needs to be saved; take away grace, and there is no way to save it.'" Just as merits and rewards had a positive role in the life of the justified, so also did the law. It was a corollary of the Protestant doctrine of justification by faith alone that "the gospel is in conflict with the law," the fourth draft decree asserted. There was debate about this phraseology, as well as about the addition of the statement that Christ "is also a Lawgiver." Eventually the first statement was changed to read, "as though the gospel were a bare and absolute promise of eternal life, without the condition of observing the commandments," while the second became: "If anyone says that Christ Jesus was given to men by God [only] as a Redeemer in whom they are to trust, and not also as a Lawgiver whom they are to obey, let him be anathema."

Although it could well have been part of the consideration of original sin, the problem of free will received the attention of the council chiefly in connection

Leo X.*Ex.Dom.*36 (Denzinger-Schönmetzer 361)

CTrid.*Decr.just.*I.10 (*CT* 5:387)

ap.CTrid.*Act.*28.vi.1546 (*CT* 5:280)

Crz.ap.CTrid.*Act.*12.vii.1546 (*CT* 5:329)

Pasch.ap.CTrid.*Act.*7.vii.1546 (*CT* 5:304)

See p. 283 above

Salm.ap.CTrid.*Act.*26.vi.1546 (*CT* 5:276)

Serip.*Just.*2.2 (*CT* 12:618); Serip.ap.CTrid.*Act.*13.vii.1546 (*CT* 5:334)

Patav.*Just.*2 (*CT* 12:605)

CTrid.6.*Decr.*1.5 (Alberigo-Jedin 672)

See pp. 149–50 above

with the doctrine of justification. The first draft of the decree quoted the papal condemnation to support its own rejection of Luther's doctrine of the bondage of the will: man did prepare himself for justification by his free will, but he did so only when God prepared, converted, inclined, and opened his heart. Even earlier in the debate, there were only four members of the theological commission who found it possible to say, with the Reformers, "that free will is in the position of being purely passive, and in no way active, with regard to justification"; as the summary of the debate observed, "they do not seem to speak in a sufficiently Catholic manner." Within the boundaries of what was "Catholic," however, there was a plurality of choices. "God does not justify a man," according to Bishop Antonio de la Cruz, "unless that man first justifies himself. . . . God first moves a man, but the man concurs with his own free will." There was, according to another bishop, "a twofold movement of the free will in the justification of the sinner," toward God and away from sin. Another participant, Alfonso Salmerón, on the basis of the familiar distinction between infant and adult, urged that for the latter "there is required a concurrence of the free will to believe the things that have been revealed." Seripando, pointing out that the human will could resist grace and then asking "Can a man consent to the call of God by the same free will?" replied: "Of course he can, but not unless [the will] has been aided, healed, and set free by divine grace." And another Augustinian, who was to be Seripando's successor, described "the movement of the will preceding justification" as taking place "when grace moves the free will." To steer a middle course within this plurality of choices, the definition asserted that "man himself neither does absolutely nothing while receiving the inspiration [of the Holy Spirit], since he can also reject it; nor yet is he able by his own free will and without the grace of God to move himself to righteousness in [God's] sight."

One other correlative of the doctrine of justification was the certitude of salvation. It was so, at any rate, for the Reformers, both because of Luther's quest for a gracious God, out of which the Reformation had come, and because of Calvin's doctrine of predesti-

See pp. 229–32 above

Mont.ap.CTrid.*Act.* 17.xii.
1546 (*CT* 5:727)

Mir.ap.CTrid.*Act*.18.x.1546
(*CT* 5:552)
Pach.ap.CTrid.*Act*.17.xii.1546
(*CT* 5:727)
Tap.*Orat*.10.14 (Mylius 2:377)

CTrid.*Act*.vii.1546 (*CT* 5:393)

CTrid.*Decr.just*.I.18 (*CT* 5:
390)
Mart.ap.CTrid.*Act*. 13.viii.
1546 (*CT* 5:406)
CTrid.*Act*.15.–26.x.1546 (*CT*
5:523–632)

Maz.ap.CTrid.*Act*.21.x.1546
(*CT* 5:581–90)
CTrid.*Act*.17.xii.1546 (*CT* 5:
727 28)
Thos.Aq.*S.T*.2.1.112.5 (*Ed.
Leon*.7:326–27)
ap.CTrid.*Act*.16.x.1546;19.x.
1546;21.x.1546 (*CT* 5:546;560,
564;588);Caj.*Summul*.D (1530:
F4r);Caj.*Purg*.2 (Lyons 1:117)

Rom.8:38–39 (Vulg.);2 Cor.
12:9
Pol.*Conc*.47 (1562:27v–28r)
Lun.ap.CTrid.*Act*.15.x.1546
(*CT* 5:525–26);Pach.ap.CTrid.
*Act*.9.xi.1546 (*CT* 5:642–43)

Nav.ap.CTrid.*Act*.19.x.1546
(*CT* 5:559)
ap.CTrid.*Act*.17.viii.1546 (*CT*
5:409)

ap.CTrid.*Act*.28.viii.1546 (*CT*
5:418–19)

CTrid.*Act*.9.i.1547 (*CT* 5:773)

CTrid.6.*Decr*.1.9 (Alberigo-
Jedin 674)

nation, to which it had led. In Roman Catholic theology, by contrast, such certitude had "almost nothing to do with the doctrine of justification," as the presiding bishop of the council (soon to become Pope Julius III) observed on the basis of the debates. Nevertheless, now that the Protestants had taken the position that the believer not only could, but should, be certain of salvation, they were to be condemned above all for this, and the council had the obligation to deal with the issue; for such a "certainty" was "alien to the Scriptures." It was, "generally speaking, approved by all" when, already in July 1546, the first form of the decree spoke out against "the error by which it is asserted that the justified not only conjecture, but know for certain, that they are predestined and are in God's grace," along with the related error "that all who are justified are obliged to believe this firmly and certainly"; still, "those who want to discuss" the matter were to have an opportunity to do so. This they did, in conjunction with the question of imputed righteousness (although the more perceptive recognized that the two questions were quite distinct), and then in a special session only on certitude. Many of them cited the statement of Thomas Aquinas that, except by special revelation, "no one can know whether he has sanctifying grace," although it was possible to know and to hope "conjecturally, on the basis of signs." The proviso about special revelation covered the declarations of "certitude" and "sufficiency" in Paul (which Cardinal Pole, for one, was willing to apply generally to all believers) and, at the insistence of the Franciscans, the case of Francis of Assisi. It was possible to speak of a "certainty of knowledge" or of a "certainty of faith" or of a "moral certainty"; the first of these was definitely impossible "in the ordinary course of events [secundum legem communem]," the third definitely possible. The issue was the second, whether without a special revelation "someone can know for certain, with the certainty of faith, that he is in [a state of] grace"; and this was what the discussants, and then the council by its decree, denied: "No one can know with the certitude of faith, which cannot be subject to error, that he has obtained the grace of God."

## Reaffirmation of Church and Dogma

It would be a grave act of reductionism to concentrate exclusively on the new definitions of the Council of Trent, which were a response to the Reformation; although these are by far the most important for our narrative, they occupied the council only during the first year or two of its deliberations. Indeed, there is considerable historical merit to the view that the principal accomplishments of the council, even for the history of church doctrine, did not lie in its dogmatic formulations at all, but in its legislation regarding the reform and administration of the church. For example, the two requirements that every diocese assume direct responsibility for the training of the clergy and that preaching be restored to its proper place in the life of the church have led to the creation of the modern theological seminary (eventually within Protestantism in some countries as well as within Roman Catholicism in most countries)—controlled by the church, isolated from the other faculties of the university, devoted exclusively to the professional preparation of the church's servants. All of this has had far-reaching consequences for the history of doctrine from the sixteenth century to the present.

CTrid.23.*Decr.*18 (Alberigo-Jedin 750–53)

CTrid.24.*Decr.*4 (Alberigo-Jedin 763)

In addition, the Council of Trent adopted definitions of several doctrines in which, in effect, reformation of church and dogma was a reaffirmation of church and dogma as set down by "the consensus of other councils and of the fathers." Chiefly, this reaffirmation involved the sacramental system, together with some of its doctrinal implications, such as purgatory, as well as many of its disciplinary implications, such as divorce. The vicissitudes of the council—plague, war, and politics both imperial and ecclesiastical—were responsible for dragging out the discussion and promulgation of these decrees over a period of more than sixteen years, and consequently for issuing in installments what should have been a unified restatement of the Roman Catholic tradition on the sacraments: the decree on the seven sacraments was issued on 3 March 1547, but those on matrimony not until 11 November 1563.

CTrid.7.*Decr.*1.pr. (Alberigo-Jedin 684)

CTrid.7.*Decr.*1 (Alberigo-Jedin 684–86)
CTrid.24.*Decr.*1 (Alberigo-Jedin 753–59)

The turnover of participants and viewpoints made it important to identify the connection of these de-

CTrid.5.*Decr*.2.3;6.*Decr*.1.6
(Alberigo-Jedin 666;673)

See vol.3:203–4

See vol.2:277–80

ap.CTrid.*Act*.17.i.1547 (*CT* 5:
835–39)
Cen.ap.CTrid.*Act*.20.i.1547
(*CT* 5:845–46)

CFlor.(1438–45) *Decr.Arm*.5
(Alberigo-Jedin 540–41)

See vol.3:204–14

Lain.ap.CTrid.*Act*.20.i.1547
(*CT* 5:850);Patav.ap.CTrid.
*Act*.24.i.1547 (*CT* 5:852)

Cen.ap.CTrid.*Act*.4.ii.1547
(*CT* 5:876–77)

Crz.ap.CTrid.*Act*.21.ii.1547
(*CT* 5:969–70)

CTrid.13.*Decr*.6 (Alberigo-
Jedin 696);Maz.ap.CTrid.*Act*.
10.ii.1547 (*CT* 5:906)

Cerv.ap.CTrid.*Act*.6.vi.1547
(*CT* 6–I:195)

ap.CTrid.*Act*.31.v.1547 (*CT*
6–I:166–67)

Cerv.*Ep*.21.v.1547 (*CT* 11:204)

Vauch.ap.CTrid.*Act*.8.iii.1547
(*CT* 5:1010–11)

Madr.ap.CTrid.*Act*.21.ix.1551
(*CT* 7–I:144)

crees with those of the earlier sessions, which had made reference to the sacraments; this also made it imperative to affirm the connection with earlier councils, above all the Fourth Lateran Council in 1215 and the Council of Florence in 1439. Commenting on the catalogue of Protestant errors on the sacraments that had been drawn up to serve as the basis for the discussions, one Franciscan theologian recited the place where each of them had already been condemned. The "summary statement [brevissima formula]" on "the truth of the sacraments" adopted at Florence had defined as normative the outcome of the medieval development of the doctrine of the seven sacraments. Here at Trent, therefore, it was possible to condemn Protestant sacramental doctrine "because it has already been condemned at the Council of Florence." What Florence had said about the discrete sacraments was also the basis for judging Protestant deviations, whether on the Eucharist or on the concept of a sacramental character as conferred for example in confirmation by a bishop. Although the decree of the Fourth Lateran Council did not make the term "transubstantiation" immune to debate at Trent, the doctrine of the real presence confessed also in its disciplinary decrees was and remained privileged.

This broad consensus on the essential content of the Roman Catholic doctrine of the sacraments led one of the co-presidents of the council, Cardinal Cervini, to suggest that on most of the seven sacraments extended debate would be unnecessary; after having "examined the canons on the doctrine of the sacrament of the Eucharist not only as to their content, but also as to their form, word by word" (so that they were now ready for publication), the council should not "waste time in examining and resolving the content and the canons for all the sacraments." At a later session the host of the council, the cardinal bishop of Trent, echoed an earlier statement in declaring his "preference for adoring this most holy Sacrament [the Eucharist] rather than disputing about it." It became clear in the protracted debates that both the criticism of the Roman Catholic view of the sacraments by various Protestants and the unresolved pluralism of later medieval eucharistic theories would make "disputing about it" un-

CTrid.13.*Decr*.1.5 (Alberigo-Jedin 695–96)

See p. 275 above

Guer.ap.CTrid.*Act*.21.ix.1551 (*CT* 7–I:147)

Muss.ap.CTrid.*Act*.9.x.1551 (*CT* 7–I:189)

Brag.ap.CTrid.*Act*.12.iii.1552 (*CT* 7–I:455)

See vol.3:209–11

See pp. 178–80 above

ap.CTrid.*Act*.17.i.1547 (*CT* 5:838)

Ambr.Cath.ap.CTrid.*Act*.16.ii. 1547 (*CT* 5:933)

CTrid.*Act*.1.iii.1547 (*CT* 5:986–91)

CTrid.7.*Decr*.1.1.1 (Alberigo-Jedin 685)
CTrid.6.*Decr*.1.7 (Alberigo-Jedin 673)

CTrid.7.*Decr*.1.1.1;1.1.5;1.1.8 (Alberigo-Jedin 684–85)

Esq.ap.CTrid.*Act*.15.ii.1547 (*CT* 5:930);Per.ap.CTrid.*Act*. 30.vi.1562 (*CT* 8:640)

avoidable even among those who were united in their defense of the practice of "adoring" it. Protracted though the debates were, however, they likewise provided the occasion, more than the earlier discussions had, for the council to be reminded that it had imposed upon itself the limit of "condemning heresies, not of deciding the scholastic disputes"; what it was to "define," according to Bishop Musso, was "not scholastic opinions" but the teaching of the church. "The opinions of the doctors that are in controversy among Catholics" were to be voiced freely at the council, but not defined as church doctrine.

Although the historical development of the doctrine of the sacraments had proceeded from the consideration of the several sacraments—above all of baptism, the Eucharist, holy orders, and penance—to the definition of "sacraments in general" and the identification of them as seven in number, all conforming to the general definition of what made a proper sacrament, the Council of Trent was obliged by such attacks as Luther's *Babylonian Captivity* to move in the opposite direction. The first task, therefore, was a conciliar reaffirmation of the Council of Florence on the seven sacraments. The statement of Luther's opponent, Ambrosius Catharinus, that all the passages collected from the Reformers on the seven sacraments "should be condemned as heretical, since they are contrary to the usage of the Roman [Catholic] Church," may have been premature as it stood; but the thirteen canons adopted by the council after its discussions did pronounce such a condemnation, although with greater caution than had been visible in earlier formulations. Thus they repeated the content and even the language of the *Decree for the Armenians* at Florence, but likewise repeated earlier decrees at Trent by adding a condemnation of any doctrine of "faith alone" in connection with the grace of the sacraments. Putting the doctrine of the "sacraments in general" at the head of the council's doctrinal legislation on the subject made a foregone conclusion of most of the questions raised in subsequent debates about sacramentality, even though it did not, as might have been expected, make the way smooth for a comprehensive "doctrine" of the individual sacraments.

*Confut.Conf.Aug.*13 (CCath 33:110–11)

First among the Protestant errors that served as
the basis of the discussions and then of the canons
adopted on 3 March 1547 was the denial that there
were "seven sacraments of the church, neither more
nor less." Although there were numerological arguments for the church's teaching, as well as a certain
symmetry between seven mortal sins or seven virtues
and seven sacraments, both the medieval development and the Reformation debates had made the issue of dominical institution the decisive one. For as
the summary of the discussion noted, it was necessary to condemn, on the one hand, the charge "that
not all the sacraments were instituted by Christ" and,
on the other hand, the claim "that something is not
a sacrament unless it is contained in the Scriptures."
When a precise consideration of the criteria led to
the conclusion that the reference in the Gospels to
an anointing by the twelve disciples could not apply
directly to the sacrament of extreme unction and that
therefore the only reference in Scripture that did apply was James 5:14–15, which "squares very well
with the definition of a sacrament," the proof of
dominical institution had to come in an a posteriori
argument from its effects. Against the Reformation
claim that anointing and confirmation had been instituted by the church fathers, everyone agreed that
"since they are sacraments of the New Law, they are
said to have been instituted by Christ, because they
are the foundations of the church which have come
to us from Christ." The first and fundamental canon
on the sacraments read therefore: "If anyone says
that the sacraments of the New Law were not all
instituted by Jesus Christ our Lord, or that they are
either more or fewer than seven . . . , or that any
of these seven is not truly and strictly a sacrament,
let him be anathema." There was a similar "common
consensus of the Catholic Church" for the teaching
that baptism, confirmation, and ordination conferred
an indelible "character" and did not have to be repeated, as well as for the reassertion of the anti-
Donatist principle that while a valid sacrament did
require in its minister the intention to confect a sacrament of the church, it did not depend on his moral
worthiness.

ap.CTrid.*Act.*17.i.1547 (*CT* 5:835)
Pasch.ap.CTrid.*Act.*11.ii.1547 (*CT* 5:922)
Sol.ap.CTrid.*Act.*26.i.1547 (*CT* 5:857);Mrtr.ap.CTrid.*Act.*3.iii.1547 (*CT* 5:1002)

See pp. 51–52, 179, 256–57 above

ap.CTrid.*Act.*29.i.1547 (*CT* 5:867)

Mark 6:13

Rav.ap.CTrid.*Act.*23.x.1551 (*CT* 7–I:256)
ap.CTrid.*Act.*17.i.1547 (*CT* 5:838)
Apol.Conf.Aug.13.6 (Ref 293);Luth.*Capt.Bab.* (*WA* 6:567–71)

Sol.ap.CTrid.*Act.*27.i.1547 (*CT* 5:859)

CTrid.7.*Decr.*1.1.1 (Alberigo-Jedin 684)
Cpr.ap.CTrid.*Act.*21.ii.1547 (*CT* 5:969)

CTrid.7.*Decr.*1.1.9 (Alberigo-Jedin 685)
CTrid.7.*Decr.*1.2.11 (Alberigo-Jedin 686)

See pp. 92–98 above

CTrid.7.*Decr.*1.11–12 (Alberigo-Jedin 685)

CTrid.7.Decr.1.2.3 (Alberigo-Jedin 685)

See p. 178 above

CTrid.7.Decr.1.2.5;1.2.2 (Alberigo-Jedin 685)

See pp. 313–22 below
CTrid.7.Decr.1.2.12–14 (Alberigo-Jedin 686)
Serip.ap.CTrid.Act.19.ii.1547 (CT 5:963)

See p. 256 above

CTrid.7.Decr.1.2.7 (Alberigo-Jedin 685)

Thos.Aq.S.T.3.38 (Ed.Leon. 11:381–87)

Calv.Inst.(1536)4 (Barth-Niesel 1:129)

CTrid.7.Decr.1.2.1 (Alberigo-Jedin 685)

CTrid.7.Decr.1.3.1–3 (Alberigo-Jedin 686)

Within this framework of the sacramental system, baptism was the first to receive its own set of canons, attacking anyone who "says that in the Roman [Catholic] Church (which is the mother and the teacher [mater et magistra] of all the churches) there is not the true doctrine concerning the sacrament of baptism." The most fundamental of these canons, however, were not directed against Luther's sacramental theology; for according to his high doctrine of baptism and of baptismal regeneration, no less than according to the Tridentine doctrine, anyone was to be condemned who taught "that baptism is optional, that is, not necessary for salvation," or "that true and natural water is not necessary for baptism." These and other heresies condemned in the canons, above all the repudiation of infant baptism, had arisen within the Anabaptist movement, to which the debates at the council gave only occasional attention. The doctrines of the Lutheran and Reformed churches were, despite Protestant objections, the target intended by the anathema against the position that "by baptism those who have been baptized become debtors to faith alone, but not to the observance of the entire law of Christ." Despite the methodological restraints that the council had imposed on itself, one of the debates among medieval doctors did find its way into the canons, partly because it had been revived by the Protestants: the relation between Christian baptism and that of John the Baptist, which Calvin had made "exactly the same." In opposition to that view, the council anathematized the idea "that the baptism of John had the same force as the baptism of Christ."

It seemed almost anticlimactic, after the thirteen canons on the sacraments in general and the fourteen on baptism, when the council went on to promulgate three canons on confirmation. The first two of these were devoted to a defense of the sacramentality of confirmation, already asserted in the decree on the sacraments in general, the third to the identification of the bishop, rather than a "simple priest," as "the ordinary minister" of this sacrament. That set a pattern—thetical doctrine amplified by discipline, defense of the inclusion in the list of seven sacraments followed by clarification of issues arising out of

CTrid.14.*Decr*.2 (Alberigo-Jedin 710–11;713)
CTrid.23.*Decr*.1 (Alberigo-Jedin 742–44)
CTrid.24.*Decr*.1 (Alberigo-Jedin 753–59)

Pgn.ap.CTrid.*Act*.19.ix.1547 (*CT* 6–I:471)

See vol.3:211–12

CTrid.24.*Decr*.1.*Can*. (Alberigo-Jedin 755–59)

CTrid.24.*Decr*.1.1 (Alberigo-Jedin 754)

CTrid.24.*Decr*.1.2–12 (Alberigo-Jedin 754–55)

Luth.*Capt.Bab*. (*WA* 6:550–51);Luth.*Ehsach*. (*WA* 30–III:205)

Buc.*Regn.Chr*.2.15 (Strasbourg 15:152–53)

Eph.5:32(Vulg.)
CFlor.(1438–45) *Decr.Arm*. (Alberigo-Jedin 550)

Eras.*Stun.blasph*. (*LB* 9:369)
Aug.*Nupt.et concup*.1.21.23 (*CSEL* 42:236)

Serip.ap.CTrid.*Act*.22.ix.1547 (*CT* 6–II:148)

James 5:14–15

CTrid.14.*Decr*.2.1 (Alberigo-Jedin 710)

Apol.*Conf.Aug*.13.11–12 (*Bek*. 293–94)

administration and application—that the council was to follow in its definition of each of three other sacraments: extreme unction on 25 November 1551; holy orders on 15 July 1563; and, shortly before adjournment, matrimony on 11 November 1563. When, early in the deliberations on matrimony, it was suggested by the canon lawyer and bishop Sebastiano Pighino that "the positions of the Lutherans should be put under the anathema, but all other questions be treated [under the heading of] reform," that was a somewhat oversimplified reflection of this pattern, which had medieval precedent. Although the council did decree a separate set of ten "canons concerning the reform of matrimony," it also incorporated into its doctrinal canons, after one canon defining matrimony as a sacrament, eleven disciplinary canons regarding polygamy, impediments of consanguinity and affinity, divorce, and related issues. In effect, then, it followed Pighino's recommendations.

The "positions of the Lutherans" to which Pighino referred were chiefly those in which Luther had denied the sacramental definition of marriage, calling it "an external, secular matter"; Bucer, for example, had made it the proper responsibility of the state, which the Roman Catholic Church had usurped. Erasmus, too, had cited Jerome and Augustine as proof that the New Testament's use of the term "sacrament" for marriage, quoted as a proof text by the Council of Florence, did not necessarily make it a sacrament of the church. Seripando, ready as always with an apposite passage from Augustine, rejoined that matrimony met all the qualifications for a sacrament: "It has the word [of God], it has an element, and it confers a grace to which it bears a likeness." The applicability of the standard proof text for extreme unction had come in for similar criticism by the Protestants, but was now also confirmed as bearing the authority of "promulgation by James, the apostle and the brother of the Lord." For the sacramentality of ordination, which the *Apology of the Augsburg Confession* had found unobjectionable so long as it referred to "the ministry of the word," it was the "testimony of Scripture, apostolic tradition, and the unanimous consensus of the fathers" that stood as proof, with the words

2 Tim.1:6(Vulg.)

CTrid.23.Decr.1.3 (Alberigo-Jedin 742)

CTrid.23.Decr.4;Can.7 (Alberigo-Jedin 742–44)

CTrid.14.Decr.1.pr. (Alberigo-Jedin 703)

CTrid.6.Decr.14 (Alberigo-Jedin 676–77)

Apol.Conf.Aug.4.271 (Bek.214)

See p. 179 above
Bill.ap.CTrid.Act.26.x.1551
(CT 7–I:269)

Grop.ap.CTrid.Act.25.x.1551
(CT 7–I:266)

See pp. 129–30 above
Tap.ap.CTrid.Act.21.x.1551
(CT 7–I:248)

CTrid.14.Can.9 (Alberigo-Jedin 712);Castr.Haer.2 (1571:106)

CTrid.14.Decr.1.3 (Alberigo-Jedin 704)

CFlor.(1438–45) Decr.Arm. (Alberigo-Jedin 548)

See vol.3:208

ap.CTrid.Act.20.–21.ix.1551
(CT 7–I:328–30)

of Paul to Timothy about "the grace of God that is in you through the imposition of my hands" as the locus classicus. This led in turn to the reassertion of the hierarchical structure of the church and of episcopal authority as a distinct office (though not as a distinct sacrament, the episcopacy being rather the full exercise of the priesthood). Since most of the reform legislation of the council was dealing with bishops and priests, here, too, the pattern of thetical doctrine amplified by discipline obtained.

The sacrament of penance had played a unique role in the Reformation debates. As the council noted in the preface to its decree on penance, there was a "close kinship [cognatio]" between penance and justification, so that it had been obliged to treat many of the issues of penance in its earlier decree on that doctrine. That kinship was no less visible in the penitential doctrines of the Reformers, who, because absolution was "the very voice of the gospel" and was received by faith, connected it closely to justification by faith, but who also, as Eberhard Billick of Cologne observed, had manifested an ambivalence about the sacramental status of penance. Billick's colleague, Johann Gropper, stressed that "not every penance is a sacrament, but only that which comes to a completion in absolution," which the priest pronounced not by his own right but by the authority of Christ; Tapper, too, echoing Duns Scotus, identified absolution as the essential content of the sacrament. Therefore the council, in the definitive draft of its decree, called the words of the priest, "I absolve you" (which were at the same time a judicial act, according to the canons of the council), "the form of the sacrament of penance," in the Aristotelian sense of the word "form."

If absolution was the "form," then, according to the decree of the Council of Florence, "the acts of the penitent" (contrition, confession, satisfaction) were, "so to speak, the matter [quasi materia]," since every sacrament had to have both form and matter. The preliminary draft of the Tridentine decree called them simply "the matter" of the sacrament, but several participants urged the restoration of the exact words of the earlier council. There was even one theologian who objected to designating "these three" as

Per.ap.CTrid.*Act*.13.xi.1551
(*CT* 7–1:315)

CTrid.14.*Decr*.1.3;*Can*.4
(Alberigo-Jedin 703–4)

CTrid.14.*Decr*.1.1 (Alberigo-Jedin 705)

CTrid.14.*Decr*.1.5;*Can*.6–8
(Alberigo-Jedin 705–7;712)

CTrid.14.*Decr*.1.8 (Alberigo-Jedin 708)

See p. 161 above

ap.CTrid.*Act*.24.x.1555 (*CT* 7–1:264)

Grop.ap.CTrid.*Act*.25.x.1551
(*CT* 7–1:268)

Rom.8:17(Vulg.)
Guer.ap.CTrid.*Act*.6.xi.1551
(*CT* 7–1:297);Muss.ap.CTrid.
*Act*.9.xi.1551 (*CT* 7–1:305)

CTrid.14.*Can*.13 (Alberigo-Jedin 713)

See p. 135 above

ap.CTrid.*Act*.19.vi.1547 (*CT* 6–1:224)

CTrid.25.*Decr*.6 (Alberigo-Jedin 796–97)

"parts of penance as a sacrament" at all. The positive formulation adopted by the council on 25 November 1551 did restore the term "so to speak, the matter," but it also employed the term "parts of penance" for the three "acts of the penitent himself." In its canons on contrition the council did not deal with attrition at all, but in its positive doctrinal statement it did call attrition "a gift of God and an impulse of the Holy Spirit," which disposed the sinner toward the acceptance of the grace offered in the sacrament of penance; without that sacrament, however, it did not lead to justification. The second of the parts of penance, the "secret sacramental confession" of all mortal sins to a priest, was not a mere "human tradition," but a matter of "divine law" that had been observed in the church since the very beginning.

As for penitential "satisfaction," the council noted that "of all the parts of penance," it was "the one that has been most attacked in our own time" on the grounds that it detracted from the satisfaction accomplished by Christ. During the conciliar debate Gropper objected to the statement of an earlier speaker that in penance "we make satisfaction for an offense against God, therefore for guilt, not only for punishment"; on the contrary, Gropper insisted, "the offense of God is infinite and cannot be resolved by us." To mitigate the apparent contradiction between penitential satisfaction and the satisfaction of Christ's atonement, other speakers described the former as a way of "suffering together with Christ, and of having his satisfaction applied to us, so that we may at the same time be glorified together with him." And the canons of the council, to the same end, condemned the teaching that the penitential "satisfaction for sins, so far as their temporal punishment is concerned, is not in any way rendered to God through the merits of Christ." Much later, on 4 December 1563, the council, on the basis of the definition laid down by Pope Leo X, published a decree on indulgences as a power employed by the church "even in the most ancient times," but it added a warning against the abuses and the laxity that threatened "ecclesiastical discipline."

It was consistent with the history of the doctrine of the sacraments in the Middle Ages and in the Reformation when the Council of Trent devoted more consideration to the Eucharist, and over a longer period of time, than to all the other sacraments combined. The first compilation of Protestant errors on the sacraments included Luther's statement that "one sacrament cannot be of greater rank than another," since they were all founded on the same word of God. Although some felt that this should not be attributed to Luther but to Zwingli, it was obvious that among the sacraments the Eucharist did have greater rank, "especially by reason of its content." The specification of that content was the most important issue in the first stage of the conciliar discussions, for on this issue most of the others depended. The Fourth Lateran Council had specified it in its decree on transubstantiation, and at Trent this became the focus—transubstantiation as a way of expressing the consensus of the centuries that the body and blood of Christ were present "in real fact, truly, and really." In keeping with the desire it had expressed earlier, the council sought also on these issues to avoid the impression of novelty by "upholding the sense of earlier councils," which in this case meant above all Fourth Lateran.

The objections to transubstantiation were on several different grounds. From the Reformed use of Augustine's "Believe, and you have already eaten," whose authentic meaning had to be defended against those who took it to say "that Augustine denies sacramental eating," it was evident that, among the Protestant errors enumerated, that "of Zwingli, Oecolampad, and the Sacramentarians" was to teach "that in the Eucharist there is not in fact [present] the body and blood of our Lord Jesus Christ." Not the theory of transubstantiation as such, then, but the doctrine of the real presence was the point of their objection to transubstantiation. The same was true of Calvin's aspersions on the use of the words of institution as a "magic incantation." But it was necessary to consider transubstantiation in comparison with alternate theories, such as the annihilation of the elements or the Wycliffite notion of their "remanence," condemned at Constance. "Where the enemies of the truth are offended above all" in transubstantiation, noted the author of one of the most careful of the

ap.CTrid.Act.17.i.1547 (CT 5:835)

Luth.Inst.min. (WA 12:836)

Tab.ap.CTrid.Act.24.i.1547 (CT 5:852);Grop.Leyb.2 (1556:261v–262r)

Crz.ap.CTrid.Act.21.ii.1547 (CT 5:969)

See vol.3:203–4 CLater.(1215) Const.1 (Alberigo-Jedin 230)

Cons.ap.CTrid.Act.18.ii.1547 (CT 5:937) Ab.Chrys.ap.CTrid.Act.16.v. 1547 (CT 6–II:9) See pp. 290–91 above

Fosc.ap.CTrid.Act.29.ix.1551 (CT 7–I:168) Leon.ap.CTrid.Act.7.ii.1547 (CT 5:885);Lec.ap.CTrid.Act. 8.iii.1547 (CT 5:1010)

See pp. 196–97 above

Visdom.ap.CTrid.Act.9.ii.1547 (CT 5:889);Leon.ap.CTrid. Act.7.ii.1547 (CT 5:889)

Cons.ap.CTrid.Act.18.ii.1547 (CT 5:942)

ap.CTrid.Act.3.ii.1547 (CT 5:869)

Cons.ap.CTrid.Act.18.ii.1547 (CT 5:943)

See p. 190 above

Visdom.ap.CTrid.Act.9.ii.1547 (CT 5:899) Leon.ap.CTrid.Act.7.ii.1547 (CT 5:884)

Cons.ap.CTrid.*Act*.18.ii.1547
(*CT* 5:944);Per.ap.CTrid.*Act*.
26.ix.1551 (*CT* 7–I:163);Muss.
ap.CTrid.*Act*.29.ix.1551 (*CT*
7–I:171)

ap.CTrid.*Act*.3.x.1551 (*CT* 7–
I:178)

Naus.ap.CTrid.*Act*.6.x.1551
(*CT* 7–II:216–17)

Naus.ap.CTrid.*Act*.28.ix.1551
(*CT* 7–II:157)

Naus.ap.CTrid.*Act*.9.x.1551
(*CT* 7–II:227)

ap.CTrid.*Act*.19.ix.1551 (*CT*
7–I:125)

CTrid.13.*Decr*.4;*Can*.2
(Alberigo-Jedin 695;697)

See vol.3:188–90

presentations on the subject, "is the new and, as they say, portentous term"; but the same objections could be (and had been) raised to such nonbiblical terms as "homoousios."

Another and no less scholarly theologian, the bishop of Vienna, took vigorous exception to the proposed statement in the canon that "our fathers and the universal Catholic Church most appropriately call this change [of the elements] 'transubstantiation.'" For, he added, "it is not sufficiently clear just how ancient those fathers of ours are who used this term 'transubstantiation,' nor is it certain that the universal Catholic Church designated this miraculous change of bread and wine 'transubstantiation.'" While he acknowledged that "since the beginning of the church there has scarcely been a more general and universal" council than the Fourth Lateran, he had nevertheless come to the conclusion that the outside pressure of heresy rather than the inherent appropriateness of the term had been responsible for that council's adoption of "transubstantiation." One of his colleagues suggested that the term be mentioned, but that "it does not appear to be a matter of faith" in itself, despite its use by the Councils of the Lateran and of Florence. The definitive language of the decree of 11 October 1551 seems to have taken account of these problems; for it affirmed the "change of the entire substance" of bread and wine into the substance of the body and blood of Christ, adding that "this change has conveniently and appropriately been called transubstantiation by the holy Catholic Church," and it employed similar language in the canon. Thus it reaffirmed the reality of the presence, and together with it the validity of transubstantiation as the church's way of confessing that presence.

The real presence and the sacrifice of the Mass had long been intertwined both in the rule of prayer and in the rule of faith, and it was to the sacrifice that the council turned from its consideration of transubstantiation and the presence (although almost eleven years elapsed between the decrees on the two eucharistic doctrines). Already in 1547 Seripando and others had compiled at least two sets of "articles of the heretics on the sacrifice of the Mass" to serve as the basis for

ap.CTrid.*Act*.29.vii.1547 (*CT* 6–I:321–23);Serip.ap.CTrid. *Act*.iv.1547 (*CT* 6–I:323–25)

See pp. 179,200–201 above

ap.CTrid.*Act*.3.i.1552 (*CT* 7–I:747)

Guer.ap.CTrid.*Act*.7.i.1552 (*CT* 7–I:447)

John 1:29

See vol.3:137 ap.CTrid.*Act*.20.i.1552 (*CT* 7–I:478)

Tap.ap.CTrid.*Act*.8.xii.1551 (*CT* 7–II:370;374) Acts 2:42

Cons.ap.CTrid.*Act*.9.viii.1547 (*CT* 6–I:350)

See p. 310 below

Caj.*Miss.sac*.3 (Lyons 3:286); Muss.ap.CTrid.*Act*.9.i.1552 (*CT* 7–I:449) Tap.ap.CTrid.*Act*.8.xii.1551 (*CT* 7–II:377)

Cons.ap.CTrid.*Act*.9.viii.1547 (*CT* 6–I:350);Herv.ap.CTrid. *Act*.17.viii.1547 (*CT* 6–I:370)

Cons.ap.CTrid.*Act*.9.viii.1547 (*CT* 6–I:350)

discussion and definition. As the earlier controversy had made clear, it was the objection of Protestants—no less of those who accepted the real presence than of those who denied it—that calling the Mass a sacrifice inevitably detracted from the uniqueness of the sacrifice on the cross and that it attributed to human works what was the sole achievement of divine grace in Christ. The council fathers, in meeting this objection, concentrated above all on the relation between the sacrifice of Calvary and the sacrifice of the Mass. A draft decree of 3 January 1552 employed the "language of these two sacrifices, because, although the sacrificial victim [hostia] is one and the same . . . , the mode of existence and of being offered is diverse." In response to the criticism, voiced by the archbishop of Granada but shared by others, "The sacrifice should be defined as one, not two," a revised draft declared: "The same sacrificial victim of the body and blood of Christ is offered in the Mass that was immolated on the cross, the same lamb [of God] and not another; it is one Christ that is sacrificed everywhere, and he is one and the same high priest for both, he who is victim and priest at the same time."

Because of the propensity of theologians for finding evidence in Scripture to support their own particular ideas, it was difficult—but also unnecessary—to argue the case for the Mass as sacrifice on a purely biblical basis. The reference of the Book of Acts to the "breaking of bread" and the language of Dionysius the Areopagite proved that the offering of the sacrifice of the Mass for the dead came "from an apostolic tradition." In the epistles of Paul (which included, of course, the Epistle to the Hebrews) there was frequent reference to "the sacrifice of Christ, yet not a word about it in the Supper, but always on the cross. Nevertheless Christ instituted both the sacrament and the sacrifice in the Supper when he said, 'This do.'" The "doing" in this command did not refer to "eating" or "drinking," since "the primary use [of the Eucharist] is to be sacrificed and offered"; that was what the verb meant in both Greek and Latin. The "eating" of the sacrificial victim followed the "immolating," in the Eucharist as in the Passover; "but we do not eat the Christ immolated on the cross, therefore it must be

Lain.ap.CTrid.*Act*.7.xii.1551
(*CT* 7–I:380)

Ps.110:4(Vulg.)

Tap.ap.CTrid.*Act*.8.xii.1551
(*CT* 7–II:374);Lain.ap.CTrid.
*Act*.7.xii.1551 (*CT* 7–II:381)

Grop.ap.CTrid.*Act*.14.xii.1551
(*CT* 7–II:445)
Caj.*Miss.sac*.6 (Lyons 3:287);
Caj.*Euch*.9 (Lyons 2:145)

Grop.ap.CTrid.*Act*.14.xii.1551
(*CT* 7–II:447);Tap.ap.CTrid.
*Act*.8.xii.1551 (*CT* 7–II:375)

Lain.ap.CTrid.*Act*.7.xii.1551
(*CT* 7–I:382)
Chrys.*Heb*.17.3 (*PG* 63:131)

ap.CTrid.*Act*.9.xii.1551
(*CT* 7 II:536)

Lain.ap.CTrid.*Act*.17.ii.1547
(*CT* 5:934)

Jedin (1949) 4–I:341

ap.CTrid.*Act*.3.ii.1547 (*CT* 5:
870)

Cons.ap.CTrid.*Act*.18.ii.1547
(*CT* 5:955);Pg.*Cont*.7 (1541–I:
168v)

See p. 123 above

Lain.ap.CTrid.*Act*.17.ii.1547
(*CT* 5:935)
Cons.ap.CTrid.*Act*.18.ii.1547
(*CT* 5:956)

Ab.Chrys.ap.CTrid.*Act*.16.v.
1547 (*CT* 6–II:11)

the one immolated in the Eucharist." Similarly, the word of the psalm, "You are a priest for eternity according to the order of Melchizedek," could not refer to the sacrifice on the cross or to a sacrifice offered once for all at the Last Supper, but must mean "the offering in the Eucharist, which happens perpetually." In spite of this distinction, there was a unity of the sacrifice in the New Testament, on the cross and in the Mass, as Cajetan had shown. Thus "the sacrifice of the Mass is, so far as that which is offered is concerned, nothing other than the sacrament of the body and blood of Christ," differing from it only in the manner of presentation and the effect. For that reason "there is no conflict between the sacrifice of the Eucharist and the sacrifice of the cross, for the former derives its power from the latter and is the benefit accomplished by it; therefore it does not detract from the suffering of Christ, but enhances it." As Chrysostom had said, the sacrifice of the Mass was an "exemplar" of the sacrifice on Calvary and was one with it; it did not detract from that eternal sacrifice, but "because we do not offer our own offering, but that of Christ, we do not by our offering make null and void the offering of Christ."

The reaffirmation of the real presence as originally affirmed in the decree of Fourth Lateran on transubstantiation, combined as it was with the Tridentine view of the authority of church and tradition, which "cannot err," made it relatively easy to dispose of the doctrinal, as distinguished from the practical and political, issues raised by the administration of the Eucharist under only one kind. "The question of the chalice was highly politicized," and there were many pragmatic arguments on both sides. Hussite and Protestant demands for the chalice had been listed in the catalogue of errors on the doctrine of the Eucharist, despite the awareness of differences between East and West. Cusanus, in his response to the Hussites, had defended the right of the church "to change, in accordance with the exigency of the times, both the ritual and the interpretation of Scripture." Undeniably, Scripture seemed to favor the use of both species, so that "we shall never be able to convince them on the basis of Holy Scripture." But Augustine's concept

See pp. 196–97 above

Lomb.ap.CTrid.Act.11.ii.1547
(CT 5:919)

Grop.Leyb.4 (1556:342r)

Pg.Cont.7 (1541–I:160v)

CTrid.21.Decr.1.2 (Alberigo-
Jedin 727)

CConst.(1414–18)13
(Alberigo-Jedin 419)

CTrid.21.Can.3;Decr.3
(Alberigo-Jedin 727)

Pach.ap.CTrid.Act.28.v.1546
(CT 5:166);Mrl.Pecc.orig.4
(CT 12:557)

ap.CTrid.Act.7.vi.1546 (CT 5:
197)
CTrid.Act.14.vi.1546 (CT 5:
223)

See p. 45 above

of spiritual eating, which Protestants were fond of citing, also refuted the demand for communion under both kinds. Among the various defenses for the practice of communion under one kind, one of the most effective, especially in response to Protestantism, was the historical observation that it had begun as a consequence of a demand by the laity to be protected from spilling the sacred species in the chalice, thus on the basis of "a certain consensus of the faithful of Christ." That consensus of the faithful was one of what the final decree called the "just causes and reasons that laymen, and clerics when not confecting [the Sacrament], should communicate only under the single species of the bread." Against the charge that such communion was incomplete, the council reaffirmed the teaching of the Council of Constance that "the total and complete Christ" was present under both kinds in the Eucharist and could be "received under either species alone."

None of this was new, but it did need to be reaffirmed in response to the Protestant alternatives. Yet several of the doctrinal issues raised by the Reformation, although they figured prominently in the interconfessional debates, were relegated by the Council of Trent to some later forum for adjudication and will therefore have to concern us in the final volume of this work. The formula about the sources of revelation was in effect a decision not to decide, and the problem was left to be dealt with by polemics and then addressed again (and left undecided again) at the First Vatican Council in 1870 and the Second Vatican Council in 1962–65. The doctrine of the immaculate conception of the Virgin Mary arose during the debates over original sin as an unavoidable implication. When one of the draft decrees spoke of original sin as transmitted "to the entire human race in accordance with its universal law," the mariological implications of this statement led to its deletion and, eventually, to a new paragraph at the end of the decree, specifying that it was not the council's intention to include Mary in its assertion of the universality of original sin and citing the constitutions on the Virgin promulgated by Pope Sixtus IV in 1477 and 1483, but still stopping short of defining the immaculate conception as a dogma

CTrid.7.*Decr.*1.6 (Alberigo-Jedin 667)

CTrid.25.*Decr.*4.2 (Alberigo-Jedin 785)

Pol.*Sum.pont.*32 (1569:95r);
Pol.*Conc.*2 (1562:2v–3r)

binding, as an article of faith, on the entire church. That would not come until 8 December 1854, with the bull *Ineffabilis Deus* of Pope Pius IX. And despite the pragmatic solution of the ecclesiological question represented by the mere fact of its having been convoked by the pope, the council did not, by its general admonition of "obedience" to the pope, come to a definitive pronouncement on the problem of the relative authority of pope and council in matters of doctrine, nor on the issue of the infallibility of the pope. That, too, would have to wait until the First—and the Second—Vatican Council.

# 6

# Challenges to
# Apostolic Continuity

Luth.ap.*Disp.Lips.* (WA 2:323)

See pp. 270–74 above

See pp. 176–77 above

Luth.*Alb.Pr.* (WA 30–III:552)

Blngr.*Assert.orth.* (1534:5r)

Calv.*Scand.* (Barth-Niesel 2: 205;191–92)

See vol.1:108–20

Acts 2:42

2 Tim.1:14;1 Tim.6:20(Vulg.)
See vol.1:333–39

When Luther, in the name of the authority of Scripture as the word of God, asserted such doctrines as justification by faith alone, defying the contrary authority of church fathers, councils, and popes, all of whom could err and had erred, the defenders of the faith identified themselves with the continuity of the Catholic Church, built upon the rock of Peter. Then, when Zwingli and his successors, in the name of the authority of Scripture as the word of God, denied the identity between the body of Christ in the Lord's Supper and the body born of Mary, Luther and his followers affirmed the continuity of the Catholic doctrine of the real presence, taught by the ancient and medieval church. And then, when the Radicals of the Reformation, who took such "delight in the novelty of things," rejected infant baptism or the trinitarian creeds in the name of the authority of Scripture as the word of God, Calvin and his colleagues stressed "the continuity of the ages" as assured by "the transmission of the true doctrine of faith" through the Catholic centuries. Apostolic continuity was a standard around which several different—and opposing—theological armies could rally.

Continuity with the apostles had been such a standard since the ancient church. It was said of the primitive Christian community that "they continued steadfastly in the apostles' doctrine," maintaining "custody of the good deposit." By that "deposit," according to Vincent of Lérins in the fifth century, the apostle meant "the riches of the Catholic faith,

Vinc.Ler.*Comm*.22.27 (Moxon 87)

See vol.2:10–16

Eus.*H.e*.1.1.1 (*GCS* 9:6)

See vol.1:119

Iren.*Haer*.3.1.1 (Harvey 2:2)
Iren.*Haer*.3.2.2 (Harvey 2:7–8)

Iren.*Haer*.3.3.1 (Harvey 2:8–9)

Williams (1962) 846

Gritsch (1967)

Schwindt (1924)

inviolate and unadulterated." To the Eastern Orthodox Church of Byzantium, this was the changeless truth of salvation. The first history of the church, that of Eusebius, opened its account with the words, "the successions from the holy apostles," affirming the apostolic continuity of the institutions and teachings of the true churches. One of the most important formulations of the three criteria of this apostolic continuity was that of Irenaeus around the end of the second century: the revelation that the apostles had "handed down to us in the Scriptures as the pillar and bulwark of our faith"; the doctrinal and creedal "tradition that is derived from the apostles"; and the ecclesiastical structure represented by "those who were by the apostles instituted bishops in the churches, and . . . the succession of these men in our times," particularly at Rome. The Catholic doctrine of apostolic continuity, Eastern and Western, was based on the assumption that these three criteria were valid, that they were harmonious and interdependent, and that they were somehow verifiable.

Each of these assumptions came into question in the period of the Reformation, with the result that each of these three criteria of apostolic continuity (and all of them together as a complex of authority) faced unprecedented challenges. Principally those challenges came from the left wing of the Reformation, which, as its leading scholarly interpreter has put it, was not a "reformation" in the same sense of the word as the other movements we have been describing in the preceding three chapters, but "a radical break from the existing institutions and theologies in the interrelated drives to restore primitive Christianity, to reconstruct, and to sublimate." In many ways that radical break was an anticipation of the very critiques of orthodoxy and apostolic continuity that were to come from modern thought in the eighteenth, nineteenth, and twentieth centuries, so that the full implications of these challenges did not become apparent until after the period being discussed in the present volume. For that reason, the discovery that the Radical Reformer Thomas Müntzer was a "Reformer without a church" and Hans Denck the "champion of an undogmatic Christianity" has aroused great theological and his-

torical interest in the twentieth century, and understandably so; for Müntzer is seen today as in many
ways the most creative figure among the Radicals,
politically and even theologically. Yet these movements also merit some attention, not merely as an
anticipation of present-day theological concerns, but
in their own right and for their own time, principally
in the context of the history of the Reformation as
"re-formation of church and dogma," within which
a Müntzer is, as "Reformer without a church," far
less important than Menno Simons and Balthasar
Hubmaier or even Hans Denck and Faustus Socinus.

## Christian Humanism and the Authority of Revelation

The coryphaeus of Christian humanism in the sixteenth century, Desiderius Erasmus, defended the
Catholic and patristic doctrine of the freedom of the

See p.140 above

Eras.*Inq.fid.* (Thompson 72)

will against Luther and the Reformation, and he regarded himself as "orthodox." Yet he was obliged at
the same time to defend himself against the charge
that the New Learning of the Renaissance was a he-

Eras.*Pseudev.* (*LB* 10:1575)

Eras.*Apol.Pi.* (*LB* 9:1100)

retical threat to "scholastic dogmas," that it had produced the Protestant Reformation, and that he himself
was guilty of "Lutheranizing" tendencies in his doc-

Eras.*Stun.blasph.* (*LB* 9:365)

trine. That ambiguity in the doctrinal position of humanism during the fifteenth and sixteenth centuries
was evident also in that area of thought which, "if we
try to assess the positive contributions of humanist
scholarship to Renaissance theology, we must emphasize above all," namely, "their achievements in

Kristeller (1961) 79

what we might call sacred philology." To that extent
"sacred philology" does belong to the history of doctrine, although it is chiefly a chapter, and an important
one, in the history of scholarship.

By common consent, the most influential achievement of the "sacred philology" of Christian humanism
was the edition of the Greek New Testament that
Erasmus published in 1516. In principle, the idea of
applying to the text of the New Testament the same
standards of philological precision and the same methods of textual criticism that were being applied to the
classics of ancient Greece and Rome, by "calling in
the assistance of a number of manuscripts . . . very

Eras.*Nov.inst.*pr. (Allen 384)

Drp.*Ep.*1.x.1514 (Allen 304)

See pp. 263–64 above
Drp.*Ep.*27.viii.1515 (Allen 347)
Latom.*Ling.*2 (1517:17);Herb.
*Enchir.*10 (CCath 12:49)

Latom.*Ling.*1 (1517:11)

Wic.*Hag.* (1541:211v–212v)

Eras.*Hier.*II.pr. (Allen 326)

Eras.*Ep.*v.1505 (Allen 182);
Fish.*Clicht.*1.1 (1520:B1r)

Eras.*Ep.*v.1515 (Allen 337)

Gen.3:15(Vulg.)

See vol.3:71.166

old and very correct" (as Erasmus said in dedicating his edition to Pope Leo X), did not appear to be automatically suspect. The inquisitor general and cardinal archbishop of Toledo, Francisco Ximénez de Cisneros, had, at the university he founded in Alcalá de Henares (whose Latin name was "Complutum"), made possible the publication of the first printed polyglot edition of the Bible, the *Complutensian Polyglot*, including in its fifth volume the Greek New Testament, which had already left the presses in 1514, although it was not circulated until after the 1516 edition of Erasmus. One colleague did express his concern to Erasmus over an "operation . . . to correct the Scriptures, and in particular to correct the Latin copies by means of the Greek." He supported his warning by citing Augustine's universally accepted axiom about the relative authority of the (Latin) church and the Gospel, together with the schism between the Greek East and the Latin West. It was a mistake to "attribute too much to the languages," a critic urged, pointing out that while Jerome had given priority to the Hebrew text, other Western and Eastern fathers such as Hilary, Augustine, and Chrysostom had preferred the Septuagint. Because of his well-known admiration for Jerome, whose works he was editing in these same years, Erasmus was in a position to remind his readers that Jerome had corrected the translations of the Septuagint despite its almost universal acceptance, on the grounds that "scholarship," not "inspiration," was the issue; thus Erasmus could argue that correcting the Vulgate in a similar fashion was an act of loyalty to Jerome. He expressed his confidence that there could not "be any danger that everybody will forthwith abandon Christ if the news happens to get out" about variants in the Greek manuscripts or mistranslations in the Latin version.

Such confidence underestimated how profoundly the translations, as well as the mistranslations, of the Latin Vulgate had come to be identified with the authority of revelation itself. For example, the use of the feminine pronoun, "She shall crush [ipsa conteret] your head," in the first messianic prophecy had, though only gradually, become a firm proof for the mariological interpretation of those words. The Prot-

Zw.*Gen.*3:15 (*CR* 100:28);
Luth.*Gen.*3:15 (*WA* 42:143–
44);Calv.*Gen.*3:15 (*CR* 51:71)

Caj.*Mos.*Gen.3:15 (1539:33)

See vol.3:164–65; p.39 above

Luke 1:28(Vulg.)
Vall.*Annot.*Luke 1:28 (*MPPR*
5:830);Eras.*Adnot.*Luke 1:28
(*LB* 6:223)

Eras.*Obsec.Virg.Mar.* (*LB* 5:
1233–40)
Eras.*Pn.Virg.Mat.* (*LB* 5:1227–
34)

Aug.Alf.*Salv.Reg.* (*CCath* 11:
78)

See p.136 above

Matt.4:17(Vulg.)
Vall.*Annot.*Matt.3:2;Mark 1:14
(*MPPR* 5:807;824)
Vall.*Annot.*2 Cor.7:9–10
(*MPPR* 5:872)

Rom.16:25;1 Tim.3:9(Vulg.)
Vall.*Annot.*Eph.1:9;Col.1:26–
27;1 Tim.3:16 (*MPPR* 5:877;
879–80;882)
Vall.*Annot.*Matt.13:11 (*MPPR*
5:814)

Gen.2:24

Eph.5:31–32(Vulg.)

Eras.*Adnot.*Eph.5:32 (*LB* 6:
855)

estant Reformers criticized that interpretation, on philological as well as theological grounds; and once Roman Catholics had come to terms with the Hebrew text, some scholars acknowledged that "it is not said of the woman, but of her seed," meaning either the church or Christ, "that it will crush the devil's head." Another mariological proof text from the Vulgate was the angelic salutation at the annunciation: "Hail, full of grace [gratia plena]." Lorenzo Valla in his *Annotations,* and then Erasmus in his, pointed out that the Greek participle meant no more than "accepted into grace," even though Erasmus did go on to compose a *Petition to the Virgin Mary* and a *Paean to the Virgin Mother.* The defenders of the faith reacted vigorously to such tampering with the sacred text. One of the commentaries on the Salve Regina composed against Luther retorted: "To this my answer is: This is a grammarian's quibble and child's play. . . . They are giving her an obscene name and then saying that Mary is 'gracious.'"

More crucial in some ways was the rendering of terms associated with the sacramental system. Luther, with his substitution of "penitence" for "penance" as a translation of the Greek "μετάνοια," was attaching himself to Valla's philological correction of the medieval use of "Do penance" as a translation of the words of Jesus in the Gospels and as a justification of the penitential system. Conversely, the answers to Luther also had to come to terms with the philological basis of his criticism. The same was true of the term "sacramentum" itself, which was the usual rendering in Latin of the Greek "μυστήριον," although sometimes "mysterium" was used instead. Valla urged that "sacramentum" be changed to "mysterium" in a number of passages, but declined to enter into a "dispute" about whether the two terms were always identical. The most crucial translation of "μυστήριον" as "sacramentum" in the Latin Bible was probably the passage: "'For this reason a man shall leave his father and his mother and shall cling to his wife, and the two shall be in one flesh.' This is a great sacrament; I am, moreover, speaking in Christ and in the church." But if the Vulgate's use of "sacramentum" was philologically indefensible here, that raised grave questions

See p. 295 above

about the sacramentality of marriage, for which this was a decisive proof text.

Fraught as it was with all of these implications for the validity and continuity of Catholic mariological and sacramental doctrine, and of other doctrines at issue with the Reformers, the question of the authority of the Vulgate was one that Luther's opponents, too, had to face. Although there may have been some who believed "that faith is in danger if one or another error" could be pointed out in the Vulgate, it was necessary to consult "the experts in the languages, and not only in the languages, but in all the other disciplines," to determine just how reliable it was as a translation. The Reformers, meanwhile, were appealing to the original languages in their polemics against Roman Catholicism and in their conflicts with the Radicals, accusing both these parties of ignorance. So it was that the Vulgate became part of the business of the Council of Trent.

A catalogue of "abuses" connected with the use of Scripture that wanted correcting listed the existence of variants and discrepancies in the manuscripts of the Latin Bible, for which "the remedy is to have only a single edition, ancient and commonly accepted [veterem scilicet et vulgatam]," whose authority everyone would have to accept. According to Bishop Bertano, the Latin Vulgate had been accepted as the "ancient" and "authoritative" version, but he added later that this should not be taken to imply the rejection of, for example, the Septuagint. In the form that the question took when put up for debate, it included the phrase, "one edition, ancient and commonly accepted [veterem et vulgatam] in each language, namely, Greek, Hebrew, and Latin," which seems to suggest that the Latin word "vulgata" did not refer only to the Latin version of that name. But several of the council fathers objected to the mentioning of the other languages, and the decree eventually adopted by the council on 8 April 1546 declared "that of all the Latin editions of the sacred books," it should be the Vulgate, "this specific ancient and commonly accepted version [haec ipsa vetus et vulgata editio]," that was to be authoritative for both liturgical and theological uses; and "no one may dare or presume, under any pretext

Ambr. Cath. *Clav.* 1 (1543:44–56)

Las. *Inc.* (Kuyper 1:8)

Mass. *Diar. III.* 1.iii. 1546 (*CT* 1:500–501)

ap. CTrid. *Act.* 17.iii. 1546 (*CT* 5:29)

Bert. ap. CTrid. *Act.* 23.iii. 1546 (*CT* 5:37)

Bert. ap. CTrid. *Act.* 1.iv. 1546 (*CT* 5:50)

ap. CTrid. *Act.* 3.iv. 1546 (*CT* 5:66)

CTrid.Sess.4.*Decr*.2 (Alberigo-Jedin 664)

Pach.ap.CTrid.*Act*.10.xii.1546 (*CT* 5:696)

whatever, to reject it." At a later session, when a draft decree on justification quoted the Septuagint, it was urged that this be replaced by the Vulgate, "which we are to follow, according to the decree of the synod."

Among the other questions raised by the sacred philology of Christian humanism, the questions of "apostolic" authorship addressed some of the most important challenges to the authority of revelation. The Epistle to the Hebrews was an especially problematical case. Although there had been many in the early centuries who had been willing to attribute it to

Eus.*H.e*.3.38.2 (*GCS* 9:284)

Eus.*H.e*.3.3.5;6.20.3 (*GCS* 9:190;566)
ap.Eus.*H.e*.6.25.14 (*GCS* 9:580)

Eras.*Adnot*.Heb.13:24 (*LB* 6:1023–24)

Paul, there were also some, especially it seems within the church at Rome, who continued to question his authorship; Origen had concluded that "only God knows" the author. Erasmus in his *Annotations* had reopened the question, but had followed the lead of Jerome in being willing to call it Pauline. Luther, on the other hand, concluded that it was not an epistle

Luth.*Vor.N.T.* (*WA DB* 7:632)

of Paul, but he had high praise for it and kept it in the New Testament. On the Roman Catholic side, Cajetan also doubted the Pauline authorship of the book. During the debates at Trent, Erasmus, Luther,

Castr.*Ep.Hebr.* (*CT* 12:497–506)
Serip.*Libr.Scrip*.2 (*CT* 12:493–96)

and Cajetan all came in for criticism from Alphonsus de Castro, and Seripando likewise addressed himself to their views in his discourse on the canon. The decree of the council on the canon explicitly listed Hebrews as one of "the fourteen epistles of Paul the

CTrid.Sess.4.*Decr*.1 (Alberigo-Jedin 664)

apostle," and that continued to be the official position of the Pontifical Biblical Commission into the twentieth century.

The authorship of patristic writings did not call forth so official and explicit a declaration by an official

See vol.3:86

organ of the church, but, as in previous periods, it did play a significant part in the challenge to conti-

See vol.1:344–49

nuity. Because of its all-but-apostolic authority as well as because of its success at holding together a speculative mysticism and a loyalty to the hierarchy of the

See vol.3:293–94

church, the corpus of writings attributed to Dionysius the Areopagite, putative first bishop of Athens (and then of Paris), figured prominently in the discussions.

Vall.*Annot*.Acts 17:34 (*MPPR* 5:652);Vall.*Enc.Thos. Aq.* (*MPPR* 6:351)
Ambr.Cath.*Excus.disp*.3 (1521:37r)
Luth.*Capt.Bab.* (*WA* 6:562);
Calv.*Inv.rel.* (*CR* 34:444)

Valla had raised doubts about those writings during the fifteenth century, but now they had to be defended also against Luther's accusations, in which the other Reformers joined. Although Dionysius the Areopa-

Dried.*Eccl.scrip*.4 (1533:493)

Herb.*Enchir*.13 (*CCath* 12:57)
Grop.*Leyb*.1 (1556:42r);Grop.
*Antididag*.1 (1547:17v–18r)
Clicht.*Eluc.eccl*.ep.ded.;4
(1517:B2v;221r–221v);Wic.
*Hag*. (1541:215r)

Wic.*Pus*. (1534:B2v;A4v);Fish.
*Confut*.8 (1523:201);Diet.
*Phim*.8 (1532:Z1r)
Coch.*Patr.parv*.1.2 (*CT* 12:
169–70)

See pp. 178,265 above
See vol.1:346
Wic.*Cat.eccl*.13;17 (1535:Y2v;
Bb1v)

Pg.*Cont*.11 (1541–II:18r)

Grop.*Leyb*.1 (1556:43r–49r)
Clicht.*Hom*.18 (1535:164–65);
Clicht.*Oec*.1.3 (1526:12v)
Wic.*Euch*.2;3;8 (1534:C4r;
D2v;H4r)
Cons.ap.CTrid.*Act*.18.ii.1547
(*CT* 5:913)

Lomb.ap.CTrid.*Act*.11.ii.1547
(*CT* 5:913)

Coch.*Luth.art*.2 (*CCath* 18:
19);Wic.*Luth.art*. (*CCath* 18:
70–71)

Las.*Hos*.2.5 (Kuyper 1:427)

See pp.20–21 above

Trinkaus (1970) 2:741

Calv.*Inst*.(1559)2.2.4 (Barth-
Niesel 3:244–47)

Zw.*Pecc.orig*. (*CR* 92:379–80)

gite did not appear in Jerome's *Lives of Illustrious Men*, he did belong to the list of those "whom the church has approved" as church fathers. He deserved to be called an "apostolic father" (like Clement of Rome or Ignatius of Antioch) and to be held in great veneration. Because there was "no ecclesiastical writer before him except the apostles themselves," Dionysius provided important proof for the continuity of Catholic penitential practice with that of the apostolic era. He performed the same function for infant baptism, whose apostolicity Luther and Calvin were also defending against the Anabaptists. His designation of anointing as an act of "making perfect" documented its antiquity, and he was a witness for the use of chrism in ordination. His comprehensive doctrine of the Eucharist—as "communion," as a memorial and a sacrifice of thanksgiving offered by the priest, and as a proper object of adoration—made him a valuable authority for the continuity in the Catholic understanding of that sacrament since the end of the first century. And as "a disciple of Paul," he demonstrated that the doctrine of purgatory had been present in the Catholic Church since ancient times. Conversely, the philological questions being raised by Christian humanism about the true provenance of the Dionysian corpus represented yet another challenge to the claims of apostolic continuity as an unbroken chain of orthodox doctrine handed down through the fathers.

There was one other challenge to the authority of the apostolic revelation with which the Christian humanists of the fifteenth and sixteenth centuries had to deal, even though, like many of the questions being discussed in this chapter, it was not to move to the center of the church's attention until the eighteenth century. That was the issue of the uniqueness and the finality of Christian revelation itself. The concern of the humanists "to show how . . . the Gentile philosophers . . . were able to come at all close to the insights that mankind received by the manifestation of Christ" inevitably aroused the accusation that they were questioning the uniqueness of the biblical message. Similarly, Zwingli's belief that the promise of salvation extended not only to Christian and Old Testament believers, but to noble pagans, confirmed Luther's suspicion that Zwingli had himself become a heathen. Nevertheless, the most fundamental consideration of the issue of uniqueness and finality by a Christian humanist and church theologian had been composed almost a century earlier by Nicholas of Cusa, in reaction to the conquest of Constantinople by Islamic invaders in 1453. While lamenting the catastrophe "with many sighs," Nicholas took the fall of New Rome as an occasion to reflect on the finality and authority of Christian revelation, in a treatise entitled *Reconciliation between the World Religions [De pace fidei],* in which his doctrine of "catholic concordance" found its counterpart in a quest for "the concord of religions."

There had, according to Cusanus, never been a nation that did not worship God and did not acknowledge him as absolute; but the difference between the true and the false worship of God lay in this, that true worship knew God to be ineffable and transcendent while false worship confused God with his works. The various world religions used various names for the one who was beyond all naming and beyond all knowing. For "the names that are attributed to God are derived from creatures, although he is ineffable in himself and transcends all that can be named or spoken." There was, then, only one religion within and behind the variety in forms of worship among the world religions. It was the purpose of this apologetic to prove that "Christ is the one who is presupposed by all who hope to achieve final happiness," regardless of whether they used the name "Christ" or not. In this sense there was already "one faith that is common to all who are living, a faith in the one almighty God and in the Holy Trinity." Having learned from Dionysius the Areopagite that "the trinitary and the unitary divine name" referred to a Deity "above names," he addressed to Muslims an interpretation of the dogma of the Trinity that was intended to be consistent with their monotheism, and he gave a sympathetic interpretation to pagan efforts to go beyond the polytheism of the Olympian gods to the one true God. All those who theologized or philosophized, whatever their terminology, were aiming for this one truth. Thus "all men, as creatures of one single Creator, are

---

Luth. *Wort.* (WA 23:69)

Nicol. Cus. *Pac.fid.* 1
(Heidelberg 7:3)

See pp. 98–110 above

Nicol. Cus. *Doct.ign.* 1.7
(Heidelberg 1:14)

Nicol. Cus. *Abscond.*
(Heidelberg 4:6)
Nicol. Cus. *Pac.fid.* 1
(Heidelberg 7:6); Nicol. Cus.
*Serm.* 1.1 (Heidelberg 16:4)

Nicol. Cus. *Pac.fid.* 7
(Heidelberg 7:20–21)

Nicol. Cus. *Pac.fid.* 1
(Heidelberg 7:7)

Nicol. Cus. *Pac.fid.* 13
(Heidelberg 7:41)

Nicol. Cus. *Serm.* 2.1
(Heidelberg 16:25–26)

See vol. 1:347–48
Dion. Ar. *D.n.* 13.3 (*PG* 3:980–81)

Nicol. Cus. *Alcor.* 2.3 (Faber 1:134v)

Nicol. Cus. *Dat.patr.lum.* 1
(Heidelberg 4:70–71); Nicol.
Cus. *Pac.fid.* 6 (Heidelberg 7:16)

Nicol. Cus. *Fil.* 5 (Heidelberg 4:59)

Nicol.Cus.*Serm.*4.1
(Heidelberg 16:62–63)

concordant in their nature, and therefore also in the worship of God." While such a daring effort by a Christian humanist to formulate a "trinitarian universalism" may have made sense in a church where the authority of revelation, the divine institution of the ecclesiastical structure, and the correctness of the orthodox dogma of the Trinity were presuppositions that were still being affirmed by everyone, or almost everyone, all of that would change when each of these components of apostolic continuity came under increasing challenge, first from the Radicals of the Reformation and eventually from the thinkers of the eighteenth century, including the theologians among them. One of these, Gotthold Ephraim Lessing, was both the rediscoverer of *Reconciliation between the World Religions* and the author of *Nathan the Wise*, one of the most eloquent and subtle pleas for such "reconciliation" in the eighteenth or in any other century.

## Spirit versus Structure

See p. 175 above

Luther's indifference to the traditional issues of church structure, which to his critics on many sides seemed cavalier, helped to make it possible for his followers to accommodate themselves to systems of ecclesiastical organization ranging from state church to free church and from a retention of the historic episcopate to (at least theoretical) congregationalism, with doctrine rather than polity as the decisive principle separating them from all others. On the other hand, as an eminent Calvin scholar has put it, "more than Luther, Zwingli, or Cranmer, Calvin was a high churchman, if by that term is meant one who reveres the Church as the one divine institution endowed with, and testifying to, the grace of Christ. He has a correspondingly high doctrine of the ministry and its

McNeill (1954) 216–17

authority." The presbyterian form of church government which many (though by no means all) Reformed churches eventually adopted was the embodiment of what appears to have been Calvin's own view of the

Calv.*Inst.*(1559)4.4.10 (Barth-Niesel 5:67–68)
Calv.*Ord.eccl.* (Barth-Niesel 2: 329)

structure closest to the New Testament pattern; but this was not a normative doctrinal question for him, although it became one for some of his followers, especially during the seventeenth century.

Clasen (1972) 30

See pp. 272–73 above

Bender (1950) 210

Hub.*Str.* (*QFRG* 29:340)
Dnk.*Mic.*3:1–3 (*QFRG* 24–III:55)
Menn.*Chr.gl.* (Herrison 86)
Ob.Phil.*Bek.*pr. (*BRN* 7:110);
Menn.*Gell.Fab.*2 (Herrison 261–62)

Friedman (1967) 49

Dnk.*Wid.*pr. (*QFRG* 24–II:105)

Williams (1957) 31

Hub.*Tf.*2 (*QFRG* 29:127);
Menn.*Fund.*3 (Meihuizen 25)

Menn.*Bek.* (Herrison 463)

Nevertheless, it was neither Luther nor Calvin nor even the Anglican Reformers, but the Radicals lumped together by their opponents as "the 'marvelous and manifold divisions and bands' of Anabaptists," who put forward, as the fundamental issue of their own version of "Reformation as re-formation," the challenge to the supposed apostolic structure of the church and the substitution for it of a restored form of truly apostolic church life. As its Roman Catholic opponents were constantly pointing out, the entire Reformation was capable of pitting Spirit against structure; but because "that which the Reformation actually originally intended they aimed to accomplish," the Anabaptists made this antithesis constitutive. All the Protestant parties claimed to be "Christians and good Evangelicals," but meanwhile each was "persecuting the other," and the genuine meaning of "Evangelical" was lost. The Anabaptists conceded that they themselves were divided into many "sects." They were, moreover, reluctant to issue "writings of dogmatic content": their most moving documents were saints' lives and accounts of martyrdom, not creeds or systematic theologies. Nevertheless, they did undertake, often under persecution, to expose their deepest convictions "in the form of articles, as far as this is possible." As a group they did so above all in the seven articles of the *Schleitheim Confession* of 1527, which "more succinctly than any other document sum up the distinctive convictions of Evangelical Anabaptism." In the next generation several individual theologians actually wrote full-length books of doctrine, most notably Menno Simons himself in the second and definitive edition of *The Foundation of Christian Doctrine* (1558), Dirk Philipsz in an *Enchiridion* (1564), and Peter Walpot in *The Book of Articles* (1577). From these sources, when combined with many of their more topical statements of faith, it is possible to identify their distinctive understanding of what a truly apostolic Reformation entailed.

Many of the accents familiar from the language of the other Reformers are audible here as well: the definition of the gospel as the forgiveness of sins; the repetition of the refrain "by grace alone" as the heart of the Christian message; the declaration that one's

Dnk.*Bös.* (*QFRG* 24–II:32)

Hub.*Tf.*4 (*QFRG* 29:144–45)

ap.*Disp.Zof.*3 (1532:27v)
Greb.*Prot.* (*CR* 90:368–69);ap.
Zw.*Hub.*1 (*CR* 91:604);ap.
*Disp.Zof.*11 (1532:135r)
Calv.*Hes.* (*CR* 37:487);Rdly.
Br.*decl.* (Moule 107–8)

See pp. 191–93 above
Hub.*Str.* (*QFRG* 29:346);Hub.
*Gespr.Zw.*4 (*QFRG* 29:202);
Menn.*Fund.*5 (Meihuizen 45)

Flac.*Clar.not.*39 (1549:E6v–
E7r);Las.*Hos.*2.5 (Kuyper 1:
426)

*Succ.Anab.*1;18 (*BRN* 7:22;68)

Luth.*Schmal.Art.*3.8 (*Bek.*
454);Calv.*Sad.* (Barth-Niesel 1:
465)

ap.*Disp.Zof.*2 (1532:15r)

Menn.*Bek.*6 (Herrison 469)
Walp.*Art.*2.132 (*QFRG* 34:
165)

Menn.*Doop.* (Herrison 405);
Menn.*Nw.Geb.* (Herrison 126)

See p. 263 above

Hub.*Urt.*1.pr.;2.pr. (*QFRG*
29:228;242);Hub.*Ax.*16
(*QFRG* 29:89)

Zw.*Tf.* (*CR* 91:318–24);*Conf.*
*Mans.*1.1 (Schlüsselburg 12:71)
Hub.*Gespr.Zw.*5 (*QFRG* 29:
207)
Aug.*Bapt.*4.24.31 (*CSEL* 51:
259)
Menn.*Gell.Fab.*3.7 (Herrison
271);Menn.*Doop.* (Herrison
408;428);Menn.*Fund.*6
(Meihuizen 70–71)
Menn.*Oors.* (Herrison 450);
Menn.*Doop.* (Herrison 414–
15);Menn.*Fund.*5 (Meihuizen
39)

faith determined what kind of salvation one would have; the exaltation of the word, will, and commandment of God as supreme over all human words, including those of the church in its traditions. This made their separation from the other Reformers all the more poignant. Thus the Reformed spokesmen at the Reformed-Anabaptist disputation in Zofingen (near Bern) agreed that they were "one in the chief points of the articles of faith" and differed on "externals." But the Anabaptists insisted on enforcing the sole authority of Scripture even more consistently and on implementing the Reformed parallelism of the two sacraments by applying to baptism the same definition of "sign" that Zwingli had applied to the Lord's Supper (and in his early thought also to baptism). In spite of being "one," therefore, the two parties could not be united. Roman Catholic polemics, despite the preponderance of Protestant over Roman Catholic theologians in the ranks of the conflict against the Anabaptists, went on tracing the origins of Anabaptism to Luther, but Luther and Calvin both charged that the pope and the Anabaptists were essentially alike in their subjectivism, while the Anabaptists for their part charged that there was no difference between "the papists and the Lutherans" and that "the Lord's Supper of the preachers" in the established churches, whether Reformed or Roman Catholic, was "false" and "perverted."

What had perverted the sacraments and the church, among "Evangelicals" no less than among "papists," was an apostasy from "the pure and chaste doctrine of the holy apostles." Augustine's classic statement about the gospel and the church had to be inverted to read: "If I did not believe the gospel, I would never believe the church, since the church is built on the gospel and not the gospel on the church." Augustine, from whom Protestants derived their claim to "apostolic authority" for infant baptism, should have heeded this himself when he presumed to ascribe such authority to whatever was "held by the entire church"; the same was true of Origen and of many other church fathers. Truly "apostolic" was whatever was laid down in "the teaching of Jesus Christ and of the apostles," regardless of "all the doctors and learned men" who

Menn.*Doop.* (Herrison 420);
Hub.*Erb.*3 (*QFRG* 29:81)
Drk.Phil.*Enchir.*4 (*BRN* 10:
95);Hub.*Gespr.Zw.*1 (*QFRG*
29:180)
Hub.*Ketz.*30 (*QFRG* 29:99–
100)

Matt.15:9
Menn.*Nw.Geb.* (Herrison 125)

Ob.Phil.*Bek.* (*BRN* 7:121)

Hub.*Bn.* (*QFRG* 29:369);
Hub.*Gespr.Zw.*pr. (*QFRG* 29:
172)

Menn.*Nw.Geb.* (Herrison 124)

Frnk.*Br.* (Rembert 219)

Hub.*Erb.*3 (*QFRG* 29:81)

Menn.*Doop.*pr. (Herrison 398)
Luke 12:32
Eph.2:20
Menn.*Fund.*7 (Meihuizen 77–
78);Menn.*Doop.*pr. (Herrison
399–400)

See pp. 271–72 above

Succ.*Anab.*conc. (*BRN* 7:78)

Dnk.*Bös.* (*QFRG* 24–II:42)

Menn.*Sup.* (Herrison 329)

Menn.*Ps.25:*22 (Herrison 176)

Menn.*Ps.25:*19 (Herrison 174)

Menn.*Doop.* (Herrison 415)

Dnk.*Wid.*7 (*QFRG* 24–II:108);
Dnk.*Ges.* (*QFRG* 24–II:54)
Hub.*Schl.*7 (*QFRG* 29:73);
Hub.*Lr.*2 (*QFRG* 29:320)

Sib.*Art.*5 (Böhmer 31);Drk.
Phil.*Enchir.*5 (*BRN* 10:205–
48);Menn.*Fund.*10 (Meihuizen
107–16)

Menn.*Bek.*2 (Herrison 464–
67);Menn.*Las.*2 (Herrison 534)

might have taught otherwise "ever since the time of the apostles." Despite the supposed authority of these "many hundreds of years," it was necessary to identify "the natural light" of human reason, not the word of God, as the source of such tradition, which therefore fell under the censure of Christ's denunciation of "the commandments of men." Therefore the church, "the true church of Christ and of the apostles," together with all the sacraments, had been "lost for a long time." So had all the articles of true apostolic doctrine. One of the Radicals went so far as to declare: "I believe that the outward church of Christ, including all its gifts and sacraments, because of the breaking in and laying waste of Antichrist right after the death of the apostles, went up into heaven and lies concealed in the Spirit and in truth. I am thus quite certain that for fourteen hundred years now there has existed no gathered church nor any sacrament." The culprit was the tradition of church fathers and councils, of ancient customs and usages, of canon lawyers and scholastic theologians.

"Against the majority of the doctors or scholars" of Christian history they pitted the only authentic "doctors of the community or congregation of Christ," the apostles. The true church was a "little flock" and had always been in the minority; but because it was "built on the foundation of the apostles and prophets," it was "a pure and clean gathering, a holy church." In opposition to such notions of a "hidden" and holy church, Roman Catholic polemics asserted the apostolic succession of bishops, but this defense of "Christendom so-called," which was a church "only in name," manifested the contrast between the realm of "Antichrist" and the "apostolic church," which was "the true Christian church." From the time of the apostles the church had "gradually degenerated" into a reliance on "outward works," of which ecclesiastical "ceremonies" were the ones on which men came to rely the most and "images" the ones that most blatantly manifested their idolatry. Rather than "apostolic succession," it was "apostolic mission [sendinge]" that was at issue between the Anabaptists and their opponents: to be "apostolic" was to be "sent," as the apostles and Christ himself had been "sent." This was

Succ.*Anab*.14 (*BRN* 7:54)

Rom.10:15

Zw.*Tf.* (*CR* 91:304);ap.*Disp. Zof.*2 (1532:13r)

Menn.*Gell.Fab.2* (Herrison 240)

Drk.Phil.*Enchir.*5 (*BRN* 10: 209–11)
Menn.*Oors.* (Herrison 441)

Ob.Phil.*Bek.* (*BRN* 7:125)

Hub.*Tf.* (*QFRG* 29:134)

Hub.*Bn.* (*QFRG* 29:370)
Menn.*Doop.* (Herrison 411);
Menn.*Chr.gl.* (Herrison 78)
Calv.*Anab.2* (*CR* 35:66);Calv.
*Rom.*7:25 (Parker 155);Zw.*Tf.*
pr. (*CR* 91:206–9);Zw.*Hub.*1
(*CR* 91:591)
Hub.*Gespr.Zw.*1 (*QFRG* 29:
175);Menn.*Las.*2 (Herrison
538)
Rdly.*Conf.Ltmr.*2.3 (*PS* 39:
120)
Luth.*Wied.* (*WA* 26:144–74);
*Conf Mans.*int. (Schlüsselburg
12:70);Ec.*Ev.*Trin.1 (1530–II:
84v)

Sib.*Art.*1 (Böhmer 29)

Hub.*Tf.* (*QFRG* 29:153)
Drk.Phil.*Enchir.*1 (*BRN* 10:
81);Menn.*Nw.Geb.* (Herrison
125–26)
Menn.*Fund.*5 (Meihuizen 36–
57)

Menn.*Doop.* (Herrison 425–
33)

Hub.*Gespr.Zw.*2 (*QFRG* 29:
182);Hub.*Lr.*1 (*QFRG* 29:
313);Drk.Phil.*Enchir.*1 (*BRN*
10:69)

Col.2:11–13
Las.*Sacr.* (Kuyper 1:173–79);
Zw.*Gen.*17:10 (*CR* 100:106)

Hub.*Gespr.Zw.*1 (*QFRG* 29:
175;179–80)
Dnk.*Bek.*2 (*QFRG* 24–II:23)

a response to the accusation that although no one was to preach without being "sent," the Anabaptists were only invading churches where the word of God had already been preached. Still there was this difference: the apostles had been called "without specific human means," while ministers now were ordinarily called through means, that is, "by God and by his congregations"—but not by secular rulers. Yet sometimes it might happen that an authentic Anabaptist minister might be "sent and called . . . by his own inspiration." Despite the difference, the threefold content of the "mission" was the same: "preaching," "faith," and "external baptism." The true church, "gathered in the Spirit," had to be separate from the "carnal church," which was a "sect." That separation, which Calvin and others took to be based on the Anabaptists' presumption of moral perfection about their church (a charge that Anabaptist theologians vehemently rejected), was in many ways the fundamental point of difference.

Yet the point of difference most often remarked by various opponents was, as the name "Anabaptist" indicates, the practice of baptizing those who had already been baptized as infants in the other churches. The *Schleitheim Confession* identified infant baptism as "the highest and chief abomination of the pope" as well as of the Protestant churches. With all their boasts of apostolic continuity, the defenders of infant baptism could not document a continuity for this practice. The true "apostolic church" followed Christ's command and baptized only believing adults. Menno called the fifth chapter of his *Foundation* "Apostolic Baptism" and devoted the final chapter of his *Christian Baptism* to the topic "How the Holy Apostles Practiced Baptism in Water," namely, by restricting it to those who had first come to faith through the word of God. "Inward baptism" by the Holy Spirit was to precede "outward baptism" with water. The parallel between circumcision and baptism, which was being used to support infant baptism, did not refer to "outward baptism" at all, but to "inward baptism." Because man was "by nature unclean in body and soul," outward baptism by itself was useless. Thus the age-old mutual dependence between the doctrine of orig-

See vol.1:290–92;316–18

Hub.*Rech*.12 (*QFRG* 29:473)
Hub.*Will*.1.pr. (*QFRG* 29:
381);Hub.*Rech*.6–7 (*QFRG*
29:466–69)

Hub.*Kind*.1 (*QFRG* 29:263)
Acts 2:38(Vulg.)

See vol.1:291

Luth.*Kl.Kat*.4.6 (*Bek*.515)
Hub.*Tf*.4 (*QFRG* 29:137)

Hub.*Tf*.6 (*QFRG* 29:155);
Hub.*Gespr.Zw*.4 (*QFRG* 29:
201)

Menn.*Doop*. (Herrison 429)

Menn.*Fund*.6 (Meihuizen 63)

Menn.*Doop*. (Herrison 404)
*Cat.Heid*.74 (Niesel 166);
Blngr.*Sum*.8.5 (1556:146r)

Matt.28:19–20

Drk.Phil.*Enchir*.1 (*BRN* 10:70)
Hub.*Tf*.3 (*QFRG* 29:128);
Hub.*Lr*.pr. (*QFRG* 29:307);
Hub.*Gespr.Zw*.2 (*QFRG* 29:
184)

Hub.*Form.Tf*. (*QFRG* 29:352)

Hub.*Bn*. (*QFRG* 29:375)

Hub.*Str*. (*QFRG* 29:345)

See pp. 215–16 above

Hub.*Lr*.1 (*QFRG* 29:316–17)

Hub.*Form.Tf*. (*QFRG* 29:350)

*Sib.Art*.1–3 (Böhmer 28–30)
Menn.*Gell.Fab*.5.9 (Herrison
294)
Menn.*Excom*.1;2.1 (Herrison
339;473)

inal sin and the practice of infant baptism was broken: Hubmaier attacked Zwingli for underestimating the power of original sin and attacked Luther for underestimating the power of free will; but he attacked both of them, and the entire tradition with them, for teaching that a baptism administered involuntarily to infants was the cure for original sin. The biblical terminology about baptism "for the remission of sins," which had, in conjunction with the practice of infant baptism, helped to establish original sin as a doctrine, did not mean that, in Luther's words, "baptism effects forgiveness of sins," but that baptism bore testimony to "the inward yes in the heart," which did effect it. As for the fate of children who died before being able to give that "inward yes," Hubmaier confessed: "I can neither pronounce [them] saved, nor can I damn them. I leave all of that to the judgment of God." Menno felt able to be more specific and more hopeful, affirming that children did have the promise of eternal life and did have a share in the covenant, but denying that this participation in the covenant was a ground for baptizing them, as for example the *Heidelberg Catechism* contended.

In his "ordinance and institution of Christian baptism" Christ had prescribed the order to be followed for apostolic baptism: first the word, then hearing, then change of life, and only then baptism. After baptism there followed the continuing discipline of the church. Hubmaier used the word "sacrament" to refer to "the baptismal vow [Tauffglübd]" rather than to the rite, and a "violator of the sacrament" was someone who broke this vow; it was from this that the power and the duty of church discipline proceeded. Reformed ecclesiology, by contrast with Lutheran, had eventually elevated discipline to the status of a mark of the church, alongside the word and the sacraments; but Anabaptist ecclesiology went significantly further, inserting discipline into the text of the Apostles' Creed and assigning to it a quasi-sacramental function. The first three articles of the *Schleitheim Confession* were: "Baptism"; "The Ban"; "Breaking of Bread." The Protestant churches, filled with worldly people, admitted that excommunication was an "apostolic" imperative, but would not practice it. Yet

Hub.*Str.* (QFRG 29:339)

Matt.18:15–18

without it baptism and the Lord's Supper were "vain, useless, and without fruit." The passage in the Gospels prescribing the process of excommunication was, to the Anabaptists, proof that sinners were to be excluded from the church; to their Reformed opponents, it was proof also that there would always be sinners in the church. This passage set forth what Anabaptists regarded as the steps of the process, from private admonition to public exclusion and "shunning." It was essential to remember, however, that those whom the church banned by this process had in fact excommunicated themselves, and that so solemn a condemnation was to be reserved for truly grave offenses, "not for [stealing] six shillings' worth of hazelnuts."

ap.*Disp.Zof.*3 (1532:28r–36r)

Hub.*Str.* (QFRG 29:341–42);
Hub.*Bn.* (QFRG 29:372);
Hub.*Rech.*23 (QFRG 29:485–86)

Menn.*Verm.* (Herrison 634)

Hub.*Lr.*1 (QFRG 29:317);
Hub.*Bn.* (QFRG 29:376)

Excommunication and church discipline had to be such a serious matter because Christian "discipleship [Nachfolge]" was serious business. What a modern editor has called "Hans Denck's motto" stated: "No one can truly know [Christ] unless he follows [nachvolge] Him in his life. And no one can follow Him except insofar as he knows Him first." There could not be genuine baptism until after repentance and such discipleship had become a reality. That was "the way of the cross." Christ's summons, "Follow me," served as the axiomatic answer to the question of authorization for the "mission" of the Anabaptists and as evidence that "all Scripture points to the necessity of separation from the world and of 'participation in the divine nature.'" The theme of participation in the nature of God recurred in the writings of the Anabaptists as a way of setting their view of salvation apart from that of the Protestant churches. The corollary of "discipleship [Nachfolge]" was "passivity [Gelassenheit]." Peter Walpot entitled the third of his five articles of faith: "True Passivity and the Christian Community of Goods." For all Christians were "in some measure like Christ" through their willingness to surrender themselves in self-sacrifice. Therefore the "sword," which was the topic of the sixth article of the *Schleitheim Confession,* was not proper for Christians to wield, any more than it had been for Christ in the Garden of Gethsemane. The bitter lesson of the debacle of "Christian revolution" at Münster in

Fellmann (1955) 2:45

Dnk.*Bös.* (QFRG 24–II:45)

ap.*Disp.Zof.*11 (1532:132v)

Menn.*Ps.25:13* (Herrison 170)

Matt.9:9

ap.*Disp.Zof.*2 (1532:15v)

2 Pet.1:4

See p. 255 above

Menn.*Geest.Ver.* (Herrison 182);Dnk.*Bös.* (QFRG 24–II:39)

Walp.*Art.*3 (QFRG 34:175–238)

Dnk.*Bös.* (QFRG 24–II:37)

Sib.*Art.*6 (Böhmer 31–33)
Menn.*Jan.Leyd.* (Herrison 628)

Matt.26:51–52

Menn.Ont.1 (Herrison 487–98)
Menn.Jan.Leyd. (Herrison 629)

Hub.Rech.1 (QFRG 29:461–62)
Dnk.Ord.8 (QFRG 24–II:97);
Dnk.Wid.3 (QFRG 24–II:107)

Menn.Chr.gl. (Herrison 78)
Sib.Art.7 (Böhmer 33)

Matt.5:34
Sib.Art.6 (Böhmer 32);Dnk.
Lieb. (QFRG 24–II:85)
Rom.13:4

Dnk.Bös. (QFRG 24–II:30)

Hub.Tf.pr. (QFRG 29:120)

Dnk.Mic.3:5–7 (QFRG 24–III:58)

Dnk.Ges. (QFRG 24–II:59)

Dnk.Wid.1 (QFRG 24–II:106)

Bainton (1937) 46

1535 had taught the Anabaptists that Christ himself, not his followers, would destroy his enemies. This "passivity" did not imply, as the Lutheran Reformers seemed to be saying, that a mere passive faith was sufficient. For faith meant "being obedient to the word of God," and Luther was wrong in condemning the Epistle of James. Concretely, the twin imperatives of discipleship and passivity required that Christians, in obedience to Christ's explicit command, "swear not at all" and take no oaths, moreover that they not serve as magistrates in the government, since that would require them to "bear the sword": they were to be obedient to the government, to the point of martyrdom, but they were not to exercise government or wage war.

Yet "passivity" was a principle not only of Christian morality but of theology and even of hermeneutics: "Every saying of God [in Scripture] must be heard" by each "in accordance with the measure of his passivity [Gelassenheit]." The best way to interpret Scripture was not necessarily through a scholarly understanding of Hebrew and Greek. It was, above all, the radical Anabaptist Hans Denck who pushed the antithesis of Spirit versus structure to the point of setting the Spirit into antithesis also with "the false, literal understanding of Scripture." Anyone who did not have the Spirit but sought to understand Scripture, he insisted, would find darkness rather than light, not alone in the Old Testament but also in the New; conversely, "anyone who genuinely has the truth can take account of it without any Scripture." Distinguishing between Scripture and the word of God, he declared that while he valued "Holy Scripture above all human treasures," it was still inferior to "the word of God, which is living, powerful, and eternal"; for the word of God was God himself, Spirit and not letter, "written without pen and paper." "Salvation," he concluded, "is not bound to Scripture." Such a radicalization of the antithesis between Spirit and structure was a hermeneutical principle that by no means all Anabaptists shared—since, for example, "Menno was a biblical literalist" in some ways—but it did give dramatic expression to their willingness to defy tradition in the name of the word of God and the power of the Spirit, even if the content of that tradition were the letter of Scripture itself.

Yet if it was good and proper, in the name of the authentic "apostolic church," to oppose all the structures of continuity by which the church for more than a millennium had been identifying itself as "apostolic," namely, the "apostolic succession" of the episcopate and ultimately the "apostolic tradition" of infant baptism itself, what was to prevent such opposition from attacking, in the name of the authentic "apostolic church," the very dogmas of the Councils of Nicea and Chalcedon, the "apostolic doctrine" by which the church for more than a millennium had been identifying itself as orthodox? The opponents of the Anabaptists among the more traditional Protestants, and the opponents of the more traditional Protestants among the Roman Catholics, had suspected all along that this would be the inevitable outcome of such a theological method. In refutation of such calumnies, Balthasar Hubmaier referred to "the confession of the foundation of the universal Christian church [gemainer Cristenlichen kirchen]" about Christ, meaning presumably the Nicene and Chalcedonian confessions, and Dirk Philipsz even taught the doctrine of "Filioque." Menno Simons could propound an orthodox summary of the doctrines of the person and the work of Christ, and he opposed Zwinglian Christology on the grounds that it taught "two Sons in Christ," in some Nestorian fashion. In opposition to this he set an orthodox trinitarian confession and a Christology that he deemed to be orthodox, although it taught that Christ had not taken his flesh from Abraham's seed but had become man "not of the womb [of Mary] but in her womb." Hans Denck, on the other hand, gave to one of the chapters of a doctrinal statement the title "On the Trinity, the Unity, and the Single Threeness of God," but then said nothing about the Trinity in the chapter itself. If Scripture alone was to decide what was authentically apostolic, and if the church had fallen away from the apostolic norm when it allied itself with the secular arm in the person of the emperor Constantine, it was difficult to avoid the conclusion that the Nicene Creed, adopted by a church council over which Constantine presided,

Hub.*Rech*.11 (*QFRG* 29:472)

Drk.Phil.*Enchir*.1 (*BRN* 10:63)

Menn.*Ps.25*:19 (Herrison 174)

Menn.*Chr.gl.* (Herrison 79–80)

Menn.*Belyd.* (Herrison 387–91)

Menn.*Las*.1 (Herrison 528–29)

Menn.*Las*.1 (Herrison 531)

Dnk.*Ord*.10 (*QFRG* 24–II:99–100)

See vol.1:202

Gr.Paw.Roz.ter. (BPP B-2:97);
Soc.Cat.fr. (BFP 1:684)

itself had to be a product of this "fall of the church," engineered by Satan, rather than a valid summary, written in the fourth century and still normative in the sixteenth century, of the apostolic faith proclaimed in the first century.

### Repudiation of Trinitarian Dogma

Luther and Calvin had gone on affirming the orthodox creeds of the ancient church and professing their adherence to the dogmas of the Trinity and of the person of Christ as these had been formulated by, respectively, the Councils of Nicea and Chalcedon.

See p. 177 above

Luther's insistence on the centrality of the gospel, as the message of the salvation given in Jesus Christ, led him to interpret the ancient creeds as "setting forth all that we are to expect and receive from God." Al-

Luth.Dtsch.Kat.2.1 (Bek.646)

though the text of the creeds concentrated on the doctrine of the person of Christ rather than on the doctrine of the work of Christ, giving an account of the relation between the Son and the Father but not so much as referring to justification, Luther transposed the creeds into an exposition of the saving work of Christ and of its application, through justification

See pp. 160–61 above

by faith, to believers now. In the interest of the doctrine of the real presence in the Lord's Supper, moreover, he and his followers developed and elaborated a doctrine of the relation between the two natures in

See pp. 158–60 above

Christ that matched or exceeded, for metaphysical complexity, that of the ancient Alexandrian theolo-

See vol.1:226–77;vol.2:37–90
Calv.Hes. (CR 37:476)

gians. Calvin and his followers denounced this christology as a grotesque betrayal of "sola Scriptura," but Calvin had given the Nicene dogma of the Trinity a more thoroughgoing biblical documentation than it had received since the patristic era. Obviously Calvin saw no inconsistency between his insistence on the sole authority of the word and will of God expressed in Scripture and his defense, against Michael Servetus and George Blandrata, of the orthodox dogma of the

Calv.Trin. (CR 36:457–644)
Calv.Inst.(1536)2 (Barth-Niesel 1:74)
Calv.Inst.(1536)2 (Barth-Niesel 1:75)
Luth.Latom. (WA 7:117)

Trinity, including the nonscriptural "novelty" of its traditional terminology. He had expressed the wish that this terminology could be "buried," as Luther had spoken of "hating the word 'homoousios'"; but the attempt by some defenders of the faith to take such obiter dicta as evidence of antitrinitarian hetero-

Coch. *Phil.* 1.2.6 (1534:C3r–C4v)

doxy could not stand up in the face of the unimpeachable conformity of the Reformation confessions to the creeds of Nicea and Chalcedon.

But the specter raised by the Roman Catholic "domino theory" was the prospect of a more consistent and hence more radical application of the principal of "sola Scriptura"—one that would cut itself loose from the doctrinal tradition in practice, not only in principle, and that would therefore no longer lead to such orthodox dogmatic conclusions—as well as of a doctrine of "justification by faith alone" for which the trinitarian definition of the person of Christ at Nicea and Chalcedon would no longer be necessary.

See pp. 267–68 above

Dav. *Def.* 15.6 (*BFP* 2:737); Górski (1929) 107–37

That specter became a reality in the "war against the Trinity" declared by the Unitarians or antitrinitarians of the Reformation, beginning during the lifetimes of the magisterial Reformers with the tragic figure of Servetus and with Blandrata and continuing a generation or two later with Faustus Socinus and the Socinians, who gave the movement its principal doctrinal exposition in the form of the *Racovian Catechism* (whose original Polish version appeared in 1605 and whose definitive Latin edition was published in 1680) as its official "confession."

Soc. *Conc. Chr.* Matt. 5:16 (*BFP* 1:9–10)

Serv. *Dial.* 1 (*ChristRest* 241); Soc. *Conc. Chr.* Matt. 5:24 (*BFP* 1:16)
Serv. *Dial.* 2 (*ChristRest* 283), Serv. *Trin.* 2 (*ChristRest* 55); Serv. *Fid. just.* 1.2 (*ChristRest* 301)
See pp. 154–55 above

Soc. *Rom.* 7 (*BFP* 1:89)
Soc. *Prol. Ev. Joh.* pr. (*BFP* 1:75)
Gr. Paw. *Roz. ter.* (*BPP* B-2:45–49)

Soc. *Cat.* (*BFP* 1:655); Serv. *Trin. err.* 1.44 (1721:32r)
Serv. *Fid. just.* 3.1 (*ChristRest* 337); Soc. *Serv.* 4.11 (*BFP* 2:237–38)

Gr. Paw. *Praw. smr.* pr. (*BPP* B-3:29)

Soc. *Serv.* 1.2 (*BFP* 2:124)
Serv. *Fid. just.* 1.2 (*ChristRest* 297); Soc. *Serv.* 4.4;4.9 (*BFP* 2:219;230)

Soc. *Serv.* 3.10 (*BFP* 2:211)

These Unitarians set themselves against both Roman Catholicism and Protestantism, rejecting such Roman Catholic ideas as the cult of the saints and purgatory, but objecting no less vehemently to such Protestant ideas as predestination, the bondage of the human will, and Luther's teaching, on the basis of Romans 7, that the justified believer was "righteous and a sinner at the same time." They joined Luther and Calvin in asserting "sola Scriptura," but rejected "essence" and "homoousios" as "a mere human fabrication, which is in no way conformable to Holy Writ." They also joined in teaching the Reformation doctrine of justification by faith alone; yet they dissociated this not only from the orthodox dogmas of the Trinity and the person of Christ, propounded by "the Antichrist" Athanasius, but even from the orthodox doctrine of the atonement: it was faith itself, defined as "trust," that was "imputed," not "the righteousness of Christ," just as in turn there was no "imputation" of man's sin to Christ. And, as if in substantiation of the warnings of the "domino theory" about the consequences of denying the Roman Catholic doctrine of the sacraments, Socinus declared that as transubstantiation, "which was once thought of as the most divine mystery of the Christian religion, has now been shown to be idolatry," so the dogmas of Nicea and Chalcedon, "these monstrous figments about our God and about his Christ, which at this time are believed to be sacrosanct . . . and the most important mysteries of our religion," would be recognized in their true light and be repudiated. Confronted with such a "new appearance" of "the same old heresies," Bullinger warned that it was not enough to declare loyalty to the sole authority of Scripture, which even the Arians had done; one was obliged as well to set forth an interpretation of Scripture that was simultaneously "native" to the text and "congruous with the articles of the faith." Calvin complained that those who were attacking ancient dogma were not only heretical but "ignorant" of the patristic tradition; but Servetus claimed to be defending "the older traditions of the apostles" and of the earliest church fathers against the later tradition of the Council of Nicea, while Socinus complained that the prologue to the Gospel of John "has, as far as I know, never until now been correctly expounded by anyone."

Although Anselm's definition of the atonement as an act of satisfaction rendered by the death of Christ to the violated justice of God was not, strictly speaking, a dogma of the church, it had so firmly established itself that Bullinger, for example, could treat it as the common property of Roman Catholics and Protestants, with the divergence between them consisting in their views on what "satisfaction," if any, was rendered by penitents over and above that of Christ. Because Anselm's treatise had first presupposed, and then had proceeded to substantiate, the orthodox Chalcedonian dogma of the person of Christ as the God-man, it came to be seen—only in the Latin West, naturally—as the necessary implication of Chalcedon and hence, in the phrase of one of the opponents of Socinus, as "the common and orthodox doctrine." To this designation Socinus retorted in his book *Jesus Christ the Savior*, which has been called his "most

Soc.*Prol.Ev.Joh.* (*BFP* 1:84); *Cat.Rac.*6.4 (1580:124)

Blngr.*Assert.orth.* (1534:7r)

See p. 265 above

Blngr.*Dec.*5.1 (1552:275r)

Calv.*Ep.Pol.* (*CR* 37:648);Calv. *Nob.Pol.* (*CR* 37:358)

Serv.*Trin.err.*2.5;1.41 (1721: 48r;29r)

Soc.*Prol.Ev.Joh.* (*BFP* 1:81)

See vol.3:144

Blngr.*Ggn.*4 (1551:12–13)

original and most important contribution to systematic theology," that the authentically "orthodox doctrine" was not the theory of satisfaction at all. One chapter of the *Racovian Catechism* was devoted to the death of Christ, and one section of the *Catechism* of Socinus bore the heading, "Refutation of the Vulgar Doctrine about the Satisfaction of Christ for Our Sins": Such a doctrine, Socinus charged, detracted from "the power and authority, or at any rate from the goodness and mercy of God" by maintaining that God either would not or could not forgive sins by sheer mercy. Christ was not "the price for our sins," nor did he "placate" the wrath of God. Rather, he "showed and taught the way of salvation," but he also "declared" the love of God and "confirmed" it by his miracles and by his death and resurrection. The principal New Testament text on the doctrine of the atonement did not portray Christ as reconciling God to the world, but as "reconciling the world to [God]." As Socinus reminded his readers, Calvin himself had said that "the salvation of all of us rests on mercy." Contrary to Anselm's theory, therefore, there was no opposition between the mercy and the justice of God, and so no "satisfaction" was necessary. Many of the same strictures applied also to such doctrines of the atonement as that of Hugo Grotius, who had proposed fundamental revisions of the satisfaction theory; for the biblical language underlying every theory of the atonement was, in any case, a "metaphor," not a literal description. The title "mediator" meant "a messenger and go-between [internuntius] and an interpreter," not someone "who effects peace between God and men."

Since, according to the orthodox tradition, Christ was what he was in order to do what he did, a revision of the Anselmic doctrine of his work required a corresponding revision of the Nicene-Chalcedonian doctrine of his person. If it was the work of Christ only to reveal divine mercy, not to make that mercy possible by reconciling it with divine justice, then, as Bernard had pointed out to Abelard, Christ no longer needed to be the "Son of God" in the sense in which orthodox dogma had used the title. For to be "called the Son of the Most High," as the angel of the an-

Wilbur (1946) 392
Soc.*Serv.*1.1 (*BFP* 2:121)

*Cat.Rac.*6.8 (1680:141–54)

Soc.*Cat.* (*BFP* 1:665–67)

Soc.*Ep.Joh.*5:1;2:2 (*BFP* 1:231; 165)

Dav.*Def.*18.3 (*BFP* 2:743)

Soc.*Serv.*1.3 (*BFP* 2:127–28)
2 Cor.5:19

Soc.*Serv.*1.8 (*BFP* 2:137);Soc.*Cat.* (*BFP* 1:666)

Soc.*Serv.*1.1 (*BFP* 2:121)
Calv.*Inst.*(1559)1.10.2 (Barth-Niesel 3:87)

Soc.*Serv.*1.1 (*BFP* 2:123);*Cat. Rac.*6.8 (1680:147)
Soc.*Serv.*3.1 (*BFP* 2:186)

See pp. 360–61 below
Soc.*Serv.*3.4;3.6 (*BFP* 2:197; 204)

Soc.*Serv.*2.2 (*BFP* 2:146)

Soc.*Cat.* (*BFP* 1:666);Soc.*Serv.* 1.7 (*BFP* 2:135);Gr.Paw.*Roz. ter.* (*BPP* B-2:31)

See p. 161 above

See vol.3:129

Serv.*Ep.Calv.*1 (*ChristRest* 577)

Luke 1:32

Matt.5:9
Soc.*Conc.Chr.*Matt.5:9 (*BFP*
1:4)

Soc.*Cat.* (*BFP* 1:655)

Serv.*Ep.Calv.*3 (*ChristRest*
581)

Serv.*Trin.err.*1.30 (1721:21r)
Soc.*Cat.* (*BFP* 1:652);Soc.*Cat.
fr.* (*BFP* 1:684–85)
Rej.*Post.*2.Trin. (*BPP* B-14:
148v)

Calv.*Ep.Pol.* (*CR* 37:647)
Calv.*Bland.* (*CR* 37:331);
Blngr.*Assert.orth.* (1534:16r–
16v);Blngr.*Dec.*4.6 (1552:229v)

Soc.*Cat.* (*BFP* 1:655)

Serv.*Trin.err.*1.44 (1721:32r)

Soc.*Resp.Dav.*1;9.4 (*BFP* 2:
718;728)

Soc.*Prol.Ev.Joh.*pr. (*BFP* 1:77)

See vol.1:175

Soc.*Cat.fr.* (*BFP* 1:686–88)

Crll.*Op.exeg.*Phil.2:6 (*BFP* 3:
506)

See vol.1:255–56

Serv.*Trin.err.*1.25 (1721:18v–
19r);Serv.*Trin.*1 (*ChristRest*
19–22)
Soc.*Resp.Dav.*14.1 (*BFP* 2:
735);Soc.*Cat.* (*BFP* 1:653–54)

nunciation prophesied that Jesus would be, or to be "called sons of God," as Jesus promised that "peace-makers" would be, did not, according to Socinus, pertain to "substance" or "essence," but was a mere "appellation." The substantial and essential interpretation of such titles had resulted in "that monstrosity of three realities," that "imaginary Trinity, three beings in one nature," which was in fact not trinitarianism but tritheism. One God and three persons, was, unavoidably, a "contradiction," which "perhaps even the angels" would have difficulty comprehending. Nonbiblical terms such as "homoousios," which, despite continuing misgivings about "formulas remote from the usage of Scripture," Calvin and his colleagues had gone on employing, were "a mere human figment, not in keeping with Holy Writ . . . and also altogether repugnant to sound reason." Servetus had pointed out that there was "not one word to be found in the whole Bible" about such notions as Trinity, person, and homoousios. Socinus joined him in denouncing a theological method that had to resort to "formulas of speaking that are utterly unknown to the sacred writers," although Socinus eventually had to denounce the literalism of his coreligionists who refused to go beyond the ipsissima verba of the Bible.

This polemic against orthodox trinitarianism as unscriptural began with the premise that, if the dogmas were correct, "Holy Writ would certain have taught them somewhere in a manner that is clear, obvious, and free of verbal complications and ambiguities." The biblical foundation for the dogmas had been provided in the ancient church by several sets of passages from the Old Testament as well as the New Testament: passages of adoption, passages of identity, passages of distinction, and passages of derivation. In its repudiation of trinitarian dogma, therefore, Unitarianism had to undertake a thorough exegetical review of these and related passages.

Because of its statement that a special name and status had been "given" to the man Jesus, Philippians 2:5–11 could be read as a passage of adoption: it did not refer to a status which Christ possessed by "nature," but to a "power" that had been "given to him and conferred upon him." He remained "subordi-

Soc.*Resp.Dav.*8.3 (*BFP* 2:726);
Soc.*Prol.Ev.Joh.* (*BFP* 1:80)
1 Cor.15:24
Crll.*Op.exeg.*1 Cor.15:24 (*BFP* 2:331–35)

Mel.*Enarr.symb.Nic.* (*CR* 23:217)

Soc.*Prol.Ev.Joh.* (*BFP* 1:75–85)

Serv.*Trin.err.*1.29 (1721:20v–21r)

Serv.*Ep.Calv.*1 (*ChristRest* 578)
Soc.*Cat.* (*BFP* 1:662);*Cat.Rac.* 4.1 (1680:28–29)

Soc.*Prol.Ev.Joh.* (*BFP* 1:78)
Gr.Paw.*Roz.ter.* (*BPP* B-2:35)
See vol.1:181–83
Serv.*Trin.*2 (*ChristRest* 65;88–89)

Soc.*Var.loc.* (*BFP* 1:142);Soc.*Cat.fr.* (*BFP* 1:686–88)

See vol.1:184–86

Matt.28.19–20

See vol.1:211–17
Soc.*Cat.fr.* (*BFP* 1:684)

Serv.*Trin.*5 (*ChristRest* 187);
Soc.*Cat.* (*BFP* 1:652)
Gr.Paw.*Praw.smr.* (*BPP* B-3:80)
*Cat.Rac.*6.6 (1680:134)

*Cat.Rac.*4.1 (1680:26)

Serv.*Trin.*1 (*ChristRest* 22)

nate" to God the Father, but he received from the Father "an equality of power" with him. This he would, however, eventually "surrender" back to the Father. Among the passages of identity "scattered everywhere throughout the prophetic and apostolic Scriptures" according to orthodox theologians, the prologue of the Gospel of John occupied a unique position, and so Socinus devoted a special treatise to this one passage. Servetus had conceded that its opening verse was "the single exception" to his rule that "all the Scriptures from first to last speak of the man Christ himself," not of some preexistent being, but he still identified the "Logos" of the prologue with Jesus the man. Socinus maintained this identification of the Logos as "the very man Christ Jesus," arguing that the title "the Word" did not refer to his ontological nature but to his office as the one who "expounded the evangelical word of his Father." The Old Testament passages of distinction such as Genesis 19:24 and Psalm 110 did not prove a "metaphysical equality between these incorporeal realities," while the "Let us make" of Genesis 1:26 reflected nothing more than a usage common to all languages, by which someone spoke to himself in the plural and in the subjunctive. As a term of derivation for Christ, "Spirit" had, already in the early church, yielded to the overriding authority of the baptismal formula and had become almost exclusively the title of the third person of the Trinity. But now that there was "no room for the question of whether there are several persons in God," the term could not refer to "a third metaphysical reality" but had to apply to the divine essence itself in its affinity with the human spirit and in its "power or efficacy."

The entire method of trinitarian exegesis was "repugnant to Scripture"; it was "an invention of Satan," which, by distorting "the passages of Scripture that speak about equality with God, but are in fact far removed from the conflicts of our own age," had "alienated the minds of men from the knowledge of the true Christ and presented us with a tripartite God." The fundamental passage of all on the entire question of the Trinity was, of course, the Shema of Deuteronomy 6:4: "Hear, O Israel, the Lord our God is one

See vol.2:199–215

Soc. *Cat.* (*BFP* 1:652)

Soc. *Cat.fr.* (*BFP* 1:682)

Serv. *Ep. Calv.*6;7 (*ChristRest* 588;594)

Serv. *Trin.*3 (*ChristRest* 107)

John 10:30(Vulg.)
Aug. *Trin.*4.9.12 (*CCSL* 50: 177–78);Aug. *Ev.Joh.*71.2 (*CCSL* 36:506)

Serv. *Trin.err.*1.33 (1721:23r)

Serv. *Ep. Calv.*1 (*ChristRest* 579)

John 3:13(var.)
See p. 160 above
Oec. *Ev.Joh.*15 (1533:60r)

Serv. *Trin.err.*2.1–2 (1721:44v–46r);Serv. *Trin.*2 (*ChristRest* 72–73)

Serv. *Var.loc.* (*BFP* 1:146);Serv. *Cat.* (*BFP* 1:674)

Eras. *Adnot.*John 3:13 (*LB* 6:352)

Lord." Its doctrine that the essence of God was numerically one necessarily implied that there could likewise be "numerically only one person in God, and by no means more than one," for only on the basis of the Shema could the first commandment and the remainder of the Decalogue carry any force. God was one and was unchangeable: no trinitarian dogma about "incarnation" or "procession" could revise that, and nothing in the books of the New Testament could be interpreted in such a way as to contradict this absolute monotheism. When Augustine took the use of the neuter in the words of Christ, "I and the Father are one [unum]," as proof for a oneness of nature but a plurality of persons, Servetus replied that "'one' in the neuter has reference not to singleness, but to oneness in mind. . . . To take 'one [unum]' in Scripture for 'one nature' is more metaphysical than Christian; indeed, it is foreign to the Scriptures." Such were the complications and excessive subtleties of the traditional exegesis. On the other hand, "if you take it as your starting point that Christ is the one toward whom all passages of Scripture tend, then everything will be easy."

Eventually, at least some of the passages of Scripture proved to be not so easy as all that. In the conflicts between Lutheran and Reformed theologians over the ubiquity of the human nature and the body of Christ, the verse in which Christ said to Nicodemus, "No one has ascended into heaven but he who descended from heaven, the Son of man, who is in heaven," had been a crux of interpretation; for it appeared to be saying that the humanity of Christ was in heaven, as well as being on earth in the presence of Nicodemus, and it could even be construed as saying that the humanity of Christ had "descended from heaven" along with his divinity and was therefore in some way itself preexistent. While accepting the textual variant, "who is in heaven," as genuine, as Servetus also had, Socinus insisted that it must be a "trope." But "even if we wish to take the words of Christ . . . in this passage without a trope, they must be read, not as 'who is in heaven,' but as 'who was in heaven,'" which was how Erasmus and others had said that the Greek present participle was to be translated here. What Socinus substituted for the trinitarian dogma of the preexistent Logos was a theory that, he had to grant, none of the Gospels mentioned: "Christ, after he was born as man but before he began to undertake the task imposed on him by God his Father, was in heaven, through the plan and action of God, and remained there for some time in order to hear from God himself" all that he was in turn to reveal to his disciples.

Far more troublesome, also within the Unitarian community, was the classic text from Philippians 2, above all its climactic verses, which did appear to affirm that Christ was to be worshiped: "that at the name of Jesus every knee should bow, in heaven and on earth and under the earth, and every tongue confess that Jesus Christ is Lord, to the glory of God the Father." Employing, alongside the principle of biblical authority, the principle that the rule of prayer should determine the rule of faith, the early church had argued, on the basis of the worship of Christ as stated in this passage and in others, that Christ was one in being with the Father and hence was deserving of such worship. With the Unitarian denial of this status, so their opponents contended, they should also, to be consistent, discontinue the practice of worshiping Christ. Socinus did warn of "the danger of idolatry among believers in Christ," defining it as "treating Christ with greater honor than is his due, namely, honor that is clearly divine, and requesting from him those things that can and should be requested from God alone."

From such warnings some of the associates of Socinus, whose spokesman was Francis Dávid, took the formula of Christ in introducing the Lord's Prayer, "Pray then like this: 'Our Father who art in heaven,'" to be an exclusionary principle, which required "that no one except God the Father be worshiped." For only the Father was truly God, who, in his public attestation at the transfiguration of Christ, had commanded "that Christ be listened to, not that he be worshiped." A sound method of biblical exegesis would substantiate this position. Even when Stephen, the first martyr, prayed, at his death, "Lord Jesus, receive my spirit," in an evident parallel to the words of Jesus at his own death, "Father, into thy hands I commit my spirit,"

Soc.*Cat.* (*BFP* 1:675)

Phil.2:10–11

See vol.1:339

See vol.1:238–42

Calv.*Inst.*(1559)1.13.24 (Barth-Niesel 3:143–44)

Soc.*Cat.* (*BFP* 1:669)

Dav.*Def.*17.1 (*BFP* 2:740)
Matt.6:9

Dav.*Def.*15.2 (*BFP* 2:736)

Matt.17:5
Dav.*Def.*2.4 (*BFP* 2:718)

Dav.*Def.*8.5 (*BFP* 2:727)
Acts 7:59

Gr.Paw.*Praw.smr.* (*BPP* B-3:76)
Luke 23:46

Dav.*Def.*2.2 (*BFP* 2:718)
Dav.*Def.*12.4;15.6;16.9 (*BFP* 2:734;737;739)

the parallel was not to be taken to mean that either the Father or Christ was equally a proper object of worship; for Stephen's prayer was, in fact though not in language, "addressed not to Christ, but to God the Father." To go on worshiping Christ, therefore, would be a liturgical relapse into a trinitarian dogma that had been exegetically discredited.

Soc.*Resp.Dav.*18.9 (*BFP* 2:745)
Soc.*Resp.Dav.*17.1 (*BFP* 2:740)
Soc.*Conc.Chr.* (*BFP* 1:61)
Soc.*Cat.fr.* (*BFP* 1:686–88)
Soc.*Resp.Dav.*19.1;23.3;27.4 (*BFP* 2:745;755;763)
Soc.*Resp.Dav.*4.1 (*BFP* 2:721–22)
Soc.*Resp.Dav.*19.6 (*BFP* 2:747);Soc.*Prol.Ev.Joh.* (*BFP* 1:80)
Phil. 2:11
Rev.19:10;22:9
Cypr.*Bon.pat.*24 (*CSEL* 3:415)
Soc.*Cat.fr.* (*BFP* 1:681)
Isa.42:8
Just.*Dial.*65 (Goodspeed 172–73)
Soc.*Resp.Dav.*21.10 (*BFP* 2:752)
John 5:27
Soc.*Var.loc.* (*BFP* 1:147)
Soc.*Resp.Dav.*21.1 (*BFP* 2:749)
Soc.*Resp.Dav.*12.2 (*BFP* 2:733)

Socinus answered that it was Dávid and his colleagues who had relapsed, into the "extremely grave error" of the old trinitarian logic of maintaining that worship of Christ necessarily implied the Nicene doctrine of "homoousios." The introductory formula of the Lord's Prayer was not intended to specify who was to be worshiped, but how the Father was to be worshiped; in fact, it taught that "when Christ is worshiped, it is the Father who is being worshiped, on account of the subordination of Christ to God the Father." Honest exegesis could not evade a confrontation with passages that seemed to prove the opposite position. The issue was not whether it was necessary, according to Scripture, that Christ be worshiped, but whether it was permissible, and whether there were clear passages in Scripture that spoke of the worship of Christ. The second chapter of Philippians was in many ways "the most appropriate" of such passages, since it specified that "the worship addressed to Christ" took place "to the glory of God the Father." The words of the angel in the Apocalypse, "Worship God," read, according to a variant recorded by Cyprian, "Worship Jesus the Lord." Even the word of God in Isaiah, "My glory I give to no other," could, as Justin Martyr had already shown, be interpreted to mean that God gave his glory to no one except Christ. Because the authority of Christ had been "given" to him by the Father, it "necessarily" followed that "the Son of God, who is Christ, is not eternal" and yet at the same time that "he is to be worshiped." In sum, the worship of Christ did not detract from the glory of God the Father; to the contrary, "it is possible to worship Christ for no other reason than that it is obligatory to worship the Father."

In theological intent as well as in exegetical method, this repudiation of the trinitarian dogma continued to presuppose the unique authority of the biblical rev-

Gr.Paw.*Praw.smr.* (*BPP* B-3: 73)

Soc.*Prol.Ev.Joh.* (*BFP* 1:78)
Soc.*Auct.Scrip.*1 (*BFP* 1:265)

*Cat.Rac.*1.2 (1680:6–8)
*Cat.Rac.*1.1 (1680:2–3);Soc.
*Auct.Scrip.*3 (*BFP* 1:275–76)

Soc.*Auct.Scrip.*1.2 (*BFP* 1:268–69)
Williams (1962) 751

Dant.*Par.*24

Soc.*Auct.Scrip.*6 (*BFP* 1:280)

Soc.*Cat.* (*BFP* 1:653)

Acts 4:12

Soc.*Cat.fr.* (*BFP* 1:679–80)

elation and the absolute necessity of Jesus Christ. It was impossible for those who accepted Christianity, now purified of the alien metaphysics that had been imposed upon it through trinitarianism, to harbor any doubts about the authority of Scripture, Old Testament and New, or about its "sufficiency." There was ample rational evidence to support this authority, together with the testimony of the early church fathers as collected by Eusebius. Later testimony came from such a "great lay theologian" as Dante, to whom Socinus devoted an entire chapter of his book *The Authority of Holy Scripture.* The authority of Scripture was central because without a knowledge of Christ "it is impossible for us either to know or to observe the will of God that has been revealed to us through that same Christ." Of course it was impossible to pry into "the inner secrets of God" himself or to understand his mysterious will "also for those who do not know Christ"; but "whatever God may have in mind for them," it remained true that "there is no other name under heaven given among men by which we must be saved." But like the other challenges to continuity, even the repudiation of trinitarian dogma would look very different in the modern period, when it was no longer possible to take all of these presuppositions for granted.

# 7

# Confessional
# Dogmatics
# In a Divided
# Christendom

On the foundations—or from the debris—of the six-teenth-century Reformation and its doctrinal defini-tions, the separated churches of Western Christendom, already in the sixteenth century but especially in the seventeenth, constructed their several systems of confessional dogmatics, each a simulacrum of that "one, holy, catholic, and apostolic" tradition to which, in one way or another, they all still pledged allegiance. As a consequence of what had happened to all of the "confessional" churches—Roman Catholic, Lu-theran, and Reformed (including Anglican)—in the century between the *Ninety-Five Theses* in 1517 and the *Canons* of the Synod of Dort in 1618–19, the universal tradition of orthodoxy was increasingly being filtered through, and identified with, the particular traditions represented by the doctrinal formularies that had come out of Reformation controversies. Thus, in response to the charge that Luther was "the pope of Protestants" and to the challenge, "Let Protestants show how he was called, when and by whom, to such an excellent and gracious vocation!" Lutheran dog-matics acquired a new chapter entitled "The Call of Luther." Here it sought to assert his authority by demonstrating that his Reformation was not a private matter, but had come by the intervention of divine providence. At the same time it argued, in opposition to Roman Catholic theologians, that Luther's call was "legitimate" even by their standards (as they had ac-knowledged by not raising this challenge until long after "the beginning of the Reformation and its con-

Stapl.*Ret*.4 (*ERL* 308–II:114r)

Stapl.*Fort*.2.1 (*ERL* 163:91v–92r)

Bald.*Art.Smal*.1.23 (1605:B1r)

Grh.*Loc*.23.8 (Cotta 12–II:125–36)

Tit.*Eccl*.11 (1653:C2v–C3v)

Quen.*Theol*.4.12.2.3 (1715–
II:1515)

Grh.*Loc*.23.8 (Cotta 12–
II:130)

Wolf.*Eut.Luth*.5.14 (1680:K1r)

troversies"); and, in opposition to left-wing Protestantism, that "Luther everywhere appeals to a regular and mediated call, and never lays claim to immediate revelations or an immediate call."

Like the first chapter of this volume, therefore, the final chapter describes a situation of doctrinal pluralism. Yet there is one decisive difference. The doctrinal pluralism of the fourteenth and fifteenth centuries had its outcome in the church doctrine of the sixteenth as defined by the several confessional groups, and therefore a treatment of it in some detail was essential to an understanding of that outcome. The doctrinal pluralism of the seventeenth century, on the other hand, presupposed the church doctrine of the sixteenth century. Except for the *Westminster Confession of Faith*, the further definitions of church doctrine in which this doctrinal pluralism issued within the period covered by this volume were only of quasi-confessional significance (as was the case with the Lutheran *Repeated Consensus* of 1655), or at best of secondary or even tertiary "confessional" standing (as was the case with the Calvinistic *Helvetic Consensus* of 1675 and the Roman Catholic papal constitution *Cum occasione* of 1653)—in comparison with the *Book of Concord*, the *Canons of the Synod of Dort*, and the *Decrees and Canons of the Council of Trent*. Other developments, such as the Marian dogmas promulgated in 1854 and 1950 and the actions of the First and Second Vatican Councils, will be the subject of the fifth and final volume of this work, in which we shall also consider the crisis of orthodoxy, beginning with Pietism, Puritanism, and Jansenism. For each of the doctrines being discussed in this final chapter, there appeared, at or near the end of the seventeenth century, some decisive event or theologian or book portending that crisis.

Although the churches may have refused to do so together, nevertheless they were together in having to come to doctrinal terms with the Reformation settlements. Doctrines that had often taken the form they did in response to a specific attack now stood as permanent monuments when the original occasion for them was largely forgotten. For example, the mediating language of Article X of the *Augsburg Confes-*

Conf.Aug.10.1 (Bek.64)

Confut.Conf.Aug.10 (CCath 33:100–101)

See pp. 185–86 above

Hutt.Conc.56 (1690:1418–20)
Mentz.Thes.theol.1.25 (1612–I:B1r)

Bell.Lib.Conc.2.36 (Fèvre 7:129)

See pp. 288–89 above

Hazelton (1974) 203

Grh.Interp.25 (1663:9–10)

Bell.Dich.dott.cris.2 (Fèvre 12:284)
Quen.Theol.4.7.1.7 (1715–II:1300–1301); see p. 240 above, p. 368 below

Keck.Syst.1.8 (1615:134)

sion on the presence of the body and blood of Christ "under the form of bread and wine" in the Eucharist had been acceptable to the Roman Catholic authors of the *Confutation of the Augsburg Confession,* and with the revisions and interpretations of its author had become acceptable to Calvin as well. But the Lutheran dogmaticians of the seventeenth century had to explain why, however it may have sounded, this language did not teach the doctrine of transubstantiation, and on the other hand, why Calvin and his followers were not entitled to claim it either. Their Roman Catholic contemporaries were compelled to show that the language of the *Confutation* did not mean approval of Lutheran eucharistic doctrine as it now stood. For all the confessional churches, moreover, this task of understanding and elaborating the doctrines established in the Reformation settlements frequently meant that the doctrines acquired a greater complexity in the process. Trent had been able to dismiss the problem of certainty as largely a Protestant aberration; but in the seventeenth century Roman Catholic thought had to carry the problem beyond the rather simplistic Tridentine formulas, producing various new answers to it, including that of Blaise Pascal, whose "search for truth reached a fulfilling incompleteness in faith."

None of the doctrines discussed in this chapter belonged only to the confession with which it is being identified here: No Christian "as such" could deny that the biblical writers were "amanuenses of the Holy Spirit"; every theologian taught that the incarnation of the Logos in the humanity of Christ was, with the Trinity, one of the two "principal mysteries of the faith"; even the opponents of "covenant theology" had to have a doctrine of covenant; and the doctrine of the gifts of grace and of their distinction from those of nature was the common property of all of Western Christendom. Nevertheless, it was the primary identification of each of these doctrines with one specific denomination that was to shape much of its future history. Despite their theological differences, Roman Catholicism and "magisterial" Protestantism were in at least formal agreement, against the Radicals, that the mark of authentic doctrine was its continuity with

Grh.*Conf.cath*.2.5.4 (1662–II:864–65)

apostolic revelation (whether contained only in Scripture or available also in the church as a second source), and consequently its unchangeability. On the Roman Catholic side, Jacques Bénigne Bossuet in his *History of the Variations of the Protestant Churches*, published at the end of this period, in 1688, and on the Protestant side, the Lutheran theologian Johann Gerhard in his *Catholic Confession* of fifty years earlier, each laid claim to that continuity and unchangeability for

Boss.*Hist.var*.pr.2–3 (Lachat 14:1–2);Grh.*Conf.cath*.2.5.4 (1662–II:879–91)

the doctrine of his own church and accused the other side of fluctuation and inconstancy.

In principle, then, no one would admit to a "development of doctrine." Some of the most profound doctrinal changes during the seventeenth and eighteenth centuries occurred within the Reformed churches. The Roman Catholic critics of Lutheranism

Bell.*Lib.Conc*.2.1 (Fèvre 7:109)

Bai.*Eccl*.2 (Gerberon 461); Stapl.*Fort*.1.5 (*ERL* 163:27r)

could point to its lack of a truly international base and sometimes characterized all Protestant "heresy" as being accepted only "in some little corner" somewhere, rather than throughout the ecumenical church. By contrast, Reformed theologians had the right to emphasize the international and pluralistic character

Keck.*Syst*.3.6 (1615:306) Ames.*Coron*.1.9;5.12 (1632:61–66;493 502); see p. 236 above

of their communion. Although it was quoted as an authority on various doctrines, the *Belgic Confession*, for example, was not a comprehensive confessional norm for all the Reformed churches that would have corresponded to the *Augsburg Confession* for Lutheranism and to the *Canons and Decrees of the Council of Trent* for Roman Catholicism; that circumstance, too, provided a theological context that encouraged such development. The outcome was the proliferation of confessions, creeds, platforms and other statements of faith in the Church of England and especially in its "Puritan" offshoots during the seventeenth and eighteenth centuries, which will concern us in our final volume. For it proved to be true here above all that "the medieval principle of uniformity could not be reconciled with the inveterate tendency of the Ref-

P.Miller (1959) 51–52

ormation to produce constant variety" and constant doctrinal development, alongside the continuing insistence on a uniform and orthodox doctrine.

## The Prolegomena of Dogmatics

The seventeenth century was the period in the history of Christian doctrine during which the prolegomena of dogmatics came to assume a dominant position. Unquestionably, the increasing attention of contemporary philosophy to epistemological issues contributed to this preoccupation, but there were internal forces within the theological situation itself that made it necessary to reopen the question of "God and the ways of knowing." One of the most prominent of these was polemics. For example, the most important work of the most important theologian of the Counter-Reformation, Robert Bellarmine, was entitled *Disputations on the Controversies over the Christian Faith against the Heretics of This Time,* published in four volumes just before the opening of the seventeenth century. Similarly, the thorough and influential dogmatics of the Lutheran theologian Johann Andreas Quenstedt bore the title *Didactico-Polemical Theology,* and many of its chapter headings were determined by the conflict with other systems of dogmatics. But also the more moderate Johann Gerhard, who was celebrated for his "sweetness" of language and who lamented the "iniquitous" situation that "those who will someday celebrate victory together in heaven disagree here on earth," could attack Calvinism for its supposed affinities with Arianism, Nestorianism, and even Mohammedanism. Although he quoted Calvin and Beza approvingly on the authority of Scripture, Gerhard rejected the suggestion that Lutheranism and Calvinism shared the same fundamental beliefs and differed only in their application of these beliefs to the issues in controversy.

Indeed, there was a persistent effort to find ever new battlegrounds. For example, the Reformed doctrine of angels (which had tended, as had the Lutheran doctrine, to repeat medieval thought, though with less detail) came in for attack above all because of its interpretation of the doctrine of the fall of the evil angels in the light of the Calvinist views of predestination and reprobation. Calvinist theologians agreed with their Lutheran and Roman Catholic opponents about the basic definition of a heretic and about the necessity of polemics (including the need to leave it to theo-

Daniélou (1957)
Mol.*Sum.haer.maj.* (Stegmüller 394–438)

Feur.*Grh.* (1638:27)

Grh.*Med.sac.*36 (1633:165)

Grh.*Disp.*2.12 (1665:558–60)
Grh.*Interp.*172 (1663:80)

Grh.*Disp.*2.12 (1655:581);Bald.*Anath.*5.106 (1700:G2r)

Trtn.*Inst.*7 (1688–I:594–625)
See vol.3:293–98
Keck.*Syst.*1.7 (1615:129);
Polan.*Syntag.*5.13 (1617:285–86)

Bucan.*Inst.*36. (1605:420);Brn.*Doct.foed.*2.4.9 (1688:149);
Heid.*Corp.theol.*5.21 (1700–I:155)
Deutsch.*Ang.*3.38 (1659:C3v)

Martn.*Sum.op.*6 (1612:95);
Polan.*Syntag.*7.22 (1617:549)
Dan.*Haer.* (1580:1);Aret.*Act.* 15 (1590:71r)
Calv.*Inst.* (1559)4.9.5 (Barth-Niesel 5:154);Bald.*Anath.*2.27 (1700:B3r)

logical experts). "It is not enough," Lambert Daneau insisted, "to speak and confess the true doctrines, unless you also refute false doctrines." They did not always agree, of course, about the identification of the "false doctrines." It was particularly the possible implications of the Lutheran doctrine of the real presence that aroused Daneau's concern.

Although the polemical stance of the theologians in the seventeenth century compelled all of them to emphasize their theological differences, they did have much in common, both theologically and philosophically. It was to be expected that a Roman Catholic theologian should praise the works of Thomas Aquinas as "brighter than the sun"; but amid all their aspersions upon "the artificial science, or rather confusion of philosophy and theology, which they peddle under the name of 'scholastic theology,'" Protestant theologians were sometimes obliged to commend the scholastics. All of them employed a method of presenting Christian doctrine that was principally "scholastic" (or, perhaps, "neo-scholastic"), and it is quite accurate to point out "a certain similarity which such a [Protestant scholastic] position shared with that of Aquinas." In fact, the German Reformed dogmatician Johann Heinrich Alsted went so far as to call one of his principal books, published in 1618, *Scholastic Theology*. Yet even when it did not say so in its title, the *System* or *Loci* or *Institutes* of a seventeenth-century theologian, like the *Summa* of a thirteenth-century thinker, was primarily an effort to make sense of a received body of doctrine, and only secondarily (if at all) to formulate "new" doctrine. Thus all the major confessional churches had, by the beginning of the seventeenth century, elected "reaffirmation" as their way of preserving their particular form of the Reformation.

This willingness to accept the outcome of the Reformation as permanent stood in tension with the continuing obligation to affirm the unity of the church and to work for its reunion. The most noteworthy doctrinal consideration of the question of unity was precipitated by the proposal of Georg Calixtus, whom strict confessionalists denounced as "the author of all the troubles in the Protestant churches." Because all

Dan.*Haer.* (1580:1)

Dan.*Haer.* (1580:76–77)

Bell.*Scrip.eccl.*2 (Fèvre 12:450)

Heid.*Corp.theol.*1.59–60
(1700–I:18);Grh.*Conf.cath.*1.2.
15 (1662–I:612–24)

Aret.*Loc.*77 (1617:438)

Platt (1982) 139

Alst.*Theol.schol.* (1618)

Wolt.*Eut.Luth.*2.17 (1680:D4r)

Calx.*Conc.eccl.*3 (1655:A2r)

Calx.*Conc.eccl.*4 (1655:A2r)

Tit.*Eccl.*5 (1653:A4v)
Calx.*Conc.eccl.*10 (1655:A4v)

Calx.*Conc.eccl.*8 (1655:A4r)
Schüssler (1961) 78

See pp.203–12, 262–74 above

Tavard (1959) 245

See pp. 276–77 above

Stapl.*Ant.ev.*Matt.15:2 (1595–1:98)

Matt.15:2

three confessions (leaving out the Radicals) laid claim to continuity with the fathers and councils of the ancient church, Calixtus insisted that Roman Catholicism "no longer" had a valid claim to "a monopoly of apostolic truth." Distinguishing between those doctrines that were "necessary for salvation" and those that were not, as well as between the content of those doctrines and the language in which they had been stated, he attempted to formulate a "consensus of the first five centuries" that would serve as the dogmatic basis for a reconciliation of the churches. The major theologians and creeds of those centuries had been explicitly biblical in their teachings, so that a reaffirmation of loyalty to them would transcend the Reformation controversies over Scripture and tradition. The dogmas of the Trinity and the person of Christ, affirmed by all on the basis of the Apostles' Creed, were to be at the center of the consensus, and an Augustinian synthesis in which the teachings of the major Protestant Reformers and of the Council of Trent could all find room would roll back the controversies to a "status quo ante." Calixtus's proposal provided much of the agenda for the ill-fated "colloquy of charity [colloquium charitativum]" held in 1645 at Thorn (Toruń) in Poland between Roman Catholics, Calvinists, and Lutherans.

The Colloquy of Thorn failed because of both ecclesiastical and secular politics. Doctrinally it came to grief over the question of authority, which already in the sixteenth century had repeatedly become primary in the interpretation of Christian doctrine. The question became, if anything, more pronounced now, as "most controversialists of the Counter-Reformation . . . misread the 'new synthesis,' the concept of two sources of faith, into the Tridentine decree" on Scripture and tradition. As Stapleton put it, quoting the decree of the Council of Trent, the apostles had handed on "traditions to us partly written in epistles, partly not written." There were two principles of authority and two sources of revelation; and that was "the greatest possible difference" between the status of "the traditions of the elders," which the apostles could neglect, and the "unwritten traditions of the church," which subsequent generations were forbidden to neglect. In an extended interpretation of the crucial text in the Gospel, "I have yet many things to say to you, but you cannot bear them now. When the Spirit of truth comes, he will guide you into all the truth," he argued that the traditions of the church fathers were not "figments of their own imagination," but the fulfillment of this promise of Christ. The tradition also clarified which of the precepts and examples of the New Testament were not binding on later generations. For "sola Scriptura" inevitably led to inconsistency, as when Protestants insisted on it and then went on affirming traditional prerogatives for the Virgin Mary that were not explicitly stated in Scripture but only in tradition. Christians were to believe what the church believed.

To the Protestants, this doctrine of tradition was an argument in a circle. The church believed what it did on the basis of the word of God, "testifying" to it but not "establishing" it. For "the authority of Scripture does not uniquely or necessarily depend on the testimony of the church, neither in terms of itself, that is, with regard to its inherent constitution, nor in terms of us, that is, with regard to its recognition and manifestation." The church fathers were to be read as they had intended, "as lights but not as divine authorities [lumina, non autem numina]." In addition, the term "tradition" was itself equivocal, some traditions were divine, some apostolic, some ecclesiastical. Among these last, some were consistent with Scripture and therefore worthy of assent; thus Scripture explicitly required assent to the virgin birth of Christ, but only permitted assent to the idea of the perpetual virginity of Mary. As for the promise of the Spirit, that was fulfilled when, after "an extremely brief interval" during which the early church had to rely on unwritten tradition (as had the people of Israel before Moses), the New Testament was written. Scripture contained "the whole counsel of God," and therefore everything necessary for salvation was "sufficiently, fully, and perfectly set down in the canonical books."

As in the sixteenth century, such statements laid Protestants open to a Roman Catholic charge of self-contradiction on the issue of canonicity. For if, as

John 16:12–13

Stap.*Ant.ev.*John 16:12–13 (1595–II:253–64)

Stapl.*Ret.*1 (*ERL* 308–I:7r) Stapl.*Count.*4.1 (*ERL* 311:412v)

See p. 261 above

Bell.*Brev.apol.* (Fèvre 7:143) Bell.*Dott.cris.brev.* (Fèvre 12:266)

Calx.*Epit.theol.*1 (1661:10–11)

Trel.*Schol.inst.*1 (1606:6)

Quen.*Theol.*1.4.2.8 (1715 I:129)

Keck.*Syst.*1.9 (1615:169) Grh.*Conf.cath.*1.2.13 (1662 I:450–52);Grh.*Interp.*87 (1663:36) Trel.*Schol.inst.*1 (1606:16); Aret.*Loc.*84 (1617:478–83)

Martn.*Sum.op.*1 (1612:25–27) Aret.*Ev.*Matt.15:2;Mark 7:3 (1587–I:100r–100v;II:21v)

Krom.*Trad.*1.34 (1665:C3r); Heid.*Corp.theol.*17.18 (1700–II:10)

Ames.*Scrip.*15 (1646:7)

Krom.*Trad.*1.1 (1665:A3r)

Heid.*Corp.theol.*2.1–2 (1700–I:23)

Acts 20:27

Keck.*Syst.*1.8 (1615:142–44)

See pp. 266–67 above

Chil.*Rel.Prot.*2.27 (1727:45–46)

Bell.*Scrip.eccl.*1 (Fèvre 12:351)

Bell.*Cont.*6.1.3 (Fèvre 3:56)

Trel.*Schol.inst.*1 (1606:6)

Ames.*Bell.*1.1.6 (1626–I:88)

Krom.*Trad.*1.21 (1665:B4r)

Holl.*Exam.*prol.3.35
(1741:138)
Br.*Comp.*prol.2.34 (Walther
1:138);Brn.*Doct.foed.*1.1.2
(1688:15–16);Trtn.*Inst.*2.6
(1688–I:100)

Trel.*Schol.inst.*1 (1606:8–9)
Bucan.*Inst.*4.8 (1605:39)

Ratschow (1964) 1:63

Myl.ap.Holl.*Exam.*prol.2.27
(1741:60–62)

Grh.*Interp.*149 (1663:66)

they could not deny, it had been the church that had decided which books belonged to the canon of Scripture and which did not, it was fatuous to speak of this Scripture as possessing "sole" authority. It was "heretics" who rejected as "extracanonical" the Books of the Maccabees, which belonged to the Christian canon, if not to the Jewish. To this Roman Catholic argument it was possible to reply that the authority of the church did not "establish" the canon but only "witnessed" to it; conversely, there was "no instance in the Christian church of an apocryphal book being admitted as Holy Scripture unless the authority of traditions had prepared the way for it." Authentically canonical Scripture was self-verifying: it "testifies to its authority by its innate [insita] efficacy, which operates in our hearts with the concurrence of the Holy Spirit." At the same time it was necessary to set this inner testimony apart from the "enthusiasm" of Reformation Radicals, who were accused of claiming to possess the witness of the Holy Spirit apart from the word of God. The Apocrypha, "having been constituted by human authority," did not possess this self-authenticating force; rather, they manifested the kinds of errors of which true Scripture was free.

The charge of self-contradiction also arose in connection with the status of the Reformation confessions. For although "the treatment and evaluation of the creeds is by no means uniform," the elevation of the confessions (above all, of the *Augsburg Confession* within Lutheranism) to the status of an enforceable "norm" of public teaching appeared to be inconsistent with "sola Scriptura." The inconsistency received further confirmation when a theologian declared that "because the *Augsburg Confession* rests upon the altogether firm foundation of the Holy Scriptures, we can and should, with full right, call it 'inspired by God.'" Later apologists explained that the word "inspired," which came from 2 Timothy 3:16, was being used here in a broader sense, but that in the strict sense it applied only to Scripture, in which all dogma was contained. Even apart from the notion of an "inspiration" of the *Augsburg Confession*, however, the very concept of the confessions as a "norm" was difficult to harmonize with the Reformers' attack on normative "tradition." Instead of saying, as orthodox Lutherans did, that the creeds and confessions of the church were to be accepted "because [quia] they agree with Scripture," some Reformed theologians preferred to speak of an acceptance of creeds and confessions, including the Apostles' Creed, "insofar as [quatenus] they agree with Scripture"; but others seemed no less willing than were their Roman Catholic opponents to invoke the Apostles' Creed as an apostolic authority.

Grh.*Disp*.8.23 (1655:169)

Polan.*Syntag*.1.17 (1617:24)
Grh.*Disp*.8.23 (1655:169)

Bell.*Dott.cris.brev.* (Fèvre 12:262)
Aret.*Act*.2:42 (1590:23r);Calx.*Conc.eccl*.22 (1655:B3r);Chil.*Rel.Prot*.4.15;4.65 (1727:143;165)

In his *Judgment of the So-Called "Book of Concord"* of 1585, Bellarmine put it to the descendants of the Protestant Reformation that they could not have it both ways: Either they had to enforce "sola Scriptura" in relation to their own confessions, or they had to admit that they too were elevating tradition to a position alongside Scripture. One way out of the dilemma was to distinguish between two kinds of "norm": the confessions were a "norm that is itself subject to another norm [norma normata]," namely, to Scripture, which was alone the "norm that decides [norma normans]." Despite Bellarmine's objections to enforced subscription, it was "permissible for a superior magistrate to oblige someone who is a living member of the church and who plans to carry out the office of public teaching in it to subscribe to the symbolical books with an oath."

Br.*Comp*.prol.2.34 (Walther 1:139)

Bell.*Brev.apol.* (Fèvre 7:139)

Holl.*Exam*.prol.2.28 (1741:62–63)

In the sense in which we are defining "doctrine" throughout this work, which includes the requirement that a doctrine be "confessed" as well as "believed" and "taught," there was much less development of doctrine during the seventeenth century than there had been during the sixteenth or would be during the nineteenth and twentieth centuries. Yet between the Reformation debates, where it was "believed" and "taught," and the First Vatican Council, where it was eventually "confessed," the doctrine of papal infallibility attained during the seventeenth century much of the form and clarity it needed. Christ had, according to Bellarmine, conferred on Peter two privileges: the personal privilege of not being able ever to lose the true faith; and the official privilege of not being able ever to teach contrary to the faith. Only the second was passed on to his successors. "The pope

See vol.1:1–7

See pp. 269–73 above

Bai.*Infall.* (Gerberon 486)

Bell.*Cont*.3.4.3 (Fèvre 2:81)

Stapl.*Ret.*4 (*ERL* 308–II:11v)
See pp. 269–72 above
Stapl.*Ret.*4 (*ERL* 308–II:2r)
Grh.*Conf.cath.*1.2.2 (1662–
I:172–73)
See vol.2:150–53
Stapl.*Ret.*4 (*ERL* 308–II:112r–
113r)
Bell.*Cont.*3.4.11 (Fèvre 2:102–
3)

Stapl.*Count.*3.5 (*ERL*
311:218v–219v)
Stapl.*Ant.ev.*Matt.10:2 (1595–
I:66)

Grh.*1.Pet.*prol. (1692:7)

Stapl.*Ret.*1 (*ERL* 308–I:19r)

Stapl.*Ret.*2 (*ERL* 308–I:49r)
Bell.*Dott.cris.brev.* (Fèvre
12:262);Bell.*Dich.dott.cris.*3.9
(Fèvre 12:293);Boss.*Hist.var.*
15.13 (Lachat 15:59–61)
*Apol.Conf.Aug.*7.23 (*Bek.*239)

Bell.*Lib.Conc.*2.34 (Fèvre
7:128)

Ames.*Bell.*1.3.6 (1629–I:231–
46)

Aret.*Loc.*57 (1617:313)
Grh.*Conf.cath.*2.5.3 (1662–
II:834–35);Tit.*Eccl.*9
(1653:B4r)
Calx.*Epit.theol.*3 (1661:197)
Trel.*Schol.inst.*2 (1606:157–
60);Ghd.*Loc.*22.7 (Cotta 10:
81–104)
Bald.*Art.Smal.*19.13 (1605-
XIX:A3r);Calov.*Art.fid.*1.1.4
(1684:12;14)
Keck.*Syst.*3.6 (1615:306)

Huls.*Vet.nov.test.*7.10
(1714:D4v)

See p. 263 above

Holl.*Exam.*prol.3 (1741:133)
Chil.*Rel.Prot.*2.97 (1727:46);
Huls.*Vet.nov.test.*7.17 (1714:
E2v)

Quen.*Theol.*1.4.2.8 (1715–I:
136)

Bucan.*Inst.*4.25 (1605:46)

as the head of the church can never err," Stapleton declared; "that is, he can never decree anything erroneous or contrary to the faith, he can never deliver any false doctrine to the church contrary to the faith." That was the meaning of Christ's promises to Peter. The case of the alleged heresy of Pope Honorius I, which by now had become common knowledge, either was based on a Greek forgery, or was derived from a misinterpretation of the documents, or pertained only "to his own person," not to "the see of Rome both in his time and ever after," which was "always clear of this heresy." In the lists of the apostles Peter was always first, as Protestants had to concede, and "the confirmation of doctrine" was the prerogative of the church of Rome, "at this day the most ancient church in Christendom." The "Catholic Church" in the creeds was none other than the Roman Catholic Church. It was a calumny when the *Apology of the Augsburg Confession* accused the pope of claiming the authority to "abolish Scripture by his leave."

Protestant exegesis was, of course, opposed to this argumentation. The church militant here on earth could err and had erred; it was pretentious for the papacy to lay claim to infallibility, indefectibilty, and catholicity. These pertained to the true catholic church, which was invisible. There was a true visible church; but Lutherans could assert that "our church, and not the Roman papal church, is the true, holy, and apostolic church," and Calvinists that "our church . . . is called 'the orthodox church.'" Although the Reformers had "received the Old and New Testaments from the papal church, which did not err in this tradition," that did not confirm the notion of the authority of the church over the Bible. The formula of Augustine about the relation of the gospel to the church, though "trite" by now, continued to be a way of demanding an answer from the Protestants. They paraphrased Augustine's statement to mean: "As long as I was a Manichean, I would not have believed the gospel unless the authority of the church had moved me, or rather admonished me [commovisset, vel commonuisset]." They insisted that Augustine was speaking about himself before his conversion, or at any rate about himself as an individual, but was not prescribing

Heid.*Corp.theol.*2.16;2.29
(1700–I:29;31)

Grh.*Conf.cath.*2.1.5 (1662–
II:213)

Trtn.*Inst.*2.6 (1686–I:104)

See p. 350 below

Cons.*Helv.*1–3 (Niemeyer
730–31);Trel.*Schol.inst.*1
(1606:5);Martn.*Sum.op.*1
(1612:1–38)

See pp. 207–8 above

Grh.*Conf.cath.*2.1.3 (1662–II:
161–92);Grh.*Interp.*21;63
(1663:8;25);Calov.*Art.fid.*1.2.9
(1684:43–46);Ames.*Bell.*1.1.4
(1629–I:42–48);Heid.*Corp.
theol.*2.83 (1700–I:46)

Keck.*Syst.*1.9 (1615:162–63)

2 Tim.3:16

Preus (1955) 27

this for everyone as a rule for believing the authority of Scripture; besides, Augustine was referring here to the church as the external means by which he had come to faith, not as "the infallible principle of believing." Roman Catholic teaching also devoted itself to clarifying biblical inspiration and to defending such a theological-isagogical position as the Mosaic authorship of the Pentateuch against its gainsayers, including some who arose within Roman Catholic ranks.

Yet the very differences between Roman Catholicism and Protestantism on the locus of authority tended to make such issues more important for Calvinists and Lutherans, whose continued and intensified concentration on the question of authority led to the expansion of the Protestant doctrine of Scripture into a major chapter (often the first chapter) of their new statements of faith and of their dogmatics. This was a doctrine for which, during the seventeenth century, it became more difficult than it had been earlier to identify differences, even of emphasis, between the two principal Protestant communions, as Lutheran theology began to match, and in some instances to overtake, Reformed theology in its doctrine of the verbal inspiration of the Bible. One difference lay in the treatment of the doctrine of the clarity (or "perspicuity") of Scripture; both affirmed it against Roman Catholic claims that Scripture was obscure and needed the church to interpret it, but some Reformed theologians, for example Bartholomaeus Keckermann, qualified this by asserting that Scripture "can easily be understood . . . , at any rate by the elect."

Both Lutheran and Reformed dogmaticians defined inspiration "as the act whereby God conveyed to man both the content of that which He wished to be written for man's sake and the very words expressing that content." Therefore "canonical Sacred Scripture," according to this doctrine of inspiration as Quenstedt defined it, "is the infallible truth, free of any error; or, to say the same thing in another way, in canonical Sacred Scripture there is no lie, no falsehood, not even the tiniest of errors [nullus vel minimus error], either in content or in words. Rather, each and every thing contained in it is altogether true, be it dogmatic or moral or historical, chronological, topographical, or onomastic. It is neither possible nor permissible to attribute to the amanuenses of the Holy Spirit any ignorance, lack of thought, or forgetfulness, or any lapse of memory, in recording Holy Writ." That formulation, which could be duplicated from the dogmatics of many other Lutheran theologians, can also be matched from Reformed theologians, who taught that "under the inspiration of God the writers simply could not err. . . . neither in important matters nor in trivial ones [levioribus]"; for "if we acknowledge any errors of any sort in the Scriptures, we no longer believe the Holy Spirit to be their author." The genealogies of Scripture had to come from the Holy Spirit, and the miracle stories had to be true. God was the true author of Scripture. The biblical writers were "merely amanuenses," to whom it was "dictated." This meant that "considered in a contributory sense, . . . as it functions in the natural domain, man's will did not produce Scripture but was utterly passive." But it was important to remember that at the same time "subjectively and materially the will of the writers was active in the writing of Scripture." Hence they could not "in their writing have strayed from the facts because of some weakness of memory or of thought processes, nor from the [right] word because of inexperience or imprudence; but all the words that are contained in Holy Writ as signs ought to be accepted and held . . . to be the words of the Holy Spirit."

When "the individual words" of Scripture were described as, quite literally, "the words of the Holy Spirit," that pertained in the strict sense only to the original languages—and to the original manuscripts, all of them now lost. "The language in which the Old Testament was written by the prophets, and the books of the New Testament by the evangelists and apostles, is the only authentic language in the Holy Scriptures," Gerhard maintained. "Therefore," he continued, "only the Hebrew and Greek languages in Holy Scripture are the authentic ones." For only these original languages were "the fountain of Israel." The polemical point of this insistence was the need to respond to the Council of Trent, which at its fourth session had raised the Latin Vulgate to an authoritative position

Quen.*Theol.*1.4.2.5 (1715–I:112)

Ames.*Scrip.*1.5 (1646:2);Trel.*Schol.inst.1* (1606:5)

Heid.*Corp.theol.*2.37 (1700–I:33)
Aret.*Loc.*127 (1617:722–23);
Aret.*Ev.*Matt.1:1–17 (1587–I:tr-7v);Aret.*Act.*2:13 (1590:16r–16v)
Bucan.*Inst.*4.2 (1605:37);Aret.*Loc.*49 (1617:261)

Bucan.*Inst.*4.12 (1605:41)

Preus (1970) 288

Cocc.*S.T.*4.41 (1665:50)

Martn.*Sum.op.*1 (1612:17–18);
Keck.*Syst.*1.8 (1615:150–51);
Brn.*Doct.foed.*1.1.4 (1688:33)
Chil.*Rel.Prot.*2.27 (1727:45);
Grh.*Disp.* (1655:1309)

Grh.*Loc.*1.13 (Cotta 2:252);
Feur.*Grh.* (1638:20–21);Grh.*Interp.*95 (1663:38–39);Grh.*Conf.cath.*2.1.2 (1662–II:65)
Ps.68:26

Ames.*Bell.*1.1.3 (1629–I:23–29)

See pp. 309–10 above

Polan.*Syntag*.1.42 (1617:83–90);Keck.*Syst*.1.8 (1615:152)
See pp. 306–9 above

Trtn.*Inst*.2.15 (1688–I:144–48);Ames.*Bell*.1.13 (1629–I:23–29)

Ames.*Bell*.1.13 (1629–I:20)

Polan.*Syntag*.1.41 (1617:83)

Luth.*Jud*. (*WA* 11:320–25)

Grh.*Conf.cath*.2.1.2 (1662–II:103–6);Grh.*1.Pet*.2:24 (1692:141);Trtn.*Inst*.2.14 (1688:140–44);Martn.*Sum.op*.1 (1612:14)

Grh.*1.Pet*.2:24 (1692:141)

*Cons.Helv*.3.11 (Niemeyer 731)

Stapl.*Ret*.3 (*ERL*:308–I:58r)

Martn.*Sum.op*.1 (1612:17–18)
Polan.*Syntag*.1.41 (1617:83)
Keck.*Syst*.1.8 (1615:151);
Ames.*Bell*.1.1.3 (1629–I:20)

See pp. 306–10 above

in the church. Although some Roman Catholic theologians of the seventeenth century were taking the words of the council to mean only that the Vulgate was superior to "all other Latin versions," not that it was on the same level as the Hebrew and Greek originals, others ascribed a normative status to the translations and interpretations contained in it. Repeating the criticisms of the Vulgate as a translation, which Erasmus and other humanists had voiced, Protestant theologians distinguished between the originals of the Bible, to which alone the adjective "inspired by God" applied unequivocally, and the Vulgate or any other translation. Among such translations, however, the Septuagint created special problems; for the writers of the New Testament—and therefore the Holy Spirit, who had employed those writers as his "amanuenses"—had repeatedly quoted the Septuagint. They had done so also in some passages such as Isaiah 7:14, where the translation "virgin" was, according to Jewish scholars, incorrect because it was more specific than the Hebrew original allowed. During the seventeenth century Protestant theology had at its disposal a vast amount of scholarship in the Semitic languages and even in rabbinic learning, which it used to good advantage in defending that rendering of Isaiah 7:14. Such a defense of the correctness of the Septuagint as employed by the New Testament did not extend to the version as a whole, but only to those renderings that had been "approved and sanctified by the Holy Spirit" in inspiring the New Testament writers. A special problem came from the discrepancies between the chronologies of the Hebrew original and the Septuagint. Although it had occupied in the Greek East a place analogous to that of the Vulgate in the Latin West (with the difference, of course, that for the East the original of the Greek New Testament had always been the authoritative text), the Septuagint, like the Vulgate, had not been divinely inspired but had only been "worked out by human industry" on the basis of the verbally inspired original and was corrupt in many passages.

Such questions of "sacred philology" were unavoidable for a doctrine that extended divine inspiration to the very words of Scripture. Under the providence of

Matt.5:18

Holl.*Exam*.prol.3.42 (1741: 144)

Keck.*Syst*.1.8 (1615:150–51)

Trtn.*Inst*.2.11.8 (1688–I:125)

Matt.6:13;Grh.*Conf.cath*.2.1.2 (1662:97–99);Polan.*Syntag*.1.38 (1617:81)

Luke 2:14

Aret.*Ev*.Luke 2:14 (1587– II:54v)

Eras.*Adnot*.1 John 5:5 (*LB* 6: 1079–81)

Luth.*DB* (1522) 1 John 5:7 (*WA DB* 7:338 [628–29])

Heid.*Corp.theol*.4.33 (1700–I: 118);Polan.*Syntag*.1.38 (1617: 81)
Hier.*Pr.ep.can.* (*PL* 29:827–31)

Quen.*Theol*.1.9.2.1 (1715– I:497)

Grh.*Disp*.(1655:1293–1394)

Grh.*Loc*.1.16 (Cotta 2:278)

God, the promise of Christ that "not an iota, not a dot will pass from the law" had been fulfilled in the preservation of the complete text of the inspired Scripture. In principle, that doctrine ought also to have encouraged a rigorous application of the methods of textual criticism in order to eliminate from the text any human accretions that might have crept in to adulterate its "authenticity." In practice, however, there was evident a reluctance to acknowledge as inauthentic a text that had become familiar or useful. This applied not only to the doxology of the Lord's Prayer, or to such a passage as the song of the Christmas angels, in which Protestant exegetes and translators preferred "good will to men" to the better-attested reading, "to men of good will"; but especially to the so-called Johannine Comma of 1 John 5:7: "For there are three that bear record in heaven, the Father, the Word, and the Holy Spirit; and these three are one."

On the basis of the manuscript evidence available to him, Erasmus had eliminated the passage from his first edition of the Greek New Testament in 1516, but had restored it in later editions, responding to a storm of protest and to further textual evidence that was produced—quite literally, produced—in support of the text. Luther's translation of the New Testament into German, being based on the 1516 edition of Erasmus, did not contain the passage. Although the weight of the textual evidence against it was seemingly overwhelming, the proof it supplied for the Trinity made an attack on its authenticity seem to be an attack on the dogma. Therefore the Reformed theologian Johann Heinrich Heidegger, citing Jerome, and the Lutheran theologians Johann Gerhard and Johann Andreas Quenstedt argued that the real corruption of the Greek text had been its "erasure by the fraud of the Arians," not its addition by orthodox fathers. In a lengthy disputation on the question, Gerhard marshaled the evidence of manuscripts and versions in an effort to show this, and in his systematic theology he reaffirmed its authenticity. A parallel issue of philology was the status of the Hebrew vowel points in the Old Testament, which had not been added to the consonantal text until well into the Christian era, after Hebrew had ceased being a spoken language. Arguing

Holl.*Exam.*prol.3.43 (1741:147–50)
Polan.*Syntag.*1.37 (1617:75–76)
Brn.*Doct.foed.*1.1.4 (1605:30–32)

Cons.*Helv.*2.10 (Niemeyer 731);Heid.*Corp.theol.*2.48 (1700–I:36)

See pp. 208–9 above

Cons.*rep.* (1666:7)

Conf.*Helv.post.*1 (Niesel 222);Form.*Conc.Epit.Sum.*1 (Bek. 767)

Ames.*Scrip.*3 (1646:1)

See vol.3:255–67;284–93

Luth.*Gal.*(1535)3:10 (WA 40–I:407–8)
See vol.3:289–90

that the providence of God would not have permitted "the perfection of Scripture" to be compromised and that no language could exist without vowels, many (though by no means all) Protestant dogmaticians of the seventeenth century came out in favor of the authenticity, and thus the divine inspiration, of the Hebrew vowel points. Although the confessions of the Reformation era did not include an explicit statement of the doctrine of verbal inspiration, it now achieved some kind of status through its inclusion in the *Repeated Consensus of the Truly Lutheran Faith* of 1655, which insisted that subscription to the Lutheran confessions necessarily entailed an acceptance of the doctrine of verbal inspiration.

It is, however, a historical injustice when present-day theological detractors of the post-Reformation doctrine of verbal inspiration overlook its function as the safeguard for the Reformation principle of "sola Scriptura." In that sense, in spite of the further development that it had undergone, the doctrine could lay claim to continuity with Calvin and even with Luther, and with such Reformation confessions as the *Second Helvetic Confession* and the *Formula of Concord*, both of which had affirmed "sola Scriptura" in their opening sentences. The Calvinistic Puritan theologian William Ames gave classic expression to the principle of "sola Scriptura" in a disputation entitled *The Perfection of Holy Scripture*, and his contemporary and countryman William Chillingworth gave it epigrammatic expression in his famous rule that "the Bible only is the religion of Protestants."

As in the twelfth and thirteenth centuries, so now again in the sixteenth and seventeenth centuries, a concentration on the nature and locus of doctrinal authority was accompanied by a consideration of the problem of reason and revelation, which became the other chief topic in the prolegomena of the systems of confessional dogmatics. Partly because Luther had sometimes spoken as though he were reviving the theory of double truth, usually but mistakenly labeled "Averroist," by which a statement that was true philosophically could be false theologically (and vice versa), Protestant systematic theologians in the seventeenth century again took up the question, "Is truth single

Meis.*Phil.sob.* (1611–I:984–1004);Holl.*Exam.*prol.1.28 (1741:30–31)

See pp. 165–66 above

Jas.1:17

Pelikan (1950) 55–61

Pelikan (1947) 253–63
*Cons.Helv.*18.37–38 (Niemeyer 735–36)

Heid.*Corp.theol.* (1700–I:12,9)

Hkr.*Eccl.pol.*1.14 (1594–I:87)

Hkr.*Eccl.pol.*1.14 (1594–I:85–89)

Hkr.*Eccl.pol.*pr. (1594–I:4)

Hkr.*Eccl.pol.*1.12 (1594–I:83)

or double?" They concluded that God was the author of both philosophical and theological truth and that therefore truth had to be one. In spite of the Thomistic origin of the "five ways" of demonstrating the existence of God by natural means, the conviction that Aristotelian philosophy was also "a gift coming down from the Father of lights" provided support for the incorporation of natural proofs for various of the doctrines of the faith into their systems. Attention to "natural theology," which, almost for the first time, the *Helvetic Consensus* enshrined in a confession and which was taken up in the writings of individual theologians, stressed simultaneously its possibilities as "not without value" and its limitations as "inadequate for salvation." This provided a framework for a renewal of the apologetic enterprise, which Luther had almost totally neglected and to which even Calvin had given only passing attention.

One of the most ambitious apologetic efforts within Protestantism during this period was, a bit surprisingly, embedded in a work that was not primarily concerned with either doctrinal or philosophical theology but with church structure: *Of the Laws of Ecclesiastical Polity* by Richard Hooker, an apologia for the unique features of the Anglican settlement. Hooker acknowledged that there were many doctrines, including the Trinity, that were "in Scripture nowhere to be found by express literal mention, only deduced they are out of Scripture by collection." Yet that did not detract from "the sufficiency of Scripture unto the end for which it was instituted," so long as one recognized what that end was—and what it was not. It was the knowledge of salvation, but it was not a detailed "ordinance of Jesus Christ" about the specific arrangements of ecclesiastical polity. These were to be known from the laws of reason and nature; for "when supernatural duties are necessarily exacted, natural are not rejected as needless," and the law of God included both. Therefore it was a mistake, in the name of "a desire to enlarge the necessary use of the word of God," to hold that "only one law, the Scripture, must be the rule to direct in all things," when in fact "God hath left sundry kinds of laws unto men, and by all those laws the actions of men are in some

Hkr.*Eccl.pol.*2.pr. (1594–I:98)

Hkr.*Eccl.pol.*1.16 (1594–I:93–94)

Hkr.*Eccl.pol.*1.12 (1594–I:83)

Caj. *Comm.S.T.*1.2.3 (*Ed. Leon.* 4:32–34);Suar.*Div.sub.*1.1.13–22 (Vivès 1:3–5)

Pasc.*Pens.*233 (Braunschvicg 13:141–55)

Guardini (1966) 159

See vol.3:261–62

Rich (1953) 182

sort directed." For God had so ordered the universe that there were many kinds of law besides the biblical and ecclesiastical, "some natural, some rational, some supernatural, some politic, some finally ecclesiastical." Therefore the "laws of ecclesiastical polity" with which Hooker was dealing were not to be derived in any simplistic way from Scripture itself, but depended on an understanding of natural and rational law, for which natural and rational means of understanding were appropriate. The most significant predecessor for much of this philosophical apologetic was not John Calvin, nor even Martin Luther (despite his similar views about both law and polity), but Thomas Aquinas.

Roman Catholic polemic against the Protestant systems, therefore, found itself able to treat these shared philosophical presuppositions as a basis for the discussion of the theological differences, even on the doctrine of justification. As part of its rehabilitation of Thomism, the theology of the Counter-Reformation likewise reasserted the "five ways" of Aquinas. Yet the most innovative solution in this period for the problem of arguments for the existence of God was also provided by Roman Catholic thought, in the *Pensées* of Blaise Pascal. His "argument of the wager [argument du pari]" manifested "profound differences," but an "affinity . . . still greater," when compared with Anselm's "ontological argument" for the existence of God. It put to the doubting mind the challenge: "Either God exists, or he does not exist. But to which side shall we incline? Reason can determine nothing here." Instead, "one has to wager" and "calculate the gain and the loss of wagering whether or not God exists." Pascal urged wagering on the affirmative possibility, "without hesitation"; for "if you win, you win all; if you lose, you lose nothing." Pascal's alternative to traditional Thomism has not become a constituent part of church doctrine. But far from showing, as has been contended, that Pascal was "removed a long way from the doctrine of the Roman Church," it was a restatement in the seventeenth century of an essentially Augustinian method of argumentation, evidencing the continuing vitality within Roman Catholic thought of ways of thinking that went back, through Bonaventure and Anselm, to Augustine himself. And in that sense it does belong to the history of church doctrine as well as to the history of philosophical theology.

Pascal died in 1662. During the final third of the seventeenth century, following his death, each of the major doctrinal issues we have just been examining came in for a reconsideration that in some way gave a preview of the eighteenth, nineteenth, and twentieth centuries. On 19 March 1682, the second of *The Four Gallican Articles,* a statement of the special status of the church in France, reaffirmed the teachings of the Council of Constance, limiting the authority of the pope in relation to a general council of the church and thus heralding the debate over church and papacy that would continue unremittingly until the period during and after the Second Vatican Council. Also in the area of authority and also within Roman Catholicism, there appeared in 1678 a book entitled *Critical History of the Old Testament* by Richard Simon, who questioned the traditional ascription of the Pentateuch to Moses. In that same year Ralph Cudworth, the best known of the Cambridge Platonists, after many delays, published his *True Intellectual System of the Universe,* which combined orthodox conclusions about the relation of God and the world with a confidence in the powers of reason that could (and did) lead to radically different conclusions. And in 1692 Joseph Butler was born, who would, in 1736, write *The Analogy of Religion,* an exposition of natural theology that would stand as a monument in the modern history of apologetics. Thus the end of the seventeenth century has rightly come to be regarded as a turning point in the history of the prolegomena of dogmatics.

See p. 112 above
*Decl.cler.Gall.*2 (*Coll.Lac.* 832)

### The Humanity of Jesus Christ

The many profound similarities manifested by the various confessional churches of the seventeenth century in their concentration on the topics of theological epistemology and doctrinal authority have made it appropriate to cross denominational boundaries in treating the issues of prolegomena. On the other hand, the definitions of dogma achieved by all the confessional churches in their doctrinal formularies and church councils during the second and third generations of the Reformation era were so precise—and so particular in their differentiation from those of the other churches—that the only way to treat the development of individual doctrines in this period is to concentrate on the several churches one at a time (following the order of the central narrative in chapters 3–5) and to examine for each of them one doctrine that, as a consequence of the Reformation antitheses, became a slogan identified with that specific confessional church.

During the century or so that followed the adoption of the *Book of Conford* in 1580, the heirs of the Lutheran Reformation composed a profusion of systems of dogmatics, in which the tradition of the *Augsburg Confession*, originally set forth as a statement of concord and consensus, took its place as an exclusionary denominational norm. The familiar Reformation assertion, common to Lutheranism and Calvinism, that the bondage of the will implied "the lack of the power

Br.*Comp*.2.2.13 (Walther 2: 296)

to act correctly with regard to a spiritual good," required continued defense on several fronts. The doctrine of justification by faith as "embracing the forgiveness of sins and the imputation of the righteousness of Christ" had to be directed not only against

Grh.*Disp*.5.10 (1655:389)

Grh.*Loc*.16.54;16.35 (Cotta 7:55;7:32–33)

Roman Catholicism, as it had been from the beginning of the Reformation, but now also against Socinianism. The interpretation of the relation between the law and the gospel as "in their nature altogether [toto coelo]

Holl.*Exam*.3.2.2.11 (1741: 1030)

distinct" was seen as a major point of difference between Lutheranism and Calvinism. The Reformed equation of Lutheran and Roman Catholic views of the eucharistic presence—transubstantiation and, despite Lutheran objections to the term, "consubstan-

Brn.*Doct.foed*.4.21.22 (1688: 602;605);Brg.*Calov*.51 (1657: L3v)
Hutt.*Conc*.prol.2 (1690:U2v–Z3r)

tiation"—also called for definition and defense. In those systems, the most prominent example of doctrinal development was in some ways the doctrine of

See pp. 343–47 above

the inspiration and inerrancy of Scripture. This doctrine was also, to a great degree, a point of convergence between Lutheran dogmatics and its adversaries in both Calvinism and Roman Catholicism, although Lutheran confessionalism disputed with both of them on the interpretation of that inspired and inerrant Scripture and with Roman Catholicism on its relation to the authority of the church as well.

Far more distinctive, however, was the Lutheran development of the doctrine of the person of Christ. Christology had emerged, "in connection with the controversy on the Holy Supper" and the doctrine of the real presence in the Eucharist, as the principal dogmatic difference setting Lutheranism apart from Calvinism—although "[this is not the same as saying] that the eucharistic doctrine of the Reformers was nothing more than a derivative from their peculiar christology." Luther had already set forth a special version of the doctrine of the communication of properties that was intended to safeguard the real presence against the objection that it was precluded by the ascension of the humanity of Christ to the right hand of God. The authors of the *Formula of Concord*, especially Martin Chemnitz, had elaborated and systematized Luther's doctrine, and in the process had compiled an appendix to the *Formula*, entitled "Catalogue of Testimonies," intended to demonstrate the continuity of Lutheran christology with that of the ancient church fathers and church councils. Considered simply as an achievement of systematic and speculative "architectonics," the christology of the Lutheran dogmaticians of the seventeenth century— including the complicated and protracted conflict between the theologians of Giessen and those of Tübingen over the condition of the divine attributes of Christ during his state of humiliation or "kenosis"— belongs principally to the history of theology rather than to the history of church doctrine, also because they "almost totally bypass" the *Formula of Concord* in their presentations of this doctrine, relying instead on the "great and definitive work on the subject of the two natures of Christ" written by Chemnitz. With some modifications, largely technical and terminological, the christology of Chemnitz eventually prevailed. Nevertheless, the doctrine of the person of Christ was, together with the doctrine of the Trinity, the principal dogmatic heritage of the ancient church and the mark of continuity with it. As such, the form it took in the debates of this period is a continuation of that dogmatic development and hence a part also of the history of church doctrine.

*Form.Conc.Epit.*8.1 (*Bek.* 804)

Gollwitzer (1937) 116

See pp. 158–61 above

*Lib.Conc.*app. (*Bek.*1101–35)

Elert (1962) 229

Thomasius (1857) 429–88

Preus (1977) 97

See vol.1:256–60

Chem.*Du.nat.*24 (1580:352)

Chem.*Du.nat.*1 (1580:7)

Bucan.*Inst.*disp. (1605:1)

Hav.*Majest.*2.3 (1658:15)

See vol.1:52–54;229–32
Trel.*Schol.inst.*1 (1606:27–28)

Grh.*Loc.*4.198 (Cotta 3:485)

Heid.*Corp.theol.*3.29;3.48;17.61 (1700–I:70;79;II:30–31)

Trel.*Schol.inst.*2. (1606:57)

Polan.*Syntag.*2.32 (1617:192)

Heid.*Corp.theol.*17.61 (1700–II:30–31)

Grh.*Loc.*2.5 (Cotta 3:110–15)

Stapl.*Count.*2.12;2.13 (*ERL* 311:137r–139v;146r);Stapl.*Ret.* 4 (*ERL* 308–II:153r;174r;196r)

Hkr.*Eccl.pol.*5.52 (1594–II:110)

See vol.1:263–66

Trel.*Schol.inst.*2 (1606:55–56);
Heid.*Corp.theol.*17.40 (1700–II:19);Brn.*Doct.foed.*4.19.16 (1688:519–20)

Trtn.*Inst.*13.7 (1688–II:345–49)

Within the dogmatic development, it was the christology of "preexistence, kenosis, and exaltation" that served as the basis, as the concentration of the dogmaticians on "that celebrated dictum of Philippians 2 about 'the form of God' and 'the form of the servant'" indicates. They were concerned both with the relation of the two "natures" of Christ to each other ("nature" being a term inherited from "the usage of the ancient church") and with the relation of the two "states" of kenosis and exaltation ("state" being a term shared with Reformed christology). The kenosis of Philippians 2 could not mean "a kenosis according to the deity," since that would imply that he was "changed according to the deity"; for with patristic christology—and with their Reformed opponents—they went on taking it as a self-evident axiom that "the deity is impassible, unchangeable, and immutable." If one drew from this axiom the inference that the divine nature as such was in every sense of the word "incommunicable," that appeared to interpose serious obstacles for Lutheran christology. There were, according to Reformed teaching, two different kinds of divine attributes, the communicable and the incommunicable, and without blasphemy against the unchangeable nature of God the incommunicable attributes could not be predicated of any creature, not even of the human nature of Christ. In response to that challenge, Lutheran dogmatics was obliged to clarify its use of the technical term "unchangeable."

As the legislation of the Council of Chalcedon about church authority figured prominently in the ecclesiological debates between Roman Catholicism and Protestantism, so at the center of the christological debates between Calvinism and Lutheranism stood its confession about the two natures in Christ: "without confusion, without change, without division, without separation." This Chalcedonian quartet of terms was affirmed by Reformed as well as by Lutheran dogmaticians, all of whom quoted it, often in the original Greek, and followed up their quotation with an analysis of each term. Reformed christology had to protest that it was not violating the prohibition against dividing or separating the two natures and that therefore it was not "Nestorian," as the Lutherans charged; and

Polan.*Syntag*.6.16 (1617:376–77);Aret.*Loc*.21 (1617:114)

Dan.*Haer*. (1580:76–77);Keck.*Syst*.3.2 1615:261)

Bell.*Lib.Conc*.1.3–4 (Fèvre 7:105–7)

Wolf.*Eut.Luth*.2.19;5.8 (1680:E1r;I3v)

Holl.*Exam*.3.1.3.31 (1741:685–89)

Br.*Comp*.3.2.1.22 (Walther 3:73)

Grh.*Interp*.192 (1663:91)

Holl.*Exam*.3.1.3.36 (1741:694)

Grh.*Loc*.4.103 (Cotta 3:413)

Luke 1:35

Hutt.*Conc*.21 (1690:596)

Grh.*Disp*. (1655:908)

See vol.2:88–89

Quen.*Theol*.3.3.1.1.3 (1715–II:154)

Trel.*Schol.inst*.2 (1606:52)

Quen.*Theol*.3.3.1.1.3 (1715–II:112);Grh.*Loc*.4.112 (Cotta 3:420–21)

in its polemics it concentrated on "without confusion," charging the Lutheran theologians in turn with being "Eutychian" for the false conclusions they were drawing from ancient christological dogma—a charge in which Roman Catholic critics of the Lutheran doctrine joined. In defending themselves against the accusation of Eutychianism, Lutherans protested that they were only teaching "the real union and communication of the natures" in Christ, which was not Eutychianism but Chalcedonian orthodoxy. Therefore they were obliged to prove their fidelity to the first two terms of the formula, explaining that they did not regard "emulsion" as a fitting metaphor for the union of the two natures in Christ. Indeed, Leo's *Tome* addressed to Chalcedon had been "a forerunner of our theologians" in its doctrine of the two natures, and Gerhard set forth the confession of the Council of Chalcedon as the basis for a valid hermeneutical method of dealing with difficult passages of Scripture. Lutheran dogmatics also went on affirming that at the Council of Ephesus of 431 "the Christian Church correctly calls the holy Virgin Mary 'Theotokos,'" and that in the incarnation of the Logos her body had been sanctified by a special action of the Holy Spirit, "so that what was to be born of Mary would be holy." Lutheran theologians accused Reformed doctrine of distorting their position on this question, even as, at the same time, they quoted Bernard's rejection of the immaculate conception against the Roman Catholic doctrine of Mary.

A prominent source for Lutheran theologians in many of these discussions of the person of Christ was John of Damascus. His discussion of "activity" in Christ helped Lutheran dogmatics to explain the concept of Christ's "official work [apotelesma]." His explanation of the appropriateness of "anhypostaton" and "enhypostaton" as terms for the human nature of Christ was acceptable to Reformed theology as well, but it appeared to be especially congenial to the Lutheran way of interpreting the personal union of the two natures in the one hypostasis of Christ. "The personal union," in the formulation of Hollaz, "is the conjunction of the two natures, divine and human, subsisting in the one hypostasis of the Son of God,

Thos.Aq.*S.T.*3.2.4 (*Ed.Leon.*
11:31)

Holl.*Exam.*3.1.3.29 (1741:683)

Holl.*Exam.*3.1.3.16 (1741:671)

Holl.*Exam.*3.1.3.18 (1741:671)

Chem.*Du.nat.*18 (1580:237–
45);Aret.*Loc.*3 (1617:23)

See vol.2:67–75

See vol.2:74
Bald.*Art.Smal.*4.20 (1605-IV:
A4r)

Grh.*Disp.*15.19 (1665:660–63)

See pp. 329–31 above

See vol.1:249–51,270–74;vol.2:
83–84

Br.*Comp.*3.2.1.16 (Walther 3:
43)

Polan.*Syntag.*6.16 (1617:379);
Brn.*Doct.foed.*4.19.16 (1688:
523–27)

bringing with it a mutual and indissoluble communion of both natures"; Hollaz quoted with approval the explanation of Thomas Aquinas that when Christ was called a "composite person," this did not mean that he consisted of two essential parts, but that he was "one person in two natures." In the incarnation, the divine nature had been the active and "assuming" nature, and the human nature the passive and "assumed" nature, which did not have an existence of its own before being assumed. Hence there was a single divine hypostasis, and the human nature was "anhypostaton," without a hypostasis of its own, as well as "enhypostaton," having its subsistence in the divine hypostasis. It did, however, have a will of its own, distinct from that of the divine nature (though altogether harmonious with it), as both Lutherans and Calvinists affirmed in opposition to the heresy of Monotheletism; for, in the ancient and orthodox formula of Gregory of Nazianzus, quoted by John of Damascus, "whatever has not been assumed [by the Logos in the incarnation] has not been healed." This unity of hypostasis implied that worship addressed to the person of the God-man was not idolatry, as it would be if the human nature had an existence of its own, and that the effort of Socinus and the *Racovian Catechism* to defend such worship while denying the dogmas of the Trinity and of Christ as the God-man was altogether inconsistent.

The "mutual and indissoluble communion of both natures" had as its necessary corollary another ancient and orthodox formula, the doctrine of "the communication of properties [communicatio idiomatum]," which Johann Wilhelm Baier defined as "that by which it comes to pass that those things which, when the two natures are compared together, belong to one of them per se and formally are truly to be predicated of the other nature also." Reformed christology, by contrast, maintained that the communication pertained "not to the relation between the natures but to the person" of Christ and was a communion of properties, not of natures; therefore it was neither "a real transfusion" nor "a real donation, from which should follow that the human nature of Christ might use the divine properties as its own instru-

Ames.*Marr.*1.18 (1642:72)

Form.*Conc.S.D.*8.87 (*Bek.* 1046–47);Chem.*Du.nat.*3 (1580:49–50)

Holl.*Exam.*3.1.3.39 (1741:698)

Chem.*Du.nat.*12 (1580:166)

Form.*Conc.S.D.*8.36 (*Bek.* 1028)

Chem.*Du.nat.*13 (1580:174)

Quen.*Theol.*3.3.1.1.3 (1715–II:129)

Polan.*Syntag.*6.16 (1617:375)

1 Cor.2:8

Holl.*Exam.*3.1.3.43 (1741:701)

Acts 20:28(var.)

Br.*Comp.*1.1.30 (Walther 2:50)

ments." It was above all in its elaboration of the communication of properties that Lutheran christology broke new ground, going far beyond the original eucharistic context of Luther's christological speculations but endeavoring to keep the soteriological emphasis on the continuing presence of Jesus Christ "also according to that nature by which he is our brother and we are flesh of his flesh." The Lutheran dogmaticians of the seventeenth century followed Chemnitz and the *Formula of Concord* in distinguishing three "genera" of communication of properties; although they diverged from the *Formula of Concord* in the order of the three "genera," they all agreed with the judgment of Chemnitz: "There is clarity among us as to the teachings but not as to the terminology. But when people can agree on the substance, they should be tolerant about the terms, which only serve the doctrine."

The first of the three "genera" of communication, according to the *Formula of Concord,* meant that "any property, though it belongs only to one of the natures, is ascribed not only to the respective nature as something separate but to the entire person who is simultaneously God and man (whether he is called God or whether he is called man)"; or, in the definition of Chemnitz, "the property which belongs to the one nature is communicated or attributed to the person in the concrete." Lutheran theologians spoke of "the concreteness of the person or of a nature [concretum vel personae, vel naturae]," but the emphasis on the concrete person, which Reformed christology likewise set forth (though in a different way and for different reasons), was intended to protect this "genus" of communication from predicating suffering and mortality of the divine nature of Christ: "We do not read in Holy Writ that the deity [of Christ] was crucified, but that 'the Lord of glory' was crucified." Other such biblical statements, which spoke of the church as having been redeemed by God with "his own blood," proved that the one who did the redeeming by shedding his blood was truly God. Carelessness of language here, not unknown among orthodox church fathers and more recent theologians, could lead to the accusation of a revival of the heresy

See vol.1:104–5
Grh.*Loc*.4.198 (Cotta 3:485–86)

Holl.*Exam*.3.1.3.44 (1741:703)

Calov.*Art.fid*.3.1.8 (1684:185)
Brg.*Calov*.57 (1657:M1v)

Grh.*Loc*.4.202 (Cotta 3:490)

Br.*Comp*.3.2.1.20 (Walther 3:52)

Hav.*Majest*.4.3. (1658:27)

Mentz.*Thes.theol*.1.34–39 (1612–I:B2r–B3r)

Grh.*Conf.cath*.2.2.1 (1662–II:299–300);Hutt.*Conc*.4 (1690:169–70)
Bucan.*Inst*.27.24;28.24 (1605:200–01,291),Alst.*Theol.cat*.2.8 (1616:344);Bell.*Cont*.10.3.17 (Fèvre 4:171–73)

Quen.*Theol*.3.3.1.2.14 (1715–II:265)
Bucan.*Inst*.28.5 (1605:283);Keck.*Syst*.3.5. (1615:299)

Aret.*Ev*.Mark 16:19 (1587–II:39v);Ames.*Marr*.1.23 (1642:94)

Brn.*Doct.foed*.4.19.16 (1688:527);Keck.*Syst*.3.2 (1615:260)

of "Patripassianism" and Sabellianism. But fear of that accusation should not lead to a denial of the proposition that "the Son of God truly, really, and properly suffered, was crucified, and died"; for the statements of Scripture attested that it was not only the human nature that suffered, but the very Son of God, "Jehovah himself." Reformed writers preferred to describe such statements as "synecdoche."

"The second genus of communication [of properties] has been the subject of the gravest controversies in the church," the genus "by which the perfections that are truly divine, together with the authority and power resulting from them, the honor and the supreme glory, are communicated to the human nature of Christ in the abstract." These "perfections" or "attributes above nature and beyond nature," which had been "given" only to the human nature because the divine nature already possessed them, could be summed up in the term "majesty"; hence this came to be known as "the genus of majesty [genus majestaticum]," which Calvinism rejected. The "controversies" had arisen because it was this aspect of the Lutheran christological doctrine that was the most directly involved in the eucharistic debate, since one of the properties of majesty said to be communicated to the human nature of Christ was divine omnipresence or "ubiquity"; hence the epithet "Ubiquitarians" for the Lutherans, employed by both Reformed and Roman Catholic adversaries. After ruling out other issues as not involved here, Quenstedt formulated the issue as:"Is Christ, according to the humanity that is united with his divine and infinite person and that is exalted at the right hand of the Divine Majesty, present, in this glorious state of exaltation, to all creatures in the universe with a true, real, substantial, and efficacious omnipresence?" Reformed theologians, while acknowledging that the phrase was not metaphorical, argued that the "right hand of God" to which Christ had ascended was, "because of the status and condition of the human body, a definite reference to a place, in which Christ, by virtue of his true human body, is circumscribed"; it was not "a ubiquitary heaven." The Lutheran doctrine was "repugnant both to sound reason and to Sacred Scripture." Luther had already

See p. 160 above

Form.Conc.Epit.8.39 (Bek. 812)

Br.Comp.3.2.2.2 (Walther 3: 76)

Br.Comp.3.2.1.22 (Walther 3: 70)

Form.Conc.Epit.8.17 (Bek. 808)

Acts 20:28(var.)

Grh.Loc.4.284 (Cotta 3:557); Grh.1.Pet.4:1 (1692:567–68)

Hkr.Eccl.pol.5.52 (1594–II: 108)

Calv.Inst.(1559)4.17.32 (Barth-Niesel 5:391)

contended that the "right hand of God" was not a place, but was the majesty of God. The human nature of Christ had, moreover, been in possession of that majesty and omnipresence from the very moment of the incarnation and had not had it "restored"; but it had, during the state of humiliation or "kenosis," voluntarily "abdicated from the full use of it."

The third "genus" of the communication of properties, according to the most common classification, pertained to the "official works [apotelesmata]" of Christ: "Actions pertaining to the office of Christ do not belong to one nature singly and alone, but are common to both, inasmuch as each contributes to them that which is its own and thus each acts with the communication of the other." Hence it was called the "apotelesmatic genus." If it was the "genus of majesty" that made it "possible" or even "easy" for Christ to be present with his body and blood in the Eucharist through the communication of the property of omnipresence to his human nature, it was by the apotelesmatic "genus" that this doctrine of the person of Christ was applied to the meaning of salvation: The union of the two natures in Christ occurred so that the work of redemption, atonement, and salvation might be accomplished in, with, and through both natures of Christ. When, therefore, in accordance with the first "genus," the New Testament could attribute the redemption of the church to the blood of God, this meant that "redeeming the church" and similar actions "are official works that are predicated of Christ according to both natures; yet we do not say that Christ suffered and died according to both natures, but that Christ suffered according to the flesh, that Christ died according to the flesh."

For all the Lutheran insistence that the doctrine of the three genera of the communication of properties, and particularly the concept of a "genus of majesty," was a way of emphasizing and ennobling the authentic humanity of Jesus Christ, the critics of the doctrine in various camps saw it as a threat to the human nature. "Although they cover it up or do not notice it," Calvin had said, the expositors of Lutheran christology did in fact "deprive [Christ] of his flesh" and of his humanity. That charge was echoed in the seven-

Bucan.*Inst*.28.22 (1605:288)

Wolf.*Eut.Luth*.4.5 (1680:H4v)

Joh.D.*F.o*.3.17 (Kotter 2:156)

Chem.*Du.nat*.26 (1580:396)
See vol.2:10–12
2 Pet.1:4

Chem.*Du.nat*.20 (1580:254)

Br.*Comp*.3.2.1.22 (Walther 3:70)

See vol.3:139–44

Br.*Comp*.prol.1.32 (Walther 1:53)

See p. 161 above

Aret.*Loc*.35;136 (1617:196–202;766–67);Bell.*Cont*.11.4.1 (Fèvre 4:602)
*Apol.Conf.Aug*.4.178 (*Bek*.195)

Bell.*Cont*.11.4.13 (Fèvre 4:633);Bell.*Lib.Conc*.2.18 (Fèvre 7:122);Bell.*Dich.dott.cris*.3.4 (Fèvre 12:288–89)

Trel.*Schol.inst*.2 (1606:65)

teenth century. If the body of Christ were omnipresent, according to the reply of Bucanus to Luther and his followers, that would not glorify his human nature but abolish it. Lutherans had echoed some of the Greek fathers in speaking about a "deified human nature of Christ." But when the church fathers had used such a suspicious-sounding term as "deification" to describe the incarnation, Chemnitz explained on the basis of John of Damascus, they "did not have in mind a transmutation, commingling, conversion, abolition, or equating of the natures, but they wished by this term to describe first of all the plan of the personal union." This was in keeping with his exegesis of the Byzantine locus classicus for "deification" as a definition of salvation: It did not mean that "the essential, uncreated, and infinite attributes of the Deity" were conferred on believers, but "gracious finite gifts, in a sense, the effects of the Deity."

This high speculation about the doctrine of the person of Christ did not produce much significant effect on the doctrine of the atonement. Despite the emphasis of the "apotelesmatic genus" on the close connection between the doctrine of the person of Christ and the doctrine of the work of Christ, the entire apparatus of the three "genera" was in fact brought into the service of the Anselmic theory of salvation through the satisfaction achieved by the suffering and death of the God-man Jesus Christ, which continued to be the dominant metaphor of redemption for the Lutheran dogmaticians. This doctrine of "satisfaction" was, according to Baier, one of the "fundamental articles," denial of which would jeopardize salvation. There was, of course, continuing controversy between Roman Catholics and Protestants over the notion of penitential "satisfactions" in the church and their relation to the "satisfaction" achieved by Christ. But Robert Bellarmine was able to quote the *Apology of the Augsburg Confession* as documentation of an ecumenical consensus that the death of Christ was a "satisfaction" offered on the cross "for the guilt" of the whole human race. The reference to the whole human race did in fact represent one qualification of that ecumenical consensus. In Reformed teaching "the priestly office of Christ" could sometimes be said to consist in "rendering satisfaction to God for men,"

See pp. 237–39 above

Cons.Helv.15.32 (Niemeyer 734)

Keck.Syst.3.4 (1615:278)
See p. 343 above
Keck.Syst.1.9 (1615:162–63)

Ames.Marr.1.20 (1642:78–81)
See pp. 324–25 above
Brn.Doct.foed.3.10.6 (1688: 288)

Burm.Synop.35.19 (1687:97); Keck.Syst.2.7 (1615:237)

Quen.Theol.3.3.2.6 (1715–II: 436)

Grh.Med.sacr.11;14 (1633:44; 59)

See pp. 162–63 above

Grh.Loc.26.486 (Cotta 18: 253–54)

Franks (1918) 2:48

Grot.Sat.1 (de Groot 3:304)

Grot.Sat.1 (de Groot 3:298–99)

Grot.Sat.7 (de Groot 3:323)

Grot.Sat.7;10 (de Groot 3:323; 331–38)

but the language of the *Helvetic Consensus*, according to which Christ had "by the obedience of his death made satisfaction to God the Father in the stead of the elect," not in the stead of all humanity, was more representative. Similarly, the Protestant insistence on the clarity and perspicuity of Scripture had come to include the qualifier that only the elect could find it completely clear.

Except for that qualifier, however, the consensus was firm. The attack of the Socinians on it occasioned an ever more vigorous assertion of it as a "decree" unto itself, even though "satisfaction" did not appear "in so many words" in Scripture, since from "the fact that the word does not appear" it did not follow that "therefore the matter does not appear." Even in a devotional context, Lutherans would review the entire life of Christ as a series of satisfactions rendered to the violated justice of God. Although Luther had, by his repeated emphasis on the theme of "Christus Victor," proposed a dramatically different view of reconciliation, there is much to be said for the historical thesis that the Reformation and its aftermath had, if anything, intensified the hold of the metaphor of satisfaction on the Western doctrine of the atonement. There were occasional echoes in the Lutheran dogmaticians of Luther's rediscovery of the patristic view of the atonement; but it remained for Reformed theology, and in its less orthodox modality at that, to propose a fundamentally different alternative to the Anselmic theory of satisfaction.

It did this in the thought of Hugo Grotius, who formulated "one of the most important [theories] in the whole history of our doctrine" of the atonement. He was careful to distinguish his critique of the notion of "satisfaction" from that of Socinus: Christ did not die as a "martyr," which is where the theories of Socinus seemed to come out, but his death was in some way the cause of the forgiveness of sins. As for the theory of "satisfaction," it could, despite its nonbiblical origin, lay claim to being a "suggestive expression" of biblical language. Nevertheless, the death of Christ was not to be seen as an appeasement of the divine wrath. Rather, in the death of Christ "the end of punishment is the manifestation of retributive jus-

Grot.*Sat*.1;4 (de Groot 3:303–4;315)

Franks (1918) 2:66

tice in regard of sins." As "the work, not merely of a theologian employing juristic ideas, but of a jurist dealing with theology," the "governmental theory of the atonement" propounded by Grotius had the strength of emphasizing that God himself was the originator of the plan of salvation. But as a private theory, it did not achieve standing within the public doctrine of the church.

It could not, moreover, despite its "Arminian" provenance, come to terms with the Calvinist—and, far beyond the borders of Calvinism, the universally human—concern to safeguard the humanity of Jesus Christ. The eventual embodiment of that concern was to take a form that both Lutherans and Calvinists would, and did, regard as heretical. Our consideration of that development will have to begin with Lutheran Pietism. As we shall see, its initial form was, dogmatically speaking, harmless enough. The *Pious Desires* of Jacob Spener, the founder of Lutheran Pietism, was published in 1675; in it the theme that would be sounded in 1728 in William Law's *Serious Call to a Devout and Holy Life* made its first important appearance in post-Reformation Protestantism. Jesus Christ, the Son of God but also the brother of all humanity, issued his summons to the entire human race with an urgency and an unavoidability that was based on his profound kinship with all its members.

Troeltsch (1960) 2:717

To be sure, "Pietism remained within the Church; indeed, at the time of the Enlightenment it bound itself very closely with the relics of the old dogmatic ecclesiastical system." But it remains true at the same time that "in the first decades of the eighteenth century there sets in a decline [of the church], which affects its entire system of church doctrine, but above

Thomasius (1857) 524

all christology." For if the subjective experience of divine grace for which Spener and Pietism called was no less to find its ground in the human life of Jesus Christ, there had to be, within his own humanity, some way of exhibiting it.

In the light of the literary form of the four Gospels, could that exhibiting take any other form than a "biography" of the human Jesus? In 1694 Hermann Samuel Reimarus was born. "Before Reimarus," it has been suggested, "no one had attempted to form a historical conception of the life of Jesus"; and so "there had been nothing to prepare the world for a work of such power as that of Reimarus." By the time that power had become evident, the question of "the humanity of Jesus Christ" was transformed from a problem of Chalcedonian christology to a task of historical-critical research into the biography of Jesus. Once that happened, the modern period had begun.

Schweitzer (1961) 13–14

## The History of the Covenant

Among the major Reformation definitions of Christian doctrine, the *Canons* promulgated by the Synod of Dort were, by several decades, chronologically the latest; consequently, the line between confessional formulation and orthodox reaffirmation, which is at best ambiguous, becomes especially so here. In addition, the Reformed, Calvinist, and Anglican configuration of Christian doctrine was, in its official and public doctrine, probably the least homogeneous of the principal "confessional" parties, not only in the Anglican communion, with its ongoing commitment to a via media transcending the usual alternatives, but throughout the Reformed version of Protestantism. Nevertheless, both in the decades preceding the Synod of Dort and in those following it, Reformed dogmatics, no less than its Lutheran and Roman Catholic counterparts, was organizing the outcome of the Reformation in the form of systematic theology and relating this to the new issues of the time. The results of that task were incorporated not only in various private works of theologians and preachers but above all in one of the major statements of Reformed church doctrine, the *Westminster Confession of Faith* of 1647, and in the *Formula of the Consensus of the Helvetic Reformed Churches* (or *Helvetic Consensus*) of 1675.

Understandably, the themes of Reformed systematic theology in the seventeenth century, whether in England (and then in New England) or on the Continent, continued to repeat many of the issues that had predominated in the sixteenth century. The prohibition of images by the second commandment (according to the Reformed numbering of the commandments) was still valid, in spite of Bellarmine's restatement of the classic case for the Christian

See pp. 216–17 above
Ex.20:4
Martn.*Sum.op.*4;8 (1612:81–84;162–66);Alst.*Theol.cat.*3.4 (1616:596)

Ames.*Bell.*2.6.5 (1629–II:246)
Brn.*Doct.foed.*3.9.3 (1688: 270–71)

See p. 320 above
Martn.*Sum.op.*10 (1612:184–86);Aret.*Loc.*108 (1617:602–9)

Hkr.*Eccl.pol.*5.57 (1594–II: 127)

Aret.*Loc.*76 (1617:427)

Trel.*Schol.inst.*3 (1606:183)

Keck.*Syst.*3.4 (1615:293)

Heid.*Corp.theol.*5.25 (1700–I: 156)

Ames.*Marr.*1.25 (1642:108)

Keck.*Syst.*3.1 (1615:243)
Aret.*Loc.*6 (1617:36)

Trel.*Schol.inst.*2 (1606:29)

See pp. 220–21 above

use of images, but the arguments for the immaculate conception of the Virgin Mary were still invalid. The Anabaptist polemic against oaths added to the Reformed theological agenda a defense of their legitimacy. It was repeatedly necessary to urge, in opposition to both Roman Catholic and Lutheran dogma, that the sacraments, or rather "the sacramental signs," offered grace, but did "not by their nature confer grace on all." In opposition to Roman Catholic teaching about the freedom of the will, Reformed as well as Lutheran thinkers went on insisting that it pertained only to "natural good," not to "supernatural good." Calvin was, of course, the most prominent Reformed authority with whom critics and defenders alike had to come to terms; but others among the Reformed church fathers (for example, Zacharias Ursinus, especially, it would seem, because of his connection with the *Heidelberg Catechism*) were also authorities to whom theologians would appeal.

As in the first generation and at the Synod of Dort, however, the most controversial doctrinal issue to which orthodox Reformed dogmaticians were obliged to address themselves in their apologias and systems, as well as in their new confessions, was double predestination—or, perhaps to be more precise, election, predestination, and reprobation. There were some who were willing to allow that "the predestination of men is of two kinds, election and reprobation," and hence that "reprobation is the predestinating of certain men" to damnation. But others argued that "in its precise meaning, the term 'predestination' does not include reprobation, but by its nature refers [only] to election to eternal life," and that therefore "it is not speaking precisely to say that 'God has predestined some men to damnation,'" since "Scripture does not call the wicked 'predestined.'" The source of the ambiguity lay in the usage of the word "predestination" itself, which, in the usage both of the Bible and of the church, sometimes applied to divine providence (by now a separate chapter of dogmatics and a separate article in the *Westminster Confession*) rather than only to election.

To answer the persistent accusation that the doctrine of the sovereignty of God and predestination

Polan.*Syntag.*4.6 (1617:238–39;242)

Aret.*Ev.*John 2:4 (1587–II:151r)
Aret.*Loc.*6 (1617:34–35);Heid.*Corp.theol.*5.10 (1700–I:150)

Calv.*Inst.*(1559)2.12.5 (Barth-Niesel 3:442–43)

Keck.*Syst.*1.9 (1615:166)

Heid.*Corp.theol.*5.4 (1700–I:148)

Ames.*Marr.*1.7 (1642:23)

Keck.*Syst.*1.6 (1615:99)

Eph.3.11
Cons.*Helv.*4.12 (Niemeyer 731)

Brn.*Doct.foed.*2.4.9 (1688:143)

Keck.*Syst.*1.6 (1615:99–100)
Polan.*Syntag.*5.1 (1617:256);
Ames.*Marr.*1.25 (1642:105)

Trtn.*Inst.*4.18 (1688–I:459)

Heid.*Corp.theol.*5.16 (1700–I:152–53)

Bucan.*Inst.*36.3 (1605:419)

Polan.*Syntag.*4.6 (1617:242)

Rom.9:16

implied a kind of "Stoic fatalism," it was best to avoid the term "fate," which was not only subject to misunderstanding but was "inane," particularly if applied to the life of Christ. God was sovereign, but he was not despotic; the divine will was absolute, but it was not arbitrary. That distinction underlay the systematization of the doctrine of decrees, for which there was ample precedent in the later recensions of Calvin's *Institutes.* Although "decree" also applied to official acts of church legislation, it was above all with the divine decrees that theology concerned itself. A decree was "an act of God by which, according to his utterly free will and by an immutable counsel and intention, he has defined and concluded, for the demonstration of his glory, all the things outside himself that are to be in the future, together with their causes, operations, circumstances, and manner, how they should come into being and exist"; a more concise definition identified a decree as "his determinate purpose of effecting all things by his almighty power and according to his counsel."

A decree was an act of God, not merely a "faculty," and it could be called, as it was in the New Testament, an "eternal purpose [propositum saeculorum]"; yet, "strictly speaking, the decrees of God should not be counted among his works," since a decree was an immanent act within the Godhead, while the "works" of God were "the execution of the decree." Again, while "strictly speaking, there cannot, as seen formally and from God's side, be an order" of God's various decrees, it was appropriate to frame a doctrine "on the order of God's decrees." According to one widely accepted formulation of the order, God had decreed the following, and in this sequence: "to reveal his glory"; "to create the world"; "to preserve and govern the world"; and "to select some in Christ . . . and to leave others in their sins and condemn them." A somewhat different arrangement distinguished between foreknowledge, counsel or decree, predestination, and election. These decrees could be called "necessary," on the grounds that whatever God had decreed from eternity could not but happen; for, quoting the locus classicus, "It depends not upon man's will or exertion, but upon God's mercy," Reformed theologians insisted that God had the right to choose whomever he pleased, since "without [grace] our will can accomplish absolutely nothing."

Aret. Loc.25 (1617:150)

Much of this theology of decrees, which could easily be expanded from other seventeenth-century sources, was little more than the transposition of the teachings of Calvin and the first generations of Reformed theologians into the key of orthodox Protestant dogmatics, with its attendant philosophical apparatus, differing from those generations chiefly by its systematic precision but not by the substance of its doctrine. What set the seventeenth century (and its anticipation in the sixteenth) apart was its concentration on "the execution of the decree" rather than on the "decree" itself. Much of the language of Scripture, even if interpreted in a predestinarian way, had addressed in the first instance "the execution of the decree" and not the "decree" as such: although it was legitimate to extrapolate backwards from the execution to the decree, the data of the biblical text were historical, not metaphysical. The *Westminster Confession* devoted its third chapter to the topic, "Of God's Eternal Decree," as had many Reformed confessions before it; but in its seventh chapter, "Of God's Covenant with Man," it went beyond those confessions, for "here for the first time a confession makes the doctrine of the covenant authoritatively binding for a major church."

Keck. Syst.3.1 (1615:245)

West. Conf.3 (Müller 549–53)

West. Conf.7 (Müller 558–60)

Schrenk (1923) 82

Such a consideration of time and history did not imply, to orthodox Calvinists, that the eternal decrees of God were in any manner conditioned by what was to be the human and historical response to them. Some Lutheran theologians, in order to obviate the notion of an absolute and arbitrary predestination, taught that "we have been elected on the basis of [ex] our divinely foreseen faith, as this finally takes hold of the merit of Christ," and had also based reprobation on God's foreknowledge of unbelief; the question was a matter of lively interest among Roman Catholic theologians, too. Reformed theologians opposed this explanation as Pelagian and Arminian: faith was the effect of predestination, not its basis or efficient cause; for even Christ was not the meritorious cause of predestination or the foundation that preceded election,

Heid. Corp.theol.5.11 (1700–I: 151)

Quen. Theol.3.2.2.4 (1715–II: 52)
Calov. Art.fid.3.2.41 (1684: 333–37)

Suar. Praed.2.23.4 (Vivès 1: 432)
Ames. Coron.1.6;1.10 (1632: 47;68–71);Keck. Syst.3.1 (1615: 246–49);Heid. Corp.theol.5.42 (1700–I:167)

Polan. Syntag.4.9 (1617:247)

Cons.Helv.5.14 (Niemeyer
731–32)

Dan.Haer. (1580:114);Polan.
Syntag.4.6 (1617:241);Heid.
Corp.theol.5.66 (1700–I:179)

Polan.Syntag.4.10 (1617:252)

Heid.Corp.theol.5.59 (1700–I:
174-75

Brn.Doct.foed.2.4.9 (1688:150)

Calv.Inst.(1559)2.12.5 (Barth-
Niesel 3:442–43)

Keck.Syst.3.1 (1615:244)

Heid.Corp.theol.5.34–35
(1700–I:160–61)

Heid.Corp.theol.5.26 (1700–I:
157)

Heid.Corp.theol.24.1 (1700–II:
377)

Ames.Coron.5.2 (1632:401)

Ames.Marr.1.25 (1642:105)

Keck.Syst.3.1 (1615:245)

but was himself "the elect one." Nevertheless, if the decree of reprobation laid down by God before human history, and therefore uncaused, was not in itself the cause of sin within human history and therefore was not, strictly speaking, the cause of damnation either, then it was necessary to identify human sin within history as the cause of damnation in the concrete, if not of reprobation in the abstract.

Therefore the most unavoidable of the questions raised by the orthodox Calvinistic doctrine of decrees—whether or not the twofold decree of election and reprobation took account of the fall of Adam and Eve— made some consideration of time and history essential for the explication of what was implied by reprobation. There were two principal alternatives in the treatment of this question, usually identified as the supralapsarian and the infralapsarian (or sublapsarian): the first, "with regard to the end, namely, eternal life," did not make a consideration of the fall a necessary part of the decree, because "the fall was not a means toward this end, but rather a hindrance," and, at least according to some systems, "the very creation and fall of man were predestined by God"; the second, since the decree involved "redemption and regeneration," concluded that "the decree of election did necessarily include an awareness and a consideration of the fall," on the grounds that, in some sense, as Johann Heinrich Heidegger put it, redemption was a "response" to sin and the fall.

Heidegger went so far as to make "election" and "covenant [testamentum]" synonyms, bringing the two concepts together, for example, in his teaching that "those who truly participate in the covenant [vere foederati]" were the ones who would persevere to the end. Other Reformed theologians, such as William Ames, also discussed the interrelation between the two concepts. Ames sought to make clear that there was "only one act of will in God properly," because he was eternal, and therefore "only one decree about the end and means"; nevertheless, "after our manner of conceiving, God in order of intention doth will the end before the means, although in order of execution he willeth the means first before their direction to the end." Thus there was a symmetry between what God had decreed in eternity and what he conferred in time, as the language of the New Testament made clear. The ambiguous relation between the doctrine of predestination and the doctrine of providence, which had been a problem for Reformed theology since the *Institutes* of John Calvin, did nevertheless demonstrate the symmetry. According to some, the term "providence" could refer to "an eternal decree of God about everything that was to be in the future"; others, while acknowledging that there was biblical warrant for this usage, regarded it as "not precise," preferring to reserve the word for "the act itself of conserving and directing" within history, not for the prehistorical and pretemporal "decree to conserve and govern things." Similarly, there were some textbooks of theology which, following the precedent of the *Heidelberg Catechism,* were arranged in such a way as to consider the doctrine of election as part of their discussion of ecclesiology.

This method of treating the doctrine of election was consistent with the "marrow" of covenant theology. Already at the end of the sixteenth century, the Scottish theologian Robert Rollock asserted: "The whole of God's word has to do with some covenant, for God does not communicate to man unless it be through a covenant." Arguing that without the doctrine of the covenant, "no context of Holy Scripture can be explained solidly, no doctrine of theology can be treated properly, no controversy can be decided accurately," Johann Heinrich Alsted characterized that doctrine as "the scope of the catechism" and proceeded to review all the other doctrines of systematic theology in its light. Entitling his book *The Doctrine of Covenants, or the System of Didactic and Elenctic Theology,* Johann Braunius made the covenant the organizing principle of his dogmatics. It was, according to yet another Reformed dogmatician, "the marrow and the center of all of Holy Scripture," to which, as "the norm and form," everything contained in Scripture was to be referred. And even a theologian who declined to devote a special chapter to it because he regarded the term as metaphorical and because he did not agree that it consituted "some sort of peculiar and essential doctrine in theology" had nevertheless to affirm that "the doctrine which theologians make a practice of

Aret.*Act*.2:47 (1590:24v)

See p. 220 above
Aret.*Loc*.5–6 (1617:28–40)
Heb. 11:40
Polan.*Syntag*.6.1 (1617:333)

Acts 2:23

Keck.*Syst*.1.7 (1615:114)

See p. 218 above
Cat.*Heid*.54 (Niesel 162)

Alst.*Theol.cat*.2.11 (1619:379)

Roll. *Voc.eff*.2 (1597)

Alst.*Theol.cat*.1.2 (1619:28–29)

Brn.*Doct.foed*.3.8.1 (1688:246)

Heid.*Corp.theol*.9.4–5 (1700–I:302)

treating under the heading 'covenant' is scattered throughout the whole doctrine of the work of Christ, as well as throughout the doctrines of our justification and sanctification."

Because of its prominence in the language of the Bible, the idea of covenant did not, of course, belong only to Reformed theology: the Counter-Reformation theologian Thomas Stapleton used it to prove that the promises of "the old covenant or testament" were not confined to "that earthly inheritance of the land of Canaan"; and the vigorously anti-Calvinistic Abraham Calovius argued on the basis of the idea of covenant that there had been justification by faith already in the Old Testament, even though he attacked the Reformed "federal theology." Yet it was here that the idea now truly came into its own. Its secular or jurisprudential meaning aside, the theological definition, on which most Reformed theologians could agree, was: "A covenant of God is an agreement between God and man, for the purpose of attaining the summum bonum"; or, more amply, "a pact or agreement of God with man, by which God, by the eminent right that he has and by his singular goodness, promises eternal life under certain conditions and seals it by certain signs and, as it were, pledges." These seals of the covenant were the sacraments. But God and man were not equals in the covenant: God stipulated and promised salvation and eternal life to man, while man "adstipulated" and "restipulated" by pledging his faith in God and his faithfulness to the covenant.

There was, however, considerably less agreement about the precise number and nomenclature of the series of covenants that God had made with the human race. The *Westminster Confession* distinguished two such covenants, together with a subset of two stages in the second covenant: "the covenant of works, wherein life was promised to Adam, and in him to his posterity, upon condition of perfect and personal obedience"; and "the covenant of grace" in Christ, which "was differently administered in the time of the law and in the time of the gospel." Amandus Polanus, in his version of the two covenants, added the view that God had "repeated the covenant [of works] with

Keck.*Syst.*33.3 (1615:268)

Stapl.*Fort.*1.3 (*ERL*163:16v)

Calov.*Art.fid.*3.2.8 (1684:266)
Calov.*Art.fid.*3.4.6 (1684:348–52)

Brn.*Doct.foed.*3.8.1 (1688:249)

Heid.*Corp.theol.*9.8 (1700–I:303);Bucan.*Inst.*22.1 (1605:221)

Trel.*Schol.inst.*2 (1606:95)

Heid.*Corp.theol.*9.11 (1700–I:304)

Cocc.*S.T.*15.41.14 (1665:426)

Gen. 3:15

Polan.*Syntag.*6.33 (1617:451–52)

Armstrong (1969) 142

Amyr.*Thes.*2 (*Thes.Salm.* 1:212)

Heid.*Corp.theol.*9.14 (1700–I:305–6)

Bucan.*Inst.*22.30 (1605:231)

*Cons.Helv.*25.57 (Niemeyer 738)

Heid.*Corp.Theol.*9.15 (1700–I:306)

the people of Israel through Moses," although the covenant of grace had meanwhile begun with the promise of "the seed of the woman" to Adam and Eve after the fall, a covenant that was in turn divided between "the old covenant of grace" before Christ and "the new covenant of grace" after Christ. There were still only two covenants, but they overlapped in such a way as to suggest the possibility that there were in fact three.

That possibility became a reality in the covenant theology of "the school of Saumur" and of Moses Amyraldus (Moïse Amyraut), which "must be regarded as the device seized upon and employed by [them] . . . to correct what they considered to be the unhealthy emphases of orthodox Calvinism." Here, too, the basis was a distinction between two kinds of covenant: an absolute covenant (like the covenant with Noah, which was not contingent upon the actions of the human partner) and a conditional covenant (which was in some way contingent also upon the human response). It was chiefly with this latter that Christian doctrine was to deal. "There are," according to Amyraldus, "three such [conditional] divine covenants mentioned in Scripture: first, that which was contracted in the earthly Paradise and which ought to be called *natural;* second, the one which God transacted in a special way with Israel and which is called *legal;* and third, that which is called *gracious* and which is set forth in the gospel."

Heidegger rejected this "novel hypothesis of Amyraldus"; Bucanus called it "madness" and "false imagination"; and the *Helvetic Consensus* came out unequivocally against "the doctrine of those who try to pass off on us [cudunt] three covenants." Against it they all reasserted the two covenants of works and of grace: "The covenant of works is the pact of God with Adam in the state of integrity, as the head of the entire human race. By it He stipulated from man the perfect obedience of the works of the law, and He promised him eternal life in heaven on the condition of that obedience; but He threatened eternal death to him if he transgressed. For his part, man promised perfect obedience in response to God and His stipulation." The covenant of works could also be called

Cocc.S.T.8.22 (1665:269–78);
Brn.Doct.foed.3.8.2 (1688:
250–53)

Heid.Corp.theol.9.20 (1700–I:
307–8)
Brn.Doct.foed.3.8.2 (1688:
250–51)

Cocc.S.T.13.31 (1665:350–59)

Heid.Corp.theol.11.2 (1700–I:
371–72)

Martn.Sum.op.4 (1612:75)

Cocc.S.T.8.22.19 (1665:271)

Burm.Synop.31.1 (1687–II:4);
Brn.Doct.foed.3.10.4 (1688:
274)

Heid.Corp.theol.11.33 (1700–
I:384)

Brn.Doct.foed.3.10.4 (1688:
274–75)

Alst.Theol.cat.1.2 (1619:29)

West.Conf.7.3 (Müller 559)

Cons.Helv.23.51 (Niemeyer
738)

Polan.Syntag.6.46 (1617:489)

either "legal" (including both natural law and positive law) or "natural"; these were not two distinct successive covenants, as Amyraldus and the school of Saumur tried to make them, but two aspects of the same covenant of works, which God had established with the entire human race through Adam, as representative man, and "also [through] Eve herself." It was the sin of Adam and Eve that rendered the covenant of works useless as a means of justification, but the interruption of the covenant of works did not remove the obligation of obedience to the law: law and gospel were not contrary to each other in the sense that one of them overthrew the other, but there was nevertheless a vast difference between them. The interruption caused by human sin did, however, remove forever the stipulation of the original covenant, namely, the promise of eternal life on the condition of the performance of the works of the law. Attacking the Socinians for trying to change both the Old Testament and the New Testament into "a legalistic covenant of works" and attacking the Pelagians and Roman Catholics for "perverting and abolishing the covenant of grace" in much the same way, the expositors of orthodox covenant theology enumerated the similarities and differences between the two covenants: both were expressions of a "voluntary condescension on God's part," but they presented mankind with opposite ways of attaining salvation.

"The gracious covenant of God," as Alsted defined it, "is that by which God promised his grace and eternal salvation to all who believe in Christ, on the condition of faith and the new obedience, but granted to them by him freely." To such definitions the *Westminster Confession* added the further elucidation that the promise was given "unto all those that are ordained unto life," or, as the *Helvetic Consensus* put it more directly, "only to those who are elect in Christ, the second Adam." The ultimate purpose of the covenant of grace was the same as the ultimate purpose of both election and reprobation: the declaration of God's supreme goodness, mercy, and justice. "There are not," therefore, the *Westminster Confession* insisted, "two covenants of grace differing in substance, but one and the same" single, eternal covenant, whether

*West.Conf.*7.6 (Müller 560)

Bucan.*Inst.*22.14 (1605:227)
Jer.31:31–32
Bucan.*Inst.*22.15 (1605:227–28)

Polan.*Syntag.*6.45–47 (1617: 488–89)

Trel.*Schol.inst.*2 (1606:54)
Alst.*Theol.cat.*1.2 (1619:32–36)

Polan.*Syntag.*6.16 (1617:394)

Heid.*Corp.theol.*11.29 (1700 I:383)

Cocc.*S.T.*15.41.4 (1665:423–24)

Martn.*Sum.op.*26 (1612:503)
Heid.*Corp.theol.*11.50 (1700–I:392)

Cocc.*S.T.*17.52 (1665:530–37)

Schrenk (1923) 127

Cons.*Helv.*24.52 (Niemeyer 738)

in the Old Testament or in the New Testament. In the Old Testament it entailed "earthly blessings" as a means of teaching about "the heavenly inheritance," and it was more burdensome and more obscure than it would become in the New. In the New Testament, "when Christ the substance [of the covenant of grace] was exhibited," there were still temporal "accessories" in addition to the "spiritual and eternal goods" that God granted, and thus "a physical covenant into which God has entered with men."

The covenant of grace was carried out through the incarnation; for if God and man were to become one in the covenant, God and man had to become one in the person of Christ, who was "the nucleus of the covenant of grace." The ratification of that eternal covenant was the primary purpose of his death on the cross, which, "because of the more abundant merit and worthiness" of Christ, exceeded what had originally been give to Adam in creation. The satisfaction rendered by Christ for human sin and God's acceptance of that satisfaction rendered null and void the power of the law to curse and punish those who had passed over into the covenant of grace, although the obligation to strive for a life in accordance with the law was not null and void. As "signs and seals of the covenant of grace," the sacraments of the New Testament declared and applied its grace to all those who were truly participants in the covenant.

The special significance of this era of Reformed church doctrine lay in its theological interpretation of the history of the covenant, in "the historically animated revitalization" of the theological interpretation of God's dealing with his people, which it substituted for traditional Reformed "systematics" and its preoccupation with God's prehistorical plan. For the historical schematization of what the *Helvetic Consensus* called "the diversity of times" and "the diversity of economies" in the various "periods" now became part of systematic theology. "Although the free and saving covenant of God hath been only one from the beginning," Ames explained, "yet the manner of the application . . . hath been diverse, according to the ages in which the church hath been gathered." And he concluded: "In this variety there hath been always a

Ames.*Marr*.1.38 (1642:170)

Heid.*Corp.theol*.9.4 (1700–I: 302)
Heid.*Corp.theol*.12–13 (1700–I:417–54);Brn.*Doct.foed*.4.16.1 (1688:391)

Ames.*Marr*.1.38 (1642:171)

P.Miller (1956) 53

Ames.*Marr*.1.39 (1642:175)

progress from the more imperfect to the more perfect." It was the task of Christian doctrine to study and compare these "ages in which the church hath been gathered" and to identify the distinctive features of this "progress." A consideration of "the flux and succession of the times" had to be incorporated into the very methodology of theology and into the structure of church doctrine. In the first instance, of course, that applied to the history of salvation recounted in the Bible, in which Ames, together with many others, specified one "manner of administration" of the covenant of grace before Moses, and another from Moses to Christ, but went on to distinguish as well "some difference of the dispensation from Adam to Abraham" in comparison with "that which was after Abraham until Moses." From Adam to Abraham; from Abraham to Moses; from Moses to Christ—these were the principal stages of the "progress from the more imperfect to the more perfect" in the history of the covenant of grace as Ames charted it.

"The difference between Calvin and the so-called Calvinists of the early seventeenth century," the leading scholar of Puritan thought has suggested, "cannot be more vividly illustrated than by a comparison of the *Institutes* with such a representative book as Ames's *Medulla*." Yet in this interpretation of the "dispensations" (or "economies") of the history of salvation, Ames was still very restrained. He presupposed, and concluded with, the thesis that "the administration of the covenant from [the time when] Christ [was] exhibited to the end of the world" would be "without end or alteration, because it is perfect"; therefore there was "not another [dispensation] to be expected, to which it should give place as to the more perfect." This stress on the finality of the New Testament dispensation and the consequent dismissal of the authority of the history since Christ was consistent with the Protestant view that the entire definitive revelation was contained in Scripture rather than in Scripture and subsequent tradition. But the radical Puritanism that grew out of Reformed theology in England—and in New England—was to precipitate a series of crises by its further development of the doctrine of the covenant and of the scheme of "dispensations."

Meanwhile, however, theologians on all sides had, ever since the Reformation and even before, been invoking the authority of history and tradition in their doctrinal discussions, both positive and polemical, and had thus accorded a status to history that appeared to be inconsistent with a dismissal of its authority. It was not surprising when Stapleton, who translated Bede's *Ecclesiastical History of the English People* into English, called upon the authority of this "learned and holy countryman of ours" to prove that the authentic religion of England was Roman Catholicism, not Anglican Protestantism; for everyone had to acknowledge "the virtue of holy Saint Bede, which properly commendeth an historiographer." But in the seventeenth century "the centre of theological gravity was shifting from the Bible into the field of ecclesiastical history"; and, once invoked, historical research would not always so easily bend itself to the authority of church doctrine. Already in the sixteenth century Aretius had pointed out, in opposition to those who demanded total unanimity "even in the minutiae" of church doctrine, that this was impossible and absurd. For anyone who examined "the history both of the church and of philosophy" would discover that there had never been a time when such unanimity and conformity to a single standard of doctrine had prevailed among "the teachings of all the doctors." Bossuet took the evidence of this pluralism in the doctrinal history of Protestantism as proof that it could not represent the unchanging truth of divine revelation, as Roman Catholicism did by its adherence to the one true faith. Thus it was permissible to be a historical relativist about the doctrinal position of other churches and their theologians, but not about one's own. In the seventeenth century it was the special concern of Calixtus to rescue the Vincentian canon of "that which has been believed everywhere, at all times, and by everyone" from this relativism, which was already manifesting itself as the outcome of historical study.

Just as the seventeenth century was ending, in 1699, there was published a radical work of historiography bearing the title *Nonpartisan History of the Church and of Heretics from the Beginning of the New Testament to 1688*, by Gottfried Arnold, who sought to

Stapl.*Fort.*2.1 (*ERL* 163:91r)

Stapl.*Pr.Bed.* (1565:2r)

O.Chadwick (1957) 4

Aret.*Loc.*58 (1617:319)

Boss.*Hist.var.*pr.2–3 (Lachat 4: 1–2)

See vol.1:333–39

Calx.*Pr.Vinc.Ler.* (1629:31)

Arn.*Hist.*1.5.5;1.4.8 (1699: 239;186–87)

Arn.*Hist.*1.4.7 (1699:174)

Hirsch (1960) 2:355

demonstrate that "orthodoxy" did not have the right to claim for itself the continuity of the centuries, which had just as often belonged to "heresy." And in 1694 Johann Lorenz von Mosheim was born; often called the father of critical ecclesiastical history, "he deliberately extricated church history from theology." Together with other critical historians of the eighteenth-century Enlightenment, Arnold and Mosheim would, by their research into "the history of the covenant" since the New Testament, bring into being one of the major intellectual and religious forces that fundamentally transformed the very definition of Christian doctrine in modern culture.

## The Gifts of Grace

Between the Council of Trent and the end of the seventeenth century, the theologians of the Roman Catholic Church were engaged in carrying out two closely related, but nevertheless quite distinct assignments: consolidating the doctrinal achievements of the council as a reaffirmation, against the teachings of the Protestant Reformers, of the authentic tradition of the church; and clarifying, within the household of faith, some of the theological inconsistencies that had been inherited from the doctrinal pluralism of previous centuries but had been left unresolved by the council. Several times the Council of Trent had been on the verge of confusing the two assignments, and each time it had been warned off from what was regarded as a dangerous course of action. Only the first assignment was its proper business, while the disputes among scholastic theologians were best left to the scholastic theologians themselves. On the whole, accordingly, Trent had observed the distinction between the consolidation of church doctrine and the clarification of doctrinal theology.

See p. 275 above

See p. 292 above

In addition to their defense of the nature and the locus of authority in the church, particularly the relation between the authority of Scripture and the authority of tradition, the theologians of the Counter-Reformation performed the assignment of consolidation by rehearsing the topics raised by the Reformers and developed by the first two generations of anti-Protestant polemicists. As the issue with which it had

Bell.*Indulg*.2.1 (Fèvre 7:57)

Stapl.*Tr.Thom*.3.4 (1588–II:
47–48)

Stapl.*Count*.4.13 (*ERL* 311:
524v)

Bai.*Sacr*.4 (Gerberon 214–15)
Bell.*Cont*.10.2.24 (Fèvre 4:
109)
Stapl.*Ret*.2 (*ERL* 308–I:41r–
43r)

See pp. 310–11 above
Bell.*Scrip.eccl*.2 (Fèvre 12:360)
Bell.*Cont*.10.2.3 (Fèvre 4:65–
66)

Stapl.*Count*.4.1 (*ERL* 311:
411v)

Bell.*Dich.dott.cris*.9 (Fèvre 12:
317–18)

Pi.V.*Ex. om*. (van Eijl 767–75)

all begun, the problem of indulgences was unavoidable. The errors and inadequacies of Protestant teaching about the sacraments, over which Thomas More had contended with Luther, were especially prominent in the polemics. By denying the real presence in the Eucharist, the "sacramentary sect" of Calvin had "conveyed away this best dish" and now proposed "to feed God's people with a piece of bare bread instead of Christ's most precious body." Thus he had depressed the sacraments into little more than didactic tools. Although Calvin claimed the testimony of Christian antiquity, and especially of Augustine, for this teaching, "the authority of the fathers"—for example, of Dionysius the Areopagite, whose authenticity was still being defended—proved the antiquity of the Roman Catholic doctrine of the real presence. It was above all the intimate connection between the sacraments and divine grace that was at issue. There was a fundamental contradiction in the Protestant position on this connection. For if God was as sovereign as, for example, the Calvinists in their doctrine of predestination made him out to be, by what right could they then maintain that "God cannot give the effect of grace to external sacraments"? Man did not have an incorporeal nature like that of the angels, and hence he needed sacraments to confer grace on him, above all the Eucharist, which contained not only grace itself but the very "author of grace and of every good, Christ our Lord himself."

As the doctrine of grace dominated the "consolidation," so it was also the most important topic of the "clarification." In the immediate aftermath of the Council of Trent, Michael Baius (Michel de Bay) restated a strongly Augustinian position on the doctrines of sin and grace, thus launching a protracted discussion of Augustinian theology. Despite the condemnation of the propositions of Baius by Pope Pius V in 1657, Cornelius Jansen renewed the protest against what he took to be the rampant Pelagianism and Semi-Pelagianism of the time, analyzing and refuting these trends with great erudition and care in his three-volume work, *Augustinus*, published in 1640, shortly after his death. That, too, was condemned, when, in 1653, Pope Innocent X issued his constitution *Cum*

Inn. X. *Cum occas.* (Argentré 3: 261–62)

*occasione*. These official proscriptions of extreme Augustinianism appeared to some to be putting the public doctrine of the church on the side of those whom Baius and Jansen had been attacking, most notably Louis Molina, whose *Harmony of Free Will with the Gifts of Grace* of 1588 was an extended apologia for the freedom of the will before and during conversion and thus for the positive role of "aids to grace [auxilia gratiae]." But the magisterium of the church, after a papal commission had reviewed the issues for a decade, left much of the question open by decreeing instead, in 1607, that none of the parties in the dispute should condemn any of the others. This decree "did not give Molinism the rights of citizenship in the church, but did give it guest privileges."

Paul. V. *Form.* 5. ix. 1607 (Schneemann 292–93)

Stegmüller (1935) 63

The status of the public doctrine of the church, as that which was not only "believed" and "taught" but

See vol. 1:3–7

Suar. *Praed.* 2.13.1 (Vivès 1: 386)

"confessed," about the entire range of issues connected with the gifts of grace was itself an important issue in these controversies. On many of those issues, it had to be acknowledged, "there is little that can be adduced from the councils and the fathers that is de-

Suar. *Grat.* 6.12.11 (Vivès 9:74)

See vol. 1:327–29

Boss. *Def. trad.* 2.5.17 (Lachat 4:190–92)
CAraus. (529) *Can.* 22 (*CCSL* 148–II:61)

Jans. *Aug.* 2.2.3.23 (1640–I: 535–42)

Bai. *Lib. arb.* 10 (Gerberon 85); Nun. *Conc.* 10;21 (Beltrán 390; 403); Ban. *Apol.* 1.20.4 (Beltrán 199)

cisive or even very persuasive." Therefore the Synod of Orange, held a century after the death of Augustine to reaffirm his teachings against Pelagianism and Semi-Pelagianism, had a standing that was special but also problematical. Because it had decreed that "no one has anything of himself except lies and sin," Jansen could, and did, quote it in support of his position, as Molina's opponents could quote others of its decrees as proof that Molina and the theologians who were exalting human freedom over divine grace were in fact Neo-Pelagians, or at any rate Semi-Pelagians. Although the Synod of Orange had been a provincial synod, not an ecumenical council, Francisco Suárez, whose defense of the doctrine of freedom was bringing upon him the accusation of Molinism, nevertheless ascribed to its canons, including the problematical

CAraus. (529) *Can.* 6 (*CCSL* 148–II:57)

ones, "an infallible authority of faith," on the grounds that they had been "so to speak, 'antecedently' confirmed by papal authority," since much of their con-

Suar. *Grat.* prol. 6.1–2 (Vivès 7: 307–8)
Suar. *Praed.* 2.13.5 (Vivès 1: 387–88); Suar. *Grat.* 1.21.6;1.21. 10 (Vivès 7:470;471–72)

tent had come from the Holy See. Then he had to bring the difficult canons of Orange into line with what he was defending as church doctrine. For the

Pasc.*Poss.comm.*1
(Braunschvicg 11:156–66)

Suar.*Grat.*5.33.1 (Vivès 8:553)

Mol.*Grat.*109.7;111.2;114.5
(Stegmüller 87;178;182)

See vol.1:339; p. 281 above

Aug.*Persev.*23.63 (*PL* 45:1031–32)

Pasc.*Poss.comm.*7
(Braunschvicg 11:213–18)
Ban.*Apol.*1.10 (Beltrán 160–64)

Bai.*Mer.op.*2.8 (Gerberon 42)

Jans.*Aug.*1.5.10 (1640–I:262)

Jans.*Aug.*2.pr.27 (1640–II:59–62)

Pasc.Aug. (Braunschvicg 11:151–52);Ban.*Mont.*5 (Beltrán 105)

determination of what that church doctrine was, however, the legislation of the Council of Trent was unique. Although there had been previous councils that had spoken on the doctrine of grace, "among the ecumenical and legitimate councils it alone has declared and defined this matter in detail, as though editing into a summa what the popes and earlier councils had handed down as tradition." Hence Molina, too, recognized various elements of the Thomistic doctrine of grace, which had been declared and defined at Trent, as doctrines that were now "binding as a matter of faith [de fide]."

Because the ecumenical councils of the church had, from the beginning, so much less to say about the doctrines of sin and of grace than about the dogmas of God and of Christ, the question of the doctrinal import of the church's worship had, ever since the ancient church, played a prominent role in the debates over the doctrine of man. When the evidence of church fathers and theologians on this doctrine appeared to be ambiguous, Augustine appealed to "the prayers which the church has always used and will use," in which the church confessed "that the good which we do not hold except by our own will, we nevertheless do not hold unless [the Lord] works it in us to will it." The Roman Catholic Augustinians of the sixteenth and seventeenth centuries made use of the same appeal now, citing "the daily prayers of the church" as authoritative on the efficacy of grace. The church prayed even for those of the departed who had died unmarked by any taint of public scandal; thereby it was affirming their need for a grace that was unmerited. Such liturgical proof texts were evidence of "the Catholic faith as this has been manifested in the prayers of the church" and as it had been unquestionably "believed" and explicitly "taught," though perhaps it may not have been formally "confessed." Together with "Paul and Augustine, [who are] the matrix and the source of all the conclusions that can be formed about grace," this evidence from the rule of prayer could help to confirm the authoritative rule of faith against the latter-day "remnants of the errors of Pelagius."

The formulation of the doctrine of grace involved

both of the assignments of theology, consolidation in opposition to those without and clarification in dialogue with those within. It was necessary to affirm this "Catholic doctrine against the heretics, above all Luther and Calvin." Prominent though the doctrine of grace had been in Luther's theology, he had denied that justification took place through the infusion of grace but had attributed it to the imputation of the righteousness of Christ for the forgiveness of sins. Against this Molina and Suárez found it appropriate to quote the definition at the Council of Trent, which had expressly rejected the limitation of justification to forgiveness. It was, however, especially for his doctrine of the bondage of the will that Luther was singled out in this discussion. That doctrine and its implications provided Molina with the argument he needed for his own assertion that the freedom of the will was a necessary constituent of the Catholic doctrine of grace, as well as for the converse of that proposition: "The freedom of the will must be preserved so that in all things the grace of the Giver may stand out." For the prevenient grace of God and the free will of man were not antitheses, but were "two parts of a single integrated cause of the act of believing." One of Molina's concerns was to obviate the necessity of positing, in addition to this "particular aid of prevenient grace," a second special act of divine aid by which the free will would be enabled to elicit acts of faith, hope, love, and repentance.

For their part, Molina's opponents and the other neo-Augustinians needed to disengage their reassertions of the primary of grace from Luther's. When Baius declared that without grace the free will was good only for sin, that sounded dangerously like an echo of Luther, but he went on to specify that there was a genuine free will and that it was aided by grace; or, in the Thomistic-Augustinian formula of Domingo Báñez, "the efficacy of divine aid, as it comes from the Holy Spirit, does not destroy liberty, but perfects it." The familiar harmonization of grace and free will accomplished by Bernard of Clairvaux exhibited the proper balance between Manicheism and Pelagianism. In opposition to Pelagianism, Bellarmine insisted that all human labors were in vain unless God

Suar.*Praed*.3.10.1 (Vivès 1: 482)

See pp.145–47 above

Mol.*Grat*.110.2 (Stegmüller 118)

See pp. 283–85 above
Mol.*Conc*.14.46.11 (Rabeneck 281);Suar.*Grat*.7.11.8 (Vivès 98:175)

See pp. 140–41 above

Mol.*Grat*.113.3 (Stegmüller 159)

Mol.*Conc*.14.23.4 (Rabeneck 149)

Mol.*Conc*.14.37.2 (Rabeneck 225)

Mol.*Conc*.14.39.1–2 (Rabeneck 240)

Pasc.*Prob.gr.* (Braunschvicg 11: 133)

Bai.*Prim.just*.2.8 (Gerberon 70–71)

Ban.*Apol*.1.14.3 (Beltrán 176)

See p. 287 above

Ban.*Apol*.3.4.1 (Beltrán 287)
Bell.*Dich.dott.cris*.4.4 (Fèvre 12:300)

added his concurrent grace, for man "can do nothing for the sake of which God may be said to grant him grace." At the same time, the gratuitous character of forgiveness did not, as the *Apology of the Augsburg Confession* maintained, preclude the presence of certain actions in the person that only "predisposed" to grace though they did not "merit" it.

Although Calvin was sometimes lumped with Luther as opposed to the Catholic doctrine of the relation between the gifts of grace and the freedom of the will, it was especially the apparent determinism of his doctrines of predestination and reprobation that earned him the opposition of Roman Catholic theologians. Even Baius, concerned though he was about what he regarded as the Semi-Pelagianism of his time, joined in that opposition: As not all "the doctors of the Catholic faith" were equal, so it was with heretics as well; and Calvin was one of the worst. The very foundation of Calvin's theology was false and contrary to the Catholic faith. The problem was that, as Calvin himself had claimed, there was considerable documentation for his doctrine in the fathers of that Catholic faith. Therefore it was necessary to rescue Augustine from the doctrine of predetermination that both Calvin and certain Roman Catholics seemed to be reading into his statements and even to rescue Gregory the Great from the doctrine of double predestination that seemed to be implicit in his explanation of the biblical locus classicus on the universal salvific will of God. It was equally necessary on all sides to find some explanation for the language of Chrysostom, who appeared to favor the extreme Pelagian position in the powers he ascribed to the unaided free will of man.

A crucial problem in the doctrine of predestination—not only for Calvin and his heirs, but for all Augustinians, including those within Roman Catholicism—was the relation between divine foreknowledge and predestination. Suárez was sure that these two terms, as they were used together in Romans 8:29, were not synonyms. How, then, was the predestinating action of God, to salvation or to reprobation, connected with his absolute foreknowledge of both sin and virtue, including faith? The case

Bell.*Cont.*14.6.4 (Fèvre 6:115)

Apol.*Conf.Aug.*4.152 (Bek. 190)

Stapl.*Ant.ev.*Luke 7:47 (1595–I:360)

Bell.*Bai.*10 (Galeota 316);Suar. *Grat.*prol.5.7 (Vivès 7:267–71)

Suar.*Grat.*5.29.2;4.3.1 (Vivès 8:538;272)

Bai.*Sacr.*1 2 (Gerberon 212–13)

Suar.*Grat.*4.3.10 (Vivès 8:275)

See pp. 224–25 above

Pasc.*Aug.* (Braunschvicg 11:153)

Suar.*Grat.*5.43 (Vivès 8:609–14)

See vol. 3:89

1 Tim 2:4
Suar.*Praed.*4.1.1 (Vivès 1:485–86)
Boss.*Def.trad.*2.5.5 (Lachat 4:171–72);Suar.*Praed.*2.8 (Vivès 1:367–72);Mol.*Conc.*14.23.14 (Rabeneck 147–48);Ban.*Apol.* 3.22–25 (Beltrán 325–30)

Suar.*Praed.*1.6.2 (Vivès 1:249)

of reprobation was the easier one, for it was possible to base it, at least in the case of adults, on a "hypothetical [ex hypothesi] foreknowledge of sin, though not of the particular sins of individuals"; hence it was permissible to say that "the foreknowledge of future sins precedes predestination—not only our predestination, but that of Christ, who is the head of those who have been predestined," although even that foreknowledge was not "absolute" in the sense that it took away free will. Contrary to what Calvin, and before him Wycliffe, had taught, predestination itself did not impose that kind of necessity. This desire to protect liberty against necessity lead Molina to assert that God foreknew something because by free will it would happen, but that it was not correct to say that it happened because God foreknew it. Diego Nuño quoted Augustine in proof of the opposite: Molina was contradicting both Thomas and Augustine. Together with his opponents, Molina did acknowledge, on the basis of Thomas and Augustine, that the number as well as the specific identity of the predestinated was already fixed. But, partly it would seem because of the Calvinist doctrine of the decrees of predestination, Roman Catholic theologians of the various parties in this period all remained committed to the extrication of the Catholic and Augustinian doctrine from any implications of "fate" or "necessity."

Yet the obligation for Roman Catholic thinkers to deal with the problematics of the gifts of grace in this period came at least as much from within their own church as from Luther and Calvin. Suárez found it necessary to respond to Molina on the question of the need for grace. Similarly, after referring to the heretical teachings of Luther and Calvin, he added: "It would be possible at this point also to discuss some of the articles of Michael Baius"; but he went on to point out that "because he was a Catholic man and did not err pertinaciously, he should not be counted among the heretics." Others were less gentle. Jansen, whose *Augustinus* was in the main a comparative examination of the teachings of Augustine, Pelagius, and the Semi-Pelagians, did occasionally let it be known that those whom he really had in mind were "the many recent thinkers, who without any ambiguity set forth the

---

Suar.*Praed*.5.6.8 (Vivès 1:514)

Mol.*Conc*.23.8.14 (Rabeneck 515)

Mol.*Praed*.23.4–5.1.9 (Stegmüller 306)

Suar.*Praed*.3.9.1–3 (Vivès 1: 479–80)

Nun.*Conc*.1.23.1 (Beltrán 399);Ban.*Apol*.1.23.1 (Beltrán 210–11)

Mol.*Praed*.23.7 (Stegmüller 331);Ban.*Mont*.3 (Beltrán 105)

Suar.*Grat*.5.24.18 (Vivés 8: 515);Jans.*Aug*.1.5.15 (1640–I: 282)

Suar.*Grat*.3.81 (Vivès 8:31)

Suar.*Grat*.prol.5.7.11 (Vivès 7: 271)

position that man, by the powers of his nature, is able
to dispose himself to grace." This was "that celebrated
question" among the scholastics whether if someone
did what lay within him God would inevitably confer
his grace. Augustine's answer to the question, according to Jansen, was clearly in the negative. But
Suárez insisted, in his response to Baius, that this was
a misreading of Augustine.

Suárez himself defined grace as "a gift granted over
and above nature and everything owed to nature"; or,
in Bellarmine's terminology, grace was "that which is
neither owed nor granted as a compensation or a reward, but is donated gratis and freely." Jansen's definition included this element, but added, on the basis
of the word of Jesus in the Gospel that "apart from
me you can do nothing," that grace was also "altogether necessary for every good work." An "aid to
grace [auxilium gratiae]," which was in many ways
the central issue of the controversies within Roman
Catholic theology during the sixteenth and seventeenth centuries, could be defined as "some sort of
supernatural gift freely granted to a man, by which
in some way he is aided to do good." Grace could
also be divided into "operating" grace ("that special
aid by which God operates in ourselves without ourselves, that is, without the concurrence of our free
will") and "cooperating" grace (by which "our free
will is aided so that it may freely cooperate with God").
It was, also according to Molina, heretical to deny
that this unearned "operating" grace was necessary
before there could be any true love of God. Once
again, the Pauline (and, by now, Augustinian) formula, "it depends not upon man's will or exertion,
but upon God's mercy," demanded clarification: Molina saw it as reinforcing the need for cooperation between divine grace and human free will; Jansen took
it to be directed explicitly against those "who set down
certain conditions for the operations of divine grace
or mercy"; and Suárez, citing the authority of Gregory Nazianzus, sought to have it both ways by urging that the free will was a "proximate cause" of
conversion, but that "it is not to be attributed to the
will in the same way as it is to grace."

All of these theologians of grace identified them-

Jans.*Aug.*1.8.17 (1640–I:521)

Jans.*Aug.*3.1.5 (1640–II:17–24)

See p. 130 above

Suar.*Grat.*1.21.1 (Vivès 1:468–69)

Sur.*Grat.*prol.3.1.3;3.2.4 (Vivès 7:130;134)

Bell.*Bai.*1 (Galeota 171)

John 15:5

Jans.*Aug.*1.6.3 (1640–I:337)

Suar.*Grat.*5.1.2 (Vivès 8:387)

Suar.*Grat.*3.1.1 (Vivès 8:4)
Pasc.*Poss.comm.*4 (Braunschvicg 11:193–94)

Mol.*Grat.*111.2 (Stegmüller 129),Mol.*Conc.*14.36.1 (Rabeneck 223)

Mol.*Grat.*109.3 (Stegmüller 50)

Rom. 9:16

Mol.*Conc.*14.42.6–8 (Rabeneck 263–65)

Jans.*Aug.*3.2.24 (1640-III:201)

Suar.*Grat.*5.31.3–4 (Vivès 8:544–45)

selves as Augustinians of one sort or another and questioned the legitimacy of such an identification for their opponents. But whatever this identification may have meant in the past, it now had to take primary account of two writings of Augustine. One of these, present of course already in the Middle Ages but made prominent by both Renaissance and Reformation, was the *Confessions,* which obliged them to include as part of their theological discussions some consideration of the subjective and experiential element in the life of grace. In its debates on the certainty of faith and the certainty of salvation, the Council of Trent had attacked the Calvinist idea that one could be subjectively certain of election and had declared, on the basis of Thomas Aquinas, that such certainty could come only by private revelation. Addressing the question of whether it was possible to experience the gifts of grace, Molina cited the precedent of Augustine, as well as that of Mary Magdalene, as evidence that grace could indeed be the content of a subjective experience. Like the fathers at Trent, he was obliged to deal with such statements of Scripture as the statement of Paul, "I am certain." But elsewhere he explained that "even if we do experience the assent of faith itself, we nevertheless do not know whether it proceeds from an acquired faith or from an infused one," and he distinguished his understanding of the certitude of faith from the Lutheran definition of faith as "knowledge, assent, and trust."

The other Augustinian treatise that demanded treatment was his first significant response to Pelagianism, *On the Merits and the Remission of Sins,* in which he had begun to consider a problem that was to become far more prominent as the Pelagian controversy progressed, the relation between grace as a gift and the biblical language about "merit" and "reward." The problem had repeatedly surfaced during the Reformation controversies. Now Baius made it the topic of a special treatise of his own, in which he maintained that if Adam and Eve had not sinned, eternal life would have been a reward to them, but that for a fallen humanity it could not; therefore, as Molina also affirmed, "merits themselves are the gifts of grace," and in that sense eternal life now was both a reward

See pp. 19–22 above

Boss.*Hist.var.*9.4 (Lachat 14: 357)

See pp. 288–89 above

See p. 131 above
Mol.*Conc.*14.44.2 (Rabeneck 267)

Mol.*Grat.*112.5 (Stegmüller 154)

Rom. 8:38 (Vulg.)

Mol.*Grat.*109.1 (Stegmüller 33)

Mol.*Conc.*14.38.6 (Rabeneck 229)

Pasc.*Poss.comm.*3 (Braunschvicg 11:187–88)

See pp. 145–46, 259 above

Bai.*Mer.op.*1.4 (Gerberon 29)
Mol.*Grat.*113.8 (Stegmüller 171)
Bai.*Mer.op.*1.6 (Gerberon 31)

See p. 287 above
Mol.*Grat.*114.1 (Stegmüller 174)

Stapl.*Ant.ev.*Matt.5:12 (1595–I:31)

See pp. 38–50 above

O'Connor (1958) 490

Pasc.*Prov.*9 (Braunschvicg 5:191–96)

ap.Pi.V.*Ex om.*73 (van Fijl 775)

Suar.*Grat.*6.2.16 (Vivès 7:292–93);Bell.*Bai.*13 (Galeota 375)

Bell.*Cont.*14.4.15 (Fèvre 5:373)

Mol.*Conc.*25.1.12 (Rabeneck 565)
Ecclus.31:10

Mol.*Conc.*14.53.4 (Rabeneck 400)

Mol.*Grat.*109.8;109.10 (Stegmüller 95;116)

and a gift. The entire concept of merit and reward, as formulated at Trent, needed to be reasserted. The promise of God was free and unmerited. But once God had promised, he had bound himself by that promise, and in that sense he "owed" what he had freely promised: he granted it as a reward, because he could not be untrue to himself.

Unavoidably, any consideration of the gifts of grace during the sixteenth and seventeenth centuries had to take account of the development, during the fourteenth and fifteenth centuries, of the doctrine of the relation between grace and original sin in the Virgin Mary. "The sixteenth century," it has been said, "had multiplied the symbolic expressions of the Immaculate Conception. It was the genius of the seventeenth to express the mystery with all possible perfection." Because of its prominence in this period, Pascal devoted the ninth of the *Provincial Letters* to a critique of the distortions to which Marian devotion was subject, and one of the propositions of Baius condemned by papal decree asserted that "no one, except for Christ, is without original sin," and that "therefore the Blessed Virgin died because of the sin contracted from Adam, and all her afflictions in this life were, as in the case of other saints, punishments for sin, whether actual or original." Suárez explained that it was the latter part of this statement that had been condemned, since, in the present status of defined church doctrine, the statement that the Virgin had been born with original sin was not officially subject to condemnation. Bellarmine gave a fuller explanation of the status in three propositions: it was not a binding article of faith that Mary was conceived without orginal sin; that opinion, however, must not under any circumstances be adjudged heretical; it was not presumptuous, but pious and far more probable, to hold this opinion in preference to its alternative. To Molina, Mary was the prime instance of a conferral of grace independent of the use of free will, as well as, on the other hand, of the biblical description of someone "who had the power to transgress and did not transgress" because of her free will; she was also, "according to the more probable opinion," the only exception to the universality of original sin. Regardless of the philological objections of Erasmus, Calvin, and others, the angelic salutation to Mary did mean that she was "full of grace," because she possessed "the gifts of the Holy Spirit in the highest possible degree."

The most fundamental of all the several distinctions involved in the history of this doctrine was that between grace and nature, with which, for example, Molina opened his *Treatise on Grace* and on which Baius was no less dependent. It had been codified by Augustine and by his disciples, such as Prosper of Aquitaine, and had achieved its definitive formulation in Thomas Aquinas: "Grace does not abolish nature, but completes it." The distinction did not imply at all that only "grace" was a divine gift, while "nature" was a human achievement. For Augustine himself had often said "that even nature is true grace, that is, a free gift" of God, not conditional on works. It was a misunderstanding of this relation between nature and grace that had led Pelagius into his errors. He had denied "that some assistance of grace . . . was necessary to the will of the first man for him to live right." Curiously, it was now against the Reformers, vigorously anti-Pelagian though they were, that this principle had to be reasserted. At the same time, they needed to be reminded of the other pole of the relation between nature and grace. Divine grace was needed to make human nature whole and to render it acceptable to God, but nevertheless there remained such a thing as natural morality. Grace and faith were not needed to make an act morally good. Or, in Molina's words, "There cannot be a meritorious act apart from grace and love, but there can be a morally good act apart from grace and love and even apart from faith." But could the man performing such acts in a purely natural state also have, by his own free will, a natural desire for the grace of God, and did that desire in any way predispose him to grace?

On the answer to that question depended the entire structure of the Augustinian doctrine of grace as it had developed in the Western church. In a series of actions during the second half of the seventeenth century, beginning with *Cum occasione* in 1653 and climaxing in *Unigenitus Dei Filius* in 1713, the teaching

See p. 308 above
Luke 1:28 (Vulg.)
Stapl.*Ant.ev.*Luke 1:28 (1595–I:335)
Bell.*Dich.dott.cris.*5 (Fèvre 12: 302–3)

Mol.*Grat.*109.pr. (Stegmüller 19–21)

Bai.*Prin.just.*1.8 (Gerberon 59)

Bai.*Princ.just.*1.10 (Gerberon 61)

See vol.3:285

Jans.*Aug.*2.3.1.20 (1640–I:778)

Suar.*Grat.*prol.3.2.2. (Vivès 7: 133)

Jans.*Aug.*1.2.7 (1640–I:111–14)

Bell.*Cont.*13.1.5 (Fèvre 5:179)

Clem.XI.*Unig.*2 (Argentré 3: 462)
Bell.*Bai.*9 (Galeota 287)
Suar.*Grat.*1.6.6 (Vivès 7:387)

Mol.*Grat.*109.1 (Stegmüller 37)

Mol.*Conc.*14.45.11 (Rabeneck 275)

Inn.X.*Cum occas.* (Argentré 3: 261–62)
Clem.XI.*Unig.* (Argentré 3: 461–76)

office of the Roman Catholic Church spoke out against Jansen's reinterpretation of the Augustinian doctrine. What had begun as a series of individual restatements of Augustine was now in the process of becoming a distinct dogmatic position and an entire party within the church: the problem of Jansen's *Augustinus* had been replaced by the problem of Augustinian Jansenism, a doctrinal movement, but also a literary and political movement, whose repercussions were to be decisive for the relation between Christian doctrine and modern culture in the eighteenth century. Together with Pietism and Puritanism, therefore, Jansenism must form the starting point for our discussion of that relation.

Pasc.*Prov.*2 (Braunschvicg 4: 164)

# Selected
# Secondary Works

## GENERAL

Burckhardt, Jacob. *The Civilization of the Renaissance in Italy.* 2 vols. Introduction by Benjamin Nelson and Charles Trinkaus. New York, 1958.

Burdach, Konrad. *Reformation Renaissance Humanismus.* 2d ed. Berlin and Leipzig, 1926. A provocative attempt at a redefinition.

Cassirer, Ernst, et al., eds. *The Renaissance Philosophy of Man.* Chicago, 1948.

——. *The Individual and the Cosmos in Renaissance Philosophy.* Translated with an introduction by Mario Domandi. Reprint edition. New York, 1979.

Dilthey, Wilhelm. *Weltanschauung und Analyse des Menschen seit Renaissance und Reformation.* Stuttgart, 1957. One of the most profound of general works on the period.

Eisenstein, Elizabeth L. *The Printing Press as an Agent of Change: Communication and Cultural Transformation in Early Modern Europe.* Cambridge, 1979.

Elton, G. R., ed. *The Reformation.* Volume 2 of *The New Cambridge Modern History.* Cambridge, 1962.

Gilson, Etienne. *History of Christian Philosophy in the Middle Ages.* New York, 1955.

Harnack, Adolf von. *Lehrbuch der Dogmengeschichte.* 3 vols. 5th ed. Tübingen, 1931–32.

Herzog, Johann Jakob, and Hauck, Albert, eds. *Realencyklopädie für protestantische Theologie und Kirche.* 3d ed. 22 vols. Leipzig, 1896–1909.

Hirsch, Emanuel. *Geschichte der neuern evangelischen Theologie im Zusammenhang mit den allgemeinen Bewegungen des europäischen Denkens.* 5 vols. Gütersloh, 1960. Although it begins where this volume ends, this work is important for the entire period of this volume as well.

Joachimsen, Paul. *Die Reformation als Epoche der deutschen Geschichte.* Munich, 1951. One of the general interpretations of the Reformation to which this volume is the most indebted.

Kretzmann, Norman; Kenny, Anthony; and Pinborg, Jan. *The Cambridge History of Later Medieval Philosophy: From the Rediscovery of Aristotle to the Disintegration of Scholasticism, 1100–1600.* Cambridge, 1982. This thousand-page volume treats many of the thinkers with whom we are also concerned here, albeit for their philosophical rather than for their doctrinal significance.

Kristeller, Paul Oskar. *Renaissance Thought: The Classic, Scholastic, and Humanist Strains.* New York, 1961.

Landgraf, Artur Michael. *Dogmengeschichte der Frühscholastik.* 4 vols. Regensburg, 1952–56.

Leff, Gordon. *Heresy in the Later Middle Ages: The Relation of Heterodoxy to Dissent c. 1250–c. 1450.* 2 vols. Manchester, 1967.

McNeill, John Thomas. *The History and Character of Calvinism.* 2d ed. New York, 1957.

Möhler, Johann Adam. *Symbolik: oder Darstellung der dogmatischen Gegensätze der Katholiken und Protestanten nach ihren öffentlichen Bekenntnisschriften.* Edited by Josef Rupert Geiselmann. 2 vols. Darmstadt, 1958–61. In the voluminous and ephemeral literature of "comparative symbolics," perhaps the most abiding of essays.

Oakley, Francis. *The Western Church in the Later Middle Ages.* Ithaca, 1979.

Oberman, Heiko Augustinus. *The Harvest of Medieval Theology: Gabriel Biel and Late Medieval Nominalism.* Cambridge, Mass., 1963.

———. *Masters of the Reformation: The Emergence of a New Intellectual Climate in Europe.* Translated by Dennis Martin. Cambridge, 1981. The reinterpretation of the sixteenth century in the light of the fourteenth and fifteenth centuries is probably the most important trend in contemporary Reformation study.

Ozment, Steven E. *The Age of Reform, 1250–1550: An Intellectual and Religious History of Late Medieval and Reformation Europe.* New Haven, 1980. A balanced and comprehensive account of the period.

Pauck, Wilhelm. "Nationalism and European Christianity." In *Environmental Factors in Christian History,* edited by John Thomas McNeill, Matthew Spinka, and Harold R. Willoughby, pp. 286–303. Chicago, 1939.

———. *The Heritage of the Reformation.* 2d ed. New York, 1961.

Pelikan, Jaroslav. *From Luther to Kierkegaard: A Study in the History of Theology.* Saint Louis, 1950.

Ritschl, Otto. *Dogmengeschichte des Protestantismus: Grundlagen und Grundzüge der theologischen Gedanken- und Lehrbildung in den protestantischen Kirchen.* 4 vols. Leipzig and Göttingen, 1908–27. The first to be successful in carrying the definition of "the history of dogma" beyond the age of the Reformation

Schaff, Philip. *The History of the Creeds.* Volume 1 of *The Creeds of Christendom.* 3 vols. New York, 1919.

Schottenloher, Karl. *Bibliographie zur deutschen Geschichte im Zeitalter der Glaubensspaltung, 1517–1585.* 6 vols. Leipzig, 1933–40.

Seeberg, Reinhold. *Lehrbuch der Dogmengeschichte.* 4th rev. ed. 4 vols. Basel, 1953–54.

Spitz, Lewis W. *The Religious Renaissance of the German Humanists.* Cambridge, Mass., 1963.

Thomasius, Gottfried. *Die Dogmengeschichte des Mittelalters und der Reformationszeit.* Erlangen, 1876.

Trinkaus, Charles. *In Our Image and Likeness: Humanity and Divinity in Italian Humanist Thought.* 2 vols. Chicago, 1970.

Troeltsch, Ernst. *The Social Teaching of the Christian Churches.* 2 vols. Introduction by H. Richard Niebuhr. Translated by Olive Wyon. New York, 1960.

Vacant, Jean-Michel-Alfred, et al., eds. *Dictionnaire de théologie catholique.* 15 vols. Paris, 1903–50.

Warfield, Benjamin Breckenridge. *Calvin and Augustine.* Philadelphia, 1956.

## 1. DOCTRINAL PLURALISM IN THE LATER MIDDLE AGES

Balić, Charles. *De debito peccati originalis in B. Virgine Maria: investigationes de doctrina quam tenuit Ioannes Duns Scotus.* Rome, 1941.

―――. *Ioannes Duns Scotus et historia Immaculatae Conceptionis.* Rome, 1955.

―――. "The Life and Works of John Duns Scotus." In *John Duns Scotus, 1265–1965,* edited by John K. Ryan and Bernardine M. Bonansea, pp. 1–27. Washington, 1965. Together with his edition of the several versions of Scotus on the *Sentences,* these works of Balić have transformed the study of Scotus and Scotism, especially in the doctrines of grace and of Mary.

Beumer, Johannes. "Augustinismus und Thomismus in der theologischen Prinzipien-lehre des Aegidius Romanus." *Scholastik* 32 (1957): 542–60.

Bloomfield, Morton. *"Piers Plowman" as a Fourteenth Century Apocalypse.* New Brunswick, N.J., 1961.

Bouwsma, William James. "The Two Faces of Humanism: Stoicism and Augustinianism in Renaissance Thought." In *Itinerarium italicum: The Profile of the Italian Renaissance in the Mirror of Its European Transformation, Dedicated to Paul Oskar Kristeller,* edited by Heiko Augustinus Oberman and Thomas A. Brady, Jr., pp. 3–60. Leiden, 1975.

Buescher, Gabriel. *The Eucharistic Teaching of William Ockham.* Saint Bonaventure, N.Y., 1950. A defense of Ockham's essential orthodoxy.

Burr, David. "Scotus and Transubstantiation." *Mediaeval Studies* 34 (1972): 336–50.

Callaey, Fredegand. "L'influence et la diffusion de l'*Arbor Vitae* d'Ubertin de Casale." *Revue d'histoire ecclésiastique* 17 (1921): 533–46.

Callus, Daniel Angelo Philip. *The Condemnation of St Thomas at Oxford.* 2d ed. London, 1955.

Capelle, B. "L'Exultet' pascal, oeuvre de Saint Ambroise." In *Miscellanea Giovanni Mercati,* pp. 219–46. Rome, 1946.

Colasanti, Giovanni. "I Ss. Cuori di Gesu e di Maria nell *Arbor Vitae* (1305) di Ubertino da Casale, O. Min." *Miscellanea Francescana* 59 (1959): 30–69.

Courtenay, William J. "Nominalism and Late Medieval Thought: A Bibliographical Essay." *Theological Studies* 33 (1972): 716–34. A guide to the vast and burgeoning literature.

―――. *Adam Wodeham: An Introduction to His Life and Writings.* Leiden, 1978.

Damerau, Rudolf. *Die Abendmahlslehre des Nominalismus, insbesondere die des Gabriel Biel.* Giessen, 1963.

Dettloff, Werner. *Die Lehre von der acceptatio divina bei Johannes Duns Scotus mit besonderer Berücksichtigung der Rechtfertigungslehre.* Werl, 1954. The effects of "voluntarism" on soteriology.

Di Fonzo, Laurentius. "La Mariologia de S. Bernardino da Siena, O.F.M. Conv." *Miscellanea Francescana* 47 (1947): 3–102.

Douglass, E. Jane Dempsey. *Justification in Late Medieval Preaching: A Study of John Geiler of Keiserberg.* Leiden, 1966.

Eckermann, Willigis. *Wort und Wirklichkeit: Das Sprachverständnis in der Theologie Gregors von Rimini und sein Weiterwirken in der Augustinerschule.* Würzburg, 1978.

Ehrle, Franz. "Der Kampf um die Lehre des hl. Thomas von Aquin in den ersten fünfzig Jahren nach seinem Tod." *Zeitschrift für katholische Theologie* 37 (1913): 266–318.

Emmen, Aquilin. "Heinrich von Langenstein und die Diskussion über die Empfängnis Mariens." In *Theologie in Geschichte und Gegenwart: Festschrift Michael Schmaus,* pp. 625–50. Munich, 1957. The still undefined state of the doctrine.

Ernst, Wilhelm. *Gott und Mensch am Vorabend der Reformation: Eine Untersuchung zur Moral-philosophie und -theologie bei Gabriel Biel.* Leipzig, 1922.

Farthing, John Lee. "Post Thomam: Images of St. Thomas Aquinas in the Academic Theology of Gabriel Biel." Ph.D. dissertation, Duke University, 1978.

Feckes, Karl. *Die Rechtfertigungslehre des Gabriel Biel und ihre Stellung innerhalb der nominalistischen Schule.* Münster, 1925.

Gerosa, Pietro Paolo. *Umanesimo cristiano del Petrarca: influenza agostiniana, attinenze medievali.* Turin, 1966. A critique of efforts to "secularize" Petrarch's thought.

Glorieux, Palémon. "Les Correctoires." *Recherches de théologie ancienne et médiévale* 14 (1947): 287–304. The anti-Thomist treatises of the thirteenth and fourteenth centuries.

Harapin, Th. "O predestinacij Kristovoj po nauci Bl. Ivana Duns Skota" [On the predestination of Christ according to the teaching of Blessed John Duns Scotus]. *Collectanea Franciscana Slavica,* pp. 267–310. Šibenik, 1935.

Heynck, Valens. "Der richterliche Charakter des Busssakraments nach Johannes Duns Scotus." *Franziskanische Studien* 47 (1965): 339–414.

Kristeller, Paul Oskar. "Augustine and the Early Renaissance." *Review of Religion* 8 (1944): 339 58.

Leff, Gordon. *Bradwardine and the Pelagians: A Study of His "De causa dei" and Its Opponents.* Cambridge, 1957.

—————. *Gregory of Rimini: Tradition and Innovation in Fourteenth Century Thought.* New York, 1961.

Levi, Giulio Augusto. "Pensiero classico e pensiero cristiano nel 'Secretum' e nella 'Familiari' del Petrarca." *Atene e Roma* 35 (1933): 63–82.

Lorenzin, Paschal. *Mariologia Iacobi a Varagine, O.P.* Rome, 1951.

McCue, James F. "The Doctrine of Transubstantiation from Berengar through Trent: The Point at Issue." *Harvard Theological Review* 61 (1968): 385–430. A solid and useful survey.

McGinn, Bernard, ed. *Visions of the End: Apocalyptic Traditions in the Middle Ages.* New York, 1979.

Maglione, Rocco. *Il concetto di conversione eucaristica in Egidio Romano.* Benevento, 1941. Pluralism in eucharistic theory.

Mandonnet, Pierre. *Mélanges Thomistes.* Paris, 1923.

Manselli, Raoul. *La "Lectura super Apocalipsim" di Pietro di Giovanni Olivi: Ricerche sull' escatologismo medioevale.* Rome, 1955.

Minges, Parthenius. *Die Gnadenlehre des Duns Scotus auf ihren angeblichen Pelagianismus und Semipelagianismus geprüft.* Münster, 1906. An early effort at reinterpretation.

Nolan, Kieran. *The Immortality of the Soul and the Resurrection of the Body according to Giles of Rome: A Historical Study of a 13th Century Theological Problem.* Rome, 1967.

Oakley, Francis. "Natural Law, the *Corpus Mysticum,* and Consent in Conciliar Thought from John of Paris to Matthias Ugonius." *Speculum* 56 (1981): 786–810.

Oberman, Heiko Augustinus. *Archbishop Thomas Bradwardine: A Fourteenth Century Augustinian.* Utrecht, 1957.

—————. "Fourteenth Century Religious Thought: A Premature Profile." *Speculum* 53 (1978): 80–93.

Ozaeta, José María. *La unión hipostática según Egidio Romano.* El Escorial, 1965.

Ozment, Steven E. *Homo Spiritualis: A Comparative Study of the Anthropology of Johannes Tauler, Jean Gerson and Martin Luther (1509–16)*. Leiden, 1969.

Pannenberg, Wolfhart. *Die Prädestinationslehre des Duns Skotus im Zusammenhang der scholastischen Lehrentwicklung*. Göttingen, 1954.

Roensch, Frederick James. *Early Thomistic School*. Dubuque, Iowa, 1964.

Schwamm, Hermann. *Das göttliche Vorherwissen bei Duns Skotus und seinen ersten Anhängern*. Innsbruck, 1934. Especially valuable for its extensive references to manuscript material from the early Scotist school.

Sedlák, Jan. *Táborské traktáty eucharistické* [Taborite eucharistic tracts]. Brno, 1918.

Seeberg, Reinhold. *Die Theologie des Johannes Duns Scotus: Eine dogmengeschichtliche Untersuchung*. Leipzig, 1900.

Smalley, Beryl. "The Bible and Eternity: John Wyclif's Dilemma." *Journal of the Warburg and Courtauld Institutes* 17 (1964): 73–89.

Steneck, Nicholas H. *Science and Creation in the Middle Ages: Henry of Langenstein (d. 1397) on Genesis*. Notre Dame, Ind., 1976.

Trapp, D. "Augustinian Theology of the 14th Century." In *Augustiniana*, edited by F. Roth and N. Teeuwen, pp. 146–274. New York, 1956.

Trinkaus, Charles. "Erasmus, Augustine, and the Nominalists." *Archiv für Reformationsgeschichte* 66 (1976): 3–32.

———, and Oberman, Heiko Augustinus, eds. *The Pursuit of Holiness*. Leiden, 1974.

Tumminello, G. *L'immacolata concezione di Maria et la scuola Agostiniana del secolo XIV*. Rome, 1942.

Vignaux, Paul. *Justification et prédestination au XIVe siècle: Duns Scot, Pierre d'Auriole, Guillaume d'Occam, Grégoire de Rimini*. Paris, 1934.

Zugaj, Marianus. "Assumptio B. M. Virginis in *Arbor Vitae Crucifixae Jesu* (a. 1305) Fr. Ubertini de Casali, O.Min." *Miscellanea Francescana* 46 (1946): 124–56.

Zumkeller, Adolar. "Die Augustinerschule des Mittelalters." *Analecta Augustiniana* 27 (1964): 167–262.

## 2. ONE, HOLY, CATHOLIC, AND APOSTOLIC?

Antonazzi, Giovanni. "Lorenzo Valla e la Donazione di Constantino nel secolo XV." *Rivista di storia della Chiesa in Italia* 4 (1950): 191–225.

Arquillière, Henri Xavier. *Le plus ancien traité de l'Église: Jacques de Viterbe "De regimine christiano."* Paris, 1926.

Bartoš, František Michalek. *Literární činnost M. Jakoubka ze Stříbra* [The literary activity of Master Jakoubek ze Stříbra]. Prague, 1925.

———. *Čechy v době Husové* [Bohemia in the age of Hus]. Prague, 1947.

———. *Petr Chelčický, duchovní otec Jednoty bratrské* [Peter Chelčický, the spiritual father of the Unitas Fratrum]. Prague, 1958.

Bernheim, Ernst. "Politische Begriffe des Mittelalters im Lichte der Anschauungen Augustins." *Deutsche Zeitschrift für Geschichtswissenschaft* 8 (1896): 1–23.

Betts, Reginald Robert. *Essays in Czech History*. London, 1969. An especially helpful chapter (pp. 132–59): "English and Czech Influences on the Hussite Movement."

Buytaert, Eligius. "Circa doctrinam Duns Scoti de traditione et de Scriptura adnotationes." *Antonianum* 40 (1965): 346–62.

Congar, Yves. "Aspects ecclésiologiques de la querelle entre mendiants et séculiers dans la seconde moitié du XIIIe siècle et le debut du XIVe." *Archives d'histoire doctrinale et littéraire du moyen âge* 36 (1961): 35–151.

Frank, Karl Suso. "Vita apostolica. Ansätze zur apostolischen Lebensform in der alten Kirche." *Zeitschrift für Kirchengeschichte* 82 (1971): 145–66.

Franzen, August. "Daz Konzil der Einheit. Einigungsbemühungen und konziliare Gedanken auf dem Konstanzer Konzil. Die Dekrete 'Haec sancta' und 'Frequens.'" In *Das Konzil von Konstanz: Beiträge zu seiner Geschichte und Theologie*, edited by August Franzen and Wolfgang Müller, pp. 69–112. Freiburg, 1964.

Gewirth, Alan. *Marsilius of Padua and Medieval Political Philosophy.* New York, 1951. The chapter entitled "The People's Church" (pp. 260–302) is especially pertinent.

Grauert, Hermann von. "Konrads von Megenberg Chronik und sein 'Planctus ecclesiae in Germaniam.'" *Historisches Jahrbuch* 22 (1901): 631–87.

Graus, František. "The Crisis of the Middle Ages and the Hussites." In *The Reformation in Medieval Perspective*, edited by Steven E. Ozment, pp. 76–103. Chicago, 1971.

Grégoire, Réginald. *Bruno de Segni exégète médiéval et théologien monastique.* Spoleto, 1965.

Heimpel, Hermann. *Dietrich von Niem (ca. 1340–1418).* Münster, 1932.

Hendrix, Scott H. "In Quest of the *Vera Ecclesia:* The Crises of Late Medieval Ecclesiology." *Viator* 7 (1976): 347–78.

Hopkins, Jasper. *A Concise Introduction to the Philosophy of Nicholas of Cusa.* Minneapolis, 1978.

Hurley, M. "'Scriptura Sola': Wyclif and His Critics." *Traditio* 16 (1960): 275–352.

Jacob, E. F. *Essays in the Conciliar Epoch.* 3d ed. Notre Dame, Ind., 1963.

Jourdain, Charles Marie Gabriel. *Un ouvrage inédit de Gilles de Rome en faveur de la Papauté.* Paris, 1858.

Kalivoda, Robert, and Kolesnyk, A. *Das hussitische Denken im Lichte seiner Quellen.* Berlin, 1969.

Kaminsky, Howard, et al. "Master Nicholas of Dresden: The Old Color and the New. Selected Works Contrasting the Primitive Church and the Roman Church." *Transactions of the American Philosophical Society*, n.s. 55, pt. 1 (1965): 3–93.

Kantorowicz, Ernst Hartwig. *The King's Two Bodies: A Study in Mediaeval Political Theology.* Princeton, 1957.

Kern, Fritz. *Humana Civilitas: Staat, Kirche und Kultur.* Leipzig, 1913.

Krämer, Werner. *Konsens und Rezeption: Verfassungsprinzipien der Kirche im Basler Konziliarismus.* Münster, 1980.

Krchňák, Aloysius. *De vita et operibus Ioannis de Ragusio.* Rome, 1960.

―――. *Čechové na basilejském sněmu* [The Czechs at the Council of Basel]. Rome, 1967.

Kropatschek, Friedrich. *Das Schriftprinzip der lutherischen Kirche.* Volume 1: *Die Vorgeschichte: Das Erbe des Mittelalters.* Leipzig, 1904.

Kybal, Vlastimil. *M. Jan Hus: život a učení* [Master John Hus: life and teachings]. 2 vols. Prague, 1923–26. Volume 2 (in two parts) is the most complete available summary of the theology of Hus.

Lambert, Malcolm David. *Franciscan Poverty: The Doctrine of the Absolute Poverty of Christ and the Apostles in the Franciscan Order, 1210–1323.* London, 1961. Unlike many other modern works, this study takes seriously the doctrinal issues in the Franciscan movement.

Lapparent, P. de. "La question du commentaire sur la Bulle 'Unam sanctam.'" *Archives d'histoire doctrinale et littéraire du Moyen-âge* 13 (1940–42): 121–51.

Leclercq, Jean. *Jean de Paris et l'ecclésiologie du XIIIe siècle.* Paris, 1942.

Macek, Jan. *Tábor v husitském revolučním hnutí* [Tabor in the Hussite revolutionary movement]. 2d ed. Prague, 1955–56.

McFarlane, K. B. *John Wycliffe and the Beginnings of English Nonconformity.* London, 1952.

McGinn, Bernard. "Angel Pope and Papal Antichrist." *Church History* 47 (1978): 155–73.

McGrade, Arthur S. *The Political Thought of William of Ockham: Personal and Institutional Principles.* Cambridge, 1974.

Monahan, Arthur P. *John of Paris on Royal and Papal Power.* New York, 1974.

Morrall, John Brimyard. *Gerson and the Great Schism.* Manchester, 1960.

Morrissey, Thomas E. "Franciscus Zabarella (1360–1417): Papacy, Community, and Limitations upon Authority." In *Reform and Authority in the Medieval and Reformation Church,* edited by Guy Fitch Lytle, pp. 37–54. Washington, 1981.

Oakley, Francis. *The Political Thought of Pierre d'Ailly: The Voluntarist Tradition.* New Haven, 1964.

Oberman, Heiko Augustinus. *Forerunners of the Reformation: The Shape of Late Medieval Thought Illustrated by Key Documents.* New York, 1966.

Pacaut, Marcel. *La théocratie. L'église et le pouvoir au moyen âge.* Paris, 1957.

Pascoe, L. B. *Jean Gerson: Principles of Church Reform.* Leiden, 1972.

Poulet, F. *La pauvreté et les pauvres dans l'oeuvre de Gerson.* Paris, 1963.

Preuss, Hans. *Die Vorstellungen vom Antichrist im späteren Mittelalter, bei Luther und in der konfessionellen Polemik.* Leipzig, 1906.

Rauh, H. D. *Das Bild des Antichrists im Mittelalter: Von Tyconius zum deutschen Symbolismus.* Münster, 1972.

Rivière, Jean. *Le problème de l'église et de l'état au temps de Philippe le Bel: Étude de théologie positive.* Louvain and Paris, 1926.

———. "Une première 'Somme' du pouvoir pontifical: Le Pape chez Augustin d'Ancone." *Revue des sciences religieuses* 18 (1938): 149–83.

Scholz, Richard. *Die Publizistik zur Zeit Philipps des Schönen und Bonifaz VIII.* Stuttgart, 1903.

———. *Unbekannte kirchenpolitische Streitschriften aus der Zeit Ludwigs des Bayern (1327–1354): Analysen.* Rome, 1911.

Schüssler, Hermann. *Der Primat der heiligen Schrift als theologisches und kanonistisches Problem im Spätmittelalter.* Wiesbaden, 1977.

Sigmund, Paul E. *Nicholas of Cusa and Medieval Political Thought.* Cambridge, Mass., 1963.

Spinka, Matthew. "Peter Chelčický, the Spiritual Father of the Unitas Fratrum." *Church History* 12 (1943): 271–91.

———. *John Hus' Concept of the Church.* Princeton, 1966.

———, ed. *Advocates of Reform: From Wyclif to Erasmus.* Philadelphia, 1958.

Spitzer, Leo. *Classical and Christian Ideas of World Harmony: Prolegomena to an Interpretation of the Word "Stimmung."* Baltimore, 1963.

Stickler, Alfons M. "Papal Infallibility—a Thirteenth-Century Invention." *Catholic Historical Review* 60 (1974): 427–41.

Stinger, Charles L. *Humanism and the Church Fathers: Ambrogio Traversari (1386–1439) and Christian Antiquity in the Italian Renaissance.* Albany, 1977.

Tierney, Brian. *Foundations of the Conciliar Theory: The Contribution of the Medieval Canonists from Gratian to the Great Schism.* Cambridge, 1955.

———. *Origins of Papal Infallibility: 1150–1350.* Leiden, 1972.

Ullmann, Walter. *Origins of the Great Schism.* London, 1949.

Vooght, Paul de. "Le conciliarisme aux conciles de Constance et de Bâle." In *Le concile et les conciles,* edited by Bernard Botte, pp. 143–81. Paris, 1960.

———. *L'hérésie de Jean Hus.* Louvain, 1960.

———. *Jacobellus de Stříbro (†1429), premier théologien du hussitisme.* Louvain, 1972.

Watts, Pauline Moffatt. *Nicolaus Cusanus: A Fifteenth-Century Vision of Man.* Leiden, 1982.

Weinstein, Donald. *Savonarola and Florence: Prophecy and Patriotism in the Renaissance.* Princeton, 1970.

Wilks, Michael J. *The Problem of Sovereignty in the Later Middle Ages: The Papal Monarchy with Augustinus Triumphus and the Publicists.* Cambridge, 1963.

Xiberta y Roqueta, Bartolomé Maria. *Guiu Terrena, carmelita de Perpinyà.* Barcelona, 1932.

Zeman, Jarold Knox. *The Hussite Movement: A Bibliographical Guide.* Ann Arbor, 1977.

## 3.  THE GOSPEL AS THE TREASURE OF THE CHURCH

Althaus, Paul. *The Theology of Martin Luther.* Translated by Robert C. Schultz. Philadelphia, 1966.

Aulén, Gustaf. *Christus Victor: An Historical Study of the Three Main Types of the Idea of Atonement.* Translated by A. G. Hebert. Reprinted with an introduction by Jaroslav Pelikan. New York, 1969.

Bainton, Roland H. *Here I Stand: A Life of Martin Luther.* New York, 1950.

Barth, Karl. "Ansatz und Ansicht in Luthers Abendmahlslehre." In *Die Theologie und die Kirche,* 2:26–75. Munich, 1928.

Billing, Einar. *Our Calling.* Translated by Conrad Bergendoff. Rock Island, Ill., 1952.

Bornkamm, Heinrich. *Luther's World of Thought.* Translated by Martin H. Bertram. Saint Louis, 1958.

———. *Luther and the Old Testament.* Translated by Eric W. and Ruth C. Gritsch. Philadelphia, 1969.

Boyle, Marjorie O'Rourke. *Erasmus on Language and Method in Theology.* Toronto, 1977.

Carlson, Edgar Martin. *The Reinterpretation of Luther.* Philadelphia, 1948.

Clebsch, William A. *England's Earliest Protestants, 1520–35.* New Haven, 1964.

Ebeling, Gerhard. *Evangelische Evangelienauslegung.* Munich, 1942.

———. *Luther: An Introduction to His Thought.* Translated by R. A. Wilson. Philadelphia, 1970.

———. *Lutherstudien.* 2 vols. Tübingen, 1971–77.

Books that are rich in insight and information.

Elert, Werner. *The Structure of Lutheranism.* Translated by Walter A. Hansen. Foreword by Jaroslav Pelikan. Saint Louis, 1962.

Engelland, Hans. *Melanchthon: Glauben und Handeln.* Munich, 1931.

Frank, Franz Hermann Reinhold. *Die Theologie der Konkordienformel historisch-dogmatisch entwickelt und beleuchtet.* 4 vols. Erlangen, 1858–65.

Fraenkel, Peter. *Testimonia Patrum: The Function of the Patristic Argument in the Theology of Philip Melanchthon.* Geneva, 1961.

Gerrish, Brian A. *Grace and Reason: A Study in the Theology of Luther.* Oxford, 1962.

Grane, Leif. *Contra Gabrielem: Luthers Auseinandersetzung mit Gabriel Biel in der disputatio contra scholasticam theologiam 1517.* Translated by Elfriede Pump. Copenhagen, 1962.

———. *Die Confessio Augustana: Einführung in die Hauptgedanken der lutherischen Reformation.* Translated by Eberhard Harbsmeier. Göttingen, 1970.

Haikola, Lauri. *Gesetz und Evangelium bei Matthias Flacius Illyricus: Eine Untersuchung zur lutherischen Theologie vor der Konkordienformel.* Lund, 1952.

Headley, John. *Luther's View of Church History.* New Haven, 1963.

Hermann, Rudolf. *Luthers These "Gerecht und Sünder zugleich."* Gütersloh, 1960.

Hoffman, Bengt R. *Luther and the Mystics: A Re-Examination of Luther's Spiritual Experience and His Relationship to the Mystics.* Minneapolis, 1976.

Holl, Karl. *Luther.* Volume 1 of *Gesammelte Aufsätze zur Kirchengeschichte.* 7th ed. Tübingen, 1948. The fountainhead of the modern study of Luther's theology.

Joachimsen, Paul. "Loci communes: Eine Untersuchung zur Geistesgeschichte des Humanismus und der Reformation." *Jahrbuch der Luther-Gesellschaft* 8 (1926): 27–97.

Kattenbusch, Ferdinand. *Luthers Stellung zu den ökumenischen Symbolen.* Giessen, 1883. Despite its being a century old, still the best treatment of this vital topic.

Köstlin, Julius. *The Theology of Luther in Its Historical Development and Inner Harmony.* Translated by Charles E. Hay. 2 vols. Philadelphia, 1895–97.

Link, W. *Das Ringen Luthers um die Freiheit der Theologie von der Philosophie.* Munich, 1940.

Maurer, Wilhelm. "Melanchthons Anteil am Streit zwischen Luther und Erasmus." *Archiv für Reformationsgeschichte* 49 (1958): 99–115.

Messner, Joachim. *Kirchliche Ueberlieferung und Autorität im Flaciuskreis: Studien zu den Marburger Zenturien.* Berlin, 1964.

Moldaenke, Günther. *Schriftverständnis und Schriftdeutung im Zeitalter der Reformation.* Vol. 1: *Matthias Flacius Illyricus.* Stuttgart, 1936.

Nagel, Wilhelm Ernst. *Luthers Anteil an der Confessio Augustana.* Gütersloh, 1930.

Noth, Gottfried. *Grundlinien der Theologie des Martin Chemnitz.* N.p., 1930.

Oberman, Heiko Augustinus. "Facientibus Quod in se est Deus non Denegat Gratiam: Robert Holcot, O.P., and the Beginnings of Luther's Theology." In *The Reformation in Medieval Perspective,* edited by Steven E. Ozment, pp. 19–41. Chicago, 1971.

Patton, Hugh. *The Efficacy of Putative Attrition in the Doctrine of Theologians of the XVI and XVII Centuries.* Rome, 1966.

Pelikan, Jaroslav. *Luther the Expositor: Introduction to the Reformer's Exegetical Writings.* Companion volume to *Luther's Works: American Edition.* Saint Louis, 1959.

———. *Obedient Rebels: Catholic Substance and Protestant Principle in Luther's Reformation.* New York, 1964.

———. "Adolf von Harnack on Luther." In *Interpreters of Luther: Essays in Honor of Wilhelm Pauck,* edited by Jaroslav Pelikan, pp. 253–74. Philadelphia, 1968.

Pesch, Otto Hermann. *Die Theologie der Rechtfertigung bei Martin Luther und Thomas von Aquin.* Mainz, 1967.

Pfürtner, Stephen. *Luther and Aquinas on Salvation.* Translated by Edward Quinn. Foreword by Jaroslav Pelikan. New York, 1964.

Preger, Wilhelm. *Matthias Flacius Illyricus und seine Zeit.* 2 vols. Erlangen, 1859–61.

Prenter, Regin. *Spiritus Creator.* Translated by John M. Jensen. Philadelphia, 1953.

———. *Der barmherzige Richter: Justitia Dei passiva in Luthers "Dictata super Psalterium."* Aarhus, 1961.

Rietschel, Ernst. *Das Problem der sichtbar-unsichtbaren Kirche bei Luther.* Leipzig, 1932.

Rupp, E. Gordon. *The Righteousness of God: Luther Studies.* New York, 1954.

Scheel, Otto. *Martin Luther: Vom Katholizismus zur Reformation.* 3d ed. 2 vols. Leipzig, 1921–30.

Schlink, Edmund. *Theology of the Lutheran Confessions.* Translated by Paul F. Koehneke and Herbert J. A. Bouman. Philadelphia, 1961.

Schubert, Hans von. *Bekenntnisbildung und Religionspolitik (1524–1534).* Gotha, 1910.

Seebass, Gottfried. *Das reformatorische Werk des Andreas Osiander.* Nuremberg, 1967.

Seeberg, Erich. *Luthers Theologie: Motive und Ideen.* 2 vols. Göttingen and Stuttgart, 1929–37.

Steinmetz, David C. *Luther and Staupitz: An Essay in the Intellectual Origins of the Protestant Reformation.* Durham, 1980.

Strauss, Gerald. *Luther's House of Learning: Indoctrination of the Young in the German Reformation.* Baltimore, 1978.

Tentler, Thomas N. *Sin and Confession on the Eve of the Reformation.* Princeton, 1977.

Vajta, Vilmos, ed. *Luther und Melanchthon: Referate des 2. Internationalen Lutherforschungskongresses.* Göttingen, 1961.

Vignaux, Paul. *Luther, commentateur des Sentences.* Paris, 1935.

Vogelsang, Erich. *Die Anfänge der Christologie Luthers nach der ersten Psalmenvorlesung.* Berlin, 1929.

Wolf, Ernst. *Peregrinatio.* 2 vols. Munich, 1962.

## 4. The Word and the Will of God

Barth, Karl. *The Heidelberg Catechism for Today.* Translated by Shirley C. Guthrie, Jr. Richmond, 1964. Historical learning combined with theological insight.

Barth, Peter. *Das Problem der natürlichen Theologie bei Calvin.* Munich, 1935.

Baker, J. Wayne. *Heinrich Bullinger and the Covenant: The Other Reformed Tradition.* Athens, Ohio, 1980.

Bartel, Oskar. *Jan Łaski.* Volume 1: *1499–1556.* Warsaw, 1955.

Bicknell, Edward John. *A Theological Introduction to the Thirty-Nine Articles.* 3d ed. London, 1955. The ambiguous situation of the *Thirty-Nine Articles* as a "Reformed" confession, discussed also by Martin Schmidt.

Bizer, Ernst. *Studien zur Geschichte des Abendmahlstreits im 16. Jahrhundert.* Darmstadt, 1962.

Bohatec, Josef. *Calvin und das Recht.* Feudingen, 1954. Especially profound in its discussion of "natural law."

————. *Budé und Calvin: Studien zur Gedankenwelt des französischen Frühhumanismus.* Graz, 1950.

Bray, John S. *Theodor Beza's Doctrine of Predestination.* Niewkoop, 1975.

Brunner, Peter. *Vom Glauben bei Calvin.* Tübingen, 1925.

Courvoisier, Jacques. *La notion d'église chez Bucer dans son développement historique.* Paris, 1933.

Davies, Rupert E. *The Problem of Authority in the Continental Reformers.* London, 1946.

Dowey, Edward A., Jr. *The Knowledge of God in Calvin's Theology.* New York, 1952. Illuminates many issues in Calvin's thought.

Eells, Hastings. *Martin Bucer.* New Haven, 1931.

Forstmann, H. Jackson. *Word and Spirit: Calvin's Doctrine of Biblical Authority.* Stanford, 1962.

Ganoczy, Alexandre. *Calvin théologien de l'église et du ministère.* Paris, 1964.

Gerrish, Brian A. "John Calvin on Luther." In *Interpreters of Luther,* edited by Jaroslav Pelikan, pp. 67–96. Philadelphia, 1968.

Gestrich, Christoph. *Zwingli als Theologe: Glaube und Geist beim Zürcher Reformator.* Zurich, 1967.

Greenslade, Stanley Lawrence. "English Versions of the Bible, 1515–1611." In *The Cambridge History of the Bible: The West from the Reformation to the Present Day,* edited by Stanley Lawrence Greenslade. Cambridge, 1963.

Greschat, Martin. "Der Bundesgedanke in der Theologie des späten Mittelalters." *Zeitschrift für Kirchengeschichte* 81 (1970): 44–63. The medieval background of a Reformed theme.

Grützmacher, Richard H. *Wort und Geist: Eine historische und dogmatische Untersuchung zum Gnadenmittel des Wortes.* Leipzig, 1902.

Hauck, Wilhelm-Albert. *Die Erwählten: Prädestination und Heilsgewissheit nach Calvin.* Gütersloh, 1950.

Hollweg, Walter. *Heinrich Bullingers Hausbuch: Eine Untersuchung über die Anfänge der reformierten Predigtliteratur.* Neukirchen, 1956.

————. *Neue Untersuchungen zur Geschichte und Lehre des Heidelberger Katechismus.* 2 vols. Neukirchen, 1961–68.

Kickel, Walter. *Vernunft und Offenbarung bei Theodor Beza: Zum Problem des Verhältnisses von Theologie, Philosophie und Staat.* Neukirchen, 1967.

Köhler, Walter. *Zwingli und Luther: Ihr Streit über das Abendmahl nach seinen politischen und religiösen Beziehungen.* 2 vols. Leipzig, 1924–53. One of the most important studies of how Protestantism divided.

Krusche, Werner. *Das Wirken des Heiligen Geistes nach Calvin.* Göttingen, 1957.

Lang, August. *Der Evangelienkommentar Martin Butzers und die Grundzüge seiner Theologie.* Leipzig, 1900.

————. *Der Heidelberger Katechismus.* Leipzig, 1913.

Locher, Gottfried W. *Zwingli's Thought: New Perspectives.* Leiden, 1981.

McDonnell, Kilian. *John Calvin, the Church, and the Eucharist.* Princeton, 1967. A sympathetic interpretation by a Roman Catholic theologian.

McLelland, Joseph C. *The Visible Words of God: An Exposition of the Sacramental Theology of Peter Martyr Vermigli A.D. 1500–1562.* Glasgow, 1957.

McNeill, John Thomas. "The Church in Sixteenth-Century Reformed Theology." *Journal of Religion* 22 (1942): 251–69.

————. "The Doctrine of the Ministry in Reformed Theology." *Church History* 12 (1943): 77–97.

————, ed. John Calvin. *Institutes of the Christian Religion.* 2 vols. Philadelphia, 1960. The leading interpreter of Calvin and Calvinism in English-speaking scholarship.

Niesel, Wilhelm. *The Theology of Calvin.* Translated by H. Knight. Philadelphia, 1956. Probably the best systematic treatment.

Parker, Thomas Henry Louis. *The Doctrine of the Knowledge of God: A Study in Calvin's Theology.* Grand Rapids, Mich., 1959.

Pauck, Wilhelm. *Das Reich Gottes auf Erden: Utopie und Wirklichkeit.* Berlin, 1928.

Pollet, Jacques V. *Huldrych Zwingli et la Reforme en Suisse.* Paris, 1963.

Potter, George Richard. *Zwingli.* Cambridge, 1976.

Raitt, Jill. *The Eucharistic Theology of Theodore Beza: Development of the Reformed Doctrine.* Chambersburg, Pa., 1972.

Schmidt, Martin. "Die Kirche von England als Gegenstand der Konfessionskunde." In *Erneuerung der Einen Kirche: Arbeiten aus Kirchengeschichte und Konfessionskunde Heinrich Bornkamm zum 65. Geburtstag gewidmet,* pp. 82–114. Göttingen, 1966.

Schweizer, Alexander. *Die protestantischen Zentraldogmen in ihrer Entwicklung innerhalb der reformierten Kirche.* 2 vols. Zurich, 1854–56.

Smits, L. *Saint Augustin dans l'oeuvre de Jean Calvin.* 2 vols. Assen, 1957–58.

Staedtke, Joachim. *Die Theologie des jungen Bullinger.* Zurich, 1962.

————. *Heinrich Bullinger Bibliographie: Beschreibendes Verzeichnis der gedruckten Werke von Heinrich Bullinger.* Zurich, 1972.

————, and Locher, Gottfried W. *Glauben und Bekennen: 400 Jahre Confessio Helvetica Posterior: Akademische Feier.* Bern, 1966.

Strohl, Henri. *Bucer, humaniste chrétien.* Paris, 1939.

Stuermann, Walter E. *A Critical Study of Calvin's Concept of Faith.* Tulsa, 1952.

Torrance, Thomas F. *Calvin's Doctrine of Man.* London, 1949.

————, ed. *The School of Faith: The Catechisms of the Reformed Church.* New York, 1959.

Van Buren, Paul. *Christ in Our Place: The Substitutionary Character of Calvin's Doctrine of Reconciliation.* Grand Rapids, Mich., 1957.

Wallace, Ronald S. *Calvin's Doctrine of the Word and Sacrament.* Edinburgh, 1953.

Walton, Robert C. *Zwingli's Theocracy.* Toronto, 1967.

Warfield, Benjamin Breckenridge. *Calvin and Calvinism.* New York, 1931.

Wendel, François. *Calvin: The Origins and Development of His Religious Thought.* Translated by Philip Mairet. New York, 1963.

Wernle, Paul. *Calvin.* Volume 3 of *Der evangelische Glaube nach den Hauptschriften der Reformatoren.* Tübingen, 1919.

## 5. THE DEFINITION OF ROMAN CATHOLIC PARTICULARITY

Braunisch, Reinhard. *Die Theologie der Rechtfertigung im "Enchiridion" (1538) des Johannes Gropper.* Münster, 1974.

Douglas, Richard M. *Jacopo Sadoleto, 1477–1547: Humanist and Reformer.* Cambridge, Mass., 1959.

Fenlon, D. *Heresy and Obedience in Tridentine Italy: Cardinal Pole and the Counter Reformation.* Cambridge, 1972.

Geiselmann, J. R. "Das Missverständnis über das Verhältnis von Schrift und Tradition in der katholischen Theologie." *Una Sancta* 11 (1956): 131–50.

Giuriato, A. M. *Le tradizioni nella IV Sessio del Concilio di Trento.* Vicenza, 1942.

Gollob, H. *Friedrich Nausea: Probleme der Gegenreformation.* Vienna, 1952.

Gottler, Joseph. *Der heilige Thomas von Aquin und die vortridentinischen Thomisten über die Wirkungen des Busssakraments.* Freiburg, 1904.

Hefner, J. *Die Entstehungsgeschichte des Trienter Rechtfertigungsdekretes.* Paderborn, 1909.

Hennig, Gerhard. *Cajetan und Luther: Ein historischer Beitrag zur Begegnung von Thomismus und Reformation.* Stuttgart, 1966.

Herte, Adolf. *Das katholische Lutherbild im Bann der Lutherkommentare des Cochläus.* 3 vols. Münster, 1943.

Iserloh, Ernst. *Die Eucharistie in der Darstellung des Johannes Eck.* Münster, 1950.

———. *Der Kampf um die Messe in den ersten Jahrzehnten der Auseinandersetzung mit Luther.* Münster, 1951.

Jedin, Hubert. *Katholische Reformation oder Gegenreformation: Ein Versuch zur Klärung der Begriffe nebst einer Jubiläumsbetrachtung über das Tridentiner Konzil.* Lucerne, 1946.

———. *Papal Legate at the Council of Trent: Cardinal Seripando.* Translated by F. C. Eckhoff. Saint Louis, 1947.

———. *Geschichte des Konzils von Trient.* 4 vols. in 5. Freiburg, 1949–75. (English translation by Ernest Graf: *A History of the Council of Trent.* Saint Louis, 1957–.) Indispensable.

Koch, W. "Das Trienter Konzilsdekret De peccato originali." *Theologische Quartalschrift* 95 (1913): 430–50, 532–64; 96 (1914): 101–23.

Kross, A. "Die Lehre von der Unbefleckten Empfängnis auf dem Konzil von Trient." *Zeitschrift für katholische Theologie* 28 (1904): 758–66.

Laemmer, Hugo. *Die vortridentinisch-katholische Theologie des Reformationszeitalters.* Berlin, 1858.

Lauchert, Friedrich, *Die italienischen literarischen Gegner Luthers.* Freiburg, 1912.

Lauriers, G. des. "St. Augustin et la question de la certitude de la grâce au Concile de Trent." In *Augustinus Magister,* 1:1051–67. Paris, 1954.

Lennerz, H. "Das Konzil von Trient und theologische Schulmeinungen." *Scholastik* 4 (1929): 38–53.

McConica, James. *English Humanists and Reformation Politics under Henry VIII and Edward VI.* Oxford, 1965.

Maichle, A. *Der Kanon der biblischen Bücher und das Konzil von Trient.* Freiburg, 1929.

Marius, Richard C. "Thomas More and the Heretics." Ph.D. dissertation, Yale University, 1962.

O'Malley, John W. *Giles of Viterbo on Church and Reform: A Study in Renaissance Thought.* Leiden, 1968.

Ortigues, Edmond. "Écritures et traditions apostoliques au Concile de Trente." *Recherches de science religieuse* 36 (1949): 271–99.

Pas, P. "La doctrine de la double justice au Concile de Trente." *Ephemerides Theologicae Lovanienses* 30 (1954): 5–53.

Penagos, L. "La doctrina del peccato original en el Concilio de Trento." In *Miscellanea Comillas* 4 (1945): 127–273.

Polman, Pontien. *Die polemische Methode der ersten Gegner der Reformation*. Münster, 1931.

———. *L'élément historique dans la controverse religieuse du XVIe siècle*. Gembloux, 1932.

Rückert, Hanns. *Die Rechtfertigungslehre auf dem Tridentinischen Konzil*. Bonn, 1925.

———. *Die theologische Entwicklung Gasparo Contarinis*. Bonn, 1926.

Schenk, W. *Reginald Pole*. London, 1950.

Schreiber, Georg, ed. *Das Weltkonzil von Trient: Sein Werden und Wirken*. 2 vols. Freiburg, 1951. Contains specific articles on various decrees, e.g., on Scripture (1:359–80) and on justification (1:117–43).

Schutte, Anne Jacobson. *Peter Paul Vergerio: The Making of an Italian Reformer*. Geneva, 1977.

Schweizer, J. *Ambrosius Catharinus Politus*. Münster, 1910.

Simoncelli, Paolo. *Il case Reginald Pole: Eresìa e santità nelle polemiche religiose del cinquecento*. Rome, 1977.

Stakemeier, E. *Der Kampf um Augustinus auf dem Tridentinum*. Paderborn, 1937.

Stupperich, Robert. *Der Humanismus und die Wiedervereinigung der Konfessionen*. Leipzig, 1936.

Tjernagel, Neelak Serawlook. *Henry VIII and the Lutherans: A Study in Anglo-Lutheran Relations from 1521 to 1547*. Saint Louis, 1965.

Wedewer, J. *Johann Dietenberger*. Freiburg, 1888.

Wicks, Jared. *Cajetan Responds: A Reader in Reformation Controversy*. Washington, 1978.

## 6. CHALLENGES TO APOSTOLIC CONTINUITY

Bainton, Roland H. *David Joris: Wiedertäufer und Kämpfer für Toleranz im 16. Jahrhundert*. Translated by Hajo Holborn and Annemarie Holborn. Leipzig, 1937.

———. *Hunted Heretic: The Life and Death of Michael Servetus, 1511–1553*. 2d ed. Boston, 1960. The discussion of the Trinity (pp. 21–56) is clear and cogent.

Baumann, Clarence. *Gewaltlosigkeit im Taüfertum: Eine Untersuchung zur theologischen Ethik des oberdeutschen Täufertums der Reformationszeit*. Leiden, 1968.

Beachy, Alvin. *The Concept of Grace in the Radical Reformation*. Nieuwkoop, 1977.

Bender, Harold S. *Conrad Grebel (ca. 1498–1526): The Founder of the Swiss Brethren*. Goshen, Ind., 1950. Basic.

———. "Anabaptist Theology of Discipleship." *Mennonite Quarterly Review* 24 (1950): 25–32.

———. "The Pacifism of the Sixteenth-Century Anabaptists." *Church History* 24 (1955): 119–31.

Blanke, Fritz. "Betrachtungen zum ältesten Täuferbekenntnis." *Archiv für Reformationsgeschichte* 37 (1940): 240–49. A study of the *Schleitheim Confession*.

Bornkamm, Heinrich. "Äusserer und innerer Mensch bei Luther und den Spiritualisten." In *Imago Dei: Beiträge zur theologischen Anthropologie*, edited by Heinrich Bornkamm, pp. 85–109. Giessen, 1932.

Burgevin, Frederick H. *"Cribratio Alchorani": Nicholas Cusanus's Criticism of the Koran in the Light of His Philosophy of Religion.* New York, 1969.

Chevalier, Philippe, et al., eds. *Dionysiaca: Recueil donnant l'ensemble des traductions latines des ouvrages attribués au Denys de l'Aréopage.* 2 vols. Paris, 1937–50.

Chmaj, Ludwik. *Faust Socyn, 1539–1604.* Warsaw, 1963.

Clasen, Claus-Peter. *Anabaptism: A Social History, 1515–1618.* Ithaca, 1972.

Cohn, Norman. *The Pursuit of the Millennium. Revolutionary Messianism in Medieval and Reformation Europe and Its Bearing on Modern Totalitarian Movements.* 2d ed. New York, 1961.

Davis, Kenneth Ronald. *Anabaptism and Asceticism: A Study in Intellectual Origins.* Scottsdale, Pa., 1974.

Edwards, Mark U. *Luther and the False Brethren.* Stanford, 1975.

Elliger, Walter. *Thomas Müntzer: Leben und Werk.* Göttingen, 1975.

Emmi, B. "Il decreto tridentino sulla Vulgata nei commenti della prima polemica protestanto-cattolica." *Angelicum* 30 (1953): 107–30.

Fast, Heinold. *Heinrich Bullinger und die Täufer.* Weierhof, 1959.

Fellmann, Walter, ed. Hans Denck. *Schriften.* 3 vols. Gütersloh, 1955–60.

Friedmann, Robert, ed. *Glaubenszeugnisse oberdeutscher Taufgesinnten,* vol. 2. Gütersloh, 1967.

———. "Schleitheim Confession (1527) and Other Doctrinal Writings of the Swiss Brethren in a Hitherto Unknown Edition." *Mennonite Quarterly Review* 16 (1942):82–98.

Gerdes, Hayo. *Luthers Streit mit den Schwärmern um das rechte Verständnis des Gesetzes Mose.* Göttingen, 1955.

Glawe, Walther. *Sebastian Francks unkirchliches Christentum: Für oder wider Kirche und Dogma?* Leipzig, 1912.

Górski, Konrad. *Grzegorz Pawel z Brzezin: Monografja z dziejow polskiej literatury arjanskiej XVI wieku* [Gregory Paul of Brzezin: a monograph from the history of the Polish Arian literature of the sixteenth century]. Cracow, 1929.

Gritsch, Eric W. *Thomas Müntzer: Reformer without a Church.* Philadelphia, 1967.

Hegler, Alfred. *Geist und Schrift bei Sebastian Franck: Eine Studie zur Geschichte des Spiritualismus in der Reformationszeit.* Freiburg, 1892. Still an important monograph.

Hershberger, Guy F., ed. *The Recovery of the Anabaptist Vision: A Sixtieth Anniverary Tribute to Harold S. Bender.* Scottsdale, Pa., 1957.

Hillerbrand, Hans Joachim. *Die politische Ethik des oberdeutschen Täufertums: Eine Untersuchung zur Religions- und Geistesgeschichte des 16. Jahrhunderts,* Leiden, 1962.

———. *A Bibliography of Anabaptism, 1520–1630.* Elkhart, Ind., 1962.

———. *A Fellowship of Discontent.* New York, 1967.

Holeczek, Heinz. *Humanistische Bibelphilologie als Reformproblem bei Erasmus von Rotterdam, Thomas More und William Tyndale.* Leiden, 1975.

Klaassen, Walter. "Spiritualization in the Reformation." *Mennonite Quarterly Review* 37 (1963): 67–78.

Kot, Stanislaw. *Socinianism in Poland: The Social and Political Ideas of the Polish Antitrinitarians in the Sixteenth and Seventeenth Centuries.* Translated by Earl Morse Wilbur. Boston, 1957.

Krahn, Cornelius. *Menno Simons (1496–1561): Ein Beitrag zur Geschichte und Theologie der Taufgesinnten.* Karlsruhe, 1936.

Littell, Franklin H. *The Anabaptist View of the Church*. 2d ed. Boston, 1958.

Loescher, John R. *The Divine Community: Trinity, Church, and Ethics in Reformation Theologies*. Kirksville, Missouri, 1981.

Martini, Magda. *Fausto Socino et la pensée socinienne*. Paris, 1967.

*The Mennonite Encyclopedia: A Comprehensive Reference Work on the Anabaptist-Mennonite Movement*. 4 vols. Scottsdale, Pa., 1955–59.

Neumann, Gerhard J. "'Rechtfertigung' und 'Person Christi' als dogmatische Glaubensfragen bei den Täufern der Reformationszeit." *Zeitschrift für Kirchengeschichte* 70 (1959): 62–75.

Nigg, Walter. *Das Buch der Ketzer*. Zurich, 1949.

Oyer, John S. *Lutheran Reformers against Anabaptists: Luther, Melanchthon, and Menius, and the Anabaptists of Central Germany*. The Hague, 1964.

Pelikan, Jaroslav. "Negative Theology and Positive Religion: A Study of Nicholas Cusanus *De pace fidei*." In *The Via Negativa*, supplementary number of *Prudentia*, pp. 65–78. Aukland, 1981.

Rees, Thomas, ed. *The Racovian Catechism, with Notes and Illustrations*. London, 1818.

Sachsse, Carl. *D. Balthasar Hubmaier als Theologe*. Berlin, 1914. Reprint edition. Aalen, 1973.

Schwindt, Adolf. *Hans Denck: Ein Vorkämpfer undogmatischen Christentums*. Schlachtern, 1924.

Sider, Ronald J. *Andreas Bodenstein von Karlstadt: The Development of His Thought, 1517–1525*. Leiden, 1974.

Stauffer, Ethelbert. "The Anabaptist Theology of Martyrdom." *Mennonite Quarterly Review* 19 (1945): 179–214.

Tedeschi, J. A., ed. *Italian Reformation Studies in Honor of Laelius Socinus*. Florence, 1965.

Wenger, John Christian. "The Schleitheim Confession of Faith." *Mennonite Quarterly Review* 19 (1945): 243–53.

———. *The Doctrines of the Mennonites*. Scottsdale, Pa., 1950.

———, ed. *The Complete Writings of Menno Simons, c. 1496–1561*. Scottsdale, Pa., 1956.

Wilbur, Earl Morse. *A History of Unitarianism: Socinianism and Its Antecedents*. Cambridge, Mass., 1946.

———. *A Bibliography of the Pioneers of the Socinian-Unitarian Movement in Modern Christianity in Italy, Switzerland, Germany, Holland*. Rome, 1950.

———. *A History of Unitarianism in Transylvania, England, and America*. Cambridge, Mass., 1952.

———, ed. *The Two Treatises of Servetus on the Trinity*. Cambridge, Mass., 1932.

Williams, George Huntston, ed. *Spiritual and Anabaptist Writers*. Philadelphia, 1957.

———. *The Radical Reformation*. Philadelphia, 1962.

———. *The Polish Brethren: Documentation of the History and Thought of Unitarianism in the Polish-Lithuanian Commonwealth and in the Diaspora, 1601–1685*. Boston, 1976–79.
Marks a turning point in the historiography of the "left wing of the Reformation."

Zeman, Jarold Knox. *The Anabaptists and the Czech Brethren in Moravia, 1526–1628: A Study of Origins and Contacts*. Foreword by Jaroslav Pelikan. The Hague, 1969.

Zuck, Lowell H. "Abortive Counter Revolt within the Reformation." *Church History* (1957): 221–26.

## 7. Confessional Dogmatics in a Divided Christendom

Achutegui, P. S. *La universalidad del conocimiento de Dio en los paganos: Segun los primeros teologos de la Compañia de Jésus, 1534–1648.* Madrid, 1951.

Althaus, Paul. *Die Prinzipien der deutschen reformierten Dogmatik im Zeitalter der aristotelischen Scholastik.* Leipzig, 1914.

Armstrong, Brian G. *Calvinism and the Amyraut Heresy: Protestant Scholasticism and Humanism in Seventeenth-Century France.* Madison, Wis., 1969. A thorough and informative monograph.

Baur, Jorg. *Die Vernunft zwischen Ontologie und Evangelium: Eine Untersuchung zur Theologie Johann Andreas Quenstedts.* Gütersloh, 1962.

Bizer, Ernst. *Frühorthodoxie und Rationalismus.* Zurich, 1963.

Bornkamm, Heinrich. *Mystik, Spiritualismus und die Anfänge des Pietismus.* Giessen, 1926.

Chadwick, Owen. *From Bossuet to Newman: The Idea of Doctrinal Development.* Cambridge, 1957.

Cremeans, Charles David. *The Reception of Calvinistic Thought in England.* Urbana, Ill., 1949.

Daniélou, Jean. *God and the Ways of Knowing.* Translated by W. Roberts. New York, 1957.

Díez-Alegría, J. *El desarrollo de la doctrina de la Ley Natural en Luis de Molina y en los maestros de la Universidad de Evora de 1565 a 1591.* Madrid, 1951.

Engel, Peter. *Die eine Wahrheit in der gespalteten Christenheit: Untersuchungen zur Theologie Georg Calixts.* Göttingen, 1976.

Eschweiler, Karl. "Die Philosophie der spanischen Spätscholastik auf den deutschen Universitäten des siebzehnten Jahrhunderts." In *Gesammelte Aufsätze zur Kulturgeschichte Spaniens,* edited by Heinrich Finke, 1:251–325. Münster, 1928.

Fatio, Olivier. *Méthode et théologie: Lambert Daneau et les debuts de la scolastique réformée.* Geneva, 1976.

Faulenbach, Heiner. *Die Struktur der Theologie des Amandus Polanus von Polansdorf.* Zurich, 1967.

————. *Weg und Ziel der Erkenntnis Christi: Eine Untersuchung zur Theologie des Johannes Coccejus.* Neukirchen, 1973.

Franks, Robert S. *A History of the Doctrine of the Work of Christ in Its Ecclesiastical Development.* 2 vols. New York, 1918.

Gass, Wilhelm. *Die Geschichte der protestantischen Dogmatik in ihrem Zusammenhange mit der Theologie überhaupt.* 4 vols. Berlin, 1854–67.

Geiger, N. *Die Basler Kirche und Theologie im Zeitalter der Hochorthodoxie.* Zurich, 1952.

Giacon, C. *La seconda scolastica.* 3 vols. Milan, 1944–50.

Gollwitzer, Helmut. *Coena Domini: Die altlutherische Abendmahlslehre in ihrer Auseinandersetzung mit dem Calvinismus dargestellt an der lutherischen Frühorthodoxie.* Munich, [1937].

Guardini, Romano. *Pascal for Our Time.* Translated by Brian Thompson. New York, 1966.

Hägglund, Bengt. *Die Heilige Schrift und ihre Deutung in der Theologie Johann Gerhards: Eine Untersuchung über das altlutherische Schriftverständnis.* Lund, 1951.

Hazelton, Roger. *Blaise Pascal: The Genius of His Thought.* Philadelphia, 1974.

Heim, Karl. "Zur Geschichte des Satzes von der doppelten Wahrheit." *Glaube und Leben,* pp. 73–97. Berlin, 1926.

Heppe, Heinrich. *Dogmatik des deutschen Protestantismus im sechzehnten Jahrhundert.* Gotha, 1857.

———. *Die Dogmatik der evangelisch-reformierten Kirche.* Edited by Ernst Bizer. Neukirchen, 1935. The Reformed counterpart to the compilations of Schmid and Ratschow (see below).

Hillerdal, Gunnar. *Reason and Revelation in Richard Hooker.* Lund, 1962.

Jansen, François Xavier. *Baius et le Baianisme.* Louvain, 1927.

Hupfeld, Renatus. *Die Etihk Johann Gerhards: Ein Beitrag zum Verständnis der lutherischen Ethik.* Berlin, 1908.

Kirste, Reinhard. *Das Zeugnis des Geistes und das Zeugnis der Schrift: Das testimonium Spiritus Sancti internum als hermeneutisch-polemischer Zentralbegriff bei Johann Gerhard in der Auseinandersetzung mit Robert Bellarmin.* Göttingen, 1976.

Knappen, Marshall M. *Tudor Puritanism: A Chapter in the History of Idealism.* Chicago, 1939.

Leube, Hans. *Die Reformideen in der deutschen lutherischen Kirche zur Zeit der Orthodoxie.* Leipzig, 1924.

———. *Kalvinismus und Luthertum im Zeitalter der Orthodoxie.* Volume 1: *Der Kampf um die Herrschaft im protestantischen Deutschland.* Leipzig, 1928.

Lewalter, Ernst. *Spanisch-jesuitische und deutsch-lutherische Metaphysik des 17. Jahrhunderts.* Hamburg, 1935. Philosophical affinities despite dogmatic differences.

Lubac, Henri de. *Surnaturel.* Paris, 1946. The relation between nature and grace.

Miel, Jan. *Pascal and Theology.* Baltimore, 1969. Emphasizes the theological Augustinianism of Pascal's thought.

Miller, Perry. *Errand into the Wilderness.* Cambridge, Mass., 1956. "The Marrow of Puritan Divinity" (pp. 48–98) is the central chapter of the book.

Nuttall, Geoffrey F. *The Holy Spirit in Puritan Faith and Experience.* Oxford, 1946.

O'Connell, Marvin R. *Thomas Stapleton and the Counter Reformation.* New Haven, 1964.

O'Connor, Edward Dennis, ed. *The Dogma of the Immaculate Conception: History and Significance.* Notre Dame, Ind., 1958.

Pelikan, Jaroslav. "Natural Theology in David Hollaz." *Concordia Theological Monthly* 18 (1947): 253–63.

———. "The Origins of the Object-Subject Antithesis in Lutheran Dogmatics." *Concordia Theological Monthly* 21 (1950): 94–104.

———. "The Evolution of the Historical." Chapter 2 of *Historical Theology: Continuity and Change in Christian Doctrine,* pp. 33–67. New York, 1971.

Petersen, Peter. *Geschichte der aristotelischen Philosophie im protestantischen Deutschland.* Leipzig, 1921.

Platt, John. *Reformed Thought and Scholasticism: The Arguments for the Existence of God in Dutch Theology, 1575–1650.* Leiden, 1982.

Preus, Robert D. *The Inspiration of Scripture: A Study of the Theology of the Seventeenth Century Lutheran Dogmaticians.* Mankato, Minn., 1955.

————. *The Theology of Post-Reformation Lutheranism: A Study of Theological Prolegomena.* Saint Louis, 1970.

————. "The Influence of the Formula of Concord on the Later Lutheran Orthodoxy." In *Discord, Dialogue, and Concord: Studies in the Lutheran Reformation's Formula of Concord,* edited by Lewis W. Spitz and Wenzel Lohff, pp. 86–101. Philadelphia, 1977.

Ratschow, Carl Heinz. *Lutherische Dogmatik zwischen Reformation und Aufklärung.* Gütersloh, 1964–.

Rich, Arthur. *Pascals Bild vom Menschen: Eine Studie uber die Dialektik von Natur und Gnade in den "Pensées."* Zurich, 1953.

Russell, Conrad. "Arguments for Religious Unity in England, 1530–1650." *Journal of Ecclesiastical History* 18 (1967): 201–26.

Ryan, E. A. *The Historical Scholarship of Saint Bellarmine.* New York, 1936.

Ryan, John K. "The Reputation of St. Thomas among English Protestant Thinkers of the Seventeenth Century." *New Scholasticism* 22 (1948): 1–33, 126–208.

Scharlemann, Robert P. *Thomas Aquinas and John Gerhard.* New Haven, 1964.

Schenke, Friedrich. *Der Kirchengedanke Johann Gerhards und seiner Zeit.* Gütersloh, 1931.

Schleiff, Arnold. *Die Selbstkritik der lutherischen Kirchen im 17. Jahrhundert.* Berlin, 1937.

————. "Sprachphilosophie und Inspirationstheorie im Denken des 17. Jahrhunderts." *Zeitschrift für Kirchengeschichte* 57 (1938): 133–52.

Schmid, Heinrich. *The Doctrinal Theology of the Lutheran Church.* Translated by Charles Augustus Hay and Henry Eyster Jacobs. Reprint edition. Minneapolis, [1961].

Schrenk, Gottlob. *Gottesreich und Bund im älteren Protestantismus, vornehmlich bei Johannes Coccejus.* Gütersloh,1923. Schrenk's book did much to illumine the early history of covenant theology.

Schüssler, Hermann. "*Georg Calixt, Theologie und Kirchenpolitik: Eine Studie zur Ökumenizität des Luthertums.* Wiesbaden, 1961.

Schweitzer, Albert. *The Quest of the Historical Jesus: A Critical Study of Its Progress from Reimarus to Wrede.* Translated by W. Montgomery. Reprint edition. New York, 1961.

Servière, Joseph de la. *La théologie de Bellarmin.* 2d ed. Paris, 1909.

Sprunger, Keith L. *The Learned Doctor William Ames: Dutch Backgrounds of English and American Puritanism.* Urbana, Ill., 1972.

Staehelin, Ernst. *Amandus Polanus von Polansdorf.* Basel, 1955.

Stegmüller, Friedrich. *Zur Gnadenlehre des jungen Suarez.* Freiburg, 1933.

————. *Geschichte des Molinismus.* Münster, 1935.

Tavard, George H. *Holy Writ or Holy Church: The Crisis of the Protestant Reformation.* New York, 1959.

Thomasius, Gottfried. "Geschichte der lutherischen Christologie." in *Christi Person und Werk,* 2:307–526. 2d ed. Erlangen, 1857.

Troeltsch, Ernst. *Vernunft und Offenbarung bei Johann Gerhard und Melanchthon.* Göttingen, 1891. This monograph by Troeltsch inaugurated not only his own scholarly career but a new interest in seventeenth-century theology.

Wallmann, Johannes. *Der Theologiebegriff bei Johann Gerhard und Georg Calixt.* Tübingen, 1961.

Weber, Hans Emil. *Die philosophische Scholastik des deutschen Protestantismus im Zeit-alter der Orthodoxie.* Leipzig, 1907.

————. *Der Einflusss der protestantischen Schulphilosophie auf die orthodox-lutherische Dogmatik.* Leipzig, 1908.

————. *Reformation, Orthodoxie, und Rationalismus.* 2 vols. in 3. Gütersloh, 1937–51. Unfortunately, left unfinished.

# Index

## Biblical

# General

THE CHRISTIAN TRADITION, Volume 4

*Designed by Joseph Alderfer.*
*Composed by the University of Chicago*
*Printing Department*
*in Linotron Garamond with display lines*
*in Foundry American Garamond.*
*Printed and bound by the Maple–Vail*
*Manufacturing Group*
*on Warren's Olde Style.*
*Bound in Joanna Arrestox Vellum and*
*stamped in green and gold.*

*The symbol on the cover is adapted from*
*the coat of arms that Martin Luther*
*designed for himself.*
*In the original version a black cross appears on a*
*red heart that is placed at the center of a white rose;*
*the rose is on a sky-blue field, and the whole device*
*is encircled by a golden ring.*